Lecture Notes in Computer

Edited by G. Goos, J. Hartmanis and

Springer

Berlin
Heidelberg
New York
Barcelona
Hong Kong
London
Milan
Paris
Singapore
Tokyo

David Sands (Ed.)

Programming Languages and Systems

10th European Symposium on Programming, ESOP 2001
Held as Part of the Joint European Conferences
on Theory and Practice of Software, ETAPS 2001
Genova, Italy, April 2-6, 2001
Proceedings

 Springer

Series Editors

Gerhard Goos, Karlsruhe University, Germany
Juris Hartmanis, Cornell University, NY, USA
Jan van Leeuwen, Utrecht University, The Netherlands

Volume Editor

David Sands
Chalmers University of Technology and Göteborg University
Department of Computing Science
412 96 Göteborg, Sweden
E-mail: dave@cs.chalmers.se

Cataloging-in-Publication Data applied for

Die Deutsche Bibliothek - CIP-Einheitsaufnahme

Programming languages and systems : proceedings / 10th European
Symposium on Programming, ESOP 2001, held as part of the Joint
European Conferences on Theory and Practice of Software, ETAPS 2001,
Genova, Italy, April 2 - 6, 2001. David Sands (ed.). - Berlin ;
Heidelberg ; New York ; Barcelona ; Hong Kong ; London ; Milan ; Paris ;
Singapore ; Tokyo : Springer, 2001
   (Lecture notes in computer science ; Vol. 2028)
   ISBN 3-540-41862-8

CR Subject Classification (1998): D.3, D.1-2, F.3-4, E.1

ISSN 0302-9743
ISBN 3-540-41862-8 Springer-Verlag Berlin Heidelberg New York

Springer-Verlag Berlin Heidelberg New York
a member of BertelsmannSpringer Science+Business Media GmbH

http://www.springer.de

© Springer-Verlag Berlin Heidelberg 2001
Printed in Germany

Typesetting: Camera-ready by author, data conversion by PTP-Berlin, Stefan Sossna
Printed on acid-free paper   SPIN: 10782434   06/3142   5 4 3 2 1 0

Foreword

ETAPS 2001 was the fourth instance of the European Joint Conferences on Theory and Practice of Software. ETAPS is an annual federated conference that was established in 1998 by combining a number of existing and new conferences. This year it comprised five conferences (FOSSACS, FASE, ESOP, CC, TACAS), ten satellite workshops (CMCS, ETI Day, JOSES, LDTA, MMAABS, PFM, RelMiS, UNIGRA, WADT, WTUML), seven invited lectures, a debate, and ten tutorials.

The events that comprise ETAPS address various aspects of the system development process, including specification, design, implementation, analysis, and improvement. The languages, methodologies, and tools which support these activities are all well within its scope. Different blends of theory and practice are represented, with an inclination towards theory with a practical motivation on one hand and soundly-based practice on the other. Many of the issues involved in software design apply to systems in general, including hardware systems, and the emphasis on software is not intended to be exclusive.

ETAPS is a loose confederation in which each event retains its own identity, with a separate program committee and independent proceedings. Its format is open-ended, allowing it to grow and evolve as time goes by. Contributed talks and system demonstrations are in synchronized parallel sessions, with invited lectures in plenary sessions. Two of the invited lectures are reserved for "unifying" talks on topics of interest to the whole range of ETAPS attendees. The aim of cramming all this activity into a single one-week meeting is to create a strong magnet for academic and industrial researchers working on topics within its scope, giving them the opportunity to learn about research in related areas, and thereby to foster new and existing links between work in areas that were formerly addressed in separate meetings.

ETAPS 2001 was hosted by the Dipartimento di Informatica e Scienze dell'Informazione (DISI) of the Università di Genova and was organized by the following team:

Egidio Astesiano (General Chair)
Eugenio Moggi (Organization Chair)
Maura Cerioli (Satellite Events Chair)
Gianna Reggio (Publicity Chair)
Davide Ancona
Giorgio Delzanno
Maurizio Martelli

with the assistance of Convention Bureau Genova. Tutorials were organized by Bernhard Rumpe (TU München). Overall planning for ETAPS conferences is the responsibility of the ETAPS Steering Committee, whose current membership is:

Egidio Astesiano (Genova), Ed Brinksma (Enschede), Pierpaolo Degano (Pisa), Hartmut Ehrig (Berlin), José Fiadeiro (Lisbon), Marie-Claude Gaudel (Paris), Susanne Graf (Grenoble), Furio Honsell (Udine), Nigel Horspool (Victoria), Heinrich Hußmann (Dresden), Paul Klint (Amsterdam), Daniel Le Métayer (Rennes), Tom Maibaum (London), Tiziana Margaria (Dortmund), Ugo Montanari (Pisa), Mogens Nielsen (Aarhus), Hanne Riis Nielson (Aarhus), Fernando Orejas (Barcelona), Andreas Podelski (Saarbrücken), David Sands (Göteborg), Don Sannella (Edinburgh), Perdita Stevens (Edinburgh), Jerzy Tiuryn (Warsaw), David Watt (Glasgow), Herbert Weber (Berlin), Reinhard Wilhelm (Saarbrücken)

ETAPS 2001 was organized in cooperation with

the Association for Computing Machinery
the European Association for Programming Languages and Systems
the European Association of Software Science and Technology
the European Association for Theoretical Computer Science

and received generous sponsorship from:

ELSAG
Fondazione Cassa di Risparmio di Genova e Imperia
INDAM - Gruppo Nazionale per l'Informatica Matematica (GNIM)
Marconi
Microsoft Research
Telecom Italia
TXT e-solutions
Università di Genova

I would like to express my sincere gratitude to all of these people and organizations, the program committee chairs and PC members of the ETAPS conferences, the organizers of the satellite events, the speakers themselves, and finally Springer-Verlag for agreeing to publish the ETAPS proceedings.

January 2001   Donald Sannella
                                        ETAPS Steering Committee chairman

Preface

This volume contains the 28 papers presented at ESOP 2001, the Tenth European Symposium on Programming, which took place in Genova, Italy, April 4–6, 2001. The ESOP series began in 1986, and addresses both practical and theoretical issues in the design, specification, and analysis of programming languages and systems.

The call for ESOP 2001 encouraged papers addressing (but not limited to)

- Programming paradigms (including functional, logic, concurrent, and object-oriented) and their integration;
- Semantics with applications to the development of correct, secure, and efficient software and systems;
- Advanced type systems, program analysis, program transformation.

The volume begins with two invited contributions. The first contribution belongs to ETAPS as a whole, and accompanies the "unifying" ETAPS invited talk given by Luca Cardelli. The second contribution is from the ESOP invited speaker, John Mitchell. The remaining 26 papers were selected by the program committee from the 76 submissions, and include one short paper which accompanied a tool-demo presentation.

Each submission was reviewed by at least three referees, and papers were selected in the latter stages of a two week discussion phase. My thanks to the members of the program committee and other referees for their hard work. Thanks also to Christian Probst for help with the conference management software, and to Don Sannella for steering the ETAPS ship so smoothly.

January 2001   David Sands

Organization

Program Chair

David Sands   Chalmers and Göteborg University, Sweden

Program Committee

Martín Abadi	Bell Labs, USA
Radhia Cousot	CNRS and École Polytechnique, France
Mads Dam	KTH Kista, Sweden
Andrew D. Gordon	Microsoft Research, UK
Robert Harper	CMU Pittsburgh, USA
Nevin Heintze	Bell Labs, USA
Daniel Le Métayer	Trusted Logic, France
Florence Maraninchi	Grenoble I/Verimag, France
Catuscia Palamidessi	Penn State, USA
Mooly Sagiv	Tel-Aviv University, Israel
David Sands	Chalmers and Göteborg University, Sweden
Peter Sestoft	KVL and ITU Copenhagen, Denmark
Harald Søndergaard	The University of Melbourne, Australia

Additional Referees

Johan Agat
Karine Altisen
Pierre Berlioux
Bruno Blanchet
Valentin Bonnard
Glenn Bruns
Michele Bugliesi
Luca Cardelli
Giuseppe Castagna
Jan Cederquist
Thomas Colcombet
Seth Copen Goldstein
Agostino Cortesi
Patrick Cousot
Karl Crary
Olivier Danvy
Ewen Denney
Nachum Dershowitz
Nurit Dor
Tyson Dowd
Conal Elliot
Martin Elsman
Jérôme Feret
Cedric Fournet
Pascal Fradet
Nissim Francez
Lars-Åke Fredlund
Stephen Freund
Roberto Giacobazzi
Pabla Giambiagi
Kevin Glynn
Gregor Goessler
Orna Grumberg

Dilian Gurov
Jörgen Gustavsson
Thomas Hallgren
Gregoire Hamon
John Hannan
Fritz Henglein
Charles Hymans
Daniel Jackson
Thomas Jensen
Mark P. Jones
Simon Jones
Jan Jurjens
Per Kreuger
John Lamping
Cosimo Laneve
Julia Lawall
Peter Lee
Bjorn Lisper
Francesco Logozzo
Renaud Marlet
Andres Martinelli
Damien Massé
Laurent Mauborgne
Antoine Miné
David Monniaux
Laurent Mounier
Lee Naish
Xavier Nicollin
Thomas Noll
Martin Odersky
Richard O'Keefe
Dino Oliva
Catherine Oriat

Gordon Pace
Joachim Parrow
Simon Peyton Jones
Frank Pfenning
François Pottier
K. V. S. Prasad
Elisa Quintarelli
C.R. Ramakrishnan
Francesco Ranzato
Julian Rathke
Jakob Rehof
Jon Riecke
Hanne Riis Nielson
Claudio Russo
Andrei Sabelfeld
Francesca Scozzari
Ran Shaham
Vitaly Shmatikov
Zoltan Somogyi
Fausto Spoto
Peter J. Stuckey
Martin Sulzmann
Mario Südholt
Tommy Thorn
Frank Valencia
Bjorn Victor
Ramesh Viswanathan
Jan Vitek
Jose-Luis Vivas
David Walker
Eran Yahav
Amiram Yehudai
Gianluigi Zavattaro

Table of Contents

A Query Language Based on the Ambient Logic

Luca Cardelli[1] and Giorgio Ghelli[2]

[1] Microsoft Research, 1 Guildhall Street, Cambridge, UK
[2] Università di Pisa, Dipartimento di Informatica, Corso Italia 40, Pisa, Italy

Abstract. The ambient logic is a modal logic proposed to describe the structural and computational properties of distributed and mobile computation. The structural part of the ambient logic is, essentially, a logic of labeled trees, hence it turns out to be a good foundation for query languages for semistructured data, much in the same way as first order logic is a fitting foundation for relational query languages. We define here a query language for semistructured data that is based on the ambient logic, and we outline an execution model for this language. The language turns out to be quite expressive. Its strong foundations and the equivalences that hold in the ambient logic are helpful in the definition of the language semantics and execution model.

1 Introduction

This work arises from the unexpected convergence of studies in two different fields: mobile computation and semistructured data.

Unstructured collections, or unstructured data, are collections that do not respect a predefined schema, and hence need to carry a description of their own structure. These are called *semistructured* when one can recognize in them some degree of homogeneity. This partial regularity makes semistructured collections amenable to be accessed through query languages, but not through query languages that have been designed to access fully structured databases. New languages are needed that are able to tolerate the data irregularity, and that can be used to query, at the same time, both data and structure. Semistructured collections are usually modeled in terms of labeled graphs, or labeled trees [3].

The ambient logic is a modal logic proposed to describe the structural and computational properties of distributed and mobile computation [10]. The logic comes equipped with a rich collection of logical implications and equivalences. The structural part of the ambient logic is, essentially, a logic designed to describe properties of labeled trees. It is therefore a good foundation for query languages for semistructured data, much in the same way as first order logic is a fitting foundation for relational query languages. First order logic is a logic of predicates (i.e. relations) and therefore it is particularly suitable to describe relational data. But, to describe tree-shaped data, we need a more suitable logic: a logic of trees or graphs.

This is an invited paper.

D. Sands (Ed.): ESOP 2001, LNCS 2028, pp. 1–22, 2001.

Here we define a query language for semistructured data that is based on the ambient logic, and we outline an execution model for this language. The language turns out to be quite expressive. Its strong foundations and the equivalences that hold in the ambient logic are helpful in the definition of the language semantics and execution model.

The paper is structured as follows. In this section we present a preview of the query language, and compare it with related proposals. In Section 2 we define the tree data model. In Section 3 we present the logic, upon which the query language, defined in Section 4, is defined. In Section 5 we present the evaluation model. In Section 6 we draw some conclusions.

1.1   A Preview

Consider the following bibliography, expressed in the syntax of our language TQL, which we explain in detail later. Informally, $a[F]$ represents a piece of data labeled a with contents F. The contents can be a collection of similar pieces of data, separated by "$|$". When the collection is empty, we can omit the brackets, so that, for example, $POPL[\ ]$ can be written as $POPL$.

The bibliography below consists of a set of references all labeled *article*. Each entry contains a number of *author* fields, a *title* field, and possibly other fields.

$ARTICLES =$

    article[*author*[*Cardelli*] | *author*[*Gordon*] | *title*[*Anytime_Anywhere*]
        | *conference*[*POPL*] | *year*[*2000*]
        | *keyword*[*Ambient_Calculus*] | *keyword*[*Logic*]] |

    article[*author*[*Cardelli*] | *title*[*Wide_Area_Computation*]
        | *booktitle*[*ICALP*] | *year*[*1999*] | *pages*[*403-444*] | *publisher*[*SV*]] |

    article[*author*[*Ghelli*] | *author*[*Pierce*] | *title*[*Bounded_Existentials*]
        | *journal*[*TCS*] | *year*[*1998*]]

Suppose we want to find all the papers in $ARTICLES$ where one author is *Cardelli*; then we can write the following query:

    from $ARTICLES \vDash .article[X]$
               $X \vDash .author[Cardelli]$
    select *paper*[X]

The query consists of a list of *matching expressions* contained between *from* and *select*, and a *reconstruction expression*, following *select*. The matching expressions bind X with every piece of data that is reachable from the root $ARTICLES$ through an *article* path, and such that a path *author* goes from X to *Cardelli*; the answer is *paper*[*author*[*Cardelli*] | *author*[*Gordon*] | ...] | *paper*[*author*[*Cardelli*] | *title*[*Wide Area Computation*] | ...], i.e. the first two articles in the databases, with the outer *article* rewritten as *paper*.

This query language is characterized by the fact that a matching expression is actually a logic expression combining matching and logical operators. For example, the following query combines path expressions and logical implication

($\Rightarrow$) to retrieve papers with no other author then *Cardelli*. Informally, **T** matches anything, hence the second condition says: if X is an author, then it is *Cardelli*.

$$\text{from} \quad ARTICLES \vDash .article[X]$$
$$\phantom{\text{from} \quad} X \vDash .author[\mathbf{T}] \Rightarrow .author[Cardelli]$$
$$\text{select} \quad X$$

Moreover, queries can be nested, giving us the power to restructure the collection, as we explain later.

1.2   Comparisons with Related Proposals

In this paper we describe a logic, a query language, and an abstract evaluation mechanism.

The tree logic can be compared with standard first order formalizations of labelled trees. Using the terminology of [3], we can encode a labeled tree with a relation *Ref(source:OID, label:Λ, destination:OID)*. The nodes of the tree are the OIDs (Object IDentifiers) that appear in the *source* and *destination* columns, and any tuple in the relation represents an edge, with label *label*. Of course, such a relation can represent a graph as well as a tree. It represents a forest if *destination* is a key for the relation, and if there exists an order relation on the OIDs such that, in any tuple, the *source* strictly precedes the *destination*.

First order formulas defined over this relation already constitute a logical language to describe tree properties. Trees are represented here by the OID of their root. We can say that, for example, "the tree x is $a[]$" by saying:

$$\exists y. \ Ref(x,a,y) \wedge (\forall y',y''. \ \neg Ref(y,y',y'')) \wedge (\forall x',x''. \ x'' \neq y \Rightarrow \neg Ref(x,x',x''))$$

There are some differences with our approach. First, our logic is 'modal', which means that a formula $\mathcal{A}$ is always about one specific 'subject', that is the part of the database currently being matched against $\mathcal{A}$. First order logic, instead, does not have an implicit subject: one can, and must, name a subject. For example, our modal formula $a[]$ implicitly describes the 'current tree', while its translation into first order logic, given above, gives a name x to the tree it describes.

Being 'modal' is neither a merit nor a fault, in itself; it is merely a difference. Modality makes it easier to decribe just one tree and its structure, whereas it makes it more difficult to describe a relationship between two different trees.

Apart from modality, another feature of the ambient logic is that its fundamental operators deal with one-step paths ($a[\mathcal{A}]$) and with the composition of trees ($\mathcal{A} \mid \mathcal{A}'$), whereas the first order approach describes everything in terms of one-step paths ($Ref(o1,a,o2)$). Composition is a powerful operator, at least for the following purposes:

- it makes it easy to describe record-like structures both partially ($b[] \mid c[] \mid \mathbf{T}$ means: contains $b[]$, $c[]$, and possibly more fields) and completely ($b[] \mid c[]$ means: contains $b[], c[]$ and only $b[], c[]$); complete descriptions are difficult in the path based approach;
- it makes it possible to bind a variable to 'the rest of the record', as in 'X is everything but the title': $paper[title[\mathbf{T}] \mid X]$.

The query language we described derives its essential *from-select* structure from set-theoretics comprehension, in the SQL tradition, and this makes it similar to other query languages for semistructured data, such as StruQL [14,15], Lorel [5,18], XML-QL [13], Quilt [11], and, to some extent, YATL [12]. An in-depth comparison between the XML-QL, YATL, and Lorel languages is carried out in [16], based on the analysis of thirteen typical queries. In [17] we wrote down those same queries in TQL; the result of this comparison is that, for the thirteen queries in [16], their TQL expression is very similar to the corresponding XML-QL, with a couple of exceptions. First, those XML-QL queries that, in [16], are expressed using Skolem functions, have to be expressed in a different way in TQL, since we do not have Skolem functions in the current version of TQL. However, our Skolem-free version of these queries is not complex. Second, XML-QL does not seem to have a general way of expressing universal quantification, and this problem shows up in the query that asks for pairs of books with the same set of authors; this is rather complex to express in XML-QL, but it is not difficult in TQL. Another related class of queries that are simpler to express using TQL are those related to the non-existence of paths, such as 'find all the papers with no title' or 'find all the papers whose only author, if any, is Ghelli'. Lorel does not have these problems, since it allows universal quantification. Quilt and XDuce [19] are Turing complete, hence are more expressive than the other languages we cited here.

One important feature of TQL is that it has a clean semantic interpretation, which pays off in several ways. First, the semantics should make it easier to prove the correctness and completeness of a specific implementation. Moreover, it simplifies the task of proving equivalences between different logic formulas or queries. To our knowledge, no such formal semantics has been defined for YATL. The semantics of Lorel has been defined, but looks quite involved, because of their extensive use of coercions.

2   Information Trees

We represent semistructured data as *information trees*. In this section we first define information trees, then we give a syntax to denote them, and finally we define an equivalence relation that determines when two different expressions denote the same information tree.

2.1   Information Trees

We represent labeled trees as nested multisets; this corresponds, of course, to unordered trees. Ordered trees (e.g. XML data) could be represented as nested lists. This option would have an impact on the logic, where the symmetric $\mathcal{A} \mid \mathcal{B}$ operator could be replaced by an asymmetric one, $\mathcal{A}; \mathcal{B}$. This change might actually simplify some aspects of the logic, but in this paper we stick to the original notion of unordered trees from [10], which also matches some recent directions in XML [1].

For a given set of *labels* Λ, we define the set $\mathcal{IT}$ of information trees, ranged over by I, as the smallest collection such that:

- the empty multiset, $\{\}$, is in $\mathcal{IT}$;
- if m is in Λ and I is in $\mathcal{IT}$ then the singleton multiset $\{\langle m, I \rangle\}$ is in $\mathcal{IT}$;
- $\mathcal{IT}$ is closed under multiset union $\biguplus_{j \in J} M(j)$, where J is an index set, and $M \in J \to \mathcal{IT}$.

2.2 Information Terms

We denote finite information trees by the following syntax of information term (info-terms), borrowed from the ambient calculus [9]. We define a function $\llbracket F \rrbracket$ mapping the info-term F to the denoted information tree. To this aim, we define three operators, $\mathbf{0}$, $m[\_]$ and $|$, on the domain of the information trees, which we use to interpret the corresponding operations on info-terms.

Info-terms and their information tree meaning

$F ::= \quad$ info-term
$\quad \mathbf{0} \qquad$ denoting the empty multiset
$\quad m[F] \quad$ denoting the multiset $\{\langle m, F \rangle\}$
$\quad F \mid F \quad$ denoting multiset union

$$
\begin{aligned}
\llbracket \mathbf{0} \rrbracket &=_{def} \mathbf{0} & &=_{def} \{\} \\
\llbracket m[F] \rrbracket &=_{def} m[\llbracket F \rrbracket] & &=_{def} \{\langle m, \llbracket F \rrbracket \rangle\} \\
\llbracket F' \mid F'' \rrbracket &=_{def} \llbracket F' \rrbracket \mid \llbracket F'' \rrbracket & &=_{def} \llbracket F' \rrbracket \uplus \llbracket F'' \rrbracket
\end{aligned}
$$

We use Π to denote the set of all terms generated by this grammar, also using parentheses for precedence. We often abbreviate $m[\mathbf{0}]$ as $m[]$, or as m. We assume that Λ includes the disjoint union of each basic data type of interest (integers, strings...), hence $5[\mathbf{0}]$, or 5, is a legitimate info-term. We assume that "$|$" associates to the right, i.e. $F \mid F' \mid F''$ is read $F \mid (F' \mid F'')$.

2.3 Congruence over Info-Terms

The interpretation of info-terms as information trees induces an equivalence relation $F \equiv F'$ on info-terms. This relation is called *info-term congruence*, and it can be axiomatized as follows.

Congruence over info-terms

$F \equiv F$
$F' \equiv F \Rightarrow F \equiv F'$
$F \equiv F', F' \equiv F'' \Rightarrow F \equiv F''$
$F \equiv F' \Rightarrow m[F] \equiv m[F']$
$F \equiv F' \Rightarrow F \mid F'' \equiv F' \mid F''$
$F \mid \mathbf{0} \equiv F$
$F \mid F' \equiv F' \mid F$
$(F \mid F') \mid F'' \equiv F \mid (F' \mid F'')$

This axiomatization of congruence is sound and complete with respect to the information tree semantics. That is, $F \equiv F'$ if and only if F and F' represent the same information tree.

2.4   Information Trees, OEM Trees, UnQL Trees

We can compare our information trees with two popular models for semistructured data: OEM data [24] and UnQL trees [6]. The first obvious difference is that OEM and UnQL models can be used to represent both trees and graphs, while here we focus only on trees. We are currently working on extending our model to include labeled graphs as well, but we prefer to focus on the simpler issue of trees, which is rich enough to warrant a separate study.

UnQL trees are characterized by the fact that they are considered modulo bisimulation, which essentially means that information trees are seen as sets instead of multisets. For example, $m[n[] \mid n[]]$ is considered the same as $m[n[]]$; hence UnQL trees are more abstract, in the precise sense that they identify more terms than we do.

On the other hand, information trees are more abstract than OEM data, since OEM data can distinguish a DAG from its tree-unfolding.

3   The Tree Logic

In this section we present the tree logic. The tree logic is based on Cardelli and Gordon's modal ambient logic, defined with the aim of specifying spatial and temporal properties of the mobile processes that can be described through the ambient calculus [10]. The ambient logic is particularly attractive because it is equipped with a large set of logical laws for tree-like structures, in particular logical equivalences, that can provide a foundation for query rewriting rules and query optimization.

We start here from a subset of the ambient logic as presented in [10], but we enrich it with information tree variables, label comparison, and recursion.

3.1   Formulas

The syntax of the tree logic formulas is presented in the following table.

The symbol $\sim$, in the label comparison clause, stands for any label comparison operator chosen in a predefined family Θ; we will assume that Θ at least contains equality, the SQL string matching operator *like*, and their negations. The positivity condition on the recursion variable ξ means that an even number of negations must be traversed in the path that goes from each occurrence of ξ to its binder.

Formulas:

$\eta ::=$		label expression
	n	label constant
	x	label variable

$\mathcal{A}, \mathcal{B} ::=$	formula
$\mathbf{0}$	empty tree
$\eta[\mathcal{A}]$	location
$\mathcal{A} \mid \mathcal{B}$	composition
$\mathbf{T}$	true
$\neg \mathcal{A}$	negation
$\mathcal{A} \wedge \mathcal{B}$	conjunction
$\mathcal{X}$	tree variable
$\exists x.\mathcal{A}$	quantification over label variables
$\exists \mathcal{X}.\mathcal{A}$	quantification over tree variables
$\eta \sim \eta'$	label comparison
ξ	recursion variable
$\mu\xi.\mathcal{A}$	recursive formula (least fixpoint); ξ may appear only positively

The interpretation of a formula $\mathcal{A}$ is given by a semantic map $[\![\mathcal{A}]\!]_{\rho,\delta}$ that maps $\mathcal{A}$ to a set of information trees, with respect to the valuations ρ and δ. The valuation ρ maps label variables x to labels (elements of Λ) and tree variables $\mathcal{X}$ to information trees, while δ maps recursion variables ξ to sets of information trees.

Formulas as sets of information trees

$$
\begin{aligned}
[\![\mathbf{0}]\!]_{\rho,\delta} &=_{def} \{\mathbf{0}\} \\
[\![\eta[\mathcal{A}]]\!]_{\rho,\delta} &=_{def} \{\rho(\eta)[I] \mid I \in [\![\mathcal{A}]\!]_{\rho,\delta}\} \\
[\![\mathcal{A} \mid \mathcal{B}]\!]_{\rho,\delta} &=_{def} \{I \mid I' \mid I \in [\![\mathcal{A}]\!]_{\rho,\delta}, I' \in [\![\mathcal{B}]\!]_{\rho,\delta}\} \\
[\![\mathbf{T}]\!]_{\rho,\delta} &=_{def} \mathcal{IT} \\
[\![\neg\mathcal{A}]\!]_{\rho,\delta} &=_{def} \mathcal{IT} \setminus [\![\mathcal{A}]\!]_{\rho,\delta} \\
[\![\mathcal{A} \wedge \mathcal{B}]\!]_{\rho,\delta} &=_{def} [\![\mathcal{A}]\!]_{\rho,\delta} \cap [\![\mathcal{B}]\!]_{\rho,\delta} \\
[\![\mathcal{X}]\!]_{\rho,\delta} &=_{def} \{\rho(\mathcal{X})\} \\
[\![\exists x.\mathcal{A}]\!]_{\rho,\delta} &=_{def} \bigcup_{n \in \Lambda} [\![\mathcal{A}]\!]_{\rho[x \mapsto n],\delta} \\
[\![\exists \mathcal{X}.\mathcal{A}]\!]_{\rho,\delta} &=_{def} \bigcup_{I \in \mathcal{IT}} [\![\mathcal{A}]\!]_{\rho[\mathcal{X} \mapsto I],\delta} \\
[\![\eta \sim \eta']\!]_{\rho,\delta} &=_{def} \text{if } \rho(\eta) \sim \rho(\eta') \text{ then } \mathcal{IT} \text{ else } \emptyset \\
[\![\mu\xi.\mathcal{A}]\!]_{\rho,\delta} &=_{def} \bigcap \{S \subseteq \mathcal{IT} \mid S \supseteq [\![\mathcal{A}]\!]_{\rho,\delta[\xi \mapsto S]}\} \\
[\![\xi]\!]_{\rho,\delta} &=_{def} \delta(\xi)
\end{aligned}
$$

This style of semantics makes it easier to define the semantics of recursive formulas. Some consequences of the semantic definition are detailed shortly.

$[\![\mathbf{0}]\!]_{\rho,\delta}$ is the singleton $\{\mathbf{0}\}$. $[\![\eta[\mathcal{A}]]\!]_{\rho,\delta}$ contains the information tree $m[I]$, if $m = \rho(\eta)$ and I is in $[\![\mathcal{A}]\!]_{\rho,\delta}$. (We assume that ρ maps any label in Λ to itself, so that we can apply ρ to η even when η is not a variable.) For each I in $[\![\mathcal{A}]\!]_{\rho,\delta}$ and I' in $[\![\mathcal{B}]\!]_{\rho,\delta}$, $[\![\mathcal{A} \mid \mathcal{B}]\!]_{\rho,\delta}$ contains the information tree $I \mid I'$. $[\![\mathbf{T}]\!]_{\rho,\delta}$ is the set of all information trees (while its negation $\mathbf{F}$ denotes the empty set). $[\![\neg\mathcal{A}]\!]_{\rho,\delta}$ is the complement of $[\![\mathcal{A}]\!]_{\rho,\delta}$ with respect to the set of all information trees $\mathcal{IT}$. I is in $[\![\mathcal{A} \wedge \mathcal{B}]\!]_{\rho,\delta}$ if it is in $[\![\mathcal{A}]\!]_{\rho,\delta}$ and in $[\![\mathcal{B}]\!]_{\rho,\delta}$. I is in $[\![\exists x.\mathcal{A}]\!]_{\rho,\delta}$ if there exists some value n for x such that I is in $[\![\mathcal{A}]\!]_{\rho[x \mapsto n],\delta}$. Here $\rho[x \mapsto n]$ denotes the subtitution that maps x to n and otherwise coincides with ρ. $[\![\eta \sim \eta']\!]_{\rho,\delta}$ is the set $\mathcal{IT}$ if the comparison holds, else it is the empty set. $[\![\mu\xi.\mathcal{A}]\!]_{\rho,\delta}$ is the least fixpoint (with respect to set inclusion) of the monotonic function that maps any set of information trees S to $[\![\mathcal{A}]\!]_{\rho,\delta[\xi\mapsto S]}$.

The meaning of a variable $\mathcal{X}$ is given by the valuation ρ. Valuations connect our logic to pattern matching; for example, $[\![m[n[\mathbf{0}]]]\!]$ is in $[\![x[\mathcal{X}]]\!]_{\rho,\delta}$ if ρ maps x to m and $\mathcal{X}$ to $[\![n[\mathbf{0}]]\!]$. The process of finding all possible ρ's such that $I \in [\![\mathcal{A}]\!]_{\rho,\delta}$ is our logic-based way of finding all possible answers to a query with respect to a database I.

We say that F *satisfies* $\mathcal{A}$ *under* ρ, δ, when the information tree $[\![F]\!]$ is in the set $[\![\mathcal{A}]\!]_{\rho,\delta}$, and then we write $F \vDash_{\rho,\delta} \mathcal{A}$:

$$F \vDash_{\rho,\delta} \mathcal{A} =_{def} [\![F]\!] \in [\![\mathcal{A}]\!]_{\rho,\delta}$$

Satisfaction enjoys the following properties, which are easily derived and help making the above semantic definition more explicit. These properties may form the basis of a matching algorithm of F against $\mathcal{A}$.

Some properties of satisfaction

$$
\begin{aligned}
F \vDash_{\rho,\delta} \mathbf{0} &\Leftrightarrow F \equiv \mathbf{0} \\
F \vDash_{\rho,\delta} \eta[\mathcal{A}] &\Leftrightarrow \exists F'. \ F \equiv \rho(\eta)[F'] \ \wedge \ F' \vDash_{\rho,\delta} \mathcal{A} \\
F \vDash_{\rho,\delta} \mathcal{A} \mid \mathcal{B} &\Leftrightarrow \exists F', F''. \ F \equiv F' \mid F'' \ \wedge \ F' \vDash_{\rho,\delta} \mathcal{A} \ \wedge \ F'' \vDash_{\rho,\delta} \mathcal{B} \\
F \vDash_{\rho,\delta} \mathbf{T} & \\
F \vDash_{\rho,\delta} \neg\mathcal{A} &\Leftrightarrow \neg(F \vDash_{\rho,\delta} \mathcal{A}) \\
F \vDash_{\rho,\delta} \mathcal{A} \wedge \mathcal{B} &\Leftrightarrow F \vDash_{\rho,\delta} \mathcal{A} \ \wedge \ F \vDash_{\rho,\delta} \mathcal{B} \\
F \vDash_{\rho,\delta} \exists x.\mathcal{A} &\Leftrightarrow \exists m \in \Lambda. \ F \vDash_{\rho[x\mapsto m],\delta} \mathcal{A} \\
F \vDash_{\rho,\delta} \exists \mathcal{X}.\mathcal{A} &\Leftrightarrow \exists I \in \mathcal{IT}. \ F \vDash_{\rho[\mathcal{X}\mapsto I],\delta} \mathcal{A} \\
F \vDash_{\rho,\delta} \eta \sim \eta' &\Leftrightarrow \rho(\eta) \sim \rho(\eta') \\
F \vDash_{\rho,\delta} \mu\xi.\mathcal{A} &\Leftrightarrow F \vDash_{\rho,\delta} \mathcal{A}\{\xi \leftarrow \mu\xi.\mathcal{A}\} \\
F \vDash_{\rho,\delta} \mathcal{X} &\Leftrightarrow [\![F]\!] = \rho(\mathcal{X}) \\
F \vDash_{\rho,\delta} \xi &\Leftrightarrow [\![F]\!] \in \delta(\xi)
\end{aligned}
$$

3.2 Some Derived Formulas

As usual, negation allows us to define many useful derived operators, as described in the following table.

Derived formulas:

$$
\begin{aligned}
\eta[\Rightarrow \mathcal{A}] &=_{def} \neg(\eta[\neg\mathcal{A}]) & \mathcal{A} \parallel \mathcal{B} &=_{def} \neg(\neg\mathcal{A} \mid \neg\mathcal{B}) \\
\mathbf{F} &=_{def} \neg\mathbf{T} & \mathcal{A} \vee \mathcal{B} &=_{def} \neg(\neg\mathcal{A} \wedge \neg\mathcal{B}) \\
\forall x.\mathcal{A} &=_{def} \neg(\exists x.\neg\mathcal{A}) & \forall \mathcal{X}.\mathcal{A} &=_{def} \neg(\exists \mathcal{X}.\neg\mathcal{A}) \\
\nu\xi.\mathcal{A} &=_{def} \neg(\mu\xi.\neg\mathcal{A}\{\xi \leftarrow \neg\xi\})
\end{aligned}
$$

$F \vDash m[\Rightarrow \mathcal{A}]$ means that 'it is not true that, for some F', $F \equiv m[F']$ and not $F' \vDash \mathcal{A}$', i.e. 'if F has the shape $m[F']$, then $F' \vDash \mathcal{A}$'. To appreciate the difference between $m[\mathcal{A}]$ and its dual $m[\Rightarrow \mathcal{A}]$, consider the following statements.

- F is an article where *Ghelli* is an author: $F \vDash article[author[Ghelli]|\mathbf{T}]$
- If F is an article, then *Ghelli* is an author: $F \vDash article[\Rightarrow author[Ghelli]|\mathbf{T}]$

$F \vDash \mathcal{A} \parallel \mathcal{B}$ means that 'it is not true that, for some F' and F'', $F \equiv F' \mid F''$ and $F' \vDash \neg\mathcal{A}$ and $F'' \vDash \neg\mathcal{B}$', which means: for *every* decomposition of F into $F' \mid F''$, *either* $F' \vDash \mathcal{A}$ *or* $F'' \vDash \mathcal{B}$. To appreciate the difference between the $|$ and the $\parallel$ operators, consider the following statements.

- There exists a composition of F into F' and F'', such that F' satisfies $article[\mathcal{A}]$, and F'' satsfies $\mathbf{T}$; i.e., there is an article inside F that satisfies $\mathcal{A}$: $F \vDash article[\mathcal{A}] \mid \mathbf{T}$
- For every decomposition of F into F' and F'', either F' satisfies $article[\Rightarrow \mathcal{A}]$, or F'' satisfies $\mathbf{F}$; i.e., every article inside F satisfies $\mathcal{A}$: $F \vDash article[\Rightarrow \mathcal{A}] \parallel \mathbf{F}$

The dual of the least fixpoint operator $\mu\xi.\mathcal{A}$ is the greatest fixpoint operator $\nu\xi.\mathcal{A}$. For example $\mu\xi.\xi$ is equivalent to $\mathbf{F}$, while $\nu\xi.\xi$ is equivalent to $\mathbf{T}$. More interestingly, $\mu\xi.\mathbf{0} \vee m[\xi]$ describes every information tree that matches $m[m[\ldots m[]]]$, and, on finite trees, it is equivalent to $\nu\xi.\mathbf{0} \vee m[\xi]$. However, if we consider infinite trees, the distinction between least and greatest fixpoint becomes more important. For example, the infinite tree $m[m[\ldots]]$ satisfies $\nu\xi.\mathbf{0} \vee m[\xi]$, but does not satisfy $\mu\xi.\mathbf{0} \vee m[\xi]$. When we consider only finite trees, as we do here, the μ and ν operators are quite similar in practice, since most interesting formulas have a single fixpoint.

Satisfaction over the derived operators enjoys the following properties, most of which are easily derived from the definition, while others are more subtle. For example, the properties of greatest fixpoints include a coinduction principle. Again, these properties may form the basis for a matching algorithm.

Some properties of satisfaction for derived formulas

$$\neg F \vDash_{\rho,\delta} \mathbf{F}$$
$$F \vDash_{\rho,\delta} \eta[\Rightarrow \mathcal{A}] \Leftrightarrow \forall F'. (F \equiv \rho(\eta)[F'] \Rightarrow F' \vDash_{\rho,\delta} \mathcal{A})$$
$$F \vDash_{\rho,\delta} \mathcal{A} \parallel \mathcal{B} \Leftrightarrow \forall F',F''. F \equiv F' \mid F'' \Rightarrow (F' \vDash_{\rho,\delta} \mathcal{A} \vee F'' \vDash_{\rho,\delta} \mathcal{B})$$
$$F \vDash_{\rho,\delta} \mathcal{A} \vee \mathcal{B} \Leftrightarrow F \vDash_{\rho,\delta} \mathcal{A} \vee F \vDash_{\rho,\delta} \mathcal{B}$$
$$F \vDash_{\rho,\delta} \forall x.\mathcal{A} \Leftrightarrow \forall m \in \Lambda. F \vDash_{\rho[x \mapsto m],\delta} \mathcal{A}$$
$$F \vDash_{\rho,\delta} \forall \mathcal{X}.\mathcal{A} \Leftrightarrow \forall I \in \mathcal{IT}. F \vDash_{\rho[\mathcal{X} \mapsto I],\delta} \mathcal{A}$$
$$F \vDash_{\rho,\delta} \nu\xi.\mathcal{A} \Leftrightarrow F \vDash_{\rho,\delta} \mathcal{A}\{\xi \leftarrow \nu\xi.\mathcal{A}\}$$
$$F \vDash_{\rho,\delta} \nu\xi.\mathcal{A} \Leftrightarrow \exists \mathcal{B}. F \vDash_{\rho,\delta} \mathcal{B} \wedge \forall F'. F' \vDash_{\rho,\delta} \mathcal{B} \Rightarrow F' \vDash_{\rho,\delta} \mathcal{A}\{\xi \leftarrow \mathcal{B}\}$$

Many logical equivalences have been derived for the ambient logic, and are inherited by the tree logic. We list some of them here. These equivalences could be exploited by a query logical optimizer.

Some equations

$\eta[\mathcal{A}]$	$\Leftrightarrow \eta[\mathbf{T}] \wedge \eta[\Rightarrow \mathcal{A}]$	$\eta[\Rightarrow \mathcal{A}]$	$\Leftrightarrow \eta[\mathbf{T}] \Rightarrow \eta[\mathcal{A}]$
$\eta[\mathbf{F}]$	$\Leftrightarrow \mathbf{F}$	$\eta[\Rightarrow \mathbf{T}]$	$\Leftrightarrow \mathbf{T}$
$\eta[\mathcal{A} \wedge \mathcal{A}']$	$\Leftrightarrow \eta[\mathcal{A}] \wedge \eta[\mathcal{A}']$	$\eta[\Rightarrow \mathcal{A} \vee \mathcal{A}']$	$\Leftrightarrow \eta[\Rightarrow \mathcal{A}] \vee \eta[\Rightarrow \mathcal{A}']$
$\eta[\mathcal{A} \vee \mathcal{A}']$	$\Leftrightarrow \eta[\mathcal{A}] \vee \eta[\mathcal{A}']$	$\eta[\Rightarrow \mathcal{A} \wedge \mathcal{A}']$	$\Leftrightarrow \eta[\Rightarrow \mathcal{A}] \wedge \eta[\Rightarrow \mathcal{A}']$

$$\eta[\exists x.\mathcal{A}] \quad \Leftrightarrow \exists x.\eta[\mathcal{A}] \ (x \neq \eta) \qquad \eta[\Rightarrow \forall x.\mathcal{A}] \quad \Leftrightarrow \forall x.\eta[\Rightarrow \mathcal{A}] \ (x \neq \eta)$$
$$\eta[\forall x.\mathcal{A}] \quad \Leftrightarrow \forall x.\eta[\mathcal{A}] \ (x \neq \eta) \qquad \eta[\Rightarrow \exists x.\mathcal{A}] \quad \Leftrightarrow \exists x.\eta[\Rightarrow \mathcal{A}] \ (x \neq \eta)$$
$$\eta[\exists \mathcal{X}.\mathcal{A}] \quad \Leftrightarrow \exists \mathcal{X}.\eta[\mathcal{A}] \qquad \eta[\Rightarrow \forall \mathcal{X}.\mathcal{A}] \quad \Leftrightarrow \forall \mathcal{X}.\eta[\Rightarrow \mathcal{A}]$$
$$\eta[\forall \mathcal{X}.\mathcal{A}] \quad \Leftrightarrow \forall \mathcal{X}.\eta[\mathcal{A}] \qquad \eta[\Rightarrow \exists \mathcal{X}.\mathcal{A}] \quad \Leftrightarrow \exists \mathcal{X}.\eta[\Rightarrow \mathcal{A}]$$
$$\mathcal{A} \mid \mathcal{A}' \quad \Leftrightarrow \mathcal{A}' \mid \mathcal{A} \qquad \mathcal{A} \parallel \mathcal{A}' \quad \Leftrightarrow \mathcal{A}' \parallel \mathcal{A}$$
$$(\mathcal{A} \mid \mathcal{A}') \mid \mathcal{A}'' \Leftrightarrow \mathcal{A} \mid (\mathcal{A}' \mid \mathcal{A}'') \qquad (\mathcal{A} \parallel \mathcal{A}') \parallel \mathcal{A}'' \Leftrightarrow \mathcal{A} \parallel (\mathcal{A}' \parallel \mathcal{A}'')$$
$$\mathcal{A} \mid \mathbf{F} \quad \Leftrightarrow \mathbf{F} \qquad \mathcal{A} \parallel \mathbf{T} \quad \Leftrightarrow \mathbf{T}$$
$$\mathbf{T} \mid \mathbf{T} \quad \Leftrightarrow \mathbf{T} \qquad \mathbf{F} \parallel \mathbf{F} \quad \Leftrightarrow \mathbf{F}$$
$$\mathcal{A} \mid (\mathcal{A}' \vee \mathcal{A}'') \Leftrightarrow (\mathcal{A} \mid \mathcal{A}') \vee (\mathcal{A} \mid \mathcal{A}'') \qquad \mathcal{A} \parallel (\mathcal{A}' \wedge \mathcal{A}'') \Leftrightarrow (\mathcal{A} \parallel \mathcal{A}') \wedge (\mathcal{A} \parallel \mathcal{A}'')$$
$$\mathcal{A} \mid \exists x.\mathcal{A}' \quad \Leftrightarrow \exists x.\mathcal{A} \mid \mathcal{A}' \ (x \notin FV(\mathcal{A})) \ \mathcal{A} \parallel \forall x.\mathcal{A}' \quad \Leftrightarrow \forall x.\mathcal{A} \parallel \mathcal{A}' \ (x \notin FV(\mathcal{A}))$$
$$\mathcal{A} \mid \forall x.\mathcal{A}' \quad \Leftrightarrow \forall x.\mathcal{A} \mid \mathcal{A}' \ (x \notin FV(\mathcal{A})) \ \mathcal{A} \parallel \exists x.\mathcal{A}' \quad \Leftrightarrow \exists x.\mathcal{A} \parallel \mathcal{A}' \ (x \notin FV(\mathcal{A}))$$

3.3 Path Formulas

All query languages for semistructured data provide some way of retrieving all data that is reachable through a *path* described by a regular expression. The tree logic is powerful enough to express this kind of queries. We show this fact here by defining a syntax for path expressions, and showing how these expressions can be translated into the logic. This way, we obtain also a more compact and readable way of expressing common queries, like those outlined in the previous section.

Consider the following statement: $\mathcal{X}$ is some article found in the *ARTICLES* collection, and some author of $\mathcal{X}$ is *Cardelli*. We can express it in the logic using the $m[\mathcal{A}] \mid \mathbf{T}$ pattern as:

$$ARTICLES \vDash article[\mathcal{X} \wedge (author[Cardelli] \mid \mathbf{T})] \mid \mathbf{T}$$

Using the special syntax of path expressions, we express the same condition as follows.
$$ARTICLES \vDash .article(\mathcal{X}).author[Cardelli]$$

Our path expressions support also the following features:

– Universally quantified paths: $\mathcal{X}$ is an article and *every* author of $\mathcal{X}$ is Cardelli.
$$ARTICLES \vDash .article(\mathcal{X})!author[Cardelli]$$

– Label negation: $\mathcal{X}$ is an article where *Ghelli* is the value of a field, but is not the author.
$$ARTICLES \vDash .article(\mathcal{X}).(\neg author)[Ghelli]$$

– Path disjunction: $\mathcal{X}$ is an article that either deals with SSD or cites some paper $\mathcal{Y}$ that only deals with SSD.
$$ARTICLES \vDash .article(\mathcal{X})(.keyword \vee .cites.article(\mathcal{Y})!keyword)[SSD]$$

– Path iteration (Kleene star): $\mathcal{X}$ is an article that either deals with SSD, or from which you can reach, through a chain of citations, an article that deals with SSD.
$$ARTICLES \vDash .article(\mathcal{X})(.cites.article)^{*}.keyword[SSD]$$

- Label matching: there exists a path through which you can reach some field $\mathcal{X}$ whose label contains e and *mail* (% matches any substring).

$$ARTICLES \vDash (.\%)^*(.\%e\%mail\%)[\mathcal{X}]$$

We now define the syntax of paths and its interpretation.

Path formulas:

$\alpha ::=$	label matching expression
η	matches any n such that n *like* η
$\neg\alpha$	matches whatever α does not match
$\beta ::=$	path element
$.\alpha$	some edge matches α
$!\alpha$	each edge matches α
$p, q ::=$	path
β	elementary path
pq	path concatenation
p^*	Kleene star
$p \vee q$	disjunction
$p(\mathcal{X})$	naming the tree at the end of the path

A path-based formula $p[\mathcal{A}]$ can be translated into the tree logic as shown below. We first define the tree formula $Matches(x, \alpha)$ as follows:

$$Matches(x, \eta) \quad =_{def} x \ like \ \eta$$
$$Matches(x, \neg\alpha) =_{def} \neg Matches(x, \alpha)$$

Path elements are interpreted by a translation, $[\![\_]\!]^p$, into the logic, using the patterns $m[\mathcal{A}] \mid \mathbf{T}$ and $m[\Rightarrow \mathcal{A}] \parallel \mathbf{F}$ that we have previously presented:

$$[\![.\alpha[\mathcal{A}]]\!]^p =_{def} (\exists x.Matches(x, \alpha) \ \wedge \ x[[\![\mathcal{A}]\!]^p]) \mid \mathbf{T}$$
$$[\![!\alpha[\mathcal{A}]]\!]^p =_{def} (\forall x.Matches(x, \alpha) \ \Rightarrow \ x[\Rightarrow [\![\mathcal{A}]\!]^p]) \parallel \mathbf{F}$$

General paths are interpreted as follows. $p^*[\mathcal{A}]$ is recursively interpreted as 'either $\mathcal{A}$ holds here, or $p^*[\mathcal{A}]$ holds after traversing p'. Target naming $p(\mathcal{X})[\mathcal{A}]$ means: at the end of p you find $\mathcal{X}$, and $\mathcal{X}$ satisfies $\mathcal{A}$; hence it is interpreted using logical conjunction. Formally, path interpretation is defined as shown below; path interpretation translates all non-path operators as themselves, as exemplified for $\mathbf{T}$ and $\mid$.

$$
\begin{array}{llll}
[\![pq[\mathcal{A}]]\!]^p & =_{def} [\![p[q[\mathcal{A}]]]\!]^p & [\![p^*[\mathcal{A}]]\!]^p & =_{def} \mu\xi.\mathcal{A} \ \vee \ [\![p[\xi]]\!]^p \\
[\![(p \vee q)[\mathcal{A}]]\!]^p & =_{def} [\![p[\mathcal{A}]]\!]^p \ \vee \ [\![q[\mathcal{A}]]\!]^p & [\![p(\mathcal{X})[\mathcal{A}]]\!]^p & =_{def} [\![p[\mathcal{X} \ \wedge \ \mathcal{A}]]\!]^p \\
[\![\mathbf{T}]\!]^p & =_{def} \mathbf{T} & [\![\mathcal{A} \mid \mathcal{A}']\!]^p & =_{def} [\![\mathcal{A}]\!]^p \mid [\![\mathcal{A}']\!]^p
\end{array}
$$

3.4   Tree Logic and Schemas

Path formulas explore the vertical structure of trees. Our logic can also express easily horizontal structure, as is common in schemas for semistructured data. (E.g. in XML DTDs, XDuce [19] and XMLSchema [1]. However, the present version of our logic deals directly only with unordered structures.)

For example, we can extract the following regular-expression-like sublanguage, inspired by XDuce types. Every expression of this language denotes a set of information trees:

0	the empty tree
$\mathcal{A} \mid \mathcal{B}$	an $\mathcal{A}$ next to a $\mathcal{B}$
$\mathcal{A} \vee \mathcal{B}$	either an $\mathcal{A}$ or a $\mathcal{B}$
$n[\mathcal{A}]$	an edge n leading to an $\mathcal{A}$
$\mathcal{A}^* =_{def} \mu\xi.\ 0 \vee (\mathcal{A} \mid \xi)$	a finite multiset of zero or more $\mathcal{A}$'s
$\mathcal{A}^+ =_{def} \mathcal{A} \mid \mathcal{A}^*$	a finite multiset of one or more $\mathcal{A}$'s
$A? =_{def} 0 \vee \mathcal{A}$	optionally an $\mathcal{A}$

In general, we believe that a number of proposals for describing the shape of semistructured data can be embedded in our logic. Each such proposal usually comes with an efficient algorithm for checking membership or other properties. These efficient algorithms, of course, do not fall out automatically from a general framework. Still, a general frameworks such as our logic can be used to compare different proposals.

4   The Tree Query Language

In this section we build a full query language on top of the logic we have defined.

4.1   The Query Language

A query language should feature the following functionalities:

- binding and selection: a mechanism to select values from the database and to bind them to variables;
- construction of the result: a mechanism to build a result starting from the bindings collected during the previous stage.

Our Tree Query Language (TQL) uses the tree logic for binding and selection, and tree building operations to construct the result. Logical formulas $\mathcal{A}$ are as previously defined.

TQL queries:

$Q ::=$	query
from $Q \models \mathcal{A}$ *select* Q'	valuation-collecting query
$\mathcal{X}$	matching variable
0	empty result

$Q \mid Q$	composition of results
$\eta[Q]$	nesting of result
$f(Q)$	tree function, for any f in a fixed set Φ

We allow some tree functions f, chosen from a set Φ of functions of type $\mathcal{IT} \to \mathcal{IT}$, to appear in the query. For example:

- *count(I)*, which yields a tree $n[\mathbf{0}]$, where n is the cardinality of the multiset I;
- *op(I)*, where *op* is a commutative, associative integer function with a neutral element; if all the pairs in I have a shape $n[I']$, where n is a natural number, then *op(I)* combines all the n's using the *op* operation obtaining the integer r, and returns $r[\mathbf{0}]$.

In practice, these functions would include user-defined functions written in an external programming language.

4.2   Query Semantics

The semantics of a query is defined in the following table. The interesting case is the one for *from $Q \vDash A$ select Q'*. In this case, the subquery Q' is evaluated once for each valuation ρ' that extends the input valuation ρ and such that $[\![Q]\!]_\rho \in [\![A]\!]_{\rho', \epsilon}$; all the resulting trees are then combined using the $\mid$ operator. The notation $\rho'^{\mathbf{V}'} \supseteq \rho^{\mathbf{V}}$ means that $\mathbf{V}' \supseteq \mathbf{V}$ and that $\rho'^{\mathbf{V}'}$ and $\rho^{\mathbf{V}}$ coincide over $\mathbf{V}$. For $F \in R^{\mathbf{V}} \to \mathcal{IT}$, we define $Par_{\rho^{\mathbf{V}} \in R^{\mathbf{V}}} \; F(\rho^{\mathbf{V}}) =_{def} \biguplus_{\rho^{\mathbf{V}} \in R^{\mathbf{V}}} F(\rho^{\mathbf{V}})$, where $\uplus$ is multiset union, namely the information tree operator that is used to interpret $\mid$.

Query semantics

$[\![\mathcal{X}]\!]_{\rho^{\mathbf{V}}}$	$= \rho^{\mathbf{V}}(\mathcal{X})$
$[\![\mathbf{0}]\!]_{\rho^{\mathbf{V}}}$	$= \mathbf{0}$
$[\![Q \mid Q']\!]_{\rho^{\mathbf{V}}}$	$= [\![Q]\!]_{\rho^{\mathbf{V}}} \mid [\![Q']\!]_{\rho^{\mathbf{V}}}$
$[\![m[Q]]\!]_{\rho^{\mathbf{V}}}$	$= m[[\![Q]\!]_{\rho^{\mathbf{V}}}]$
$[\![x[Q]]\!]_{\rho^{\mathbf{V}}}$	$= \rho^{\mathbf{V}}(x)[[\![Q]\!]_{\rho^{\mathbf{V}}}]$
$[\![f(Q)]\!]_{\rho^{\mathbf{V}}}$	$= f([\![Q]\!]_{\rho^{\mathbf{V}}})$
$[\![\textit{from } Q \vDash A \textit{ select } Q']\!]_{\rho^{\mathbf{V}}}$	
	$= Par_{\rho'^{\mathbf{V}'} \in \{\rho'^{\mathbf{V}'} \mid \mathbf{V}'=\mathbf{V} \cup FV(A), \; \rho'^{\mathbf{V}'} \supseteq \rho^{\mathbf{V}}, \; [\![Q]\!]_{\rho^{\mathbf{V}}} \in [\![A]\!]_{\rho'^{\mathbf{V}'}, \epsilon}\}} \; [\![Q']\!]_{\rho'^{\mathbf{V}'}}$

According to this semantics, the result of a query *from $Q' \vDash A$ select Q''* can be an infinite multiset. Therefore, in a nested query, the database Q' can be infinite, even if we start from a finite initial database. Obviously, one would not like this to happen in practice. One possible solution is to syntactically restrict Q' to a variable $\mathcal{X}$. Another solution is to have a static or dynamic check on the finiteness of the result; one such option is dicussed in Section 4.4.

4.3   Examples of Queries

We explain the query operators through examples. As in Section 1.1, we abbreviate a query

$$\text{from } Q \vDash \mathcal{A} \text{ select from } Q' \vDash \mathcal{A}' \text{ select } Q''$$

as

$$\text{from } Q \vDash \mathcal{A}, \; Q' \vDash \mathcal{A}' \text{ select } Q'' \; .$$

The database *ARTICLES* is the one given in Section 1.1.

All papers whose only author (if any) is *Cardelli* can be retrieved by the following query (where we use $\mathcal{X} \wedge \ldots$ as an alternative to a nested binder $\mathcal{X} \vDash \ldots$):

$$\text{from} \quad ARTICLES \vDash \; .article[\mathcal{X} \wedge \, !author[Cardelli]] \quad select \quad \mathcal{X}$$

We may use disjunction to find both *e-mails* and *emails* inside some *author* field.

$$\text{from} \quad ARTICLES \vDash \; .article[.author[.e\text{-}mail[\mathcal{X}] \vee .email[\mathcal{X}]]]$$
$$select \quad e\text{-}mail[\mathcal{X}]$$

Using recursion, we look for *e-mail* at the current level or, recursively, at any inner nesting level.[1]

$$\text{from} \quad ARTICLES \vDash \; \mu\xi. \; .e\text{-}mail[\mathcal{X}] \vee .email[\mathcal{X}] \vee \exists x. \; .x[\xi]$$
$$select \quad e\text{-}mail[\mathcal{X}]$$

The following query binds two label variables y and z to the label and the content of a field $y[z]$, where z is '*like %Ghelli%*' (*like* matches '%' to any substring). Recursion may be used to look for such fields at any depth.

$$\text{from} \quad ARTICLES \vDash \; .article[.y[z] \wedge z \text{ like } \%Ghelli\%]$$
$$select \quad found[label[y] \mid content[z]]$$

Query nesting allows us to restructure data. For example, the following query rearranges papers according to their year of publication: for each year $\mathcal{X}$ (outer *from*), it collects all the papers of that year. The composition $Year[\mathcal{X}] \mid \mathcal{Z}$ binds $\mathcal{Z}$ to all fields but the year; this way of collecting all the siblings except one is impossible, or difficult, in most other query languages.

$$\text{from} \quad ARTICLES \vDash .article[.Year[\mathcal{X}]]$$
$$select \quad publications\_by\_year[\; Year[\mathcal{X}]$$
$$\mid \; (from \; ARTICLES \vDash .article[Year[\mathcal{X}] \mid \mathcal{Z}]$$
$$select \; article[\mathcal{Z}] \;)$$
$$]$$

Relational-style join queries can be easily written in TQL either by matching the two data sources with two logical expressions that share some variables (equijoins) or by exploiting the comparison operators. Universal quantification can be expressed both on label and tree variables; more examples can be found in [17].

---

[1] When every $\mathcal{X}$ is inside an $m[]$ operator, like in this example, recursion is guaranteed to terminate, but we still have enough flexibility to express complex queries, such as queries that evaluate boolean circuits [22].

4.4   Safe Queries

It is well-known that disjunction, negation, and universal quantification create 'safety' problems in logic-based query languages. The same problems appear in our query language.

Consider for example the following query:

$$from \ \ db \vDash (author[\mathcal{X}] \vee autore[\mathcal{Y}]) \mid \mathbf{T} \ \ select \ \ author[\mathcal{X}] \mid autore[\mathcal{Y}]$$

Intuitively, every entry in db that is an *author* binds $\mathcal{X}$ but not $\mathcal{Y}$, and vice-versa for *autore* entries. Formally, both situations generate an infinite amount of valuations; for example, if $\rho(db) = author[m[]]$, then $\{\rho' \mid [\![db]\!]_\rho \in [\![\mathcal{A}]\!]_{\rho',\epsilon}\}$ is the infinite set

$$\{(db \mapsto author[m[]], \ \mathcal{X} \mapsto m[], \ \mathcal{Y} \mapsto I) \mid I \in \mathcal{IT}\} \ .$$

Negation creates a similar problem. Consider the following query.

$$from \ \ db \vDash \neg author[\mathcal{X}] \ \ select \ \ notauthor[\mathcal{X}]$$

Its binder, with respect to the above input valuation, generates the following infinite set of bindings:

$$\{(db \mapsto author[m[]], \ \mathcal{X} \mapsto I) \mid I \in \mathcal{IT}, I \neq m[]\}\} \ ,$$

and the query has the following infinite result:

$$\{notauthor[I] \mid I \in \mathcal{IT}, I \neq m[]\} \ .$$

These queries present two different, but related, problems:

- their semantics depends on the sets Λ and $\mathcal{IT}$ of all possible labels and information trees;
- their semantics is infinite.

We say that a query is safe when its semantics is finite. Query safety is known to be undecidable for the relational tuple calculus [4], and we suspect it is undecidable for our calculus too. However, as in relational calculi, it is not difficult to devise some sufficient syntactical conditions for safety, and to solve the non-safety problem by restricting the language to the syntactically safe queries. A different way to solve the problem is to allow unsafe queries, and to design a query processor for them. Our semantics accounts for unsafe queries, since it does not restrict the set of valuations generated by a binder to be finite, nor does it restrict the query answer to be finite.

5   Query Evaluation

In this section we define a query evaluation procedure. This procedure is really a refined semantics of queries, which is intermediate in abstraction between the semantics of Section 4.2 and an implementation algorithm. It is based on an algebra of trees and tables that is suggestive of realistic implementations, and may be seen as a specification of such implementations. In Pisa we have realized one such implementation, which is described in [23,8].

The query evaluation procedure is based on the manipulation of sets of valuations. These sets, unfortunately, may be infinite. For a real implementation, one must typically find a finite representation of infinite sets. Moreover, at the level of query manipulations, one would like to push negation to the leaves, introducing dualized logical operators as indicated in the first table in Section 3.2. These dualized operators also become part of an implementation. We do not deal here with the possible ways of finitely representing these infinite sets, or how to implement operators over them. In [23,8], though, we describe a technique for finitely representing sets of valuations in terms of a finite disjunction of a set of conjunctive constraints over the valuations, in the style of [20,21].

Any practical implementation of a query language is based on the use of particular efficiently implementable operators, such as relational join and union. We write our query evaluation procedure in this style as much as possible, but we naively use set complement to interpret negation, and we do not deal with dualized operators.

Our query evaluation procedure shows how to directly evaluate a query to a resulting set of trees. In database technology, instead, it is typical to translate the query into an expression over algebraic operators (which, in [23,8] and in XML Query Algebra [2], include also operators such as if-then-else, iteration and fixpoint). These expressions are first syntactically manipulated to enhance their performance, and finally evaluated. We ignore here issues of translation and manipulation of intermediate representations.

The core of the query evaluation problem is binder evaluation. A binder evaluation procedure takes an information tree I and a formula $\mathcal{A}$, that is used as a pattern for matching against I. The procedure takes also a valuation ρ and returns the set of all the valuations for the free variables of $\mathcal{A}$ that are not in the domain of ρ.

To describe the procedure, we first introduce an algebra over tables. Tables are sets of valuations (here called rows). We then use this algebra to define the evaluation procedure.

5.1   The Table Algebra

Let $\mathbf{V} = V_1, ..., V_n$ be a finite set of variables, where each variable V_i is either an information tree variable $\mathcal{X}$, whose universe $U(\mathcal{X})$ is defined to be the set $\mathcal{IT}$ of all information trees, or a label variable x, whose universe $U(x)$ is defined to be the set Λ of all labels.

A row with schema $\mathbf{V}$ is a function that maps each V_i to an element of $U(V_i)$; we use $\rho^{\mathbf{V}}$ as a meta-variable to range over rows with schema $\mathbf{V}$ (or just ρ when $\mathbf{V}$ is clear from context). A table with schema $\mathbf{V}$ is a set of rows over $\mathbf{V}$; we use $\mathcal{T}^{\mathbf{V}}$ for the set of tables with schema $\mathbf{V}$, and $R^{\mathbf{V}}$ as a meta-variable to range over $\mathcal{T}^{\mathbf{V}}$. When $\mathbf{V}$ is the empty set, we have only one row over $\mathbf{V}$, which we denote with ϵ; hence we have only two tables with schema $\emptyset$, the empty one, $\emptyset$, and the singleton, $\{\epsilon\}$. We use $\mathbf{1^V}$ to denote the largest table with schema $\mathbf{V}$, i.e. the set of all rows with schema $\mathbf{V}$.

The table algebra is based on five primitive operators: union, complement, product, projection, and restriction, each carrying schema information. They correspond to the standard operations of relational algebra.

The operators of table algebra:

$$R^{\mathbf{V}} \cup^{\mathbf{V}} R'^{\mathbf{V}} =_{def} R^{\mathbf{V}} \cup R'^{\mathbf{V}} \subseteq \mathbf{1^V}$$

$$Co^{\mathbf{V}}(R^{\mathbf{V}}) =_{def} \mathbf{1^V} \setminus R^{\mathbf{V}} \subseteq \mathbf{1^V}$$

$$\mathbf{V'} \cap \mathbf{V} = \emptyset: \quad R^{\mathbf{V}} \times^{\mathbf{V}, \mathbf{V'}} R'^{\mathbf{V'}} =_{def} \{\rho; \rho' \mid \rho \in R^{\mathbf{V}}, \ \rho' \in R'^{\mathbf{V'}}\} \subseteq \mathbf{1}^{\mathbf{V} \cup \mathbf{V'}}$$

$$\mathbf{V'} \subseteq \mathbf{V}: \quad \prod_{\mathbf{V'}}^{\mathbf{V}} R^{\mathbf{V}} =_{def} \{\rho' \mid \rho' \in \mathbf{1^{V'}}, \ \exists \rho \in R^{\mathbf{V}}. \ \rho \supseteq \rho'\} \subseteq \mathbf{1^{V'}}$$

$$FV(\eta, \eta') \subseteq \mathbf{V}: \quad \sigma_{\eta \sim \eta'}^{\mathbf{V}} R^{\mathbf{V}} =_{def} \{\rho \mid \rho \in R^{\mathbf{V}}, \ \rho_+^{\mathbf{V}}(\eta) \sim \rho_+^{\mathbf{V}}(\eta')\} \subseteq \mathbf{1^V}$$

The table union $R^{\mathbf{V}} \cup^{\mathbf{V}} R'^{\mathbf{V}}$ is defined as the set-theoretic union of two tables with the same schema $\mathbf{V}$.

The table complement $Co^{\mathbf{V}}(R^{\mathbf{V}})$ is defined as the set-theoretic difference $\mathbf{1^V} \setminus R^{\mathbf{V}}$.

If $R^{\mathbf{V}}$ and $R'^{\mathbf{V'}}$ are two tables whose schemas are disjoint, their table cartesian product $R^{\mathbf{V}} \times^{\mathbf{V}, \mathbf{V'}} R'^{\mathbf{V'}}$ is defined as the set containing all rows obtained by concatenating each row of $R^{\mathbf{V}}$ with each row of $R'^{\mathbf{V'}}$. The result has schema $\mathbf{V} \cup \mathbf{V'}$.

If $\mathbf{V'}$ is a subset of $\mathbf{V}$, the projection $\prod_{\mathbf{V'}}^{\mathbf{V}} R^{\mathbf{V}}$ is defined as the set of all rows in $R^{\mathbf{V}}$ restricted to the variables in $\mathbf{V'}$.

Let $\rho_+^{\mathbf{V}}$ be the function that coincides with $\rho^{\mathbf{V}}$ over $\mathbf{V}$, and maps every $\eta \notin \mathbf{V}$ to η. If $FV(\eta, \eta') \subseteq \mathbf{V}$, then the restriction $\sigma_{\eta \sim \eta'}^{\mathbf{V}} R^{\mathbf{V}}$ is the set

$$\{\rho^{\mathbf{V}} \mid \rho^{\mathbf{V}} \in R^{\mathbf{V}} \ and \ \rho_+^{\mathbf{V}}(\eta) \sim \rho_+^{\mathbf{V}}(\eta')\} \ ,$$

where $\sim$ is a label comparison operator, as in Section 3.

We will also use some derived operators, defined in the following table.

Table algebra, derived operators:

$$\mathbf{V} \subseteq \mathbf{V'}: Ext_{\mathbf{V'}}^{\mathbf{V}}(R^{\mathbf{V}}) =_{def} R^{\mathbf{V}} \times^{\mathbf{V}, \mathbf{V'} \setminus \mathbf{V}} \mathbf{1}^{\mathbf{V'} \setminus \mathbf{V}} \subseteq \mathbf{1^{V'}}$$

$$R^{\mathbf{V}} \cap^{\mathbf{V}} R'^{\mathbf{V}} =_{def} Co^{\mathbf{V}}(Co^{\mathbf{V}}(R^{\mathbf{V}}) \cup^{\mathbf{V}} Co^{\mathbf{V}}(R'^{\mathbf{V}})) \subseteq \mathbf{1^V}$$

$$R^{\mathbf{V}} \bowtie^{\mathbf{V}, \mathbf{V'}} R'^{\mathbf{V'}} =_{def} Ext_{\mathbf{V} \cup \mathbf{V'}}^{\mathbf{V}}(R^{\mathbf{V}}) \cap^{\mathbf{V} \cup \mathbf{V'}} Ext_{\mathbf{V} \cup \mathbf{V'}}^{\mathbf{V'}}(R'^{\mathbf{V'}}) \subseteq \mathbf{1}^{\mathbf{V} \cup \mathbf{V'}}$$

$$R^{\mathbf{V}} \oplus^{\mathbf{V}, \mathbf{V'}} R'^{\mathbf{V'}} =_{def} Ext_{\mathbf{V} \cup \mathbf{V'}}^{\mathbf{V}}(R^{\mathbf{V}}) \cup^{\mathbf{V} \cup \mathbf{V'}} Ext_{\mathbf{V} \cup \mathbf{V'}}^{\mathbf{V'}}(R'^{\mathbf{V'}}) \subseteq \mathbf{1}^{\mathbf{V} \cup \mathbf{V'}}$$

$$\mathbf{V'} \subseteq \mathbf{V}: \coprod_{\mathbf{V'}}^{\mathbf{V}} R^{\mathbf{V}} =_{def} Co^{\mathbf{V'}}(\prod_{\mathbf{V'}}^{\mathbf{V}} Co^{\mathbf{V}}(R^{\mathbf{V}})) \subseteq \mathbf{1^{V'}}$$

The operator $R^{\mathbf{V}} \bowtie^{\mathbf{V}, \mathbf{V'}} R'^{\mathbf{V'}}$ is well-known in the database field. It is called 'natural join', and can be also defined as follows: the set containing all rows obtained by concatenating each row ρ in $R^{\mathbf{V}}$ with those rows ρ' in $R'^{\mathbf{V'}}$ such that ρ and ρ' coincide over $\mathbf{V} \cap \mathbf{V'}$. One important property of natural join is that it always yields finite tables when is applied to finite tables, even if its definition uses the extension operator. Moreover, the optimization of join has been extensively studied; for this reason we will use this operator, rather than extension plus intersection, in the definition of our query evaluation procedure.

Outer union $R^{\mathbf{V}} \oplus^{\mathbf{V},\mathbf{V}'} R'^{\mathbf{V}'}$ and co-projection $\coprod_{\mathbf{V}'}^{\mathbf{V}} R^{\mathbf{V}}$ are useful for treating the dualized operators.

Outer union is dual to join, in the following sense:

$$R^{\mathbf{V}} \oplus^{\mathbf{V},\mathbf{V}'} R'^{\mathbf{V}'} = Co^{\mathbf{V} \cup \mathbf{V}'}(Co^{\mathbf{V}}(R^{\mathbf{V}}) \bowtie^{\mathbf{V},\mathbf{V}'} Co^{\mathbf{V}'}(R'^{\mathbf{V}'}))$$

Projection and co-projection are both left-inverse of extension:

$$\prod_{\mathbf{V}}^{\mathbf{V}'}(Ext_{\mathbf{V}'}^{\mathbf{V}}(R^{\mathbf{V}})) = R^{\mathbf{V}}$$
$$\coprod_{\mathbf{V}}^{\mathbf{V}'}(Ext_{\mathbf{V}'}^{\mathbf{V}}(R^{\mathbf{V}})) = R^{\mathbf{V}}$$

However, they represent two different ways of right-inverting extension:

$$\prod_{\mathbf{V}'}^{\mathbf{V}} R^{\mathbf{V}} = \bigcap \{ R'^{\mathbf{V}'} \mid Ext_{\mathbf{V}}^{\mathbf{V}'}(R'^{\mathbf{V}'}) \supseteq R^{\mathbf{V}} \}$$
$$\coprod_{\mathbf{V}'}^{\mathbf{V}} R^{\mathbf{V}} = \bigcup \{ R'^{\mathbf{V}'} \mid Ext_{\mathbf{V}}^{\mathbf{V}'}(R'^{\mathbf{V}'}) \subseteq R^{\mathbf{V}} \}$$

5.2   Query Evaluation

We specify here an evaluation procedure $\mathcal{Q}(Q)_\rho$ that, given a query Q and a row ρ that specifies a value for each free variable of Q, evaluates the corresponding information tree. A closed query *"from $Q \vDash \mathcal{A}$ select Q'"* is evaluated by first evaluating Q to an information tree I. The pair $I, \mathcal{A}$ is then evaluated to yield a table $R^{\mathbf{V}}$ whose schema contains all the free variables in $\mathcal{A}$. Finally, Q' is evaluated once for each row ρ of $R^{\mathbf{V}}$; all the resulting information trees are combined using $|$, to obtain the query result. This process is expressed in the last case of the table below.

The first part of the table describes how a quadruple $I, \mathcal{A}, \rho^{\mathbf{V}}, \gamma$ is evaluated by a binder evaluation procedure $\mathcal{B}$ to return a table with schema $\mathcal{S}(\mathcal{A}, \mathbf{V}, \hat{\gamma})$. The schema function $\mathcal{S}$ is specified in the table that follows, and enjoys the property that $\mathcal{S}(\mathcal{A}, \mathbf{V}, \hat{\epsilon}) = FV(\mathcal{A}) \setminus \mathbf{V}$. Here γ is an environment that maps recursion variables ξ to functions from information trees to tables. We assume that γ is always given together with a schema $\hat{\gamma}$ mapping recursion variables to sets of variables $\mathbf{V}$, such that $\gamma(\xi) \in \mathcal{IT} \to \mathcal{T}^{\hat{\gamma}(\xi)}$.

The notation $\{(x \mapsto n)\}$ represents a table that contains only the row that maps x to n, and similarly for $\{(\mathcal{X} \mapsto I)\}$.

Binder and query evaluation

$\mathcal{B}(I, \mathbf{0})_{\rho^{\mathbf{V}}, \gamma}$	$=$	if $I = \mathbf{0}$ then $\{\epsilon\}$ else $\emptyset$	
$\mathcal{B}(I, n[\mathcal{A}])_{\rho^{\mathbf{V}}, \gamma}$	$=$	if $I = n[I']$ then $\mathcal{B}(I', \mathcal{A})_{\rho^{\mathbf{V}}, \gamma}$ else $\emptyset$	
$\mathcal{B}(I, x[\mathcal{A}])_{\rho^{\mathbf{V}}, \gamma}$	$=$	$\mathcal{B}(I, \rho^{\mathbf{V}}(x)[\mathcal{A}])_{\rho^{\mathbf{V}}, \gamma}$	if $x \in \mathbf{V}$
$\mathcal{B}(I, x[\mathcal{A}])_{\rho^{\mathbf{V}}, \gamma}$	$=$		if $x \notin \mathbf{V}$

$$\text{if } I = n[I'] \text{ then } \{(x \mapsto n)\} \bowtie^{\{x\}, \, \mathcal{S}(\mathcal{A}, \mathbf{V}, \hat{\gamma})} \mathcal{B}(I', \mathcal{A})_{\rho\mathbf{v}, \gamma} \text{ else } \emptyset$$

$$\mathcal{B}(I, \mathcal{A} \mid \mathcal{B})_{\rho\mathbf{v}, \gamma} =$$
$$\bigcup_{I', I'' \in \{I', I'' \mid I' \mid I'' = I\}}^{\mathcal{S}(\mathcal{A} \mid \mathcal{B}, \mathbf{V}, \hat{\gamma})} (\mathcal{B}(I', \mathcal{A})_{\rho\mathbf{v}, \gamma} \bowtie^{\mathcal{S}(\mathcal{A}, \mathbf{V}, \hat{\gamma}), \, \mathcal{S}(\mathcal{B}, \mathbf{V}, \hat{\gamma})} \mathcal{B}(I'', \mathcal{B})_{\rho\mathbf{v}, \gamma})$$

$$\mathcal{B}(I, \mathbf{T})_{\rho\mathbf{v}, \gamma} \quad = \quad \{\epsilon\}$$

$$\mathcal{B}(I, \neg \mathcal{A})_{\rho\mathbf{v}, \gamma} \quad = \quad Co^{\mathcal{S}(\mathcal{A}, \mathbf{V}, \hat{\gamma})}(\mathcal{B}(I, \mathcal{A})_{\rho\mathbf{v}, \gamma})$$

$$\mathcal{B}(I, \mathcal{A} \wedge \mathcal{B})_{\rho\mathbf{v}, \gamma} = \mathcal{B}(I, \mathcal{A})_{\rho\mathbf{v}, \gamma} \bowtie^{\mathcal{S}(\mathcal{A}, \mathbf{V}, \hat{\gamma}), \, \mathcal{S}(\mathcal{B}, \mathbf{V}, \hat{\gamma})} \mathcal{B}(I, \mathcal{B})_{\rho\mathbf{v}, \gamma}$$

$$\mathcal{B}(I, \mathcal{X})_{\rho\mathbf{v}, \gamma} \quad = \quad \text{if } I = \rho^{\mathbf{V}}(\mathcal{X}) \text{ then } \{\epsilon\} \text{ else } \emptyset \qquad\qquad \text{if } \mathcal{X} \in \mathbf{V}$$

$$\mathcal{B}(I, \mathcal{X})_{\rho\mathbf{v}, \gamma} \quad = \quad \{(\mathcal{X} \mapsto I)\} \qquad\qquad\qquad\qquad\qquad \text{if } \mathcal{X} \notin \mathbf{V}$$

$$\mathcal{B}(I, \exists \mathcal{X}. \, \mathcal{A})_{\rho\mathbf{v}, \gamma} = \prod_{\mathcal{S}(\mathcal{A}, \mathbf{V}, \hat{\gamma}) \backslash \{\mathcal{X}\}}^{\mathcal{S}(\mathcal{A}, \mathbf{V}, \hat{\gamma})} \mathcal{B}(I, \mathcal{A})_{\rho\mathbf{v}, \gamma}$$

$$\mathcal{B}(I, \exists x. \, \mathcal{A})_{\rho\mathbf{v}, \gamma} = \prod_{\mathcal{S}(\mathcal{A}, \mathbf{V}, \hat{\gamma}) \backslash \{x\}}^{\mathcal{S}(\mathcal{A}, \mathbf{V}, \hat{\gamma})} \mathcal{B}(I, \mathcal{A})_{\rho\mathbf{v}, \gamma}$$

$$\mathcal{B}(I, \eta \sim \eta')_{\rho\mathbf{v}, \gamma} = \sigma_{\rho_+^{\mathbf{V}}(\eta) \sim \rho_+^{\mathbf{V}}(\eta')}^{\mathcal{S}(\eta \sim \eta', \mathbf{V}, \hat{\gamma})} \mathbf{1}^{\mathcal{S}(\eta \sim \eta', \mathbf{V}, \hat{\gamma})}$$

$$\mathcal{B}(I, \mu\xi.\mathcal{A})_{\rho\mathbf{v}, \gamma} = Fix(\lambda M \in \mathcal{IT} \to \mathcal{T}^{\mathcal{S}(\mu\xi.\mathcal{A}, \mathbf{V}, \hat{\gamma})}.\lambda \mathcal{Y}.\mathcal{B}(\mathcal{Y}, \mathcal{A})_{\rho\mathbf{v}, \gamma[\xi \mapsto M]})(I)$$

$$\mathcal{B}(I, \xi)_{\rho\mathbf{v}, \gamma} \quad = \quad \gamma(\xi)(I)$$

$$\mathcal{Q}(\mathcal{X})_{\rho\mathbf{v}} \qquad\qquad\qquad = \rho^{\mathbf{V}}(\mathcal{X})$$

$$\mathcal{Q}(\mathbf{0})_{\rho\mathbf{v}} \qquad\qquad\qquad = \mathbf{0}$$

$$\mathcal{Q}(Q \mid Q')_{\rho\mathbf{v}} \qquad\qquad = \mathcal{Q}(Q)_{\rho\mathbf{v}} \mid \mathcal{Q}(Q')_{\rho\mathbf{v}}$$

$$\mathcal{Q}(m[Q])_{\rho\mathbf{v}} \qquad\qquad = m[\mathcal{Q}(Q)_{\rho\mathbf{v}}]$$

$$\mathcal{Q}(x[Q])_{\rho\mathbf{v}} \qquad\qquad = \rho^{\mathbf{V}}(x)[\mathcal{Q}(Q)_{\rho\mathbf{v}}]$$

$$\mathcal{Q}(f(Q))_{\rho\mathbf{v}} \qquad\qquad = f(\mathcal{Q}(Q)_{\rho\mathbf{v}})$$

$$\mathcal{Q}(\textit{from } Q \vDash \mathcal{A} \textit{ select } Q')_{\rho\mathbf{v}} = \text{let } I = \mathcal{Q}(Q)_{\rho\mathbf{v}} \text{ and } R^{FV(\mathcal{A}) \backslash \mathbf{V}} = \mathcal{B}(I, \mathcal{A})_{\rho\mathbf{v}, \epsilon}$$
$$\text{in } Par_{\rho' \in R^{FV(\mathcal{A}) \backslash \mathbf{V}}} \, \mathcal{Q}(Q')_{(\rho\mathbf{v} ; \rho')}$$

The schema function $\mathcal{S}$

$$\mathcal{S}(\mathbf{0}, \mathbf{V}, \Gamma) \quad = \quad \emptyset$$

$$\mathcal{S}(n[\mathcal{A}], \mathbf{V}, \Gamma) \quad = \quad \mathcal{S}(\mathcal{A}, \mathbf{V}, \Gamma)$$

$$\mathcal{S}(x[\mathcal{A}], \mathbf{V}, \Gamma) \quad = \quad \mathcal{S}(\mathcal{A}, \mathbf{V}, \Gamma) \cup (\{x\} \backslash \mathbf{V})$$

$$\mathcal{S}(\mathcal{A} \mid \mathcal{B}, \mathbf{V}, \Gamma) \quad = \quad \mathcal{S}(\mathcal{A}, \mathbf{V}, \Gamma) \cup \mathcal{S}(\mathcal{B}, \mathbf{V}, \Gamma)$$

$$\mathcal{S}(\mathbf{T}, \mathbf{V}, \Gamma) \quad = \quad \emptyset$$

$$\mathcal{S}(\neg \mathcal{A}, \mathbf{V}, \Gamma) \quad = \quad \mathcal{S}(\mathcal{A}, \mathbf{V}, \Gamma)$$

$$\mathcal{S}(\mathcal{A} \wedge \mathcal{B}, \mathbf{V}, \Gamma) = \mathcal{S}(\mathcal{A}, \mathbf{V}, \Gamma) \cup \mathcal{S}(\mathcal{B}, \mathbf{V}, \Gamma)$$

$$\mathcal{S}(\mathcal{X}, \mathbf{V}, \Gamma) \quad = \quad \{\mathcal{X}\} \backslash \mathbf{V}$$

$$\mathcal{S}(\exists \mathcal{X}. \, \mathcal{A}, \mathbf{V}, \Gamma) = \mathcal{S}(\mathcal{A}, \mathbf{V}, \Gamma) \backslash \{\mathcal{X}\}$$

$$\mathcal{S}(\exists x. \, \mathcal{A}, \mathbf{V}, \Gamma) = \mathcal{S}(\mathcal{A}, \mathbf{V}, \Gamma) \backslash \{x\}$$

$$\mathcal{S}(\eta \sim \eta', \mathbf{V}, \Gamma) = FV(\eta, \eta') \backslash \mathbf{V}$$

$$\mathcal{S}(\mu\xi.\mathcal{A}, \mathbf{V}, \Gamma) \quad = \quad \mathcal{S}(\mathcal{A}, \mathbf{V}, \Gamma[\xi \mapsto \emptyset])$$

$$\mathcal{S}(\xi, \mathbf{V}, \Gamma) \quad = \quad \Gamma(\xi)$$

Since the rule for comparisons $\eta \sim \eta'$ is subtle, we expand here some special cases.

Some special cases of comparison evaluation

$$\mathcal{B}(I, x \sim x')_{\rho \mathbf{V}, \gamma} = \sigma^{\{x, x'\}}_{x \sim x'} \mathbf{1}^{\{x, x'\}} \qquad \text{if } x \notin \mathbf{V}, x' \notin \mathbf{V}$$

$$\mathcal{B}(I, x \sim x')_{\rho \mathbf{V}, \gamma} = \sigma^{\{x\}}_{x \sim \rho \mathbf{V}(x')} \mathbf{1}^{\{x\}} \qquad \text{if } x \notin \mathbf{V}, x' \in \mathbf{V}$$

$$\mathcal{B}(I, x \sim x')_{\rho \mathbf{V}, \gamma} = \sigma^{\emptyset}_{\rho \mathbf{V}(x) \sim \rho \mathbf{V}(x')} \mathbf{1}^{\emptyset} \qquad \text{if } x \in \mathbf{V}, x' \in \mathbf{V}$$

$$\mathcal{B}(I, x \sim n)_{\rho \mathbf{V}, \gamma} = \sigma^{\{x\}}_{x \sim n} \mathbf{1}^{\{x\}} \qquad \text{if } x \notin \mathbf{V}$$

$$\mathcal{B}(I, n \sim n')_{\rho \mathbf{V}, \gamma} = \sigma^{\emptyset}_{n \sim n'} \mathbf{1}^{\emptyset} \quad (\textit{i.e. if } n \sim n' \textit{ then } \{\epsilon\} \textit{ else } \emptyset)$$

Lemma 1.

$$\mathcal{S}(\mu \xi. \mathcal{A}, \mathbf{V}, \hat{\gamma}) = \mathcal{S}(\mathcal{A}, \mathbf{V}, \hat{\gamma}[\xi \mapsto \mathcal{S}(\mu \xi. \mathcal{A}, \mathbf{V}, \hat{\gamma})])$$
$$\mathcal{B}(I, \mathcal{A})_{\rho \mathbf{V}, \gamma} \in \mathcal{T}^{\mathcal{S}(\mathcal{A}, \mathbf{V}, \hat{\gamma})}.$$

Lemma 2. *Let $\mathcal{A}$ be a formula, $\mathbf{V}$ be a set of variables, let Ξ be a set $\{\xi_i\}^{i \in I}$ of recursion variables that includes those that are free in $\mathcal{A}$, and let γ be a function defined over Ξ such that, for every ξ_i, $\gamma(\xi_i) \in \mathcal{IT} \to \mathcal{T}^{\hat{\gamma}(\xi_i)}$, where $\hat{\gamma}(\xi_i)$ is disjoint from $\mathbf{V}$. then:*

$$\forall \rho \in \mathbf{1}^{\mathbf{V}}, I \in \mathcal{IT}. \; \mathcal{B}(I, \mathcal{A})_{\rho \gamma} = \{\rho' \mid \rho' \in \mathbf{1}^{\mathcal{S}(\mathcal{A}, \mathbf{V}, \hat{\gamma})}, \; I \in [\![\mathcal{A}]\!]_{(\rho'; \rho), \bar{\gamma}(\rho')}\}$$

where $\bar{\gamma}(\rho) = \lambda \xi : \Xi. \{I \mid \rho \in \gamma(\xi)(I)\}$.

The following proposition states that the query evaluation procedure is equivalent to the query semantics of Section 4.2. The proof uses Lemma 2 in the from-select case.

Proposition 1. $\forall Q, \; \mathbf{V} \supseteq FV(Q), \; \rho^{\mathbf{V}}. \; \mathcal{Q}(Q)_{\rho \mathbf{V}} = [\![Q]\!]_{\rho \mathbf{V}}$

6   Conclusions and Future Directions

We have defined a query language that operates on information represented as unordered trees. One can take different views of how information should be represented. For example as ordered trees, as in XML, or as unordered graphs, as in semistructured data. We believe that each choice of representation would lead to a (slightly different) logic and a query language along the lines described here. We are currently looking at some of these options.

There are currently many proposals for regular pattern languages for semistructured data, many having in common the desire to describe tree shapes and not just linear paths. Given the expressive power of general recursive formulas $\mu \xi. \mathcal{A}$, we believe we can capture many such proposals, even though an important part of those proposals is to describe efficient matching techniques.

In this study we have exploited a subset of the ambient logic. The ambient logic, and the calculus, also offer operators to specify and perform tree updates [7]. Possible connections with semistructured data updates should be explored.

An implementation of TQL is currently being carried out, based on the implementation model we described. The current prototype can be used to query XML documents accessible through files or through web servers.

Acknowledgements. Andrew D. Gordon contributed to this work with many useful suggestions. Giorgio Ghelli was partially supported by "Ministero dell'Università e della Ricerca Scientifica e Tecnologica", project DATA-X, by Microsoft Research, and by the E.U. workgroup APPSEM.

References

1. XML schema. Available from http://www.w3c.org, 2000.
2. XML query. Available from http://www.w3c.org, 2001.
3. S. Abiteboul, P. Buneman, and D. Suciu. *Data on the WEB: From Relations to Semistructured Data and XML*. Morgan Kaufmann, San Mateo, CA, October 1999.
4. S. Abiteboul, R. Hull, and V. Vianu. *Foundations of Databases*. Addison-Wesley, Reading, MA, 1995.
5. Serge Abiteboul, Dallan Quass, Jason McHugh, Jennifer Widom, and Janet L. Wiener. The Lorel query language for semistructured data. *International Journal on Digital Libraries*, 1(1):68–88, 1997.
6. P. Buneman, S. B. Davidson, G. G. Hillebrand, and D. Suciu. A query language and optimization techniques for unstructured data. In *Proc. of the 1996 ACM SIGMOD International Conference on Management of Data (SIGMOD), Montreal, Quebec, Canada*, pages 505–516, 4–6 June 1996. *SIGMOD Record* 25(2), June 1996.
7. L. Cardelli. Semistructured computation. In *Proc. of the Seventh Intl. Workshop on Data Base Programming Languages (DBPL)*, 1999.
8. L. Cardelli and G. Ghelli. Evaluation of TQL queries. Available from http://www.di.unipi.it/~ghelli/papers.html, 2001.
9. L. Cardelli and A. D. Gordon. Mobile ambients. In *Proceedings FoSSaCS'98*, volume 1378 of *LNCS*, pages 140–155. Springer-Verlag, 1998. Accepted for publication in *Theoretical Computer Science*.
10. L. Cardelli and A. D. Gordon. Anytime, anywhere: Modal logics for mobile ambients. In *Proc. of Principles of Programming Languages (POPL)*. ACM Press, January 2000.
11. D. Chamberlin, J. Robie, and D. Florescu. Quilt: An XML query language for heterogeneous data sources. In *Proc. of Workshop on the Web and Data Bases (WebDB)*, 2000.
12. Sophie Cluet, Claude Delobel, Jérôme Siméon, and Katarzyna Smaga. Your mediators need data conversion. In *Proc. of ACM SIGMOD International Conference on Management of Data (SIGMOD)*, 1998.
13. A. Deutsch, D. Florescu M. Fernandez, A. Levy, and D. Suciu. A query language for XML. In *Proc. of the Eighth International World Wide Web Conference*, 1999.
14. M. Fernandez, D. Florescu, A. Levy, and D. Suciu. A query language and processor for a web-site management system. In *Proc. of Workshop on Management of Semistructured Data, Tucson*, 1997.

15. Mary Fernandez, Daniela Florescu, Jaewoo Kang, Alon Levy, and Dan Suciu. Catching the boat with Strudel: experiences with a web-site management system. In *Proc. of ACM SIGMOD International Conference on Management of Data (SIGMOD)*, pages 414–425, 1998.

16. Mary Fernandez, J. Siméon, P. Wadler, S. Cluet, A. Deutsch, D. Florescu, A. Levy, D. Maier, J. McHugh, J. Robie, D. Suciu, and J. Widom. XML query languages: Experiences and exemplars. Available from http://www-db.research.bell-labs.com/user/simeon/xquery.ps, 1999.

17. G. Ghelli. TQL as an XML query language. Available from http://www.di.unipi.it/~ghelli/papers.html, 2001.

18. R. Goldman, J. McHugh, and J. Widom. From semistructured data to XML: Migrating the lore data model and query language. In *Proc. of Workshop on the Web and Data Bases (WebDB)*, pages 25–30, 1999.

19. B.C. Pierce H. Hosoya. XDuce: A typed XML processing language (preliminary report). In *Proc. of Workshop on the Web and Data Bases (WebDB)*, 2000.

20. P. Kanellakis. Tutorial: Constraint programming and database languages. In *Proc. of the 14th Symposium on Principles of Database Systems (PODS), San Jose, California*, pages 46–53. ACM Press, 1995.

21. G. Kuper, L. Libkin, and J. Paredaens. *Constraint Databases*. Springer-Verlag, Berlin, 2000.

22. F. Neven and T. Schwentick. Expressive and efficient pattern languages for tree-structured data. In *Proc. of the 19th Symposium on Principles of Database Systems (PODS)*, 2000.

23. F. Pantaleo. Realizzazione di un linguaggio di interrogazione per XML. Tesi di Laurea del Dipartimento di Informatica dell'Università di Pisa, 2000.

24. Y. Papakonstantinou, H.G. Molina, and J. Widom. Object exchange across heterogeneous information sources. *Proc. of the eleventh IEEE Int. Conference on Data Engineering, Birmingham, England*, pages 251–260, 1996.

Probabilistic Polynomial-Time Process Calculus and Security Protocol Analysis

John C. Mitchell

Stanford University
Stanford, CA 94305
http://www.stanford.edu/~jcm

Abstract. We propose a formal framework for analyzing security protocols. This framework, which differs from previous logical methods based on the Dolev-Yao model, is based on a process calculus that captures probabilistic polynomial time. Protocols are written in a restricted form of π-calculus and security is expressed as a form or *observational equivalence*, a standard relation from programming language theory that involves quantifying over possible additional processes that might interact with the protocol. Using an asymptotic notion of probabilistic equivalence, we may relate observational equivalence to polynomial-time statistical tests. Several example protocols have been analyzed. We believe that this framework offers the potential to codify and automate realistic forms of protocol analysis. In addition, our work raises some foundational problems for reasoning about probabilistic programs and systems.

1 Summary

This invited lecture for ESOP '01 will describe an approach to security protocol analysis based on a probabilistic polynomial-time process calculus and asymptotic observational equivalence. The work has been carried out in collaboration with P. Lincoln, M. Mitchell, A. Scedrov, A. Ramanathan, and V. Teague. Some of the basic ideas are described in [LMMS98], with a description of a simplified form of the process calculus appearing in [MMS98] and further example protocols considered in [LMMS99]. The closest technical precursor is the Abadi and Gordon spi-calculus [AG99,AG98] which uses observational equivalence and channel abstraction but does not involve probability or computational complexity bounds; subsequent related work is cited in [AF01], for example. Prior work on CSP and security protocols, e.g., [Ros95,Sch96], also uses process calculus and security specifications in the form of equivalence or related approximation orderings on processes. Slides from this talk will be available on the author's web site at http://www.stanford.edu/~jcm.

2 Protocols

Protocols based on cryptographic primitives are commonly used to protect access to computer systems and to protect transactions over the Internet. Two well-known examples are the Kerberos authentication scheme [KNT94,KN93], used

D. Sands (Ed.): ESOP 2001, LNCS 2028, pp. 23–29, 2001.

to manage encrypted passwords, and the Secure Sockets Layer [FKK96], used by Internet browsers and servers to carry out secure internet transactions. In recent years, a variety of methods have developed for analyzing and reasoning about such protocols. These approaches include specialized logics such as BAN logic [BAN89], special-purpose tools designed for cryptographic protocol analysis [KMM94], and theorem proving [Pau97a,Pau97b] and model-checking methods using general purpose tools [Low96,Mea96,MMS97,Ros95,Sch96].

Although there are many differences among existing formal approaches, most use the same basic model of adversary capabilities. This model, apparently derived from [DY83] and views expressed in [NS78], treats cryptographic operations as "black-box" primitives. For example, encryption is generally considered a primitive operation, with plaintext and ciphertext treated as atomic data that cannot be decomposed into sequences of bits. In most uses of this model, as explained in [MMS97,Pau97a,Sch96], there are specific rules for how an adversary can learn new information. For example, if the decryption key is sent over the network "in the clear", it can be learned by the adversary. However, it is not possible for the adversary to learn the plaintext of an encrypted message unless the entire decryption key has already been learned. Generally, the adversary is treated as a nondeterministic process that may attempt any possible attack, and a protocol is considered secure if no possible interleaving of actions results in a security breach. The two basic assumptions of this model, perfect cryptography and nondeterministic adversary, provide an idealized setting in which protocol analysis becomes relatively tractable.

While there have been significant accomplishments using this model, the assumptions inherent in the standard model also make it possible to "verify" protocols that are in fact susceptible to attack. For example, the model does not allow the adversary to learn a decryption key by guessing, since then some nondeterministic execution would allow a correct guess, and all protocols relying on encryption would be broken. However, in some real cases, adversaries can learn some bits of a key by statistical analysis, and can then exhaustively search the remaining (smaller) portion of the key space. Such an attack is simply not considered by the model described above, since it requires both knowledge of the particular encryption function involved and also the use of probabilistic methods.

Our goal is to develop an analysis framework that can be used to explore interactions between protocols and cryptographic primitives. We are also interested in devising specifications of cryptographic primitives such as oblivious transfer and selective decommittment. Our framework uses a language for defining communicating probabilistic polynomial-time processes [MMS98]. We restrict processes to probabilistic polynomial time since the adversary is represented by an arbitrary context, written in the process calculus. Limiting the running time of an adversary allows us to lift other restrictions on the behavior of an adversary. Specifically, an adversary may send randomly chosen messages, or perform arbitrary probabilistic polynomial-time computation on messages overheard on the network. In addition, we treat messages as sequences of bits and allow specific encryption functions such as RSA or DES to be written in full as part of a protocol. An important feature of this framework is that we can analyze probabilistic as well as deterministic encryption functions and protocols. Without a probabilistic framework, it would not be possible to analyze an encryption function such as ElGamal [ElG85], for example, for which a single plaintext may have more than one ciphertext.

Security properties of a protocol P may be formulated by writing an idealized protocol Q so that, intuitively, for any adversary M, the interactions between M and P have the same observable behavior as the interactions between M and Q. This intuitive description may be formalized by using observational equivalence (also called observational congruence), a standard notion from the study of programming languages. Namely, two processes (such as two protocols) P and Q are observationally equivalent, written $P \simeq Q$, if any program $\mathcal{C}[P]$ containing P has the same observable behavior as the program $\mathcal{C}[Q]$ with Q replacing P. The reason observational equivalence is applicable to security analysis is that it involves quantifying over all possible adversaries, represented by the environments, that might interact with the protocol participants. In our asymptotic formulation, observational equivalence between probabilistic polynomial-time processes coincides with the traditional notion of indistinguishability by polynomial-time statistical tests [Lub96,Yao82], a standard way of characterizing cryptographically strong pseudo-random number generators.

The remainder of this short document presents the key definitions, as reference for the author's invited talk.

3   Process Calculus

The protocol language consists of a set of *terms*, or sequential expressions that do not perform any communication, and *processes*, which can communicate with one another. The process portion of the language is a restriction of standard π-calculus [MPW92]. All computation done by a process is expressed using terms. Since our goal is to model probabilistic polynomial-time adversaries by quantifying over processes definable in our language, it is essential that all functions definable by terms lie in probabilistic polynomial time. Although we use pseudo-code to write terms in this paper, we have developed an applied, simply-typed lambda calculus which exactly captures the probabilistic polynomial-time terms [MMS98].

The syntax of processes is given by the following grammar:

$$
\begin{array}{lll}
P ::= & \mathbf{0} & \text{(termination)} \\
& \nu_{c_{q(|n|)}}.(P) & \text{(private channel)} \\
& c_{q(|n|)}(x).P & \text{(input)} \\
& c_{q(|n|)}\langle T \rangle & \text{(output)} \\
& [T = T].P & \text{(match)} \\
& P \mid P & \text{(parallel composition)} \\
& !_{q(|n|)}.P & \text{($q(|n|)$-fold replication)}
\end{array}
$$

Polynomials appear explicitly in the syntax of processes in two places, in channel names and in replication. In a channel name $c_{q(|n|)}$, the polynomial

$q(|n|)$ associated with the channel c indicates that for some value n of the security parameter, channel c can carry values of $q(|n|)$ bits or fewer. This restriction on the size of natural numbers that are communicated from one process to another is needed to maintain the polynomial-time restriction on process computations. Replication $!_{q(|n|)}.P$ results in $q(|n|)$ copies of process P, where n is again the security parameter. For simplicity, after fixing n when we evaluate a process P, we replace all subexpressions of P of the form $!_{q(|n|)}.R$ with $q(|n|)$ copies of R in parallel. We also assume that all channel names and variable names are α-renamed apart.

The operational semantics of this process calculus is fairly intricate, due to probabilistic considerations and the desire to keep communication on a private channel from biasing the probabilities associated with externally observable communication on public channels. In brief, executing a process step begins with *outer evaluation* of any terms. In a process $[T_1 = T_2].P$, for example, we evaluate terms T_1 and T_2 before possibly performing any communication inside P. Similarly, execution of $c_{q(|n|)}\langle T\rangle$ begins with the evaluation of the term T, and execution of $P\,|\,Q$ with the outer-evaluation of both P and Q.

Once a process is outer-evaluated, a set of eligible communication pairs is selected. The set of *schedulable processes* $S(P)$ is defined inductively by

$$
\begin{aligned}
S(\mathbf{0}) &= \emptyset \\
S(\nu_{c_{p(|n|)}}.(Q)) &= S(Q) \\
S(c_{p(|n|)}(x).Q) &= \{c_{p(|n|)}(x).Q\} \\
S(c_{p(|n|)}\langle T\rangle) &= \{c_{p(|n|)}\langle T\rangle\} \\
S(Q_1 \mid Q_2) &= S(Q_1) \cup S(Q_2)
\end{aligned}
$$

Since P is outer-evaluated prior to computing $S(P)$, we do not need to consider the case $P \equiv [T_1 = T_2].Q$. Note that every process in $S(P)$ is either waiting for input or ready to output. The set of *communication triples* $C(P)$ is

$$\{\langle P_1, P_2, Q_{P_1,P_2}[\;\;]\rangle \mid P_i \in S(P), P_1 \equiv c_{p(|n|)}\langle a\rangle, P_2 \equiv c_{p(|n|)}(x).R, P \equiv Q_{P_1,P_2}[P_1,P_2]\}$$

and the set of *eligible processes* $E(P)$ is defined by

$$
E(P) = \begin{cases} C(P)|_{\text{private channels}} & \text{if there is a possible private communication} \\ C(P)|_{\text{public channels}} & \text{otherwise .} \end{cases}
$$

The reason for this definition, explained intuitively in [LMMS99], is to keep communication on a private channel from biasing the probabilities associated with externally observable communication on public channels. Once a set of eligible processes have been determined, a computation step of P proceeds by selecting one communication triple from $E(P)$ at random and performing the resulting communication step.

4   Equivalence

An *observation* is a test on a specific public channel for a specific natural number. More precisely, let Obs be the set of all pairs $\langle i, c_{p(|n|)} \rangle$ where i is a natural number and $c_{p(|n|)}$ is a public channel. If, during an evaluation of process expression P, the scheduler selects the communication triple

$$\langle c_{p(|n|)} \langle i \rangle, c_{p(|n|)}(x).P', Q_{c_{p(|n|)} \langle i \rangle, c_{p(|n|)}(x).P'} \rangle$$

we will say that the observable $\langle i, c_{p(|n|)} \rangle \in Obs$ *occurs* and write $P \rightsquigarrow \langle i, c_{p(|n|)} \rangle$.

A process P may contain the security parameter n, as described above. We will write P_m to signify that the parameter n is assigned the natural number m. A *process family* $\mathcal{P}$ is the set $\langle P_i | i \in \mathbb{N} \rangle$. Since contexts may contain the process parameter n, we can define the *context family* $\mathcal{C}[\ ]$ analogously.

If $\mathcal{P}$ and $\mathcal{Q}$ are two process families, then $\mathcal{P}$ and $\mathcal{Q}$ are *observationally equivalent*, written write that $\mathcal{P} \cong \mathcal{Q}$, if

$$\forall q(x).\forall \mathcal{C}[\ ].\forall o \in Obs. \exists n_o. \forall n > n_o :$$

$$\left| \mathrm{Prob}(C[P] \rightsquigarrow o) - \mathrm{Prob}(C[Q] \rightsquigarrow o) \right| \leq \frac{1}{q(n)}$$

where $\mathcal{C}[\ ]$ indicates a context family and $q(x)$ an everywhere-positive polynomial.

It is straightforward to check that $\cong$ is an equivalence relation. Moreover, we believe that this formal definition reasonably models the ability to distinguish two processes by feasible intervention and observation. If $P = \{P_n\}_{n \geq 0}$ is a scheme for generating pseudorandom sequences of bits, and $Q = \{Q_n\}_{n \geq 0}$ consists of processes that generate truly random bits (e.g., by calls to our built-in random-bit primitive), then our definition of observational equivalence corresponds to a standard notion from the study of pseudorandomness and cryptography (see, e.g., [Lub96,Yao82]). Specifically, $P \simeq Q$ iff P and Q pass the same polynomial-time statistical tests.

5   Applications and Future Directions

An example authentication protocol, proposed by Bellare and Rogaway [BR94], is discussed in [LMMS99]. However, the proof of security of this protocol that is presented in [LMMS99] is ad hoc, and relies on specific syntactic similarities between the protocol and its specification. In the future, we hope to develop more powerful systematic proof methods for observational congruence. Since there has been little prior work on complexity-bounded probabilistic process formalisms and asymptotic equivalence, one of our near-term goals is to better understand the forms of probabilistic reasoning that would be needed to carry out more rigorous protocol analysis.

References

[AF01]   M. Abadi and C. Fournet. Mobile values, new names, and secure communication. In *28th ACM Symposium on Principles of Programming Languages*, pages 104–115, 2001.

[AG98]   M. Abadi and A. Gordon. A bisimulation method for cryptographic protocol. In *Proc. ESOP'98, Springer Lecture Notes in Computer Science*, 1998.

[AG99]   M. Abadi and A. Gordon. A calculus for cryptographic protocols: the spi calculus. *Information and Computation*, 143:1–70, 1999. Expanded version available as SRC Research Report 149 (January 1998).

[BAN89]   M. Burrows, M. Abadi, and R. Needham. A logic of authentication. *Proceedings of the Royal Society, Series A*, 426(1871):233–271, 1989. Also appeared as SRC Research Report 39 and, in a shortened form, in ACM Transactions on Computer Systems 8, 1 (February 1990), 18-36.

[BR94]   M. Bellare and P. Rogaway. Entity authentication and key distribution. In *Advances in Cryptology - CRYPTO '93, Lecture Notes in Computer Science, Vol. 773*, 1994.

[DY83]   D. Dolev and A. Yao. On the security of public-key protocols. *IEEE Transactions on Information Theory*, 2(29), 1983.

[ElG85]   T. ElGamal. A public-key cryptosystem and a signature scheme based on discrete logarithms. *IEEE Transactions on Information Theory*, IT-31:469–472, 1985.

[FKK96]   A. Freier, P. Karlton, and P. Kocher. The SSL protocol version 3.0. `draft-ietf-tls-ssl-version3-00.txt`, November 18 1996.

[KMM94]   R. Kemmerer, C. Meadows, and J. Millen. Three systems for cryptographic protocol analysis. *J. Cryptology*, 7(2):79–130, 1994.

[KN93]   J.T. Kohl and B.C. Neuman. The Kerberos network authentication service (version 5). Internet Request For Comment RFC-1510, September 1993.

[KNT94]   J.T. Kohl, B.C. Neuman, and T.Y. Ts'o. *The evolution of the Kerberos authentication service*, pages 78–94. IEEE Computer Society Press, 1994.

[LMMS98]   P.D. Lincoln, J.C. Mitchell, M. Mitchell, and A. Scedrov. A probabilistic poly-time framework for protocol analysis. In *ACM Conf. Computer and Communication Security*, 1998.

[LMMS99]   P.D. Lincoln, J.C. Mitchell, M. Mitchell, and A. Scedrov. Probabilistic polynomial-time equivalence and security protocols. In *FM'99 World Congress On Formal Methods in the Development of Computing Systems*, 1999.

[Low96]   G. Lowe. Breaking and fixing the Needham-Schroeder public-key protocol using CSP and FDR. In *2nd International Workshop on Tools and Algorithms for the Construction and Analysis of Systems*. Springer-Verlag, 1996.

[Lub96]   M. Luby. *Pseudorandomness and Cryptographic Applications*. Princeton Computer Science Notes, Princeton University Press, 1996.

[Mea96]   C. Meadows. Analyzing the Needham-Schroeder public-key protocol: a comparison of two approaches. In *Proc. European Symposium On Research In Computer Security*. Springer Verlag, 1996.

[MMS97]   J.C. Mitchell, M. Mitchell, and U. Stern. Automated analysis of cryptographic protocols using Murφ. In *Proc. IEEE Symp. Security and Privacy*, pages 141–151, 1997.

[MMS98]   J. Mitchell, M. Mitchell, and A. Scedrov. A linguistic characterization of bounded oracle computation and probabilistic polynomial time. In *IEEE Symp. Foundations of Computer Science*, 1998.

[MPW92]   R. Milner, J. Parrow, and D. Walker. A calculus of mobile processes, part i. *Information and Computation*, 100(1):1–40, 1992.

[NS78]   R.M. Needham and M.D. Schroeder. Using encryption for authentication in large networks of computers. *Communications of the ACM*, 21(12):993–999, 1978.

[Pau97a]   L.C. Paulson. Mechanized proofs for a recursive authentication protocol. In *10th IEEE Computer Security Foundations Workshop*, pages 84–95, 1997.

[Pau97b]   L.C. Paulson. Proving properties of security protocols by induction. In *10th IEEE Computer Security Foundations Workshop*, pages 70–83, 1997.

[Ros95]   A. W. Roscoe. Modelling and verifying key-exchange protocols using CSP and FDR. In *8th IEEE Computer Security Foundations Workshop*, pages 98–107. IEEE Computer Soc Press, 1995.

[Sch96]   S. Schneider. Security properties and CSP. In *IEEE Symp. Security and Privacy*, 1996.

[Yao82]   A. Yao. Theory and applications of trapdoor functions. In *IEEE Foundations of Computer Science*, pages 80–91, 1982.

A Systematic Approach to Static Access Control

François Pottier[1], Christian Skalka[2], and Scott Smith[2]

[1] INRIA Rocquencourt, Francois.Pottier@inria.fr
[2] The Johns Hopkins University, {ces,scott}@cs.jhu.edu

Abstract. The Java JDK 1.2 Security Architecture includes a dynamic mechanism for enforcing access control checks, so-called *stack inspection*. This paper studies type systems which can statically guarantee the success of these checks. We develop these systems using a new, systematic methodology: we show that the security-passing style translation, proposed by Wallach and Felten as a *dynamic* implementation technique, also gives rise to *static* security-aware type systems, by composition with conventional type systems. To define the latter, we use the general HM(X) framework, and easily construct several constraint- and unification-based type systems. They offer significant improvements on a previous type system for JDK access control, both in terms of expressiveness and in terms of readability of inferred type specifications.

1 Introduction

The Java Security Architecture [2], found in JDK 1.2 and later, includes mechanisms to protect systems from operations performed by untrusted code. These access control decisions are enforced by *dynamic* checks. Our goal is to make some or all of these decisions *statically*, by extensions to the type system. Thus, access control violations will be caught at compile-time rather than run-time. Furthermore, types (whether inferred or programmer-supplied) will constitute a specification of the security policy.

A Brief Review of the JDK Security Architecture. For lack of space, we cover the JDK security architecture in a cursory manner here; see [2,13,8] for more detailed background. To use the access control system, the programmer adds `doPrivileged` and `checkPrivilege` commands to the code. At run-time, a `doPrivileged` command adds a flag to the current stack frame, enabling a particular privileged operation. The flag is implicitly eliminated when the frame is popped. When a privilege is checked via a `checkPrivilege` command, the stack frames are searched most to least recent. If a frame is encountered with the desired flag, the search stops and the check succeeds. Additionally, each stack frame is annotated with its owner (the owner of the method being invoked), and all stack frames searched by the above algorithm must be owned by some principal authorized for the privilege being checked. This keeps illicit code, invoked by the trusted codebase when `doPrivileged` is on the stack, from performing the privileged operation.

D. Sands (Ed.): ESOP 2001, LNCS 2028, pp. 30–45, 2001.
© Springer-Verlag Berlin Heidelberg 2001

Our Framework. This paper follows up on an initial access control type system presented by the last two authors in [8] and places emphasis on a more modular approach to type system construction. The previous paper developed the security type system *ab initio*. In this paper, we reduce the security typing problem to a conventional typing problem using a translation-based method inspired by [5]. We use a standard language of row types [7] to describe sets of privileges. We also re-use the HM(X) framework [3,9], which allows a wide variety of type systems to be defined in a single stroke, saves some proof effort, and (most importantly) shows that our custom type systems arise naturally out of a standard one.

In addition to these methodological enhancements, this paper improves upon its predecessor in several other ways. In particular, [8] was based on subtyping constraints, whereas one of the type systems presented here uses row unification alone; this makes it more efficient and leads to more concise types. Also, the calculus studied in this paper allows for dynamic test-and-branch on whether a privilege is enabled. Lastly, because our new approach relies on HM(X), we can easily provide `let`-polymorphism.

We begin by defining a simplified model of the Java JDK 1.2 security architecture. It is a λ-calculus, called λ_{sec}, equipped with a non-standard operational semantics that includes a specification of stack inspection. In order to construct a static type system for λ_{sec}, we translate it into a standard λ-calculus, called λ_{set}. The translation is a security-passing style transformation [13]: it implements stack inspection by passing around sets of privileges at run-time. For this purpose, λ_{set} is equipped with built-in notions of set and set operations.

Then, we define a type system for λ_{set}. Because λ_{set} is a standard λ-calculus, we are able to define our type system as a simple instance of the HM(X) framework [3]. In fact, by using this framework a whole family of type systems may be succinctly defined, each with different costs and benefits. In order to give precise types to λ_{set}'s built-in set operations, our instance uses set types, defined as a simplification of Rémy's record types [7].

Lastly, we show that any type system for λ_{set} gives rise through the translation to a type system for λ_{sec}. The latter's correctness follows immediately from the former's, provided the translation itself is correct. This is quite easy to show, since the property does not involve types at all.

2   The Source Language λ_{sec}

This section defines λ_{sec}, a simplified model of the JDK 1.2 security architecture. It is a λ-calculus equipped with a notion of code ownership and with constructs for enabling or checking privileges. Its grammar is given in Fig. 1.

We assume given notions of *principals* and *resources* (the latter also known as *privileges*), taken from arbitrary sets $\mathcal{P}$ and $\mathcal{R}$. We use p and r to range over principals and resources, respectively, and P and R to range over sets thereof.

We assume given a fixed *access credentials list* $\mathcal{A}$. It is a function which maps every principal $p \in \mathcal{P}$ to a subset of $\mathcal{R}$. We let $\mathcal{A}^{-1}$ denote its "inverse", that is,

$$p \in \mathcal{P}, P \subseteq \mathcal{P} \qquad\qquad\qquad\qquad\qquad\qquad principals$$
$$r \in \mathcal{R}, R \subseteq \mathcal{R} \qquad\qquad\qquad\qquad\qquad\qquad resources$$
$$\mathcal{A} \in \mathcal{P} \to 2^{\mathcal{R}} \qquad\qquad\qquad\qquad access\ credentials$$

$$v ::= \lambda x.f \qquad\qquad\qquad\qquad\qquad\qquad\qquad\qquad values$$
$$e ::= x \mid \lambda x.f \mid e\,e \mid \text{let } x = e \text{ in } e \mid \text{letpriv } r \text{ in } e \mid \qquad expressions$$
$$\qquad \text{checkpriv } r \text{ for } e \mid \text{testpriv } r \text{ then } e \text{ else } e \mid f$$
$$f ::= p.e \qquad\qquad\qquad\qquad\qquad\qquad signed\ expressions$$

$$E ::= [] \mid E\,e \mid v\,E \mid \text{let } x = E \text{ in } e \mid \qquad evaluation\ contexts$$
$$\qquad \text{letpriv } r \text{ in } E \mid p.E$$

Fig. 1. Grammar for λ_{sec}

the function which maps a resource $r \in \mathcal{R}$ to $\{p \in \mathcal{P} \mid r \in \mathcal{A}(p)\}$. Without loss of generality, we assume the existence of a fixed principal p_0 such that $\mathcal{A}(p_0) = \varnothing$.

A signed expression $p.e$ behaves as the expression e endowed with the authority of principal p. Notice how the body of every λ-abstraction is required to be a signed expression – thus, every piece of code must be vouched for by some principal. The construct letpriv r in e allows an authorized principal to enable the use of a resource r within the expression e. The construct checkpriv r for e asserts that the use of r is currently enabled. If r is indeed enabled, e is evaluated; otherwise, execution fails. The construct testpriv r then e_1 else e_2 dynamically tests whether r is enabled, branching to e_1 or e_2 if this holds or fails, respectively.

2.1   Stack Inspection

The JDK 1.2 determines whether a resource is enabled by literally examining the runtime stack, hence the name *stack inspection*. We give a simple specification of this process by noticing that stacks are implicitly contained in *evaluation contexts*, whose grammar is defined in Fig. 1. Indeed, a context defines a path from the term's root down to its active redex, along which one finds exactly the security annotations which the JDK 1.2 would maintain on the stack, that is, code owners p and enabled resources r.

To formalize this idea, we associate a finite string of principals and resources, called a *stack*, to every evaluation context E. The right-most letters in the string correspond to the most recent stack frames.

$$\text{stack}([]) = \epsilon \qquad\qquad\qquad \text{stack}(E\,e) = \text{stack}(E)$$
$$\text{stack}(v\,E) = \text{stack}(E) \qquad \text{stack}(\text{let } x = E \text{ in } e) = \text{stack}(E)$$
$$\text{stack}(\text{letpriv } r \text{ in } E) = r.\text{stack}(E) \qquad\qquad \text{stack}(p.E) = p.\text{stack}(E)$$

Then, Fig. 2 defines stack inspection, with $S \vdash r$ meaning access to resource r is allowed by stack S, and $S \vdash P$ meaning some principal in P is the most recent owner on S. This specification corresponds roughly to Wallach's [13, p. 71]. We write $E \vdash r$ for $\text{stack}(E) \vdash r$.

$$\frac{r \in \mathcal{A}(p) \quad S \vdash r}{S.p \vdash r} \qquad \frac{S \vdash r}{S.r' \vdash r} \qquad \frac{S \vdash \mathcal{A}^{-1}(r)}{S.r \vdash r} \qquad \frac{S \vdash P}{S.r \vdash P} \qquad \frac{p \in P}{S.p \vdash P}$$

Fig. 2. Stack inspection algorithm

2.2 Operational Semantics for λ_{sec}

The operational semantics of λ_{sec} is defined by the following reduction rules:

$$
\begin{aligned}
E[(\lambda x.f)\, v] &\to E[f[v/x]] \\
E[\text{let } x = v \text{ in } e] &\to E[e[v/x]] \\
E[\text{checkpriv } r \text{ for } e] &\to E[e] & \text{if } E \vdash r \\
E[\text{testpriv } r \text{ then } e_1 \text{ else } e_2] &\to E[e_1] & \text{if } E \vdash r \\
E[\text{testpriv } r \text{ then } e_1 \text{ else } e_2] &\to E[e_2] & \text{if } \neg(E \vdash r) \\
E[\text{letpriv } r \text{ in } v] &\to E[v] \\
E[p.v] &\to E[v]
\end{aligned}
$$

The first two rules are standard. The next rule allows checkpriv r for e to reduce into e only if stack inspection succeeds (as expressed by the side condition $E \vdash r$); otherwise, execution is blocked. The following two rules use stack inspection in a similar way to determine how to reduce testpriv r then e_1 else e_2; however, they never cause execution to fail. The last two rules state that security annotations become unnecessary once the expression they enclose has been reduced to a value. In a Java virtual machine, these rules would be implemented simply by popping stack frames (and the security annotations they contain) after executing a method.

This operational semantics constitutes a concise, formal description of Java stack inspection in a higher-order setting. It is easy to check that every closed term either is a value, or is reducible, or is of the form $E[\text{checkpriv } r \text{ for } e]$ where $\neg(E \vdash r)$. Terms of the third category are *stuck*; they represent access control violations. An expression e is said to *go wrong* if and only if $e \to^\star e'$, where e' is a stuck expression, holds.

3   The Target Calculus λ_{set}

We now define a standard calculus, λ_{set}, to be used as the target of our translation. It is a λ-calculus equipped with a number of constants which provide set operations, and is given in Fig. 3. We will use $e.r$, $e \vee R$ and $e \wedge R$ as syntactic sugar for $(._r\, e)$, $(\vee_R\, e)$ and $(\wedge_R\, e)$, respectively.

The constant R represents a constant set. The construct $e.r$ asserts that r is an element of the set denoted by e; its execution fails if that is not the case. The construct $e \vee R$ (resp. $e \wedge R$) allows computing the union (resp. intersection) of the set denoted by e with a constant set R. Lastly, the expression $?_r\, e\, f\, g$

$$
\begin{aligned}
e &::= x \mid v \mid e\,e \mid \mathrm{let}\,x = e\,\mathrm{in}\,e && \textit{expressions} \\
v &::= \lambda x.e \mid R \mid \cdot_r \mid ?_r \mid \vee_R \mid \wedge_R && \textit{values} \\
E &::= [] \mid E\,e \mid v\,E \mid \mathrm{let}\,x = E\,\mathrm{in}\,e && \textit{evaluation contexts}
\end{aligned}
$$

Fig. 3. Grammar for λ_{set}

dynamically tests whether r belongs to the set R denoted by e, and accordingly invokes f or g, passing R to it. The operational semantics for λ_{set} is as follows:

$$
\begin{aligned}
(\lambda x.e)\,v &\to e[v/x] \\
\mathrm{let}\,x = v\,\mathrm{in}\,e &\to e[v/x] \\
R.r &\to R && \text{if } r \in R \\
?_r\,R &\to \lambda f.\lambda g.(f\,R) && \text{if } r \in R \\
?_r\,R &\to \lambda f.\lambda g.(g\,R) && \text{if } r \notin R \\
R_1 \vee R_2 &\to R_1 \cup R_2 \\
R_1 \wedge R_2 &\to R_1 \cap R_2 \\
E[e] &\to E[e'] && \text{if } e \to e'
\end{aligned}
$$

Again, an expression e is said to *go wrong* if and only if $e \to^{\star} e'$, where e' is a stuck expression, holds.

4   Source-to-Target Translation

A translation of λ_{sec} into λ_{set} is defined in Fig. 4. The distinguished identifiers s and $\_$ are assumed not to appear in source expressions. Notice that s may appear free in translated expressions. Translating an (unsigned) expression requires specifying the current principal p.

One will often wish to translate an expression under minimal hypotheses, i.e. under the initial principal p_0 and a void security context. To do so, we define $(\!|\,e\,|\!) = [\![e]\!]_{p_0}[\varnothing/s]$. Notice that s does not appear free in $(\!|\,e\,|\!)$. If e is closed, then so is $(\!|\,e\,|\!)$.

$$
\begin{aligned}
[\![x]\!]_p &= x \\
[\![\lambda x.f]\!]_p &= \lambda x.\lambda s.[\![f]\!] \\
[\![e_1\,e_2]\!]_p &= [\![e_1]\!]_p\,[\![e_2]\!]_p\,s \\
[\![\mathrm{let}\,x = e_1\,\mathrm{in}\,e_2]\!]_p &= \mathrm{let}\,x = [\![e_1]\!]_p\,\mathrm{in}\,[\![e_2]\!]_p \\
[\![\mathrm{letpriv}\,r\,\mathrm{in}\,e]\!]_p &= \mathrm{let}\,s = s \vee (\{r\} \cap \mathcal{A}(p))\,\mathrm{in}\,[\![e]\!]_p \\
[\![\mathrm{checkpriv}\,r\,\mathrm{for}\,e]\!]_p &= \mathrm{let}\,\_ = s.r\,\mathrm{in}\,[\![e]\!]_p \\
[\![\mathrm{testpriv}\,r\,\mathrm{then}\,e_1\,\mathrm{else}\,e_2]\!]_p &= ?_r\,s\,(\lambda s.[\![e_1]\!]_p)\,(\lambda s.[\![e_2]\!]_p) \\
[\![f]\!]_p &= [\![f]\!] \\
[\![p.e]\!] &= \mathrm{let}\,s = s \wedge \mathcal{A}(p)\,\mathrm{in}\,[\![e]\!]_p
\end{aligned}
$$

Fig. 4. Source-to-Target Translation

The idea behind the translation is simple: the variable s is bound at all times to the set of currently enabled resources. Every function accepts s as an extra parameter, because it must execute within its caller's security context. As a result, every function call has s as its second parameter. The constructs letpriv r in e and $p.e$ cause s to be locally bound to a new value, reflecting the new security context; more specifically, the former enables r, while the latter disables all privileges not in $\mathcal{A}(p)$. The constructs checkpriv r for e and testpriv r then e_1 else e_2 are implemented simply by looking up the current value of s. In the latter, s is re-bound, within each branch, to the *same* value. This may appear superfluous at first sight, but has an important impact on typing, because it allows s to be given a different (more precise) type within each branch.

This translation can be viewed as a generalization of Wallach's security-passing style transformation [13] to a higher-order setting. Whereas they advocated this idea as an implementation technique, with efficiency in mind, we use it only as a vehicle in the proof of our type systems. Here, efficiency is not at stake. Our objective is only to define a correct translation, that is, to prove the following:

Theorem 4.1. *If $e \to^\star v$, then $(\!|e|\!) \to^\star (\!|v|\!)$. If e goes wrong, then $(\!|e|\!)$ goes wrong. If e diverges, then $(\!|e|\!)$ diverges.*

The proof is divided in two steps. First, we define a new stack inspection algorithm, which walks the stack forward instead of backward, and computes, at each step, the set of currently enabled resources. Then, we show that the translation implements this algorithm, interleaved with the actual code. Both proof steps are straightforward, and we omit them here for brevity.

5   Types for λ_{set}

We define a type system for the target calculus as an instance of the parametric framework HM(X) [3,9]. HM(X) is a generic type system in the Hindley-Milner tradition, parameterized by an abstract constraint system X. Sect. 5.1 briefly recalls its definition. Sect. 5.2 defines a specific constraint system called SETS, yielding the type system HM(SETS). Sect. 5.3 extends HM(SETS) to the entire language λ_{set} by assigning types to its primitive operations. Sect. 5.4 states type safety results and discusses a couple of choices.

5.1   The System HM(X)

The system HM(X) is parameterized by a *sound term constraint system X*, i.e. by notions of *types τ*, *constraints C*, and *constraint entailment* $\Vdash$, which must satisfy a number of axioms [3].

Then, a *type scheme* is a triple of a set of quantifiers $\bar{\alpha}$, a constraint C, and a type τ (which, in this paper, must be of kind *Type*; see Sect. 5.2), written $\sigma ::= \forall \bar{\alpha}[C].\tau$. A *type environment* Γ is a partial mapping of program variables to type schemes. A *judgement* is a quadruple of a satisfiable constraint C, a

VAR
$$\frac{\Gamma(x) = \forall\bar\alpha[D].\tau \qquad C \Vdash \exists\bar\alpha.D}{C,\Gamma \vdash x : \forall\bar\alpha[D].\tau}$$

SUB
$$\frac{C,\Gamma \vdash e : \tau \qquad C \Vdash \tau \leq \tau'}{C,\Gamma \vdash e : \tau'}$$

ABS
$$\frac{C,(\Gamma;x:\tau) \vdash e : \tau'}{C,\Gamma \vdash \lambda x.e : \tau \to \tau'}$$

APP
$$\frac{C,\Gamma \vdash e_1 : \tau_2 \to \tau \qquad C,\Gamma \vdash e_2 : \tau_2}{C,\Gamma \vdash e_1\,e_2 : \tau}$$

LET
$$\frac{C,\Gamma \vdash e_1 : \sigma \qquad C,(\Gamma;x:\sigma) \vdash e_2 : \tau}{C,\Gamma \vdash \text{let } x = e_1 \text{ in } e_2 : \tau}$$

$\forall$ INTRO
$$\frac{C \wedge D,\Gamma \vdash e : \tau \qquad \bar\alpha \cap \mathrm{fv}(C,\Gamma) = \varnothing}{C \wedge \exists\bar\alpha.D,\Gamma \vdash e : \forall\bar\alpha[D].\tau}$$

$\forall$ ELIM
$$\frac{C,\Gamma \vdash e : \forall\bar\alpha[D].\tau}{C \wedge D,\Gamma \vdash e : \tau}$$

$\exists$ INTRO
$$\frac{C,\Gamma \vdash e : \sigma \qquad \bar\alpha \cap \mathrm{fv}(\Gamma,\sigma) = \varnothing}{\exists\bar\alpha.C,\Gamma \vdash e : \sigma}$$

Fig. 5. The system $\mathrm{HM}(X)$

$$
\begin{array}{lr}
\tau ::= \alpha,\beta,\ldots \mid \tau \to \tau \mid \{\tau\} \mid r : \tau; \ \tau \mid \partial\tau \mid c & \textit{types} \\
c ::= \mathbf{NA} \mid \mathbf{Pre} \mid \mathbf{Abs} \mid \mathbf{Either} & \textit{capabilities} \\
C ::= \mathbf{true} \mid C \wedge C \mid \exists\alpha.C \mid \tau = \tau \mid \tau \leq \tau \mid \text{if } c \leq \tau \text{ then } \tau \leq \tau & \textit{constraints}
\end{array}
$$

Fig. 6. SETS Grammar

type environment Γ, an expression e and a type scheme σ, written $C,\Gamma \vdash e : \sigma$, derivable using the rules of Fig. 5. These rules correspond to those given in [9].

The following type safety theorem is proven in [3] with respect to a denotational presentation of the call-by-value λ-calculus with `let`. We have proved a syntactic version of it, in the style of [14], which better suits our needs.

Theorem 5.1. *If* $C,\Gamma \vdash e : \sigma$ *holds, then* e *does not go wrong.*

5.2   The Constraint System SETS

In order to give precise types to the primitive set operations in λ_{set}, we need specific types and constraints. Together with their logical interpretation, which defines their meaning, these form a constraint system called SETS.

The syntax of types and constraints is defined in Fig. 6. The type language features a *set* type constructor $\{\cdot\}$, the two standard *row* constructors [7], and four *capability* constructors. Capabilities tell whether a given element may appear in a set (**Pre**), may not appear in it (**Abs**), may or may not appear in it (**Either**), or whether this information is irrelevant, because the set itself is unavailable (**NA**). For instance, the singleton set $\{r\}$ will be one (and the only)

$$\frac{\alpha \in \mathcal{V}_k}{\alpha : k} \qquad \frac{\tau, \tau' : Type}{\tau \to \tau' : Type} \qquad \frac{\tau : Row_\varnothing}{\{\tau\} : Type} \qquad \frac{\tau : Cap \qquad r \notin R \\ \tau' : Row_{R \cup \{r\}}}{(r : \tau \,;\, \tau') : Row_R} \qquad \frac{\tau : Cap}{\partial \tau : Row_R}$$

$$c : Cap \qquad \vdash \textbf{true} \qquad \frac{\vdash C_1, C_2}{\vdash C_1 \wedge C_2 \\ \vdash \text{if } C_1 \text{ then } C_2} \qquad \frac{\vdash C}{\vdash \exists \alpha.C} \qquad \frac{\tau, \tau' : k}{\vdash \tau = \tau' \\ \vdash \tau \leq \tau'}$$

Fig. 7. Kinding rules

value of type $\{r : \textbf{Pre} \,;\, \partial \textbf{Abs}\}$. The constraint language offers standard equality and subtyping constraints, as well as a form of conditional constraints. Sample uses of these types and constraints will be shown in Sect. 5.3.

To ensure that only meaningful types and constraints can be built, we immediately equip them with *kinds*, defined by $k ::= Cap \mid Row_R \mid Type$, where R ranges over finite subsets of $\mathcal{R}$. For every kind k, we assume given a distinct, denumerable set of *type variables* $\mathcal{V}_k$. We use $\alpha, \beta, \gamma, \ldots$ to represent type variables. From here on, we consider only *well-kinded* types and constraints, as defined in Fig. 7. The purpose of these rules is to guarantee that every constraint has a well-defined interpretation within our model, whose definition follows.

To every kind k, we associate a mathematical structure $[\![k]\!]$. $[\![Cap]\!]$ is the set of all four capabilities. Given a finite set of resources $R \subseteq \mathcal{R}$, $[\![Row_R]\!]$ is the set of total, almost constant functions from $\mathcal{R} \setminus R$ into $[\![Cap]\!]$. (A function is *almost constant* if it is constant except on a finite number of inputs.) In short, Row_R is the kind of rows which do *not* carry the fields mentioned in R; $Row_\varnothing$ is the kind of complete rows. $[\![Type]\!]$ is the free algebra generated by the constructors $\to$, with signature $[\![Type]\!] \times [\![Type]\!] \to [\![Type]\!]$, and $\{\cdot\}$, with signature $[\![Row_\varnothing]\!] \to [\![Type]\!]$.

Each of these structures is then equipped with an ordering. Here, a choice has to be made. If we do *not* wish to allow subtyping, we merely define the ordering on every $[\![k]\!]$ as equality. Otherwise, we proceed as follows. First, a lattice over $[\![Cap]\!]$ is defined, whose least (resp. greatest) element is **NA** (resp. **Either**), and where **Abs** and **Pre** are incomparable. This ordering is then extended, pointwise and covariantly, to every $[\![Row_R]\!]$. Finally, it is extended inductively to $[\![Type]\!]$ by viewing the constructor $\{\cdot\}$ as covariant, and the constructor $\to$ as contravariant (resp. covariant) in its first (resp. second) argument.

We may now give the interpretation of types and constraints within the model. It is parameterized by an *assignment* ρ, i.e. a function which, for every kind k, maps $\mathcal{V}_k$ into $[\![k]\!]$. The interpretation of types is obtained by extending ρ so as to map every type of kind k to an element of $[\![k]\!]$, as follows:

$$\rho(\tau \to \tau') = \rho(\tau) \to \rho(\tau') \qquad\qquad \rho(\{\tau\}) = \{\rho(\tau)\}$$
$$\rho(r : \tau \,;\, \tau')(r) = \rho(\tau) \qquad\qquad \rho(r : \tau \,;\, \tau')(r') = \rho(\tau')(r') \qquad (r \neq r')$$
$$\rho(\partial \tau)(r) = \rho(\tau) \qquad\qquad\qquad \rho(c) = c$$

$$\frac{}{\rho \vdash \mathbf{true}} \qquad \frac{\rho \vdash C_1 \qquad \rho \vdash C_2}{\rho \vdash C_1 \wedge C_2} \qquad \frac{\rho = \rho'\,[\alpha] \qquad \rho' \vdash C}{\rho \vdash \exists \alpha.C}$$

$$\frac{\rho(\tau) = \rho(\tau')}{\rho \vdash \tau = \tau'} \qquad \frac{\rho(\tau) \leq \rho(\tau')}{\rho \vdash \tau \leq \tau'} \qquad \frac{c \leq \rho(\tau) \Rightarrow \rho \vdash \tau' \leq \tau''}{\rho \vdash \text{if } c \leq \tau \text{ then } \tau' \leq \tau''}$$

Fig. 8. Interpretation of constraints

Fig. 8 defines the constraint satisfaction predicate $\cdot \vdash \cdot$, whose arguments are an assignment ρ and a constraint C. (The notation $\rho = \rho'\,[\alpha]$ means that ρ and ρ' coincide except possibly on α.) *Entailment* is defined as usual: $C \Vdash C'$ (read: C entails C') holds iff, for every assignment ρ, $\rho \vdash C$ implies $\rho \vdash C'$.

We refer to the type and constraint logic, together with its interpretation, as SETS. More precisely, we have defined two logics, where $\leq$ is interpreted as either equality or as a non-trivial subtype ordering. We will refer to them as SETS$^=$ and SETS$^\leq$, respectively. Both are sound term constraint systems [3].

5.3 Dealing with the Primitive Operations in λ_{set}

The typing rules of HM(X) cover only the λ-calculus with **let**. To extend HM(SETS) to the whole language λ_{set}, we must assign types to its primitive operations. Let us define an initial type environment Γ_1 as follows:

$$R : \{R : \mathbf{Pre}\,;\ \partial\mathbf{Abs}\}$$
$$._r : \forall \beta.\{r : \mathbf{Pre}\,;\ \beta\} \to \{r : \mathbf{Pre}\,;\ \beta\}$$
$$\vee_R : \forall \beta\bar{\gamma}.\{R : \bar{\gamma}\,;\ \beta\} \to \{R : \mathbf{Pre}\,;\ \beta\}$$
$$\wedge_R : \forall \beta\bar{\gamma}.\{R : \bar{\gamma}\,;\ \beta\} \to \{R : \bar{\gamma}\,;\ \partial\mathbf{Abs}\}$$
$$?_r : \forall \alpha\beta\gamma.\{r : \gamma\,;\ \beta\} \to (\{r : \mathbf{Pre}\,;\ \beta\} \to \alpha) \to (\{r : \mathbf{Abs}\,;\ \beta\} \to \alpha) \to \alpha$$

Here, α, β, γ range over type variables of kind *Type*, *Row$_\star$*, *Cap*, respectively. We abuse notation: if R is $\{r_1, \ldots, r_n\}$, then $R : c$ denotes $r_1 : c\,;\ \ldots\,;\ r_n : c$, and $R : \bar{\gamma}$ denotes $r_1 : \gamma_1\,;\ \ldots\,;\ r_n : \gamma_n$.

None of the type schemes in Γ_1 carry constraints. If we wish to take advantage of conditional constraints, we must refine the type of $?_r$. Let Γ_2 be the initial type environment obtained by replacing the last binding in Γ_1 with

$$?_r : \forall \bar{\alpha}\bar{\beta}\gamma[C].\{r : \gamma\,;\ \beta\} \to (\{r : \mathbf{Pre}\,;\ \beta_1\} \to \alpha_1) \to (\{r : \mathbf{Abs}\,;\ \beta_2\} \to \alpha_2) \to \alpha$$
$$\text{where } C = \quad \text{if } \mathbf{Pre} \leq \gamma \text{ then } \beta \leq \beta_1 \wedge \text{ if } \mathbf{Abs} \leq \gamma \text{ then } \beta \leq \beta_2$$
$$\wedge \text{ if } \mathbf{Pre} \leq \gamma \text{ then } \alpha_1 \leq \alpha \wedge \text{ if } \mathbf{Abs} \leq \gamma \text{ then } \alpha_2 \leq \alpha$$

Here, the input and output of each branch (represented by β_i and α_i, respectively) are linked to the input and output of the whole construct (represented by β and α) through conditional constraints. Intuitively, this means that the security requirements and the return type of a branch may be entirely ignored unless the branch seems liable to be taken. (For more background on conditional constraints, the reader is referred to [1,4].)

5.4   The Type Systems $\mathcal{S}_i^{rel}$

Sect. 5.2 describes two constraint systems, SETS$^=$ and SETS$^\le$. Sect. 5.3 defines two initial typing environments, Γ_1 and Γ_2. These choices give rise to four related type systems, which we refer to as $\mathcal{S}_i^{rel}$, where rel and i range over $\{=, \le\}$ and $\{1, 2\}$, respectively. Each of them offers a different compromise between accuracy, readability and cost of analysis. In each case, Theorem 5.1 may be extended to the entire language λ_{set} by proving a simple δ-*typability* [14] lemma, i.e. by checking that Γ_i correctly describes the behavior of the primitive operations. The proofs are straightforward and are not given here.

Despite sharing a common formalism, these systems may call for vastly different implementations. Indeed, every instance of $\mathrm{HM}(X)$ must come with a constraint resolution algorithm. $\mathcal{S}_1^=$ is a simple extension of the Hindley-Milner type system with rows, and may be implemented using unification [6]. $\mathcal{S}_2^=$ is similar, but requires conditional (i.e. delayed) unification constraints, adding some complexity to the implementation. $\mathcal{S}_1^\le$ and $\mathcal{S}_2^\le$ require maintaining subtyping constraints, usually leading to complex implementations.

In the following, we lack the space to describe all four variants. Therefore, we will focus on $\mathcal{S}_1^=$. Because it is based on unification, it is efficient, easy to implement, and yields readable types. We conjecture that, thanks to the power of row polymorphism, it is flexible enough for many practical uses (see Sect. 7.3).

6   Types for λ_{sec}

6.1   Definition

Sect. 5 defined a type system, $\mathcal{S}_i^{rel}$, for λ_{set}. Sect. 4 defined a translation of λ_{sec} into λ_{set}. Composing the two automatically gives rise to a type system for λ_{sec}, also called $\mathcal{S}_i^{rel}$ for simplicity, whose safety is a direct consequence of Theorems 4.1 and 5.1.

Definition 6.1. *Let e be a closed λ_{sec} expression. By definition, $C, \Gamma \vdash e : \sigma$ holds if and only if $C, \Gamma \vdash (\!| e |\!) : \sigma$ holds.*

Theorem 6.2. *If $C, \Gamma \vdash e : \sigma$ holds, then e does not go wrong.*

Turning type safety into a trivial corollary was the main motivation for basing our approach on a translation. Indeed, because Theorem 4.1 concerns untyped terms, its proof is straightforward. (The δ-typability lemmas mentioned in Sect. 5.3 do involve types, but are typically very simple.) A direct type safety proof would be non-trivial and would duplicate most of the steps involved in proving $\mathrm{HM}(X)$ correct.

6.2   Reformulation: Derived Type Systems

Definition 6.1, although simple, is not a direct definition of typing for λ_{sec}. We thus will give rules which allow typing λ_{sec} expressions without explicitly translating them into λ_{set}. These so-called *derived* rules can be obtained in a rather systematic way from the definition of $\mathcal{S}_i^{rel}$ and the definition of the translation. (In fact, it would be interesting to formally automate the process.)

In these rules, the symbols τ and ς range over types of kind *Type*; more specifically, ς is used to represent some security context, i.e. a set of available resources. The symbols ρ and φ range over types of kind *Row$_\star$* and *Cap*, respectively. The $\star$ symbol in the rules indicates an irrelevant principal. In the source-to-target translation, all functions are given an additional parameter, yielding types of the form $\tau_1 \to \varsigma_2 \to \tau_2$. To recover the more familiar and appealing notation proposed in [8], we define the macro $\tau_1 \xrightarrow{\varsigma_2} \tau_2 =_{def} \tau_1 \to \varsigma_2 \to \tau_2$.

Fig. 9 gives derived rules for $\mathcal{S}_1^=$, the simplest of our type systems. There, all

$$\text{VAR} \quad \frac{\Gamma(x) = \sigma}{p, \varsigma, \Gamma \vdash x : \sigma} \qquad\qquad \text{ABS} \quad \frac{\star, \varsigma_2, (\Gamma; x : \tau_1) \vdash f : \tau_2}{p, \varsigma_1, \Gamma \vdash \lambda x.f : \tau_1 \xrightarrow{\varsigma_2} \tau_2}$$

$$\text{APP} \quad \frac{p, \varsigma, \Gamma \vdash e_1 : \tau_2 \xrightarrow{\varsigma} \tau \qquad p, \varsigma, \Gamma \vdash e_2 : \tau_2}{p, \varsigma, \Gamma \vdash e_1\, e_2 : \tau}$$

$$\text{LET} \quad \frac{p, \varsigma, \Gamma \vdash e_1 : \sigma \qquad p, \varsigma, (\Gamma; x : \sigma) \vdash e_2 : \tau}{p, \varsigma, \Gamma \vdash \text{let } x = e_1 \text{ in } e_2 : \tau}$$

$$\forall\,\text{INTRO} \quad \frac{p, \varsigma, \Gamma \vdash e : \tau \qquad \bar{\alpha} \cap \text{fv}(\varsigma, \Gamma) = \varnothing}{p, \varsigma, \Gamma \vdash e : \forall \bar{\alpha}.\tau}$$

$$\forall\,\text{ELIM} \quad \frac{p, \varsigma, \Gamma \vdash e : \forall \bar{\alpha}.\tau}{p, \varsigma, \Gamma \vdash e : \tau[\bar{\tau}/\bar{\alpha}]}$$

$$\text{LETPRIV}^- \quad \frac{p, \{\rho\}, \Gamma \vdash e : \tau \qquad r \notin \mathcal{A}(p)}{p, \{\rho\}, \Gamma \vdash \text{letpriv } r \text{ in } e : \tau}$$

$$\text{LETPRIV}^+ \quad \frac{p, \{r : \mathbf{Pre}\,;\, \rho\}, \Gamma \vdash e : \tau \qquad r \in \mathcal{A}(p)}{p, \{r : \varphi\,;\, \rho\}, \Gamma \vdash \text{letpriv } r \text{ in } e : \tau}$$

$$\text{CHECKPRIV} \quad \frac{p, \{r : \mathbf{Pre}\,;\, \rho\}, \Gamma \vdash e : \tau}{p, \{r : \mathbf{Pre}\,;\, \rho\}, \Gamma \vdash \text{checkpriv } r \text{ for } e : \tau}$$

$$\text{TESTPRIV} \quad \frac{p, \{r : \mathbf{Pre}\,;\, \rho\}, \Gamma \vdash e_1 : \tau \qquad p, \{r : \mathbf{Abs}\,;\, \rho\}, \Gamma \vdash e_2 : \tau}{p, \{r : \varphi\,;\, \rho\}, \Gamma \vdash \text{testpriv } r \text{ then } e_1 \text{ else } e_2 : \tau}$$

$$\text{OWN} \quad \frac{p, \{r_1 : \varphi_1\,;\, \ldots\,;\, r_n : \varphi_n\,;\, \partial\mathbf{Abs}\}, \Gamma \vdash e : \tau \qquad \mathcal{A}(p) = \{r_1, \ldots, r_n\}}{\star, \{r_1 : \varphi_1\,;\, \ldots\,;\, r_n : \varphi_n\,;\, \rho\}, \Gamma \vdash p.e : \tau}$$

Fig. 9. Typing rules for λ_{sec} derived from $\mathcal{S}_1^=$

constraints are equations. As a result, all type information can be represented in term form, rather than in constraint form [9]. We exploit this fact to give a simple presentation of the derived rules. Type schemes have the form $\forall \bar{\alpha}.\tau$, and judgements have the form $p, \varsigma, \Gamma \vdash e : \sigma$.

To check that these derived rules are correct, we prove the following lemmas:

Lemma 6.3. $p, \varsigma, \Gamma \vdash e : \sigma$ *holds iff* **true**, $(\Gamma_1; \Gamma; s : \varsigma) \vdash [\![e]\!]_p : \sigma$ *holds.*

Lemma 6.4. $p_0, \{\partial \mathbf{Abs}\}, \Gamma \vdash e : \sigma$ *holds iff* **true**, $(\Gamma_1; \Gamma) \vdash (\![e]\!) : \sigma$ *holds.*

Together, Theorem 6.2 and Lemma 6.4 show that, if a closed λ_{sec} expression e is well-typed according to the rules of Fig. 9, under the initial principal p_0 and the empty security context $\{\partial \mathbf{Abs}\}$, then e cannot go wrong.

Derived rules for each member of the $\mathcal{S}_i^{rel}$ family can be given in a similar way. The same process can also be used to yield type inference rules, rather than the logical typing rules shown here.

7   Examples

7.1   Basic Use of Security Checks

Imagine an operating system with two kinds of processes, root processes and user processes. Killing a user process is always allowed, while killing a root process requires the privilege *killing*. At least one distinguished principal *root* has this privilege. The system functions which perform the killing are implemented by *root*, as follows:

$$kill = \lambda(p : process).root.\mathsf{checkpriv}\ killing\ \mathrm{for}\ \dots() \quad - kill\ the\ process$$
$$killIfUser = \lambda(p : process).root.\dots() \quad - kill\ the\ process\ if\ it\ is\ user\text{-}level$$

In system $\mathcal{S}_1^=$, these functions receive the following (most general) types:

$$kill : \forall \beta.process \xrightarrow{\{killing:\mathbf{Pre}\ ;\ \beta\}} unit$$
$$killIfUser : \forall \beta.process \xrightarrow{\{\beta\}} unit$$

The first function can be called only if it can be statically proven that the privilege *killing* is enabled. The second one, on the other hand, can be called at any time, but will never kill a root process. To complement these functions, it may be desirable to define a function which provides a "best attempt" given the current (dynamic) security context. This may be done by dynamically checking whether the privilege is enabled, then calling the appropriate function:

$$tryKill = \lambda(p : process).root.$$
$$\mathsf{testpriv}\ killing\ \mathrm{then}\ kill(p)\ \mathrm{else}\ killIfUser(p)$$

This function is well-typed in system $S_1^=$. Indeed, within the first branch of the testpriv construct, it is statically known that the privilege *killing* must be enabled; this is why the sub-expression *kill(p)* is well-typed. The inferred type shows that *tryKill* does not have any security requirements:

$$tryKill : \forall\beta.process \xrightarrow{\{\beta\}} unit$$

7.2   Security Wrappers

A library writer often needs to surround numerous internal functions with "boilerplate" security code before making them accessible. To avoid redundancy, it seems desirable to allow the definition of generic *security wrappers*. When applied to a function, a wrapper returns a new function which has the same computational meaning but different security requirements.

Assume given a principal p such that $\mathcal{A}(p) = \{r, s\}$. Here are two wrappers likely to be of use to this principal:

$$enable_r = \lambda f.p.\lambda x.p.\text{letpriv } r \text{ in } f\, x$$
$$require_r = \lambda f.p.\lambda x.p.\text{checkpriv } r \text{ for } f\, x$$

In system $S_1^=$, these wrappers receive the following (most general) types:

$$enable_r : \forall \ldots .(\alpha_1 \xrightarrow{\{r:\mathbf{Pre}\,;\,s:\gamma_1\,;\,\partial\mathbf{Abs}\}} \alpha_2) \xrightarrow{\{\beta_1\}} (\alpha_1 \xrightarrow{\{r:\gamma_2\,;\,s:\gamma_1\,;\,\beta_2\}} \alpha_2)$$
$$require_r : \forall \ldots .(\alpha_1 \xrightarrow{\{r:\mathbf{Pre}\,;\,s:\gamma_1\,;\,\partial\mathbf{Abs}\}} \alpha_2) \xrightarrow{\{\beta_1\}} (\alpha_1 \xrightarrow{\{r:\mathbf{Pre}\,;\,s:\gamma_1\,;\,\beta_2\}} \alpha_2)$$

These types are very similar; they may be read as follows. Both wrappers expect a function f which allows that r be enabled ($r : \mathbf{Pre}$), i.e. one which *either* requires r to be enabled, *or* doesn't care about its status. (Indeed, as in ML, the type of the actual argument may be more general than that of the formal.) They return a new function with identical domain and codomain (α_1, α_2), which works regardless of r's status (*enable_r* yields $r : \gamma_2$) or requires r to be enabled (*require_r* yields $r : \mathbf{Pre}$). The new function retains f's expectations about s ($s : \gamma_1$). f must not require any further privileges ($\partial\mathbf{Abs}$), because it is invoked by p, which enjoys privileges r and s only.

These polymorphic types are very expressive. Our main concern is that, even though the privilege s is not mentioned in the *code* of these wrappers, it does appear in their *type*. More generally, every privilege in $\mathcal{A}(p)$ may show up in the type of a function written on behalf of principal p, which may lead to very verbose types. An appropriate type abbreviation mechanism may be able to address this problem; this is left as a subject for future work.

7.3   Advanced Examples

We lack space to cover numerous more subtle features of the type systems; let us give only some brief comments.

In Sect. 7.1, our use of testpriv was easily seen to be correct, because the sensitive action $kill(p)$ was performed within its lexical scope. Matters become more delicate when testpriv is used to yield a function (or, in Java, an object), whose security requirements *depend* on the test's outcome, and which is later invoked outside its scope. Conditional constraints are then required to track the dependency and prove that the function invocation is safe. It is not clear whether this idiom is a critical one to support in practice, and the question may be answerable only through experiment.

In Sect. 7.2, we pointed out that it is legal to pass $enable_r$ a function f which doesn't care about the status of r, provided the type of f is *polymorphic* in r's status, as in

$$\forall \gamma . \alpha_1 \xrightarrow{\{r:\gamma\,;\,\beta\}} \alpha_2$$

If, on the other hand, it is monomorphic (because f is λ-bound rather than let-bound), as in

$$\alpha_1 \xrightarrow{\{r:\textbf{Either}\,;\,\beta\}} \alpha_2$$

then the application ($enable_r\ f$) becomes well-typed only if subtyping is available, i.e. if **Pre** is a subtype of **Either**. We expect this situation to be infrequent, although this remains to be confirmed.

8   Discussion

Extension to a Full-Featured Language. Many features of the Java language or environment are not addressed in this theoretical study. In particular, Java views privileges as first-class objects, making static typing problematic. In our model, privileges are identifiers, and expressions cannot compute privileges. In the case of Java, it is an open question whether a completely static mechanism can be devised. If not, it may be desirable to take a soft typing approach [1].

Related Work. The security-passing style translation described in Sect. 4 is monadic. Monadic type systems have been used to analyze the use of impure language features in otherwise pure languages [11]. However, as deplored in [11], there is still "a need to create a new effect system for each new effect". In other words, we apparently cannot readily re-use the work on monadic type systems in our setting. In fact, our work may be viewed as a *systematic* construction of an "effect" type system adapted to our particular effectful programming language.

Several researchers have proposed ways of defining efficient, provably correct compilation schemes for languages whose security policy is expressed by a *security automaton*. Walker [12] defines a source language, equipped with such a security policy, then shows how to compile it into a dependently-typed target language, whose type system, by encoding assertions about security states, guarantees that no run-time violations will occur. Walker first builds the target type system, then defines a typed translation. On the opposite, our approach consists in first defining an untyped translation, then letting the source type system arise from it. Thiemann's approach to security automata [10] is conceptually much closer to ours: he also starts with an untyped security-passing translation, whose output he then feeds through a standard program specializer, in order to automatically obtain an optimizing translation.

Our paper shares some motivations with these works; however, our aim was not only to gain performance by eliminating many dynamic checks, but also to define a programming discipline. This requires security types to be available not only at the level of compiled code, as in Walker's work, but also in the source code itself.

References

[1] Alexander S. Aiken, Edward L. Wimmers, and T. K. Lakshman. Soft typing with conditional types. In *Principles of Programming Languages*, pages 163–173, January 1994. URL: http://http.cs.berkeley.edu/~aiken/ftp/popl94.ps.

[2] Li Gong. Java security architecture (JDK1.2).
URL: http://java.sun.com/products/jdk/1.2/docs/guide/security/spec/
security-spec.doc.html, October 1998.

[3] Martin Odersky, Martin Sulzmann, and Martin Wehr. Type inference with constrained types. *Theory and Practice of Object Systems*, 5(1):35–55, 1999. URL: http://www.cs.mu.oz.au/~sulzmann/publications/tapos.ps.

[4] François Pottier. A 3-part type inference engine. In Gert Smolka, editor, *Proceedings of the 2000 European Symposium on Programming (ESOP'00)*, volume 1782 of *Lecture Notes in Computer Science*, pages 320–335. Springer Verlag, March 2000. URL: http://pauillac.inria.fr/ fpottier/publis/fpottier-esop-2000.ps.gz.

[5] François Pottier and Sylvain Conchon. Information flow inference for free. In *Proceedings of the the Fifth ACM SIGPLAN International Conference on Functional Programming (ICFP'00)*, pages 46–57, September 2000.
URL: http://pauillac.inria.fr/ fpottier/publis/fpottier-conchon-icfp00.ps.gz.

[6] Didier Rémy. Extending ML type system with a sorted equational theory. Technical Report 1766, INRIA, Rocquencourt, BP 105, 78153 Le Chesnay Cedex, France, 1992. URL:
ftp://ftp.inria.fr/INRIA/Projects/cristal/Didier.Remy/eq-theory-on-types.ps.gz.

[7] Didier Rémy. Projective ML. In *1992 ACM Conference on Lisp and Functional Programming*, pages 66–75, New-York, 1992. ACM Press. URL:
ftp://ftp.inria.fr/INRIA/Projects/cristal/ Didier.Remy/lfp92.ps.gz.

[8] Christian Skalka and Scott Smith. Static enforcement of security with types. In *Proceedings of the the Fifth ACM SIGPLAN International Conference on Functional Programming (ICFP'00)*, pages 34–45, Montr al, Canada, September 2000. URL: http://www.cs.jhu.edu/~ces/papers/secty_icfp2000.ps.gz.

[9] Martin Sulzmann, Martin Müller, and Christoph Zenger. Hindley/Milner style type systems in constraint form. Research Report ACRC–99–009, University of South Australia, School of Computer and Information Science, July 1999. URL: http://www.ps.uni-sb.de/~mmueller/papers/hm-constraints.ps.gz.

[10] Peter Thiemann. Enforcing security properties using type specialization. In David Sands, editor, *Proceedings of the 2001 European Symposium on Programming (ESOP'01)*, Lecture Notes in Computer Science. Springer Verlag, April 2001.

[11] Philip Wadler and Peter Thiemann. The marriage of effects and monads. Submitted to *ACM Transactions on Computational Logic*. URL: http://cm.bell-labs.com/cm/cs/who/wadler/papers/ effectstocl/effectstocl.ps.gz.

[12] David Walker. A type system for expressive security policies. In *Conference Record of POPL'00: The 27th ACM SIGPLAN-SIGACT Symposium on Principles of Programming Languages*, pages 254–267, Boston, Massachusetts, January 2000. URL: http://www.cs.cornell.edu/home/walker/papers/sa-popl00_ps.gz.

[13] Dan S. Wallach. *A New Approach to Mobile Code Security*. PhD thesis, Princeton University, January 1999. URL: http://www.cs.princeton.edu/sip/pub/dwallach-dissertation.html.

[14] Andrew K. Wright and Matthias Felleisen. A syntactic approach to type soundness. *Information and Computation*, 115(1):38–94, November 1994. URL: http://www.cs.rice.edu/CS/PLT/Publications/ic94-wf.ps.gz.

Secure Information Flow and CPS

Steve Zdancewic and Andrew C. Myers

Cornell University, Ithaca NY 14853, USA
{zdance,andru}@cs.cornell.edu

Abstract. *Security-typed languages* enforce secrecy or integrity policies by type-checking. This paper investigates continuation-passing style as a means of proving that such languages enforce non-interference and as a first step towards understanding their compilation. We present a low-level, secure calculus with higher-order, imperative features. Our type system makes novel use of *ordered linear continuations*.

1 Introduction

Language based mechanisms for enforcing secrecy or integrity policies are attractive because, unlike ordinary access control, static information flow can enforce end-to-end policies. These policies require that data be protected despite being manipulated by programs with access to various covert channels. For example, such a policy might prohibit a personal finance program from transmitting credit card information over the Internet even though the program needs Internet access to download stock market reports. To prevent the finance program from illicitly transmitting the private information (perhaps cleverly encoded), the compiler checks that the information flows in the program are admissible.

There has been much recent work on formulating Denning's original lattice model of information-flow control [9] in terms of type systems for static program verification [1,16,20,21,25,26,27,30,32]. The desired security property is *non-interference* [14], which states that high-security data is not observable by low-security computation. Nevertheless, secure information flow in the context of higher-order languages with imperative features is not well understood.

This paper proposes the use of continuation-passing style (CPS) translations [8,12,28] as a means of ensuring non-interference in imperative, higher-order languages. There are two reasons for using CPS. First, CPS is a vehicle for proving a non-interference result, generalizing previous work by Smith and Volpano [30]. Second, CPS is useful for representing low-level programs [4,18], which opens up the possibility of verifying the security of compiler output via typed assembly language [18] or proof-carrying code [22].

This research was supported by DARPA Contract F30602-99-1-0533, monitored by USAF Rome Laboratory. The U.S. Government is authorized to reproduce and distribute reprints for Government purposes, notwithstanding any copyright annotation thereon. The views and conclusions contained herein are those of the authors and should not be interpreted as necessarily representing the official policies or endorsement of DARPA, AFRL, or the U.S. Government.

D. Sands (Ed.): ESOP 2001, LNCS 2028, pp. 46–61, 2001.

We observe that a naive approach to providing security types for an imperative CPS language yields a system that is too conservative: secure programs (in the non-interference sense) are rejected. To rectify this problem, we introduce *ordered linear continuations*, which allow information flow control in the CPS target language to be made more precise. The ordering property of linear continuations is crucial to the non-interference argument, which is the first such theorem for a higher-order, imperative language.

As with previous non-interference results for call-by-value languages [16,20], the theorem holds only for programs that halt regardless of high-security data. Consequently, termination channels can arise, but they leak at most one bit per run on average, we consider them acceptable. There are other channels not captured by this notion of non-interference: high-security data can alter the running time of the program or change its memory consumption. Non-interference holds despite these apparent information leaks because the language itself provides no means for observing these resources (for instance, access to the system clock). Recent work attempts to address such covert channels [3].

The next section shows why a naive type system for secure information flow is too restrictive for CPS and motivates the use of ordered linear continuations. Section 3 presents the target language, its operational semantics, and the novel features of its type system. The non-interference theorem is proved in Section 4, and Section 5 demonstrates the viability of this language as a low-level calculus by showing how to CPS translate a higher-order, imperative language. We conclude with some discussion and related work in Section 6.

2   CPS and Security

Type systems for secrecy or integrity are concerned with tracking dependencies in a program [1]. One difficulty is *implicit flows*, which arise from the control flow of the program. Consider the code fragment A in Figure 1. There is an implicit flow between the value stored in x and the value stored in y, because examining the contents of y after the program has run gives information about the value in x. There is no information flow between x and z, however. This code is secure even when x and y are high-security variables and z is low-security. (In this paper, *high security* means "high secrecy" or "low integrity." Dually, *low security* means "low secrecy" or "high integrity.")

Fragment B illustrates the problem with CPS translation. It shows the code from A after control transfer has been made explicit. The variable k is bound to the continuation of the if, and the jump is indicated by the application k $\langle \rangle$. Because the invocation of k has been lifted into the branches of the conditional, a naive type system for information flow will conservatively require that the body of k not write to low-security memory locations: The value of x would apparently be observable by low-security code. Program B is rejected because k writes to a low-security variable, z.

However, this code *is* secure: There is no information flow between x and z in B because the continuation k is invoked in both branches. As example C shows, if

```
(A)    if x then { y := 1; } else { y := 2; }
       z := 3; halt;

(B)    let k = (λ⟨⟩. z := 3; halt) in
       if x then { y := 1; k ⟨⟩; } else { y := 2; k ⟨⟩; }

(C)    let k = (λ⟨⟩. z := 3; halt) in
       if x then { y := 1; k ⟨⟩; } else { y:= 2; halt; }

(D)    letlin k = (λ⟨⟩. z := 3; halt) in
       if x then { y := 1; k ⟨⟩; } else { y:= 2; k ⟨⟩; }

(E)    letlin k0 = (λ⟨⟩. halt) in
       letlin k1 = (λk. z := 1; k ⟨⟩) in
       letlin k2 = (λk. z := 2; k ⟨⟩) in
       if x then { letlin k = (λ⟨⟩. k1 k0) in k2 k }
            else { letlin k = (λ⟨⟩. k2 k0) in k1 k }
```

Fig. 1. Examples of Information Flow in CPS

k is *not* used in one of the branches, then information about x can be learned by observing z. Linear type systems [2,13,33,34] can express exactly the constraint that k is used in both branches. By making k's linearity explicit, the type system can use the additional information to recover the precision of the source program analysis. Fragment D illustrates our simple approach: In addition to a normal let construct, we include letlin for introducing linear continuations. The program D certifies as secure even when z is a low-security variable, whereas C does not.

Although linearity allows for more precise reasoning about information flow, linearity alone is unsafe in the presence of first-class linear continuations. In example E, continuations k0, k1, and k2 are all linear, but there is an implicit flow from x to z because z lets us observe the *order* in which k1 and k2 are invoked. It is thus necessary to regulate the ordering of linear continuations.

It is simpler to make information flow analysis precise for the source language because the structure of the language limits control flow. For example, it is known that both branches of a conditional return to a common merge point. This knowledge can be exploited to obtain less conservative analysis of implicit flows, but the standard CPS transformation loses this information by unifying all forms of control to a single mechanism. In our approach, the target language still has a single underlying control transfer mechanism (examples B and D execute exactly the same code), but information flow can be analyzed with the same precision as in the source.

3   The Secure CPS Calculus

The target is a call-by-value, imperative language similar to those found in the work on Typed Assembly Language [6,18], although its type system is inspired by previous language-based security research [16,20,32]. This section describes the secure CPS language, its operational behavior, and its static semantics.

Types

$\ell, \mathsf{pc} \in \mathcal{L}$

$\tau ::= \text{int} \mid 1 \mid \sigma \text{ ref} \mid [\mathsf{pc}](\sigma, \kappa) \to 0$

$\sigma ::= \tau_\ell$

$\kappa ::= 1 \mid (\sigma, \kappa) \to 0$

Values and Primitive Operations

$bv ::= n \mid \langle\rangle \mid L^\sigma \mid \lambda[\mathsf{pc}]f(x{:}\sigma, y{:}\kappa).\,e$

$v ::= x \mid bv_\ell$

$lv ::= \langle\rangle \mid y \mid \lambda\langle\mathsf{pc}\rangle(x{:}\sigma, y{:}\kappa).\,e$

$prim ::= v \mid v \oplus v \mid \mathbf{deref}(v)$

Expressions

$e ::= \mathbf{let}\ x = prim\ \mathbf{in}\ e$

$\mid \mathbf{let}\ x = \mathbf{ref}^\sigma_\ell\ v\ \mathbf{in}\ e$

$\mid \mathbf{set}\ v := v\ \mathbf{in}\ e$

$\mid \mathbf{letlin}\ y = lv\ \mathbf{in}\ e$

$\mid \mathbf{let}\ \langle\rangle = lv\ \mathbf{in}\ e$

$\mid \mathbf{if0}\ v\ \mathbf{then}\ e\ \mathbf{else}\ e$

$\mid \mathbf{goto}\ v\ v\ lv$

$\mid \mathbf{lgoto}\ lv\ v\ lv$

$\mid \mathbf{halt}^\sigma\ v$

Fig. 2. Syntax for the Secure CPS Language

3.1 Syntax

The syntax for the secure CPS language is given in Figure 2. Elements of the lattice of security labels, $\mathcal{L}$, are ranged over by meta-variables ℓ and pc. We reserve the meta-variable pc to suggest that the security label corresponds to information learned by observing the program counter. The $\sqsubseteq$ operator denotes the lattice ordering, with the join operation given by $\sqcup$, and least element $\perp$.

Types fall into two syntactic classes: security types, σ, and linear types, κ. Security types are the types of ordinary values and consist of a base-type component, τ, annotated with a security label, ℓ. Base types consist of integers, unit, references, and continuations (written $[\mathsf{pc}](\sigma, \kappa) \to 0$). Correspondingly, base values, bv, include integers, n, a unit, $\langle\rangle$, type-annotated memory locations, L^σ, and continuations, $\lambda[\mathsf{pc}]f(x{:}\sigma, y{:}\kappa).\,e$. All computation occurs over secure values, v, which are base values annotated with a security label. Variables, x, range over values. We adopt the notation $\mathsf{label}(\tau_\ell) = \ell$, and extend the join operation to security types: $\tau_\ell \sqcup \ell' = \tau_{(\ell \sqcup \ell')}$.

An ordinary continuation $\lambda[\mathsf{pc}]f(x{:}\sigma, y{:}\kappa).\,e$ is a piece of code (the expression e) that accepts a non-linear argument of type σ and a linear argument of type κ. Continuations may recursively invoke themselves using the variable f. The notation $[\mathsf{pc}]$ indicates that this continuation may be called only from a context in which the program counter carries information of security at most pc. To avoid unsafe implicit flows, the body of the continuation may create effects only observable by principals able to read data with label pc.

Linear values are either unit, variables, or linear continuations, which contain code expressions parameterized by non-linear and linear arguments just like ordinary continuations. Unlike ordinary continuations, linear continuations may not be recursive[1], but they may be invoked from any calling context; hence linear types do not require any pc annotation. The syntax $\langle\mathsf{pc}\rangle$ serves to distinguish

---

[1] A linear continuation k may be discarded by a recursive ordinary continuation that loops infinitely, passing itself k. Precise terminology for our "linear" continuations would be "affine" to indicate that they may, in fact, never be invoked.

linear continuation values from non-linear ones. As for ordinary continuations, the label pc restricts the continuation's effects.

The primitive operations include binary arithmetic ($\oplus$), dereference, and a means of copying secure values. Program expressions consist of a sequence of let bindings for primitive operations, reference creation, and imperative updates (via set). The letlin construct introduces a linear continuation, and the expression let $\langle\rangle$ = lv in e, necessary for type-checking but operationally a no-op, eliminates a linear unit before executing e. Straight-line code sequences are terminated by conditional statements, non-local transfers of control via goto (for ordinary continuations) or lgoto (for linear continuations), or halt.

3.2 Operational Semantics

The operational semantics (Figure 3) are given by a transition relation between machine configurations of the form $\langle M, \text{pc}, e\rangle$. Memories, M, are finite partial maps from typed locations to closed values. The notation $M[L^\sigma \leftarrow v]$ denotes the memory obtained from M by updating the location L^σ to contain the value v of type σ. A memory is *well-formed* if it is closed under the dereference operation and each value stored in the memory has the correct type. The notation $e\{v/x\}$ indicates capture-avoiding substitution of value v for variable x in expression e.

The label pc in a machine configuration represents the security level of information that could be learned by observing the location of the program counter. Instructions executed with a program-counter label of pc are restricted so that they update only to memory locations with labels more secure than pc. For example, [E3] shows that it is valid to store a value to a memory location of type σ only if the security label of the data joined with the security labels of the program counter and the reference itself is lower than label(σ), the security clearance needed to read the data stored at that location. Rules [E6] and [E7] show how the program-counter label changes after branching on data of security level ℓ. Observing which branch is taken reveals information about the condition variable, and so the program counter must have the higher security label pc $\sqcup$ ℓ.

As shown in rules [P1]–[P3], computed values are stamped with the pc label. Checks like the one on [E3] prevent illegal information flows. The two let rules ([E1] and [E4]) substitute the bound value in the rest of the program.

Operationally, the rules for goto and lgoto are very similar—each causes control to be transferred to the target continuation. They differ in their treatment of the program-counter label, as seen in rules [E8] and [E9]. Ordinary continuations require that the pc before the jump be bounded above by the label associated with the body of the continuation, preventing implicit flows. Linear continuations instead cause the program-counter label to be restored (potentially lowered) to that of the context in which they were declared.

3.3 Static Semantics

The type system for the secure CPS language enforces the linearity and ordering constraints on continuations and guarantees that security labels on values are re-

$[P1]$ $\langle M, \text{pc}, bv_\ell \rangle \Downarrow bv_{\ell \sqcup \text{pc}}$ $[P2]$ $\langle M, \text{pc}, n_\ell \oplus n'_{\ell'} \rangle \Downarrow (n[\![\oplus]\!] n')_{\ell \sqcup \ell' \sqcup \text{pc}}$

$[P3]$ $$\frac{M(L^\sigma) = bv_{\ell'}}{\langle M, \text{pc}, \text{deref}(L^\sigma_\ell) \rangle \Downarrow bv_{\ell \sqcup \ell' \sqcup \text{pc}}}$$

$[E1]$ $$\frac{\langle M, \text{pc}, prim \rangle \Downarrow v}{\langle M, \text{pc}, \text{let } x = prim \text{ in } e \rangle \longmapsto \langle M, \text{pc}, e\{v/x\} \rangle}$$

$[E2]$ $$\frac{\ell \sqcup \text{pc} \sqsubseteq \text{label}(\sigma) \quad L^\sigma \notin Dom(M)}{\langle M, \text{pc}, \text{let } x = \text{ref}^\sigma_{\ell'} \, bv_\ell \text{ in } e \rangle \longmapsto \langle M[L^\sigma \leftarrow bv_{\ell \sqcup \text{pc}}], \text{pc}, e\{L^\sigma_{\ell' \sqcup \text{pc}}/x\} \rangle}$$

$[E3]$ $$\frac{\ell \sqcup \ell' \sqcup \text{pc} \sqsubseteq \text{label}(\sigma) \quad L^\sigma \in Dom(M)}{\langle M, \text{pc}, \text{set } L^\sigma_\ell := bv_{\ell'} \text{ in } e \rangle \longmapsto \langle M[L^\sigma \leftarrow bv_{\ell \sqcup \ell' \sqcup \text{pc}}], \text{pc}, e \rangle}$$

$[E4]$ $\langle M, \text{pc}, \text{letlin } y = lv \text{ in } e \rangle \longmapsto \langle M, \text{pc}, e\{lv/y\} \rangle$

$[E5]$ $\langle M, \text{pc}, \text{let } \langle \rangle = \langle \rangle \text{ in } e \rangle \longmapsto \langle M, \text{pc}, e \rangle$

$[E6]$ $\langle M, \text{pc}, \text{if0 } 0_\ell \text{ then } e_1 \text{ else } e_2 \rangle \longmapsto \langle M, \text{pc} \sqcup \ell, e_1 \rangle$

$[E7]$ $\langle M, \text{pc}, \text{if0 } n_\ell \text{ then } e_1 \text{ else } e_2 \rangle \longmapsto \langle M, \text{pc} \sqcup \ell, e_2 \rangle \quad (n \neq 0)$

$[E8]$ $$\frac{\text{pc} \sqsubseteq \text{pc}' \quad v = (\lambda[\text{pc}']f(x{:}\sigma, y{:}\kappa).e)_\ell \quad e' = e\{v/f\}\{bv_{\ell' \sqcup \text{pc}}/x\}\{lv/y\}}{\langle M, \text{pc}, \text{goto } (\lambda[\text{pc}']f(x{:}\sigma, y{:}\kappa).e)_\ell \, bv_{\ell'} \, lv \rangle \longmapsto \langle M, \text{pc}' \sqcup \ell, e' \rangle}$$

$[E9]$ $\langle M, \text{pc}, \text{lgoto } (\lambda\langle \text{pc}'\rangle(x{:}\sigma, y{:}\kappa).e) \, bv_\ell \, lv \rangle \longmapsto \langle M, \text{pc}', e\{bv_{\ell \sqcup \text{pc}}/x\}\{lv/y\} \rangle$

Fig. 3. Expression Evaluation

spected. Together, these restrictions rule out illegal information flows and impose enough structure on the language for us to prove a non-interference property.

As in other mixed linear–non-linear type systems [31], two separate type contexts are used. Γ is a finite partial map from non-linear variables to security types, whereas K is an *ordered* list (with concatenation denoted by ",") mapping linear variables to their types. The order in which continuations appear in K defines the order in which they are invoked: Given $K = \bullet, (y_n{:}\kappa_n), \ldots, (y_1{:}\kappa_1)$, the continuations will be executed in the order $y_1 \ldots y_n$. The context Γ admits the usual weakening and exchange rules (which we omit), but K does not. The two contexts are separated by $\|$ in the judgments to make them more distinct, and $\bullet$ denotes an empty context.

Figures 4 and 5 show the rules for type-checking. The judgment form $\Gamma \vdash v : \sigma$ says that ordinary value v has security type σ in context Γ. Linear values may mention linear variables and so have judgments of the form $\Gamma \parallel K \vdash lv : \kappa$. Primitive operations may not contain linear variables, but the security of the value produced depends on the program-counter: $\Gamma [\text{pc}] \vdash prim : \sigma$ says that in context Γ where the program-counter label is bounded above by pc, $prim$ computes a value of type σ. Similarly, $\Gamma \parallel K [\text{pc}] \vdash e$ means that expression e is

$$[TV1] \quad \overline{\Gamma \vdash n_\ell : \text{int}_\ell}$$

$$[TV2] \quad \overline{\Gamma \vdash \langle\rangle_\ell : 1_\ell}$$

$$[TV3] \quad \overline{\Gamma \vdash L_\ell^\sigma : \sigma \text{ ref}_\ell}$$

$$[TV4] \quad \overline{\Gamma \vdash x : \sigma} \; \Gamma(x) = \sigma$$

$$f, x \notin Dom(\Gamma)$$
$$\sigma' = ([\text{pc}](\sigma, \kappa) \to 0)_\ell$$
$$\Gamma, f : \sigma', x : \sigma \parallel y : \kappa \; [\text{pc}] \vdash e$$
$$[TV5] \quad \overline{\Gamma \vdash (\lambda[\text{pc}]f(x : \sigma, y : \kappa). e)_\ell : \sigma'}$$

$$[TV6] \quad \frac{\Gamma \vdash v : \sigma \quad \vdash \sigma \leq \sigma'}{\Gamma \vdash v : \sigma'}$$

$$[S1] \quad \frac{\text{pc}' \sqsubseteq \text{pc} \quad \vdash \sigma' \leq \sigma \quad \vdash \kappa' \leq \kappa}{\vdash [\text{pc}](\sigma, \kappa) \to 0 \quad \leq \quad [\text{pc}'](\sigma', \kappa') \to 0}$$

$$[S2] \quad \frac{\vdash \tau \leq \tau' \quad \ell \sqsubseteq \ell'}{\vdash \tau_\ell \leq \tau'_{\ell'}}$$

$$[TL1] \quad \overline{\Gamma \parallel \bullet \vdash \langle\rangle : 1}$$

$$[TL2] \quad \overline{\Gamma \parallel y : \kappa \vdash y : \kappa}$$

$$x \notin Dom(\Gamma), y \notin Dom(K)$$
$$\kappa' = (\sigma, \kappa) \to 0$$
$$\Gamma, x : \sigma \parallel y : \kappa, K \; [\text{pc}] \vdash e$$
$$[TL3] \quad \overline{\Gamma \parallel K \vdash \lambda\langle\text{pc}\rangle(x : \sigma, y : \kappa). e : \kappa'}$$

Fig. 4. Value and Linear Value Typing

type-safe and contains no illegal information flows in the type context $\Gamma \parallel K$, when the program-counter label is at most pc. In the latter two forms, pc is a conservative approximation to the information affecting the program counter.

The rules for checking ordinary values, $[TV1]$–$[TV6]$ shown in Figure 4, are, for the most part, standard. A value cannot contain free linear variables because discarding (or copying) it would break linearity. A continuation type contains the pc label used to check its body (rule $[TV5]$). The lattice ordering on security labels lifts to a subtyping relationship on values (rule $[S2]$). Continuations exhibit the expected contravariance (rule $[S1]$). We omit the obvious reflexivity and transitivity rules. Reference types are invariant, as usual.

Linear values are checked using rules $[TL1]$–$[TL3]$. They may safely mention free linear variables, but the variables must not be discarded or reordered. Thus, unit checks only in the empty linear context (rule $[TL1]$), and a linear variable checks only when it is alone in the context (rule $[TL2]$). In a linear continuation (rule $[TL3]$), the linear argument, y, is the tail of the stack of continuations yet to be invoked. Intuitively, this judgment says that the continuation body e must invoke the continuations in K before jumping to y.

The rules for primitive operations ($[TP1]$–$[TP3]$ in Figure 5) require that the calculated value have security label at least as restrictive as the current pc, reflecting the "label stamping" behavior of the operational semantics. Values read through deref (rule $[TP3]$) pick up the label of the reference as well, which prevents illegal information flows due to aliasing.

Rule $[TE4]$ illustrates how the conservative bound on the security level of the program-counter is propagated: The label used to check the branches is the label before the test, pc, joined with the label on the data being tested, ℓ. The rule for goto, $[TE8]$, restricts the program-counter label of the calling context, pc, joined with the label on the continuation itself, ℓ, to be less than the program-counter label under which the body was checked, pc'. This prevents

$[TP1]$
$$\frac{\Gamma \vdash v : \sigma \quad \mathsf{pc} \sqsubseteq \mathsf{label}(\sigma)}{\Gamma\,[\mathsf{pc}] \vdash v : \sigma}$$

$[TP2]$
$$\frac{\Gamma \vdash v : \mathsf{int}_\ell \quad \Gamma \vdash v' : \mathsf{int}_\ell \quad \mathsf{pc} \sqsubseteq \ell}{\Gamma\,[\mathsf{pc}] \vdash v \oplus v' : \mathsf{int}_\ell}$$

$[TP3]$
$$\frac{\Gamma \vdash v : \sigma\ \mathsf{ref}_\ell \quad \mathsf{pc} \sqsubseteq \mathsf{label}(\sigma \sqcup \ell)}{\Gamma\,[\mathsf{pc}] \vdash \mathtt{deref}(v) : \sigma \sqcup \ell}$$

$[TE1]$
$$\frac{\Gamma\,[\mathsf{pc}] \vdash prim : \sigma \quad \Gamma, x{:}\sigma \parallel \mathrm{K}\,[\mathsf{pc}] \vdash e}{\Gamma \parallel \mathrm{K}\,[\mathsf{pc}] \vdash \mathtt{let}\ x = prim\ \mathtt{in}\ e}$$

$[TE2]$
$$\frac{\Gamma \vdash v : \sigma \quad \mathsf{pc} \sqsubseteq \ell \sqcup \mathsf{label}(\sigma) \quad \Gamma, x{:}\sigma\ \mathsf{ref}_\ell \parallel \mathrm{K}\,[\mathsf{pc}] \vdash e}{\Gamma \parallel \mathrm{K}\,[\mathsf{pc}] \vdash \mathtt{let}\ x = \mathtt{ref}_\ell^\sigma\ v\ \mathtt{in}\ e}$$

$[TE3]$
$$\frac{\Gamma \vdash v : \sigma\ \mathsf{ref}_\ell \quad \Gamma \parallel \mathrm{K}\,[\mathsf{pc}] \vdash e \quad \Gamma \vdash v' : \sigma \quad \mathsf{pc} \sqcup \ell \sqsubseteq \mathsf{label}(\sigma)}{\Gamma \parallel \mathrm{K}\,[\mathsf{pc}] \vdash \mathtt{set}\ v := v'\ \mathtt{in}\ e}$$

$[TE4]$
$$\frac{\Gamma \vdash v : \mathsf{int}_\ell \quad \Gamma \parallel \mathrm{K}\,[\mathsf{pc} \sqcup \ell] \vdash e_i}{\Gamma \parallel \mathrm{K}\,[\mathsf{pc}] \vdash \mathtt{if0}\ v\ \mathtt{then}\ e_1\ \mathtt{else}\ e_2}$$

$[TE5]$
$$\frac{\Gamma \parallel \mathrm{K}_2 \vdash \lambda\langle\mathsf{pc}'\rangle(x{:}\sigma, y{:}\kappa).\,e' : (\sigma, \kappa) \to 0 \quad \mathsf{pc} \sqsubseteq \mathsf{pc}' \quad \Gamma \parallel \mathrm{K}_1, y{:}(\sigma, \kappa) \to 0\,[\mathsf{pc}] \vdash e}{\Gamma \parallel \mathrm{K}_1, \mathrm{K}_2\,[\mathsf{pc}] \vdash \mathtt{letlin}\ y = \lambda\langle\mathsf{pc}'\rangle(x{:}\sigma, y{:}\kappa).\,e'\ \mathtt{in}\ e}$$

$[TE6]$
$$\frac{\Gamma \vdash v : \sigma \quad \mathsf{pc} \sqsubseteq \mathsf{label}(\sigma)}{\Gamma \parallel \bullet\,[\mathsf{pc}] \vdash \mathtt{halt}^\sigma\ v}$$

$[TE7]$
$$\frac{\Gamma \parallel \mathrm{K}_1 \vdash lv : 1 \quad \Gamma \parallel \mathrm{K}_2\,[\mathsf{pc}] \vdash e}{\Gamma \parallel \mathrm{K}_1, \mathrm{K}_2\,[\mathsf{pc}] \vdash \mathtt{let}\ \langle\rangle = lv\ \mathtt{in}\ e}$$

$[TE8]$
$$\frac{\Gamma \vdash v : ([\mathsf{pc}'](\sigma, \kappa) \to 0)_\ell \quad \Gamma \vdash v' : \sigma \quad \Gamma \parallel \mathrm{K} \vdash lv : \kappa \quad \mathsf{pc} \sqcup \ell \sqsubseteq \mathsf{pc}' \quad \mathsf{pc} \sqsubseteq \mathsf{label}(\sigma)}{\Gamma \parallel \mathrm{K}\,[\mathsf{pc}] \vdash \mathtt{goto}\ v\ v'\ lv}$$

$[TE9]$
$$\frac{\Gamma \parallel \mathrm{K}_2 \vdash lv : (\sigma, \kappa) \to 0 \quad \Gamma \vdash v : \sigma \quad \Gamma \parallel \mathrm{K}_1 \vdash lv' : \kappa \quad \mathsf{pc} \sqsubseteq \mathsf{label}(\sigma)}{\Gamma \parallel \mathrm{K}_1, \mathrm{K}_2\,[\mathsf{pc}] \vdash \mathtt{lgoto}\ lv\ v\ lv'}$$

Fig. 5. Primitive Operation and Expression Typing

implicit information flows from propagating into function bodies. Likewise, the values passed to a continuation (linear or not) must pick up the calling context's pc (via the constraint $\mathsf{pc} \sqsubseteq \mathsf{label}(\sigma)$) because they carry information about the context in which the continuation was invoked.

The rule for `halt`, $[TE6]$, requires an empty linear context, indicating that the program consumes all linear continuations before stopping. The σ annotating `halt` is the type of the final output of the program; its label should be constrained by the security clearance of the user of the program.

The rules for `letlin`, $[TE5]$, and `lgoto`, $[TE9]$, manipulate the linear context to enforce the ordering property on continuations. For `letlin`, the linear context is split into K_1 and K_2. The body e is checked under the assumption that the new continuation, y, is invoked before any continuation in K_1. Because y invokes the continuations in K_2 before its linear argument (as described above for rule $[TL3]$), the ordering $\mathrm{K}_1, \mathrm{K}_2$ in subsequent computation will be respected. The rule for `lgoto` works similarly.

Linear continuations capture the pc (or a more restrictive label) of the context in which they are introduced, as shown in rule $[TE5]$. Unlike the rule for `goto`, the rule for `lgoto` does not constrain the pc, because the linear continuation *restores* the program-counter label to the one it captured. Because linear continuations capture the pc of their introduction context, we make the mild assumption that *initial programs* introduce all linear continuation values (not variables) via letlin. During execution this constraint is not required, and programs in the image of the translation satisfy this property.

This type system is sound with respect to the operational semantics [36]. The proof is, for the most part, standard, following in the style of Wright and Felleisen [35]. We simply state the lemmas necessary for the discussion of the non-interference result of the next section.

Lemma 1 (Subject Reduction). *If* $\bullet \parallel K [pc] \vdash e$ *and* M *is a well-formed memory such that* $Loc(e) \subseteq Dom(M)$ *and* $\langle M, pc, e \rangle \longmapsto \langle M', pc', e' \rangle$, *then* $\bullet \parallel K [pc'] \vdash e'$ *and* M' *is a well-formed memory such that* $Loc(e') \subseteq Dom(M')$.

Lemma 2 (Progress). *If* $\bullet \parallel \bullet [pc] \vdash e$ *and* M *is well-formed and* $Loc(e) \subseteq Dom(M)$, *then either* e *is of the form* halt$^\sigma$ v *or there exist* M', pc', *and* e' *such that* $\langle M, pc, e \rangle \longmapsto \langle M', pc', e' \rangle$

Note that Subject Reduction holds for terms containing free occurrences of linear variables. This fact is important for proving that the ordering on linear continuations is respected. The Progress lemma (and hence Soundness) applies only to closed programs, as usual.

4   Non-interference

This section proves a non-interference result for the secure CPS language, generalizing Smith and Volpano's preservation-style argument [30]. A technical report [36] gives a detailed account of our approach in a more expressive language.

Informally, the non-interference result shows that low-security computations are not able to observe high-security data. Here, "low-security" refers to the set of security labels $\sqsubseteq \zeta$, where ζ is an arbitrary point in $\mathcal{L}$, and "high-security" refers to labels $\not\sqsubseteq \zeta$. The proof shows that high-security data and computation can be arbitrarily changed without affecting the value of any computed low-security result. Furthermore, memory locations visible to low-security observers (locations storing data labeled $\sqsubseteq \zeta$) are also unaffected by high-security values.

Non-interference reduces to showing that two programs are equivalent from the low-security perspective. Given a program e_1 that operates on high- and low-security data, it suffices to show that e_1 is low-equivalent to the program e_2 that differs from e_1 in its high-security computations.

How do we show that e_1 and e_2 behave the same from the low-security point of view? If $pc \sqsubseteq \zeta$, meaning that e_1 and e_2 may perform actions visible to low observers, they necessarily must perform the same computation on low-security values. Yet e_1 and e_2 may differ in their behavior on high-security data and still be equivalent from the low perspective. To show their equivalence, we should find substitutions γ_1 and γ_2 containing the relevant high-security data such that

$e = \gamma_1(e)$ and $e_2 = \gamma_2(e)$—both e_1 and e_2 look the same after factoring out the high-security data.

On the other hand, when $\mathsf{pc} \not\sqsubseteq \zeta$, no matter what e_1 and e_2 do their actions should not be visible from the low point of view; their computations are irrelevant. The operational semantics guarantee that the program-counter label is monotonically increasing *except* when a linear continuation is invoked. If e_1 invokes a linear continuation causing pc to fall below ζ, e_2 must follow suit; otherwise the low-security observer can distinguish them. The ordering on linear continuations forces e_2 to invoke the same low-security continuation as e_1.

The crucial invariant maintained by well-typed programs is that it is possible to factor out (via substitutions) the relevant high-security values and those linear continuations that reset the program-counter label to be $\sqsubseteq \zeta$.

Definition 1 (Substitutions). *For context Γ, let $\gamma \models \Gamma$ mean that γ is a finite map from variables to closed values such that $Dom(\gamma) = Dom(\Gamma)$ and for every $x \in Dom(\gamma)$ it is the case that $\bullet \vdash \gamma(x) : \Gamma(x)$.*

For linear context K, write $\Gamma \vdash k \models K$ to indicate that k is a finite map of variables to linear values (with free variables from Γ) with the same domain as K and such that for every $y \in Dom(k)$ we have $\Gamma \parallel \bullet \vdash k(y) : K(y)$.

Substitution application, written $\gamma(e)$, indicates the capture-avoiding substitution of the value $\gamma(x)$ for free occurrences of x in e, for each x in the domain of γ ($k(e)$ is defined similarly).

Linear continuations that set the pc label $\not\sqsubseteq \zeta$ may appear in low-equivalent programs, because, from the low-security point of view, they are not relevant.

Definition 2 (letlin Invariant). *A term satisfies the letlin invariant if every linear continuation expression $\lambda\langle \mathsf{pc}\rangle(x:\sigma, y:\kappa).\,e$ appearing in the term is either in the binding position of a letlin or satisfies $\mathsf{pc} \not\sqsubseteq \zeta$.*

If substitution k contains only low-security linear continuations and $k(e)$ is a closed term such that e satisfies the letlin invariant, then all the low-security continuations not letlin-bound in e must be obtained from k. This invariant ensures that k factors out all of the relevant continuations from $k(e)$.

Extending these ideas to values, memories, and machine configurations we obtain the definitions below:

Definition 3 (ζ-Equivalence).

$\Gamma \vdash \gamma_1 \approx_\zeta \gamma_2$	*If $\gamma_1, \gamma_2 \models \Gamma$ and for every $x \in Dom(\Gamma)$ it is the case that $\mathsf{label}(\gamma_i(x)) \not\sqsubseteq \zeta$ and $\gamma_i(x)$ satisfies the letlin invariant.*
$\Gamma \parallel K \vdash k_1 \approx_\zeta k_2$	*If $\Gamma \vdash k_1, k_2 \models K$ and for every $y \in Dom(K)$ it is the case that $k_1(y) \equiv_\alpha k_2(y) = \lambda\langle \mathsf{pc}\rangle(x:\sigma, y':\kappa).\,e$ such that $\mathsf{pc} \sqsubseteq \zeta$ and e satisfies the letlin invariant.*
$v_1 \approx_\zeta v_2 : \sigma$	*If there exist $\Gamma, \gamma_1,$ and γ_2 plus terms $v_1' \equiv_\alpha v_2'$ such that $\Gamma \vdash \gamma_1 \approx_\zeta \gamma_2$, and $\Gamma \vdash v_i' : \sigma$ and $v_i = \gamma_i(v_i')$ and each v_i' satisfies the letlin invariant.*

$M_1 \approx_\zeta M_2$ *If for all $L^\sigma \in Dom(M_1) \cup Dom(M_2)$ if $\mathsf{label}(\sigma) \sqsubseteq \zeta$, then*
        $L^\sigma \in Dom(M_1) \cap Dom(M_2)$ and $M_1(L^\sigma) \approx_\zeta M_2(L^\sigma) : \sigma$.

Definition 4 (Non-Interference Invariant). *The non-interference invariant is a predicate on machine configurations, written $\Gamma \parallel K \vdash \langle M_1, \mathsf{pc}_1, e_1 \rangle \approx_\zeta \langle M_1, \mathsf{pc}_2, e_2 \rangle$ that holds if the following conditions are all met:*

  (i)   *There exist substitutions $\gamma_1, \gamma_2, k_1, k_2$ and terms e'_1 and e'_2 such that $e_1 = \gamma_1(k_1(e'_1))$ and $e_2 = \gamma_2(k_2(e'_2))$.*
  (ii) *Either (a) $\mathsf{pc}_1 = \mathsf{pc}_2 \sqsubseteq \zeta$ and $e'_1 \equiv_\alpha e'_2$ or (b) $\Gamma \parallel K [\mathsf{pc}_1] \vdash e'_1$ and $\Gamma \parallel K [\mathsf{pc}_2] \vdash e'_2$ and $\mathsf{pc}_i \not\sqsubseteq \zeta$.*
  (iii) *$\Gamma \vdash \gamma_1 \approx_\zeta \gamma_2$ and $\Gamma \parallel K \vdash k_1 \approx_\zeta k_2$*
  (iv) *$Loc(e_1) \subseteq Dom(M_1)$ and $Loc(e_2) \subseteq Dom(M_2)$ and $M_1 \approx_\zeta M_2$.*
  (v)   *Both e'_1 and e'_2 satisfy the* `letlin` *invariant.*

Our proof is a preservation argument showing that the Non-Interference Invariant holds after each transition. When the pc is low, equivalent configurations execute in lock step (modulo high-security data). After the program branches on high-security information (or jumps to a high-security continuation), the two programs may temporarily get out of sync, but during that time they may affect only high-security data. If the program counter drops low again (via a linear continuation), both computations return to lock-step execution.

We first show that ζ-equivalent configuration evaluate in lock step as long as the program counter has low security.

Lemma 3 (Low-pc Step). *Suppose $\Gamma \parallel K \vdash \langle M_1, \mathsf{pc}_1, e_1 \rangle \approx_\zeta \langle M_2, \mathsf{pc}_2, e_2 \rangle$, $\mathsf{pc}_1 \sqsubseteq \zeta$ and $\mathsf{pc}_2 \sqsubseteq \zeta$. If $\langle M_1, \mathsf{pc}_1, e_1 \rangle \longmapsto \langle M'_1, \mathsf{pc}'_1, e'_1 \rangle$, then $\langle M_2, \mathsf{pc}_2, e_2 \rangle \longmapsto \langle M'_2, \mathsf{pc}'_2, e'_2 \rangle$ and there exist Γ' and K' such that $\Gamma' \parallel K' \vdash \langle M'_1, \mathsf{pc}'_1, e'_1 \rangle \approx_\zeta \langle M'_2, \mathsf{pc}'_2, e'_2 \rangle$.*

Proof. (Sketch) We omit the details due to space constraints. Reason by cases on the security of the value used in the transition—if it's label is $\sqsubseteq \zeta$, α-equivalence implies both programs behave identically, otherwise, we extend the substitutions corresponding to Γ' to contain the differing high-security data.   □

Next, we prove that linear continuations do indeed get called in the order described by the linear context.

Lemma 4 (Linear Continuation Ordering). *Assume $K = y_n : \kappa_n, \ldots, y_1 : \kappa_1$, each κ_i is a linear continuation type, and $\bullet \parallel K [\mathsf{pc}] \vdash e$. If $\bullet \vdash k \models K$, then in the evaluation starting from any well-formed configuration $\langle M, \mathsf{pc}, k(e) \rangle$, the continuation $k(y_1)$ will be invoked before any other $k(y_i)$.*

Proof. The operational semantics and Subject Reduction are valid for open terms. Progress, however, does not hold for open terms. Evaluate the open term e in the configuration $\langle M, \mathsf{pc}, e \rangle$. If the computation diverges, none of the y_i's ever reach an active position, and hence are not invoked. Otherwise, the computation must get stuck (it can't halt because Subject Reduction implies that all configurations are well-typed; the `halt` expression requires an empty linear context). The stuck term must be of the form `lgoto` y_i v lv, and because it is well-typed, rule [TE9] implies that $y_i = y_1$.   □

We use the ordering lemma to prove that equivalent high-security configurations eventually return to equivalent low-security configurations.

Lemma 5 (High-pc Step). *If $\Gamma \parallel K \vdash \langle M_1, pc_1, e_1 \rangle \approx_\zeta \langle M_2, pc_2, e_2 \rangle$ and $pc_i \not\sqsubseteq \zeta$, then $\langle M_1, pc_1, e_1 \rangle \longmapsto \langle M_1', pc_1', e_1' \rangle$ implies that either e_2 diverges or $\langle M_2, pc_2, e_2 \rangle \longmapsto^* \langle M_2', pc_2', e_2' \rangle$ and there exist Γ' and K' such that $\Gamma' \parallel K' \vdash \langle M_1', pc_1', e_1' \rangle \approx_\zeta \langle M_2', pc_2', e_2 \rangle$.*

Proof. (Sketch) By cases on the transition step of the first configuration. Because $pc_1 \not\sqsubseteq \zeta$ and all rules except [*E9*] increase the program-counter label, we may choose zero steps for e_2 and still show that $\approx_\zeta$ is preserved. Condition (ii) holds via part(b). The other invariants follow because all values computed and memory locations written to must have labels higher than pc_1 (and hence $\not\sqsubseteq \zeta$). Thus, the only memory locations affected are high-security: $M_1' \approx_\zeta M_2 = M_2'$. Similarly, [*TE5*] forces linear continuations introduced by e_1 to have $pc \not\sqsubseteq \zeta$. Substituting them in e_1 maintains clause (vi) of the invariant.

Now consider the case for [*E9*]. Let $e_1 = \gamma_1(k_1(e_1''))$, then $e_1'' = \text{lgoto } lv \ v_1 \ lv_1$ for some lv. If lv is not a variable, clause (vi) ensures that the program counter in lv's body is $\not\sqsubseteq \zeta$. Pick 0 steps for the second configuration as above. Otherwise, if lv is a variable, y, then [*TE9*] guarantees that $K = K', y : \kappa$. By assumption, $k_1(y) = \lambda\langle pc \rangle (x : \sigma, y' : \kappa'). e$, where $pc \sqsubseteq \zeta$. Assume e_2 does not diverge. By the ordering lemma, $\langle M_2, pc_2, e_2 \rangle \longmapsto^* \langle M_2', pc_2', \text{lgoto } k_2(y) \ v_2 \ lv_2 \rangle$. Simple induction on the length of this transition sequence shows that $M_2 \approx_\zeta M_2'$, because the program counter may not become $\sqsubseteq \zeta$. Thus, $M_1' = M_1 \approx_\zeta M_2 \approx_\zeta M_2'$. By invariant (iii), $k_2(y) \equiv_\alpha k_1(y)$. Furthermore, [*TE9*] requires that $\text{label}(\sigma) \not\sqsubseteq \zeta$. Let $\Gamma' = \Gamma, x : \sigma$, $\gamma_1' = \gamma_1\{x \mapsto \gamma_1(v_1) \sqcup pc_1\}$, $\gamma_2' = \gamma_2\{x \mapsto \gamma_2(v_2) \sqcup pc_2\}$; take k_1' and k_2' to be the restrictions of k_1 and k_2 to the domain of K', and choose $e_1' = \gamma_1'(k_1'(e))$ and $e_2' = \gamma_2'(k_2'(e))$. All of the necessary conditions are satisfied as is easily verified via the operational semantics.   □

Finally, we use the above lemmas to prove non-interference. Assume a program that computes a low-security value has access to high-security data. Arbitrarily changing the high-security data does not affect the program's result.

First, some convenient notation for the initial continuation: Let $stop(\tau_\ell)$: $\kappa_{stop} = \lambda\langle\bot\rangle(x : \tau_\ell, y : 1). \text{let } \langle\rangle = y \text{ in halt}^{\tau_\ell} \ x$ where $\kappa_{stop} = (\tau_\ell, 1) \to 0$.

Theorem 1 (Non-interference). *Suppose $x : \sigma \parallel y : \kappa_{stop} \ [\bot] \vdash e$ for some initial program e. Further suppose that $\text{label}(\sigma) \not\sqsubseteq \zeta$ and $\bullet \vdash v_1, v_2 : \sigma$. Then*

$$\langle \emptyset, \bot, e\{v_1/x\}\{stop(\text{int}_\zeta)/y\} \rangle \longmapsto^* \langle M_1, \zeta, \text{halt}^{\text{int}_\zeta} \ n_{\ell_1} \rangle$$
and
$$\langle \emptyset, \bot, e\{v_2/x\}\{stop(\text{int}_\zeta)/y\} \rangle \longmapsto^* \langle M_2, \zeta, \text{halt}^{\text{int}_\zeta} \ m_{\ell_2} \rangle$$

implies that $M_1 \approx_\zeta M_2$ and $n = m$.

Proof. It is easy to verify that

$$x : \sigma \parallel y : \kappa_{stop} \vdash \langle \emptyset, \bot, e\{v_1/x\}\{stop(\text{int}_\zeta)/y\} \rangle \approx_\zeta \langle \emptyset, \bot, e\{v_2/x\}\{stop(\text{int}_\zeta)/y\} \rangle$$

by letting $\gamma_1 = \{x \mapsto v_1\}$, $\gamma_2 = \{x \mapsto v_2\}$, and $k_1 = k_2 = \{y \mapsto stop(\text{int}_\zeta)\}$. Induction on the length of the first expression's evaluation sequence, using the Low- and High-pc Step lemmas plus the fact that the second evaluation sequence terminates implies that $\Gamma \parallel K \vdash \langle M_1, \zeta, \text{halt}^{\text{int}_\zeta}\, n_{\ell_1} \rangle \approx_\zeta \langle M_2, \zeta, \text{halt}^{\text{int}_\zeta}\, m_{\ell_2} \rangle$. Clause (iv) of the Non-interference Invariant implies that $M_1 \approx_\zeta M_2$. Soundness implies that $\ell_1 \sqsubseteq \zeta$ and $\ell_2 \sqsubseteq \zeta$. This means, because of clause (iii), that neither n_{ℓ_1} nor m_{ℓ_2} are in the range of γ_i'. Thus, the integers present in the halt expressions do not arise from substitution. Because $\zeta \sqsubseteq \zeta$, clause (ii) implies that $\text{halt}^{\text{int}_\zeta}\, n_{\ell_1} \equiv_\alpha \text{halt}^{\text{int}_\zeta}\, m_{\ell_2}$, from which we obtain $n = m$ as desired.   □

5   Translation

This section presents a CPS translation for a secure, imperative, higher-order language that includes only the features essential to demonstrating the translation. Its type system is adapted from the SLam calculus [16] to follow our "label stamping" operational semantics. The judgment $\Gamma \vdash_{\text{pc}} e : s$ shows that expression e has source type s under type context Γ, assuming the program-counter label is bounded above by pc.

Source types are similar to those of the target, except that instead of continuations there are functions. Function types are labeled with their *latent effect*, a lower bound on the security level of memory locations that will be written to by that function. The type translation, following previous work on typed CPS conversion [15], is given in terms of three mutually recursive functions: $(-)^*$, for base types, $(-)^+$ for security types, and $(-)^-$ to linear continuation types:

$$\text{int}^* = \text{int} \qquad (s\ \text{ref})^* = s^+\ \text{ref} \qquad (s_1 \xrightarrow{\ell} s_2)^* = [\ell](s_1^+, s_2^-) \to 0$$
$$t_\ell^+ = (t^*)_\ell \qquad s^- = (s^+, 1) \to 0$$

Figure 6 shows the term translation as a type-directed map from source typing derivations to target terms. For simplicity, we present an un-optimizing CPS translation, although we expect that first-class linear continuations will support more sophisticated translations, such as tail-call optimization [8]. To obtain the full translation of a closed term e of type s, we use the initial continuation from Section 4: letlin stop = $stop(s^+)$ in $[\![\emptyset \vdash_\ell e : s]\!]$stop.

The basic lemma for establishing correctness of the translation is proved by induction on the typing derivation of the source term. This result also shows that the CPS language is at least as precise as the source.

Lemma 6 (Type Translation). $\Gamma \vdash_\ell e : s \Rightarrow \Gamma^+ \parallel y : s^-\ [\ell] \vdash [\![\Gamma \vdash_\ell e : s]\!]y$.

6   Related Work

The constraints imposed by linearity can be seen as a form of resource management [13], in this case limiting the set of possible future computations. Linear continuations have been studied in terms of their category theoretic semantics [11] and also as a computational interpretation of classical logic [5]. Polakow and Pfenning have investigated the connections between ordered linear-logic,

$$[\![\Gamma, x:s' \vdash_{\mathsf{pc}} x : s' \sqcup \mathsf{pc}]\!]y \Rightarrow \mathtt{lgoto}\ y\ x\ \langle\rangle$$

$$\left[\!\!\left[\dfrac{\Gamma, f:s, x:s_1 \vdash_{\mathsf{pc'}} e : s_2}{\Gamma \vdash_{\mathsf{pc}} (\mu f(x:s_1).e)_\ell : s \sqcup \mathsf{pc}} \right]\!\!\right]y \Rightarrow \begin{cases} \mathtt{lgoto}\ y\ (\lambda[\mathsf{pc'}]f(x:s_1^+, y':s_2^-). \\ \quad [\![\Gamma, f:s, x:s_1 \vdash_{\mathsf{pc'}} e : s_2]\!]y')_\ell\ \langle\rangle \end{cases}$$

$$\left[\!\!\left[\begin{array}{c} \Gamma \vdash_{\mathsf{pc}} e : s \\ \Gamma \vdash_{\mathsf{pc}} e' : s_1 \\ \ell \sqsubseteq \mathsf{pc'} \sqcap \mathrm{label}(s_1) \\ \hline \Gamma \vdash_{\mathsf{pc}} (e\ e') : s_2 \end{array} \right]\!\!\right]y \Rightarrow \begin{cases} \mathtt{letlin}\ k_1 = \lambda\langle\mathsf{pc}\rangle(f:s^+, y_1:1). \\ \quad \mathtt{let}\ \langle\rangle = y_1\ \mathtt{in} \\ \quad \mathtt{letlin}\ k_2 = \lambda\langle\mathsf{pc}\rangle(x:s_1^+, y_2:1). \\ \quad\quad \mathtt{let}\ \langle\rangle = y_2\ \mathtt{in} \\ \quad\quad \mathtt{goto}\ f\ x\ y \\ \quad \mathtt{in}\ [\![\Gamma \vdash_{\mathsf{pc}} e' : s_1]\!]k_2 \\ \mathtt{in}\ [\![\Gamma \vdash_{\mathsf{pc}} e : s]\!]k_1 \end{cases}$$

$$\left[\!\!\left[\begin{array}{c} \Gamma \vdash_{\mathsf{pc}} e : \mathsf{int}_\ell \\ \Gamma \vdash_{\mathsf{pc'}} e_i : s' \\ \ell \sqsubseteq \mathsf{pc'} \\ \hline \Gamma \vdash_{\mathsf{pc}} \mathtt{if0}\ e\ \mathtt{then} \\ e_1\ \mathtt{else}\ e_2 : s' \end{array} \right]\!\!\right]y \Rightarrow \begin{cases} \mathtt{letlin}\ k_1 = \lambda\langle\mathsf{pc}\rangle(x:\mathsf{int}_\ell^+, y_1:1). \\ \quad \mathtt{let}\ \langle\rangle = y_1\ \mathtt{in} \\ \quad \mathtt{if0}\ x\ \mathtt{then}\ [\![\Gamma \vdash_{\mathsf{pc'}} e_1 : s']\!]y \\ \quad\quad\quad \mathtt{else}\ [\![\Gamma \vdash_{\mathsf{pc'}} e_2 : s']\!]y \\ \mathtt{in}\ [\![\Gamma \vdash_{\mathsf{pc}} e : \mathsf{int}_\ell]\!]k_1 \end{cases}$$

$$\left[\!\!\left[\begin{array}{c} \Gamma \vdash_{\mathsf{pc}} e : s'\ \mathsf{ref}_\ell \\ \Gamma \vdash_{\mathsf{pc}} e' : s' \\ \ell \sqsubseteq \mathrm{label}(s') \\ \hline \Gamma \vdash_{\mathsf{pc}} e := e' : s' \end{array} \right]\!\!\right]y \Rightarrow \begin{cases} \mathtt{letlin}\ k_1 = \lambda\langle\mathsf{pc}\rangle(x_1:s'\ \mathsf{ref}_\ell^+, y_1:1). \\ \quad \mathtt{let}\ \langle\rangle = y_1\ \mathtt{in} \\ \quad \mathtt{letlin}\ k_2 = \lambda\langle\mathsf{pc}\rangle(x_2:s'^+, y_2:1). \\ \quad\quad \mathtt{let}\ \langle\rangle = y_2\ \mathtt{in} \\ \quad\quad \mathtt{set}\ x_1 := x_2\ \mathtt{in} \\ \quad\quad \mathtt{lgoto}\ y\ x_2\ \langle\rangle \\ \quad \mathtt{in}\ [\![\Gamma \vdash_{\mathsf{pc}} e' : s']\!]k_2 \\ \mathtt{in}\ [\![\Gamma \vdash_{\mathsf{pc}} e : s'\ \mathsf{ref}_\ell]\!]k_1 \end{cases}$$

Fig. 6. CPS Translation (Here $s = (s_1 \xrightarrow{\mathsf{pc'}} s_2)_\ell$, and the k_i's and y_i's are fresh.)

stack-based abstract machines, and CPS [24]. Linearity also plays a role in security types for process calculi such as the π-calculus [17]. Because the usual translation of the λ-calculus into the π-calculus can be seen as a form of CPS translation, it might be enlightening to investigate the connections between security in process calculi and low-level code.

CPS translation has been studied in the context of program analysis [10,23]. Sabry and Felleisen observed that increased precision in some CPS data flow analyses is due to duplication of analysis along different execution paths [29]. They also note that some analyses "confuse continuations" when applied to CPS programs. Our type system distinguishes linear from non-linear continuations to avoid confusing "calls" with "returns." More recently, Damian and Danvy showed that CPS translation can improve binding-time analysis in the λ-calculus [7], suggesting that the connection between binding-time analysis and security [1] warrants more investigation.

Linear continuations appear to be a higher-order analog to *post-dominators* in a control-flow graph. Algorithms for determining post-dominators (see Muchnick's text [19]) might yield inference techniques for linear continuation types.

Conversely, linear continuations might yield a type-theoretic basis for correctness proofs of optimizations based on post-dominators.

Understanding secure information flow in low-level programs is essential to providing secrecy of private data. We have shown that explicit ordering of continuations can improve the precision of security types. Ordered linear continuations constrain the uses of continuations so that implicit flows of information can be controlled more accurately. These constraints also make possible our noninterference proof, the first of its kind for a higher-order, imperative language.

Many thanks to James Cheney, Dan Grossman, François Pottier, Stephanie Weirich, and Lantian Zheng for their comments on drafts of this paper. Thanks also to Jon Riecke for many interesting discussions about the SLam calculus.

References

1. Martín Abadi, Anindya Banerjee, Nevin Heintze, and Jon Riecke. A core calculus of dependency. In *Proc. 26th ACM Symp. on Principles of Programming Languages (POPL)*, pages 147–160, 1999.
2. Samson Abramsky. Computational interpretations of linear logic. *Theoretical Computer Science*, 111:3–57, 1993.
3. Johan Agat. Transforming out timing leaks. In *Proc. 27th ACM Symp. on Principles of Programming Languages (POPL)*, January 2000.
4. Andrew Appel. *Compiling with Continuations*. Cambridge University Press, 1992.
5. Gavin Bierman. A classical linear lambda calculus. *Theoretical Computer Science*, 227(1–2):43–78, 1999.
6. Karl Crary, David Walker, and Greg Morrisett. Typed memory management in a calculus of capabilities. In *Proc. 26th ACM Symp. on Principles of Programming Languages (POPL)*, pages 262–275, 1999.
7. Daniel Damian and Olivier Danvy. Syntactic accidents in program analysis: On the impact of the CPS transformation. In *Proc. 5th ACM SIGPLAN International Conference on Functional Programming (ICFP)*, pages 209–220, 2000.
8. Olivier Danvy and Andrzej Filinski. Representing control: A study of the CPS transformation. *Mathematical Structures in Computer Science*, 2:361–391, 1992.
9. Dorothy E. Denning and Peter J. Denning. Certification of Programs for Secure Information Flow. *Comm. of the ACM*, 20(7):504–513, July 1977.
10. J. Mylaert Filho and G. Burn. Continuation passing transformations and abstract interpretation. In *Proc. First Imperial College, Department of Computing, Workshop on Theory and Formal Methods*, 1993.
11. Andrzej Filinski. Linear continuations. In *Proc. 19th ACM Symp. on Principles of Programming Languages (POPL)*, 1992.
12. Cormac Flanagan, Amr Sabry, Bruce F. Duba, and Matthias Felleisen. The essence of compiling with continuations. In *Proceedings of the ACM '93 Conference on Programming Language Design and Implementation*, 1993.
13. Jean-Yves Girard. Linear logic. *Theoretical Computer Science*, 50:1–102, 1987.
14. J. A. Goguen and J. Meseguer. Security policies and security models. In *Proc. IEEE Symposium on Security and Privacy*, pages 11–20, April 1982.
15. Robert Harper and Mark Lillibridge. Explicit polymorphism and CPS conversion. In *Proc. 20th ACM Symp. on Principles of Programming Languages (POPL)*, 1993.
16. Nevin Heintze and Jon G. Riecke. The SLam calculus: Programming with secrecy and integrity. In *Proc. 25th ACM Symp. on Principles of Programming Languages (POPL)*, San Diego, California, January 1998.

17. Kohei Honda, Vasco Vasconcelos, and Nobuko Yoshida. Secure information flow as typed process behaviour. In *Proc. of the 9th European Symposium on Programming*, volume 1782 of *Lecture Notes in Computer Science*, pages 180–199. Springer, 2000.
18. Greg Morrisett, David Walker, Karl Crary, and Neal Glew. From system F to typed assembly language. *ACM Transactions on Programming Languages and Systems*, 21(3):528–569, May 1999.
19. Steven S. Muchnick. *Advanced Compiler Design and Implementation*. Morgan Kaufmann Publishers, 1997.
20. Andrew C. Myers. JFlow: Practical mostly-static information flow control. In *Proc. 26th ACM Symp. on Principles of Programming Languages (POPL)*, San Antonio, TX, USA, January 1999.
21. Andrew C. Myers and Barbara Liskov. A decentralized model for information flow control. In *Proc. 17th ACM Symp. on Operating System Principles (SOSP)*, pages 129–142, Saint-Malo, France, 1997.
22. George C. Necula. Proof-carrying code. In *Proc. 24th ACM Symp. on Principles of Programming Languages (POPL)*, pages 106–119, January 1997.
23. Flemming Nielson. A denotational framework for data flow analysis. *Acta Informatica*, 18:265–287, 1982.
24. Jeff Polakow and Frank Pfenning. Properties of terms in continuation-passing style in an ordered logical framework. In J. Despeyroux, editor, *2nd Workshop on Logical Frameworks and Meta-languages*, Santa Barbara, California, June 2000.
25. François Pottier and Sylvain Conchon. Information flow inference for free. In *Proc. 5th ACM SIGPLAN International Conference on Functional Programming (ICFP)*, pages 46–57, 2000.
26. Andrei Sabelfeld and David Sands. A PER model of secure information flow in sequential programs. In *Proceedings of the European Symposium on Programming*. Springer-Verlag, March 1999. LNCS volume 1576.
27. Andrei Sabelfeld and David Sands. Probabilistic noninterference for multi-threaded programs. In *Proceedings of the 13th IEEE Computer Security Foundations Workshop*. IEEE Computer Society Press, July 2000.
28. Amr Sabry and Matthias Felleisen. Reasoning about programs in continuation-passing style. *Lisp and Symbolic Computation: An International Journal*, 1993.
29. Amr Sabry and Matthias Felleisen. Is continuation-passing useful for data flow analysis? In *Proc. SIGPLAN '94 Conference on Programming Language Design and Implementation*, pages 1–12, 1994.
30. Geoffrey Smith and Dennis Volpano. Secure information flow in a multi-threaded imperative language. In *Proc. 25th ACM Symp. on Principles of Programming Languages (POPL)*, San Diego, California, January 1998.
31. David N. Turner and Philip Wadler. Operational interpretations of linear logic. *Theoretical Computer Science*, 2000. To Appear.
32. Dennis Volpano, Geoffrey Smith, and Cynthia Irvine. A sound type system for secure flow analysis. *Journal of Computer Security*, 4(3):167–187, 1996.
33. Philip Wadler. Linear types can change the world! In M. Broy and C. Jones, editors, *Programming Concepts and Methods*. North Holland, 1990.
34. Philip Wadler. A taste of linear logic. In *Mathematical Foundations of Computer Science*, volume 711 of *Lecture Notes in Computer Science*. Springer-Verlag, 1993.
35. Andrew K. Wright and Matthias Felleisen. A syntactic approach to type soundness. *Information and Computation*, 115(1):38–94, 1994.
36. Steve Zdancewic and Andrew C. Myers. Confidentiality and integrity with untrusted hosts. Technical Report 2000-1810, Cornell University, 2000.

Enforcing Safety Properties Using Type Specialization

Peter Thiemann

Universität Freiburg
thiemann@informatik.uni-freiburg.de

Abstract. Type specialization can serve as a powerful tool in enforcing safety properties on foreign code. Using the specification of a monitoring interpreter, polyvariant type specialization can produce compiled code that is guaranteed to obey a specified safety policy. It propagates a security state at compile-time and generates code for each different security state. The resulting code contains virtually no run-time operations on the security state, at the price of some code duplication. A novel extension of type specialization by intersection types limits the amount of code duplication considerably, thus making the approach practical.

A few years back, mobile code was merely an exciting research subject. Meanwhile, the situation has changed dramatically and mobile code is about to invade our everyday lives. Many applications load parts of their code —or even third-party extension modules— from the network and run it on the local computer. Web browsers are the most prominent of these applications, but many others (*e.g.*, mobile agents) are gaining importance quickly.

The advent of these applications and related incidents has brought an increasing awareness of the problems involved in executing foreign and potentially hostile programs. Clearly, it should be guaranteed that foreign code does not compromise the hosting computer, by crashing the computer (data integrity), by accessing/modifying data that it is not supposed to access (memory integrity) or —more generally— by using resources that it is not supposed to use. A generally accepted way of giving this guarantee is to execute the code in a *sand box*. Conceptually, a sand box performs monitored execution. It tracks the execution of foreign code and stops it if it attempts an illegal sequence of actions. A property that can be enforced in this way is called a *safety property*.

Such sand box environments have been conceived and implemented with widely different degrees of sophistication. The obvious approach to such a sand box is to perform monitoring by interpreting the code. However, while the approach is highly flexible it involves a large interpretation overhead. Another approach, taken by the JDK [14], is to equip strategic functions in a library with calls to a security manager. A user-provided instantiation of the security manager is then responsible to keep track of the actions and to prevent unwanted actions. The latter approach is less flexible, but more efficient. Java solves the problem of data and memory integrity statically by subjecting all programs to a bytecode verification process [18].

D. Sands (Ed.): ESOP 2001, LNCS 2028, pp. 62–76, 2001.

Related Work

The Omniware approach [35, 1, 19] guarantees memory integrity by imposing a simple program transformation on programs in assembly language. The transformation confines a foreign module to its own private data and code segment. The approach is very efficient, but of limited expressiveness.

Schneider [31] shows that all and only safety properties can be decided by keeping track of the execution history. The history is abstracted into a (not necessarily finite) state automaton. The SASI project implemented this idea [17] for x86-assembly language and for JVM bytecode. Both allow for a separate specification of a state automaton and rely on an ad-hoc code transformation to integrate the propagation of the state with the execution of the program.

Evans and Twyman [8] have constructed an impressive system that takes a specification of a safety policy and generates a transformed version of the Java run-time classes. Any program that uses the transformed classes is guaranteed to obey the specified safety policy.

Necula and Lee [23, 25, 22, 24] have developed a framework in which compiled machine programs can be combined with an encoding of a proof that the program obeys certain properties (for example, a safety policy). The resulting *proof-carrying code* is sent to a remote machine, which can check the proof locally against the code, to make sure that it obeys the safety policy. This has been pursued further by Appel and others [20, 2].

Kozen [16] has developed a very light-weight version of proof-carrying code. He has built a compiler that includes hints to the structure of the compiled program in the code. A receiver of such instrumented code can verify the structural hints and thus obtain confidence that the program preserves memory integrity.

Typed assembly language (TAL) [21] provides another avenue to generating high-level invariants for low-level code. Using TAL can guarantee type safety and memory integrity. TAL programs include extensive type annotations that enable the receiver to perform type checking effectively.

Wallach and Felten [37] coined the term security-passing style for a transformation that makes explicit the systematic extension of functions by an extra parameter encoding a security property. This idea has been pursued by a number of works, including the present one.

Colcombet and Fradet [4] propose to transform code received from a foreign principal, guided by a safety policy. The transformed code propagates a run-time encoding of a security state which is checked at run-time to avoid illegal actions.

Walker [36] presents a sophisticated type system that can encode the passing of the security state on the type-level. The type system enables powerful optimizations. However, a separate transformation system must be implemented and lemmas about the security policy must be proven separately and fed into the system to enable optimizing transformations.

Pottier and others [28] use a transformation to security-passing style as a starting point to generate a security-aware type system from a standard type system. They do not consider the implementation of the transformation.

Implementing program transformations by program specialization has been proposed by Turchin and Glück [34, 9] and put into practice by Glück, Jørgensen, and others [11, 10, 32].

Syntax

$Exp \ni$ $e ::= v \mid (\text{if } e\ e\ e) \mid \mathsf{0}(e\ldots e) \mid e@(e\ldots e)$

$Value \ni$ $v ::= x \mid a \mid \text{fix } x(x\ldots x)e$

evaluation contexts $C ::= (\text{if } [\,]\ e\ e) \mid \mathsf{0}(v\ldots[\,]\ e\ldots) \mid [\,]@(e\ldots e) \mid v@(v\ldots[\,]\ e\ldots)$

security states $\sigma \in \Sigma$

base-type constants $a \in Base$

primitive operators $\mathsf{0} \in Op$

types $\tau ::= \text{BaseType} \mid (\tau,\ldots,\tau) \to \tau$

Operational semantics

$$\sigma, (\text{if true } e_1\ e_2) \;\to\; \sigma, e_1$$
$$\sigma, (\text{if false } e_1\ e_2) \;\to\; \sigma, e_2$$
$$\sigma, \mathsf{0}(a_1\ldots a_n) \qquad \to \delta(\mathsf{0})(\sigma, a_1\ldots a_n), v \quad \text{if } v = [\![\mathsf{0}]\!](a_1,\ldots,a_n) \text{ is defined}$$
$$\sigma, (\text{fix } x_0(x_1\ldots x_n)e)@(v_1\ldots v_n) \to \sigma, e[x_0 \mapsto \text{fix } x_0(x_1\ldots x_n)e, x_i \mapsto v_i]$$

If $\sigma, e \to \sigma', e'$ then $\sigma, C[e] \to \sigma', C[e']$.

Fig. 1. The source language

Contributions. The present work demonstrates that previous ad-hoc approaches to enforcing safety properties by program transformation can be expressed uniformly using partial evaluation. This simplifies their theoretical development and their implementation considerably since partial evaluation technology is reused.

After introducing the source language, security automata, and type specialization, Section 2 gives a naive implementation of monitored execution using an instrumented interpreter for a simply-typed call-by-value lambda calculus.

In Section 3, we define a translation into a two-level lambda calculus. Type specialization [12] of the resulting two-level terms can remove (in certain cases) all run-time operations on the security state. Specialization creates variants of user code tailored to particular security states. They must be drawn from a finite set for our approach to work.

In Section 4, we introduce a novel extension of type specialization by intersection types and subtyping. It avoids unnecessary code duplication, thus making our approach practical. Our prototype implementation automatically performs all example optimizations from Walker's paper [36].

Technical results are the correctness proofs of the translation and the non-standard compilation performed by type specialization. They guarantee the safety of the translated and the compiled code. We have proved correct our extension of type specialization, which amounts to proving subject reduction [13].

1   Prerequisites

The source language. is a simply-typed call-by-value lambda calculus with constants, conditionals, and primitive operations on base types (see Fig. 1).

Each primitive operation, 0, can change the current security state. The value of $\texttt{fix } x_0(x_1 \ldots x_n)e$ is a recursively defined function. Write $\lambda(x_1 \ldots x_n)e$ if x_0 does not appear in e, and $\texttt{let } x = e_1 \texttt{ in } e_2$ for $(\lambda(x)e_2)@(e_1)$. The typing rules defining the judgement $\Gamma \vdash e : \tau$ are standard.

Each primitive operation, $0 : \text{BaseType}^n \to \text{BaseType}$, comes with a partial semantic function $[\![0]\!] \in \text{BaseType}^n \hookrightarrow \text{BaseType}$ and a total state transition function, $\delta : Op \to \Sigma \times \text{BaseType}^n \to \Sigma$, which models the change of the (security-) state on application of the operation. The semantics of the language is given in structural operational style. It maps a pair of a (security-) state, σ, and a closed term to a new state and closed term.

Each reduction sequence $\sigma_0, e_0 \to \sigma_1, e_1, \to \ldots$ gives rise to a potentially infinite sequence $\boldsymbol{\sigma} = (\sigma_0, \sigma_1, \ldots)$ of states (a trace). Write $\sigma_0, e_0 \downarrow \sigma', v$ if there is a finite sequence of reductions, $\sigma_0, e_0 \to \sigma_1, e_1 \to \ldots \to \sigma', v$.

Eta-value conversion is the reflexive, transitive, symmetric, and compatible closure of eta-value reduction: $\texttt{fix } x_0(x_1, \ldots, x_n)v@(x_1, \ldots, x_n) \to_{\eta v} v$ where $x_0, x_1, \ldots, x_n$ are distinct variables not occurring free in v.

A security automaton. is a tuple $\mathcal{S} = (\Sigma, Op, Value, \delta, \sigma_0, bad)$ [36] where

- Σ is a countable set of states;
- Op is a finite set of operation symbols;
- $Value$ is a countable set of values;
- $\delta : Op \to \Sigma \times Value^* \to \Sigma$ is a total function with $\delta(0)(bad, x_1 \ldots x_n) = bad$ (state transition function);
- $\sigma_0 \in \Sigma$ is the initial state; and
- $bad \in \Sigma$ is the sink state with $\sigma_0 \neq bad$.

A safety policy is a set of finite and infinite traces that obeys certain restrictions [31]. A reduction sequence is acceptable if its associated trace is contained in the policy. Schneider [31] has shown that all safety policies can be modeled by a security automaton.

A closed term e_0 is *safe* with respect to $\mathcal{S}$ and some $\sigma_0 \in \Sigma \setminus \{bad\}$ if either there exist $\sigma' \in \Sigma$ and $v \in Value$ such that $\sigma_0, e_0 \downarrow \sigma', v$ and $\sigma' \neq bad$ or the trace of σ_0, e_0 is infinite. It is safe with respect to $\mathcal{S}$ if it is safe with respect to the initial state σ_0.

A typical example is the policy that no network **send** operation happens after a **read** operation from a local file. The transition functions are the identity functions for all primitive operations except **send** and **read**.

$$\Sigma = \{\textit{before-read}, \textit{after-read}, \textit{bad}\} \qquad \sigma_0 = \textit{before-read}$$

σ	$\delta(\textbf{read})(\sigma, \textit{file})$	$\delta(\textbf{send})(\sigma, \textit{data})$	$\delta(0)(\sigma, y_1 \ldots y_n)$
before-read	after-read	before-read	before-read
after-read	after-read	bad	after-read
bad	bad	bad	bad

The program $(\lambda(x)\textbf{read}(\textit{file}))@(\textbf{send}(\textit{data}))$ is safe (with respect to σ_0) due to the trace (*before-read, before-read, after-read*). It is not safe with respect to *after-read*: the corresponding trace is (*after-read, bad, bad*).

The program $(\lambda(x)\textbf{send}(\textit{data}))@(\textbf{read}(\textit{file}))$ is not safe with respect to any state: it generates the unacceptable traces (*before-read, after-read, bad*) and (*after-read, after-read, bad*).

Type specialization. [12] transforms a source expression into a specialized expression *and* its specialized type. The type contains all the compile-time information. If there is no run-time information left then the specialized expression becomes trivial, indicated by •, and can be discarded.

In contrast, traditional partial evaluation techniques [15] rely on non-standard interpretation or evaluation of a source program to perform as many operations on compile-time data as possible. They propagate compile-time data using compile-time values. Once a traditional specializer generates a specialized expression, it loses all further information about it. This leads to the *well-formedness restriction* in binding-time analysis: if a function is classified as a run-time value, then so are its arguments and results.

Since type specialization relies on type inference, there is no well-formedness restriction: compile-time and run-time data may be arbitrarily mixed.

Figure 2 defines type specialization as a judgement $\Gamma \vdash e \rightsquigarrow e' : \tau'$, that is, in typing context Γ the two-level term e specializes to specialized term e' with specialized type τ'. In a two-level term, constants are always compile-time values, variables may be bound to compile-time or run-time values, `lift` converts a compile-time constant into a run-time constant, and `poly` and `spec` control polyvariance (see below). The operation $e_1 + e_2$ is an example primitive operation. For simplicity, we formalize only single-argument functions.

Here is an example specialization of the term $(\underline{\lambda}x.\mathtt{lift}\ x)\underline{@}4$:

$$\frac{\dfrac{\dfrac{x \rightsquigarrow x' : S\{4\} \vdash x \rightsquigarrow x' : S\{4\}}{x \rightsquigarrow x' : S\{4\} \vdash \mathtt{lift}\ x \rightsquigarrow 4 : Int}}{\emptyset \vdash \underline{\lambda}x.\mathtt{lift}\ x \rightsquigarrow \lambda x'.4 : S\{4\} \to Int} \quad \emptyset \vdash 4 \rightsquigarrow \bullet : S\{4\}}{\emptyset \vdash (\underline{\lambda}x.\mathtt{lift}\ x)\underline{@}4 \rightsquigarrow (\lambda x'.4)@\bullet : Int}$$

The typing expresses the compile-time value 4 as a singleton type, $S\{4\}$.

There are two significant changes with respect to Hughes's presentation [12]. First, Hughes's two-level terms obey a simple type discipline. It ensures that the specializer never confuses compile-time and run-time values. However, it does not guarantee that the two-level term specializes successfully. Moreover, the specializer discovers errors of this kind anyway while inferring specialized types. Therefore, we have dropped this set of typing rules.

Second, Hughes's presentation hardwires the processing of singleton types into the rule for compile-time addition. Instead, we have formalized compile-time addition through conversion rules for singleton types. This choice simplifies the specification of extensions considerably, as demonstrated in Sec. 4.

For brevity, our formalization does not include compile-time functions, which are expanded at compile-time before their specialized type is inferred. Their addition is exactly as in Hughes's work [12,13] and is orthogonal to the problems discussed in the present paper.

The `poly` and `spec` constructs [12] introduce and eliminate polyvariant values. A polyvariant value is a set of specialized terms indexed by their specialized types. The type specializer employs a numeric encoding of the index in its output. It implements the rules using backtracking.

Syntax of two-level language

Terms
$$e ::= x \mid n \mid e\overline{+}e \mid \overline{\textbf{if}}\ e\ \overline{\textbf{then}}\ e\ \overline{\textbf{else}}\ e \mid \overline{\textbf{fix}}\ x(x)e \mid e\overline{@}e \mid \textbf{poly}\ e \mid$$
$$\textbf{lift}\ e \mid e\underline{+}e \mid \underline{\textbf{if}}\ e\ \underline{\textbf{then}}\ e\ \underline{\textbf{else}}\ e \mid \underline{\textbf{fix}}\ x(x)e \mid e\underline{@}e \mid \textbf{spec}\ e$$

Specialized terms $e' ::= \bullet \mid x \mid n \mid e'{+}e' \mid \textbf{if}\ e'\ \textbf{then}\ e'\ \textbf{else}\ e' \mid$
$$e'@e' \mid \textbf{fix}\ x(x)e' \mid (e', \ldots, e') \mid \pi_i(e')$$

Specialized types $\tau' ::= S\{n\} \mid Int \mid \tau' \to \tau' \mid \tau'{+}\tau' \mid \tau' \times \ldots \times \tau'$

Typing contexts $\Gamma ::= \emptyset \mid \Gamma, x \leadsto e' : \tau'$

Equality on specialized types

$$\tau' = \tau' \qquad \frac{\tau_1' = \tau_2' \quad \tau_2' = \tau_3'}{\tau_1' = \tau_3'} \qquad \frac{\tau_1' = \tau_2'}{\tau_2' = \tau_1'} \qquad \frac{\tau_1' = \tau_2' \quad \tau_3' = \tau_4'}{\tau_1' \to \tau_3' = \tau_2' \to \tau_4'}$$

$$\frac{\tau_1' = \tau_2' \quad \tau_3' = \tau_4'}{\tau_1'{+}\tau_3' = \tau_2'{+}\tau_4'} \qquad S\{n_1\}{+}S\{n_2\} = S\{n_1 + n_2\}$$

Inference rules of type specialization

$$\Gamma, x \leadsto e' : \tau', \Gamma' \vdash x \leadsto e' : \tau' \qquad \Gamma \vdash n \leadsto \bullet : S\{n\} \qquad \frac{\Gamma \vdash e \leadsto e' : S\{n\}}{\Gamma \vdash \textbf{lift}\ e \leadsto n : Int}$$

$$\frac{\Gamma \vdash e_1 \leadsto e_1' : \tau_1' \quad \Gamma \vdash e_2 \leadsto e_2' : \tau_2'}{\Gamma \vdash e_1\overline{+}e_2 \leadsto \bullet : \tau_1'{+}\tau_2'} \qquad \frac{\Gamma \vdash e_1 \leadsto e_1' : Int \quad \Gamma \vdash e_2 \leadsto e_2' : Int}{\Gamma \vdash e_1\underline{+}e_2 \leadsto e_1'{+}e_2' : Int}$$

$$\frac{\Gamma \vdash e_0 \leadsto e_0' : S\{0\} \quad \Gamma \vdash e_1 \leadsto e_1' : \tau'}{\Gamma \vdash \overline{\textbf{if}}\ e_0\ \overline{\textbf{then}}\ e_1\ \overline{\textbf{else}}\ e_2 \leadsto e_1' : \tau'} \qquad \frac{\Gamma \vdash e_0 \leadsto e_0' : S\{1\} \quad \Gamma \vdash e_2 \leadsto e_2' : \tau'}{\Gamma \vdash \overline{\textbf{if}}\ e_0\ \overline{\textbf{then}}\ e_1\ \overline{\textbf{else}}\ e_2 \leadsto e_2' : \tau'}$$

$$\frac{\Gamma \vdash e_0 \leadsto e_0' : Int \quad \Gamma \vdash e_1 \leadsto e_1' : \tau' \quad \Gamma \vdash e_2 \leadsto e_2' : \tau'}{\Gamma \vdash \underline{\textbf{if}}\ e_0\ \underline{\textbf{then}}\ e_1\ \underline{\textbf{else}}\ e_2 \leadsto \textbf{if}\ e_0'\ \textbf{then}\ e_1'\ \textbf{else}\ e_2' : \tau'}$$

$$\frac{\Gamma, x_0 \leadsto x_0' : \tau_2' \to \tau_1', x_1 \leadsto x_1' : \tau_2' \vdash e \leadsto e' : \tau_1'}{\Gamma \vdash \underline{\textbf{fix}}\ x_0(x_1)e \leadsto \textbf{fix}\ x_0'(x_1')e' : \tau_2' \to \tau_1'}$$

$$\frac{\Gamma \vdash e_1 \leadsto e_1' : \tau_2' \to \tau_1' \quad \Gamma \vdash e_2 \leadsto e_2' : \tau_2'}{\Gamma \vdash e_1\underline{@}e_2 \leadsto e_1'@e_2' : \tau_1'}$$

$$\frac{\Gamma \vdash e \leadsto e' : \tau_1' \quad \tau_1' = \tau_2'}{\Gamma \vdash e \leadsto e' : \tau_2'}$$

$$\frac{(\forall 1 \leq i \leq n)\Gamma \vdash e \leadsto e_i' : \tau_i'}{\Gamma \vdash \textbf{poly}\ e \leadsto (e_1', \ldots, e_n') : \tau_1' \times \ldots \times \tau_n'} \qquad \frac{\Gamma \vdash e \leadsto e' : \tau_1' \times \ldots \times \tau_n'}{\Gamma \vdash \textbf{spec}\ e \leadsto \pi_i(e') : \tau_i'}$$

Fig. 2. Standard type specialization

Hughes [13] has proved the correctness of type specialization by specifying two reduction relations, one for two-level terms, $\to_{tt}$, and one for specialized terms, $\to_{sp}$, (see Fig. 3) and then proving a result like this:

Proposition 1 (Simulation). *If $\Gamma \vdash e_1 \leadsto e_1' : \tau'$ and $e_1 \to_{tt} e_2$ then there exists e_2' such that $\Gamma \vdash e_2 \leadsto e_2' : \tau'$ and $e_1' \to_{sp}^* e_2'$.*

As in Hughes's paper [13], the proof relies on a number of substitution lemmas (see Section 4), which are all easy to prove.

Reduction for two-level terms

$$n_1\overline{+}n_2 \qquad \overline{} \qquad \rightarrow_{tt} (n_1 + n_2)$$
$$\overline{\texttt{if } 0 \texttt{ then}} \; e_1 \; \overline{\texttt{else}} \; e_2 \rightarrow_{tt} e_1$$
$$\overline{\texttt{if } 1 \texttt{ then}} \; e_1 \; \overline{\texttt{else}} \; e_2 \rightarrow_{tt} e_2$$
$$(\overline{\texttt{fix}} \; f(x)e_1)\overline{@}e_2 \qquad \rightarrow_{tt}$$
$$\qquad e_1[f \mapsto \overline{\texttt{fix}} \; f(x)e_1, x \mapsto e_2]$$
$$\texttt{spec} \; (\texttt{poly} \; e) \qquad \rightarrow_{tt} e$$
$$\texttt{lift } n_1 \underline{+} \texttt{lift } n_2 \qquad \rightarrow_{tt} \texttt{lift } (n_1 + n_2)$$
$$\underline{\texttt{if } 0 \texttt{ then}} \; e_1 \; \underline{\texttt{else}} \; e_2 \rightarrow_{tt} e_1$$
$$\underline{\texttt{if } 1 \texttt{ then}} \; e_1 \; \underline{\texttt{else}} \; e_2 \rightarrow_{tt} e_2$$
$$(\underline{\texttt{fix}} \; x_0(x_1)e_1)\underline{@}e_2 \qquad \rightarrow_{tt}$$
$$\qquad e_1[x_0 \mapsto \underline{\texttt{fix}} \; x_0(x_1)e_1, x_1 \mapsto e_2]$$

Reduction for specialized terms

$$n_1 + n_2 \qquad \rightarrow_{sp} (n_1 + n_2)$$
$$\texttt{if } 0 \texttt{ then } e'_1 \texttt{ else } e'_2 \rightarrow_{sp} e'_1$$
$$\texttt{if } 1 \texttt{ then } e'_1 \texttt{ else } e'_2 \rightarrow_{sp} e'_2$$
$$(\texttt{fix } x_0(x_1)e'_1)@e'_2 \qquad \rightarrow_{sp}$$
$$\qquad e'_1[x_0 \mapsto \texttt{fix } x_0(x_1)e'_1, x_1 \mapsto e'_2]$$
$$\pi_i(e'_1, \ldots, e'_n) \qquad \rightarrow_{sp} e'_i$$

Fig. 3. Notions of reduction

$$||\text{BaseType}|| = \text{BaseType}$$
$$||(\tau_1, \ldots, \tau_n) \rightarrow \tau|| = (\Sigma, ||\tau_1||, \ldots, ||\tau_n||, (\Sigma, ||\tau||) \rightarrow \textbf{Ans}) \rightarrow \textbf{Ans}$$
$$|\tau| = (\Sigma, (\Sigma, ||\tau||) \rightarrow \textbf{Ans}) \rightarrow \textbf{Ans}$$

$$||\emptyset|| = \emptyset$$
$$||\Gamma, x : \tau|| = ||\Gamma||, x : ||\tau||$$

$$||x|| = x$$
$$||a|| = a$$
$$||\texttt{fix } x_0(x_1 \ldots x_n)e|| = \texttt{fix } x_0(\sigma, x_1, \ldots, x_n, x_{n+1})|e|(\sigma, x_{n+1})$$

$$|v|(\sigma, c) = c(\sigma, ||v||)$$
$$|(\texttt{if } e_1 \; e_2 \; e_3)|(\sigma, c) = |e_1|(\sigma, \lambda(\sigma_1, y_1).\texttt{if } y_1 \texttt{ then } |e_2|(\sigma_1, c) \texttt{ else } |e_3|(\sigma_1, c))$$
$$|O(e_1 \ldots e_n)|(\sigma, c) = |e_1|(\sigma, \lambda(\sigma_1, y_1). \ldots. |e_n|(\sigma_{n-1}, \lambda(\sigma_n, y_n).$$
$$\qquad \texttt{let } \sigma' = \delta(O)(\sigma_n, y_1 \ldots y_n) \texttt{ in}$$
$$\qquad \texttt{if } \sigma' = \textit{bad} \texttt{ then halt() else } c(\sigma', O(y_1, \ldots, y_n))) \ldots)$$
$$|e_0@(e_1 \ldots e_n)|(\sigma, c) = |e_0|(\sigma, \lambda(\sigma_0, y_0).|e_1|(\sigma_0, \lambda(\sigma_1, y_1). \ldots. |e_n|(\sigma_{n-1}, \lambda(\sigma_n, y_n).$$
$$\qquad y_0@(\sigma_n, y_1, \ldots, y_n, c)) \ldots))$$

Fig. 4. Translation that enforces a security policy

2   Enforcing a Policy by Interpretation

A simple way to enforce safe execution is to incorporate a security automaton into an interpreter or a translation. Before attempting a primitive operation, a translated program steps the security state and checks whether the result is *bad*.

Figure 4 shows a translation to continuation-passing and state-passing style [30], augmented by stepping and testing of the security state. The translation makes explicit the flow of control and of the current security state. Using **Ans** as the type of answers, the translation acts on types as follows.

Proposition 2. *If* $\Gamma \vdash e : \tau$ *then* $||\Gamma|| \vdash |e| : |\tau|$.

The translated program never violates the security policy if the operations $\delta(O)$ on the explicit state do not affect the state component in the operational semantics. Formally, let $\mathcal{S}' = (\Sigma, Op', Value, \delta', \sigma_0, bad)$ with $Op' = Op \cup \{\delta(O) \mid O \in Op\} \cup \{\texttt{halt}\}$ (regarding $\delta(O)$ as the name of a new primitive) and, for all $O \in Op$, $\delta'(O) = \delta(O)$ and $\delta'(\delta(O))(v_\sigma, v_1 \ldots v_n) = v_\sigma$. Let $[\![\texttt{halt}]\!]() = a$, a fixed constant signaling an error.

A translated expression is safe with respect to $\mathcal{S}'$ and arbitrary σ.

Proposition 3. *If* $\sigma, |e|(\sigma, \lambda(\sigma, y)y) \downarrow \sigma', v'$ *then* $\sigma' \neq bad$.

If the original term delivers a result without entering a bad state then so does the translated term.

Proposition 4. *Suppose* $\sigma, e \downarrow \sigma', v$. *If* $\sigma' \neq bad$ *then* $\sigma, |e|(\sigma, \lambda(\sigma, y)y) \downarrow \sigma', ||v||$.

If evaluation of the translated term leads to non-termination or to an undefined primitive operation then so does evaluation of the source term.

Proposition 5. *If there exist no* σ' *and* v' *such that* $\sigma, |e|(\sigma, \lambda(\sigma, y)y) \downarrow \sigma', v'$ *then there exist no* σ' *and* v' *such that* $\sigma, e \downarrow \sigma', v'$.

Using this naive translation yields inefficient programs because every use of a primitive operation is preceded by a run-time check of the security state.

3   Compiling Policies by Type Specialization

To submit the translation to a specializer, we retarget it to a two-level language, indicating compile-time by overlining and run-time by underlining. Type specialization [12] of the translated terms can remove the state component, σ, and the corresponding run-time checks completely, in certain cases.

We consider the two-level translation as an interpreter and specialize it with respect to a source program. The specialized program can be shown to be safe in two steps: Prove that translated programs are safe, and appeal to the correctness of the specializer (Prop. 1) to see that the specialized programs are safe.

3.1   First Steps

Specialization potentially generates code variants for each different security state. Hence, it is only applicable if the set of states is finite. For further simplification, we initially assume that the transition function *does not* depend on the arguments but only on the name of the primitives. Hence, the compile-time transition function, $\overline{\delta}$, is well-defined and gives the full information:

- $\overline{\delta}(O)(\overline{\sigma}) := \overline{\sigma}'$ if $\forall y_1 \ldots y_n.\delta(O)(\sigma, y_1, \ldots, y_n) = \sigma'$,
- $\overline{\delta}(O)(\overline{\sigma}) := bad$ if $\forall \sigma'.\exists y_1 \ldots y_n.\delta(O)(\sigma, y_1, \ldots, y_n) \neq \sigma'$.

Hence, the state becomes a compile-time value and all operations thereon can be computed at compile-time. Figure 5 defines the translation. It follows the basic strategy of Danvy and Filinski's one-pass translation to continuation-passing style [7, 6]. It avoids introducing administrative redexes by converting

$$
\begin{aligned}
\|\mathrm{BaseType}\|_e &= \mathrm{BaseType} \\
\|(\tau_1, \ldots, \tau_n) \to \tau\|_e &= \underline{\mathrm{poly}} \ (\overline{\Sigma}, \|\tau_1\|_e, \ldots, \|\tau_n\|_e, \underline{\mathrm{poly}} \ (\overline{\Sigma}, \|\tau\|_e) \underline{\to} \mathbf{Ans}) \underline{\to} \mathbf{Ans} \\
|\tau|_e &= (\overline{\Sigma}, (\overline{\Sigma}, \|\tau\|_e) \overline{\Rightarrow} \underline{\mathbf{Ans}}) \overline{\Rightarrow} \underline{\mathbf{Ans}} \\[4pt]
\|\emptyset\|_e &= \emptyset \\
\|\Gamma, x : \tau\|_e &= \|\Gamma\|_e, x : \|\tau\|_e \\[4pt]
\|x\|_e &= x \\
\|a\|_e &= a \\
\|\mathtt{fix} \ x_0(x_1 \ldots x_n)e\|_e &= \underline{\mathrm{poly}} \ \underline{\mathtt{fix}} \ x_0(\overline{\sigma}, x_1, \ldots, x_n, x_{n+1}) \\
& \qquad |e|_e \overline{@}(\overline{\sigma}, \overline{\lambda}(\overline{\sigma}, y).\mathtt{spec} \ x_{n+1} \underline{@}(\overline{\sigma}, y)) \\[4pt]
|v|_e(\overline{\sigma}, c) &= c \overline{@}(\overline{\sigma}, \|v\|_e) \\
|(\mathtt{if} \ e_1 \ e_2 \ e_3)|_e(\overline{\sigma}, c) &= |e_1|_e \overline{@}(\overline{\sigma}, \overline{\lambda}(\overline{\sigma}_1, y_1). \\
& \qquad \underline{\mathtt{if}} \ y_1 \ \underline{\mathtt{then}} \ |e_2|_e \overline{@}(\overline{\sigma}_1, c) \ \underline{\mathtt{else}} \ |e_3|_e \overline{@}(\overline{\sigma}_1, c)) \\[4pt]
|0(e_1 \ldots e_n)|_e(\overline{\sigma}_0, c) &= |e_1|_e(\overline{\sigma}_0, \overline{\lambda}(\overline{\sigma}_1, y_1)). \ldots |e_n|_e(\overline{\sigma}_{n-1}, \overline{\lambda}(\overline{\sigma}_n, y_n). \\
& \qquad \overline{\mathtt{let}} \ \overline{\sigma}' = \overline{\delta}(0)(\overline{\sigma}_n) \ \overline{\mathtt{in}} \\
& \qquad \overline{\mathtt{if}} \ \overline{\sigma}' = bad \ \overline{\mathtt{then}} \ \underline{\mathtt{halt}}() \ \overline{\mathtt{else}} \\
& \qquad \overline{\mathtt{let}} \ y = \underline{O}(y_1, \ldots, y_n) \ \overline{\mathtt{in}} \ c \overline{@}(\overline{\sigma}', y)) \ldots) \\[4pt]
|e_0@(e_1 \ldots e_n)|_e(\overline{\sigma}, c) &= |e_0|_e \overline{@}(\overline{\sigma}, \overline{\lambda}(\overline{\sigma}_0, y_0). \\
& \qquad |e_1|_e \overline{@}(\overline{\sigma}_0, \overline{\lambda}(\overline{\sigma}_1, y_1)). \ldots |e_n|_e \overline{@}(\overline{\sigma}_{n-1}, \overline{\lambda}(\overline{\sigma}_n, y_n). \\
& \qquad \mathtt{spec} \ y_0 \underline{@}(\overline{\sigma}_n, y_1, \ldots, y_n, \underline{\mathrm{poly}} \ \underline{\lambda}(\overline{\sigma}, y).c \overline{@}(\overline{\sigma}, y))) \ldots))
\end{aligned}
$$

Fig. 5. Two-level translation

$$
\begin{array}{ll}
\underline{\lambda}(\sigma, \mathit{file}, c). & \underline{\mathrm{poly}} \ \underline{\lambda}(\sigma, \mathit{file}, c). \\
\overline{\mathtt{let}} \ \sigma' = \overline{\delta}(\mathrm{read})(\sigma) \ \overline{\mathtt{in}} & \overline{\mathtt{let}} \ \sigma' = \overline{\delta}(\mathrm{read})(\sigma) \ \overline{\mathtt{in}} \\
\overline{\mathtt{if}} \ \overline{=}(\sigma', bad) \ \overline{\mathtt{then}} \ \underline{\mathtt{HALT}}() \ \overline{\mathtt{else}} \quad (1) & \overline{\mathtt{if}} \ \overline{=}(\sigma', bad) \ \overline{\mathtt{then}} \ \underline{\mathtt{HALT}}() \ \overline{\mathtt{else}} \quad (2) \\
\underline{\mathtt{let}} \ y_1 = \underline{\mathrm{read}}(\mathit{file}) \ \underline{\mathtt{in}} & \underline{\mathtt{let}} \ y_1 = \underline{\mathrm{read}}(\mathit{file}) \ \underline{\mathtt{in}} \\
c \underline{@}(\sigma', y_1) & \mathtt{spec} \ (c) \underline{@}(\sigma', y_1)
\end{array}
$$

Fig. 6. Translated example

compile-time continuations to run-time ones, and vice versa, using eta-value expansion. The relevant terms are in the translation of $\mathtt{fix}$ and application: $\underline{\lambda}(\overline{\sigma}, y).c \overline{@}(\overline{\sigma}, y)$ converts the compile-time continuation c to a run-time value and $\overline{\lambda}(\overline{\sigma}, y).\mathtt{spec} \ x_{n+1} \underline{@}(\overline{\sigma}, y)$ converts the run-time continuation x_{n+1} into a compile-time one.

Both the terms for $\mathtt{fix}$ and for application contain subterms of the form $\underline{\lambda}(\overline{\sigma}, x, \ldots).\ldots$ where a run-time function has a compile-time parameter, $\overline{\sigma}$. This violates the well-formedness restriction of traditional partial evaluation [15] and is the motivation for using type specialization altogether.

3.2   Polyvariance Matters

To see, why the `poly` and `spec` annotations in the translation are required, consider a simple example term

$$\lambda(\textit{file})\textbf{read}(\textit{file}) \tag{3}$$

and its translation (1) in Fig. 6. It has specialized type

$$(S\{\textit{before-read}\}, \text{BaseType}, (S\{\textit{after-read}\}, \text{BaseType}) \underrightarrow{} \text{Ans}) \underrightarrow{} \text{Ans}$$

when called in state *before-read* and type

$$(S\{\textit{after-read}\}, \text{BaseType}, (S\{\textit{after-read}\}, \text{BaseType}) \underrightarrow{} \text{Ans}) \underrightarrow{} \text{Ans}$$

when called in state *after-read*. Since the types are different, the function cannot be used at both types at once.

To overcome this restriction, Hughes introduced polyvariance. A polyvariant expression gives rise to a tuple of specializations, one for every different type of use. Hence the translation uses `poly` $\underline{\lambda}(\overline{\sigma}, x, \ldots).\ldots$ which has specialized type $((S\{\sigma_1\}, \text{BaseType}, \ldots) \to \tau_1') \times \ldots \times ((S\{\sigma_n\}, \text{BaseType}, \ldots) \to \tau_n')$, for distinct $\sigma_1, \ldots, \sigma_n$. The set $\{\sigma_1, \ldots, \sigma_n\}$ contains only those states that actually reach a use of the polyvariant type. The specializer determines this set dynamically during specialization. A term `spec` $\ldots$ indicates an elimination point for a tuple introduced by `poly`. It selects a component of the tuple, based on the required type (*i.e.*, the state at the elimination point).

Using `poly` in the translation of (3) yields (2) in Fig. 6 with specialized type

$$\begin{aligned} &((S\{\textit{before-read}\}, \text{BaseType}, (S\{\textit{after-read}\}, \text{BaseType}) \underrightarrow{} \text{Ans}) \underrightarrow{} \text{Ans}) \\ &\times ((S\{\textit{after-read}\}, \text{BaseType}, (S\{\textit{after-read}\}, \text{BaseType}) \underrightarrow{} \text{Ans}) \underrightarrow{} \text{Ans}) \end{aligned} \tag{4}$$

and specialized code

$$\begin{aligned} &(\lambda(\textit{file}, c)\textbf{let } y_1 = \textbf{read}(\textit{file}) \textbf{ in } c@(y_1) \\ &, \lambda(\textit{file}, c)\textbf{let } y_1 = \textbf{read}(\textit{file}) \textbf{ in } c@(y_1)). \end{aligned} \tag{5}$$

3.3   Properties of the Translation

The translation preserves typing.

Proposition 6. *If $\Gamma \vdash e : \tau$ then $\|\Gamma\|_e \vdash |e|_e : |\tau|_e$.*

We state the relation to the naive translation (Fig. 4) using the function *erase*(). It maps a two-level term to a standard term by erasing all overlining and underlining annotations as well as *erase*(`lift` e) = *erase*(e), *erase*(`poly` e) = *erase*(e), and *erase*(`spec` e) = *erase*(e).

Proposition 7. $\sigma, |e|(\sigma, \lambda(\sigma, y)y) \quad \downarrow \quad \sigma', \|v\| \quad$ *if and only if* $\sigma, \textit{erase}(|e|_e)(\sigma, \lambda(\sigma, y)y) \downarrow \sigma', \textit{erase}(\|v\|_e).$

$$|0(e_1 \ldots e_n)|_1'(\overline{\sigma}_0, c)$$
$$= |e_1|_1'(\overline{\sigma}_0, \overline{\lambda}(\overline{\sigma}_1, y_1). \ldots . |e_n|_1'(\overline{\sigma}_{n-1}, \overline{\lambda}(\overline{\sigma}_n, y_n).$$
$$\underline{\mathtt{let}}\ \overline{\sigma}' = \overline{\delta}(0)(\overline{\sigma}_n)\ \underline{\overline{\mathtt{in}}}$$
$$\underline{\overline{\mathtt{if}}}\ \overline{\sigma}' \neq bad\ \underline{\overline{\mathtt{then}}}\ c\overline{\underline{@}}(\overline{\sigma}', \underline{O}(y_1, \ldots, y_n))\ \underline{\overline{\mathtt{else}}}$$
$$\underline{\mathtt{let}}\ \underline{\sigma} = \underline{\delta}(0)(\mathtt{lift}\ \overline{\sigma}_n, y_1, \ldots, y_n)\ \underline{\mathtt{in}}$$
$$\underline{\mathtt{if}}\ \underline{\sigma}{=}\mathtt{lift}\ bad\ \underline{\mathtt{then}}\ \mathtt{halt}()\ \underline{\mathtt{else}}$$
$$\underline{\overline{\mathtt{let}}}\ \{\overline{\sigma}_1', \ldots, \overline{\sigma}_r'\} = \Delta(0)(\overline{\sigma}')\ \underline{\overline{\mathtt{in}}}$$
$$\underline{\mathtt{let}}\ y = \underline{O}(y_1, \ldots, y_n)\ \underline{\mathtt{in}}$$
$$\underline{\mathtt{if}}\ \underline{\sigma}{=}\mathtt{lift}\ \overline{\sigma}_1'\ \underline{\mathtt{then}}\ c\overline{\underline{@}}(\overline{\sigma}_1', y)\ \underline{\mathtt{else}}$$
$$\underline{\mathtt{if}}\ \underline{\sigma}{=}\mathtt{lift}\ \overline{\sigma}_2'\ \underline{\mathtt{then}}\ c\overline{\underline{@}}(\overline{\sigma}_2', y)\ \underline{\mathtt{else}}$$
$$\ldots c\overline{\underline{@}}(\overline{\sigma}_r', y)) \ldots)$$

Fig. 7. Revised heterogeneous treatment of primitive operators

To relate to the compiled/specialized program, we invoke the correctness of the underlying specializer and conclude the safety of the compiled program.

Proposition 8. *Suppose* $\emptyset \vdash \mathtt{trans}\ e\ (\overline{\sigma}_0, \overline{\lambda}(\overline{\sigma}, y).y) \rightsquigarrow e' : \tau'$ *where* $\mathtt{trans}$ *is the program text defining* $|\ |_e$. *The compiled program* e' *is safe wrt.* $\sigma_0 \in \Sigma$.

Technically, Hughes's correctness proof applies to type specialization for a call-by-name lambda calculus. This does not pose problems in our case, because we are only specializing programs in continuation-passing style.

3.4   Achieving Generality

Up to now, the state transition function did not depend on the arguments to the primitives. This restriction can be removed using the revised treatment of primitive operators in Fig. 7.

The code first evaluates and checks the arguments of the operation. If it can predict a potential security violation from the pre-computed security state, $\overline{\sigma}'$, then it generates a run-time test using an implementation, $\underline{\delta}$, of the state transition function applied to the run-time constant, $\mathtt{lift}\ \overline{\sigma}_n$, and the actual arguments. The resulting run-time security state, $\underline{\sigma}$, is tested against bad at run-time. Finally, it extracts a compile-time state from $\underline{\sigma}$ using

$$\Delta(0)(\sigma) = \{\delta(0)(\sigma, y_1, \ldots, y_n) \mid y_1, \ldots, y_n \in Base\} \setminus \{bad\}$$

to estimate the set of possible non-bad outcomes of the run-time state transition $\delta(0)$ on the compile-time state $\overline{\sigma}$. Using this set, the code recovers the compile-time value from the run-time outcome of the state transition by testing the latter against all possible values and using the compile-time value in the continuation. This is essentially "The Trick" [15], a standard binding-time improving transformation. It is a further source of code duplication because the continuation c is processed for each possible outcome.

Specialized types (revised)

$$\tau' ::= \dots \mid \bigwedge [\tau' \dots \tau']$$

Kinding

$$S\{n\} : INT \qquad \frac{\tau_1' : INT \quad \tau_2' : INT}{\tau_1' + \tau_2' : INT}$$

$$\frac{\tau' : INT \quad \tau'' : INT}{\tau' \sim \tau'' : *} \qquad Int \sim Int : * \qquad \frac{\tau_1' \sim \tau_1'' : * \quad \tau_2' \sim \tau_2'' : *}{\tau_1' \to \tau_2' \sim \tau_1'' \to \tau_2'' : *}$$

$$\frac{(\forall 1 \le i,j \le n)\tau_i' \sim \tau_j' : *}{\bigwedge [\tau_1' \dots \tau_n'] : *} \qquad \frac{\tau' \sim \tau'' : *}{\tau' : *}$$

Equality relation (additional rules)

$$\frac{\tau_1' = \tau_1'' \quad \dots \quad \tau_n' = \tau_n''}{\bigwedge [\tau_1', \dots, \tau_n'] = \bigwedge [\tau_1'', \dots, \tau_n'']}$$

Subtyping relation (extending equality)

$$\frac{i \in \{1, \dots, n\}}{\bigwedge [\tau_1', \dots, \tau_n'] \le \tau_i'} \qquad \frac{(\forall 1 \le i \le n)\tau' \le \tau_i'}{\tau' \le \bigwedge [\tau_1', \dots, \tau_n']} \qquad \frac{\tau_2'' \le \tau_2' \quad \tau_1' \le \tau_1''}{\tau_2' \to \tau_1' \le \tau_2'' \to \tau_1''}$$

Additional specialization rules

$$\frac{\Gamma \vdash e \rightsquigarrow e' : \tau' \quad \tau' \le \tau''}{\Gamma \vdash e \rightsquigarrow e' : \tau''} \qquad \frac{(\forall 1 \le i \le n)\Gamma \vdash e_1 \rightsquigarrow e_1' : \tau_i' \quad \Gamma, x \rightsquigarrow x' : \bigwedge [\tau_i' \mid 1 \le i \le n] \vdash e_2 \rightsquigarrow e_2' : \tau'}{\Gamma \vdash \underline{let}\ x = e_1\ \underline{in}\ e_2 \rightsquigarrow \underline{let}\ x' = e_1'\ \underline{in}\ e_2' : \tau'}$$

Fig. 8. Type specialization with intersections and subtyping

4 Compiling Policies Using Intersection Types

The code generated from the translation (Fig. 5) can contain many identically specialized versions of a single function. This section proposes a remedy against this useless code growth.

For a concrete example, let's look again at the translation of $\lambda(\mathit{file})\mathbf{read}(\mathit{file})$ in Fig. 6, (1), its specialized types in (4) and terms in (5). Despite the difference in the specialization types, the code is identical. It turns out that the function has an *intersection type* [5, 3, 26, 27]:

$$\bigwedge \left[\begin{array}{l} (S\{\mathit{before\text{-}read}\}, \mathrm{BaseType}, (S\{\mathit{after\text{-}read}\}, \mathrm{BaseType}) \to \mathrm{Ans}) \to \mathrm{Ans}, \\ (S\{\mathit{after\text{-}read}\}, \mathrm{BaseType}, (S\{\mathit{after\text{-}read}\}, \mathrm{BaseType}) \to \mathrm{Ans}) \to \mathrm{Ans} \end{array} \right] \tag{6}$$

This observation suggests an extension of type specialization with a restricted notion of intersection types and subtyping. The restriction is that intersection types can only be formed from structurally isomorphic types that differ in singleton types, as formalized in Fig. 8 with the judgement $\tau' \sim \tau'' : *$.

In the running example, specialization with intersection types generates the same term $\lambda(\mathit{file}, c)\mathbf{let}\ y_1 = \mathbf{read}(\mathit{file})\ \mathbf{in}\ c@(y_1)$ with type (6).

The extended syntax of specialized types contains finite intersections of types. The rules defining $\tau' = \tau''$ make equality compatible with intersection. Subtyping extends equality with the usual rules for intersection and function subtyping [26].

The additional specialization rules include the standard subsumption rule, which eliminates intersection types where required. The introduction rule for intersection types requires a special <u>let</u> $x = e_1$ <u>in</u> e_2 construct because its implementation incurs considerable expense. The type specializer processes the term e_1 for each demanded type τ_i' and checks that the resulting specialized term e_1' is *identical* for each τ_i'. If that is not possible, we must revert to polyvariance and generate a new variant. Many functions are polymorphic with respect to the security state. In this case, the intersection typing generates exactly one variant.

Finally, we have to extend the simulation result (Prop. 1) to the enriched language. Since there are no new reductions, it is sufficient to extend the proofs of the substitution lemmas [13]:

Lemma 1 (Source substitution). *If $\Gamma \vdash e_1 \rightsquigarrow e_1' : \tau_1'$ and $\Gamma, x_1 \rightsquigarrow e_1' : \tau_1' \vdash e_2 \rightsquigarrow e_2' : \tau_2'$ then $\Gamma \vdash e_2[x_1 \mapsto e_1] \rightsquigarrow e_2' : \tau_2'$.*

Lemma 2 (Specialized substitution). *Let θ be a substitution that maps variables in specialized terms to specialized terms. If $\Gamma \vdash e \rightsquigarrow e' : \tau'$ then $\theta(\Gamma) \vdash e \rightsquigarrow \theta(e') : \tau'$.*

5   Conclusions

We have shown that partial evaluation techniques are well-suited to translate programs into safe programs that observe security policies specified by security automata. We have exhibited a heterogeneous approach that eliminates most run-time security checks, but can result in code duplication.

We have extended the type specializer by intersection types to avoid excessive code duplication in this approach. This refined approach automatically achieves all optimizations mentioned in Walker's work [36]. A prototype implementation, which has been used to validate the examples in this paper, can be obtained from the author.

In future work we plan to address the restriction to finite sets of security states by splitting them into compile-time and run-time components and to integrate the translation with our earlier work on run-time code generation [33]. The resulting framework will provide just-in-time enforcing compilation and it will serve for experiments with mobile code.

References

1. A.-R. Adl-Tabatabai, G. Langdale, S. Lucco, and R. Wahbe. Efficient and language-independent mobile programs. In *Proceedings of the ACM SIGPLAN '96 Conference on Programming Language Design and Implementation (PLDI)*, pages 127–136, Philadelphia, Pa., May 1996.
2. A. W. Appel and A. P. Felty. A semantics model of types and machine instructions for proof-carrying code. In Reps [29], pages 243–253.
3. F. Barbanera and M. Dezani-Ciancaglini. Intersection and union types. In T. Ito and A. Meyer, editors, *Proc. Theoretical Aspects of Computer Software*, volume 526 of *Lecture Notes in Computer Science*, Sendai, Japan, 1991. Springer-Verlag.

4. T. Colcombet and P. Fradet. Enforcing trace properties by program transformation. In Reps [29], pages 54–66.
5. M. Coppo and M. Dezani-Ciancaglini. A new type-assignment for λ-terms. *Archiv. Math. Logik*, 19(139-156), 1978.
6. O. Danvy and A. Filinski. Abstracting control. In *Proc. 1990 ACM Conference on Lisp and Functional Programming*, pages 151–160, Nice, France, 1990. ACM Press.
7. O. Danvy and A. Filinski. Representing control: A study of the CPS transformation. *Mathematical Structures in Computer Science*, 2:361–391, 1992.
8. D. Evans and A. Twyman. Flexible policy-directed code safety. In *IEEE Symposium on Security and Privacy*, Oakland, CA, May 1999.
9. R. Glück. On the generation of specializers. *Journal of Functional Programming*, 4(4):499–514, Oct. 1994.
10. R. Glück and J. Jørgensen. Generating optimizing specializers. In *IEEE International Conference on Computer Languages*, pages 183–194. IEEE Computer Society Press, 1994.
11. R. Glück and J. Jørgensen. Generating transformers for deforestation and supercompilation. In B. Le Charlier, editor, *Static Analysis*, volume 864 of *Lecture Notes in Computer Science*, pages 432–448. Springer-Verlag, 1994.
12. J. Hughes. Type specialisation for the λ-calculus; or, a new paradigm for partial evaluation based on type inference. In O. Danvy, R. Glück, and P. Thiemann, editors, *Partial Evaluation*, volume 1110 of *Lecture Notes in Computer Science*, pages 183–215, Schloß Dagstuhl, Germany, Feb. 1996. Springer-Verlag.
13. J. Hughes. The correctness of type specialisation. In G. Smolka, editor, *Proc. 9th European Symposium on Programming*, volume 1782 of *Lecture Notes in Computer Science*, pages 215–229, Berlin, Germany, Mar. 2000. Springer-Verlag.
14. Java2 platform. http://www.javasoft.com/products/, 2000.
15. N. D. Jones, C. K. Gomard, and P. Sestoft. *Partial Evaluation and Automatic Program Generation*. Prentice-Hall, 1993.
16. D. Kozen. Language-based security. Technical Report TR99-1751, Cornell University, Computer Science, June 15, 1999.
17. Úlfar Erlingsson and F. B. Schneider. SASI enforcement of security policies: A retrospective. In *Proceedings of the 1999 New Security Paradigms Workshop*, Caledon Hills, Ontario, Canada, Sept. 1999.
18. T. Lindholm and F. Yellin. *The Java Virtual Machine Specification*. Addison-Wesley, 1996.
19. S. Lucco, O. Sharp, and R. Wahbe. Omniware: A universal substrate for web programming. *WorldWideWeb Journal*, 1(1), Dec. 1995.
20. N. G. Michael and A. W. Appel. Machine instruction syntax and semantics in higher order logic. In *17th International Conference on Automated Deduction (CADE-17)*, June 2000.
21. G. Morrisett, D. Walker, K. Crary, and N. Glew. From system F to typed assembly language. In L. Cardelli, editor, *Proc. 25th Annual ACM Symposium on Principles of Programming Languages*, San Diego, CA, USA, Jan. 1998. ACM Press.
22. G. C. Necula. Proof-carrying code. In *Proceedings of the 24th ACM Symposium on Principles of Programming Languages*, Paris, France, Jan. 1997.
23. G. C. Necula and P. Lee. Safe kernel extensions without run-time checking. In *Proceedings of the Second Symposium on Operating System Design and Implementation*, Seattle, Wa., Oct. 1996.

24. G. C. Necula and P. Lee. The design and implementation of a certifying compiler. In K. D. Cooper, editor, *Proceedings of the 1998 ACM SIGPLAN Conference on Programming Language Design and Implementation (PLDI)*, pages 333–344, Montreal, Canada, June 1998. ACM. Volume 33(5) of SIGPLAN Notices.

25. G. C. Necula and P. Lee. Safe, Untrusted Agents Using Proof-Carrying Code. In G. Vigna, editor, *Mobile Agent Security*, Lecture Notes in Computer Science No. 1419, pages 61–91. Springer-Verlag: Heidelberg, Germany, 1998.

26. B. Pierce. Programming with intersection types, union types, and polymorphism. Technical Report CMU-CS-91-106, Carnegie Mellon University, Feb. 1991.

27. B. C. Pierce. Intersection types and bounded polymorphism. *Mathematical Structures in Computer Science*, 11, 1996.

28. F. Pottier, C. Skalka, and S. Smith. A systematic approach to static access control. In D. Sands, editor, *Proc. 10th European Symposium on Programming*, Lecture Notes in Computer Science, Genova, Italy, Apr. 2001. Springer-Verlag.

29. T. Reps, editor. *Proc. 27th Annual ACM Symposium on Principles of Programming Languages*, Boston, MA, USA, Jan. 2000. ACM Press.

30. J. C. Reynolds. Definitional interpreters for higher-order programming languages. In *ACM Annual Conference*, pages 717–740, July 1972.

31. F. B. Schneider. Enforceable security policies. Technical Report TR99-1759, Cornell University, Ithaca, NY, USA, July 1999.

32. M. Sperber, R. Glück, and P. Thiemann. Bootstrapping higher-order program transformers from interpreters. In *Proc. 11th Annual Symposium on Applied Computing, SAC (SAC '96)*, pages 408–413, Philadelphia, PA, Feb. 1996. ACM.

33. M. Sperber and P. Thiemann. Two for the price of one: Composing partial evaluation and compilation. In *Proc. of the ACM SIGPLAN '97 Conference on Programming Language Design and Implementation*, pages 215–225, Las Vegas, NV, USA, June 1997. ACM Press.

34. V. F. Turchin. Program tranformation with metasystem transitions. *Journal of Functional Programming*, 3(3):283–313, July 1993.

35. R. Wahbe, S. Lucco, T. E. Anderson, and S. L. Graham. Efficient software-based fault isolation. In *Proceedings of the 14th ACM Symposium on Operating Systems Principles*, pages 203–216, 1993.

36. D. Walker. A type system for expressive security policies. In Reps [29], pages 254–267.

37. D. S. Wallach and E. W. Felten. Understanding java stack inspection. In *Proceedings of 1998 IEEE Symposium on Security and Privacy*, Oakland, CA, May 1998.

Semantics and Program Analysis of Computationally Secure Information Flow

Peeter Laud[*]

FR Informatik
Universität des Saarlandes
laud@cs.uni-sb.de

Abstract. This paper presents a definition of secure information flow. It is not based on noninterference, but on computational indistinguishability of the secret inputs, when the public outputs are observed. This definition allows cryptographic primitives to be handled. This paper also presents a Denning-style information-flow analysis for programs that use encryption as a primitive operation. The proof of the correctness of the analysis is sketched.

1 Introduction

When is a program safe to run? One aspect of safety is confidentiality, which arises when the inputs and outputs of the program are partitioned into several different security classes. The typical classification of data is into public and confidential (of course, more complex classifications are also possible); for example, data that is received from or sent to a network may be treated as public, and data that is local to the site executing the program, as confidential. Our goal is to verify that an attacker who can observe the public outputs of the program cannot learn anything about the confidential inputs. In this case we say, that the program has *secure information flow*.

What does it mean that an attacker can or cannot learn anything? There exists quite a large body of literature studying different instances of secure information flow, e.g., [3,4,5,7,10,11,12,13,14,15,16]. With the notable exception of [15,16], security is defined through noninterference, i.e., it is required that the public outputs of the program do not contain any information (in the information-theoretic sense) about the confidential inputs. This corresponds to an all-powerful attacker who, in his quest to obtain confidential information, has no bounds on the resources (time and space), that it can use. Furthermore, in these definitions an "attacker" is represented by an arbitrary function, which does not even have to be a computable function; the attacker is permitted essentially arbitrary power.

The approach of defining the concept of "secure information flow" by means of an all-powerful adversary does not allow for cryptographic primitives to be treated easily, as they are usually only computationally secure, but not informa-

---

[*] Supported by Deutsche Forschungsgemeinschaft, under the Graduate Studies Program #623, "Quality Guarantees for Computer Systems"

D. Sands (Ed.): ESOP 2001, LNCS 2028, pp. 77–91, 2001.

tion-theoretically. Also, realistic adversaries are resource-bounded; hence this should be reflected in our definitions, especially if we can show that more programs are secure by this means.

The contributions of this paper are as follows:

– A definition of secure information flow that corresponds to an adversary working in probabilistic polynomial time (in the following abridged as *PPT*; where "polynomial" means polynomial in a suitable security parameter[1]). Our definition of secure information flow is stated in terms of program's inputs and outputs only, in this sense it is similar to that of Leino and Joshi [10].
– A program analysis that allows us to certify that the flow of information in the program is secure in the aforementioned sense. The programming language contains a binary operator "encrypt message x under the key k"[2]. The analysis reflects that finding the message from the cryptotext is infeasible without knowing the key.

2 Related Work

The use of program analysis to determine information flow was pioneered by Denning [4,5]. She instrumented the semantics of programs with annotations that expressed which program variables were dependent on which other program variables. The definition of secure information flow was given in terms of these instrumentations [5]. Also, she gave an accompanying program analysis.

Volpano et al. [14] gave a definition of secure information flow without using any instrumentations. They define a program to be secure if there exists a simulation of the program that operates only on the public variables and delivers the same public outputs. They also give a type system for certifying programs for secure information flow.

Leino and Joshi [10] give a definition of secure information flow that makes use of programs' inputs and outputs only. They define the program to be secure if the values of its secret inputs cannot be observed from its public outputs. Sabelfeld and Sands [13] and Abadi et al. [1] have given generalisations of this idea. However, none of these papers describes an accompanying mechanical verification tool.

Recently, Volpano and Smith [15,16] have weakened the security definition a bit (it is no longer noninterference) to handle cryptographic primitives, namely one-way functions. However, there are two ways in which their definition might be considered unsatisfactory:

– It is too restrictive in allowing the use of constructs that violate the noninterference condition.
– The notion of security is too lax (in [16] Volpano allows the adversary to find out *partial* information about the confidential input value).

---

[1] by encryption, the security parameter is related to (and often defined to be equal to) the key length

[2] also contains a nullary operator "generate a new key"

Work has also been done to define and handle the integrity properties of data (e.g. [7,11]). These questions are outside the scope of this paper.

Another work, which is not about secure information flow, but which has influenced the current paper, is that of Abadi and Rogaway [2]. They provide a computational justification of one part of the formal approach to cryptography — namely to the construction of messages from simpler ones by tupling and encryption. The construction of messages could be viewed as a straight-line program; actually, if one only considers straight-line programs, then their results subsume ours. Because of our treatment of control flow, we have seemingly more restrictions on programs than they have.

3   Syntax and Semantics

The programming language that we consider is a simple imperative programming language (the WHILE-language). Given a set **Var** of variables and a set **Op** of arithmetic, relational, boolean etc. operators, the syntax of the programs is given by the following grammar:

$$
\begin{aligned}
\mathsf{P} ::=\ & x := o(x_1, \dots, x_k) \\
\mid\ & \mathsf{P}_1; \mathsf{P}_2 \\
\mid\ & \textit{if } b \textit{ then } \mathsf{P}_1 \textit{ else } \mathsf{P}_2 \\
\mid\ & \textit{while } b \textit{ do } \mathsf{P}_1,
\end{aligned}
$$

where $b, x, x_1, \dots, x_k$ range over **Var**, o ranges over **Op** and $\mathsf{P}_1, \mathsf{P}_2$ range over programs. We assume that there are two distinguished elements in the set **Op** — a binary operator $\mathcal{E}nc$ ($\mathcal{E}nc(k, x)$ is the encryption of the message x under the key k) and a nullary operator $\mathcal{G}en$ (generating a new key).

We also make use of flowcharts as the program representation. Each node of the flowchart contains either an assignment statement or a test. Additionally, we add an extra *start-* and an extra *end-*node to the flowchart. It should be clear, how a program P is converted to a flowchart.

The semantics that we give for the programming language, is denotational in style. If **State** is the set of all possible internal states of the program, then the denotational semantics usually has the type **State** $\rightarrow$ **State**$_\perp$, i.e. it maps the initial state of the program to its final state. **State**$_\perp$:= **State** $\uplus \{\perp\}$, where $\perp$ denotes non-termination. Moreover, one usually defines **State** := **Var** $\rightarrow$ **Val**, where **Val** is the set of all possible values that the variables can take. The set **Val** is usually not specified any further.

Furthermore, for defining the semantics of programs one requires that for each operator $o \in$ **Op** of arity k its semantics $[\![o]\!] :$ **Val**$^k \rightarrow$ **Val** has already been defined. We want that $[\![\mathcal{E}nc]\!]$ and $[\![\mathcal{G}en]\!]$ satisfy certain cryptographic definitions, namely the following:

Definition 1 (from [2]). *An encryption scheme* (*Gen, Enc*) [3] *is which-key and repetition concealing, if for every PPT algorithm with two oracles* $\mathcal{A}^{(\cdot),(\cdot)}$, *the following difference of probabilities is negligible in n:*

---

[3] This tuple should also have the third component — the decryption algorithm, but we do not need it for that definition

$$\Pr\big[k, k' \leftarrow Gen(\mathbf{1}^n) \; : \; \mathcal{A}^{Enc(\mathbf{1}^n, k, \cdot), Enc(\mathbf{1}^n, k', \cdot)}(\mathbf{1}^n) = 1\big] -$$
$$\Pr\big[k \leftarrow Gen(\mathbf{1}^n) \; : \; \mathcal{A}^{Enc(\mathbf{1}^n, k, \mathbf{0}^{|\cdot|}), Enc(\mathbf{1}^n, k, \mathbf{0}^{|\cdot|})}(\mathbf{1}^n) = 1\big] \; .$$

Here $\ell(n) \in \mathbb{Z}[n]$ is a suitable *length polynomial*. An encryption system is thus which-key and repetition concealing, if no (polynomially bounded) adversary can distinguish the following two situations: There are two black boxes.

1. Given a bitstring as the input, the boxes encrypt it and return the result. They use different encryption keys.
2. The black boxes throw away their input and return the encryption of a fixed bit-string $\mathbf{0}^{\ell(n)}$. Both boxes use the same encryption key.

From this definition we see, that the structure of the semantics has to be more complicated than just having the type $\mathbf{State} \rightarrow \mathbf{State}_\perp$. The issues are:

– According to Def. 1, *Enc* and *Gen* are not functions, but are families of functions, indexed by the *security parameter* $n \in \mathbb{N}$. Hence the semantics also has to be a family of functions, mapping a program's inputs to its outputs. For each n we have to define a set $\mathbf{State}_n$ and the n-th component of semantics would map each element of $\mathbf{State}_n$ to $\mathbf{State}_{n\perp}$.
– The algorithms *Enc* and *Gen* operate over bit-strings[4]. Therefore we specify $\mathbf{State}_n := \mathbf{Var} \rightarrow \mathbf{Val}_n$ and $\mathbf{Val}_n := \{0, 1\}^{\ell(n)}$.
– Clearly no family of *deterministic* functions satisfies Def. 1; the families of functions *Gen* and *Enc* have to be *probabilistic*. Thus the semantics of programs has to be probabilistic, too. Its n-th component maps each element of $\mathbf{State}_n$ to a probability distribution over $\mathbf{State}_{n\perp}$. We denote the set of probability distributions over a set $\mathcal{X}$ by $\mathcal{D}(\mathcal{X})$.

There is one more issue. We are not interested in program runs that take too much time. The encryption scheme is defined to be secure only against polynomially bounded adversaries. Thus we are interested in only "polynomially long" program runs (i.e. the set of interesting runs may be different for different values of the security parameter). We support this discrimination by defining a previously described family of functions mapping inputs to outputs *for each path in the flowchart* from the *start*- to the *end*-node. Also, the (intuitive) meaning of $\perp$ changes. Instead of denoting non-termination it now means "control flow does not follow that path".

To sum it all up, the semantics $[\![P]\!]_{\mathrm{Path}}$ of a program P has the type $\mathbf{Path} \rightarrow \prod_{n \in \mathbb{N}}(\mathbf{State}_n \rightarrow \mathcal{D}(\mathbf{State}_{n\perp}))$, where $\mathbf{Path}$ denotes all paths in the flowchart of P from *start* to *end*. Also

– for each operator $o \in \mathbf{Op}$ of arity k the semantics of o is a family of (possibly probabilistic) functions $[\![o]\!] : \prod_{n \in \mathbb{N}}(\mathbf{Val}_n^k \rightarrow \mathcal{D}(\mathbf{Val}_n))$;
– $([\![\mathcal{G}en]\!], [\![\mathcal{E}nc]\!])$ is a which-key and repetition concealing encryption scheme.

---

[4] this is not so explicit in the above definition, but it is the standard in complexity-theoretic definitions of cryptographic primitives

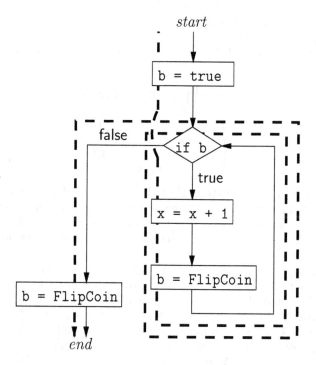

Fig. 1. Example for the semantics of paths

To explain the semantics of the program at a certain path, look at the program P in Fig. 1. Suppose that the semantics of the operator `FlipCoin` is such, that it returns either true or false with equal probability. Let the marked path be P. For each $x_{\text{init}}, b_{\text{init}} \in \mathbf{Val}_n$ we have

$$[\![P]\!]_{\text{Path}}(P)(\left\{\begin{array}{l} x \mapsto x_{\text{init}} \\ b \mapsto b_{\text{init}} \end{array}\right\}) = \left\{\begin{array}{ll} \left\{\begin{array}{l} x \mapsto x_{\text{init}} + 2 \\ b \mapsto \text{true} \end{array}\right\} \mapsto \frac{1}{8} \\ \left\{\begin{array}{l} x \mapsto x_{\text{init}} + 2 \\ b \mapsto \text{false} \end{array}\right\} \mapsto \frac{1}{8} \\ \bot \qquad\qquad\quad \mapsto \frac{3}{4} \end{array}\right\}.$$

It should be clear from this example, how $[\![P]\!]_{\text{Path}}$ is calculated. We omit the further specifications from this paper.

4   Confidentiality Definition

The confidentiality definition expresses that something holds for all (long enough) polynomially long computations. This needs an exact definition of a polynomially long computation.

Definition 2. *A function* $S : \mathbb{N} \to \mathcal{P}(\mathbf{Path})$ *is a* polynomially long path-set, *iff there exists a polynomial* $q \in \mathbb{Z}[n]$, *such that for all* n, *the length of the elements (paths) of* $S(n)$ *is not greater than* $q(n)$.

We denote the set of all polynomially long path-sets by $\mathcal{PLP}$. The set $\mathcal{PLP}$ is ordered by pointwise inclusion.

Given a program P and a polynomially long path-set $\mathcal{S}$, we can define, how P behaves on $\mathcal{S}$.

$$[\![P]\!] : \mathcal{PLP} \to \prod_{n\in\mathbb{N}}(\mathbf{State}_n \to \mathcal{D}(\mathbf{State}_{n\perp}))$$

$$[\![P]\!](\mathcal{S})(S_{n,s}) = \left\{\begin{array}{l} S_n \mapsto \sum_{P\in\mathcal{S}(n)} [\![P]\!]_{\mathrm{Path}}(P)(S_{n,s})(S_n) \\ \perp \mapsto 1 - \sum_{S_n\in\mathbf{State}_n} [\![P]\!](\mathcal{S})(S_{n,s})(S_n) \end{array}\right\},$$

where $n \in \mathbb{N}$, $S_{n,s}, S_n \in \mathbf{State}_n$. Thus the behaviour of P on a path-set is the "sum" of its behaviours on the elements of this path-set. The probability, that a final state S_n is reached over $\mathcal{S}$ is the sum of probabilities that this state is reached over the elements of $\mathcal{S}(n)$. $\perp$ means, that the control flow does not follow any path in $\mathcal{S}(n)$.

We are going to define, what it means, that certain outputs of the program do reveal something about a part (the confidential part) of the input to the program. What kind of object is this "part of the input"? In most general case it is just a family of functions $c = \{c_n\}_{n\in\mathbb{N}}$, $c_n : \mathbf{State}_n \to \{0,1\}^*$. For example, if the set of variables has been partitioned into public and confidential variables, then $c_n(S_n)$ would return a tuple consisting of the values of all confidential variables in the state S_n. As we are going to define *computational* security, we require, that c is polynomial-time computable, i.e. there exists an algorithm $\mathcal{C}$ that works in polynomial time and $\mathcal{C}(\mathbf{1}^n, S_n) = c_n(S_n)$.

Definition 3. *A part $c = \{c_n\}_{n\in\mathbb{N}}$ of the input, given to program P is recoverable from the final values of the variables in $Y \subseteq \mathbf{Var}$, given that the input to P is distributed accordingly to $D_s = \{D_{n,s}\}_{n\in\mathbb{N}}$, $D_{n,s} \in \mathcal{D}(\mathbf{State}_n)$, iff there exists a polynomial-time computable predicate $B = \{B_n\}_{n\in\mathbb{N}}$, $B_n : \{0,1\}^* \to \{0,1\}$ and a polynomially long path-set $\mathcal{S}_0 \in \mathcal{PLP}$, such that for all polynomially long path-sets $\mathcal{S} \in \mathcal{PLP}$, where $\mathcal{S} \geq \mathcal{S}_0$, there exists a PPT algorithm $\mathcal{A}$, such that for all PPT algorithms $\mathcal{B}$ the following difference is not negligible in n:*

$$\Pr\left[S_{n,s} \leftarrow D_{n,s}, S_n \leftarrow [\![P]\!](\mathcal{S})(S_{n,s}) : \mathcal{A}(\mathbf{1}^n, S_n|_Y) = B_n(c_n(S_{n,s}))\right] -$$
$$\Pr\left[S_{n,s} \leftarrow D_{n,s} : \mathcal{B}(\mathbf{1}^n) = B_n(c_n(S_{n,s}))\right] .$$

Let us explain some points of this definition a bit:

- We demand that after the program has run for long enough (but still polynomial!) time ($\exists \mathcal{S}_0 \forall \mathcal{S} \geq \mathcal{S}_0$), its behaviour "stabilises" in the sense that nothing more will become or cease to be recoverable.
- We demand that after this stabilisation, a property that is similar to the notion of semantic security (more exactly, to its negation) of encryption systems must hold for $[\![P]\!](\mathcal{S})$, with regard to c and Y. We require, that the final values of the variables in Y tell us something about c, that we did not know before. See [6, Sec. 5] (and also references therein) for the discussion of semantic security.

- The probability distribution of the inputs to the program has been made explicit in our definition. It has not usually been the case in earlier works (for example [4,11,14]), where one has *implicitly* assumed, that the input variables are independent of each other.
- The definition of recoverability is termination-sensitive, as the value S_n that is picked accordingly to $[\![P]\!](\mathcal{S})(S_{n,s})$ may also be $\perp$ (in this case define the contraction of $\perp$ to Y to be $\perp$, too). However, it is not sensitive to timing.

We say, that the program P is secure for the initial distribution D_s, if the secret part of its input is not recoverable from the final values of the set of the public variables of P.

5   Program Analysis

We suppose that we have a fixed program P, the secret part of the input c that is calculated by the algorithm $\mathcal{C}$ in polynomial time, and the initial probability distribution D_s. Before we present our analysis, let us state some further constraints to the programs and to the details of the semantics, that we have not stated before, because they had been unnecessary to give the definition of recoverability. For some of these constraints it is intuitively clear that they must be obeyed, if we talk about computational security. Some other constraints are really the shortcomings of our quite simple analysis (comparable in its power to the one in [5]) and removal of them should be the subject of further work.

- For each operator $o \in \mathbf{Op}$, the semantics of o must be computable in polynomial time, i.e. there must exist a polynomial-time algorithm $\mathcal{O}$, such that $[\![o]\!]_n(\cdot) = \mathcal{O}(\mathbf{1}^n, \cdot)$ for all n. Otherwise we could have an atomic operation "crack the key" in our programming language . . . . Thus the necessity of this constraint should be obvious.
- The probability distribution D_s must be polynomial-time constructible, i.e. there must be a PPT algorithm $\mathcal{D}$, such that the random variables $D_{n,s}$ and $\mathcal{D}(\mathbf{1}^n)$ have identical distribution for each n. Without this requirement it might be possible to use the initial distribution as an oracle of some sort and thus answer questions that a PPT algorithm should be unable to answer.
- Keys and non-keys must not be mixed, i.e., each variable in $\mathbf{Var}$ should have a type of either "key" or "data" and it is not allowed to substitute one for another. The output of $\mathcal{Gen}$ and the first input (the key) of $\mathcal{Enc}$ have the type "key", everything else has the type "data". This has several consequences:
  - One may not use data as keys. This is an obvious constraint, because it just means that the used keys must be good ones, i.e. created by $\mathcal{Gen}$. An extra constraint is that the initial values of the variables of type "key" must be good keys, too.
  - One may not use keys as data. This is a shortcoming of our analysis, that for example [2] (almost) does not have. We believe that using their techniques it is possible to get rid of that constraint.
  - There is no decryption operator. Also a shortcoming. We believe that by building definition-use chains between encryption and decryption operators it is possible to keep track, what could be calculated from the encrypted data, and to remove the shortcoming that way.

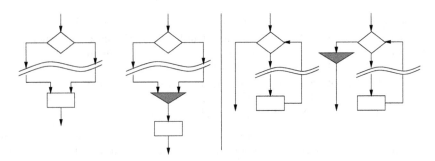

Fig. 2. Auxiliary nodes to separate control dependency regions

- At each program point, it must be statically known, which keys are equal and which are not. This is probably the biggest shortcoming of our analysis. We defer its discussion to Sec. 7. For each node N of the flowchart and each variable k with type "key", we let $\mathsf{E}(N, k) \subseteq \mathbf{Var}$ denote the set of keys that are equal to k at the node N. If the program satisfies this requirement, then one can compute E easily by using the methods of alias analysis, see, for example [9, Sec. 4.2.1 and 4.2.2]. Note that this requirement also generates a constraint on D_s, similar to the case of requiring good keys.
- The program P must run in expected polynomial time. Although our security definition is termination sensitive, our analysis is not.

To handle the implicit flows more comfortably, we add dummy nodes (we call them *merge*-nodes) to the flowchart in those places where the control dependency regions end. Figure 2 explains adding *merge*-nodes to branches and while-loops. In this way the starts and ends of the control dependency regions are marked in the flowchart (starts with *if*, ends with *merge*) and we do not have to treat the edges going from one control dependency region to another differently from those that start and end inside the same region.

The type of the analysis $\mathcal{W}$ is $Node \to \mathcal{P}_{\mathrm{U}}(\mathcal{P}(\widetilde{\mathbf{Var}}))$, where $Node$ is the set of the nodes in the flowchart and $\widetilde{\mathbf{Var}} = \mathbf{Var} \cup Node_{if}$, where $Node_{if} \subset Node$ is the set of all *if*-nodes. Here $\mathcal{P}_{\mathrm{U}}(\mathcal{X})$, where $\mathcal{X}$ is a partially ordered set, denotes the set of all such subsets of $\mathcal{X}$ that are upper closed. We will also make use of an operator $\mathsf{cl}_{\mathrm{U}}(\cdot)$ which, when applied to a subset of a partially ordered set, returns its upper closure.

$Y \in \mathcal{W}(N)$, where $N \in Node$ and $Y \subseteq \widetilde{\mathbf{Var}}$ means that the analysis has determined that at node N the secret part of the input of the program may be recoverable from the values of the variables in $Y \cap \mathbf{Var}$, if one also takes into account that at the nodes in $Y \cap Node_{if}$ the branch leading to the node N was chosen. Actually the *if*-nodes in Y are used to track the implicit flow from the boolean variables that guard them. A better explanation can be given after presenting the transfer functions for *if*- and *merge*-nodes. The analysis may erroneously report that the secret part of the input is recoverable from Y, when in reality it isn't. However, the analysis may not err to the other side.

We continue with presenting the transfer functions $[\![N]\!]_{\text{abstr}}$, where $N \in \textit{Node}$. The type of these functions is obviously $\mathcal{P}_U(\mathcal{P}(\widetilde{\mathbf{Var}})) \to \mathcal{P}_U(\mathcal{P}(\widetilde{\mathbf{Var}}))$. We start by giving two auxiliary functions (of the same type). Let $x \in \widetilde{\mathbf{Var}}$, $X, Y \subseteq \widetilde{\mathbf{Var}}$, $\mathcal{X} \in \mathcal{P}_U(\mathcal{P}(\widetilde{\mathbf{Var}}))$.

$$\text{kill}\big[x\big](\mathcal{X}) = \text{cl}_U(\{Z \mid Z \in \mathcal{X}, x \notin Z\})$$
$$\text{flow}\big[X \Rightarrow Y\big](\mathcal{X}) = \text{cl}_U(\mathcal{X} \cup \{(Z \backslash X) \cup \{v\} \mid Z \in \mathcal{X}, v \in Y\})$$

The meaning of the function $\text{kill}\big[x\big]$ should be obvious. The function $\text{flow}\big[X \Rightarrow Y\big]$ describes the flow of information from the variables in X to the variables in Y. It says, that if an adversary can find something from the values of the variables in the set Z, then after the information has flown, the properties of the values of the variables in $Z \cap X$, that the adversary makes use of, may also be derivable from the value of some variable in Y.

- The node N is labeled with $x := o(x_1, \dots, x_k)$, where $o \neq \mathcal{E}nc$. Assume w.l.o.g. that x is different from $x_1, \dots, x_k$.

$$[\![N]\!]_{\text{abstr}} = \text{flow}\big[\{x_1, \dots, x_k\} \Rightarrow \{x\}\big] \circ \text{kill}\big[x\big]$$

- The node N is labeled with $x := \mathcal{E}nc(k, y)$. We again assume that $x \neq y$. Let $K \subseteq \mathbf{Var}$, such that all variables in K have the type "key". Define one more auxiliary function

$$\text{flow}\big[X \overset{K}{\Rightarrow} Y\big](\mathcal{X}) = \text{cl}_U(\mathcal{X} \cup \{(Z \backslash X) \cup \{v, k\} \mid Z \in \mathcal{X}, v \in Y, k \in K\}),$$

which describes the flow of information from X to Y, during which it becomes encrypted with some key from the set K.

$$[\![N]\!]_{\text{abstr}} = \text{flow}\big[\{y\} \overset{\text{E}(N,k)}{\Rightarrow} \{x\}\big] \circ \text{kill}\big[x\big]$$

- The node N is labeled with *if* b.

$$[\![N]\!]_{\text{abstr}} = \text{flow}\big[\{b\} \Rightarrow \{N\}\big]$$

- The node N is a *merge*-node. Let the corresponding *if*-node be N_{if}. Let $\mathbf{Var}_{\text{asgn}} \subseteq \mathbf{Var}$ be the set of variables that are assigned to somewhere between N_{if} and N.

$$[\![N]\!]_{\text{abstr}} = \text{kill}\big[N_{\text{if}}\big] \circ \text{flow}\big[\{N_{\text{if}}\} \Rightarrow \mathbf{Var}_{\text{asgn}}\big]$$

Here we see how the implicit flow from a boolean variable to those variables, assigning to which it controls, is taken care of. ($b \Rightarrow N_{\text{if}} \Rightarrow \mathbf{Var}_{\text{asgn}}$)
- The transfer function for the *end*-node is the identity function.
- The node N is the *start*-node. What should be our initial analysis information? It must describe the initial probability distribution D_s. For example, if the secret part c of the input is just the values of the variables from the set $\mathbf{Var}_{\text{conf}}$ and according to D_s, all input variables are independent of each other, the initial analysis information must be at least

$\mathsf{cl}_U(\{\{x\} \mid x \in \mathbf{Var}_{conf}\})$. In general case (and formally), if $Y_1, \dots, Y_l \subseteq \mathbf{Var}$ and there exist a polynomial-time computable predicate $B = \{B_n\}_{n\in\mathbb{N}}$ and a PPT algorithm with an oracle $\mathcal{A}^{(\cdot)}$, such that for each PPT algorithm $\mathcal{B}$ there exists an i, $1 \leq i \leq l$, such that

$$\Pr\left[S_{n,s} \leftarrow D_{n,s} \; : \; \mathcal{A}^{\mathcal{B}(\mathbf{1}^n)}(\mathbf{1}^n, i, S_{n,s}|_{Y_i}) = B(c_n(S_{n,s}))\right] -$$
$$\Pr\left[S_{n,s} \leftarrow D_{n,s} \; : \; \mathcal{B}(\mathbf{1}^n) = B(c_n(S_{n,s}))\right]$$

is not negligible in n, then at least one of the sets $Y_1, \dots, Y_l$ must be an element of the initial analysis information.

The set $\mathcal{P}_U(\mathcal{P}(\widetilde{\mathbf{Var}}))$ is obviously ordered by inclusion and the least upper bound is the set union. This completes the specification of the data flow analysis.

6 Proof of Correctness

Theorem 1. *Let* P *be a program in the* WHILE-*language, let* **Var** *be its set of variables and* N_{end} *be the node labeled with* end *in its flowchart. Let* c *be the secret part of the input to* P, *let* D_s *be the probability distribution of the input, let* $Y \subseteq \mathbf{Var}$. *Let the requirements in the beginning of Sec. 5 be satisfied and let* $\mathcal{W}$ *be the program analysis for* P, c *and* D_s. *If* c *is recoverable from the final values of the variables in* Y, *given that the input to* P *is distributed accordingly to* D_s, *then* $Y \in \mathcal{W}(N_{end})$.

The theorem thus says that if one can find out something about the secret input when observing certain outputs, then the analysis reports that these outputs give away secret information.

We define some auxiliary notions to present a technical lemma. Let $\overline{\mathcal{W}}$: $\mathcal{P}(\mathbf{Var}) \to \mathcal{P}_U(\mathcal{P}(\mathbf{Var}))$ be such, that $\overline{\mathcal{W}}(X)$, where $X \subseteq \mathbf{Var}$, equals $\mathcal{W}(N_{end})$ if we take $\mathcal{W}(N_{start})$ to be equal to $\mathsf{cl}_U(\{X\})$ and calculate $\mathcal{W}(N_{end})$ by the analysis given in the previous section. Thus $\overline{\mathcal{W}}(X)$ is the set of sets of variables that are "caused to be" in the analysis result for N_{end} by the presence of X in the initial analysis information. For $Y \subseteq \mathbf{Var}$ let $\mathcal{M}(Y) := \{X \subseteq \mathbf{Var} \mid Y \in \overline{\mathcal{W}}(X)\}$ and let $\overline{\mathcal{M}}(Y)$ be the set of all maximal elements of $\mathcal{M}(Y)$.

Lemma 1. *Let* P *be a program. Let its flowchart be annotated with the assumptions about the equality of keys (i.e. let* E *be fixed). Let* $q \in \mathbb{Z}[n]$ *and let* $S \in \mathcal{PLP}$ *be such, that a path* P *belongs to* $S(n)$ *iff* $|P| \leq q(n)$.

There exist PPT algorithms $\{\mathcal{A}_X\}_{X\subseteq\mathbf{Var}}$, *such that*

- *the input of* $\mathcal{A}_X(\mathbf{1}^n, \cdot)$ *is a function of type* $X \to \mathbf{Val}_n$;
- *the output of* $\mathcal{A}_X(\mathbf{1}^n, \cdot)$ *is either* $\perp$ *or a set* $Z \subseteq \mathbf{Var}$ *and a function* f : $Z \to \mathbf{Val}_n$.

For all initial probability distributions $D_s = \{D_{n,s}\}_{n \in \mathbb{N}}$, which satisfies the annotations of the program and for which the expected running time of the program is bounded by the polynomial q, for all subsets $Y \subseteq \mathbf{Var}$ and all PPT algorithms $\mathcal{D}$ the following difference is negligible in n:

$$\Bigl(\sum_{X \in \overline{\mathcal{M}}(Y)} \Pr\bigl[S_{n,s} \leftarrow D_{n,s}, (Z, f) \leftarrow \mathcal{A}_X(\mathbf{1}^n, S_{n,s}|_X) \; : $$

$$Y \subseteq Z \wedge \mathcal{D}(\mathbf{1}^n, S_{n,s}, f|_Y) = 1 \bigr] \Bigr) - $$

$$\Pr\bigl[S_{n,s} \leftarrow D_{n,s}, S_n \leftarrow [\![P]\!](\mathcal{S})(S_{n,s}) \; : \; \mathcal{D}(\mathbf{1}^n, S_{n,s}, S_n|_Y) = 1 \bigr] \; . $$

The lemma is proved by induction over the syntax of the WHILE-language.

The above lemma states an indistinguishability result ([6, Sec. 5] discusses the relationship between semantic security and indistinguishability). Intuitively, the lemma claims that if we know only some of the program's input variables, then we can still simulate the run of the program, by computing only the values of the variables that only depend on the values of known input variables. The final set of variables, whose values the algorithm knows at the end of the program, may depend on the chosen branches at *if*-nodes. Also, the lemma claims that the sets Z that the algorithms $\mathcal{A}_X$ output, are in average not too small — for each $Y \subseteq \mathbf{Var}$ there are sets $X \subseteq \mathbf{Var}$, for which $\mathcal{A}_X$ outputs $Z \supseteq Y$ with significant probability. Moreover, we can recreate the distribution $(S_{n,s}, S_n|_Y)$, where $S_{n,s}$ is the initial and S_n the corresponding final state of the program, with the help of the algorithms $\mathcal{A}_X$ (at least for a computationally bounded observer).

$\mathcal{A}_X$ works by executing the program (by following its flowchart). If the next statement is $x = o(x_1, \ldots, x_k)$ and the algorithm currently knows $x_1, \ldots, x_k$, then it will also know x, otherwise it will forget x, except for encryptions, where the algorithm randomly generates unknown inputs. At statement *if* b, if $\mathcal{A}_X$ currently knows b, then it will enter the right branch, otherwise it will jump directly to the corresponding *merge* and forget the variables in $\mathbf{Var}_{\mathrm{asgn}}$.

Proof (of the theorem). Suppose that the secret part c is recoverable from the final values of Y. According to the definition of recoverability, there exists an algorithm $\mathcal{A}$ that does that. The lemma provides us with the algorithms $\{\mathcal{A}_X\}_{X \subseteq \mathbf{Var}}$. For each $X \subseteq \mathbf{Var}$ we construct an algorithm $\mathcal{A}'^{(\cdot)}_X$ as follows: on input $(\mathbf{1}^n, f_0)$ we first run $\mathcal{A}_X$ on the same input, which gives us a set Z and a function $f : Z \to \mathbf{Val}_n$. We then check whether $Y \subseteq Z$ and

- if true, return $\mathcal{A}(\mathbf{1}^n, f|_Y)$;
- if false, invoke the oracle and return whatever it returns.

Let $\{Y_1, \ldots, Y_l\}$ be the set $\overline{\mathcal{M}}(Y)$. Let $\mathcal{A}'^{(\cdot)}$ be an algorithm, that on input $(\mathbf{1}^n, i, f_0)$, where $1 \leq i \leq l$ runs the algorithm $\mathcal{A}'^{(\cdot)}_{Y_i}$ on $(\mathbf{1}^n, f_0)$. Let $\mathcal{B}$ be any PPT algorithm. We now claim that the following difference is negligible in n:

$$\left(\sum_{i=1}^{l}\Pr\left[S_{n,s}\leftarrow D_{n,s}\ :\ \mathcal{A}'^{(\cdot)}(\mathbf{1}^n,i,S_{n,s}|_{Y_i})=B(c_n(S_{n,s}))\right]\right)-$$

$$\left(\Pr\left[S_{n,s}\leftarrow D_{n,s},S_n\leftarrow[\![P]\!](\mathbb{S})(S_{n,s})\ :\ \mathcal{A}(\mathbf{1}^n,S_n|_Y)=B_n(c_n(S_{n,s}))\right]+\right.$$

$$\left.(l-1)\Pr\left[S_{n,s}\leftarrow D_{n,s}\ :\ \mathcal{B}(\mathbf{1}^n)=B_n(c_n(S_{n,s}))\right]\right)\ .$$

Thus there exists an i that $\Pr\left[S_{n,s}\leftarrow D_{n,s}\ :\ \mathcal{A}^{\mathcal{B}(\mathbf{1}^n)}(\mathbf{1}^n,i,S_{n,s}|_{Y_i})=B(c_n(S_{n,s}))\right]$ is greater or equal or only negligibly less than

$$\frac{1}{l}\Pr\left[S_{n,s}\leftarrow D_{n,s},S_n\leftarrow[\![P]\!](\mathbb{S})(S_{n,s})\ :\ \mathcal{A}(\mathbf{1}^n,S_n|_Y)=B_n(c_n(S_{n,s}))\right]+$$

$$\frac{l-1}{l}\Pr\left[S_{n,s}\leftarrow D_{n,s}\ :\ \mathcal{B}(\mathbf{1}^n)=B_n(c_n(S_{n,s}))\right]$$

but this is significantly greater than $\Pr\left[S_{n,s}\leftarrow D_{n,s}:\mathcal{B}(\mathbf{1}^n)=B(c_n(S_{n,s}))\right]$. Thus there exists a j, such that Y_j is in the initial analysis information. But $Y\in\overline{\mathcal{W}}(Y_j)$ and thus $Y\in\mathcal{W}(N_{end})$.

The claim follows from

$$\sum_{i=1}^{l}\Pr\left[S_{n,s}\leftarrow D_{n,s}\ :\ \mathcal{A}'^{(\cdot)}(\mathbf{1}^n,i,S_{n,s}|_{Y_i})=B(c_n(S_{n,s}))\right]=$$

$$\sum_{X\in\overline{\mathcal{M}}(Y)}\Pr\left[S_{n,s}\leftarrow D_{n,s},(Z,f)\leftarrow\mathcal{A}_X(\mathbf{1}^n,S_{n,s}|_X)\ :\right.$$

$$\left.Y\subseteq Z\wedge\mathcal{A}(\mathbf{1}^n,f|_Y)=B(c_n(S_{n,s}))\right]+$$

$$\sum_{X\in\overline{\mathcal{M}}(Y)}\Pr\left[S_{n,s}\leftarrow D_{n,s},(Z,f)\leftarrow\mathcal{A}_X(\mathbf{1}^n,S_{n,s}|_X):Y\not\subseteq Z\wedge\mathcal{B}(\mathbf{1}^n)=B(c_n(S_{n,s}))\right].$$

The lemma gives that the first summand is only negligibly different from

$$\Pr\left[S_{n,s}\leftarrow D_{n,s},S_n\leftarrow[\![P]\!](\mathbb{S})(S_{n,s})\ :\ \mathcal{A}(\mathbf{1}^n,S_n|_Y)=B_n(c_n(S_{n,s}))\right]\ .$$

The second summand equals

$$\sum_{X\in\overline{\mathcal{M}}(Y)}\Pr\left[S_{n,s}\leftarrow D_{n,s}\ :\ \mathcal{B}(\mathbf{1}^n)=B(c_n(S_{n,s}))\right]-$$

$$\sum_{X\in\overline{\mathcal{M}}(Y)}\Pr\left[S_{n,s}\leftarrow D_{n,s},(Z,f)\leftarrow\mathcal{A}_X(\mathbf{1}^n,S_{n,s}|_X):Y\subseteq Z\wedge\mathcal{B}(\mathbf{1}^n)=B(c_n(S_{n,s}))\right],$$

where, according to the lemma, the second sum differs only negligibly from $\Pr\left[S_{n,s}\leftarrow D_{n,s}:\mathcal{B}(\mathbf{1}^n)=B(c_n(S_{n,s}))\right]$ (and the first is $|\overline{\mathcal{M}}(Y)|=l$ times that).

```
k1 := gen_key()
if b then
  k2 := k1
else
  k2 := gen_key()
x := enc(k1, y)
```

Knowing the equality of keys

```
k1 := gen_key()
if b then
  k2 := k1
else
  k2 := gen_key()
x1 := enc(k1, y1)
x2 := enc(k2, y2)
```

Knowing, which key was used

Fig. 3. Example programs

7   Discussion

We have presented an analysis that, for a certain class of programs, can decide whether these programs have computationally secure information flow. As an example consider the program consisting of a single statement x := enc(k, y). Suppose that the variables k and y are secret and x is public. In this case, our analysis finds that the initial value of y can be recovered from the final value of y or from the final values of x and k. However, both of these possibilities require the knowledge of some secret output, and thus the program does not leak the value of y.

Our analysis reports, that nothing about the initial value of y can be found from the final value of x. On the other hand, the initial value of y obviously interferes with the final value of x and thus an analysis using non-interference as its security criterion must reject this program.

Statically knowing which keys are equal. We require that at all program points we can statically answer the question "Which variables of type 'key' are equal?" The reason for this requirement is that, by having a cryptotext and a key, it is usually possible to determine whether this cryptotext was produced with this key, because the encryption usually involves padding the message in a certain way, see, for example, [8]. At least our definitions allow this determination to be possible. As an example of using this information, see the program in the left of the Fig. 3. In this case, the adversary can find the initial value of b from the final values of x and k2, which our analysis does not reflect. The adversary has to check whether x was generated by encrypting with k2 or not. The requirement placed on E guarantees that this extra information is already statically known.

Intuitively, it may seem that as k2 is assigned to at statements whose execution is controlled by b, the variable k2 should be recorded to be dependent on b after the if-then-else-statement. Actually k2 is just a newly generated key at this place, thus, according to our semantics, it is not dependent on anything. On the other hand, *the pair* $\langle k1, k2 \rangle$ depends on b. Unfortunately we are not yet able to handle such dependencies.

Still, we believe that even the class of programs satisfying all the constraints given in the beginning of Sec. 5 is interesting enough — and moreover, big enough — to contain realistic programs.

Requiring which-key and repetition concealedness. The question naturally arises, why do we require such properties from the cryptosystem that we use. The example in the right of Fig. 3 shows that which-key concealedness is indeed necessary (at least when we use the analysis presented in Sec. 5). If the encryption was not which-key concealing, then the adversary might be able to determine whether x1 and x2 were encrypted under the same key or not. This allows him to find the initial value of b. The analysis does not account for this. A similar example would show the necessity of repetition-concealedness. Although Abadi and Rogaway [2] show that which-key concealedness is not hard to achieve, it would be interesting to study what could be done (how should the analysis look like) with weaker encryption primitives — especially with ones that are not repetition-concealing.

Modeling secure information flow with noninterference. It is easy to write down an information-theoretic analogue to the definition of recoverability — it would look similar to Cohen's [3] strong dependency, especially to its deductive viewpoint. One can also give similar program analysis and prove the corresponding correctness result. The analysis $\mathcal{W}_{\mathrm{NI}}$ would look identical to $\mathcal{W}$; the only difference would be the absence of the special handling of encryption. The correctness proof would actually be simpler than the one presented in Sec. 6 — the lemma 1 would be easier to state, because the entities $\mathcal{A}_X$, $X \subseteq \mathbf{Var}$, would not be constrained to be PPT algorithms.

Comparison to Denning's and Myers's abstract semantics. Observing the analysis $\mathcal{W}_{\mathrm{NI}}$, we see that the minimal elements of $\mathcal{W}_{\mathrm{NI}}(N) \in \mathcal{P}_{\mathrm{U}}(\mathcal{P}(\widetilde{\mathbf{Var}}))$ are all one-element sets. Thus, we could replace the set $\mathcal{P}_{\mathrm{U}}(\mathcal{P}(\widetilde{\mathbf{Var}}))$ with $\mathcal{P}(\widetilde{\mathbf{Var}})$ (by identifying the set $\mathrm{cl}_{\mathrm{U}}(\{\{x_1\}, \ldots , \{x_k\}\}) \in \mathcal{P}_{\mathrm{U}}(\mathcal{P}(\widetilde{\mathbf{Var}}))$ with the set $\{x_1, \ldots , x_k\} \in \mathcal{P}(\widetilde{\mathbf{Var}})$). We continue by replacing $\mathcal{P}(\widetilde{\mathbf{Var}})$ with $\widetilde{\mathbf{Var}} \rightarrow \{L, H\}$ by considering the characteristic functions $\mathcal{X}_{\{x_1, \ldots , x_k\}} : \widetilde{\mathbf{Var}} \rightarrow \{0, 1\}$ and identifying $0 \equiv L$, $1 \equiv H$. This gives us Denning's and Denning's [5] information flow analysis for the two-element lattice of security classes, also stated in their terms.

On covert flows. Our analysis is not termination-sensitive — it does not detect that a program's secret inputs may affect whether it terminates. Actually, termination is an issue if the security of the information flow is defined through noninterference. When using our definition, one needs to detect whether the program runs in polynomial time or not. Reitman and Andrews [12] have presented an axiomatic approach for checking the security of information flow, their method is termination sensitive and the way it has been made termination-sensitive is very explicit. Thus we should be able to apply their ideas to our analysis to make it termination-sensitive (or "superpolynomial-running-time-sensitive") as well. Another possible covert channel that we do not address is how long the program runs and what can be detected from its timing behaviour.

Acknowledgements. We are thankful to Reinhard Wilhelm and Thomas W. Reps. Their comments have certainly made this paper more readable.

References

1. Abadi, M., Banerjee, A., Heintze, N., Riecke, J.G.: A Core Calculus of Dependency. In proc. of the 26th ACM SIGPLAN-SIGACT Symposium on Principles of Programming Languages, San Antonio, TX, January 20–22, 1999, ACM Press, pp. 147–160, 1999.

2. Abadi, M., Rogaway, P.: Reconciling Two Views of Cryptography (The Computational Soundness of Formal Encryption). In: van Leeuwen, J., Watanabe, O., Hagiya, M., Mosses, P.D., Ito, T. (eds.): proc. of the International Conference IFIP TCS 2000 Sendai, Japan, August 17-19, 2000 (LNCS 1872), Springer-Verlag pp. 3–22, 2000.

3. Cohen, E.: Information Transmission in Sequential Programs. In: DeMillo, R.A., Dobkin, D.P., Jones, A.K., Lipton, R.J. (eds.): Foundations of Secure Computation. Academic Press, pp. 297–335. 1978.

4. Denning, D.E.: A Lattice Model of Secure Information Flow. Communications of the ACM **19**(5), pp. 236–243, 1976.

5. Denning, D.E., Denning, P.: Certification of Programs for Secure Information Flow. Communications of the ACM **20**(7), pp. 504–513, 1977.

6. Goldreich, O.: The Foundations of Modern Cryptography. In: Kaliski, B. (ed.): proc. of CRYPTO '97, Santa Barbara, CA, August 17–21, 1997 (LNCS 1294), Springer-Verlag, pp. 46–74, 1997.

7. Heintze, N., Riecke, J.G.: The SLam Calculus: Programming with Secrecy and Integrity. In proc. of the 25th ACM SIGPLAN-SIGACT Symposium on Principles of Programming Languages, San Diego, CA, January 19–21, 1998, ACM Press, pp. 365–377, 1998.

8. Kaliski, B., Staddon, J.: PKCS #1: RSA Cryptography Standard. Version 2.0. RSA Laboratories, September 1998.

9. Landi, W.: Interprocedural Aliasing in the Presence of Pointers. PhD thesis, Rutgers University, 1992.

10. Leino, K.R.M., Joshi, R.: A Semantic Approach to Secure Information Flow. In: Jeuring, J. (ed.): proc. of "Mathematics of Program Construction, MPC'98", Marstrand, Sweden, June 15–17, 1998 (LNCS 1422), Springer-Verlag, 254–271, 1998.

11. Myers, A.C.: JFlow: Practical Mostly-Static Information Flow Control. In proc. of the 26th ACM SIGPLAN-SIGACT Symposium on Principles of Programming Languages, San Antonio, TX, January 20–22, 1999, ACM Press, pp. 228–241, 1999.

12. Reitman, R.P., Andrews, G.R.: Certifying information flow properties of programs: an axiomatic approach. In proc. of the 6th Annual ACM Symposium on Principles of Programming Languages, San Antonio, TX, January 1979, ACM Press, pp. 283–290, 1979.

13. Sabelfeld, A., Sands, D.: A Per Model of Secure Information Flow in Sequential Programs. In: Swierstra, S.D. (ed.): proc. of the 8th European Symposium on Programming, ESOP'99, Amsterdam, The Netherlands, 22-28 March, 1999 (LNCS 1576), Springer-Verlag, pp. 40–58, 1999.

14. Volpano, D., Smith, G., Irvine, C.: A Sound Type System for Secure Flow Analysis. Journal of Computer Security **4**(2,3), pp. 167–187, 1996.

15. Volpano, D., Smith, G.: Verifying secrets and relative secrecy. In proc. of the 27th ACM SIGPLAN-SIGACT Symposium on Principles of Programming Languages, Boston, MA, January 19–21, 2000, ACM Press, pp. 268–276, 2000.

16. Volpano, D.: Secure Introduction of One-way Functions. In proc. of the 13th IEEE Computer Security Foundations Workshop. Cambridge, UK, July 3–5, 2000.

Encoding Intensional Type Analysis

Stephanie Weirich[*]

Department of Computer Science, Cornell University
Ithaca, NY 14850
sweirich@cs.cornell.edu

Abstract. Languages for intensional type analysis permit ad-hoc polymorphism, or run-time analysis of types. However, such languages require complex, specialized constructs to support this operation, which hinder optimization and complicate the meta-theory of these languages. In this paper, we observe that such specialized operators need not be intrinsic to the language, and in fact, their operation may be simulated through standard encodings of iteration in the polymorphic lambda calculus. Therefore, we may more easily add intensional analysis operators to complicated languages via translation, instead of language extension.

1 Introduction

Consider a well-known inductive datatype (presented in Standard ML syntax [14] augmented with explicit polymorphism):

```
datatype Tree = Leaf | Node of Tree * Tree
Treerec : ∀a. Tree -> a -> ( a * a -> a ) -> a
```

Leaf and Node are introduction forms, used to create elements of type Tree. The function Treerec is an elimination form, iterating computation over an element of type Tree, creating a fold or a catamorphism. It accepts a base case (of type a) for the leaves and an inductive case (of type a * a -> a) for the nodes . For example, we may use Treerec to define a function to display a Tree. First, we explicitly instantiate the return type a with [string]. For the leaves, we provide the string "Leaf", and for the nodes we concatenate (with the infix operator ^) the strings of the subtrees.

```
val showTree = fn x : Tree =>
  Treerec [string] x
    "Leaf"
    (fn (s1:string, s2:string) => "Node(" ^ s1 ^ "," ^ s2 ")")
```

[*] This paper is based on work supported in part by the National Science Foundation under Grant No. CCR-9875536. Any opinions, findings and conclusions or recommendations expressed in this publication are those of the author and do not reflect the views of this agency.

D. Sands (Ed.): ESOP 2001, LNCS 2028, pp. 92–106, 2001.

As `Tree` is an inductive datatype, it is well known how to encode it in the polymorphic lambda calculus [1]. The basic idea is to encode a `Tree` as its elimination form — a function that iterates over the tree. In other words, a `Leaf` is a function that accepts a base case and an inductive case and returns the base case. Because we do not wish to constrain the return type of iteration, we abstract it, explicitly binding it with Λa.

```
val Leaf = Λa. fn base:a => fn ind:a * a -> a => base
```

Likewise, a `Node`, with two subtrees x and y, selects the inductive case, passing it the result of continuing the iteration through the two subtrees.

```
val Node (x:Tree) (y:Tree) =
    Λa. fn base:a  => fn ind:a * a -> a =>
        ind (Treerec [a] x base ind) (Treerec [a] y base ind)
```

However, as all of the iteration is encoded into the data structure itself, the elimination form only needs to pass it on.

```
val Treerec = Λa. fn x : Tree => fn base : a =>
                  fn ind  : a * a -> a => x [a] base ind
```

Consequently, we may write `Node` more simply as

```
val Node (x:Tree) (y:Tree) =
    Λa. fn base:a  => fn ind:a * a -> a =>
        ind (x [a] base ind) (y [a] base ind)
```

Now consider another inductive datatype:

```
datatype Type = Int | Arrow of Type * Type
Typerec : ∀a. Type -> a -> ( a * a -> a ) -> a
```

Ok, so we just changed the names. However, this datatype (or at least the introductory forms of it) is quite common in typed programming languages. It is the inductive definition of the types of the simply-typed lambda calculus.

$$\tau ::= int \mid \tau \to \tau$$

Just as we may write functions in ML to create and manipulate `Trees`, in some languages, we may write functions (or *type constructors*) that create and manipulate `Types`. These functions over `Types` must themselves be typed (we use the word *kind* for the types of types). If we use `Type` (notated by Ω) as the base kind, we get what is starting to look like the syntax of the kinds and type constructors of Girard's language F_ω [8].

(kinds)	$\kappa ::= \Omega \mid \kappa \to \kappa$
(type constructors)	$\tau ::= int \mid \tau \to \tau \mid \alpha \mid \lambda\alpha{:}\kappa.\tau \mid \tau\tau$

The language λ_i^{ML} [9] adds the elimination form *Typerec* to this type constructor language. Because *Typerec* may determine the *structure* of an abstract

$$(kinds) \qquad\qquad \kappa ::= \Omega \mid \kappa_1 \rightarrow \kappa_2$$

$$(type\ constructors) \quad c,\tau ::= \alpha \mid \lambda\alpha{:}\kappa.c \mid c_1 c_2 \mid int \mid \tau_1 \rightarrow \tau_2 \mid$$
$$\mid \ Typerec[\kappa] \ \tau \ c_i \ c_{\rightarrow}$$

$$(types) \qquad\qquad \sigma ::= T(\tau) \mid R(\tau) \mid \sigma_1 \rightarrow \sigma_2 \mid \forall\alpha{:}\kappa.\sigma$$

$$(terms) \qquad\qquad e ::= i \mid x \mid \lambda x{:}\sigma.e \mid e_1 e_2$$
$$\mid \ \Lambda\alpha{:}\kappa.e \mid e[c] \mid R_i \mid R_{\rightarrow}$$
$$\mid \ typerec[c] \ e \ e_i \ e_{\rightarrow}$$

Fig. 1. Syntax of of the source language, λ_R

type, its operation is called *intensional analysis*. Furthermore, λ_i^{ML} also allows the definition of a fold over a Type to create a *term*, with the special term *typerec*. With this term, λ_i^{ML} supports run-time type analysis, as the identities of type constructors affect run-time execution. For example, just as we defined a function to print out trees, we can define a function to print out types at run time.

```
val showType = Λa:Ω.
    typerec [string] a
        "int"
        (fn (s1:string, s2:string) => "(" ^ s1 ^ " -> " ^ s2 ^ ")")
```

Even though the type constructor *Typerec* and the term *typerec* are very specialized operators in λ_i^{ML}, they are just folds over an inductive data structure. And just as we can encode folds over Trees in the polymorphic lambda calculus, we can encode folds over Types. Note that to encode the type constructor *Typerec*, we will need to add kind polymorphism to the type constructor language.

In the rest of this paper, we will demonstrate how to encode a language with intensional type analysis operators into a variant of F_ω augmented with kind polymorphism. The fact that such an encoding exists means that the specialized operators *typerec* and *Typerec* do not need to be an intrinsic part of a programming language for it to support intensional type analysis. Therefore, we may more easily add these operators to complicated languages via a translation semantics, instead of through language extension.

The rest of the paper is organized as follows. Formal descriptions of the source and target languages appear in Section 2, and we present the embedding between them in Section 3. Section 4 describes the limitations of the translation and discusses when one might want an explicit iteration operator in the target language. Section 5 discusses related work and concludes.

Constructor *Typerec*	Term *typerec*
Formation	*Formation*

$$\frac{\Delta \vdash \tau : \Omega \qquad \Delta \vdash c_i : \kappa \qquad \Delta \vdash c_\rightarrow : \kappa \rightarrow \kappa \rightarrow \kappa}{\Delta \vdash \mathit{Typerec}[\kappa]\ \tau\ c_i\ c_\rightarrow\ : \kappa}$$

$$\frac{\Delta; \Gamma \vdash c : \Omega \rightarrow \Omega \qquad \Delta; \Gamma \vdash e : R(\tau) \qquad \Delta; \Gamma \vdash e_i : T(c(\mathit{int})) \qquad \Delta; \Gamma \vdash e_\rightarrow : \forall \alpha{:}\Omega.\forall \beta{:}\Omega.\ T(c\alpha \rightarrow c\beta \rightarrow c(\alpha \rightarrow \beta))}{\Delta; \Gamma \vdash \mathit{typerec}[c]\ e\ e_i\ e_\rightarrow\ : T(c\tau)}$$

Constructor equivalence	*Operational semantics*

$$\Delta \vdash \mathit{Typerec}[\kappa]\ \mathit{int}\ c_i\ c_\rightarrow = c_i : k$$

$$\mathit{typerec}[c]\ R_i\ e_i\ e_\rightarrow \mapsto e_i$$

$$\Delta \vdash \mathit{Typerec}[\kappa](\tau_1 \rightarrow \tau_2)\ c_i\ c_\rightarrow = \\ c_\rightarrow\ (\mathit{Typerec}[\kappa]\ \tau_1\ c_i\ c_\rightarrow) \\ (\mathit{Typerec}[\kappa]\ \tau_2\ c_i\ c_\rightarrow) : k$$

$$\mathit{typerec}[c]\ (R_\rightarrow[\tau_1][\tau_2]\ v_1\ v_2)\ e_i\ e_\rightarrow \mapsto \\ e_\rightarrow[\tau_1][\tau_2]\ (\mathit{typerec}[c]\ v_1\ e_i\ e_\rightarrow) \\ (\mathit{typerec}[c]\ v_2\ e_i\ e_\rightarrow)$$

Fig. 2. *Typerec* and *typerec*

2   The Languages

Instead of directly presenting a translation of λ_i^{ML}, we instead choose as the source language Crary *et al.*'s λ_R [5]. Because we will define two elimination forms, *typerec* and *Typerec*, we will need to separate type information used at the term level for run-time type analysis from that used at the type constructor level for static type checking. The language λ_R exhibits this separation by using terms that *represent* type constructors for analysis at run time, reserving type constructors for type-level analysis. A translation from λ_i^{ML} into λ_R provides term representations (suitable for *typerec*) for each type constructor abstracted by the source program.

To avoid analyzing quantified types, the core of λ_R is a predicative variant of F_ω. The quantifier $\forall \alpha{:}\kappa.\sigma$ ranges only over "small" types which do not include the quantified types. Therefore, the syntax (Figure 1) is divided into four syntactic categories: type *constructors* described by *kinds*, and *terms* described by *types*. By convention we use the meta-variable τ for constructors of kind Ω (those equivalent to unquantified types) and c for arbitrary constructors. A constructor τ of kind Ω may be explicitly coerced to a type with $T(\tau)$.

The semantics of λ_R includes judgments for type constructor formation $\Delta \vdash c : k$, type constructor equality $\Delta \vdash c_1 = c_2 : k$, type formation $\Delta \vdash \sigma$, type equality $\Delta \vdash \sigma_1 = \sigma_2$, term formation $\Delta; \Gamma \vdash e : \sigma$ and small-step operational semantics $e \mapsto e'$. In these judgments, Δ and Γ are contexts describing the kinds and types of the free constructor and term variables.

The semantics of the type constructor *Typerec* and term *typerec* appears in Figure 2. Unlike λ_i^{ML}, the argument to *typerec* is a term representing a type constructor, not the type constructor itself. The type $R(\tau)$ describes such a term representing τ. The type is singular; for any τ, only one term inhabits $R(\tau)$. Therefore, once the identity of a term of type $R(\tau)$ is determined, so is the identity of τ. For example, if $x : R(\alpha)$ and x matches the representation of the type int, denoted R_i, then we know α must be int.

Arrow types in λ_R are represented by the $R_\rightarrow$ term. This term requires the two types of the subcomponents of the arrow type and the two terms representing those types.

$$R_\rightarrow : \forall\alpha{:}\Omega.\forall\beta{:}\Omega.\, R(\alpha) \to R(\beta) \to R(\alpha \to \beta)$$

For example, the type $int \to int$ is represented by the term

$$R_\rightarrow[int][int]\, R_i\, R_i$$

One extremely useful property of $typerec$ not illustrated by the showType example from Section 1, is that the types of the e_i and $e_\rightarrow$ branches to $typerec$ may depend on the identity of the analyzed type. If the argument to $typerec$ is a term of type $R(\tau)$, the result type of the expression is $T(c\tau)$, where c may be an arbitrary type constructor. (The $typerec$ term is annotated by c to permit syntax-directed type checking.) However, instead of requiring that the e_i be of type $T(c\tau)$, it may be of type $T(c\,int)$, reflecting the fact that in e_i branch we know τ is int. Likewise, the return type of the $e_\rightarrow$ is $T(c(\alpha \to \beta))$, for some α and β.

There are several differences between λ_R presented in this paper and the language of Crary $et\ al.$ [5]. To simplify presentation, this version is call-by-name instead of call-by-value. Also, here the result of $typerec$ is annotated with a type constructor, instead of a type. However, we make two essential changes to support the embedding presented in this paper. First, we prevent R-types from appearing as an argument to $typerec$ or $Typerec$, by making R a part of the type language, and not a type constructor. We discuss in the next section why this restriction is necessary.

Second, although $typerec$ and $Typerec$ usually define a primitive recursive fold over kind Ω (also called a $paramorphism$ [12,11]), in this language we replace these operators with their iterative cousins (which define $catamorphisms$). The difference between iteration and primitive recursion is apparent in the kind of $c_\rightarrow$ and the type of $e_\rightarrow$. With primitive recursion, the arrow branch receives four arguments: the two subcomponents of the arrow constructor and two results of continuing the fold through these subcomponents. In iteration, on the other hand, the arrow branch receives only two arguments, the results of the continued fold.[1] We discuss this restriction further in Section 4.1.

The remainder of the static and operational semantics for this language, and for the primitive recursive versions, $typerec^{pr}$ and $Typerec^{pr}$, appear in Appendices A.1 and B. For space reasons, we omit the formation rules for types and type constructors, as they may be inferred from the rules for equality.

---

[1] Because we cannot separate type constructors passed for static type checking, from those passed for dynamic type analysis in λ_i^{ML}, we $must$ provide the subcomponents of the arrow type to the arrow branch of $typerec$. Therefore, we cannot define an iterative version of $typerec$ for that language.

$$(kinds) \quad \kappa \ ::= \ \Omega \mid \kappa_1 \to \kappa_2 \mid \chi \mid \forall \chi.\kappa$$

$$(con's) \quad c,\tau ::= \ \alpha \mid \lambda\alpha{:}\kappa.c \mid c_1 c_2 \mid \Lambda\chi.c \mid c[\kappa]$$
$$\mid \ int \mid \tau_1 \to \tau_2 \mid \forall\alpha{:}\kappa.\tau$$

$$(terms) \quad e \ ::= \ i \mid x \mid \lambda x{:}\tau.e \mid e_1 e_2$$
$$\mid \ \Lambda\alpha{:}\kappa.e \mid e[c]$$

Fig. 3. Syntax of the target language, λU^-

The target language of the translation is λU^-, the language F_ω augmented with kind polymorphism at the type constructor level (Figure 3). As the target language is impredicative, both types and type constructors are in the same syntactic class. In Section 4.2 we discuss why we might want alternate target languages not based on impredicative polymorphism. The static and operational semantics of λU^- appear in Appendices A.2 and C.

3   The Translation

The translation of λ_R into λU^- can be thought of as two separate translations: A translation of the kinds and constructors of λ_R into the kinds and constructors of λU^- and a translation of the types and terms of λ_R into the constructors and terms of λU^-. For reference, the complete translation appears in Figure 4.

3.1   Defining Iteration

To define the translation of *Typerec* we use the traditional encoding of inductive datatypes in impredicative polymorphism. As before, we encode τ, of kind Ω as its elimination form: a function that chooses between two given branches — one for c_i, one for $c_\to$. Then $Typerec[\kappa] \ \tau \ c_i \ c_\to$ can be implemented with

$$[\![\tau]\!][\![\kappa]\!] \ [\![c_i]\!] \ [\![c_\to]\!]$$

As τ is of kind type, we define $[\![\Omega]\!]$ to reflect the fact that $[\![\tau]\!]$ must accept an arbitrary kind and the two branches.

$$[\![\Omega]\!] = \forall\chi.\chi \to (\chi \to \chi \to \chi) \to \chi$$

Accordingly, the encoding of the type constructor *int* just returns its first argument (the kinds of the arguments have been elided)

$$[\![int]\!] = (\Lambda\chi.\lambda\iota.\lambda\alpha.\iota)$$

Now consider the constructor equality rule when the argument to *Typerec* is an arrow type. The translation of the arrow type constructor $\to$, should apply the second argument (the $c_\to$ branch) to the result of continuing the recursion through the two subcomponents.

$$[\![\tau_1 \to \tau_2]\!] = \Lambda\chi.\lambda\iota.\lambda\alpha.\alpha([\![\tau_1]\!][\chi] \ \iota \ \alpha)([\![\tau_2]\!][\chi] \ \iota \ \alpha)$$

A critical property of this translation is that it preserve the equivalences that exist in the source language. For example, one equivalence we must preserve from the source language is that

$$[\![Typerec[\kappa] \ (\tau_1 \to \tau_2) \ c_i \ c_\to]\!] = [\![c_\to(Typerec[\kappa] \ \tau_1 \ c_i \ c_\to)(Typerec[\kappa] \ \tau_2 \ c_i \ c_\to)]\!]$$

If we expand the left side, we get

$$(\Lambda\chi.\lambda\iota.\lambda\alpha.\alpha([\![\tau_1]\!][\chi] \ \iota \ \alpha)([\![\tau_2]\!][\chi] \ \iota \ \alpha)) \ [\![\kappa]\!] \ [\![c_i]\!] \ [\![c_\to]\!]$$

This term is then β-equivalent to the expansion of the right hand side.

$$[\![c_\to]\!] \ ([\![\tau_1]\!][\![\kappa]\!][\![c_i]\!][\![c_\to]\!]) \ ([\![\tau_2]\!][\![\kappa]\!][\![c_i]\!][\![c_\to]\!])$$

Because type constructors are a separate syntactic class from types, we must define $[\![T(\tau)]\!]$, the coercion between them. We convert $[\![\tau]\!]$ of kind $[\![\Omega]\!]$ into a λU^- constructor of kind Ω using the iteration built into $[\![\tau]\!]$.

$$[\![T(\tau)]\!] = [\![\tau]\!] \ [\Omega] \ int \ (\lambda\alpha{:}\Omega.\lambda\beta{:}\Omega.\alpha \to \beta)$$

For example,

$$\begin{aligned}[\![T(int)]\!] &= [\![int]\!][\Omega] \ int \ (\lambda\alpha{:}\Omega.\lambda\beta{:}\Omega.\alpha \to \beta) \\ &= (\Lambda\chi.\lambda\iota.\lambda\alpha.\iota)[\Omega] \ int \ (\lambda\alpha{:}\Omega.\lambda\beta{:}\Omega.\alpha \to \beta) \\ &=_\beta int \end{aligned}$$

We use a very similar encoding for *typerec* at the term level, as we do for *Typerec*. Again, we wish to apply the translation of the argument to the translation of the branches, and let the argument select between them.

$$[\![typerec[c]e \ e_i \ e_\to]\!] \quad \text{as} \quad [\![e]\!] \ [\![c]\!] \ [\![e_i]\!] \ [\![e_\to]\!]$$

The translations of R_i and $R_\to$ are analogous to those of the type constructors *int* and $\to$. However, there is a subtle point about the definition of $R(\tau)$, the type of the argument to *typerec*. To preserve typing, we define $[\![R(\tau)]\!]$ as:

$$\begin{aligned}\forall\gamma{:}[\Omega \to \Omega].[\![T(\gamma \ int)]\!] \\ \to [\![\forall\alpha{:}\Omega.\forall\beta{:}\Omega. \ T(\gamma\alpha) \to T(\gamma\beta) \to T(\gamma(\alpha \to \beta))]\!] \\ \to [\![T(\gamma\tau)]\!]\end{aligned}$$

Here we see why R cannot be a type constructor; if it were, we would have an additional branch for it in the translation of T mapping the R constructor to the R type. So the definition would be

$$[\![T(\tau)]\!] = [\![\tau]\!] \ [\Omega] \ int \ (\lambda\alpha{:}\Omega.\lambda\beta{:}\Omega.\alpha \to \beta) \ (\lambda\alpha{:}\Omega. \ R(\alpha)) \qquad (WRONG)$$

causing the definition of $[\![R(\tau)]\!]$ to be recursive.

Kind Translation

$$[\![\Omega]\!] \qquad\qquad\qquad = \forall\chi.\chi \to (\chi \to \chi \to \chi) \to \chi$$
$$[\![\kappa_1 \to \kappa_2]\!] \qquad\qquad = [\![\kappa_1]\!] \to [\![\kappa_2]\!]$$

Constructor Translation

$$[\![\alpha]\!] \qquad\qquad\qquad = \alpha$$
$$[\![\lambda\alpha{:}\kappa.c]\!] \qquad\qquad = \lambda\alpha{:}[\![\kappa]\!].[\![c]\!]$$
$$[\![c_1 c_2]\!] \qquad\qquad\quad = [\![c_1]\!]\,[\![c_2]\!]$$
$$[\![int]\!] \qquad\qquad\qquad = \Lambda\chi.\lambda\iota{:}\chi.\lambda\alpha{:}\chi \to \chi \to \chi.\iota$$
$$[\![\tau_1 \to \tau_2]\!] \qquad\qquad = \Lambda\chi.\lambda\iota{:}\chi.\lambda\alpha{:}\chi \to \chi \to \chi.$$
$$\qquad\qquad\qquad\qquad \alpha\,([\![\tau_1]\!]\,[\chi]\,\iota\,\alpha)\,([\![\tau_2]\!]\,[\chi]\,\iota\,\alpha)$$
$$[\![Typerec[\kappa]\,\tau\,c_i\,c_{\to}]\!] \;= [\![\tau]\!]\,[[\![\kappa]\!]]\,[\![c_i]\!]\,[\![c_{\to}]\!]$$

Type Translation

$$[\![T(\tau)]\!] \qquad\qquad\quad = [\![\tau]\!]\,[\Omega]\;int\,(\lambda\alpha{:}\Omega.\lambda\beta{:}\Omega.\alpha \to \beta)$$
$$[\![R(\tau)]\!] \qquad\qquad\quad = \forall\gamma{:}[\Omega \to \Omega].[\![T(\gamma\,int)]\!]$$
$$\qquad\qquad\qquad\qquad \to [\![\forall\alpha{:}\Omega.\forall\beta{:}\Omega.\,T(\gamma\alpha) \to T(\gamma\beta) \to T(\gamma(\alpha \to \beta))]\!]$$
$$\qquad\qquad\qquad\qquad \to [\![T(\gamma\tau)]\!]$$
$$[\![int]\!] \qquad\qquad\qquad = int$$
$$[\![\sigma_1 \to \sigma_2]\!] \qquad\qquad = [\![\sigma_1]\!] \to [\![\sigma_2]\!]$$
$$[\![\forall\alpha{:}\kappa.\sigma]\!] \qquad\qquad = \forall\alpha{:}[\![\kappa]\!].[\![\sigma]\!]$$

Term Translation

$$[\![x]\!] \qquad\qquad\qquad = x$$
$$[\![\lambda x{:}\sigma.e]\!] \qquad\qquad\, = \lambda x{:}[\![\sigma]\!].[\![e]\!]$$
$$[\![e_1 e_2]\!] \qquad\qquad\quad = [\![e_1]\!]\,[\![e_2]\!]$$
$$[\![\Lambda\alpha{:}\kappa.e]\!] \qquad\qquad = \Lambda\alpha{:}[\![\kappa]\!].[\![e]\!]$$
$$[\![e[c]]\!] \qquad\qquad\quad = [\![e]\!][[\![c]\!]]$$
$$[\![R_i]\!] \qquad\qquad\qquad = (\Lambda\gamma{:}[\Omega \to \Omega].\lambda i{:}[\![T(\gamma\,int)]\!].$$
$$\qquad\qquad\qquad\qquad \lambda a{:}[\![\forall\alpha{:}\Omega.\forall\beta{:}\Omega.\,T(\gamma\alpha) \to T(\gamma\beta) \to T(\gamma(\alpha \to \beta))]\!].i)$$
$$[\![R_{\to}]\!] \qquad\qquad\quad = \Lambda\alpha{:}[\Omega].\Lambda\beta{:}[\Omega].\lambda x_1{:}[\![R(\alpha)]\!].\lambda x_2{:}[\![R(\beta)]\!]$$
$$\qquad\qquad\qquad\qquad (\Lambda\gamma{:}[\Omega \to \Omega].\lambda i{:}[\![T(\gamma\,int)]\!].$$
$$\qquad\qquad\qquad\qquad \lambda a{:}[\![\forall\alpha{:}\Omega.\forall\beta{:}\Omega.\,T(\gamma\alpha) \to T(\gamma\beta) \to T(\gamma(\alpha \to \beta))]\!].$$
$$\qquad\qquad\qquad\qquad a\,[\alpha][\beta](x_1[\gamma]\,i\,a)\,(x_2[\gamma]\,i\,a))$$
$$[\![typerec[c]\,e\,e_i\,e_{\to}]\!] = [\![e]\!][[\![c]\!]][\![e_i]\!]\,[\![e_{\to}]\!]$$

Fig. 4. Translation of λ_R into λU^-

3.2 Properties of the Embedding

The translation presented above enjoys the following properties. Define $[\![\Delta]\!]$ as $\{\alpha{:}[\![\Delta(\alpha)]\!] \mid \alpha \in Dom(\Delta)\}$ and $[\![\Gamma]\!]$ as $\{x{:}[\![\Gamma(x)]\!] \mid x \in Dom(\Gamma)\}$.

Theorem 1 (Static Correctness).

1. $\emptyset \vdash [\![\kappa]\!]$
2. If $\Delta \vdash c : \kappa$ then $[\![\Delta]\!] \vdash [\![c]\!] : [\![\kappa]\!]$.
3. If $\Delta \vdash c = c' : \kappa$ then $[\![\Delta]\!] \vdash [\![c]\!] = [\![c']\!] : [\![\kappa]\!]$.
4. If $\Delta \vdash \sigma$ then $[\![\Delta]\!] \vdash [\![\sigma]\!] : \Omega$.
5. If $\Delta \vdash \sigma = \sigma'$ then $[\![\Delta]\!] \vdash [\![\sigma]\!] = [\![\sigma']\!] : \Omega$
6. If $\Delta; \Gamma \vdash e : \sigma$ then $[\![\Delta; \Gamma]\!] \vdash [\![e]\!] : [\![\sigma]\!]$.

Proof is by induction on the appropriate derivation.

Theorem 2 (Dynamic Correctness). *If $\emptyset \vdash e : \sigma$ and $e \mapsto e'$ then $[\![e]\!] \mapsto^*$ $[\![e']\!]$.*

Proof is by induction on $\emptyset \vdash e : \sigma$.

4 Discussion

Despite the simplicity and elegance of this encoding, it falls short for two reasons, which we discuss in this section.

4.1 Extension to Primitive Recursion

At the term level we could extend the previous definition of *typerec* to a primitive recursive version *typerec^{pr}* by providing terms of type $R(\alpha)$ and $R(\beta)$ to $e_\rightarrow$. In that case, $[\![R(\tau)]\!]$ must be a recursive definition:

$$\forall \gamma{:}[\![\Omega \rightarrow \Omega]\!].[\![T(\gamma\ int)]\!]$$
$$\rightarrow [\![\forall \alpha{:}\Omega.\forall \beta{:}\Omega.\ R(\alpha) \rightarrow R(\beta) \rightarrow T(\gamma\alpha) \rightarrow T(\gamma\beta) \rightarrow T(\gamma(\alpha \rightarrow \beta))]\!]$$
$$\rightarrow [\![T(\gamma\tau)]\!]$$

We have defined $[\![R(\tau)]\!]$ in terms of $[\![R(\alpha)]\!]$ and $[\![R(\beta)]\!]$. We might expect that a realistic term language include parameterized recursive types. In that case, the definition of *typerec^{pr}* is no more difficult than that of *typerec*; just supply the extra arguments to the arrow branch. In other words,

$$[\![R_\rightarrow]\!] = \Lambda\alpha{:}[\![\Omega]\!].\Lambda\beta{:}[\![\Omega]\!].\lambda x_1{:}[\![R(\alpha)]\!].\lambda x_2{:}[\![R(\beta)]\!].$$
$$\Lambda\gamma{:}[\![\Omega \rightarrow \Omega]\!].\lambda i.\lambda a.$$
$$a[\alpha][\beta]\ x_1\ x_2\ (x_1[\gamma]ia)(x_2[\gamma]ia)$$

However, we cannot add recursive kinds to implement primitive recursion at the type constructor level without losing decidable type checking. Even without resorting to recursive types, there is a well known technique for encoding primitive recursion in terms of iteration, by pairing the argument with the result in the iteration.[2] Unfortunately, this pairing trick only works for closed expressions, and only produces terms that are $\beta\eta$−equivalent in the target language. Therefore, at the term level, our strong notion of dynamic correctness does not hold. Using this technique, we must weaken it to:

If $\emptyset \vdash e : \sigma$ and $e \mapsto e'$ then $[\![e]\!]$ is $\beta\eta$-convertible with $[\![e']\!]$.

At the type-constructor level, $\beta\eta$-equivalence is sufficient. However, for type checking, we need the equivalence to extend to constructors with free-variables. The reason that this trick does not work is that λU^- can encode iteration over datatypes only weakly; there is no induction principle for this encoding provable in λU^-. Therefore, we cannot derive a proof of equality in the equational theory of the target language that relies on induction. This weakness has been encountered before. In fact, it is conjectured that it is impossible to encode primitive recursion in System F using $\beta\eta$-equality [22]. A stronger equational theory for λU^-, perhaps one incorporating a parametricity principle [19], might solve this problem. However, a simpler way to support primitive recursion would be to include an operator for primitive recursion directly in the language [13,18,3,4].

4.2   Impredicativity and Non-termination

Another issue with this encoding is that the target language must have impredicative polymorphism at the type and kind level. In practice, this property is acceptable in the target language. Although, impredicativity at the kind level destroys strong-normalization [2],[3] intensional polymorphism was designed for typed-compilation of Turing-complete language [9], and impredicativity at the type level is vital for such transformations as typed closure conversion. Furthermore, Trifonov *et al.* show that impredicative kind polymorphism allows the analysis of quantified types [23]. Allowing such impredicativity in the source language does not prevent this encoding; we can similarly encode the type-erasure version of their language [21].

However, the source language of this paper, λ_R, is predicative and strongly-normalizing, and the fact that this encoding destroys these properties is unsatisfactory. It seems reasonable, then, to look at methods of encoding iteration within predicative languages [16,7]. In adding iteration to the kind level, *strict positivity* (the recursively bound variable may not appear to the left of an arrow) may be required [3], to prevent the definition of an equivalent paradox.

5   Related Work and Conclusions

Böhm and Berarducci [1] showed how to to encode any covariant datatype in the polymorphic lambda calculus. A variant of this idea, called dictionary passing, was used to implement ad-hoc polymorphism in the language Haskell [17]

---

[2] See the tutorials in Meertens [11] and Mitchell [15] Section 9.3

[3] Coquand [2] originally derived a looping term by formalizing a paradox along the lines of Reynolds' theorem [20], forming an isomorphism between a set and its double power set. Hurkens [10] simplified this argument and developed a shorter looping term, using a related paradox.

through type classes [24]. In Standard ML [14], Yang [25] similarly used it to encode type-specialized functions (such as type-directed partial evaluation [6]). Because core ML does not support higher-order polymorphism, he presented his encoding within the ML module system.

At the type constructor level, Crary and Weirich [4] encoded the *Typerec* construct with a language supporting product, sum and inductive kinds. Their aim was to support type analysis in type-preserving compilation. Because various intermediate languages do not share the same type system, they needed some way to express the analysis of source-level types within the target language.

In this paper we demonstrate that all of these encodings are related, and have the implementation of iteration at their core. While intensional type analysis seems to require highly specialized operators, here we observe that it is no more complicated to include than iteration over inductive datatypes. Though we have implemented such iteration via the standard encoding into the polymorphic lambda calculus, other constructs supporting iteration suffice. In fact, alternative operations for iteration may be necessary in situations where impredicative polymorphism is not desirable.

Acknowledgments. Thanks to Robert Harper, Bratin Saha, Karl Crary and Greg Morrisett for much helpful discussion.

References

1. C. Böhm and A. Berarducci. Automatic synthesis of typed Λ-programs on term algebras. *Theoretical Computer Science*, 39:135–154, 1985.
2. Thierry Coquand. A new paradox in type theory. In Dag Prawitz, Brian Skyrms, and Dag Westerståhl, editors, *Logic, methodology and philosophy of science IX : proceedings of the Ninth International Congress of Logic, Methodology, and Philosophy of Science, Uppsala, Sweden, August 7-14, 1991*, Amsterdam, 1994. Elsevier.
3. Thierry Coquand and Christin Paulin. Inductively defined types. In P. Martin-Löf and G. Mints, editors, *COLOG-88 International Conference on Computer Logic*, volume 417 of *Lecture Notes in Computer Science*, pages 50–66, Tallinn, USSR, December 1988. Springer-Verlag.
4. Karl Crary and Stephanie Weirich. Flexible type analysis. In *1999 ACM International Conference on Functional Programming*, pages 233–248, Paris, September 1999.
5. Karl Crary, Stephanie Weirich, and Greg Morrisett. Intensional polymorphism in type erasure semantics. In *1998 ACM International Conference on Functional Programming*, volume 34 of *ACM SIGPLAN Notices*, pages 301–313, Baltimore, MD, September 1998. Extended Version is Cornell University Computer Science TR98-1721.
6. Olivier Danvy. Type-directed partial evaluation. In *Twenty-Third ACM Symposium on Principles of Programming Languages*, January 1996.
7. Peter Dybjer. Inductive sets and families in Martin-Löf's type theory and their set-theoretic semnatics. In Gerard Huet and Gordon Plotkin, editors, *Logical Frameworks*, pages 280–306. Prentice Hall, 1991.
8. Jean-Yves Girard. *Interprétation fonctionelle et élimination des coupures de l'arithmétique d'ordre supérieur*. PhD thesis, Université Paris VII, 1972.
9. Robert Harper and Greg Morrisett. Compiling polymorphism using intensional type analysis. In *Twenty-Second ACM Symposium on Principles of Programming Languages*, pages 130–141, San Francisco, January 1995.

10. A. J. C. Hurkens. A simplification of girard's paradox. In Mariangiola Dezani-Ciancaglini and Gordon Plotkin, editors, *Second International Conference on Typed Lambda Calculi and Applications, TLCA '95*, volume 902 of *Lecture Notes in Computer Science*, Edinburgh, United Kingdom, April 1995. Springer-Verlag.

11. Lambert G. L. T. Meertens. Paramorphisms. *Formal Aspects of Computing*, 4(5):413–424, 1992.

12. E. Meijer, M.M. Fokkinga, and R. Paterson. Functional programming with bananas, lenses, envelopes and barbed wire. In *FPCA91: Functional Programming Languages and Computer Architecture*, volume 523 of *Lecture Notes in Computer Science*, pages 124–144. Springer-Verlag, 1991.

13. Paul Francis Mendler. *Inductive Definition in Type Theory*. PhD thesis, Department of Computer Science, Cornell University, Ithaca, New York, September 1987.

14. Robin Milner, Mads Tofte, Robert Harper, and David MacQueen. *The Definition of Standard ML (Revised)*. The MIT Press, Cambridge, Massachusetts, 1997.

15. John C. Mitchell. *Foundations for Programming Languages*. The MIT Press, 1996.

16. C. Paulin-Mohring. Inductive definitions in the system Coq - rules and properties. In M. Bezem and J.-F. Groote, editors, *Proceedings of the conference Typed Lambda Calculi and Applications*, number 664 in Lecture Notes in Computer Science, 1993. LIP research report 92-49.

17. Simon L. Peyton Jones and J. Hughes (editors). Report on the programming language Haskell 98, a non-strict purely functional language. Technical Report YALEU/DCS/RR-1106, Yale University, Department of Computer Science, February 1999. Available from http://www.haskell.org/definition/.

18. F. Pfenning and C. Paulin-Mohring. Inductively defined types in the Calculus of Constructions. In *Proceedings of Mathematical Foundations of Programming Semantics*, volume 442 of *Lecture Notes in Computer Science*. Springer-Verlag, 1990.

19. Gordon Plotkin and Martín Abadi. A logic for parametric polymorphism. In *International Conference on Typed Lambda Calculi and Applications*, pages 361–375, 1993.

20. John C. Reynolds. Polymorphism is not set-theoretic. In *Proceedings of the International Symposium on Semantics of Data Types*, volume 173 of *Lecture Notes in Computer Science*. Springer-Verlag, 1984.

21. Bratin Saha, Valery Trifonov, and Zhong Shao. Fully reflexive intensional type analysis in type erasure semantics. In *Third Workshop on Types in Compilation*, Montreal, September 2000.

22. Zdzisław Spławski and Paweł Urzyczyn. Type fixpoints: Iteration vs. recursion. In *Fourth ACM International Conference on Functional Programming*, pages 102–113, Paris, France, September 1999.

23. Valery Trifonov, Bratin Saha, and Zhong Shao. Fully reflexive intensional type analysis. In *Fifth ACM International Conference on Functional Programming*, pages 82–93, Montreal, September 2000. Extended version is YALEU/DCS/TR-1194.

24. Philip Wadler and Stephen Blott. How to make ad-hoc polymorphism less ad-hoc. In *Sixteenth ACM Symposium on Principles of Programming Languages*, pages 60–76. ACM, 1989.

25. Zhe Yang. Encoding types in ML-like languages. In *1998 ACM International Conference on Functional Programming*, volume 34 of *ACM SIGPLAN Notices*, pages 289 – 300, Baltimore, MD, September 1998.

A   Operational Semantics

A.1 λ_R

$$(\lambda\alpha{:}x.e)e' \mapsto e[e'/x]$$

$$(\Lambda\alpha{:}\kappa.e)[c] \mapsto (e[c/\alpha])$$

$$\frac{e_1 \mapsto e_1'}{e_1 e_2 \mapsto e_1' e_2} \qquad \frac{e \mapsto e'}{e[c] \mapsto e'[c]}$$

$$\frac{}{typerec^{pr}[c]\ R_i\ e_i\ e_\rightarrow \mapsto e_i}$$

$$\frac{}{\begin{array}{l} typerec^{pr}[c]\ (R_\rightarrow[\tau_1][\tau_2]e_1\ e_2)\ e_i\ e_\rightarrow \mapsto \\ \quad e_\rightarrow[\tau_1][\tau_2]\ e_1\ e_2 \\ \quad (typerec^{pr}[c]\ e_1\ e_i\ e_\rightarrow) \\ \quad (typerec^{pr}[c]\ e_2\ e_i\ e_\rightarrow) \end{array}}$$

$$\frac{e \mapsto e'}{\begin{array}{l} typerec^{pr}[c]\ e\ e_i\ e_\rightarrow \mapsto \\ \quad typerec^{pr}[c]\ e'\ e_i\ e_\rightarrow \end{array}}$$

A.2 λU^-

$$(\lambda x{:}c.e)e' \mapsto e[e'/x]$$

$$\frac{e_1 \mapsto e_1'}{e_1 e_2 \mapsto e_1' e_2}$$

$$(\Lambda\alpha{:}\kappa.e)[c] \mapsto (e[c/\alpha])$$

$$\frac{e \mapsto e'}{e[c] \mapsto e'[c]}$$

B   Static Semantics of λ_R

B.1   Constructor Equivalence

$$\boxed{\Delta \vdash c_1 = c_2 : \kappa}$$

$$\frac{\Delta, \alpha{:}\kappa' \vdash c_1 : \kappa \qquad \Delta \vdash c_2 : \kappa' \qquad \alpha \notin Dom(\Delta)}{\Delta \vdash (\lambda\alpha{:}\kappa'.c_1)c_2 = c_1[c_2/\alpha] : \kappa}$$

$$\frac{\Delta \vdash c : \kappa_1 \to \kappa_2 \qquad \alpha \notin Dom(\Delta)}{\Delta \vdash \lambda\alpha{:}\kappa_1.c\,\alpha = c : \kappa_1 \to \kappa_2}$$

$$\frac{\Delta, \alpha{:}\kappa \vdash c = c' : \kappa'}{\Delta \vdash \lambda\alpha{:}\kappa.c = \lambda\alpha{:}\kappa.c' : \kappa \to \kappa'}$$

$$\frac{\Delta \vdash c_1 = c_1' : \kappa' \to \kappa \qquad \Delta \vdash c_2 = c_2' : \kappa'}{\Delta \vdash c_1 c_2 = c_1' c_2' : \kappa}$$

$$\frac{\Delta \vdash c_1 = c_1' : \kappa' \to \kappa \qquad \Delta \vdash c_2 = c_2' : \kappa'}{\Delta \vdash c_1 \to c_2 = c_1' \to c_2' : \Omega}$$

$$\frac{\Delta \vdash c : \kappa}{\Delta \vdash c = c : \kappa}$$

$$\frac{\Delta \vdash c' = c : \kappa}{\Delta \vdash c = c' : \kappa}$$

$$\frac{\Delta \vdash c = c' : \kappa \qquad \Delta \vdash c' = c'' : \kappa}{\Delta \vdash c = c'' : \kappa}$$

$$\frac{\Delta \vdash c_i : \kappa \qquad \Delta \vdash c_\to : \Omega \to \Omega \to \kappa \to \kappa \to \kappa}{\Delta \vdash Typerec^{pr}[\kappa](int)\,(c_i, c_\to) = c_i : \kappa}$$

$$\frac{\Delta \vdash c_1 : \Omega \qquad \Delta \vdash c_2 : \Omega \qquad \Delta \vdash c_i : \kappa \qquad \Delta \vdash c_\to : \Omega \to \Omega \to \kappa \to \kappa \to \kappa}{\begin{array}{c}\Delta \vdash Typerec^{pr}[\kappa](c_1 \to c_2)\,(c_i, c_\to) = \\ c_\to\, c_1\, c_2\, (Typerec^{pr}[\kappa]c_1\,(c_i, c_\to)) \\ (Typerec^{pr}[\kappa]c_2\,(c_i, c_\to)) : \kappa\end{array}}$$

$$\frac{\Delta \vdash c = c' : \Omega \qquad \Delta \vdash c_i = c_i' : \kappa \qquad \Delta \vdash c_\to = c_\to' : \Omega \to \Omega \to \kappa \to \kappa \to \kappa}{\begin{array}{c}\Delta \vdash Typerec^{pr}[\kappa]\, c\, (c_i, c_\to) = \\ Typerec^{pr}[\kappa]\, c'\, (c_i', c_\to') : \kappa\end{array}}$$

B.2   Type Equivalence

$$\boxed{\Delta \vdash \sigma_1 = \sigma_2}$$

$$\frac{\Delta \vdash c_1 = c_2 : \kappa}{\Delta \vdash T(c_1) = T(c_2)}$$

$$\frac{\Delta \vdash c_1 = c_2 : \kappa}{\Delta \vdash R(c_1) = R(c_2)}$$

$$\frac{\Delta \vdash \sigma_1 = \sigma_1' \qquad \Delta \vdash \sigma_2 = \sigma_2'}{\Delta \vdash \sigma_1 \to \sigma_2 = \sigma_1' \to \sigma_2'}$$

$$\overline{\Delta \vdash T(int) = int}$$

$$\frac{\Delta \vdash \sigma_1 = T(c_1) \qquad \Delta \vdash \sigma_2 = T(c_2)}{\Delta \vdash \sigma_1 \to \sigma_2 = T(c_1 \to c_2)}$$

$$\frac{\Delta, \alpha{:}\kappa \vdash \sigma = \sigma'}{\Delta \vdash \forall\alpha{:}\kappa.\sigma = \forall\alpha{:}\kappa.\sigma'}$$

$$\frac{\Delta \vdash \sigma}{\Delta \vdash \sigma = \sigma}$$

$$\frac{\Delta \vdash \sigma' = \sigma}{\Delta \vdash \sigma = \sigma'}$$

$$\frac{\Delta \vdash \sigma = \sigma' \qquad \Delta \vdash \sigma' = \sigma''}{\Delta \vdash \sigma = \sigma''}$$

B.3   Term Formation

$$\boxed{\Delta; \Gamma \vdash e : \sigma}$$

$$\overline{\Delta; \Gamma \vdash i : int}$$

$$\frac{\Gamma(x) = \sigma}{\Delta; \Gamma \vdash x : \sigma}$$

$$\frac{\Delta, \Gamma, x{:}\sigma_2 \vdash e : \sigma_1 \qquad \Delta; \Gamma \vdash \sigma_2 \qquad x \notin Dom(\Gamma)}{\Delta; \Gamma \vdash \lambda x{:}\sigma_2.e : \sigma_2 \to \sigma_1}$$

$$\frac{\Delta; \Gamma \vdash e_1 : \sigma_2 \to \sigma_1 \qquad \Delta; \Gamma \vdash e_2 : \sigma_2}{\Delta; \Gamma \vdash e_1 e_2 : \sigma_1}$$

$$\frac{\Delta; \Gamma \vdash e : \forall\alpha{:}\kappa.\sigma \qquad \Delta; \Gamma \vdash c : \kappa}{\Delta; \Gamma \vdash e[c] : \sigma[c/\alpha]}$$

$$\frac{\Delta; \Gamma, \alpha{:}\kappa \vdash e : \sigma \qquad x \notin Dom(\Gamma)}{\Delta; \Gamma \vdash \Lambda\alpha{:}\kappa.e : \forall\alpha{:}\kappa.\sigma}$$

$$\frac{\Delta; \Gamma \vdash e : \sigma_2 \qquad \Delta; \Gamma \vdash \sigma_1 = \sigma_2}{\Delta; \Gamma \vdash e : \sigma_1}$$

$$\overline{\Delta; \Gamma \vdash R_i : R(int)}$$

$$\Delta; \Gamma \vdash R_\rightarrow : \forall \alpha{:}\Omega.\forall \beta{:}\Omega.$$
$$R(\alpha) \rightarrow R(\beta) \rightarrow R(\alpha \rightarrow \beta)$$

$$\Delta; \Gamma \vdash c : \Omega \rightarrow \Omega$$
$$\Delta; \Gamma \vdash e : R(\tau)$$
$$\Delta; \Gamma \vdash e_i : T(c(int))$$
$$\Delta; \Gamma \vdash e_\rightarrow : \forall \alpha{:}\Omega.\forall \beta{:}\Omega.\ R(\alpha) \rightarrow R(\beta)$$
$$\rightarrow T(c(\alpha) \rightarrow c(\beta) \rightarrow c(\beta \rightarrow \gamma))$$
$$\overline{\Delta; \Gamma \vdash typerec^{pr}[c]\ e\ e_i\ e_\rightarrow : T(c\tau)}$$

C   Static Semantics of λU^-

C.1   Kind Formation

$$\boxed{E \vdash \kappa}$$

$$\overline{E, \chi \vdash \chi}$$

$$\overline{E \vdash \Omega}$$

$$\frac{E \vdash \kappa_1 \qquad E \vdash \kappa_2}{E \vdash \kappa_1 \rightarrow \kappa_2}$$

$$\frac{E, \chi \vdash \kappa}{E \vdash \forall \chi.\kappa}$$

C.2   Constructor Equivalence

$$\boxed{E; \Delta \vdash c = c' : \kappa}$$

$$\frac{\begin{array}{c} E; \Delta, \alpha{:}\kappa' \vdash c_1 : \kappa \\ E; \Delta \vdash c_2 : \kappa' \\ \alpha \notin Dom(\Delta) \end{array}}{E; \Delta \vdash (\lambda \alpha{:}\kappa'.c_1)c_2 = c_1[c_2/\alpha] : \kappa}$$

$$\frac{E; \Delta \vdash c : \kappa_1 \rightarrow \kappa_2\ \alpha \notin Dom(\Delta)}{E; \Delta \vdash \lambda \alpha{:}\kappa_1.c\,\alpha = c : \kappa_1 \rightarrow \kappa_2}$$

$$\frac{E; \Delta, \alpha{:}\kappa \vdash c = c' : \kappa'}{E; \Delta \vdash \lambda \alpha{:}\kappa.c = \lambda \alpha{:}\kappa.c' : \kappa \rightarrow \kappa'}$$

$$\frac{\begin{array}{c} E; \Delta \vdash c_1 = c_1' : \kappa' \rightarrow \kappa \\ E; \Delta \vdash c_2 = c_2' : \kappa' \end{array}}{E; \Delta \vdash c_1 c_2 = c_1' c_2' : \kappa}$$

$$\frac{E, \chi; \Delta \vdash c : \kappa'}{E; \Delta \vdash \Lambda\chi.c[\kappa] = c[\kappa/\chi] : \kappa'[\kappa/\chi]}$$

$$\frac{E; \Delta \vdash c : \forall \chi'.\kappa}{E; \Delta \vdash \Lambda\chi.c[\chi] = c : \forall \chi'.\kappa}$$

$$\frac{E, \chi; \Delta \vdash c = c' : \kappa}{E; \Delta \vdash \Lambda\chi.c = \Lambda\chi.c' : \forall \chi.\kappa}$$

$$\frac{E; \Delta \vdash c = c' : \forall \chi.\kappa}{E; \Delta \vdash c[\kappa] = c'[\kappa] : \kappa'[\kappa/\chi]}$$

$$\frac{\begin{array}{c} E; \Delta \vdash c_1 = c_1' : \kappa' \rightarrow \kappa \\ E; \Delta \vdash c_2 = c_2' : \kappa' \end{array}}{E; \Delta \vdash c_1 \rightarrow c_2 = c_1' \rightarrow c_2' : \Omega}$$

$$\frac{E; \Delta, \alpha{:}\kappa \vdash \sigma = \sigma'}{E; \Delta \vdash \forall \alpha{:}\kappa.\sigma = \forall \alpha{:}\kappa.\sigma'}$$

$$\frac{E; \Delta \vdash c : \kappa}{E; \Delta \vdash c = c : \kappa}$$

$$\frac{E; \Delta \vdash c' = c : \kappa}{E; \Delta \vdash c = c' : \kappa}$$

$$\frac{E; \Delta \vdash c = c' : \kappa \qquad E; \Delta \vdash c' = c'' : \kappa}{E; \Delta \vdash c = c'' : \kappa}$$

C.3   Term Formation

$$\boxed{\Delta; \Gamma \vdash e : \sigma}$$

$$\overline{\Delta; \Gamma \vdash i : int}$$

$$\frac{\Gamma(x) = \sigma}{\Delta; \Gamma \vdash x : \sigma}$$

$$\frac{\begin{array}{c} \Delta; \Gamma, x{:}\sigma_2 \vdash e : \sigma_1 \\ \Delta; \Gamma \vdash \sigma_2 \qquad x \notin Dom(\Gamma) \end{array}}{\Delta; \Gamma \vdash \lambda x{:}\sigma_2.e : \sigma_2 \rightarrow \sigma_1}$$

$$\frac{\Delta; \Gamma \vdash e_1 : \sigma_2 \rightarrow \sigma_1 \quad \Delta; \Gamma \vdash e_2 : \sigma_2}{\Delta; \Gamma \vdash e_1 e_2 : \sigma_1}$$

$$\frac{\Delta; \Gamma \vdash e : \forall \alpha{:}\kappa.\sigma \quad \Delta; \Gamma \vdash c : \kappa}{\Delta; \Gamma \vdash e[c] : \sigma[c/\alpha]}$$

$$\frac{\Delta; \Gamma, \alpha{:}\kappa \vdash e : \sigma \quad x \notin Dom(\Gamma)}{\Delta; \Gamma \vdash \Lambda \alpha{:}\kappa.e : \forall \alpha{:}\kappa.\sigma}$$

$$\frac{\Delta; \Gamma \vdash e : \sigma_2 \quad \cdot; \Delta \vdash \sigma_1 = \sigma_2 : \Omega}{\Delta; \Gamma \vdash e : \sigma_1}$$

Fusion on Languages

Roland Backhouse

University of Nottingham
rcb@cs.nott.ac.uk

Abstract. Many functions on context-free languages can be expressed
in the form of the least fixed point of a function whose definition mimics
the grammar of the given language. This paper presents the basic theory
that explains when a function on a context-free language can be defined
in this way. The contributions are: a novel definition of a regular algebra
capturing division properties, several theorems showing how complex
regular algebras are built from simpler ones, and the application of fixed
point theory and Galois connections to practical programming problems.

1   Introduction

A common technique for solving programming problems is to express the problem in terms of solving a system of mutually recursive equations. Having done so,
a number of techniques can be used for solving the equations, ranging from simple iterative techniques to more sophisticated but more specialised elimination
techniques.

A relatively straightforward and well-known example is the problem of finding
shortest paths through a graph. The distances to any one node from the nodes
in a graph can be expressed as a set of simultaneous equations, which equations
can be solved using for example Dijkstra's shortest path algorithm [Dij59]. Another, similar but much less straightforward, problem is that of finding the *edit
distance* between a word and a (context-free) language — the minimum number of edit operations required to edit the given word into a word in the given
language. In the case that the language is defined by a context-free grammar,
the problem can be solved by constructing a system of equations in the edit
distances between each segment of the given word and each nonterminal in the
given grammar [AP72]. This set of equations can then be solved using a simple
iterative technique or Knuth's generalisation [Knu77] of Dijkstra's shortest path
algorithm.

A stumbling block for the use of recursive equations is that there is often a
very big leap from a problem's specification to the algorithm for constructing the
system of simultaneous equations; the justification for the leap almost invariably
involves a *post hoc* verification of the construction. Thus, whereas methods for
solving the equations, once constructed, are well-known and understood, the
process of constructing the equations is not. The example of edit distances just
given is a good example. Indeed, the theory of context-free languages offers
many examples [JS94,JS95] — determining whether the language generated by

D. Sands (Ed.): ESOP 2001, LNCS 2028, pp. 107–121, 2001.

a given grammar is empty or not, determining the length of a shortest word in a context-free language, determining the $FIRST$ set of each of the nonterminals in a grammar, and so on.

In this paper we present a general theorem which expresses when the solution to a problem can be expressed as solving a system of simultaneous equations. We give several examples of the theorem together with several non-examples (that is, examples where the theorem is not directly applicable). The non-examples serve two functions. They highlight the gap between specification and recursive equations —we show in several cases how a small change in the specification leads to a breakdown in the solution by recursive equations— and they inform the development of a methodology for the construction of recursive equations.

Section 2 summarises the mathematical theory underlying this paper — the theory of Galois connections and fixed point calculus. The novel contribution begins in section 3. We propose a novel definition of a regular algebra, chosen so that we can encompass within one theorem many examples of programming problems, including ones involving computations on context-free grammars as well as the standard examples on finite graphs. Several theorems are presented showing how complex regular algebras can be constructed from simpler ones. Section 4 introduces the notion of a regular homomorphism and specialises the fusion theorem of section 2 in the context of regular algebras. Section 5 is about extending "measures" on the elements of a monoid to measures on the elements of a regular algebra. A measure is some function that imposes a (possibly partial) ordering on the elements of its domain. In order to apply the fusion theorem of section 4 we require that measures preserve the regular algebra structure. The main theorem in section 5 provides a simple test for when this is indeed the case for the proposed extension mechanism. The section is concluded by several non-trivial examples of measures on languages.

For space reasons, proofs, further examples and extensive references have been omitted; see `http://www.cs.nott.ac.uk/~rcb/papers` instead.

2   Galois Connections and Fixed Points

This section summarises the (standard) mathematical theory needed to understand the later sections. The notation we use follows the recommendations of Dijkstra and Scholten [DS90]. In particular, angle brackets delimit the scope of bound variables so that $\langle x{:}R{:}E \rangle$ denotes the function that maps a value x in the range given by predicate R to the value denoted by expression E. Also, function application is denoted by an infix dot.

2.1   Galois Connections and Fixed Points

Definition 1 (Galois Connection).   Suppose $\mathcal{A} = (A, \sqsubseteq)$ and $\mathcal{B} = (B, \preceq)$ are partially ordered sets and suppose $F \in A \leftarrow B$ and $G \in B \leftarrow A$. Then (F, G) is a Galois connection between $\mathcal{A}$ and $\mathcal{B}$ iff, for all $x \in B$ and $y \in A$,

$$F.x \sqsubseteq y \equiv x \preceq G.y \ .$$

We refer to F as the *lower adjoint* and to G as the *upper adjoint*.

The concept of a Galois connection was introduced by Oystein Ore in 1944 [Ore44] and was first used in computing science in 1964 [HS64]. The concept is now widely known particularly in the field of abstract interpretation [CC77, CC79]. Elementary examples of functions having Galois adjoints include negation of boolean values, the floor and ceiling functions, the maximum and minimum operators on sets of numbers, and weakest liberal preconditions.

We assume familiarity with the notion of supremum and infimum of a (monotonic) function. Following the tradition in regular algebra to denote binary suprema by the symbol "+", we use Σf to denote the supremum of f.

The following existence theorem is often used to determine that a function is indeed a lower adjoint.

Theorem 1 (Fundamental Theorem).   Suppose that $\mathcal{B}$ is a poset and $\mathcal{A}$ is a complete poset. Then a monotonic function $F \in \mathcal{A} \leftarrow \mathcal{B}$ is a lower adjoint in a Galois connection equivales F is supremum-preserving.

The next theorem on Galois connections is described by Lambek and Scott [LS86] as "the most interesting consequence of a Galois correspondence".

Theorem 2 (Unity of Opposites).   Suppose $F \in \mathcal{A} \leftarrow \mathcal{B}$ and $G \in \mathcal{B} \leftarrow \mathcal{A}$ are Galois connected functions, F being the lower adjoint and G being the upper adjoint. Then $F.\mathcal{B}$ and $G.\mathcal{A}$ are isomorphic posets. Moreover, if one of $\mathcal{A}$ or $\mathcal{B}$ is complete then $F.\mathcal{B}$ and $G.\mathcal{A}$ are also complete.

Suppose $\mathcal{A} = (A, \sqsubseteq)$ is a partially ordered set. Assuming $\mathcal{A}$ is complete, we denote the least prefix point of f by μf.

Theorem 3 (μ-fusion).   Suppose $f \in A \leftarrow B$ is the lower adjoint in a Galois connection between the complete posets $(A, \sqsubseteq)$ and $(B, \preceq)$. Suppose also that $g \in (B, \preceq) \leftarrow (B, \preceq)$ and $h \in (A, \sqsubseteq) \leftarrow (A, \sqsubseteq)$ are monotonic functions. Then

$$f.\mu g = \mu h \ \Leftarrow \ f \circ g = h \circ f \ .$$

We call this theorem μ-"fusion" because it states when application of function, f, can be "fused" with a fixed point, μg, to form a fixed point, μh. The fusion rule is the basis of so-called "loop fusion" techniques in programming: the combination of two loops, one executed after the other, into a single loop. The theorem also plays a central role in the abstract interpretation of programs — see [CC77,CC79].

2.2   Applying Fusion: Example and Non-example

This section discusses two related examples. The first is an example of how the fusion theorem is applied; the second illustrates how the fusion theorem need not be *directly* applicable. Later we return to the second example and show how it can be generalised in such a way that the fusion theorem does become applicable.

Both examples are concerned with membership of a set. So, let us consider an arbitrary set $\mathcal{U}$. For each x in $\mathcal{U}$ the predicate $(x \in)$ maps a subset P

of $\mathcal{U}$ to the boolean value true if x is an element of P and otherwise to false. The predicate ($x\in$) preserves set union. That is, for all bags $\mathcal{S}$ of subsets of $\mathcal{U}$, $x\in\cup\mathcal{S} \equiv \exists\langle P: P\in\mathcal{S}: x\in P\rangle$. According to the fundamental theorem, the predicate ($x\in$) thus has an upper adjoint. Indeed, we have, for all booleans b,

$$x\in S \Rightarrow b \equiv S \subseteq \text{if } b \rightarrow \mathcal{U} \square \neg b \rightarrow \mathcal{U}\backslash\{x\} \text{ fi }.$$

Now suppose f is a monotonic function on sets. Let μf denote its least fixed point. The fact that ($x\in$) is a lower adjoint means that we may be able to apply the fusion theorem to reduce a test for membership in μf to solving a recursive equation. Specifically

$$(x\in\mu f \equiv \mu g) \quad \Leftarrow \quad \forall\langle S:: x \in f.S \equiv g.(x\in S)\rangle .$$

That is, the recursive equation with underlying endofunction f is replaced by the equation with underlying endofunction g (mapping booleans to booleans) if we can establish the property $\forall\langle S:: x \in f.S \equiv g.(x\in S)\rangle$. An example of where this is always possible is testing whether the empty word is in the language defined by a context-free grammar. For concreteness, consider the grammar with just one nonterminal S and productions

$$S \quad ::= \quad aS \quad | \quad SS \quad | \quad \varepsilon$$

Then the function f maps set X to $\{a\}\cdot X \cup X\cdot X \cup \{\varepsilon\}$ and the function g maps boolean b to $(\varepsilon\in\{a\} \wedge b) \vee (b\wedge b) \vee \varepsilon\in\{\varepsilon\}$. Note how the definition of g has the same structure as the definition of f. Effectively set union has been replaced by disjunction and concatenation has been replaced by conjunction. Of course, g can be simplified further (to the constant function true) but that would miss the point of the example.

Now suppose that instead of taking x to be the empty word we consider any word other than the empty word. Then, the use of the fusion theorem breaks down. This is because the empty word is the only word x that satisfies the property $x \in X\cdot Y \equiv x\in X \wedge x\in Y$ for all X and Y. Indeed, taking x to be a for illustration purposes, we have

$$a \in \mu\langle X:: \{a\}\cdot X \cup X\cdot X \cup \{\varepsilon\}\rangle \equiv \text{true }, \text{ but}$$

$$\mu\langle b:: (a\in\{a\} \wedge b) \vee (b\wedge b) \vee a\in\{\varepsilon\}\rangle \equiv \text{false }.$$

This second example emphasises that the conclusion of μ-fusion demands *two* properties of f, g and h, namely that f be a lower adjoint, and that $f\circ g = h\circ f$. The rule is nevertheless very versatile since being a lower adjoint is far from being uncommon, and many algebraic properties take the form $f\circ g = h\circ f$ for some functions f, g and h. In cases when the rule is not immediately applicable we have to seek generalisations of f and/or g that do satisfy both properties. Example 9 shows how this is done in the case of the general membership test for context-free languages.

3 Regular Algebra

In this section we propose a novel definition of a regular algebra, motivated by a desire to exploit to the full the calculational properties of Galois connections. We give several examples of regular algebras and theorems showing how more regular algebras can be built up from simpler algebras.

Our view of a regular algebra is that it is the combination of a monoid (the algebra of composition) and a complete poset (the algebra of choice), with an interface between the two structures. The interface is that composition distributes through choice in all circumstances; in other words, the product operator of the monoid structure admits left and right "division" or "factorisation" operators.

Various axiomatisations of regular algebra have been given in the past, in particular several by Conway[Con71]. Conway introduced (left and right) *factors* in the context of regular languages, exploiting implicitly the fact that concatenation functions $(L\cdot)$ and $(\cdot L)$, for given language L, are both lower adjoints. Some remarkable results in his book make significant use of the existence of factors. However, Conway did not base any of his axiomatisations on this fact. Other axiomatisations (for example, Kozen [Koz91]) are too weak to encompass all the applications considered in this paper.

3.1 Definition and Examples

Our definition of a regular algebra is a combination of a monoid and a complete, universally distributive lattice.

Definition 2 (Regular Algebra). Suppose $\mathcal{A}=(A, \preceq)$ is a complete lattice. (This means that the suprema and infima of all monotonic functions exist, whatever the shape set.) Denote the binary supremum operator on $\mathcal{A}$ by $\oplus$. Then $\mathcal{A}$ is said to be *universally distributive* if, for all $a \in A$, the endofunction $(\oplus a)$ is the upper adjoint in a Galois connection of the poset $\mathcal{A}$ with itself.

A *regular algebra* is a 5-tuple $(A, \otimes, \oplus, \preceq, 0, 1)$ where

(a) $(A, \otimes, 1)$ is a monoid,

(b) $(A, \preceq, \oplus, 0)$ is a complete, universally distributive lattice with least element 0 and binary supremum operator $\oplus$,

(c) for all $a \in A$, the endofunctions $(a \otimes)$ and $(\otimes a)$ are both lower adjoints in Galois connections between $(A, \preceq)$ and itself.

The standard example of a complete, universally distributive lattice is a power set lattice — the set of subsets of a given set ordered by set inclusion. The main application of universal distributivity is predicting uniqueness of fixed points. This however will not be an issue in this paper.

Where necessary, we use the notation $(a\backslash)$ and $(/a)$ for the upper adjoints of the functions $(a\otimes)$ and $(\otimes a)$, respectively. Thus the rules are: for all x and y, $a \otimes x \preceq y \equiv x \preceq a \backslash y$ and $x \otimes a \preceq y \equiv x \preceq y/a$. The operators $\backslash$ and $/$ are called *division* operators, and we often paraphrase requirement 2(c) as *product admits (left and right) division*.

Example 1 (Bool).   The set $\mathbb{B}$ containing the boolean values true and false is the carrier of a regular algebra. The ordering is implication, summation is disjoint sum and product is conjunction. The zero of product is false and its unit is true. This algebra forms the basis of decision problems. Although very simple, we shall see in example 5 that this is not a primitive regular algebra.

Example 2 (Min Cost Algebra).   A regular algebra that occurs frequently in problems involving some cost function has carrier the set of all positive real numbers, $\mathbb{R}^{\geq 0}$, augmented with a largest element, ∞. (That is, the carrier is $\mathbb{R}^{\geq 0} \cup \{\infty\}$.) This set forms a monoid where the product operation is defined by

$$x \otimes y \quad = \quad \begin{array}{ll} \text{if} & x = \infty \vee y = \infty \;\rightarrow\; \infty \\ \square & x \neq \infty \wedge y \neq \infty \;\rightarrow\; x + y \\ \text{fi} \end{array}$$

and the unit of product is 0. Ordering its elements by the at-least relation, where by definition $\infty \geq x$ for all x, the set forms a complete, universally distributive lattice. The supremum is minimum. Henceforth, we denote the minimum of x and y by $x \downarrow y$ and their maximum by $x \uparrow y$. Moreover, the product operation admits division. The upper adjoint of $(\otimes y)$ is given by

$$z/y \quad = \quad \begin{array}{ll} \text{if} & y = \infty \;\rightarrow\; 0 \\ \square & y \neq \infty \wedge z \neq \infty \;\rightarrow\; (z-y) \uparrow 0 \\ \square & y \neq \infty \wedge z = \infty \;\rightarrow\; \infty \\ \text{fi} \quad . \end{array}$$

Example 3 (Bottleneck Algebra).   Bottleneck problems are problems with a max-min requirement. For example, if it is required to drive a high load under a number of low bridges, we want to find the maximum over all different routes of the minimum height bridge on the route. A regular algebra fundamental to bottleneck problems has carrier the set of all real numbers, augmented with largest and smallest values, ∞ and $-\infty$ respectively. The addition operator is maximum (so that the ordering relation is at-most) and the product operator is minimum. The minimum operator is easily seen to satisfy the property

$$x \downarrow y \leq z \;\equiv\; x \leq z/y \;\;, \text{ where}$$

$$z/y \;=\; \text{if } y \leq z \;\rightarrow\; \infty \;\square\; y > z \;\rightarrow\; z \text{ fi}$$

That is, the product operator in the algebra admits division.

3.2   All Solutions

When solving optimisation problems, where we are not just interested in the optimum value of the cost function, but in determining some value in the domain of solutions that optimises the cost function, we consider an algebra of pairs, where the first element is the cost and the second element is a set of values that have that cost. An algebra of pairs is also appropriate for decision problems, where a simple yes/no answer is insufficient, and when two criteria for optimality are combined. For example, we may wish to determine among all least-cost solutions to a given problem, a solution that optimises some other criterion, like size or weight. Theorem 4 is the basis for the use of regular algebra in such circumstances. The theorem details the construction of an algebra of pairs in which the pairs are ordered lexicographically. In general, it is not possible to combine arbitrary regular algebras in this way; the first algebra in the pair is assumed to be a *cost* algebra, as defined below.

Definition 3.   A *cost algebra* is a regular algebra with the property that the ordering on elements is total and, for all $y \neq \mathbf{0}$,

$$(x{\cdot}y)/y = x/y{\cdot}y = x = y{\cdot}y \backslash x = y \backslash (y{\cdot}x) \ .$$

It is easy to verify that the algebras of examples 1 and 2 are cost algebras.

Theorem 4 (Cost Algebras).   Suppose $\mathcal{R}_1$ and $\mathcal{R}_2$ are both regular algebras. Suppose further that $\mathcal{R}_1$ is a cost algebra. Define the set P to be the set of ordered pairs (x, r) where $x \in \mathcal{R}_1$, $r \in \mathcal{R}_2$ and $x = \mathbf{0}_1 \Rightarrow r = \mathbf{0}_2$. Order P lexicographically; specifically, let

$$(x, r) \preceq (y, s) \ \equiv \ x < y \ \vee \ (x = y \wedge r \sqsubseteq s)$$

where $\leq$ is the ordering in algebra $\mathcal{R}_1$, $\sqsubseteq$ is the ordering in algebra $\mathcal{R}_2$, and $\preceq$ is the ordering in P. Define the product operation on elements of P coordinatewise:

$$(x, r) \otimes (y, s) \ = \ (x{\cdot}y \ , \ r{\circ}s)$$

the products $x{\cdot}y$ and $r{\circ}s$ being the products in the appropriate algebra. Define addition by

$$
\begin{aligned}
(x, r) \oplus (y, s) \ = \quad &\text{if} \quad x < y \ \rightarrow \ (x, r) \\
&\square \quad x = y \ \rightarrow \ (x, r{+}s) \\
&\square \quad y < x \ \rightarrow \ (y, s) \\
&\text{fi} \quad .
\end{aligned}
$$

Then $(P, \otimes, \oplus, \preceq, (\mathbf{0}_1, \mathbf{0}_2), (\mathbf{1}_1, \mathbf{1}_2))$ is a regular algebra.

Example 4.   Suppose we consider a network of cities connected by a number of roads. Each road has a certain length and along each road there is a low bridge. It is required to drive a high load from one of the cities to another by an "optimum" route (a route being a sequence of connecting roads).

One criterion of optimality is that we choose, among the shortest routes, a route that maximises the minimum height of bridge along the route. A second criterion of optimality is that, among the routes that maximise the minimum height of bridge along the route, we choose a shortest route.

The construction of theorem 4 is applicable to the first criterion of optimality. The elements of the algebra are ordered pairs ($distance$, $height$). A route with "cost" (d , h) is better than a route with "cost" (e , k) if $d < e$ or $d = e$ and $h \geq k$. As this is a regular algebra, it is possible to apply the standard all-pairs path-finding algorithm to determine, for all pairs of cities, the cost of a best route between the cities.

The construction of theorem 4 is *not* applicable to the second criterion of optimality; an attempt to embed the lexicographical ordering on ($height$, $distance$) pairs in a regular algebra fails because product does not distribute through addition and optimal routes may be composed of suboptimal parts.

3.3   Vector Algebras

Recursive equations typically involve several unknowns, possibly even an infinite set of unknowns. This situation is modelled in a straightforward and standard way. We consider a collection of equations in a collection of unknowns as a single equation in a single unknown, that unknown being a vector of values. And a vector is just a function with range the carrier set of a regular algebra. The set of functions with domain some arbitrary, fixed set and range a regular algebra forms a regular algebra if we extend the operators in the range algebra pointwise.

Theorem 5 (Vector Algebras).   Suppose $\mathcal{A} = (A, \times, +, \leq, 0, 1)$ is a regular algebra and suppose $\mathcal{B} = (B, \sqsubseteq)$ is an arbitrary poset. Then $\mathcal{A} \leftarrow \mathcal{B} = (A \leftarrow B, \dot{\times}, \dot{+}, \dot{\leq}, \dot{0}, \dot{1})$ is a regular algebra, where product, addition and ordering are defined pointwise and $\dot{0}$ and $\dot{1}$ are the constant functions returning 0 and 1, respectively.

3.4   From Monoids to Regular Algebras

Some important examples of regular algebras are power set algebras. These are introduced in this section.

Lemma 1.   Every monoid can be extended to a power set regular algebra in the obvious way: monoid (A , $\cdot$, 1) is extended to a regular algebra with carrier set 2^A , partial ordering the subset relation, and multiplication extended to sets in the usual way with $\{1\}$ as the unit.

Example 5 (Bool).   The simplest possible example of a monoid has carrier $\{1\}$. The subsets of this set are the empty set and the set itself. The power set regular algebra is clearly isomorphic to the booleans. Choosing to map the empty set to false and $\{1\}$ to true, the product operation of the regular algebra is conjunction, and the addition operator is disjunction. This is example 1 discussed earlier.

Example 6.   A *language* over alphabet T is a set of words, i.e. a subset of T^*. The power set regular algebra constructed from the monoid $(T^*, \cdot, \varepsilon)$, where the infix dot denotes concatention of words and ε denotes the empty word, has carrier the set of all languages over alphabet T.

3.5   Graph Algebras

If regular algebra is to be applied to path-finding problems then it is vital that the property of being a regular algebra can be extended to graphs/matrices[1] [BC75].

Often, graphs are supposed to have finite dimensions. In the present circumstances —the assumption of a complete lattice— there is no need to impose this as a requirement. Indeed if we are to include the algebra of binary relations over some given, possibly infinite, set in the class of regular algebras then we certainly should not require graphs to have finite dimension. Other applications demand a very general definition of a graph. In the following, a *binary relation* is just a set of pairs.

Definition 4.   Suppose r is a binary relation and suppose A is a set. A *(labelled) graph of dimension r over A* is a function f with domain r and range A. Elements of relation r are called *edges*.

We will use $M_r A$ to denote the class of all labelled graphs of dimension r over A. If f is a graph and the pair (i, j) is an element of r, then $i\langle f\rangle j$ will be used to denote the application of f to the pair (i, j).

Definition 5 (Addition and Product).   Suppose $\mathcal{R} = (A, \times, +, \leq, 0, 1)$ is a regular algebra. Then zero and the addition and product operators of $\mathcal{R}$ can be extended to graphs as follows. Two graphs f and g of the same dimension r can be ordered according to the rule: for all pairs (i, j) in r, $f \stackrel{.}{\leq} g \equiv \forall\langle i, j :: i\langle f\rangle j \leq i\langle g\rangle j\rangle$. The supremum ordering is just pointwise. In particular, f and g of the same dimension r are added according to the rule: for all pairs (i, j) in r, $i\langle f \dotplus g\rangle j = i\langle f\rangle j + i\langle g\rangle j$. Two graphs f and g of dimensions r and s can be multiplied to form a graph of dimension $r{\circ}s$ according to the rule: for all pairs (i, j) in $r{\circ}s$,

$$i\langle f \dot{\times} g\rangle j \;=\; \Sigma\langle k\colon\; (i,k) \in r \wedge (k,j) \in s\colon\; i\langle f\rangle k \times k\langle g\rangle j\rangle \;\;.$$

Finally, the zero graph, denoted by $\mathbf{0}$, is defined by: for all pairs (i, j) in r, $i\langle \mathbf{0}\rangle j = 0$.

---

[1] For us, the words *graph* and *matrix* are interchangeable. In some applications "graph" is the word that is traditionally used, in others "matrix" is more conventional. For consistency we use "graph" everywhere throughout this paper.

Henceforth, we use $M_r A$ to denote the class of all graphs of dimension r over A.

Theorem 6 (Graph Algebras).   Suppose $\mathcal{R} = (A, \times, +, \le, 0, 1)$ is a regular algebra with carrier A, and suppose r is a reflexive, transitive relation. Define an ordering, addition and product operators as in definition 5. Define the unit graph, denoted by **1**, by

$$i\langle \mathbf{1} \rangle j \;=\; \text{if } i = j \to 1 \;\square\; i \ne j \to 0 \text{ fi} \;.$$

(Note that $M_r A$ is closed under the product operation and contains **1** on account of the assumptions that r is transitive and reflexive, respectively.) Then the algebra $M_r \mathcal{R} \;=\; (M_r A, \dot{\times}, \dot{+}, \dot{\le}, \mathbf{0}, \mathbf{1})$ so defined is a regular algebra.

There are several important examples of graph regular algebras. The binary relations on some set A is one example. The underlying regular algebra is the booleans $\mathbb{B}$, and the edge relation is the cartesian product $A \times A$. The relation represented by graph f is the set of pairs (i, k) such that $i\langle f \rangle k$. Graph addition corresponds to the union of relations, and graph product corresponds to the composition of relations. The divisions f/g and $f\backslash g$ are called residuals [Dil39] in the mathematics literature and weakest pre and post specifications [HH86] in the computing science literature.

Path problems on finite graphs provide additional examples of graph algebras. The standard example is shortest paths: the underlying algebra is the minimum cost algebra introduced in definition 2.

4   Regular Homomorphisms and the Main Theorem

In this section we specialise the fusion theorem of section 2 to systems of equations with the structure of a context-free grammar.

Definition 6 (Regular Homomorphism).   Let $\mathcal{R} = (R, \circ, 1_R)$ and $\mathcal{S} = (S, \cdot, 1_S)$ be monoids. Suppose m is a function with domain R and range S. Then m is said to be *compositional* if $m.(x \cdot y) \;=\; m.x \circ m.y$, for all x and y in R. Also, m is said to be a *monoid homomorphism* from $\mathcal{R}$ to $\mathcal{S}$ if m is compositional and preserves units: $m.1_R = 1_S$. Now let $\mathcal{R} = (R, \circ, \oplus, \preceq, 0_R, 1_R)$ and $\mathcal{S} = (S, \cdot, +, \le, 0_S, 1_S)$ be regular algebras. Suppose m is a function with domain R and range S. Then m is said to be a *regular homomorphism* if m is a monoid homomorphism (from $(R, \circ, 1_R)$ to $(S, \cdot, 1_S)$) and it is a lower adjoint in a Galois connection between the two orderings.

For m to be a regular homomorphism it must be compositional and preserve the unit of $\mathcal{R}$. However, the latter requirement is redundant if we restrict attention to the values in the image of R under m. After all, we have $m.x = m.(x \circ 1_R) = m.x \cdot m.1_R$ and, similarly, $m.y = m.(1_R \circ y) = m.1_R \cdot m.y$ so that $(m.R, \cdot, m.1_R)$ is a monoid, where $m.R$ denotes the image of the set R under m. In more complicated applications this observation becomes important. Formally, we combine the observation with the unity-of-opposites theorem in the following theorem.

Theorem 7 (Range Algebras).   Let $\mathcal{R} = (R, \circ, \oplus, \preceq, 0_R, 1_R)$ and $\mathcal{S} = (S, \cdot, +, \leq, 0_S, 1_S)$ be regular algebras. Suppose m is a function with domain R and range S that is compositional and is a lower adjoint in a Galois connection between the orderings. Let $m.R$ be the image of R under m and let $m^\sharp$ denote its upper adjoint. Then $m.\mathcal{R} = (m.R, \cdot, \boxplus, \leq, 0_S, m.1_R)$ is a regular algebra, where $x \boxplus y = m.(m^\sharp.x \oplus m^\sharp.y)$. Moreover, m is a regular homomorphism from $\mathcal{R}$ to $m.\mathcal{R}$.

Regular homomorphisms are lower adjoints and are compositional. These are exactly the conditions we need to apply the fusion theorem to systems of equations with the structure of a context-free grammar.

Theorem 8 (Fusion on Languages).   Suppose G is a context-free grammar, and $\mathcal{R}$ and $\mathcal{S}$ are regular algebras. Suppose also that m is a regular homomorphism from $\mathcal{R}$ to $\mathcal{S}$. Suppose g is the endofunction obtained in the obvious way from G by interpreting concatenation and choice by the product and addition operators of $\mathcal{R}$, and by giving suitable interpretations to the symbols of the alphabet. Suppose h is obtained in the same way using $\mathcal{S}$ instead of $\mathcal{R}$. (See section 2.2 for an example.) Then $m . \mu g = \mu h$.

5   Measures

On its own, theorem 8 is difficult to use because the requirement of being a regular homomorphism is quite strong. However, the sort of functions m that we usually consider are defined by extending a function on words to a function on languages. We call such functions "measures". The sort of measures we have in mind are the length of a word, the first k symbols in a word, and the edit distance of a word from some given word. For example the length function on words is extended to the length-of-a-shortest-word function on languages.

In this section we show that the standard mechanism for extending a measure to a set results in a homomorphism of regular algebras, the only condition being that we start with a measure that is compositional. This makes theorem 8 relatively easy to use.

Theorem 9 (Monoidal Extensions).   Suppose that $(M, \cdot, 1_M)$ is a monoid and that $\mathcal{R} = (R, \cdot, +, \leq, 0_R, 1_R)$ is a regular algebra. Suppose m is a function with domain M and range R. Consider the power set algebra $(2^M, \cdot, \cup, \subseteq, \phi, \{1_M\})$ as defined in theorem 1. Define *measure*, the *extension* of m to subsets of M (elements of 2^M), by $measure.S = \Sigma\langle x: x \in S: m.x \rangle$. Then *measure* is a regular homomorphism if m is compositional.

We consider several examples.

Example 7 (Test for Empty).   Suppose we wish to determine whether a language is empty or not. Consider the regular algebra $\mathbb{B}$ (definition 1). Define the measure m of a word to be **true**. Then the extension *measure* of m to

sets of words tests whether a language is empty or not. Specifically, by defini-
tion $measure.S \equiv \exists\langle u: u \in S: \text{true}\rangle$. That is, $measure.S \equiv S \neq \phi$. The measure
m is clearly compositional and so $measure$ is a regular homomorphism, and
theorem 8 can be applied.

Example 8 (Membership).   We return to the membership problem discussed
in section 2.2. Consider the regular algebra $\mathbb{B}$ (definition 1). Given a word X,
define the measure m of a word u to be $u = X$. Then the extension, $measure$,
of m to sets of words tests for membership of x in the set. Specifically, by
definition $measure.S \equiv \exists\langle u: u \in S: u = X\rangle$. That is, $measure.S \equiv X \in S$. This
measure is a regular homomorphism if measure m is compositional. But m is
compositional equivales $\varepsilon = X$. So the only example of a membership test on
sets of words that is a regular homomorphism is the so-called *nullability* test:
the test whether the empty word is in the set. So only in this case can theorem
8 be applied directly.

The next two examples involve graph algebras. Note how example 9 gener-
alises example 8.

Example 9 (General Context-Free Parsing).   The general parsing algorithm
invented by Cocke, Younger and Kasami exploits a regular homomorphism. (See
[AU72, p332] for references to the origin of the Cocke-Younger-Kasami parsing
algorithm.)

Let X be a given word and let N be the length of X. The motivating
problem is to determine whether X —the input string— is in a language L
given by some context-free grammar.

We use X to define a measure on words and then we extend the measure to
sets and then to vectors of sets. The measure of word u is a graph of Booleans
that determines which segments of X are equal to u. Specifically, let us index
the symbols of X from 0 onwards. The edge relation of the graph is the set of
pairs (i, j) such that $0 \le i \le j \le N$ and will be denoted by seg. Note that this
is a reflexive, transitive relation. For brevity we omit this constraint on i and
j from now on.

Now, with i and j satisfying $0 \le i \le j \le N$, let $X[i..j)$ denote the segment
of word X beginning at index i and ending at index $j-1$. (So $X[i..i)$ is the
empty word.) Now define[2] $m.u = \langle i, j:: X[i..j) = u\rangle$. This defines $m.u$ to be
a boolean graph with dimension the set of pairs (i, j) satisfying $0 \le i \le j \le N$.
The extension of the measure m to sets is

$$measure.S = \langle i, j:: \exists\langle u: u \in S: X[i..j) = u\rangle\rangle$$

so that

$$0\langle measure.S\rangle N \equiv X \in S \ .$$

Crucial to the correctness of the Cocke-Younger-Kasami algorithm is that m is
compositional. This is proved as follows.

[2] Recall that $\langle i, j:: X[i..j) = u\rangle$ denotes a function mapping pair (i, j) (implicitly)
satisfying $0 \le i \le j \le N$ to the boolean value $X[i..j) = u$.

$$m.u \times m.v$$

$$=\qquad\{\qquad \text{definition of } m\qquad\}$$

$$\langle i,j:: X[i..j) = u\rangle \times \langle i,j:: X[i..j) = v\rangle$$

$$=\qquad\{\qquad \text{definition of graph product in algebra } M_{seg}\mathsf{B}\qquad\}$$

$$\langle i,j:: \exists\langle k:: X[i..k) = u \wedge X[k..j) = v\rangle\rangle$$

$$=\qquad\{\qquad \text{word calculus}\qquad\}$$

$$\langle i,j:: X[i..j) = u{\cdot}v\rangle$$

$$=\qquad\{\qquad \text{definition of } m\qquad\}$$

$$m.(u{\cdot}v) \ .$$

We conclude that theorem 8 can be applied. Thus testing whether X is an element of the language generated by a context-free grammar G involves solving a system of order $N^2 \times k$ equations where k is the number of nonterminals in the grammar.

The final example is the most complicated, and requires a more complicated justification.

Example 10 (Error Repair).   A general technique for error repair when parsing languages is to compute the minimum number of edit operations required to edit the input string into a string in the language being recognised [AP72]. The technique involves a generalisation of the Cocke-Younger-Kasami algorithm, similar to the generalisation that is made when going from Warshall's transitive closure algorithm to Floyd's all-shortest-paths algorithm.

Let X be a given word (the input string) and let N be the length of X. As in example 9, we use X to define a measure on words and then we extend the measure to sets. The measure of word u is a triangular graph of numbers that determines how many edit operations are required to transform each segment of X to the word u.

Transforming one word to another involves a sequence of primitive edit operations. Initially the input index, i, is set to 0; the edit operations scan the input string from left to right, transforming it to the output string. The allowed edit operations and their effect on the input string are

- *Insert(a)* . Insert symbol a after the current symbol in the output string.
- *Delete* . Increment the index i.
- *ChangeTo(a)* . Increment the index i and add symbol a to the end of the output string.
- *OK* . Copy the symbol at index i of the input to the output. Then increment i.

(We will see that the choice of allowed edit operations is crucial to the correctness of the generalised algorithm.)

Let $dist(u,v)$ denote the minimum number of non-OK edit operations needed to transform word u into word v using a sequence of the above edit operations. Now define

$$m.u \ = \ \langle i, j :: dist(X[i..j]\,, u) \rangle \ .$$

This defines $m.u$ to be a graph of numbers. The numbers, augmented by ∞, form the min-cost regular algebra discussed in example 2. Thus graphs over numbers also form a regular algebra. Taking this as the range algebra, the extension of the measure m to sets is

$$measure.S \ = \ \langle i, j :: \ \downarrow \langle u : u \in S : dist(X[i..j]\,, u) \rangle \rangle$$

so that $0 \langle measure.S \rangle N$ is the minimum number of edit operations required to repair the word X to a word in S.

Crucial to the correctness of the generalised Cocke-Younger-Kasami algorithm is that m is compositional. This follows from

$$dist(X[i..j]\,, u \cdot v) \ = \ \downarrow \langle k :: dist(X[i..k]\,, u) + dist(X[k..j]\,, v) \rangle$$

which is a non-trivial property of the chosen collection of edit operations

To see that the property is non-trivial, suppose we extend the set of edit operations to allow the transposition of two adjacent characters. (Transposing characters is a very common error when using a keyboard.) Then the edit distance function is not compositional as, for example, $dist$ ("ab","ba") is 1 —it takes one transposition to transform the word "ab" to the word "ba"— but this is not equal to the minimum of $dist$ ("ab","b") + $dist(\varepsilon$,"a") and $dist$ ("a","b") + $dist$ ("b","a") and $dist(\varepsilon$,"b") + $dist$ ("ab","a") —which it should be if the function m were to be compositional. Indeed, computing minimal edit distances for context-free languages is very difficult if the possibility of transpositions is included in the analysis.

This is the first example where m is compositional but not a monoid homomorphism. In an algebra of graphs with underlying algebra minimum costs the (i,j)th entry in the unit graph is ∞ whenever $i \neq j$. The (i,j)th entry in $m.\varepsilon$, on the other hand, is the cost of deleting all the symbols of $X[i..j]$. This is an instance where theorem 7 is really needed. The extension $measure$ of m is indeed a regular homomorphism; its domain is the algebra over languages and its range is the algebra of graphs in the image set of $measure$.

References

[AP72]   A. V. Aho and T.G. Peterson. A minimum-distance error-correcting parser for context-free languages. *SIAM J. Computing*, 1:305–312, 1972.

[AU72]   Alfred V. Aho and Jeffrey D. Ullman. *The theory of parsing, translation and compiling*, volume 1 of *Series in Automatic Computation*. Prentice-Hall, 1972.

[BC75]   R.C. Backhouse and B.A. Carré. Regular algebra applied to path-finding problems. *Journal of the Institute of Mathematics and its Applications*, 15:161–186, 1975.

[CC77]   Patrick Cousot and Radhia Cousot. Abstract interpretation: A unifed lattice model for static analysis of programs by construction or approximation of fixpoints. In *Conference Record of the Fourth Annual ACM Symposium on Principles of Programming Languages*, pages 238–252, Los Angeles, California, January 1977.

[CC79]   Patrick Cousot and Radhia Cousot. Systematic design of program analysis frameworks. In *Conference Record of the Sixth Annual ACM Symposium on Principles of Programming Languages*, pages 269–282, San Antonio, Texas, January 1979.

[Con71] J.H. Conway. *Regular Algebra and Finite Machines*. Chapman and Hall, London, 1971.

[Dij59] E.W. Dijkstra. A note on two problems in connexion with graphs. *Numerische Mathematik*, 1:269–271, 1959.

[Dil39] R.P. Dilworth. Non-commutative residuated lattices. *Transactions of the American Mathematical Society*, 46:426–444, 1939.

[DS90]   Edsger W. Dijkstra and Carel S. Scholten. *Predicate Calculus and Program Semantics*. Texts and monographs in Computer Science. Springer-Verlag, 1990.

[HH86]   C.A.R. Hoare and Jifeng He. The weakest prespecification. *Fundamenta Informaticae*, 9:51–84, 217–252, 1986.

[HS64]   J. Hartmanis and R.E. Stearns. Pair algebras and their application to automata theory. *Information and Control*, 7(4):485–507, 1964.

[JS94]   J. Jeuring and S.D. Swierstra. Bottom-up grammar analysis — a functional formulation —. In Donald Sannella, editor, *Proceedings Programming Languages and Systems, ESOP '94*, volume 788 of *LNCS*, pages 317–332, 1994.

[JS95]   J. Jeuring and S.D. Swierstra. Constructing functional programs for grammar analysis problems. In S. Peyton Jones, editor, *Proceedings Functional Programming Languages and Computer Architecture, FPCA '95*, June 1995.

[Knu77] D.E. Knuth. A generalization of Dijkstra's shortest path algorithm. *Information Processing Letters*, 6(1):1–5, 1977.

[Koz91] Dexter Kozen. A completeness theorem for Kleene algebras and the algebra of regular events. In *Proc. 6th Annual IEEE Symp. on Logic in Computer Science*, pages 214–225. IEEE Society Press, 1991.

[LS86]   J. Lambek and P.J. Scott. *Introduction to Higher Order Categorical Logic*, volume 7 of *Studies in Advanced Mathematics*. Cambridge University Press, 1986.

[Ore44] Oystein Ore. Galois connexions. *Transactions of the American Mathematical Society*, 55:493–513, 1944.

Programming the Web with High-Level Programming Languages

Paul Graunke[1], Shriram Krishnamurthi[2],
Steve Van Der Hoeven[3], and Matthias Felleisen[4]

[1] Department of Computer Science, Rice University
[2] Department of Computer Science, Brown University
[3] ESSI, Université de Nice
[4] Department of Computer Science, Rice University

Abstract. Many modern programs provide operating system-style services to extension modules. A Web server, for instance, behaves like a simple OS kernel. It invokes programs that dynamically generate Web pages and manages their resource consumption. Most Web servers, however, rely on conventional operating systems to provide these services. As a result, the solutions are inefficient, and impose a serious overhead on the programmer of dynamic extensions.
In this paper, we show that a Web server implemented in a suitably extended high-level programming language overcomes all these problems. First, building a server in such a language is straightforward. Second, the server delivers static content at performance levels comparable to a conventional server. Third, the Web server delivers dynamic content at a much higher rate than a conventional server, which is important because a significant portion of Web content is now dynamically generated. Finally, the server provides programming mechanisms for the dynamic generation of Web content that are difficult to support in a conventional server architecture.

1 Web Servers and High-Level Operating Systems

A Web server provides operating system-style services. Like an operating system, a server runs programs (e.g., CGI scripts). Like an operating system, a server protects these programs from each other. And, like an operating system, a server manages resources (e.g., network connections) for the programs it runs.

Some existing Web servers rely on the underlying operating system to implement these services. Others fail to provide services due to shortcomings of the implementation languages. In this paper, we show that implementing a Web server in a suitably extended functional programming language is straightforward and satisfies three major properties. First, the server delivers *static* content at a performance level comparable to a conventional server. Second, the Web server delivers *dynamic* content at five times the rate of a conventional server. Considering the explosive growth of dynamically created Web pages [7], this performance improvement is important. Finally, our server provides programming mechanisms for the dynamic generation of Web content that are difficult to support in a conventional server architecture.

D. Sands (Ed.): ESOP 2001, LNCS 2028, pp. 122–136, 2001.

The basis of our experiment is MrEd [11], an extension of Scheme [15]. The implementation of the server heavily exploits four extensions: first-class *modules*, which help structure the server and represent server programs; preemptive *threads*; which are needed to execute server programs; *custodians*, which manage the resource consumption of server programs; and *parameters*, which control stateful attributes of threads. The server programs also rely on Scheme's capabilities for manipulating continuations as first-class values. The paper shows which role each construct plays in the construction of the server.

The following section is a brief introduction to MrEd. Section 3 explains the core of our server implementation. In section 4 we show how the server can be extended to support Scheme CGI scripts and illustrate how programming in the extended Scheme language facilitates the implementation of scripts. Sections 3 and 4 also present performance results. Section 5 discusses related work. The final section summarizes our ideas and presents areas for future work.

2   MrEd: A High-Level Operating System

MrEd [11] is a safe implementation of Scheme [15]; it is one of the fastest existing Scheme interpreters. Following the tradition of functional languages, a Scheme program specifies a computation in terms of values and legitimate primitive operations on values (creation, selection, mutation, predicative tests). The implementation of the server exploits traditional functional language features, such as closures and standard data structures, and also Scheme's ability to capture and restore continuations, possibly multiple times.

MrEd extends Scheme with structures, exceptions, and modules. The module system [10] permits programmers to specify *atomic units* and *compound units*. An atomic unit is a closed collection of definitions. Each unit has an import and an export signature. The import signature specifies what names the module expects as imports; the export signature specifies which of the locally defined names will become visible to the rest of the world. Units are first-class values. There are two operations on unit values: invocation and linking. A unit is invoked via the **invoke-unit/sig** special form, which must supply the relevant imports from the lexical scope. MrEd permits units to be loaded and invoked at run-time. A unit is linked—or *compounded*—via the **compound-unit/sig** mechanism. Programmers compound units by specifying a (possibly cyclic) graph of connections among units, including references to the import signature; the result is a unit.

The extended language also supports the creation of threads and thread synchronization. Figure 1 specifies the relevant primitives. Threads are created from 0-ary procedures (thunks); they synchronize via counting semaphores. For communication between parent and child threads, however, synchronization via semaphores is too complex. For this purpose, MrEd provides (thread) *parameters*. The form

(**parameterize** ([*parameter1 value1*]...) *body1*...)

sets *parameter1* to *value1* for the dynamic extent of the computation *body1* ...; when this computation ends, the parameter is reset to its original value. New threads inherit copies of their parent's parameter bindings, though the parameter values themselves are not copied. That is, when a child sets a parameter, it

tcp-listen : Nat [Nat] → Tcp-listener
;; reserves a port to accept connections, optionally specifying the
;; maximum number of clients that may wait for a connection

tcp-accept : Tcp-listener →* Input-port Output-port
;; creates I/O ports for a connection request via the listener

---

thread : (→ Void) → Thread
;; spawns a thunk as a thread

make-semaphore : Nat → Semaphore
;; creates a semaphore with specified number of tokens

semaphore-post : Semaphore → Void
;; posts a semaphore and releases waiting threads

semaphore-wait : Semaphore → Void
;; waits (and possibly suspends) for a semaphore

---

make-custodian : → Custodian
;; creates a custodian

custodian-shutdown-all : Custodian → Void
;; shuts down all threads in custodian and reclaims all resources

Fig. 1. MrEd's TCP, thread and custodian primitives

does not affect a parent; when it mutates the state of a parameter, the change is globally visible. The server deals with only two of MrEd's standard parameters: *current-custodian* and *exit-handler*. The default *exit-handler* halts the entire runtime system. Setting this parameter to another function can cause conditions that would normally exit to raise an exception or perform clean up operations.

Finally, MrEd provides a mechanism for managing resources, such as threads (with associated parameter bindings), TCP listeners, file ports, and so on. When a resource is allocated, it is placed in the care of the current *custodian*, the value of the *current-custodian* parameter. Figure 1 specifies the only relevant operation on custodians: *custodian-shutdown-all*. It accepts a custodian and reaps the associated resources: it kills the threads in its custody, closes the ports, reclaims the TCP listeners, and recursively shuts down all child custodians.

3   Serving Static Content

A basic web server satisfies HTTP requests by reading Web pages from files. High-level languages ease the implementation of such a server, while retaining efficiency comparable to widely used servers. The first subsection explains the core of our server implementation. The second subsection compares performance figures of our server to Apache [2], a widely-used, commercially-deployed server.

3.1   Implementation of the Web Server's Core

The core of a web server is a wait-serve loop. It waits for requests on a particular TCP port. For each request, it creates a thread that serves the request. Then the server recurs:[1]

```
;; server-loop : Tcp-listener → Void
(define (server-loop listener)
  (let-values ([(ip op) (tcp-accept listener)])
    (thread (lambda () (serve-connection ip op))))
  (server-loop listener))
```

For each request, the server parses the first line and the optional headers:

```
;; serve-connection : Input-port Output-port → Void
(define (serve-connection ip op)
  (let-values ([(meth url-string major-version minor-version)
                (read-request ip op)])
    (let* ([headers (read-headers ip op)]
           [url (string→url url-string)]
           [host (find-host (url-host url) headers)])
      (dispatch meth host port url headers ip op))))
```

```
;; read-request : Input-port Output-port →* Symbol String String String
;; to read a request from ip, to parse it, and to determine the
;; request method (get, put), URL, and protocol versions
;; effect: raises an exception and closes the ports, if parsing fails
(define (read-request ip op) ... )
```

A dispatcher uses this information to find the correct file corresponding to the given URL. If it can find and open the file, the dispatcher writes the file's contents to the output port; otherwise it writes an error message. In either case, it closes the ports before returning.[2]

3.2   Performance

It is easy to write compact implementations of systems with high-level constructs, but we must demonstrate that we don't sacrifice performance for abstraction. More precisely, we would like our server to serve content from files at about the same rate as Apache [2]. We believed that this goal was within

---

[1] **let-values** binds names to the values returned by multiple-valued computations such as *tcp-accept*, which returns input and output ports.

[2] The server may actually loop to handle multiple requests per connection. Our paper does not explore this possibility further.

Clients	Connections/Second								
	1kB file			10kB file			100kB file		
	MrEd	Apache	Ratio	MrEd	Apache	Ratio	MrEd	Apache	Ratio
2	967.5	1557.9	62.1%	655.1	771.6	84.9%	105.2	113.2	92.9%
4	986.7	1623.4	60.8%	772.0	1084.4	71.2%	110.2	115.7	95.2%
8	997.9	1607.0	62.1%	752.9	1099.0	68.5%	116.0	115.8	100.2%
16	982.8	1597.0	61.5%	782.6	1101.3	71.1%	116.5	116.1	100.3%
32	923.8	1551.0	59.6%	760.7	1104.0	68.9%	116.7	116.3	100.3%
64	917.6	1577.2	58.2%	787.1	1093.0	72.0%	115.1	116.5	98.8%
128	946.3	1547.8	61.1%	769.4	1104.1	69.7%	116.7	116.5	100.2%

Ratio = MrEd/Apache

The client and server software each ran on an AMD Athlon 800MHz processor with 192 Mbytes of memory, running FreeBSD 4.1.1-STABLE, connected by a standard 100 Mbit/s Ethernet connection.

Fig. 2. Performance for static content server

reach because most of the computational work involves parsing HTTP requests, reading data from disk, and copying bytes to a (network) port.[3]

To verify this conjecture, we compared our server's performance to that of Apache on files of three different sizes. For each test, the client requested a single file repeatedly. This minimized the impact of disk speed; the underlying buffer cache should keep small files in memory. Requests for different files would even out the performance numbers according to Amdahl's law because the total response time would include an extra disk access component that would be similar for both servers.

The results in figure 2 show that we have essentially achieved our goal. The results were obtained using the S-client measuring technology [5]. For the historically most common case [4]—files between six and thirteen kB—our server performs at a rate of 60% to 80% of Apache. For larger files, which are now more common due to increased uses of multimedia documents, the two servers perform at the same rate. In particular, for one and ten kB files, more than four pending requests caused both servers to consume all available CPU cycles. For the larger 100 kB files, both servers drove the network card at full capacity.

4   Dynamic Content Generation

Over the past few years, the Web's content has become increasingly dynamic. *USA Today*, for instance, finds that as of the year 2000, more than half of the Web's content is generated dynamically [7]. Servers no longer retrieve plain files

---

[3] This assumes that the server does not have a large in-memory cache for frequently-accessed documents.

from disk but use auxiliary programs to generate a document in response to a request. These Web programs often interact with the user and with databases. This section explains how small changes to the code of section 3 accommodate dynamic extensions, that the performance of the revised server is superior to that of Apache,[4] and that it supports a new programming paradigm that is highly useful in the context of dynamic Web content generation.

4.1 Simple Dynamic Content Generation

Since a single server satisfies different requests with different content generators, we implement a generator as a module that is dynamically invoked and linked into the server context. More specifically, a CGI program in our world is a unit:

(unit/sig () **(import** *cgi*ˆ) ⟨*def+exp*⟩ ... ⟨*exp*⟩)

It exports nothing; it imports the names specified in the **cgi**ˆ signature. The result of its final expression (and of the unit invocation) is an HTML page.[5]

Here is a trivial CGI program using **quasiquote** [22] to create an HTML page with **unquote** (a comma) allowing references to the *TITLE* definition.

```
(unit/sig () (import cgiˆ)
  (define TITLE "My first web page")
  '(html (head (title ,TITLE))
         (body
            (p (center ,TITLE))
            (p "Hello, World!")))))
```

The script defines a title and produces a simple Web page containing a message.

The imports of a content generator supply the request method, the URL, the optional headers, and the bindings:

```
(define-signature cgiˆ (
  method      ; (union 'get 'post 'head)
  url         ; Url
  headers     ; (listof (cons Symbol String))
  bindings    ; (listof (cons Symbol String))
  ...))
```

To add dynamic content generation to our server, we modify the *dispatch* function from section 3 to redirect requests for URLs starting with "/cgi-bin/". More concretely, instead of responding with the contents of a file, *dispatch* loads a unit from the specified location in the file system. Before invoking the unit, the function installs a new *current-custodian* and a new *exit-handler* via a **parameterize** expression:

---

[4] Apache outperforms most other servers for CGI-based content generation [1].

[5] To be precise, it generates an X-expression, which is an S-expression representation of an XML document. The server handles other media types also; we do not discuss these in this paper.

```
;; in dispatch:
...
(if (cgi-url? url)
    (let ([cust (make-custodian)])
      (parameterize
          ([current-custodian cust]
           [exit-handler (lambda (x) (custodian-shutdown-all cust))])
        (let ([cgi-program (cached-load (url-path url))])
          (output-xhtml (invoke-unit/sig cgi-program cgi^)))))
    ...)
```

The newly installed custodian is shut down on termination of the CGI script. This halts child threads, closes ports, and reaps the script's resources. The new *exit-handler* is necessary so that erronious content generators shut down only the custodian instead of the entire server.

4.2 Content Generators Are First-Class Values

Since units are first-class values in MrEd, the server can store content generators in a cache. Introducing a cache avoids some I/O overhead but, more importantly, it introduces new programming capabilities. In particular, a content generator can now maintain local state across invocations. Here is an example:

```
(let ([count 0])
  (unit/sig () (import cgi^)
    (set! count (add1 count))
    `(html (head (title "Testing Persistent State of Counter"))
           (body (p "This is a cgi generated web page.")
                 (p "The current count is " ,(number→string count))))))
```

This generator maintains a local count that is incremented each time the unit is invoked to satisfy an HTTP request. Its output is an HTML page that contains the current value of *count*.

4.3 Exchanging Values between Content Generators

In addition to maintaining persistent state across invocations, content generators may also need to interact with each other. Conventional servers force server programs to communicate via the file system or other mechanisms based on character streams. This requires marshaling and unmarshaling data, a complex and error prone process. In our server architecture, dynamic content generators can naturally exchange high-level forms of data through the common heap.

Our dynamic content generation model features a simple extension that permits multiple generators to be defined within a single lexical scope. The current unit of granularity in the implementation is a file. That is, one file may yield an expression that contains multiple generators. The expression may perform arbitrary operations to define and initialize the shared scope. To distinguish between the generators, the server's interface requires that the file return an association list of type

(listof (cons Symbol Content-generator))

For instance, a file contain two content generators:

(let* ([*data-file* ...]
    [*lock* (*make-semaphore* 1)])
  '((add . ,⟨Content-generator⟩$_1$)
  (delete . ,⟨Content-generator⟩$_2$)))

This yields two generators that share a lock to a common file. The distinguishing name in the association is treated as part of the URL in a CGI request.

4.4   Interactive Generation of Content

In a recent ICFP article [23], Christian Queinnec suggested that Web browsing in the presence of dynamic Web content generation can be understood as the process of capturing and resuming continuations.[6] For example, a user can bookmark a generated page that contains a form and (try to) complete it several times. This action corresponds to the resumption of the content generator's computation after the generation of the first form.

Ordinarily, programming this style of computation is a complex task. Each time the computation requires interaction (responses to queries, inspection of intermediate results, and so forth) from the user, the programmer must split the program into two fragments. The first generates the request for interaction, typically as a form whose processor is the remainder of the computation. The first program must store its intermediate results externally so the second program can access and use them. The staging and marshaling are cumbersome, error-prone, slow, and inhibit the reuse of existing non-CGI programs that are being refitted with Web-based interfaces. To support this common programming paradigm, our server links content generators to the three additional primitives in figure 3.

---

send/suspend : (Url → Html-page) → (*list* Method
                                                Url
                                                (listof (*cons* Symbol String))
                                                (listof (*cons* Symbol String)))
send/finish : Html-page → Void
adjust-timeout : Nat → Void

Fig. 3. Additional content generator primitives

The *send/suspend* function allows the content generator to send an HTML form to the client for further input. The function captures the continuation and suspends the computation of the content generator. When the user responds, the server resumes the continuation with four values: the request method, the URL, the optional headers, and the form bindings.

---

[6] This idea also appears in Hughes's paper on arrows [14].

To implement this functionality, *send/suspend* consumes a function of one argument. This function, in turn, consumes a unique URL and generates a form whose action attribute refers to the URL. When the user submits the form, the suspended continuation is resumed. Consider figure 4, which presents a simple example of an interactive content generator. This script implements curried multiplication, asking for one number with one HTML page at a time. The two underlined expressions represent the intermediate stops where the script displays a page and waits for the next set of user inputs. Once both sets of inputs are available it produces a page with the product.

```
(unit/sig () (import cgi^)

    ;; get-input-w/-short-form : String → (String → Html-page)
    (define (get-input-w/-short-form which-one)
       (let-values ([(method url headers bindings)
                     (send/suspend
                        (lambda ( k-url )
                          `(html (head (title ,which-one " number"))
                            (body
                               (form ((method "post") (action , k-url ))
                                  "Enter the " ,which-one " number:" nbsp
                                  (input ((type "text") (name ,which-one)))
                                  (input ((type "submit") (name "submit"))))))))))])
          (extract which-one bindings)))

    ;; string-multiply : String String → String
    ...

    `(html (head (title "Product"))
       (body (p "The product is: "
              ,(string-multiply (get-input-w/-short-form "first")
                                (get-input-w/-short-form "second")))))))
```

Fig. 4. An interactive CGI program

In general, this paradigm produces programs that naturally correspond to the flow of information between client and server. These programs are easier to match to specifications, to validate, and to maintain. The paradigm also causes problems, however. The first problem, as Queinnec points out, concerns garbage collection of the suspended continuations. By invoking *send/suspend*, a content generator hands out a reference to its current continuation. Although these references to continuations are symbolic links in the form of unique URLs, they are nevertheless references to values in the server's heap. Without further restrictions, garbage collection cannot be based on reachability. To make matters worse, these continuations also hold on to resources, such as open files or TCP connections, which the server may need for other programs.

Giving the user the flexibility to bookmark intermediate continuations and explore various choices creates another problem. Once the program finishes interacting with the user, it records the final outcome by updating persistent state on the server. These updates must happen at most once to prevent catastrophes such as double billing or shipping too many items.

Based on this analysis, our server implements the following policy. When the content generator returns or calls the *send/finish* primitive, all the continuations associated with this generator computation are released. Generators that wish to keep the continuations active can suspend instead. When a user attempts to access a reclaimed continuation, a page directs them to restart the computation. Furthermore, each instance of a content generator has a predetermined lifetime after which continuations are disposed. Each use of a continuation updates this lifetime. A running continuation may also change this amount by calling *adjust-timeout*. This mechanism for shutting down the generator only works because the reaper and the content generator's thread share the same custodian. This illustrates why custodians, or resource management in general, cannot be identified with individual threads.

4.5   Implementing Interactive Generation of Content

The implementation of the interactive CGI policy is complicated by the (natural) MrEd restriction that capturing a continuation is local to a thread and that a continuation can only be resumed by its original thread. To comply with this restriction, *send/suspend* captures a continuation, stores it in a table indexed by the current content generator, and causes the thread to wait for input on a channel. When a new request shows up on the channel, the thread looks up the matching continuation in its table and resumes it with the request information in an appropriate manner. A typical continuation URL looks like this:

```
http://www/cgi-bin/send-test.ss;id38,k3-839800468
```

This URL has two principle pieces of information for resuming computation: the thread (id38) and the continuation itself (k3). The random number at the end serves as a password preventing other users from guessing continuation URLs.

The table for managing the continuations associated with a content generator actually has two tiers. The first tier associates instance identifiers for content generators with a channel and a continuation table. This continuation table associates continuation identifiers with continuations. Here is a rough sketch:

generator instance table	
instance-id	channel × continuations-table
⋮	⋮
instance-id	channel × continuations-table

continuations table	
continuation-id	continuation
⋮	⋮
continuation-id	continuation

When a thread processes a request to resume its generator's continuation, it looks up the content generator in one table, and extracts the channel and continuation table for that generator. The server then looks up the desired continuation in this second table and passes it along with the request information and the ports for the current connection.

The two-tier structure of the tables also facilitates clean-up. When the time limit for an instance of a content generator expires or when the content generator computation terminates, the instance is removed from the generator instance table. This step, in turn, makes the continuation instance table inaccessible and thus available for garbage collection.

4.6   Performance

We expect higher performance from our Web server than from conventional servers that use the Common Gateway Interface (CGI) [19]. A conventional server starts a separate OS process for each incoming request, creating a new address space, loading code, etc. Our server eliminates these costs by avoiding the use of OS process boundaries and by caching CGI programs.

Our experiments confirm that our server handles more connections per second than CGI programs written in C. For example, for the comparison in figure 5, we clock a C program's binary in CGI and FastCGI against a Scheme script producing the same data. The table does not contain performance figures for responses of 100 kB and larger because for those sizes the network bandwidth becomes the dominant factor just as with static files.

The table also indicates that both the standard CGI implementation and our server scale much better relative to response size than FastCGI does. We conjecture that this is because FastCGI copies the response twice, and is thus much more sensitive to the response size. Of course, as computations become more intensive, the comparison becomes one of compilers and interpreters rather than of servers and their protocols. We are continuing to conduct experiments, and intend to present the additional performance measurements in a future edition of this paper.

4.7   Modularity of the Server

Web servers must not only be able to load web programs (e.g., CGI scripts) but also load new modules in order to extend their capabilities. For example, requiring password authentication to access particular URLs affects serving content

	CGI		FastCGI		MrEd Full		MrEd Lite	
Clients	1kB	10kB	1kB	10kB	1kB	10kB	1kB	10kB
8	161.1	158.7	742.7	551.6	766.5	665.9	851.4	742.6
16	157.6	156.9	728.8	547.2	759.6	659.3	847.3	727.9
32	153.4	153.1	720.7	544.4	733.8	627.4	837.8	721.4

MrEd Full is the server described in this paper. It includes the continuation reaper described at the end of section 4.4, whose implementation is currently quite inefficient. MrEd Lite disables this reaper (rendering *send/suspend* less usable), making its services more directly comparable to those of CGI and FastCGI.

Fig. 5. Performance for dynamic content generation

from files and from all dynamic content generators. In order to facilitate billing various groups hosted by the server, the administrator may find it helpful to produce separate log files for each client instead of a monolithic one. A flexibly structured server will split key tasks into separate modules, which can be replaced at link time with alternate implementations.

Apache's module system [25] allows the builder of the Web server to replace pieces of the server's response process, such as those outlined above, with with their own code. The builder installs structures with function pointers into a Chain of Command pattern [13]. Using this pattern provides the necessary extensibility but it imposes a complex protocol on the extension programmer, and it fails to provide static guarantees about program composition.

In contrast, our server is constructed in a completely modular fashion using the unit system [10]. This provides the flexibility of the Apache module system in a less ad hoc, more hierarchical manner. To replace part of how the server responds to requests, the server builder writes a compound unit that links the provided units and the replacement units together, forming an extended server. Naturally, the replacement units may link to the original units and delegate to them as desired.

Using units instead of dynamic protocols has several benefits. First, the server doesn't need to traverse chains of structures, checking for a module that wants to handle the request. Second, the newly linked server and all the replacement units are subject to the same level of static analysis as the original server. (Our soft-typing tool [9] revealed several easily corrected premature end-of-file bugs in the original server.)

5   Related Work

The performance problems of the CGI interface has led others to develop higher-speed alternatives [20,25]. In fact, one of the driving motivations behind the Microsoft .NET initiative [17] appears to be the need to improve Web server performance, partially by eliminating process boundaries.[7] Apache provides a module interface that allows programmers to link code into the server that, among other things, generates content dynamically for given URLs. However, circumventing the underlying operating system's protection mechanisms without providing an alternative within the server opens the process for catastrophic failures.

FastCGI [20] provides a safer alternative by placing each content generator in its own process. Unlike traditional CGI, FastCGI processes handle multiple requests, avoiding the process creation overhead. The use of a separate process, however, generates bi-directional inter-process communication cost, and introduces coherence problems in the presence of state. It also complicates the creation of CGI protocols that communicate higher-order data, such as that of section 4.4.

IO-Lite [21] demonstrates the performance advantages to programs that are modified to share immutable buffers instead of copying mutable buffers across protection domains. Since the underlying memory model of MrEd provides safety and immutable string buffers, our server automatically provides this memory model without the need to alter programming styles or APIs.

The problem of managing resources in long-running applications has been identified before in the Apache module system [25], in work on resource containers [6], and elsewhere. The Apache system provides a pool-based mechanism for freeing both memory and file descriptors en masse. Resource containers provide an API for separating the ownership of resources from traditional process boundaries. The custodians in MrEd provide similar functionality with a simpler API than those mentioned.

Like our server programs, Java servlets [8] are content generating code that runs in the same runtime system as the server. Passing information from one request to the processing of the next request cannot rely on storing information in instance variables since the servlet may be unloaded and re-loaded by the server. Passing values through static variables does not solve the problem either, since in some cases the server may instantiate multiple instances of the servlet on the same JVM or on different ones. Instead they provide session objects that assist the programmer with the task of manually marshaling state into and out of re-written urls, cookies, or secure socket layer connections.

The Java servlet interface allows implementations to distribute requests to multiple JVMs for automatic load balancing purposes. Lacking the subprocess management facilities of MrEd's custodians, they rely on an explicit delete method in the servlet to shut the subprocess down cooperatively. While this provides more flexibility by allowing arbitrary clean-up code, the servlet isn't guaranteed to comply.

Finally, the J-Server [24] runs atop Java extended with operating systems features. The J-Server team identified and addressed the server's need to prevent dynamic content generators from shutting down the entire server, while allowing the server to shutdown the content generators reliably. They too identified the need for generators to communicate with each other, but their solution employs

---

[7] Jim Miller, personal communication.

remote method invocation (which introduces both cost and coherence concerns) instead of shared lexical scope. Their work addresses issues of resource accounting and quality of service, which is outside the scope of this paper. Their version of Java lacks a powerful module system and first-class continuations.

6   Conclusion and Future Work

The content of the Web is becoming more dynamic. The next generation of Web servers must therefore tightly integrate and support the construction of extensible and verifiable dynamic content generators. Furthermore, they must allow programmers to write interactive, dynamic scripts in a more natural fashion than engendered by current Web scripting facilities. Finally, the servers must themselves become more extensible and customizable.

Our paper demonstrates that all these programming problems can be solved with a high-level programming language, provided it offers OS-style services in a safe manner. Our server accommodates both kinds of extensibility found in traditional servers—applications, which serve data, and extensions, which adapt the behavior of the server itself—by exploiting its underlying module system. All these features are available on the wide variety of platforms that run MrEd (both traditional operating systems and experimental kernels such as the OS/Kit [12]). The result is a well-performing Web server that accommodates natural and flexible programming paradigms without burdening programmers with platform-specific facilities or complex, error-prone dynamic protocols. We have deployed this server for our book's widely accessed web site.

Two major areas of future work involve type systems and interoperability. Research should explore how the essential additions to Scheme—dynamically linkable modules that are first-class values, threads, custodians, and parameters—can be integrated in typed functional languages such as ML and how the type system can be exploited to provide even more safety guarantees. While MrEd already permits programmers to interoperate with C programs through a foreign-function interface, we are studying the addition of and interoperation between multiple safe languages in our operating system, so programmers can use the language of their choice and reuse existing applications [16].

Acknowledgments. We thank Matthew Flatt and Darren Sanders for their assistance.

References

1. Acme Labs. Web server comparisons.
   http://www.acme.com/software/thttpd/benchmarks.html.
2. Apache. http://www.apache.org/.
3. Arlitt, M. and C. Williamson. Web server workload characterization: the search for invariants. In *ACM SIGMETRICS*, 1996.
4. Aron, M., D. Sanders, P. Druschel and W. Zwaenepoel. Scalable content-aware request distribution in cluster-based network servers. In *Annual Usenix Technical Conference*, 2000. San Diego, CA.

5. Banga, G. and P. Druschel. Measuring the capacity of a web server. In *USENIX Symposium on Internet Technologies and Systems*, December 1997.
6. Banga, G., P. Druschel and J. Mogul. Resource containers: A new facility for resource management in server systems. In *Third Symposium on Operating System Design and Implementation*, February 1999.
7. BrightPlanet. DeepWeb. `http://www.completeplanet.com/Tutorials/DeepWeb/`.
8. Coward, D. Java servlet specification version 2.3, October 2000. `http://java.sun.com/products/servlet/index.html`.
9. Flanagan, C., M. Flatt, S. Krishnamurthi, S. Weirich and M. Felleisen. Catching bugs in the web of program invariants. In *ACM SIGPLAN Conference on Programming Language Design and Implementation*, pages 23–32, May 1996.
10. Flatt, M. and M. Felleisen. Cool modules for HOT languages. In *ACM SIGPLAN Conference on Programming Language Design and Implementation*, 1998.
11. Flatt, M., R. B. Findler, S. Krishnamurthi and M. Felleisen. Programming languages as operating systems (*or*, Revenge of the Son of the Lisp Machine). In *ACM SIGPLAN International Conference on Functional Programming*, pages 138–147, September 1999.
12. Ford, B., G. Back, G. Benson, J. Lepreau, A. Lin and O. Shivers. The Flux OSKit: A Substrate for OS and Language Research. In *16th ACM Symposium on Operating Systems Principles*, October 1997. Saint-Malo, France.
13. Gamma, E., R. Helm, R. Johnson and J. Vlissides. *Design Patterns, Elements of Reusable Object-Oriented Software*. Addison-Wesley, 1994.
14. Hughes, J. Generalising monads to arrows, 1998.
15. Kelsey, R., W. Clinger and J. Rees. Revised[5] report on the algorithmic language Scheme. *ACM SIGPLAN Notices*, 33(9), October 1998.
16. Krishnamurthi, S. *Linguistic Reuse*. PhD thesis, Rice University, 2001.
17. Microsoft Corporation. `http://www.microsoft.com/net/`.
18. Mogul, J. The case for persistent connection HTTP. In *ACM SIGCOMM*, 1995.
19. NCSA. The common gateway interface. `http://hoohoo.ncsa.uiuc.edu/cgi/`.
20. Open Market, Inc. FastCGI specification. `http://www.fastcgi.com/`.
21. Pai, V. S., P. Druschel and W. Zwaenepoel. IO-lite: A unified I/O buffering and caching system. In *Third Symposium on Operating Systems Design and Implementation*, February 1999.
22. Pitman, K. Special forms in lisp. In *Conference Record of the Lisp Conference*, August 1980. Stanford University.
23. Queinnec, C. The influence of browsers on evaluators or, continuations to program web servers. In *ACM SIGPLAN International Conference on Functional Programming*, 2000.
24. Spoonhower, D., G. Czajkowski, C. Hawblitzel, C.-C. Chang, D. Hu and T. von Eicken. Design and evaluation of an extensible web and telephony server based on the J-Kernel. Technical report, Department of Computer Science, Cornell University, 1998.
25. Thau, R. Design considerations for the Apache server API. In *Fifth International World Wide Web Conference*, May 1996.

On the Completeness of Model Checking

Francesco Ranzato

Dipartimento di Matematica Pura ed Applicata
Università di Padova
Via Belzoni 7, 35131 Padova, Italy
franz@math.unipd.it

Abstract. In POPL'00, Cousot and Cousot introduced and studied a novel general temporal specification language, called $\overset{\curvearrowright}{\mu}$-calculus, in particular featuring a natural and rich time-symmetric trace-based semantics. The classical state-based model checking of the $\overset{\curvearrowright}{\mu}$-calculus is an abstract interpretation of its trace-based semantics, which, surprisingly, turns out to be incomplete, even for finite systems. Cousot and Cousot identified the temporal connectives causing such incompleteness. In this paper, we first characterize the least, i.e. least informative, refinements of the state-based model checking abstraction which are complete relatively to any incomplete temporal connective. On the basis of this analysis, we show that the least refinement of the state-based model checking semantics of (a slight and natural monotone restriction of) the $\overset{\curvearrowright}{\mu}$-calculus which is complete w.r.t. the trace-based semantics does exist, and it is essentially the trace-based semantics itself. This result can be read as stating that any model checking algorithm for the $\overset{\curvearrowright}{\mu}$-calculus abstracting away from sets of traces will be necessarily incomplete.

1 Introduction

The classical semantics of standard temporal specification languages for model checking, like CTL, μ-calculus and variations thereof, are state-based and time-asymmetric [3,6,11,12]. State-based means that, given a transition system modelling some reactive system, the semantics of a temporal formula ϕ is given by the set of states of the transition system satisfying ϕ, possibly w.r.t. some environment whenever ϕ contains free variables. Time-asymmetry refers to the asymmetric nature of the classical notion of trace in transition systems, since traces are commonly indexed on natural numbers and therefore have a finite past and an infinite future. Recently, Cousot and Cousot [6] introduced a novel general temporal specification language, called $\overset{\curvearrowright}{\mu}$-calculus, inspired from Kozen's [9] μ-calculus and featuring a time-symmetric trace-based semantics. In the $\overset{\curvearrowright}{\mu}$-calculus semantics, traces are indexed over integer numbers, i.e. both past and future are infinite, and a time reversal operator allows a uniform symmetric treatment of past and future. Traces record the present time, and hence the present state as well, by an integer number, and temporal formulae are therefore interpreted as sets of traces. The generality of the $\overset{\curvearrowright}{\mu}$-calculus stems from mixing linear and branching time modalities, and this allows to recover most standard

D. Sands (Ed.): ESOP 2001, LNCS 2028, pp. 137–154, 2001.

specification languages like CTL, CTL* and Kozen's μ-calculus as suitable fragments.

The most relevant feature in Cousot and Cousot's [6] work is in the application of the abstract interpretation methodology [4,5] to the $\widehat{\mu}$-calculus. In particular, it is shown how to derive standard state-based model checking by abstract interpretation from the trace-based semantics of the $\widehat{\mu}$-calculus. This is performed exploiting a so-called universal checking abstraction map $\alpha_M^\forall$: given a model to check M (i.e., the set of traces generated by some transition system), $\alpha_M^\forall$ abstracts a trace-interpreted $\widehat{\mu}$-calculus temporal formula ϕ to the set of present states s of M such that any (here we are considering the universal case: dually, in the existential checking abstraction "any" becomes "some") execution of M departing from the state s satisfies ϕ. Thus, the abstract domain consists of sets of states, since $\alpha_M^\forall$ abstracts sets of traces to sets of states. In particular, $\alpha_M^\forall(\phi)$ encodes a classical state-based interpretation like $\{s \in States \mid M, s \models \phi\}$, and therefore the state-based local model-checking problem of determining if a given state s in M satisfies ϕ amounts to checking whether $s \in \alpha_M^\forall(\phi)$. This abstraction map from sets of traces to sets of states compositionally induces a state-based abstract semantics $[\![\cdot]\!]^{state}$ for the $\widehat{\mu}$-calculus, which, by construction through the abstract interpretation technique, is sound w.r.t. the trace-based semantics: for any formula ϕ, $\alpha_M^\forall([\![\phi]\!]^{trace}) \supseteq [\![\phi]\!]^{state}$.

Completeness for the abstract state-based semantics in general does not hold, i.e. the containment above may be strict, even for finite systems (see [6, Counterexample (60)]). This means that trace-based and state-based model checking for the $\widehat{\mu}$-calculus, in general, are not equivalent: there exist some formula ϕ and state s such that $M, s \models_{trace} \phi$, while $M, s \not\models_{state} \phi$. The consequence of such incompleteness is that in order to deal with general temporal specifications of the $\widehat{\mu}$-calculus, model checking algorithms should handle sets of traces instead of sets of traces, and this is evidently infeasible. Moreover, Cousot and Cousot single out the sources of such incompleteness, that is, the temporal connectives of the $\widehat{\mu}$-calculus which are incomplete for the universal checking abstraction: these are the predecessor, shifting the present time one step in the past, the disjunction, and the reversal, exchanging past and future w.r.t. the present time.

Giacobazzi et al. [8] observed that completeness for an abstract interpretation, i.e. abstract domains plus abstract operations, only depends on the underlying abstract domains. Hence, this opens up the key question of making an abstract interpretation complete by minimally extending the underlying abstract domain. Following the terminology in [8], we call complete shell of an abstract domain A the most abstract, i.e. containing the least amount of information, domain, when this exists, which extends A and is complete for some operation or (fixpoint) semantics. The relevance of such concept should be clear: the complete shell of an abstract domain A characterizes exactly the least amount of information which must be added to A in order to get completeness, when this can be done. It is shown in [8] that complete shells relative to sets of concrete operations, the so-called absolute complete shells, exist under weak and reasonable hypotheses, and some constructive methods to characterize them are given.

On the other hand, for complete shells relative to fixpoint operators, it is argued that no general result of existence can be given, even under very restrictive hypotheses.

This paper analyzes the incompleteness of state-based model checking within the Cousot and Cousot [6] framework described above from the perspective of minimally making an abstract intepretation complete. We first characterize the absolute complete shells of the universal checking abstraction $\alpha_M^{\vee}$ — namely, the abstract domain of sets of states approximating the domain of sets of traces — relatively to each incomplete temporal connective, namely predecessor, disjunction and reversal. The results are quite illuminating. Completeness w.r.t. the predecessor leads to an absolute complete shell which refines sets of states to a domain of sequences indexed over natural numbers (intended to represent the past time) of sets of states. The least refinement of $\alpha_M^{\vee}$ which is complete for the reversal operator is simply a domain consisting of pairs of sets of states, where the meaning is as follows: if $\frown M$ denotes the reversal of the model M, a trace-interpreted formula ϕ is abstracted to the pair $\langle \alpha_M^{\vee}(\phi), \alpha_{\frown M}^{\vee}(\phi) \rangle$. Hence, as expected, completeness for the reversal requires an additional component taking into account the universal checking abstraction for the reversed model $\frown M$. Finally, disjunction is, somehow, the more demanding connective: the abstract domain of the corresponding absolute complete shell consists of sets of traces belonging to the model to check M, and therefore this amounts to an abstraction which essentially is the identity. Morever, this abstraction is complete for the predecessor too, and hence more concrete than its absolute complete shell mentioned above. Globally, we also characterize the absolute complete shell of $\alpha_M^{\vee}$ relatively to all[1] the temporal connectives involved by the $\widehat{\mu}$-calculus. Hence, this abstract domain must be complete both for disjunction and reversal. Actually, we show that this global absolute complete shell consists of sets of traces belonging to M or to its reversal. Thus, this abstract domain is even more close to the concrete domain of sets of generic traces.

Finally and more importantly, we faced the problem of characterizing the complete shell of the universal checking abstraction relatively to the whole trace-based concrete semantics of the $\widehat{\mu}$-calculus. In other terms, we are seeking to characterize the most abstract domain A^s extending the universal checking abstract domain of sets of states and inducing a complete abstract semantics, i.e., such that for any formula ϕ, $\alpha_{A^s}(\llbracket \phi \rrbracket^{trace}) = \llbracket \phi \rrbracket^{A^s}$. In this case, since the $\widehat{\mu}$-calculus involves (least and greatest) fixpoints, as recalled above, it should be remarked that no general result in [8] ensures the existence of such complete abstract domain. Nevertheless, it turns out that this complete shell does exist, and it coincides with the absolute complete shell relative to all the temporal connectives, namely the identity on sets of traces in M or its reversal. This complete shell therefore induces an abstract semantics which essentially is the trace-based semantics itself. Thus, the intuitive interpretation of this important

---

[1] There is a technical detail here: abstract interpretation requires concrete operations to be monotone or antitone. Thus, in the paper we consider a standard monotone restriction of the new general universal state quantification introduced in [6].

result is as follows: any semantic refinement of the state-based model checking which aims at being trace-complete for the $\widehat{\mu}$-calculus ineluctably leads to the trace-based semantics itself. Otherwise stated, any model checking algorithm for the $\widehat{\mu}$-calculus abstracting away from sets of traces will be necessarily incomplete.

2   Abstract Interpretation and Completeness

Notation. Let us first introduce some basic notation that will be used throughout the paper. Conditionals are denoted by $(b \in Bool\,?\,x\,\raisebox{-0.3ex}{\textit{¿}}\,y)$, evaluating to x when b is true and to y when b is false. Let X and Y be sets. $X \smallsetminus Y$ denotes set-difference, $X \subsetneq Y$ denotes strict inclusion, and $X \to Y$ denotes the set of total functions from X to Y. If X plays the role of some "universe" and $Y \subseteq X$ then $\neg Y \stackrel{\text{def}}{=} X \smallsetminus Y$. Given a sequence $\sigma \in \mathbb{Z} \to X$, for any $i \in \mathbb{Z}$, $\sigma_i \in X$ stands for $\sigma(i)$. Given $f : X \to X$, the i-th power of f, where $i \in \mathbb{N}$, is inductively defined as follows: $f^0 \stackrel{\text{def}}{=} \lambda x.x$; $f^{i+1} \stackrel{\text{def}}{=} \lambda x.f(f^i(x))$. $lfp(f)$ and $gfp(f)$ denote, respectively, the least and greatest fixpoint, when they exist, of an operator f on a poset. Sometimes, a poset $\langle P, \leq \rangle$ will be denoted more compactly by $P_\leq$. Given a poset $P_\leq$, the set of functions $X \to P$ becomes a poset for the pointwise ordering $\dot{\leq}$, where $f \dot{\leq} g$ iff $\forall x \in X.f(x) \leq g(x)$.

Closure Operators. The structure $\langle uco(C), \sqsubseteq, \sqcup, \sqcap, \lambda x.\top, \lambda x.x \rangle$ denotes the complete lattice of all (upper) closure operators (shortly closures) on a complete lattice $\langle C, \leq, \vee, \wedge, \top, \bot \rangle$, where $\rho \sqsubseteq \eta$ iff $\forall x \in C.\ \rho(x) \leq \eta(x)$. Throughout the paper, for any $\rho \in uco(C)$, we follow a standard notation by denoting the image $\rho(C)$ simply by ρ itself: This does not give rise to ambiguity, since one can readily distinguish the use of ρ as function or set according to the context. Let us recall that (i) each closure $\rho \in uco(C)$ is uniquely determined by the set of its fixpoints, which coincides with its image, i.e. $\rho = \{x \in C \mid \rho(x) = x\}$, (ii) $\rho \sqsubseteq \eta$ iff $\eta \subseteq \rho$, and (iii) a subset $X \subseteq C$ is the set of fixpoints of a closure iff $X = \mathcal{M}(X) \stackrel{\text{def}}{=} \{\wedge Y \mid Y \subseteq X\}$ ($\mathcal{M}(X)$ is called the Moore-closure of X; note that $\top = \wedge\varnothing \in \mathcal{M}(X)$; sometimes, we will write $\mathcal{M}_C(X)$ to emphasize the underlying complete lattice). Hence, note that, given any $X \subseteq C$, $\mathcal{M}(X)$ is the (set of fixpoints of the) greatest (w.r.t. $\sqsubseteq$) closure whose set of fixpoints contains X.

Abstract Domains. It is well known that within the standard Cousot and Cousot framework, abstract domains can be equivalently specified either by Galois connections/insertions (GCs/GIs) or by closure operators [5]. In the first case, concrete and abstract domains C and A — for simplicity, these are assumed to be complete lattices — are related by a pair of adjoint functions $\alpha : C \to A$ and $\gamma : A \to C$, compactly denoted by (α, C, A, γ), and therefore C and A may consist of objects having different representations. In the second case, instead, an abstract domain is specified as a closure operator on the concrete domain C (and this closure could be also given by means of its set of fixpoints). Thus, the closure operator approach is particularly convenient when reasoning about properties of abstract domains independently from the representation of their objects. Given a concrete domain C, we will identify $uco(C)$ with the so-called complete lattice $\mathcal{L}_C$ of abstract interpretations of C (cf. [4, Section 7] and [5, Section 8]). The ordering on $uco(C)$ corresponds precisely to the standard order used in abstract interpretation to compare abstract domains with regard to their precision: A_1 is more precise (or concrete) than A_2 iff $A_1 \sqsubseteq A_2$ in $uco(C)$. Thus, lub's $\sqcup$ and glb's $\sqcap$ on $\mathcal{L}_C$ give, respectively, the most precise abstraction and the most abstract concretization of a family of abstract domains.

Complete Abstract Interpretations. Let us succinctly recall the basic notions concerning completeness in abstract interpretation. Let $f : C \to C$ be a monotone or antitone concrete semantic function[2] occurring in some complex semantic specification, and let $f^\sharp : A \to A$ be a corresponding abstract function, where $A \in \mathcal{L}_C$. The concept of soundness is standard and well known: $\langle A, f^\sharp \rangle$ is a sound abstract interpretation — or $f^\sharp$ is a correct approximation of f relatively to A — when $\alpha_{C,A} \circ f \overset{.}{\leq}_A f^\sharp \circ \alpha_{C,A}$. On the other hand, $\langle A, f^\sharp \rangle$ is complete when equality holds, i.e. $\alpha_{C,A} \circ f = f^\sharp \circ \alpha_{C,A}$. Thus, in abstract interpretation, completeness means that the abstract semantics equals the abstraction of the concrete semantics, or, otherwise stated, that abstract computations accumulate no loss of information.

Completeness is a Domain Property. Any abstract domain $A \in \mathcal{L}_C$ induces the so-called canonical best correct approximation $f^A : A \to A$ of $f : C \to C$, defined by $f^A \overset{\text{def}}{=} \alpha_{C,A} \circ f \circ \gamma_{A.C}$. This terminology is justified by the fact that any $f^\sharp : A \to A$ is a correct approximation of f iff $f^A \sqsubseteq f^\sharp$. Consequently, any abstract domain always induces an (automatically) sound abstract interpretation. Of course, this is not in general true for completeness: not every abstract domain induces a complete abstract interpretation. However, whenever a complete abstract operation exists then the best correct approximation is complete as well. This therefore means that completeness is a property which depends on the underlying abstract domain only. As a consequence, whenever abstract domains are specified by closure operators, an abstract domain $\rho \in \mathcal{L}_C$ is defined to be complete for f if $\rho \circ f \circ \rho = \rho \circ f$. More in general, this definition of completeness can be naturally extended to a set F of semantic functions by requiring completeness for each $f \in F$. Throughout the paper, we will adopt the following useful notation: $\Gamma(C, f) \overset{\text{def}}{=} \{\rho \in \mathcal{L}_C \mid \rho \text{ is complete for } f\}$. Hence, for a set F, $\Gamma(C, F) = \cap_{f \in F} \Gamma(C, f)$.

Making Abstract Interpretations Complete. The fact that completeness is an abstract domain property opens the key question of making an abstract interpretation complete by minimally extending (or, dually, restricting: we will not touch this issue here, see [8]) the underlying abstract domain. Following [8], given a concrete interpretation $\langle C, f \rangle$ and an abstract domain $A \in \mathcal{L}_C$, the absolute

---

[2] For simplicity, we consider unary functions with the same domain and co-domain, since the extension to the general case is straightforward.

complete shell[3] of A for f, when it exists, is the most abstract domain $A^s \in \mathcal{L}_C$ which extends, viz. is more precise than, A and is complete for f. In other words, the absolute complete shell of A characterizes the least amount of information to be added to A in order to get completeness, when this can be done. Let us succinctly recall the solution to this completeness problem recently given in [8].

Let us fix the following standard notation: if $X \subseteq C$ then $\max(X) \stackrel{\text{def}}{=} \{x \in X \mid \forall y \in X. \, x \leq y \Rightarrow x = y\}$. Given a set of monotone semantic functions $F \subseteq C \rightarrow C$, the abstract domain transformer $R_F : \mathcal{L}_C \rightarrow \mathcal{L}_C$ is defined as follows:

$$R_F(\eta) \stackrel{\text{def}}{=} \mathcal{M}(\cup_{f \in F, y \in \eta} \max(\{x \in C \mid f(x) \leq y\})).$$

Theorem 2.1 ([8, Theorem 5.10, p. 388]). *Let $F \subseteq C \rightarrow C$ and $\rho \in \mathcal{L}_C$. If F is a set of continuous (i.e., preserving lub's of directed subsets) functions then the absolute complete shell of ρ for F exists, and it is given by $gfp(\lambda\eta \in uco(C).\rho \sqcap R_F(\eta))$.*

This therefore is a constructive result of existence for absolute complete shells. It turns out that $\lambda\eta.\rho \sqcap R_F(\eta) : uco(C) \rightarrow uco(C)$ is itself continuous [8, Lemma 5.11], and therefore its greatest fixpoint can be constructively obtained as ω-limit of the Kleene's iteration sequence.

3   Temporal Abstract Interpretation

In this section, we recall the key notions and definitions of Cousot and Cousot's [6] abstract interpretation-based approach to model checking.

Basic Notions. $\mathbb{S}$ is a given, possibly infinite, set of states. Discrete time is modeled by the whole set of integers and therefore paths of states are time-symmetric, in particular are infinite also in the past. Thus, $\mathbb{P} \stackrel{\text{def}}{=} \mathbb{Z} \rightarrow \mathbb{S}$ is the set of paths. An execution with an initial state s can then be encoded by repeating forever in the past the state s. A trace must keep track of the present time, and hence $\mathbb{T} \stackrel{\text{def}}{=} \mathbb{Z} \times \mathbb{P}$ is the set of traces. Finally, a (temporal) model is simply a set of traces: $\mathbb{M} \stackrel{\text{def}}{=} \wp(\mathbb{T})$ is the set of temporal models. The semantics of a temporal logic formula ϕ will be a temporal model, that, intuitively, will be the set of all and only the traces making ϕ true.

Models to check will be generated by transition systems, encoding some reactive system. The transition relation $\tau \subseteq \mathbb{S} \times \mathbb{S}$ is assumed to be total, i.e., $\forall s \in \mathbb{S}. \exists s' \in \mathbb{S}. \langle s, s' \rangle \in \tau$ and $\forall s' \in \mathbb{S}. \exists s \in \mathbb{S}. \langle s, s' \rangle \in \tau$. This is not restrictive, since any transition relation can be lifted to a total transition relation simply by adding transitions $\langle s, s \rangle$ for any state s which is not reachable or which cannot reach any state. The model generated by the transition system $\langle \mathbb{S}, \tau \rangle$ is therefore defined as $\mathcal{M}_\tau \stackrel{\text{def}}{=} \{\langle i, \sigma \rangle \in \mathbb{T} \mid i \in \mathbb{Z}, \, \forall k \in \mathbb{Z}. \langle \sigma_k, \sigma_{k+1} \rangle \in \tau\}$.

---

[3] [8] also introduces the concept of relative complete shell, and this explains the use of the adjective absolute.

3.1   Syntax and Semantics of the $\widehat{\mu}$-Calculus

The reversible $\widehat{\mu}$-calculus has been introduced by Cousot and Cousot [6] inspired by Kozen's [9] propositional μ-calculus. Actually, the $\widehat{\mu}$-calculus is a generalization of the μ-calculus, with new reversal and abstraction modalities and with a trace-based semantics. Throughout the paper, $\mathbb{X}$ will denote an infinite set of logical variables.

Definition 3.1 ([6, Definition 13]). Formulae ϕ of the reversible $\widehat{\mu}$-calculus are inductively defined as follows:

$$\phi ::= \boldsymbol{\sigma}_S \mid \boldsymbol{\pi}_t \mid X \mid \oplus \phi \mid \phi^\frown \mid \phi_1 \vee \phi_2 \mid \neg\phi \mid \boldsymbol{\mu}X.\phi \mid \boldsymbol{\nu}X.\phi \mid \forall\phi_1 : \phi_2$$

where the quantifications are as follows: $S \in \wp(\mathbb{S})$, $t \in \wp(\mathbb{S} \times \mathbb{S})$, and $X \in \mathbb{X}$. $\mathcal{L}_{\widehat{\mu}}$ denotes the set of $\widehat{\mu}$-calculus formulae. $\qquad\square$

In order to give the trace-interpreted semantics of the $\widehat{\mu}$-calculus, we preliminarly recall the necessary temporal model transformers.

Definition 3.2 ([6, Section 3]).

- For any $S \in \wp(\mathbb{S})$, $\boldsymbol{\sigma}_{\{\!|S|\!\}} \stackrel{\text{def}}{=} \{\langle i, \sigma \rangle \in \mathbb{T} \mid \sigma_i \in S\} \in \mathbb{M}$ is the S-state model, i.e., the set of traces whose current state is in S.
- For any $t \in \wp(\mathbb{S} \times \mathbb{S})$, $\boldsymbol{\pi}_{\{\!|t|\!\}} \stackrel{\text{def}}{=} \{\langle i, \sigma \rangle \in \mathbb{T} \mid (\sigma_i, \sigma_{i+1}) \in t\} \in \mathbb{M}$ is the t-transition model, i.e., the set of traces whose next step is a t-transition.
- $\oplus : \mathbb{M} \to \mathbb{M}$ is the predecessor transformer:
  $\oplus(X) \stackrel{\text{def}}{=} \{\langle i-1, \sigma \rangle \in \mathbb{T} \mid \langle i, \sigma \rangle \in X\} = \{\langle i, \sigma \rangle \in \mathbb{T} \mid \langle i+1, \sigma \rangle \in X\}$.
- $\frown : \mathbb{M} \to \mathbb{M}$ is the reversal transformer:
  $\frown(X) \stackrel{\text{def}}{=} \{\langle -i, \lambda k.\sigma_{-k} \rangle \in \mathbb{T} \mid \langle i, \sigma \rangle \in X\}$.
- $\neg : \mathbb{M} \to \mathbb{M}$ is the complement transformer:
  $\neg X \stackrel{\text{def}}{=} \mathbb{M} \setminus X$.
- Given $s \in \mathbb{S}$, $(\cdot)_{\downarrow s} : \mathbb{M} \to \mathbb{M}$ is the state projection operator:
  $X_{\downarrow s} \stackrel{\text{def}}{=} \{\langle i, \sigma \rangle \in X \mid \sigma_i = s\}$.
- $\forall : \mathbb{M} \times \mathbb{M} \to \mathbb{M}$ is the universal state closure transformer:
  $\forall(X, Y) \stackrel{\text{def}}{=} \{\langle i, \sigma \rangle \in X \mid X_{\downarrow \sigma_i} \subseteq Y\}$. $\qquad\square$

It is worth to recall that reversal and negation allow to define a number of interesting dual transformers. For example, the successor transformer is defined by $\ominus \stackrel{\text{def}}{=} \frown \circ \oplus \circ \frown$, and the existential transformer by $\exists \stackrel{\text{def}}{=} \lambda(X, Y). \neg\forall(X, \neg Y)$.

The $\widehat{\mu}$-calculus trace-based semantics goes as follows. Of course, the intuition is that a closed formula ϕ is interpreted as the set of traces which make ϕ true.

Definition 3.3 ([6, Definition 13]). $\mathbb{E} \stackrel{\text{def}}{=} \mathbb{X} \to \mathbb{M}$ is the set of environments over $\mathbb{X}$. Given $\xi \in \mathbb{E}$, $X \in \mathbb{X}$ and $N \in \mathbb{M}$, $\xi[X/N] \in \mathbb{E}$ is defined to be the environment acting as ξ in $\mathbb{X} \setminus \{X\}$ and mapping X to N. The $\widehat{\mu}$-calculus semantics $[\![\cdot]\!] : \mathfrak{L}_{\widehat{\mu}} \to \mathbb{E} \to \mathbb{M}$ is inductively and partially (because least or greatest fixpoints could not exist) defined as follows:

$$[\![\sigma_S]\!]\xi \stackrel{\text{def}}{=} \sigma_{\{S\}} \qquad\qquad [\![\phi_1 \vee \phi_2]\!]\xi \stackrel{\text{def}}{=} [\![\phi_1]\!]\xi \cup [\![\phi_2]\!]\xi$$

$$[\![\pi_t]\!]\xi \stackrel{\text{def}}{=} \pi_{\{t\}} \qquad\qquad [\![\neg\phi]\!]\xi \stackrel{\text{def}}{=} \neg([\![\phi]\!]\xi)$$

$$[\![X]\!]\xi \stackrel{\text{def}}{=} \xi(X) \qquad\qquad [\![\mu X.\phi]\!]\xi \stackrel{\text{def}}{=} lfp(\lambda N \in \mathbb{M}.[\![\phi]\!]\xi[X/N])$$

$$[\![\oplus\phi]\!]\xi \stackrel{\text{def}}{=} \oplus([\![\phi]\!]\xi) \qquad\qquad [\![\nu X.\phi]\!]\xi \stackrel{\text{def}}{=} gfp(\lambda N \in \mathbb{M}.[\![\phi]\!]\xi[X/N])$$

$$[\![\phi^\frown]\!]\xi \stackrel{\text{def}}{=} {}^\frown([\![\phi]\!]\xi) \qquad\qquad [\![\forall\phi_1 : \phi_2]\!]\xi \stackrel{\text{def}}{=} \forall([\![\phi_1]\!]\xi, [\![\phi_2]\!]\xi)$$

$\square$

Forward/Backward/State-Closed Formulae. Intuitively, a $\widehat{\mu}$-calculus formula ϕ is defined to be forward/backward/state-closed when the future/past/present only matters, that is, for all $\xi \in \mathbb{E}$, the past/future/paste&future of any trace in the semantics $[\![\phi]\!]\xi$ can be arbitrarily perturbated without affecting the semantics. This is formalized as follows.

Definition 3.4 ([6, Section 7.2]). If $\sigma, \beta \in \mathbb{P}$ and $i \in \mathbb{Z}$, then

– $\beta[_i\sigma \stackrel{\text{def}}{=} \lambda k \in \mathbb{Z}.(k < i ? \beta_k ¿ \sigma_k)$ is the prolongation of β at time i;

– $\beta_i]\sigma \stackrel{\text{def}}{=} \lambda k \in \mathbb{Z}.(k \leq i ? \beta_k ¿ \sigma_k)$ is the prolongation of β after time i.

The following operators of type $\mathbb{M} \to \mathbb{M}$ are defined:

$Fd \stackrel{\text{def}}{=} \lambda X.\{\langle i, \beta[_i\sigma\rangle \in \mathbb{T} \mid \langle i, \sigma\rangle \in X, \beta \in \mathbb{P}\}$ is the forward closure;

$Bd \stackrel{\text{def}}{=} \lambda X.\{\langle i, \beta_i]\sigma\rangle \in \mathbb{T} \mid \langle i, \sigma\rangle \in X, \beta \in \mathbb{P}\}$ is the backward closure;

$St \stackrel{\text{def}}{=} \lambda X.Fd(X) \cup Bd(X) = \lambda X.\{\langle i, \beta[_i\sigma_i]\beta'\rangle \in \mathbb{T} \mid \langle i, \sigma\rangle \in X, \beta, \beta' \in \mathbb{P}\}$ is the state closure. $\square$

It is easy to see that these actually are closure operators, i.e., $Fd, Bd, St \in uco(\mathbb{M}_\subseteq)$. Thus, $\phi \in \mathfrak{L}_{\widehat{\mu}}$ is called a forward/backward/state formula whenever, for all $\xi \in \mathbb{E}$, $[\![\phi]\!]\xi = Fd/Bd/St([\![\phi]\!]\xi)$.

The state-closed formulae actually are the classical state-formulae of CTL-like logics [3]. Moreover, path-formulae of CTL-like logics are, in this terminology, forward-closed. Actually, Cousot and Cousot [6] isolate the following fragment of the $\widehat{\mu}$-calculus called CTL$_+^\star$:

$$\phi ::= \sigma_S \mid \pi_t \mid \oplus\phi \mid \phi_1 \vee \phi_2 \mid \neg\phi \mid \phi_1 \mathbf{U}\phi_2 \mid \forall\phi$$

where $\phi_1 \mathbf{U}\phi_2 \stackrel{\text{def}}{=} \mu X.\phi_2 \vee (\phi_1 \wedge \oplus X)$ and $\forall\phi \stackrel{\text{def}}{=} \forall \boxplus (\pi_\tau) : \phi$, with $[\![\boxplus (\pi_\tau)]\!]\varnothing = \mathbb{M}_\tau$ (see [6, Section 5] for the details). It is then showed [6, Lemma (18)] that any CTL$_+^\star$ formula is forward-closed, while formulae generated by

$$\psi ::= \sigma_S \mid \psi_1 \vee \psi_2 \mid \neg\psi \mid \forall\phi$$

actually are state-closed.

3.2   Trace-Based Model Checking

It is straightforward to formulate the model checking problem within the trace-based Cousot and Cousot's framework [6]. A closed temporal specification $\phi \in \mathcal{L}_\mu$ is identified by its semantics, namely by the temporal model $[\![\phi]\!]\varnothing \in \mathbb{M}$. Thus, the universal model checking of a system $\mathcal{M}_\tau$ against a specification ϕ amounts to check whether $\mathcal{M}_\tau \subseteq [\![\phi]\!]\varnothing$. It is also useful to distinguish a dual existential model checking, where the goal is that of checking whether $[\![\phi]\!]\varnothing \cap \mathcal{M}_\tau \neq \varnothing$.

3.3   State-Based Model Checking Abstractions

The classical state-based model checking can then be understood as an abstract interpretation, roughly abstracting traces to states.

Universal Checking Abstraction. Given a model (to check) $M \in \mathbb{M}$, the universal checking abstraction map $\alpha_M^\forall : \mathbb{M} \to \wp(\mathbb{S})$ abstracts a trace-interpreted temporal specification $\phi \in \mathbb{M}$ to the set of possible (present) states s of M which universally satisfy ϕ, that is, such that if the present state of M is s then ϕ holds. The intuition is that $\alpha_M^\forall(\phi)$ encodes a standard state-based interpretation like $\{s \in \mathbb{S} \mid M, s \models \phi\}$.

The universal checking abstraction is therefore encoded by the following definition [6, Definition 45]:

$$\alpha_M^\forall(\phi) \stackrel{\text{def}}{=} \{s \in \mathbb{S} \mid M_{\downarrow s} \subseteq \phi\}.$$

Following the terminology by Müller-Olm et al. [12]: (i) the state-based global model checking problem of determining the set of present states in M that satisfy ϕ simply amounts to determining $\alpha_M^\forall(\phi)$, and (ii) the state-based local model checking problem of checking if a given state s in M satisfies ϕ amounts to checking whether $s \in \alpha_M^\forall(\phi)$.

In this context, the superset relation between states provides the right notion of approximation: if $S \subseteq \alpha_M^\forall(\phi)$ then each state in S satisfies ϕ, and therefore if $S \subseteq T$ then T can be thought of as more precise than S. Actually, $\alpha_M^\forall$ gives rise to an adjunction between $\langle \wp(\mathbb{S}), \supseteq \rangle$ and $\langle \mathbb{M}, \supseteq \rangle$, where the concretization map $\gamma_M^\forall : \wp(\mathbb{S}) \to \mathbb{M}$ is defined by: $\gamma_M^\forall(S) \stackrel{\text{def}}{=} \{\langle i, \sigma \rangle \in \mathbb{T} \mid \langle i, \sigma \rangle \in M, \ \sigma_i \in S\}$. When dealing with a model $\mathcal{M}_\tau$ generated by a transition system, by the totality hypothesis on the transition relation τ, we have that for any $s \in \mathbb{S}$, $\mathcal{M}_{\tau \downarrow s} \neq \varnothing$. This implies that $\gamma_{\mathcal{M}_\tau}^\forall$ is 1-1, and therefore $(\alpha_{\mathcal{M}_\tau}^\forall, \langle \mathbb{M}, \supseteq \rangle, \langle \wp(\mathbb{S}), \supseteq \rangle, \gamma_{\mathcal{M}_\tau}^\forall)$ is a GI [6, (48)]. Thus, this GI induces the following closure operator on models ordered by the superset inclusion.

Definition 3.5. $\rho_M^\forall \stackrel{\text{def}}{=} \gamma_M^\forall \circ \alpha_M^\forall \in uco(\langle \mathbb{M}, \supseteq \rangle)$ is the *universal checking closure* relative to a model $M \in \mathbb{M}$. Hence, $\rho_M^\forall = \lambda X.\{\langle i, \sigma \rangle \in M \mid M_{\downarrow \sigma_i} \subseteq X\}$.   □

Notice that for any $X \in \mathbb{M}$, $\rho_M^\forall(X) \subseteq X \cap M$, and that $\rho_M^\forall(X)$ gives the least set of traces whose $\alpha_M^\forall$-abstraction is $\alpha_M^\forall(X)$. The intuition is that $\rho_M^\forall(X)$ throws away from X all those traces $\langle i, \sigma \rangle$ either which are not in M — these traces "do not matter", since $\alpha_M^\forall(\neg M) = \varnothing$ — or which are in M but whose present state σ_i does not universally satisfy X.

Existential Checking Abstraction. Dually, the existential checking abstraction map $\alpha_M^\exists : \mathbb{M} \to \wp(\mathbb{S})$ abstracts a given trace-interpreted temporal specification $\phi \in \mathbb{M}$ to the set of possible (present) states s of the model M which existentially satisfy ϕ, that is, for which there exists at least a trace of M which satisfies ϕ and whose present state is s. This leads to the following definition [6, Definition 49]:

$$\alpha_M^\exists(\phi) \overset{\text{def}}{=} \{s \in \mathbb{S} \mid M_{\downarrow s} \cap \phi \neq \varnothing\}.$$

In this case, the subset relation formalizes the notion of approximation: if $\alpha_M^\exists(\phi) \subseteq S$ then each $s \notin S$ is such that if M is in state s then ϕ surely does not hold, and therefore any $T \supseteq S$ has to be understood as less precise than S. Thus, it can be roughly said that the existential checking abstraction is ideally useful for checking so-called safety properties of reactive systems, i.e., "bad things do not happen during executions". It turns out that $\alpha_M^\exists$ gives rise to an adjunction between $\langle \wp(\mathbb{S}), \subseteq \rangle$ and $\langle \mathbb{M}, \subseteq \rangle$, where the concretization map $\gamma_M^\exists : \wp(\mathbb{S}) \to \mathbb{M}$ is given by $\gamma_M^\exists(S) \overset{\text{def}}{=} \{\langle i, \sigma \rangle \in \mathbb{T} \mid \langle i, \sigma \rangle \in M \Rightarrow \sigma_i \in S\}$. As above, for a model $\mathcal{M}_\tau$ generated by a transition system, by the totality hypothesis, $\alpha_{\mathcal{M}_\tau}^\exists$ is onto, and hence $(\alpha_{\mathcal{M}_\tau}^\exists, \langle \mathbb{M}, \subseteq \rangle, \langle \wp(\mathbb{S}), \subseteq \rangle, \gamma_{\mathcal{M}_\tau}^\exists)$ is a GI [6, (50)]. Here, we get the following closure.

Definition 3.6. $\rho_M^\exists \overset{\text{def}}{=} \gamma_M^\exists \circ \alpha_M^\exists \in uco(\langle \mathbb{M}, \subseteq \rangle)$ is the *existential checking closure* relative to a model $M \in \mathbb{M}$. Hence, $\rho_M^\exists = \lambda X.\{\langle i, \sigma \rangle \in \mathbb{T} \mid \langle i, \sigma \rangle \in M \Rightarrow M_{\downarrow \sigma_i} \cap X \neq \varnothing\} = \lambda X.\{\langle i, \sigma \rangle \in M \mid M_{\downarrow \sigma_i} \cap X \neq \varnothing\} \cup \neg M$. $\quad\square$

Here, we have that, for any $X \in \mathbb{M}$, $X \cup \neg M \subseteq \rho_M^\exists(X)$. The intuition is that $\rho_M^\exists$ adds to X any trace which is not in M — these can be considered meaningless as far as the existential checking of M is concerned, since $\alpha_M^\exists(\neg M) = \varnothing$ — plus any trace in M whose present state existentially satisfies X.

Classical State-Based (Abstract) Semantics. Given a total transition system $\langle \mathbb{S}, \tau \rangle$ and its associated model $\mathcal{M}_\tau$, the classical state-based semantics of a temporal formula is calculationally designed as the abstract semantics induced by the model checking abstractions seen above. This is an instance of the very general abstract interpretation scheme introduced by Cousot and Cousot in [6, Section 8] in order to be language-, semantics- and abstraction-independent and to handle monotone and antitone semantic functions simultaneously. Basically, this process amounts to abstract any model transformer of Definition 3.2 by the corresponding best correct approximation induced by the checking abstraction. For example, the predecessor transformer $\oplus : \mathbb{M} \to \mathbb{M}$ is abstracted to $\alpha_{\mathcal{M}_\tau}^\forall \circ \oplus \circ \gamma_{\mathcal{M}_\tau}^\forall : \wp(\mathbb{S}) \to \wp(\mathbb{S})$, where $\alpha_{\mathcal{M}_\tau}^\forall \circ \oplus \circ \gamma_{\mathcal{M}_\tau}^\forall = \widetilde{pre}[\tau] \overset{\text{def}}{=} \lambda S \in \wp(\mathbb{S}).\{s \in \mathbb{S} \mid \forall s' \in \mathbb{S}. (s \overset{\tau}{\to} s') \Rightarrow s' \in S\}$ (cf. [6, Section 11.2]) is the best correct approximation of $\oplus$ for the GI $(\alpha_{\mathcal{M}_\tau}^\forall, \langle \mathbb{M}, \supseteq \rangle, \langle \wp(\mathbb{S}), \supseteq \rangle, \gamma_{\mathcal{M}_\tau}^\forall)$.

The general scenario is as follows. $\mathbb{E}^s \overset{\text{def}}{=} \mathbb{X} \to \wp(\mathbb{S})$ is the set of state environments. The checking abstractions $\alpha_M^\forall$ and $\alpha_M^\exists$ are extended pointwise to environments: $\dot{\alpha}_M^\forall, \dot{\alpha}_M^\exists : \mathbb{E} \to \mathbb{E}^s$, where, e.g., $\dot{\alpha}_M^\forall(\xi) \overset{\text{def}}{=} \lambda X \in \mathbb{X}.\alpha_M^\forall(\xi(X))$. The process of abstraction then compositionally leads to the following abstract state-based semantics for the $\widehat{\mu}$-calculus: $[\![\cdot]\!]_\tau^\forall, [\![\cdot]\!]_\tau^\exists : \mathcal{L}_{\widehat{\mu}} \to \mathbb{E}^s \to \wp(\mathbb{S})$. These are inductively defined as one expects, following the lines of Definition 3.3. Thus, $\llbracket\phi\rrbracket_\tau^\forall$ corresponds to the classical state interpretation of a temporal formula ϕ.

Soundness of the abstract state-based semantics is by construction: for any $\phi \in \mathcal{L}_{\widehat{\mu}}$ and $\xi \in \mathbb{E}$, $\alpha_{\mathcal{M}_\tau}^\forall(\llbracket\phi\rrbracket\xi) \supseteq \llbracket\phi\rrbracket_\tau^\forall\dot{\alpha}_{\mathcal{M}_\tau}^\forall(\xi)$ and $\alpha_{\mathcal{M}_\tau}^\exists(\llbracket\phi\rrbracket\xi) \subseteq \llbracket\phi\rrbracket_\tau^\forall\dot{\alpha}_{\mathcal{M}_\tau}^\exists(\xi)$.

3.4 Completeness Issues

In general, completeness does not hold, even when the set of states is finite, i.e., the containments above may well be strict (see the finite counterexample given in [6, Counterexample (60)]). This means, for example, that there exist a closed formula $\phi \in \mathcal{L}_{\widehat{\mu}}$ and a state $s \in \mathbb{S}$ such that $s \in \alpha_{\mathcal{M}_\tau}^\forall(\llbracket\phi\rrbracket\varnothing) \smallsetminus \llbracket\phi\rrbracket_\tau^\forall\varnothing$, and therefore trace-based and state-based model checking for ϕ are not equivalent: $\mathcal{M}_\tau, s \models_{trace} \phi$ (viz., $\mathcal{M}_{\tau\downarrow s} \subseteq \llbracket\phi\rrbracket\varnothing$), while $\mathcal{M}_\tau, s \not\models_{state}\phi$ (viz., $s \notin \llbracket\phi\rrbracket_\tau^\forall\varnothing$). Intuitively, incompleteness states that in order to deal with temporal specifications of the $\widehat{\mu}$-calculus, model checking algorithms should handle sets of traces instead that sets of traces, and this is evidently infeasible.

Cousot and Cousot [6] identified the model transformers causing such incompleteness and provided some sufficient conditions ensuring completeness. In view of Section 2, in the following, we will mostly adopt the convenient closure operator approach to abstract domains.

The first incomplete transformer for the universal checking abstraction is the predecessor operator $\oplus$, as shown in [6, Section 11.2]. In this case, the following sufficient condition holds: for all $X \in \mathbb{M}$, if $X = Fd(X)$ then $\rho_{\mathcal{M}_\tau}^\forall(\oplus(\rho_{\mathcal{M}_\tau}^\forall(X))) = \rho_{\mathcal{M}_\tau}^\forall(\oplus(X))$. In other words, the predecessor transformer is complete for any forward-closed formula to check. Of course, dually, the successor model transformer $\ominus$ is incomplete as well.

Disjunction, namely set union, is the second incomplete model transformer, as observed in [6, Section 11.6]. Here, we have that for any $X, Y \in \mathbb{M}$, if $X = St(X)$ or $Y = St(Y)$ then $\rho_{\mathcal{M}_\tau}^\forall(\rho_{\mathcal{M}_\tau}^\forall(X) \cup \rho_{\mathcal{M}_\tau}^\forall(Y)) = \rho_{\mathcal{M}_\tau}^\forall(X \cup Y)$. This means that disjunction on at least one state-closed formula turns out to be complete.

The above sufficient conditions allow to identify some meaningful complete fragments of the $\widehat{\mu}$-calculus. This is the case, for example, of the $\mu_+^\forall$-calculus considered in [6, Section 13], which is complete for the universal checking abstraction and subsumes the classical $\forall$CTL logic.

Finally, the reversal model transformer $\frown$ is also incomplete, as shown by the following example, although this is not explicitly mentioned in [6, Section 11].

Example 3.7. We follow the lines of [6, Counterexample (56)]. Let $\mathbb{S} \overset{\text{def}}{=} \{\circ, \bullet\}$ and $\tau \overset{\text{def}}{=} \{\langle\circ, \circ\rangle, \langle\bullet, \bullet\rangle, \langle\bullet, \circ\rangle\}$. We have that $\mathcal{M}_\tau = \{\langle i, \lambda k.\circ\rangle\}_{i\in\mathbb{Z}} \cup \{\langle i, \lambda k.\bullet\rangle\}_{i\in\mathbb{Z}} \cup \{\langle i, \lambda k.(k < m ? \bullet : \circ)\rangle\}_{i,m\in\mathbb{Z}}$. Let $X \overset{\text{def}}{=} \{\langle i, \sigma\rangle \mid \forall k \geq i.\sigma_k = \bullet\}$, and therefore $\frown(X) = \{\langle i, \sigma\rangle \mid \forall k \leq i.\sigma_k = \bullet\}$. Since $\mathcal{M}_{\tau\downarrow\circ} \not\subseteq X$ and $\mathcal{M}_{\tau\downarrow\bullet} = \{\langle i, \lambda k.\bullet\rangle\}_{i\in\mathbb{Z}} \cup \{\langle i, \lambda k.(k < m ? \bullet : \circ)\rangle\}_{i,m\in\mathbb{Z},i<m} \not\subseteq X$, we have that $\rho_{\mathcal{M}_\tau}^\forall(X) = \varnothing$, and hence $\rho_{\mathcal{M}_\tau}^\forall(\frown(\rho_{\mathcal{M}_\tau}^\forall(X))) = \varnothing$. Instead, it turns out that $\rho_{\mathcal{M}_\tau}^\forall(\frown(X)) = \mathcal{M}_{\tau\downarrow\bullet}$. □

Of course, a dual reasoning can be made for the existential checking abstraction: here, the incomplete model transformers are predecessor, successor, conjunction and reversal.

4   Absolute Complete Shells for Model Transformers

In this section we characterize the absolute complete shells of the checking closures for the incomplete model transformers identified in Section 3.4.

In the following, we will consider checking closures parameterized w.r.t. a generic model $M \in \mathbb{M}$ satisfying the following hypothesis.

Hypothesis 4.1. *For any universal and existential state closure, respectively $\rho_M^{\forall}$ and $\rho_M^{\exists}$, the model $M \in \mathbb{M}$ is such that $\oplus(M) = M = \ominus(M)$ and $\oplus(\frown(M)) = \frown(M) = \ominus(\frown(M))$.*

This therefore means that M and its reversal $\frown M$ are closed for forward and backward time progresses. This is obviously satisfied by any model generated by a transition system.

Remark 4.2. *Any model $\mathbb{M}_\tau \in \mathbb{M}$ generated by a transition system $\langle \mathbb{S}, \tau \rangle$ satisfies the Hypothesis 4.1.*

Predecessor. Let us first characterize the absolute complete shell of the universal checking closure for the predecessor model transformer. Since the predecessor operator is additive, this complete shell actually exists in view of Theorem 2.1, and its set of fixpoints turns out to be as follows.

Theorem 4.3. *The absolute complete shell $S_{\forall_M}^{\oplus}$ of $\rho_M^{\forall}$ for $\oplus$ exists and it is characterized by the following set of fixpoints: $\mathcal{M}_{\mathbb{M}_{\supseteq}}(\{\ominus^n(X) \mid n \in \mathbb{N}, X \in \rho_M^{\forall}\})$.*

Thus, each arbitrary union (that is Moore-closure in $\langle \mathbb{M}, \supseteq \rangle$) of arbitrary powers of the successor transformer applied to fixpoints of the universal checking closure turns out to be a fixpoint of the closure $S_{\forall_M}^{\oplus} \in uco(\langle \mathbb{M}, \supseteq \rangle)$. In other terms, in order to minimally refine the checking closure $\rho_M^{\forall}$ to a complete closure for the predecessor transformer, one must close the image of $\rho_M^{\forall}$ under the application of the inverse of the predecessor transformer, i.e., the successor.

We also provide an interesting characterization of the absolute complete shell $S_{\forall_M}^{\oplus}$ as a mapping on models. First, we need to introduce the following notion.

Definition 4.4. *Given $\langle i, \sigma \rangle \in \mathbb{T}$, $M \in \mathbb{M}$ and $k \in \mathbb{N}$, the projection $M_{\downarrow \langle i, \sigma \rangle}^{-k}$ of M at the k-th past state of $\langle i, \sigma \rangle$ is defined as follows:*

$$M_{\downarrow \langle i, \sigma \rangle}^{-k} \stackrel{\text{def}}{=} \{\langle j, \beta \rangle \in M \mid \beta_{j-k} = \sigma_{i-k}\}.$$

$\square$

The k-th past state projection of a model is therefore a generalization of the (current) state projection, since $M_{\downarrow \sigma_i} = M_{\downarrow \langle i, \sigma \rangle}^{0}$. The following result holds.

Theorem 4.5. *The absolute complete shell $S_{\forall_M}^{\oplus}$ of $\rho_M^{\forall}$ for $\oplus$ can be characterized as follows: $S_{\forall_M}^{\oplus} = \lambda X.\{\langle i, \sigma \rangle \in M \mid \exists k \in \mathbb{N}. \, M_{\downarrow \langle i, \sigma \rangle}^{-k} \subseteq X\}$.*

Thus, for any $X \in \mathbb{M}$, $S_{\forall_M}^{\oplus}(X)$ throws away from X all those traces either which are not in M or which are in M but any past or current state of the trace does not universally satisfy X. $S_{\forall_M}^{\oplus}(X)$ is actually a refinement of $\rho_M^{\forall}(X)$, since $\rho_M^{\forall}(X) \subseteq S_{\forall_M}^{\oplus}(X) \subseteq X \cap M$, and it characterizes exactly the least amount of information that must be added to $\rho_M^{\forall}(X)$ in order to be complete for the predecessor. The intuition is that while $\rho_M^{\forall}$ considers present states only (i.e., $M_{\downarrow \sigma_i} \subseteq X$), as expected, completeness for the predecessor forces to take into account any past state (i.e., $\exists k \in \mathbb{N}. M_{\downarrow \langle i, \sigma \rangle}^{-k} \subseteq X$). Thus, the basic idea is "to prolong the abstract domain $\wp(\mathbb{S})$ in the past". This leads to design the following abstract domain.

Definition 4.6. Define $\wp(\mathbb{S})^{\triangleleft} \overset{\text{def}}{=} \mathbb{Z}_{\leq 0} \to \wp(\mathbb{S})$, where $\mathbb{Z}_{\leq 0}$ is the set of nonpositive integers. $\wp(\mathbb{S})^{\triangleleft}$ is endowed with standard pointwise orderings $\dot{\subseteq}$ and $\dot{\supseteq}$, making it a complete lattice.
Given $z \in \mathbb{Z}_{\leq 0}$, $s \in \mathbb{S}$ and $M \in \mathbb{M}$, define $M_{\downarrow s}^{z} \overset{\text{def}}{=} \{\langle i, \sigma \rangle \in M \mid \sigma_{i+z} = s\}$.
The mappings $\alpha_{\forall_M}^{\oplus} : \mathbb{M} \to \wp(\mathbb{S})^{\triangleleft}$ and $\gamma_{\forall_M}^{\oplus} : \wp(\mathbb{S})^{\triangleleft} \to \mathbb{M}$ are defined as follows:

$$\alpha_{\forall_M}^{\oplus}(X) \overset{\text{def}}{=} \lambda z \in \mathbb{Z}_{\leq 0}. \{s \in \mathbb{S} \mid M_{\downarrow s}^{z} \subseteq X\};$$

$$\gamma_{\forall_M}^{\oplus}(\Sigma) \overset{\text{def}}{=} \{\langle i, \sigma \rangle \in M \mid \exists k \in \mathbb{N}. \sigma_{i-k} \in \Sigma_{-k}\}. \qquad \square$$

Corollary 4.7. $(\alpha_{\forall_M}^{\oplus}, \mathbb{M}_{\supseteq}, \wp(\mathbb{S})^{\triangleleft}_{\dot{\supseteq}}, \gamma_{\forall_M}^{\oplus})$ is a GC, and additionally a GI when $M = \mathbb{M}_\tau$ for some transition system $\langle \mathbb{S}, \tau \rangle$, inducing the closure $S_{\forall_M}^{\oplus} \in uco(\mathbb{M}_{\supseteq})$.

Hence, the above result provides a concrete representation for one possible and simple abstract domain for the closure $S_{\forall_M}^{\oplus}$. The abstract domain $\wp(\mathbb{S})_{\supseteq}$ of the universal checking abstraction $\alpha_M^{\forall}$ is refined to a domain of infinite sequences of sets of states. Such sequences are indexed over $\mathbb{Z}_{\leq 0}$, and this aims at recalling that for any $\Sigma \in \wp(\mathbb{S})^{\triangleleft}$ and $i \in \mathbb{N}$, $\Sigma_{-i} \in \wp(\mathbb{S})$ is a set of states at time $-i \in \mathbb{Z}_{\leq 0}$. Basically, $\alpha_{\forall_M}^{\oplus}$ can be viewed as the most natural "prolongation" of $\alpha_M^{\forall}$ in the past.

Example 4.8. The example [6, Counterexample (56)] has been used to show that, in general, $\alpha_M^{\forall}$ is not complete for $\oplus$. The setting has been already recalled in Example 3.7. Let $X \overset{\text{def}}{=} \{\langle i, \sigma \rangle \mid i \in \mathbb{Z}, \forall j < i. \sigma_j = \bullet\}$. It is observed in [6, Counterexample (56)] that $\varnothing = \rho_{\mathbb{M}_\tau}^{\forall}(\oplus(\rho_{\mathbb{M}_\tau}^{\forall}(X))) \subsetneq \rho_{\mathbb{M}_\tau}^{\forall}(\oplus(X))$. Instead, it is not hard to check that for $S_{\forall_{\mathbb{M}_\tau}}^{\oplus}$ completeness does hold:

$$S_{\forall_{\mathbb{M}_\tau}}^{\oplus}(\oplus(X)) =$$
$$= \mathbb{M}_{\tau \downarrow \bullet} = \{\langle i, \lambda k.\bullet \rangle \mid i \in \mathbb{Z}\} \cup \{\langle i, \lambda k.(k < m\ ?\ \bullet\ \dot{\iota}\ \circ)\rangle \mid i, m \in \mathbb{Z},\ i < m\} =$$
$$= S_{\forall_{\mathbb{M}_\tau}}^{\oplus}(\oplus(S_{\forall_{\mathbb{M}_\tau}}^{\oplus}(X))). \qquad \square$$

Disjunction. Let us turn to disjunction, i.e. union $\cup$, the second incomplete model transformer. Here again, the absolute complete shell of $\rho_M^{\forall}$ for (finite) disjunction exists by Theorem 2.1, because union on $\mathbb{M}_{\supseteq}$ is trivially additive.

Theorem 4.9. The absolute complete shell $S_{\forall_M}^{\cup}$ of $\rho_M^{\forall}$ for $\cup$ exists and it is characterized as follows:
(1) The set of fixpoints of $S_{\forall_M}^{\cup}$ is $\{X \in \mathbb{M} \mid X \subseteq M\}$;

(2) $S^{\cup}_{\forall_M} = \lambda X. X \cap M$;

(3) $S^{\cup}_{\forall_M}$ is the closure induced by the GI $(\alpha^{\cup}_{\forall_M}, \mathbb{M}_{\supseteq}, \wp(M)_{\supseteq}, \gamma^{\cup}_{\forall_M})$, where $\alpha^{\cup}_{\forall_M} \overset{\text{def}}{=} \lambda X. X \cap M$ and $\gamma^{\cup}_{\forall_M} \overset{\text{def}}{=} \lambda X. X$.

Thus, this shows that the absolute complete shell $S^{\cup}_{\forall_M}$ of the universal checking closure for the union of models is essentially the identity mapping. More precisely, given the model to check M, one simple (actually, in a natural sense, it could be termed the simplest) abstract domain equivalent to the closure $S^{\cup}_{\forall_M}$ is $\wp(M)_{\supseteq}$ endowed with the abstraction map $\lambda X. X \cap M$ which merely removes those traces which are not in M. This can be read as stating that completeness for disjunction requires all the traces in M.

Example 4.10. [6, Counterexample (58)] shows that, in general, $\alpha^{\forall}_M$ is not complete for $\cup$. The setting is still that of Example 3.7. Let $X_1 \overset{\text{def}}{=} \{\langle i, \sigma \rangle \mid i \in \mathbb{Z}, \exists k \geq i. \forall j \geq k. \sigma_j = \circ\}$ and $X_2 \overset{\text{def}}{=} \{\langle i, \sigma \rangle \mid i \in \mathbb{Z}, \forall k \geq i. \sigma_k = \bullet\}$. [6, Counterexample (58)] observes incompleteness: $\rho^{\forall}_{\mathcal{M}_\tau}(\rho^{\forall}_{\mathcal{M}_\tau}(X_1) \cup \rho^{\forall}_{\mathcal{M}_\tau}(X_2)) \subsetneq \rho^{\forall}_{\mathcal{M}_\tau}(X_1 \cup X_2)$. For the absolute complete shell $S^{\cup}_{\forall_{\mathcal{M}_\tau}}$, instead, we have that:

$S^{\cup}_{\forall_{\mathcal{M}_\tau}}(X_1) = X_1 \cap \mathcal{M}_\tau = \{\langle i, \lambda k. \circ \rangle \mid i \in \mathbb{Z}\} \cup \{\langle i, \lambda k.(k < m \ ? \ \bullet \ \raisebox{-0.3ex}{$\dot{\scriptstyle\iota}$} \ \circ) \rangle \mid i, m \in \mathbb{Z}, i \leq m\}$,

$S^{\cup}_{\forall_{\mathcal{M}_\tau}}(X_2) = X_2 \cap \mathcal{M}_\tau = \{\langle i, \lambda k. \bullet \rangle \mid i \in \mathbb{Z}\}$,

$S^{\cup}_{\forall_{\mathcal{M}_\tau}}(X_1 \cup X_2) = S^{\cup}_{\forall_{\mathcal{M}_\tau}}(X_1) \cup S^{\cup}_{\forall_{\mathcal{M}_\tau}}(X_2)$,

and this easily implies that $S^{\cup}_{\forall_{\mathcal{M}_\tau}}(S^{\cup}_{\forall_{\mathcal{M}_\tau}}(X_1) \cup S^{\cup}_{\forall_{\mathcal{M}_\tau}}(X_2)) = S^{\cup}_{\forall_{\mathcal{M}_\tau}}(X_1 \cup X_2)$.   □

Reversal. Let us consider reversal, the last incomplete model transformer. Again, the absolute complete shell of $\rho^{\forall}_M$ for the reversal exists by Theorem 2.1, because the reversal operator $\frown$ on $\mathbb{M}_{\supseteq}$ is obviously additive.

Theorem 4.11. *The absolute complete shell $S^{\frown}_{\forall_M}$ of $\rho^{\forall}_M$ for $\frown$ exists and it is characterized as follows:*

(1) *The set of fixpoints of $S^{\frown}_{\forall_M}$ is $\mathcal{M}_{\mathbb{M}_{\supseteq}}(\rho^{\forall}_M \cup \{\frown(X) \in \mathbb{M} \mid X \in \rho^{\forall}_M\})$;*

(2) $S^{\frown}_{\forall_M} = \lambda X. \rho^{\forall}_M(X) \cup \frown(\rho^{\forall}_M(\frown(X)))$;

(3) *$S^{\frown}_{\forall_M}$ is the closure operator induced by the GC $(\alpha^{\frown}_{\forall_M}, \mathbb{M}_{\supseteq}, \wp(\mathbb{S})^2_{\supseteq}, \gamma^{\frown}_{\forall_M})$, where $\alpha^{\frown}_{\forall_M} \overset{\text{def}}{=} \lambda X. \langle \alpha^{\forall}_M(X), \alpha^{\curlyvee}_M(X) \rangle$ and $\gamma^{\frown}_{\forall_M} \overset{\text{def}}{=} \lambda \langle X_1, X_2 \rangle. \gamma^{\forall}_M(X_1) \cup \gamma^{\curlyvee}_M(X_2)$.*

The above result tells us that the complete shell $S^{\frown}_{\forall_M}$ simply refines $\wp(\mathbb{S})$ to $\wp(\mathbb{S})^2$, where a model X is abstracted to the pair $\langle \alpha^{\forall}_M(X), \alpha^{\curlyvee}_M(X) \rangle$. Hence, completeness for the reversal requires an additional component taking into account the universal checking abstraction for the reversed model $\frown(M)$. Also, notice that the GC $(\alpha^{\frown}_{\forall_M}, \mathbb{M}_{\supseteq}, \wp(\mathbb{S})^2_{\supseteq}, \gamma^{\frown}_{\forall_M})$ can be also viewed as the direct (not reduced) product (see [5]) of $(\alpha^{\forall}_M, \mathbb{M}_{\supseteq}, \wp(\mathbb{S})_{\supseteq}, \gamma^{\forall}_M)$ and $(\alpha^{\curlyvee}_M, \mathbb{M}_{\supseteq}, \wp(\mathbb{S})_{\supseteq}, \gamma^{\curlyvee}_M)$.

All the Model Transformers. To conclude our analysis, we characterize the absolute complete shell of $\rho^{\forall}_M$ for the set of all the model transformers of Definition 3.2. This exists by Theorem 2.1 because all the operations are continuous, taking care of the following technicality. As far as the universal state closure transformer $\forall$ is concerned, the following restriction is needed. We just consider the unary restrictions $\lambda X.\forall(N, X) : \mathbb{M} \to \mathbb{M}$, where $N \subseteq M \cup {}^\frown(M)$, of the universal state closure transformer, because from the abstract interpretation viewpoint the binary transformer $\forall : \mathbb{M} \times \mathbb{M} \to \mathbb{M}$ is problematic. In fact, the binary operation $\forall$ is neither monotone nor antitone in its first argument, and therefore it does not give rise to a concrete binary operation suitable to abstract interpretation. On the other hand, given any $N \in \mathbb{M}$, the unary restriction $\lambda X.\forall(N, X)$ is monotone. As seen at the end of Section 3.1, this is enough to recover the standard universal state quantification. In the sequel, we will use the following compact notation: $M^* \stackrel{\mathrm{def}}{=} M \cup {}^\frown(M)$. We have the following result.

Theorem 4.12. *The absolute complete shell $S_{\forall_M}$ of $\rho_M^\forall$ for $\{\sigma_S\}_{S \in \wp(\mathbb{S})} \cup \{\pi_t\}_{t \in \wp(\mathbb{S}^2)} \cup \{\oplus, \cap, \cup, \neg, {}^\frown\} \cup \{\lambda X.\forall(N, X)\}_{N \subseteq M^*}$ exists and it is characterized as follows:*
(1) The set of fixpoints of $S_{\forall_M}$ is $\{X \in \mathbb{M} \mid X \subseteq M^*\}$;
(2) $S_{\forall_M} = \lambda X.X \cap M^*$;
(3) $S_{\forall_M}$ is the closure induced by the GI $(\alpha_{\forall_M}, \mathbb{M}_\supseteq, \wp(M^*)_\supseteq, \gamma_{\forall_M})$, where $\alpha_{\forall_M} \stackrel{\mathrm{def}}{=} \lambda X.X \cap M^*$ and $\gamma_{\forall_M} \stackrel{\mathrm{def}}{=} \lambda X.X$;
(4) $S_{\forall_M} = S_{\forall_M}^\cup \sqcap S_{\forall_M}^\frown$.

This shell must be complete both for disjunction and reversal, and therefore $S_{\forall_M}$ results to be more concrete than the corresponding shells $S_{\forall_M}^\cup$ and $S_{\forall_M}^\frown$ seen above. Actually, it turns out that $S_{\forall_M}$ is precisely the glb in $uco(\mathbb{M}_\supseteq)$ of these two shells. Thus, this globally complete abstract domain is even more close to the concrete domain of sets of generic traces, since the corresponding abstraction is just "something less" than the identity.

It is also interesting to observe that when we leave out the reversal operator, as expected, the complete shell becomes $S_{\forall_M}^\cup$, as stated by the following result.

Theorem 4.13. $S_{\forall_M}^\cup$ *is the absolute complete shell of $\rho_M^\forall$ for $\{\sigma_S\}_{S \in \wp(\mathbb{S})} \cup \{\pi_t\}_{t \in \wp(\mathbb{S}^2)} \cup \{\oplus, \cap, \cup, \neg\} \cup \{\lambda X.\forall(N, X)\}_{N \subseteq M}$.*

Existential Checking Closure. The scenario for the existential checking closure is dual to the universal case. The following statement collects the most important characterizations.

Theorem 4.14.
(1) $S_{\exists_M}^\oplus \stackrel{\mathrm{def}}{=} \lambda X.\{\langle i, \sigma \rangle \in \mathbb{T} \mid \langle i, \sigma \rangle \in M \Rightarrow (\forall k \in \mathbb{N}. M_{\downarrow\langle i, \sigma \rangle}^{-k} \cap X \neq \varnothing)\}$ is the absolute complete shell of $\rho_M^\exists$ for $\oplus$;
(2) $S_{\exists_M}^\cap \stackrel{\mathrm{def}}{=} \lambda X.X \cup \neg M$ is the absolute complete shell of $\rho_M^\exists$ for $\cap$;
(3) $S_{\exists_M}^\frown \stackrel{\mathrm{def}}{=} \lambda X.\rho_M^\exists(X) \cup {}^\frown(\rho_M^\exists({}^\frown X))$ is the absolute complete shell of $\rho_M^\exists$ for ${}^\frown$;
(4) $S_{\exists_M} \stackrel{\mathrm{def}}{=} \lambda X.X \cup \neg M^*$ is the absolute complete shell of $\rho_M^\exists$ for $\{\sigma_S\}_{S \in \wp(\mathbb{S})} \cup \{\pi_t\}_{t \in \wp(\mathbb{S}^2)} \cup \{\oplus, \cap, \cup, \neg, {}^\frown\} \cup \{\lambda X.\forall(N, X)\}_{N \subseteq M^*}$.

5   Completeness of Temporal Calculi

As already observed in Section 4, from the abstract interpretation viewpoint, the universal state closure connective $\forall$ of the full $\widehat{\mu}$-calculus is somehow problematic, because, according to Cousot and Cousot's [6] Definition 3.1, the binary connective $\forall$ can be applied without any restriction, while its semantic counterpart, the universal state closure transformer $\forall : \mathbb{M} \times \mathbb{M} \to \mathbb{M}$, is neither monotone nor antitone in its first argument. On the other hand, given any $N \in \mathbb{M}$, the unary restriction $\lambda X.\forall(N, X) : \mathbb{M} \to \mathbb{M}$ is monotone, and this is enough in order to have the standard universal state quantification: $\forall\phi \stackrel{\text{def}}{=} \forall \boxplus (\pi_\tau) : \phi$. This naturally leads to the following slight "monotone" restriction, which we call $\widehat{\mu}^-$-calculus, of the $\widehat{\mu}$-calculus.

Definition 5.1. Formulae ϕ of the $\widehat{\mu}^-$-calculus are inductively defined as follows:

$$\phi ::= \boldsymbol{\sigma}_S \mid \boldsymbol{\pi}_t \mid X \mid \oplus \phi \mid \phi^\frown \mid \phi_1 \vee \phi_2 \mid \neg\phi \mid \boldsymbol{\mu}X.\phi \mid \boldsymbol{\nu}X.\phi \mid \forall\phi$$

where $S \in \wp(\mathbb{S})$, $t \in \wp(\mathbb{S} \times \mathbb{S})$, and $X \in \mathbb{X}$. $\mathcal{L}_{\widehat{\mu}}$ denotes the set of $\widehat{\mu}^-$-calculus formulae.   □

Of course, the trace-semantics for the $\widehat{\mu}^-$-calculus is completely identical to that of the $\widehat{\mu}$-calculus given in Definition 3.3, but for the universal connective: $[\![\forall\phi]\!]\xi \stackrel{\text{def}}{=} \forall(\mathcal{M}_\tau, [\![\phi]\!]\xi)$.

The main result of this section is then stated for the $\widehat{\mu}^-$-calculus. The scenario is as follows. As seen in Section 3.3 for the universal and existential checking abstractions, any abstraction of the domain $\mathbb{M}$ of concrete temporal models, ordered by the superset or subset relation, induces an abstract semantics for the $\widehat{\mu}$-calculus, and therefore for the $\widehat{\mu}^-$-calculus. More in detail, for the universal case, given a model to check $M \in \mathbb{M}$ — which is supposed to be generated by a transition system $\langle \mathbb{S}, \tau \rangle$ — any closure operator, i.e. abstract domain, $\rho \in uco(\mathbb{M}_\supseteq)$, induces the set of abstract environments $\mathbb{E}^\rho \stackrel{\text{def}}{=} \mathbb{X} \to \rho$, and the corresponding abstract semantics $[\![\cdot]\!]^\rho : \mathcal{L}_{\widehat{\mu}} \to \mathbb{E}^\rho \to \rho$. Given an environment $\xi \in \mathbb{E}$, $\dot\rho(\xi) \stackrel{\text{def}}{=} \lambda X.\rho(\xi(X)) \in \mathbb{E}^\rho$ is the corresponding abstract environment induced by ρ. Soundness, i.e., $\forall\phi \in \mathcal{L}_{\widehat{\mu}}.\forall\xi \in \mathbb{E}. \rho([\![\phi]\!]\xi) \supseteq [\![\phi]\!]^\rho\dot\rho(\xi)$, holds by construction (cf. [6, Theorem (40)]), while completeness for ρ means that equality always holds. We therefore have the following theorem.

Theorem 5.2. $S_{\forall_M}$ *is the least (w.r.t. subset image containment) closure operator on* $\mathbb{M}_\supseteq$ *(1) complete for the $\widehat{\mu}^-$-calculus and (2) containing the universal checking closure* $\rho_M^\forall$.

It is important to stress that since the $\widehat{\mu}$-calculus involves (least and greatest) fixpoints, no general result in [8] ensures the existence of the above complete abstract domain. Nevertheless, the above result shows that this complete shell does exist, and it coincides with the absolute complete shell $S_{\forall_M}$ relative to all the temporal connectives seen in Theorem 4.12, namely the identity on sets of traces in M or its reversal. Hence, in this case, fixpoints do not affect the outcome. This complete shell induces an abstract semantics which essentially is the trace-based semantics itself. Thus, this key result can be interpreted as follows: if we want to refine the state-based model checking — i.e., the classical domain of sets of states — in order to be trace-complete for the $\widehat{\mu}$-calculus, we ineluctably get the trace-based semantics itself.

When the reversal connective is not included, analogously to Theorem 4.13 we get the following characterization.

Definition 5.3. Formulae ϕ of the μ^*-calculus are defined as follows:

$$\phi ::= \boldsymbol{\sigma}_S \mid \boldsymbol{\pi}_t \mid X \mid \oplus \phi \mid \phi_1 \vee \phi_2 \mid \neg\phi \mid \boldsymbol{\mu}X.\phi \mid \boldsymbol{\nu}X.\phi \mid \forall\phi$$

where $S \in \wp(\mathbb{S})$, $t \in \wp(\mathbb{S} \times \mathbb{S})$, and $X \in \mathbb{X}$.   □

Theorem 5.4. $S_{\forall_M}^{\cup}$ is the least (w.r.t. subset image containment) closure operator on $\mathbb{M}_{\supseteq}$ (1) complete for the μ^*-calculus and (2) containing the universal checking closure $\rho_M^{\forall}$.

The Existential Case. The situation is fully dual: we simply state the result.

Theorem 5.5. $S_{\exists_M}$ and $S_{\exists_M}^{\cup}$ are, respectively, the least (w.r.t. subset image containment) closures on $\mathbb{M}_{\subseteq}$ (1) complete, respectively, for the $\widehat{\mu}$-calculus and for the μ^*-calculus, and (2) containing the existential checking closure $\rho_M^{\exists}$.

6   Conclusion

In the context of a novel and rich temporal specification language called $\widehat{\mu}$-calculus, Cousot and Cousot [6] showed that classical state-based model checking is an abstract interpretation of the trace-based semantics for the $\widehat{\mu}$-calculus, which is incomplete. In this paper, we have characterized the least, i.e. least informative, refinement of the state-based model checking semantics of the $\widehat{\mu}$-calculus which is complete w.r.t. the trace-based semantics, and this turns out to be essentially the trace-based semantics itself.

Cousot and Cousot [6, Section 14] also showed that standard abstract model checking [2,3,7,10] using a surjective mapping from concrete states to a set of abstract states can be understood as a further step of abstraction over the state-based model checking semantics. Analogously to what has been studied in this paper, this opens the question of minimally refining abstract model checking in order to get completeness, which is a very desirable property when performing model checking for abstract models. Some recent results in this direction for ACTL* are given by Clarke et al. in [1].

Acknowledgements. I wish to thank Roberto Giacobazzi for the many helpful discussions we had on May 2000 in Place des Vosges, and Radhia Cousot for hosting me at LIX, École Polytechnique, Palaiseau, on May 2000. Special thanks to Maddie Hayes. This work has been partly supported by the Italian MURST project "Automatic program certification by asbtract interpretation".

References

1. E.M. Clarke, O. Grumberg, S. Jha, Y. Lu, and H. Veith. Counterexample-guided abstraction refinement. In *Proc. CAV'00*, LNCS 1855, pp. 154–169, 2000.
2. E.M. Clarke, O. Grumberg and D. Long. Model checking and abstraction. *ACM TOPLAS*, 16(5):1512–1542, 1994.
3. E.M. Clarke, O. Grumberg and D.A. Peled. *Model checking*. The MIT Press, 1999.
4. P. Cousot and R. Cousot. Abstract interpretation: a unified lattice model for static analysis of programs by construction or approximation of fixpoints. In *Proc. 4th ACM POPL*, pp. 238–252, 1977.
5. P. Cousot and R. Cousot. Systematic design of program analysis frameworks. In *Proc. 6th ACM POPL*, pp. 269–282, 1979.
6. P. Cousot and R. Cousot. Temporal abstract interpretation. In *Proc. 27th ACM POPL*, pp. 12–25, 2000.
7. D. Dams, O. Grumberg, and R. Gerth. Abstract interpretation of reactive systems. *ACM TOPLAS*, 16(5):1512–1542, 1997.
8. R. Giacobazzi, F. Ranzato, and F. Scozzari. Making abstract interpretations complete. *J. ACM*, 47(2):361–416, 2000.
9. D. Kozen. Results on the propositional μ-calculus. *TCS*, 27:333–354, 1983.
10. C. Loiseaux, S. Graf, J. Sifakis, A. Bouajjani, and S. Bensalem. Property preserving abstractions for the verification of concurrent systems. *Formal Methods in System Design*, 6:1–36, 1995.
11. Z. Manna and A. Pnueli. *The Temporal Logic of Reactive and Concurrent Systems Specification*. Springer-Verlag, 1992.
12. M. Müller-Olm, D. Schmidt, and B. Steffen. Model-checking: a tutorial introduction. In *Proc. SAS'99*, LNCS 1694, pp. 330–354, 1999.

Modal Transition Systems: A Foundation for Three-Valued Program Analysis

Michael Huth[1], Radha Jagadeesan[*2], and David Schmidt[**1]

[1] Computing and Information Sciences, Kansas State University,
{huth,schmidt}@cis.ksu.edu, WWW home page:
http://www.cis.ksu.edu/{~huth,~schmidt}
[2] Department of Mathematics and Computer Science, Loyola University of Chicago,
radha@cs.luc.edu, WWW home page: http://www.cs.luc.edu/~radha

Abstract. We present *Kripke modal transition systems* (Kripke MTSs),
a generalization of modal transition systems [27,26], as a foundation
for three-valued program analysis. The semantics of Kripke MTSs are
presented by means of a mixed power domain of states; soundness and
consistency are proved. Two major applications, model checking partial
state spaces and three-valued program shape analysis, are presented as
evidence of the suitability of Kripke MTSs as a foundation for three-
valued analyses.

1 Introduction

A *modal transition system* (MTS) [27,26] labels each of its state transitions
with a modality — *may* or *must* — expressing transition behaviors that *(i)*
necessarily occur (*must* modality), *(ii) possibly* occur (*may* modality), and *(iii)*
not possibly occur (*absence* of a transition). Figure 1 shows an example MTS — a
specification of a slot machine, where some behaviors of the final implementation
are fixed (the *must*-transitions) and some are uncertain (the *may*-transitions).

Conventional state-transition modellings are over-approximations made by
adding more computation paths [8,7], thereby limiting validation to safety properties ("nothing bad will happen"). MTSs, however, perform both over- and
under-approximation, admitting both safety *and* liveness properties ("something
good will happen") to be deduced. As a bonus, the outcomes of analyses of MTSs
are three-valued, meaning that validation, refutation, and conditional reasoning
can be undertaken in the framework. Abstractions of both control *and* data can
be modelled with MTSs.

The paper proceeds as follows: Section 2 reviews doubly labeled transition
systems [12] and characterizes their behaviors by logics of "liveness" and "safety."
Section 3 introduces *Kripke MTSs*, their refinement relation, and their semantics
for the modal mu-calculus [25]. Sections 4 and 5 show how to apply Kripke MTSs
to two analyses that rely on three-valued logic: *(i)* Bruns and Godefroid's partial

---

[*] Supported by NSF CCR-9901071.
[**] Supported by NSF CCR-9970679 and INT-9981558.

D. Sands (Ed.): ESOP 2001, LNCS 2028, pp. 155–169, 2001.

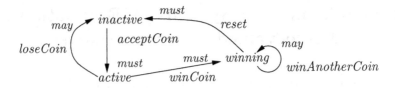

Fig. 1. Slot machine specification in modal transition format

Kripke structures [3] and extended transition systems [29,39] and *(ii)* the pointer shape-graph analysis of Sagiv, Reps, and Wilhelm [35]. Section 6 concludes.

2   Doubly Labeled Transition Systems

We begin with the definition of a *doubly labeled transition system* [12]:

Definition 1 (Doubly labeled transition systems). *A* doubly labeled transition system *(DLTS),* $\mathcal{K}$, *is a tuple* $(\Sigma_K, \text{Act}, \text{AP}, \longrightarrow, L)$, *where* Σ_K *is a set of states,* Act *is a (countable) set of action symbols,* AP *is a (countable) set of atomic propositions,* $\longrightarrow$ *is a transition relation that is a subset of* $\Sigma_K \times \text{Act} \times \Sigma_K$, *and* L *is a labeling function* $L\colon \Sigma_K \to \mathcal{P}(\text{AP})$. *We call* $\mathcal{K}$ finitely-branching *if for each* $s \in \Sigma_K$ *and* $a \in \text{Act}$, *the sets* $L(s)$ *and* $\{s' \in \Sigma_K \mid s \to^a s'\}$ *are finite.* [1]

As Figure 2 shows, each state is annotated with the set of primitive properties that hold for it. Behaviors are compared by means of *simulations*:

Definition 2 (Simulation). *Let* $\mathcal{C}$ *and* $\mathcal{A}$ *be doubly labeled transition systems, where for simplicity* $\text{Act}_C = \text{Act}_A$. *A relation,* $Q \subseteq \Sigma_C \times \Sigma_A$, *is a* simulation *if, for all* $s \in \Sigma_C, t \in \Sigma_A$, $Q(s,t)$ *holds iff: for all* $a \in \text{Act}_C$ *and* $s' \in \Sigma_C$ *with* $s \to^a s'$, *there is some* $t' \in \Sigma_A$ *with* $t \to^a t'$ *and* $Q(s',t')$.

Given $\mathcal{C}$ and $\mathcal{A}$, we can compute the greatest simulation, $\prec$, on $\Sigma_C \times \Sigma_A$, a preorder, by a standard fixed-point argument. The intuition behind a simulation is that a transition made by $\mathcal{C}$ can be "mimicked" by one in $\mathcal{A}$. In practice, one of $\mathcal{C}$ or $\mathcal{A}$ is an "implementation" and the other is its "abstraction" or "specification" or "model," which must be analyzed for correctness properties. As noted in [36], there are natural connections between simulations and Galois connections [8] on such transition systems.

Live Simulations. Simulations should respect atomic properties. A simulation, $Q \subseteq \Sigma_C \times \Sigma_A$, is a *live simulation* if $Q(s,t)$ implies $L(s) \subseteq L(t)$, for all $s \in \Sigma_C$ and $t \in \Sigma_A$. It is easy to prove that there is a greatest live simulation, $\prec_{live}$, on $\Sigma_C \times \Sigma_A$. There is a crucial connection between live simulations and modal logic:

---

[1] Making $L(s)$ finite as well prevents inconsistencies if we convert state propositions into action labels.

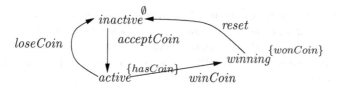

Fig. 2. Slot machine implementation as a doubly labeled transition system

Consider the following modal logic, L_{pos}, which expresses liveness or "possibility" properties [33], where $p \in \text{AP}$ and $a \in \text{Act}$:

$$\phi ::= \top \mid p \mid \phi_1 \wedge \phi_2 \mid \phi_1 \vee \phi_2 \mid \langle a \rangle \, \phi \qquad (1)$$

The diamond modality denotes the possibility of an a-transition. For a DLTS, $\mathcal{K}$, we define $\| \phi \| \subseteq \Sigma_K$ by induction on the grammar for ϕ:

$\| \top \| \stackrel{\text{def}}{=} \Sigma_K$,

$\| p \| \stackrel{\text{def}}{=} \{ s \in \Sigma_K \mid p \in L(s) \}$,

$\| \phi_1 \wedge \phi_2 \| \stackrel{\text{def}}{=} \| \phi_1 \| \cap \| \phi_2 \|$,

$\| \phi_1 \vee \phi_2 \| \stackrel{\text{def}}{=} \| \phi_1 \| \cup \| \phi_2 \|$,

$\| \langle a \rangle \, \phi \| \stackrel{\text{def}}{=} \{ s \in \Sigma_K \mid$ for some s', $s \rightarrow^a s'$ and $s' \in \| \phi \| \}$.

Proposition 1 (Logical characterization). *[18] Let $\mathcal{C}$ and $\mathcal{A}$ be finitely-branching DLTSs and $s \in \Sigma_C$, $t \in \Sigma_A$. Then $s \prec_{live} t$ iff for all $\phi \in L_{\text{pos}}$, $[s \in \| \phi \| \Rightarrow t \in \| \phi \|]$.*

Thus, to calculate liveness properties of an implementation, $\mathcal{A}$, we construct a model, $\mathcal{C}$, and calculate the greatest live simulation. Then, liveness properties that are deduced to hold for $\mathcal{C}$'s states will hold for the corresponding states in $\mathcal{A}$. Dually, we might model an implementation, $\mathcal{C}$, by an abstract model, $\mathcal{A}$, and use the latter to *refute* liveness properties of $\mathcal{C}$.

Safe simulations. The dual of a live simulation is a *safe* one: a simulation, $Q \subseteq \Sigma_C \times \Sigma_A$, is *safe* if $Q(s,t)$ implies $L(s) \supseteq L(t)$, for all $s \in \Sigma_C$ and $t \in \Sigma_A$. There is a greatest safe simulation, $\prec_{safe}$, on $\Sigma_C \times \Sigma_A$. The logic L_{nec} expresses safety or "necessarily" properties [33], where $p \in \text{AP}$ and $a \in \text{Act}$:

$$\phi ::= \top \mid p \mid \phi_1 \wedge \phi_2 \mid \phi_1 \vee \phi_2 \mid [a]\phi \qquad (2)$$

We define $\| \phi \| \subseteq \Sigma_K$ for the first four clauses in the same manner as for the logic L_{pos}, and we define $\| [a]\phi \| \stackrel{\text{def}}{=} \{ s \in \Sigma_K \mid$ for all s', $s \rightarrow^a s'$ implies $s' \in \| \phi \| \}$ as the meaning of the box modality.

Proposition 2 (Logical characterization). *Let $\mathcal{C}$ and $\mathcal{A}$ be finitely-branching DLTSs and $s \in \Sigma_C$, $t \in \Sigma_A$. Then $s \prec_{safe} t$ iff for all $\phi \in L_{\text{nec}}$, $[t \in \| \phi \| \Rightarrow s \in \| \phi \|]$.*

Thus, to calculate safety properties of an implementation, $\mathcal{C}$, we construct $\mathcal{A}$ and calculate a safe simulation. Then, safety properties that hold for $\mathcal{A}$'s states will hold for the corresponding states in $\mathcal{C}$. (This is the standard approach in *abstract interpretation* studies [8,36].) Dually, we might model an implementation, $\mathcal{A}$, by an abstract model, $\mathcal{C}$, and use the latter to *refute* safety properties of $\mathcal{A}$.

3   Modal Transition Systems

Kripke MTSs allow us to freely combine safety *and* liveness properties in property validation *and* refutation. An MTS's "loose" transitions — that is, transitions that may or may not be present in the final implementation — are labeled as *may-transitions*, and "tight" transitions, which must be preserved in the final implementation, are labeled as *must-transitions* [27]. Review Figure 1. With this intuition, every must-transition is by definition a may-transition. These ideas also apply to the atomic properties that label an MTS's states, giving us the modal version of DLTSs, which we call a *Kripke MTS*:

Definition 3 (Kripke MTS). *A Kripke MTS is a tuple $\mathcal{K} = \langle \Sigma_K, \mathsf{Act}, \mathsf{AP}, \overset{must}{\longrightarrow}, \overset{may}{\longrightarrow}, L^{must}, L^{may} \rangle$, where both $\langle \Sigma_K, \mathsf{Act}, \mathsf{AP}, \overset{must}{\longrightarrow}, L^{must} \rangle$ and $\langle \Sigma_K, \mathsf{Act}, \mathsf{AP}, \overset{may}{\longrightarrow}, L^{may} \rangle$ are DLTSs with $\overset{must}{\longrightarrow} \subseteq \overset{may}{\longrightarrow}$ and $L^{must}(s) \subseteq L^{may}(s)$, for all $s \in \Sigma_K$.*

Note the pairings: $\overset{must}{\longrightarrow}$ and L^{must} are paired, because they define a system of transitions and properties that *must* be preserved in any implementation of the Kripke MTS; $\overset{may}{\longrightarrow}$ and L^{may} are paired, because they define a system of transitions and properties that *may* be preserved in any implementation. For a Kripke MTS $\mathcal{C}$ to be a refinement of a Kripke MTS $\mathcal{A}$, it must preserve all must-aspects of $\mathcal{A}$ and it may selectively discard $\mathcal{A}$'s may-aspects:

Definition 4 (Refinement). *A refinement between Kripke MTSs $\mathcal{C}$ and $\mathcal{A}$ is a relation $Q \subseteq \Sigma_C \times \Sigma_A$ such that, for all $s \in \Sigma_C$ and $t \in \Sigma_A$, if $Q(s,t)$, then*

1. *if $t \to_a^{must} t'$, then for some $s' \in \Sigma_C$, $s \to_a^{must} s'$ and $Q(s',t')$;*
2. *if $s \to_a^{may} s'$, then for some $t' \in \Sigma_A$, $t \to_a^{may} t'$ and $Q(s',t')$;*
3. *$L^{must}(t) \subseteq L^{must}(s)$; and*
4. *$L^{may}(s) \subseteq L^{may}(t)$.*

A Kripke MTS such that $\overset{must}{\longrightarrow} = \overset{may}{\longrightarrow}$ and $L^{must} = L^{may}$ is *concrete*, that is, it is a doubly labeled transition system [12], a "final implementation." As usual, for Kripke MTSs $\mathcal{C}$ and $\mathcal{A}$, there is a greatest refinement relation $\prec_r$.

Next, consider the logic $\mathcal{L}$:

$$\phi ::= \top \mid p \mid \phi_1 \wedge \phi_2 \mid \langle a \rangle \phi \mid [a]\phi \tag{3}$$

where $p \in \mathsf{AP}$ and $a \in \mathsf{Act}$.

Definition 5 (Semantics of modal logic). *For a Kripke MTS $\mathcal{K}$ and any $\phi \in \mathcal{L}$, we define a semantics $\lVert \phi \rVert \in \mathcal{P}(\Sigma_K) \times \mathcal{P}(\Sigma_K)$, where $\mathcal{P}(\Sigma_K)$ is the powerset of Σ_K, ordered by set inclusion, and $\lVert \phi \rVert^{\mathrm{nec}}$ and $\lVert \phi \rVert^{\mathrm{pos}}$ are the projection of $\lVert \phi \rVert$ to its first and second component, respectively:*

1. $\lVert \top \rVert \stackrel{\text{def}}{=} \langle \Sigma_K, \Sigma_K \rangle$;
2. $\lVert p \rVert \stackrel{\text{def}}{=} \langle \{s \in \Sigma_K \mid p \in L^{must}(s)\}, \{s \in \Sigma_K \mid p \in L^{may}(s)\} \rangle$;
3. $\lVert \phi_1 \wedge \phi_2 \rVert \stackrel{\text{def}}{=} \langle \lVert \phi_1 \rVert^{\mathrm{nec}} \cap \lVert \phi_2 \rVert^{\mathrm{nec}}, \lVert \phi_1 \rVert^{\mathrm{pos}} \cap \lVert \phi_2 \rVert^{\mathrm{pos}} \rangle$;
4. $\lVert \langle a \rangle \phi \rVert \stackrel{\text{def}}{=} \langle \{s \in \Sigma_K \mid$ *for some* s', $s \rightarrow^a_{must} s'$ *and* $s' \in \lVert \phi \rVert^{\mathrm{nec}}\}$,
   $\{s \in \Sigma_K \mid$ *for some* s', $s \rightarrow^a_{may} s'$ *and* $s' \in \lVert \phi \rVert^{\mathrm{pos}}\} \rangle$
5. $\lVert [a]\phi \rVert \stackrel{\text{def}}{=} \langle \{s \in S \mid$ *for all* s', $s \rightarrow^a_{may} s'$ *implies* $s' \in \lVert \phi \rVert^{must}\}$,
   $\{s \in S \mid$ *for all* s', $s \rightarrow^a_{must} s'$ *implies* $s' \in \lVert \phi \rVert^{may}\} \rangle$,

The "necessarily" interpretation, $\lVert \phi \rVert^{\mathrm{nec}}$, is an under-approximation of those states for which a proposition necessarily holds true (that is, the states for which the proposition holds for all future refinements/implementations). Dually, the "possibly" interpretation, $\lVert \phi \rVert^{\mathrm{pos}}$, is an over-approximation of those states for which there is some refinement for which the proposition holds. The semantics $\lVert \phi \rVert^{\mathrm{nec}}$ is the one given by Larsen [26]; it produces this result:

Proposition 3 (Logical characterization). *[26][2] Let $\mathcal{C}$ and $\mathcal{A}$ be finitely-branching[3] Kripke MTSs and $s \in \Sigma_C$, $t \in \Sigma_A$. Then $s \prec_r t$ iff for all $\phi \in \mathcal{L}$, $[t \in \lVert \phi \rVert^{\mathrm{nec}} \Rightarrow s \in \lVert \phi \rVert^{\mathrm{nec}}]$.*

This result tells us to build an MTS, $\mathcal{A}$, that abstracts an implementation, $\mathcal{C}$. Both safety *and* liveness properties can be validated on $\mathcal{A}$, and they carry over to $\mathcal{C}$. Using the "possibly" interpretation, a new logical characterization follows, allowing us to refute safety and liveness properties of an implementation, $\mathcal{C}$, by refuting them on $\mathcal{A}$:

Proposition 4 (Logical characterization). *Let $\mathcal{C}$ and $\mathcal{A}$ be finitely-branching Kripke MTSs and $s \in \Sigma_C$, $t \in \Sigma_A$. Then $s \prec_r t$ iff for all $\phi \in \mathcal{L}$, $[s \in \lVert \phi \rVert^{\mathrm{pos}} \Rightarrow t \in \lVert \phi \rVert^{\mathrm{pos}}]$.*

Negation and Invariants. We can retain both validation and refutation on Kripke MTSs if we add negation and recursive definition to our logic, giving the modal-mu calculus [25,2], ActMu:

$$\phi ::= \top \mid p \mid Z \mid \neg\phi \mid \phi_1 \wedge \phi_2 \mid \langle a \rangle \phi \mid [a]\phi \mid \mu Z.\phi \qquad (4)$$

where p ranges over AP, Z over a (countable) set of variables, $a \in$ Act, and the bodies ϕ in $\mu Z.\phi$ are formally monotone. Disjunction ($\vee$) and implication ($\rightarrow$) are derived as $\neg(\neg\phi \wedge \neg\psi)$ and $\neg(\phi \wedge \neg\psi)$, respectively. This logic is very expressive,

---

[2] Larsen's results were proved for MTSs.
[3] For all $s \in \Sigma_K$ and $a \in$ Act, the sets $\{s' \in \Sigma_K \mid s \rightarrow^{may}_a s'\}$ and $L^{may}(s)$ are finite.

and important specification logics like CTL* can be embedded into it [10]. We require environments, ρ, mapping variables Z to elements of $\mathcal{P}(\Sigma_K) \times \mathcal{P}(\Sigma_K)$. The semantics, $\llbracket \phi \rrbracket_\rho \in \mathcal{P}(\Sigma_K) \times \mathcal{P}(\Sigma_K)$, is defined as for $\mathcal{L}$, but parametric in an environment ρ; this semantics is essentially the one in [19]. Given the must- and may-aspects of an MTS, the semantics of negation is delicate, and we follow Kelb [24] and Levi [28]. The semantics of the remaining clauses, Z and $\mu Z.\phi$, are dealt with in a standard manner:

1. $\llbracket Z \rrbracket_\rho \stackrel{\text{def}}{=} \rho(Z)$;
2. $\llbracket \neg\phi \rrbracket_\rho \stackrel{\text{def}}{=} \langle \Sigma_K \setminus \llbracket \phi \rrbracket_\rho^{\text{pos}}, \Sigma_K \setminus \llbracket \phi \rrbracket_\rho^{\text{nec}} \rangle$;
3. $\llbracket \mu Z.\phi \rrbracket_\rho$ is the least fixed point of the monotone functional
$$d \mapsto \llbracket \phi \rrbracket_{\rho[Z \mapsto d]} : \mathcal{P}(\Sigma_K) \times \mathcal{P}(\Sigma_K) \to \mathcal{P}(\Sigma_K) \times \mathcal{P}(\Sigma_K).$$

Note the semantics of negation: "*necessarily* $\neg\phi$" is "not *possibly* ϕ," and "*possibly* $\neg\phi$" is "not *necessarily* ϕ".

Theorem 1 (Soundness and consistency of semantics). *For any Kripke MTS $\mathcal{K}$, $\phi, \psi \in$ ActMu, and environment ρ:*

1. $\llbracket \phi \rrbracket_\rho^{\text{nec}} \subseteq \llbracket \phi \rrbracket_\rho^{\text{pos}}$;
2. $\llbracket \phi \wedge \neg\phi \rrbracket_\rho^{\text{nec}} = \emptyset$; and $\llbracket \phi \vee \neg\phi \rrbracket_\rho^{\text{pos}} = \Sigma_K$. That is, the semantics is consistent for $\llbracket \ \rrbracket^{\text{nec}}$ and "complete" for $\llbracket \ \rrbracket^{\text{pos}}$;
3. if $s \prec_r t$, then $t \in \llbracket \phi \rrbracket_\rho^{\text{nec}}$ implies $s \in \llbracket \phi \rrbracket_\rho^{\text{nec}}$; and $s \in \llbracket \phi \rrbracket_\rho^{\text{pos}}$ implies $t \in \llbracket \phi \rrbracket_\rho^{\text{pos}}$. That is, the semantics is sound;
4. if $\mathcal{K}$ is concrete, then $\llbracket \phi \rrbracket_\rho^{\text{nec}} = \llbracket \phi \rrbracket_\rho^{\text{pos}}$ and corresponds to the standard semantics for doubly labeled transition systems (as given for CTL* in [12]).

The semantics of negation behaves classically, that is, $\llbracket \neg\neg\phi \rrbracket = \llbracket \phi \rrbracket$ and $\llbracket \neg\langle a \rangle \phi \rrbracket = \llbracket [a]\neg\phi \rrbracket$ hold. The underlying interpretations $\llbracket \phi \rrbracket^{\text{nec}}$ and $\llbracket \phi \rrbracket^{\text{pos}}$, however, are not classical, but *three valued*, in the sense that a state, s, can possess a property, ϕ, in only three possible ways:

1. $s \in \llbracket \phi \rrbracket^{\text{nec}}$ (and hence, $s \in \llbracket \phi \rrbracket^{\text{pos}}$): "$\phi$ necessarily holds for s."
2. $s \in \llbracket \phi \rrbracket^{\text{pos}}$ and $s \notin \llbracket \phi \rrbracket^{\text{nec}}$ ($s \in \llbracket \phi \wedge \neg\phi \rrbracket^{\text{pos}}$): "$\phi$ possibly holds for s."
3. $s \notin \llbracket \phi \rrbracket^{\text{pos}}$ (hence, $s \notin \llbracket \phi \rrbracket^{\text{nec}}$): "$\phi$ does not possibly hold for s."

Note the loss of precision in the second case above: $s \in \llbracket \phi \wedge \neg\phi \rrbracket^{\text{pos}}$; there cannot be a final implementation which satisfies $\phi \wedge \neg\phi$. For the partial Kripke structures of Section 4, a more precise analysis is possible [4].

To finish the technical development, we note that the Kripke MTS semantics and its properties adapt to the scenario where Σ_K is no longer flat. For finite-state models, meanings $\llbracket \phi \rrbracket_\rho$ are elements of the mixed power domain $\mathsf{M}[\Sigma_K]$ [15,17,20].[4] This lets us adapt standard abstract interpretation studies

---

[4] Elements of $\mathsf{M}[\Sigma_K]$ are pairs $\langle H, S \rangle$, where H is a Scott-closed lower subset and S a Scott-compact upper subset of Σ_K such that H equals $\{s \in \Sigma_K \mid \exists s' \in H \cap S : s \leq s'\}$. This consistency condition replaces the inclusion requirement ($H \subseteq S$) of the discrete case.

and even lets us define and manipulate a fully abstract domain of MTSs by the isomorphism, $D \cong \prod_{a \in \mathrm{Act}} M[D]$ [20].

Abstract Kripke MTSs. Let $\mathcal{C} = (\Sigma_K, \mathrm{Act}, \mathrm{AP}, \longrightarrow, L)$ be a possibly infinite-state DLTS. Given a finite set of boolean predicates $\{p_1, p_2, \ldots, p_n\}$, we can derive a finite-state abstract Kripke MTS $\mathcal{A}$: abstract states, a, are equivalence classes of states that satisfy exactly the same predicates p_i in $\mathcal{C}$; abstract transitions are defined, as in [11], by (i) $[s] \rightarrow^a_{must} [s']$ iff for all $s_* \in [s]$, there exists $s'_* \in [s']$ such that $s_* \rightarrow^a s'_*$ and (ii) $[s] \rightarrow^a_{may} [s']$ iff there exist $s_* \in [s]$ and $s'_* \in [s']$ such that $s_* \rightarrow^a s'_*$; finally, propositions are defined as $L^{must}([s]) \stackrel{def}{=} \bigcap_{s' \in [s]} L(s')$ and $L^{may}([s]) \stackrel{def}{=} \bigcup_{s' \in [s]} L(s')$.

This refinement relationship is well behaved and induces *two* Galois connections [8], one between the concrete model $\mathcal{C}$ and the may-component of $\mathcal{A}$, and one between $\mathcal{C}$ and $\mathcal{A}$'s must-component. This phemonemon is foreshadowed by the universal ($\alpha^\forall$) and existential ($\alpha^\exists$) abstraction maps of Cousot and Cousot [9], which extract may- and must-behaviors from linear-time models.

It is immediate that $\mathcal{C}$ is a refinement of $\mathcal{A}$, giving us a sound tool for verifying *and* refuting *all* properties expressed in the modal mu-calculus. With some effort, this approach applies to refinements to non-concrete Kripke MTSs as well.

4   Abstracting Control and Data

Partial Kripke Structures. For model checking partial state spaces, Bruns and Godefroid devised *partial Kripke structures* [3]:

Definition 6. *A* partial Kripke structure[5] *is a 4-tuple,* $\mathcal{K} = (\Sigma_K, \mathrm{AP}, \longrightarrow, L)$, *where* Σ_K *is a set of states,* AP *is a set of atomic propositions,* $\longrightarrow \subseteq \Sigma_K \times \Sigma_K$ *is a set of transitions, and* $L \colon \Sigma_K \times \mathrm{AP} \to \mathbf{3}$ *is a labeling function, where* $\mathbf{3}$ *is the set* $\{\bot, \mathrm{F}, \mathrm{T}\}$ *endowed with the* information ordering $\bot \leq \mathrm{F}$ *and* $\bot \leq \mathrm{T}$.

Figure 3 depicts three partial Kripke structures with initial states s_1, s_2, and s_3, respectively [3]. We write $p = v$ at a state s to denote $L(s, p) = v$. These systems have different information regarding the truth of p at their initial states and their rightmost successor states. At their leftmost successor states, all three systems leave the truth status of p unresolved. Below, we show that these systems, their abstraction notion and temporal logic semantics are special instances of the corresponding notions for Kripke MTSs. Partial Kripke structures are related in the following fashion:

Definition 7 (Completeness order). *A* completeness order *[3] on two partial Kripke structures is a binary relation* $Q \subseteq \Sigma_C \times \Sigma_A$ *such that* $Q(s, t)$ *implies*

1. *for all* $p \in \mathrm{AP}$, $L(s, p) \leq L(t, p)$ *in the information ordering,*
2. *if* $s \longrightarrow s'$, *then there is some* $t' \in \Sigma_A$ *with* $t \longrightarrow t'$ *and* $Q(s', t')$, *and*
3. *if* $t \longrightarrow t'$, *then there is some* $s' \in \Sigma_C$ *with* $s \longrightarrow s'$ *and* $Q(s', t')$.

---

[5] We assume that these structures are finitely branching.

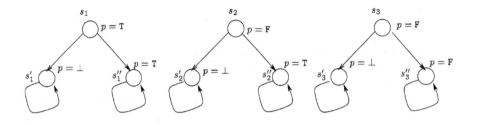

Fig. 3. Three partial Kripke structures [3]

In usual fashion, we write $s \triangleleft t$ if there is a completeness order Q in which $Q(s,t)$ holds. Properties of states of partial Kripke structures are expressed in the logic PML: $\phi ::= p \mid \neg\phi \mid \phi \wedge \phi \mid \Diamond\phi$. Bruns and Godefroid require a second, *truth ordering* on the set $\{\bot, F, T\}$ for defining a three-valued semantics for this logic: $F < \bot < T$. Denotations $[s \models \phi]$ are elements of $\{F < \bot < T\}$:

$$[s \models p] \stackrel{\text{def}}{=} L(s,p) \tag{5}$$
$$[s \models \neg\phi] \stackrel{\text{def}}{=} \text{neg}[s \models \phi]$$
$$[s \models \phi_1 \wedge \phi_2] \stackrel{\text{def}}{=} \min([s \models \phi_1], [s \models \phi_2])$$
$$[s \models \Diamond\phi] \stackrel{\text{def}}{=} \max\{[s' \models \phi] \mid s \longrightarrow s'\},$$

where neg is strict logical complement and min and max are meet and join in the truth ordering, respectively. Bruns and Godefroid logically characterize the completeness preorder: For partial Kripke structures C and A, $s \in \Sigma_C$, $t \in \Sigma_A$, $s \triangleleft t$ iff for all ϕ in PML, $[s \models \phi] \leq [t \models \phi]$ in the truth ordering.

The embedding of partial Kripke structures into Kripke MTS rests on the order-isomorphism $\Psi: (E \to \mathbf{3}) \to M[E]$ between the mixed power domain $M[E]$ and the set of all functions $E \to \mathbf{3}$, ordered pointwise in the information ordering — if E is discrete; identify a function $f: E \to \mathbf{3}$ with the pair $\Psi f \stackrel{\text{def}}{=} \langle f^{-1}\{T\}, f^{-1}\{\bot, T\}\rangle$. We then translate a partial Kripke structure, K, into the Kripke MTS, $K' = (\Sigma_K, \{*\}, \text{AP}, \longrightarrow, \longrightarrow, L^{must}, L^{may})$,[6] where the propositional component $(L^{must}(s), L^{may}(s))$ is defined as ΨL.

Proposition 5 (Correspondence of semantics). *For partial Kripke structure, K, and its Kripke MTS translation, K', for all $s \in \Sigma_K$ and ϕ in PML, $[\![\phi]\!] = \Psi(\lambda s.[s \models \phi])$. The inverse $\triangleleft^{-1}$ of the greatest completeness order $\triangleleft$ on K is the greatest refinement of its Kripke MTS translation K'.*

The full MTS formulation, unlike partial Kripke structures, allows for modalities on transitions and remains well defined when the domain of states is nonflat, making it applicable to conventional abstraction frameworks [8,7]. To illustrate

---

[6] We identify $\Sigma_K \times \Sigma_K$ with $\Sigma_K \times \{*\} \times \Sigma_K$.

model checks on such systems, consider $\phi \stackrel{\text{def}}{=} \mu Z.p \vee ([*]Z \wedge \langle * \rangle \top)$, saying "$p$ holds eventually on all paths" [2], on the systems of Figure 3.[7] Our semantics computes $s_1 \in \| \phi \|^{\text{nec}}$, since p is true at s_1; $s_2 \in \| \phi \|^{\text{pos}}$, since p may be true at s_2'; and $s_3 \notin \| \phi \|^{\text{pos}}$, since there is a path on which p is never true.

Partial Bisimulations. Partial Kripke structures abstract propositional information only. Bruns and Godefroid also studied systems that abstract state transitions, the so-called extended transition systems [3], and their partial bisimulation [29,39]:

Definition 8. *An* extended transition system (ETS)[8] *[3] is a 4-tuple $\mathcal{E} = (\Sigma_E, \mathsf{Act}, \longrightarrow, \uparrow)$, where Σ_E is a set of states, $\longrightarrow \subseteq \Sigma_E \times \mathsf{Act} \times \Sigma_E$ is a set of transitions, and $\uparrow \subseteq \Sigma_E \times \mathsf{Act}$ is a* divergence relation.

Read $s \uparrow a$ as "some of the a-transitions from s in the full model may be missing at s in the ETS" [3]. We write $s \downarrow a$ when $s \uparrow a$ fails to hold, meaning that all a-transitions from s in the full state space are present at s in the ETS.

Definition 9. *Given ETSs, $\mathcal{E}$ and $\mathcal{F}$, a* partial bisimulation *[29,39] (*divergence preorder *[3]) is a subset, Q, of $\Sigma_E \times \Sigma_F$ such that $Q(s,t)$ implies*

1. *whenever $s \rightarrow_a s'$, there exists some $t' \in \Sigma_F$ such that $t \rightarrow_a t'$ and $Q(s',t')$;*
2. *if $s \downarrow a$, then (i) $t \downarrow a$, and (ii) whenever $t \rightarrow_a t'$, there exists some $s' \in \Sigma_E$ such that $s \rightarrow_a s'$ and $Q(s',t')$.*

Every ETS has a greatest partial bisimulation, $\sqsubseteq$. We embed $\mathcal{E}$ into a Kripke MTS $\mathbf{T}[\mathcal{E}] \stackrel{\text{def}}{=} (\Sigma_E, \mathsf{Act}, \emptyset, \stackrel{must}{\longrightarrow}, \stackrel{may}{\longrightarrow}, \emptyset, \emptyset)$ by (i) $s \rightarrow_a^{must} s'$ iff $s \rightarrow_a s'$ and (ii) $s \rightarrow_a^{may} s'$ iff ($s \rightarrow_a s'$ or $s \uparrow a$). Note how $\uparrow$ makes $\mathcal{E}$ three-valued in may-transitions.

Theorem 2. *Given an ETS $\mathcal{E}$, $\mathbf{T}[\mathcal{E}]$ is an MTS satisfying, for all $s \in \Sigma_E$, $(\exists s' \in \Sigma_E: s \rightarrow_{may}^a s' \wedge s \nrightarrow_{must}^a s') \to (\forall s'' \in \Sigma_E: s \rightarrow_{may}^a s'')$. The inverse $\sqsubseteq^{-1}$ of the greatest partial bisimulation $\sqsubseteq$ on $\mathcal{E}$ is $\prec_r$, the greatest refinement on $\mathbf{T}[\mathcal{E}]$. The intuitionistic semantics for Hennessy-Milner logic in [29] corresponds to the semantics $\| \cdot \|^{\text{nec}}$ of that fragment of* ActMu *on $\mathbf{T}[\mathcal{E}]$.*

5   Abstracting Data: Shape-Based Pointer Analysis

An important form of pointer analysis is *shape analysis* [6,14,22,35,40], where the contents of heap storage is approximated by a graph whose nodes denote objects and whose arcs denote the values of the objects' fields. Local ("stack") variables that point into the heap are drawn as arcs pointing to the nodes.

Figure 4 displays the syntax of such *shape graphs*. The example in the Figure depicts an approximation to a singly linked list of length at least two: Objects are circles; a double-circled object is a "summary node," meaning that it possibly

---

[7] We use $*$ in ϕ to denote the sole action type.

[8] We assume that all such structures are finitely branching.

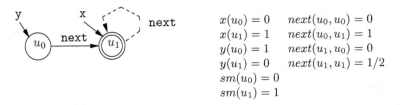

$$x(u_0) = 0 \quad next(u_0, u_0) = 0$$
$$x(u_1) = 1 \quad next(u_0, u_1) = 1$$
$$y(u_0) = 1 \quad next(u_1, u_0) = 0$$
$$y(u_1) = 0 \quad next(u_1, u_1) = 1/2$$
$$sm(u_0) = 0$$
$$sm(u_1) = 1$$

Fig. 4. Shape graph and its coding as predicates

$T[\texttt{x = y}] : x'(v) = y(v);$ all other predicates $p' = p$
$T[\texttt{x.next = y}] : next'(v_1, v_2) = next(v_1, v_2) \wedge (sm(v_1) \vee \neg x(v_1)) \vee (x(v_1) \wedge y(v_2));$
   all other $p' = p$
$T[\texttt{x = y.next}] : x'(v) = \exists v_1.y(v_1) \wedge next(v_1, v);$ all other $p' = p$
$T[\texttt{x = new Node()}] :$ let v_{new} be a fresh node, in $x'(v) = (v = v_{new});$
   all other $p'(v) = (p(v) \wedge (v \neq v_{new}))$

Effect of **x = y** on Figure 4:   Effect of **x.next = y** on Figure 4:

Fig. 5. Transfer functions on shape graphs

represents more than one concrete object. Since the objects were constructed from a class/struct that owns a **next** field, objects have **next**-labeled arcs. For discussion, the objects are named u_0 and u_1, and local variables x and y point to the objects. A solid arc denotes that a field definitely points to an object; a dotted arc means the field possibly points to it. Thus, the self-arc on u_1 must be dotted because u_1 possibly denotes multiple nodes, meaning that a **next** dereference possibly points to one of the concrete objects denoted by the node.

Shape graphs can be encoded in various ways; in Figure 4, we display a coding due to Sagiv, Reps, and Wilhelm [35], who define local-variable points-to information with unary predicates and field points-to information with binary ones. The predicates produce the answers "necessarily points to" (1), "possibly points to" (1/2), and "not points to" (0), where the values are ordered $0 \leq 1/2 \leq 1$. The predicate, sm, notes which nodes are summary nodes.

Shape graphs can be used as data values for a data-flow analysis, where a program's transfer functions transform an input shape graph to an output one. The transfer functions for assignment and object construction appear in Figure 5, where p' denotes predicate p updated by the transfer function, $T[\texttt{C}]$, for command C. The transfer functions are written as predicate-logic formulas, where conjunction is interpreted as meet; disjunction as join; and negation as strict complement. A data-flow analysis is assembled in the usual way [8,16,23, 31,32]:

1. a control-flow graph is extracted from the source program, where transfer functions annotate the arcs of the graph;
2. a finite-height sup-semilattice of data-flow values (here, based on shape graphs) is defined, where values from the semilattice will be collected at the nodes (program points) of the control-flow graph.
3. a least fixed-point calculation is undertaken on the flow equations induced by the control-flow graph.

Step 2 is the most interesting, in that a *single* shape graph might be collected at each node ("independent attribute" analysis, e.g., [40]) or a set of shape graphs might be collected ("relational" analysis, e.g., [35]). In the former case, the join operation weakens solid arcs into dotted ones when dissimilar graphs are joined; in the latter case, a bounded set union (*widening* [8]) operation is employed so that no infinite set of graphs is constructed.

Modal Shape Graphs. The dotted and solid arcs of shape graphs strongly suggest that modal transition systems lurk in the foundations, and so they do:

Definition 10 (Modal shape graph). *A* modal shape graph (MSG) *is a Kripke MTS* $\mathcal{M} \stackrel{\text{def}}{=} (\Sigma_M, \mathsf{Act}, \mathsf{AP}, \stackrel{must}{\longrightarrow}, \stackrel{may}{\longrightarrow}, L^{must}, L^{may})$, *where* AP *is a set of local variables along with the distinguished predicate,* sm, Act *is a set of field names, and* Σ_M *is a set of heap objects.*

Our modelling sets $\mathbf{x} \in L^{must}(s)$ when a solid arc shows that $\mathbf{x}$ points to object s. Similarly, $L^{may}(s)$ collects the names of local variables that possibly point to it. When s is a summary node, then $sm \in L^{must}(s)$. Of course, $\stackrel{must}{\longrightarrow}$ and $\stackrel{may}{\longrightarrow}$ model the solid and dotted field-labeled arcs, respectively. It is easy to translate shape graphs, like that in Figure 4, into MTS format:

$$\Sigma_M = \{u_0, u_1\} \qquad \mathsf{Act} = \{next\} \qquad \mathsf{AP} = \{x, y, sm\}$$
$$\stackrel{must}{\longrightarrow} = \{(u_0, next, u_1)\} \qquad \stackrel{may}{\longrightarrow} = \{(u_1, next, u_1)\}$$
$$L^{must}(u_0) = \{y\}, \quad L^{must}(u_1) = \{x, sm\}$$
$$L^{may}(u_0) = \emptyset, \quad L^{may}(u_1) = \emptyset$$

A concrete, run-time execution state is coded as a concrete modal shape graph.[9]

Transfer Functions. There is little challenge in writing the transfer functions for modal shape graphs: Given a modal shape graph $\mathcal{M}$, let $\mathcal{M}[\mathsf{C}]$ be the graph obtained from $\mathcal{M}$ by executing command C. We only specify those aspects of $\mathcal{M}[\mathsf{C}]$ that are different from $\mathcal{M}$:

1. $\mathbf{x}$ = $\mathbf{y}$: For all $s \in \Sigma_M$, $\mathbf{x} \in L[\mathsf{C}]^{must}(s)$ iff $\mathbf{y} \in L^{must}(s)$; and $\mathbf{x} \in L[\mathsf{C}]^{may}(s)$ iff $\mathbf{y} \in L^{may}(s)$.
2. $\mathbf{x}$ = $\mathbf{y}.\mathbf{n}$: For all $s \in \Sigma_M$, $\mathbf{x} \in L[\mathsf{C}]^{must}(s)$ iff $(\exists s' \in S)\, \mathbf{y} \in L^{must}(s')$ and $s' \stackrel{must}{\longrightarrow}_{\mathbf{n}} s$; and $\mathbf{x} \in L[\mathsf{C}]^{may}(s)$ iff $(\exists s' \in S)\, \mathbf{y} \in L^{may}(s')$ and $s' \stackrel{may}{\longrightarrow}_{\mathbf{n}} s$.

---

[9] Where every local variable, $\mathbf{x}$, belongs to at most one $L^{must}(s)$.

3. x.n = y: For all $s \in \Sigma_M$, (i) if $x \in L^{must}(s)$ and there is some s'' with $s \xrightarrow{must}_n s''$, then, for all $s' \in S$, $y \in L[C]^{must}(s')$ implies $s \xrightarrow{must[C]}_n s'$; and (ii) if $x \in L^{may}(s)$ and there is some s'' with $s \xrightarrow{may}_n s''$, then, for all $s' \in S$, $y \in L[C]^{may}(s')$ implies $s \xrightarrow{may[C]}_n s'$. If $sm \in L^{must}(y)$, then all transitions from y are preserved.

4. x = new Node(): Creates a fresh object that is labeled with x. Set $\Sigma_{M[C]} \stackrel{def}{=} \Sigma_M \cup \{s_{new}\}$ ($s_{new} \notin \Sigma_M$); and for all $s \in \Sigma_M$, $x \notin L[C]^{may}(s)$, and $x \in L[C]^{must}(s_{new})$.

Properties as Temporal Formulas. Once a data-flow analysis builds a shape graph, we check the graph for correctness properties that are expressible in the CTL-subset [5,10] of the modal mu-calculus. In [35], such properties are encoded in predicate logic augmented with a transitive closure operator.

Here are examples: The direction relationship [14], stating that an access path exists from the object named by x to an object named by y, is written $D(x,y) \stackrel{def}{=} EF_{next}(x \wedge EF_{next}y)$ — an object, s, has atomic property x iff x points to s. Recall that $EF_a\phi$ states, "there exists a path of a-labeled transitions such that, at some state in the future, ϕ holds true." To validate that there is *necessarily* (*possibly*) a path from s, we check if $s \in \| D(x,y) \|^{nec}$ ($s \in \| D(x,y) \|^{pos}$); to refute existence of a path, we check $s \in \| \neg D(x,y) \|^{nec}$.

The interference relationship [14], saying that pointers x and y have access paths to a common heap node, is written with *inverse* transition relationships of $\xrightarrow{must}$: $I(x,y) \stackrel{def}{=} (EF_{next^{-1}}x) \wedge (EF_{next^{-1}}y)$. We check $s \in \| I(x,y) \|^{pos}$ to see if aliasing of object s by x and y is possible.

Aliasing of pointers can be expressed: For aliasing $\stackrel{def}{=} EF_{next}(\bigvee_{x \neq y} x \wedge y)$, the formulas (a) $AG_{next} \neg$aliasing, (b) $AG_{next} \neg (x \wedge \bigvee_{x \neq y} y)$, and (c) $AG_{next} \neg (x \wedge y)$ can then be used to check: (a) the absense of any kind of aliasing; (b) that x has no alias; and that (c) x and y never point to the same heap node. (Recall that $AG_a\phi$ states, "for all a-paths, it is globally true for all states along the path, that ϕ holds.")

We can check for possibly cyclic data structures. The predicate cyclic $\stackrel{def}{=}$ $\bigvee_{x \in AP} x \wedge EX_{next}EF_{next}x$ states that a heap node is pointed to by some x that has an access path to, presumably the same, heap node pointed to by x. (Recall that $EX_a\phi$ says, "there exists an a-transition to a next state where ϕ holds.")

Improving Precision: The Embedding Theorem and *Focus* Operation. For improving the analysis's precision (e.g., "strong updates"), Sagiv, Wilhelm, and Reps employ a *focus* operation [35], which refines a shape graph into a set of shape-graph variants, such that a predicate that formerly evaluated to 1/2 ("possibly holds") in the original graph now evaluates to 0 or to 1 in every variant. The set of variants must be consistent and complete with regards to the original graph, and an Embedding Theorem is used to make this argument. A more precise, relational, data-flow analysis is the result.

Within the representation of modal shape graphs, the hypotheses of the Embedding Theorem ensure a refinement relation, and the consequences of the Theorem follow from the soundness of refinement (Theorem 1).

The *focus* operation itself defines a *cover*: A set of MTSs, $\mathcal{S}_\mathcal{A}$, *covers* an MTS, $\mathcal{A}$, iff *(i)* for all $\mathcal{K} \in \mathcal{S}_\mathcal{A}$, $\mathcal{K} \prec_r \mathcal{A}$; *(ii)* for every concrete MTS, $\mathcal{C}$, such that $\mathcal{C} \prec_r \mathcal{A}$, there exists some $\mathcal{K} \in \mathcal{S}_\mathcal{A}$ such that $\mathcal{C} \prec_r \mathcal{K}$. Any property that necessarily holds true for all the MTSs in $\mathcal{S}_\mathcal{A}$ holds true for all concrete refinements of $\mathcal{A}$; dually, any property that possibly holds for any MTS in $\mathcal{S}_\mathcal{A}$ holds true for $\mathcal{A}$; thus, $\mathcal{S}_\mathcal{A}$ is consistent and complete regarding the concrete MTSs represented by $\mathcal{A}$.

The *focus* operation in [35] generates one particular shape-graph cover by examining a may-transition reachable from a program variable and refining it to a must-transition in one graph variant, removing it in another graph variant, and splitting the transition's source or destination summary node in a third variant. Of course, there can exist other forms of *focus* operations; in all cases, a cover must be defined.

6   Conclusions

The case studies demonstrate how modal transition systems provide a foundation for development of analyses whose outcomes take the form, "necessarily" (yes), "possibly" (maybe), and "not possibly" (no). These applications go beyond the traditional use for MTSs (proving properties of loose specifications). In addition to the two examples in this paper, there are other program analyses that are neatly expressed via Kripke MTSs; two noteworthy ones are

- Whaley and Rinard's *points-to escape analysis* [40], where multi-threaded programs are analyzed for object sharing. Shape graphs are generated, where solid arcs represent assignments made by the thread being analyzed, and dotted arcs represent assignments made by other threads executing in parallel. Jackson's Z-like Alloy logic [21] is used to model check the graphs.
- Interprocedural data-flow analysis [34,36], where graphs are used to denote control flow. Those program transitions that must occur (e.g., intraprocedural transitions) are denoted by solid arcs; transitions that might occur (e.g., procedure call- and return-arcs, where the exact procedure invoked or the exact invocation point is uncertain) are denoted by may-arcs.

Other applications await discovery (e.g., cartesian abstraction in the SLAM project [1]), and the relationship of our semantic framework to earlier studies of 3-valued modal logic [13,30,37] and intuitionistic modal logic [38] deserves examination as well.

References

1. T. Ball, A. Podelski, and S. K. Rajamani. Boolean and Cartesian Abstraction for Model Checking C Programs. Personal communication, December 2000.
2. J. C. Bradfield. *Verifying Temporal Properties Of Systems*. Birkhäuser, Boston, Mass., 1991.

3. G. Bruns and P. Godefroid. Model Checking Partial State Spaces with 3-Valued Temporal Logics. In *Proceedings of the 11th Conference on Computer Aided Verification*, volume 1633 of *Lecture Notes in Computer Science*, pages 274–287. Springer Verlag, July 1999.

4. G. Bruns and P. Godefroid. Gernalized Model Checking: Reasoning about Partial State Spaces. In *Proceedings of CONCUR'2000 (11th International Conference on Concurrency Theory)*, volume 1877 of *Lecture Notes in Computer Science*, pages 168–182. Springer Verlag, August 2000.

5. J. R. Burch, E. M. Clarke, D. L. Dill K. L. McMillan, and J. Hwang. Symbolic model checking: 10^{20} states and beyond. Proceedings of the Fifth Annual Symposium on Logic in Computer Science, June 1990.

6. D. Chase, M. Wegman, and F. Zadeck. Analysis of pointers and structures. In *SIGPLAN Conf. on Prog. Lang. Design and Implementation*, pages 296–310. ACM Press, 1990.

7. E.M. Clarke, O. Grumberg, and D.E. Long. Model checking and abstraction. *ACM Transactions on Programming Languages and Systems*, 16(5):1512–1542, 1994.

8. P. Cousot and R. Cousot. Abstract interpretation: a unified lattice model for static analysis of programs. In *Proc. 4th ACM Symp. on Principles of Programming Languages*, pages 238–252. ACM Press, 1977.

9. P. Cousot and R. Cousot. Temporal abstract interpretation. In *Conference Record of the Twentyseventh Annual ACM SIGPLAN-SIGACT Symposium on Principles of Programming Languages*, pages 12–25, Boston, Mass., January 2000. ACM Press, New York, NY.

10. M. Dam. CTL* and ECTL* as Fragments of the Modal mu-Calculus. *Theoretical Computer Science*, 126:77–96, 1994.

11. D. Dams. *Abstract interpretation and partition refinement for model chec king*. PhD thesis, Technische Universiteit Eindhoven, The Netherlands, 1996.

12. R. de Nicola and F. Vaandrager. Three Logics for Branching Bisimulation. *Journal of the Association of Computing Machinery*, 42(2):458–487, March 1995.

13. M. Fitting. Many-valued modal logics. *Fundamenta Informaticae*, 17:55–73, 1992.

14. R. Ghiya and L. J. Hendren. Is it a Tree, a DAG, or a Cyclic Graph? A Shape Analysis for Heap-Directed Pointers in C. In *Proceedings of the 23rd ACM SIGPLAN-SIGACT Symposium on Principles of Programming Languages*, pages 1–15, 1996.

15. C. Gunter. The mixed power domain. *Theoretical Computer Science*, 103:311–334, 1992.

16. M. Hecht. *Flow Analysis of Computer Programs*. Elsevier, 1977.

17. R. Heckmann. Power domains and second order predicates. *Theoretical Computer Science*, 111:59–88, 1993.

18. M. C. B. Hennessy and Robin Milner. Algebraic laws for non-determinism and concurrency. *JACM*, 32:137–161, 1985.

19. M. Huth. A Unifying Framework for Model Checking Labeled Kripke Structures, Modal Transition Systems, and Interval Transition Systems. In *Proceedings of the 19th International Conference on the Foundations of Software Technology & Theoretical Computer Science*, Lecture Notes in Computer Science, pages 369–380, IIT Chennai, India, December 1999. Springer Verlag.

20. M. Huth, R. Jagadeesan, and D. Schmidt. Modal transition systems: new foundations and new applications. To appear as a KSU-CIS Techreport, August 2000.

21. D. Jackson, I. Schechter, and I. Shlyakhter. Alcoa: the alloy constraint analyzer. In *Proc. International Conference on Software Engineering*, Limerick, Ireland, 2000.

22. N.D. Jones and S. Muchnick. Flow analysis and optimization of LISP-like structures. In *Proc. 6th. ACM Symp. Principles of Programming Languages*, pages 244–256, 1979.

23. J. Kam and J. Ullman. Global data flow analysis and iterative algorithms. *J. ACM*, 23:158–171, 1976.

24. P. Kelb. Model checking and abstraction: a framework preserving both truth and failure information. Technical Report Technical report, OFFIS, University of Oldenburg, Germany, 1994.

25. D. Kozen. Results on the propositional mu-calculus. *Theoretical Computer Science*, 27:333–354, 1983.

26. K. G. Larsen. Modal Specifications. In J. Sifakis, editor, *Automatic Verification Methods for Finite State Systems*, number 407 in Lecture Notes in Computer Science, pages 232–246. Springer Verlag, June 12–14 1989. International Workshop, Grenoble, France.

27. K. G. Larsen and B. Thomsen. A Modal Process Logic. In *Third Annual Symposium on Logic in Computer Science*, pages 203–210. IEEE Computer Society Press, 1988.

28. F. Levi. A symbolic semantics for abstract model checking. In *Static Analysis Symposium: SAS'98*, volume 1503 of *Lecture Notes in Computer Science*. Springer Verlag, 1998.

29. R. Milner. A modal characterisation of observable machine behaviours. In G. Astesiano and C. Böhm, editors, *CAAP '81*, volume 112 of *Lecture Notes in Computer Science*, pages 25–34. Springer Verlag, 1981.

30. O. Morikawa. Some modal logics based on a three-valued logic. *Notre Dame J. of Formal Logic*, 30:130–137, 1989.

31. S. Muchnick and N.D. Jones, editors. *Program Flow Analysis: Theory and Applications*. Prentice-Hall, 1981.

32. F. Nielson, H. R. Nielson, and C. Hankin. *Principles of Program Analysis*. Springer Verlag, 1999.

33. A. Pnueli. Applications of temporal logic to the specification and verification of reactive systems: a survey of current trends. In J.W. de Bakker, editor, *Current Trends in Concurrency*, volume 224 of *Lecture Notes in Computer Science*, pages 510–584. Springer-Verlag, 1985.

34. T. Reps. Program analysis via graph reachability. In J. Maluszynski, editor, *Proc. Int'l. Logic Prog. Symp.'97*, pages 5–19. MIT Press, 1997.

35. M. Sagiv, T. Reps, and R. Wilhelm. Parametric Shape Analysis via 3-Valued Logic. In *Proceedings of the 26th ACM SIGPLAN-SIGACT Symposium on Principles of programming languages*, pages 105–118, January 20-22, San Antonio, Texas 1999.

36. D. A. Schmidt. Binary relations for abstraction and refinement. *Elsevier Electronic Notes in Computer Science*, November 1999. Workshop on Refinement and Abstraction, Osaka, Japan. To appear.

37. K. Segerberg. Some modal logics based on a three-valued logic. *Theoria*, 33:53–71, 1967.

38. C. Stirling. Modal logics for communicating systems. *Theoretical Computer Science*, 39:331–347, 1987.

39. D. J. Walker. Bisimulation and divergence. *Information and Computation*, 85(2):202–241, 1990.

40. J. Whaley and M. Rinard. Compositional pointer and escape analysis for Java programs. In *Proc. OOPSLA'99*, pages 187–206. ACM, 1999.

Entailment with Conditional Equality Constraints*

Zhendong Su and Alexander Aiken

EECS Department, University of California, Berkeley
{zhendong,aiken}@cs.berkeley.edu

Abstract. Equality constraints (unification constraints) have widespread use in program analysis, most notably in static polymorphic type systems. *Conditional equality constraints* extend equality constraints with a weak form of subtyping to allow for more accurate analyses. We give a complete complexity characterization of the various entailment problems for conditional equality constraints. Additionally, for comparison, we study a natural extension of conditional equality constraints.

1 Introduction

There are two decision problems associated with constraints: *satisfiability* and *entailment*. For the commonly used constraint languages in type inference and program analysis applications, the satisfiability problem is now well understood [1, 2, 8, 11, 16, 17, 20, 22, 23, 7, 6, 27]. For example, it is well-known that satisfiability of equality constraints can be decided in almost linear time (linear time if no infinite terms are allowed [21]). For entailment problems much less is known, and the few existing results give intractable lower bounds for the constraint languages they study, except for equality constraints where polynomial time algorithms exist [3, 4].

In this paper, we consider the entailment problem for *conditional equality constraints*. Conditional equality constraints extend the usual equality constraints with an additional kind of constraint $\alpha \Rightarrow \tau$, which is satisfied if $\alpha = \perp$ or $\alpha = \tau$. Conditional equality constraints have been used in a number of program analyses, such as the tagging analysis of Henglein [14], the pointer analysis proposed by Steensgaard [25], and a form of equality-based flow systems for higher order functional languages [19]. We also consider entailment for a natural extension of conditional equality constraints.

Consider the equality constraints $C_1 = \{\alpha = \beta, \beta = \gamma, \alpha = \gamma\}$. Since $\alpha = \gamma$ is implied by the other two constraints, we can simplify the constraints to $C_2 = \{\alpha = \beta, \beta = \gamma\}$. We say that "$C_1$ entails C_2", written $C_1 \vDash C_2$, which means that every solution of C_1 is also a solution of C_2. In this case we also have $C_2 \vDash C_1$, since the two systems have exactly the same solutions. In the program

---

* This research was supported in part by the National Science Foundation grant No. CCR-0085949 and NASA Contract No. NAG2-1210.

D. Sands (Ed.): ESOP 2001, LNCS 2028, pp. 170–189, 2001.

analysis community, the primary motivation for studying entailment problems comes from type systems with *polymorphic constrained types*. Such type systems combine polymorphism (as in ML [18]) with subtyping (as in object-oriented languages such as Java [10]), giving polymorphic types with associated subtyping constraints. A difficulty with constrained types is that there are many equivalent representations of the same type, and the "natural" ones to compute tend to be very large and unwieldy. For the type system to be practical, scalable, and understandable to the user, it is important to simplify the constraints associated with a type. As the example above illustrates, entailment of constraint systems is a decision problem closely related to constraint simplification.

Considerable effort has been directed at constraint simplification. One body of work considers practical issues with regard to simplification of constraints [5,7,6,27,17], suggesting heuristics for simplification and experimentally measuring the performance gain of simplifications. Another body of work aims at a better understanding how difficult the simplification problems are for various constraint logics [7,12,13]. Flanagan and Felleisen [7] consider the simplification problem for a particular form of set constraints and show that a form of entailment is PSPACE-hard. Henglein and Rehof [12,13] consider another simpler form of entailment problem for subtyping constraints. They show that structural subtyping entailment for constraints over simple types is coNP-complete and that for recursive types is PSPACE-complete, and that the nonstructual entailment for both simple types and recursive types is PSPACE-hard. A complete complexity characterization of nonstructual subtyping entailment remains open. In fact, it is an open problem whether nonstructual subtyping entailment is decidable. Thus for these different forms of constraints, the problems are intractable or may even be undecidable. In the constraint logic programming community, the entailment problems over equality constraints have been considered by Colmerauer and shown to be polynomial time decidable [3, 4, 15, 24]. Previous work leaves open the question of whether there are other constraint languages with efficiently decidable entailment problems besides equality constraints over trees (finite or infinite).

1.1   Contributions

We consider two forms of the entailment problem: *simple entailment* and *restricted entailment* (sometimes also referred to as *existential entailment* [24]), which we introduce in Section 2. Restricted entailment arises naturally in problems that compare polymorphic constrained types (see Section 2). We show there are polynomial time algorithms for conditional equality constraints for both versions of entailment. We believe these algorithms will be of practical interest. In addition, we consider restricted entailment for a natural extension of conditional equality constraints. We show that restricted entailment for this extension turns out to be coNP-complete. The coNP-completeness result is interesting because it provides a natural boundary between tractable and intractable constraint languages.

Due to space constraints, we only provide sketches of some proofs or omit them entirely. Details may be found in the full paper [26].

2   Preliminaries

We work with simple types. Our type language is

$$\tau ::= \bot \mid \top \mid \tau_1 \to \tau_2 \mid \alpha.$$

This simple language has two constants $\bot$ and $\top$, a binary constructor $\to$, and variables α ranging over a denumerable set $\mathcal{V}$ of type variables. The algorithms we present apply to type languages with other base types and type constructors. Variable-free types are *ground types*. $\mathcal{T}$ and $\mathcal{T_G}$ are the set of types and the set of ground types respectively. An *equality constraint* is $\tau_1 = \tau_2$ and a *conditional equality constraint* is $\alpha \Rightarrow \tau$. A *constraint system* is a finite conjunction of equality and conditional equality constraints. An *equality constraint system* has only equality constraints.

Let C be a constraint system and $\text{Var}(C)$ the set of type variables appearing in C. A *valuation* of C is a function mapping $\text{Var}(C)$ to ground types $\mathcal{T_G}$. We extend a valuation ρ to work on type expressions in the usual way:

$$\rho(\bot) = \bot; \quad \rho(\top) = \top; \quad \rho(\tau_1 \to \tau_2) = \rho(\tau_1) \to \rho(\tau_2)$$

A valuation ρ *satisfies* constraint $\tau_1 = \tau_2$, written $\rho \vDash \tau_1 = \tau_2$, if $\rho(\tau_1) = \rho(\tau_2)$, and it satisfies a constraint $\alpha \Rightarrow \tau$, written $\rho \vDash \alpha \Rightarrow \tau$, if $\rho(\alpha) = \bot$ or $\rho(\alpha) = \rho(\tau)$. We write $\rho \vDash C$ if ρ satisfies every constraint in C. The set of valuations satisfying a constraint system C is the solutions of C, denoted by $S(C)$. We denote by $S(C)|_E$ the set of solutions of C restricted to a set of variables E.

Definition 1 (Terms). Let C be a set of constraints. $\text{Term}(C)$ is the set of terms appearing in C: $\text{Term}(C) = \{\tau_1, \tau_2 \mid (\tau_1 = \tau_2) \in C \lor (\tau_1 \Rightarrow \tau_2) \in C\}$.

The satisfiability of equality constraints can be decided in almost linear time in the size of the original constraints using a union-find data structure [28]. With a simple modification to this algorithm for equality constraints, we can decide the satisfiability of a system of conditional equality constraints in almost linear time (see Proposition 1 below). [1]

Example 1. Here are example conditional constraints:
   a) $\alpha \Rightarrow \bot$ Solution: α must be $\bot$.
   b) $\alpha \Rightarrow \top$ Solution: α is either $\bot$ or $\top$.
   c) $\alpha \Rightarrow \beta \to \gamma$ Solution: α is either $\bot$ or a function type $\beta \to \gamma$,
                      where β and γ can be any type.

Proposition 1. Let C be any system of constraints with equality constraints and conditional equality constraints. We can decide whether there is a satisfying valuation for C in almost linear time.

---

[1] Notice that using a linear unification algorithm such as [21] does not give a more efficient algorithm, because equality constraints are added dynamically.

Proof. [Sketch] The basic idea of the algorithm is to solve the equality constraints and to maintain along with each variable a list of constraints conditionally depending on that variable. Once a variable α is unified with a non-$\bot$ value, any constraints $\alpha \Rightarrow \tau$ on the list are no longer conditional and are added as equality constraints $\alpha = \tau$. Note that a post-processing step is required to perform the occurs check. The time complexity is still almost linear since each constraint is processed at most twice. See, for example, [25] for more information.   □

In later discussions, we refer to this algorithm as CONDRESOLVE. The result of running the algorithm on C is a term dag denoted by CONDRESOLVE(C) (see Definition 5). As is standard, for any term τ, we denote the equivalence class to which τ belongs by ECR(τ).

In this paper, we consider two forms of entailment: *simple entailment*: $C \models c$, and *restricted entailment*: $C_1 \models_E C_2$, where C, C_1, and C_2 are systems of constraints, and c is a single constraint, and E is a set of *interface* variables. In the literature, $C_1 \models_E C_2$ is sometimes written $C_1 \models \exists E'.C_2$, where $E' = \text{Var}(C_2) \setminus E$.

For the use of restricted entailment, consider the following situation. In a polymorphic analysis, a function (or a module) is analyzed to generate a system of constraints [9,7]. Only a few of the variables, the *interface variables*, are visible outside the function. We would like to simplify the constraints with respect to a set of interface variables. In practice, restricted entailment is more commonly encountered than simple entailment.

Definition 2 (Simple Entailment). Let C be a system of constraints and c a constraint. We say that $C \models c$ if for every valuation ρ with $\rho \models C$, we have $\rho \models c$ also.

Definition 3 (Restricted Entailment). Let C_1 and C_2 be two constraint systems, and let E be the set of variables $\text{Var}(C_1) \cap \text{Var}(C_2)$. We say that $C_1 \models_E C_2$ if for every valuation ρ_1 with $\rho_1 \models C_1$ there exists ρ_2 with $\rho_2 \models C_2$ and $\rho_1(\alpha) = \rho_2(\alpha)$ for all $\alpha \in E$.

Definition 4 (Interface and Internal Variables). In $C_1 \models_E C_2$, variables in E are *interface variables*. Variables in $(\text{Var}(C_1) \cup \text{Var}(C_2)) \setminus E$ are *internal variables*.

Notation

- τ and τ_i denote type expressions.
- α, β, γ, α_i, β_i, and γ_i denote interface variables.
- μ, ν, σ, μ_i, ν_i, and σ_i denote internal variables.
- α denotes a generic variable, in places where we do not distinguish interface and internal variables.

For simple entailment $C \models c$, it suffices to consider only the case where c is a constraint between variables, *i.e.*, c is of the form $\alpha = \beta$ or $\alpha \Rightarrow \beta$. For simple entailment, $C \models \tau_1 = \tau_2$ if and only if $C \cup \{\alpha = \tau_1, \beta = \tau_2\} \models \alpha = \beta$, where α

Let C be a system of constraints. The following algorithm outputs a term graph representing the solutions of C.

1. Let G be the term graph $\textsc{CondResolve}(C)$.
2. For each variable α in $\text{Var}(C)$, check whether it must be $\bot$: If neither $G \cup \{\alpha = \top\}$ nor $G \cup \{\alpha = \sigma_1 \to \sigma_2\}$ is satisfiable, add $\alpha = \bot$ to G.

Fig. 1. Modified conditional unification algorithm.

and β do not appear in C and $\tau_1 = \tau_2$. The same also holds for when c is of the form $\alpha \Rightarrow \tau$.

Simple entailment also enjoys a distributive property, that is $C_1 \vDash C_2$ if and only if $C_1 \vDash c$ for each $c \in C_2$. Thus it suffices to only study $C \vDash c$. This distributive property does not hold for restricted entailment. Consider $\emptyset \vDash_{\{\alpha,\beta\}} \{\alpha \Rightarrow \sigma, \beta \Rightarrow \sigma\}$, where σ is a variable different from α and β. This entailment does not hold (consider $\rho_1(\alpha) = \top$ and $\rho_1(\beta) = \bot \to \bot$), but both the entailments $\emptyset \vDash_{\{\alpha,\beta\}} \{\alpha \Rightarrow \sigma\}$ and $\emptyset \vDash_{\{\alpha,\beta\}} \{\beta \Rightarrow \sigma\}$ hold.

Terms can be represented as directed trees with nodes labeled with constructors and variables. Term graphs (or term DAGs) are a more compact representation to allow sharing of common subterms.

Definition 5 (Term DAG). In a term DAG, a variable is represented as a node with out-degree 0. A function type is represented as a node $\to$ with out-degree 2, one for the domain and one for the range. No two different nodes in a term DAG may represent the same term (sharing must be maximal).

We also represent conditional constraints in the term graph. We represent $\alpha \Rightarrow \tau$ as a directed edge from the node representing α to the node representing τ. We call such an edge a *conditional edge*, in contrast to the two outgoing edges from a $\to$ node, which are called *structural edges*.

The following known result is applied extensively in the rest of the paper [3,4].

Theorem 1 (Entailment over Equality Constraints). Both simple entailment and restricted entailment over equality constraints can be decided in polynomial time.

3   Simple Entailment over Conditional Equality Constraints

In this section, we consider simple entailment over conditional equality constraints. Recall for $\alpha \Rightarrow \tau$ to be satisfied by a valuation ρ, either $\rho(\alpha) = \bot$ or $\rho(\alpha) = \rho(\tau)$.

Lemma 1 (Transitivity of $\Rightarrow$). Any valuation ρ satisfying $\alpha \Rightarrow \beta$ and $\beta \Rightarrow \gamma$, also satisfies $\alpha \Rightarrow \gamma$.

If both of the following cases return SUCCESS, output YES; else output NO.

1. a) Run the conditional unification algorithm in Figure 1 on $C \cup \{\alpha = \top\}$.
   If not satisfiable, then SUCCESS; else continue.
   b) Compute strongly connected components (SCC) on the conditional
   edges and merge the nodes in every SCC. This step yields a modified
   term graph.
   c) Compute congruence closure on the term graph obtained in Step 1b.
   We do not consider the conditional edges for computing congruence
   closure.
   d) If $\beta = \top$ is in the closure, SUCCESS; else FAIL.
2. a) Run the conditional unification algorithm in Figure 1 on $C \cup \{\alpha = \sigma_1 \to \sigma_2\}$, where σ_1 and σ_2 are two fresh variables not in $\mathrm{Var}(C) \cup \{\alpha, \beta\}$. If not satisfiable, then SUCCESS; else continue.
   b) Compute strongly connected components (SCC) on the conditional
   edges and merge the nodes in every SCC. This step yields a modified
   term graph.
   c) Compute congruence closure on the term graph obtained in Step 2b.
   Again, we do not consider the conditional edges for computing congruence closure.
   d) If $\beta = \sigma_1 \to \sigma_2$ is in the closure, SUCCESS; else FAIL.

Fig. 2. Simple entailment $C \vDash \alpha \Rightarrow \beta$ over conditional equality constraints.

Consider the constraints $\{\alpha \Rightarrow \top, \alpha \Rightarrow \bot \to \bot\}$. The only solution is $\alpha = \bot$. The fact that α must be $\bot$ is not explicit. For entailment, we want to make the fact that α must be $\bot$ explicit.

Assume that we have run CONDRESOLVE on the constraints to get a term graph G. For each variable α, we check whether it must be $\bot$. If both adding $\alpha = \top$ to G and $\alpha = \sigma_1 \to \sigma_2$ to G (for fresh variables σ_1 and σ_2) fail, α must be $\bot$, in which case, we add $\alpha = \bot$ to G. We repeat this process for each variable. Notice that this step can be done in polynomial time. We present this modification to the conditional unification algorithm in Figure 1.

We now present an algorithm for deciding $C \vDash \alpha = \beta$ and $C \vDash \alpha \Rightarrow \beta$ where C is a system of conditional equality constraints. Note $C \vDash \alpha = \beta$ holds if and only if both $C \vDash \alpha \Rightarrow \beta$ and $C \vDash \beta \Rightarrow \alpha$ hold. We give the algorithm in Figure 2. The basic idea is that to check $C \vDash \alpha \Rightarrow \beta$ holds we have two cases: when α is $\top$ and when α is a function type. In both cases, we require $\beta = \alpha$. The problem then basically reduces to simple entailment over equality constraints. Congruence closure is required to make explicit the implied equalities between terms involving $\to$. Computing strongly connected components is used to make explicit, for example, $\alpha = \beta$ if both $\alpha \Rightarrow \beta$ and $\beta \Rightarrow \alpha$. It is easy to see that the algorithm runs in worst case polynomial time in the size of C.

Theorem 2. The simple entailment algorithm in Figure 2 is correct.

4   Restricted Entailment over Conditional Equality Constraints

In this section, we give a polynomial time algorithm for restricted entailment over conditional constraints.

Consider the following example term graph for the constraints

$$\{\alpha_1 \Rightarrow \bot, \alpha_1 \Rightarrow \sigma_1, \alpha_2 \Rightarrow \sigma_1, \alpha_2 \Rightarrow \sigma_2, \alpha_3 \Rightarrow \sigma_2, \alpha_3 \Rightarrow \top\}.$$

Example 2.

Notice that the solutions of the constraints in Example 2 with respect to $\{\alpha_1, \alpha_2, \alpha_3\}$ are all tuples $\langle v_1, v_2, v_3 \rangle$ that satisfy

$$(v_1 = \bot \wedge v_3 = \bot) \vee (v_1 = \bot \wedge v_2 = \bot \ \wedge v_3 = \top) \vee (v_1 = \bot \wedge v_2 = \top \ \wedge v_3 = \top)$$

Now suppose we do the following: we take pairs of constraints, find their solutions with respect to $\{\alpha_1, \alpha_2, \alpha_3\}$, and take the intersection of the solutions. Let S^* denote the set of all valuations. Figure 3 shows the solutions for all the subsets of two constraints with respect to $\{\alpha_1, \alpha_2, \alpha_3\}$. One can show that the intersection of these solutions is the same as the solution for all the constraints. Intuitively, the solutions of a system of conditional constraints can be characterized by considering all pairs of constraints independently. We can make this intuition formal by putting some additional requirements on the constraints.

For simplicity, in later discussions, we consider the language without $\top$. With some extra checks, the presented algorithm can be adapted to include $\top$ in the language.

Here is the route we take to develop a polynomial time algorithm for restricted entailment over conditional constraints.

Section 4.1
> We introduce a notion of a *closed system* and show that closed systems have the property that it is sufficient to consider pairs of conditional constraints in determining the solutions of the complete system with respect to the interface variables.

Section 4.2
> We show that restricted entailment with a pair of conditional constraints can be decided in polynomial time, *i.e.*, $C \vDash_E C_= \cup \{c_1, c_2\}$ can be decided in polynomial time, where $C_=$ consists of equality constraints, and c_1 and c_2 are conditional constraints.

Section 4.3
> We show how to reduce restricted entailment to restricted entailment in terms of closed systems. In particular, we show how to reduce $C_1 \vDash_E C_2$ to $C'_1 \vDash_{E'} C'_2$ where C'_2 is closed.

Combining the results, we arrive at a polynomial time algorithm for restricted entailment over conditional constraints.

$$S(\{\alpha_1 \Rightarrow \bot, \alpha_2 \Rightarrow \sigma_1\}) = \{\langle v_1, v_2, v_3 \rangle \mid v_1 = \bot\}$$
$$S(\{\alpha_2 \Rightarrow \sigma_1, \alpha_2 \Rightarrow \sigma_2\}) = S^*$$
$$S(\{\alpha_3 \Rightarrow \sigma_2, \alpha_3 \Rightarrow \top\}) = \{\langle v_1, v_2, v_3 \rangle \mid (v_3 = \bot) \vee (v_3 = \top)\}$$
$$S(\{\alpha_1 \Rightarrow \bot, \alpha_2 \Rightarrow \sigma_1\}) = \{\langle v_1, v_2, v_3 \rangle \mid v_1 = \bot\}$$
$$S(\{\alpha_1 \Rightarrow \bot, \alpha_2 \Rightarrow \sigma_2\}) = \{\langle v_1, v_2, v_3 \rangle \mid v_1 = \bot\}$$
$$S(\{\alpha_1 \Rightarrow \bot, \alpha_3 \Rightarrow \sigma_2\}) = \{\langle v_1, v_2, v_3 \rangle \mid v_1 = \bot\}$$
$$S(\{\alpha_1 \Rightarrow \bot, \alpha_3 \Rightarrow \top\}) = \{\langle v_1, v_2, v_3 \rangle \mid (v_1 = \bot \wedge v_3 = \bot) \vee (v_1 = \bot \wedge v_3 = \top)\}$$
$$S(\{\alpha_1 \Rightarrow \sigma_1, \alpha_2 \Rightarrow \sigma_1\}) = \{\langle v_1, v_2, v_3 \rangle \mid (v_1 = \bot) \vee (v_2 = \bot) \vee (v_2 = v_3)\}$$
$$S(\{\alpha_1 \Rightarrow \sigma_1, \alpha_2 \Rightarrow \sigma_2\}) = S^*$$
$$S(\{\alpha_1 \Rightarrow \sigma_1, \alpha_3 \Rightarrow \sigma_2\}) = S^*$$
$$S(\{\alpha_1 \Rightarrow \sigma_1, \alpha_3 \Rightarrow \top\}) = \{\langle v_1, v_2, v_3 \rangle \mid (v_3 = \bot) \vee (v_3 = \top)\}$$
$$S(\{\alpha_2 \Rightarrow \sigma_1, \alpha_3 \Rightarrow \sigma_2\}) = S^*$$
$$S(\{\alpha_2 \Rightarrow \sigma_1, \alpha_3 \Rightarrow \top\}) = \{\langle v_1, v_2, v_3 \rangle \mid (v_3 = \bot) \vee (v_3 = \top)\}$$
$$S(\{\alpha_2 \Rightarrow \sigma_2, \alpha_3 \Rightarrow \sigma_2\}) = \{\langle v_1, v_2, v_3 \rangle \mid (v_2 = \bot) \vee (v_3 = \bot) \vee (v_2 = v_3)\}$$
$$S(\{\alpha_2 \Rightarrow \sigma_2, \alpha_3 \Rightarrow \top\}) = \{\langle v_1, v_2, v_3 \rangle \mid (v_3 = \bot) \vee (v_3 = \top)\}$$

Fig. 3. Solutions for all subsets of two constraints.

4.1   Closed Systems

We define the notion of a closed system and show the essential properties of closed systems for entailment. Before presenting the definitions, we first demonstrate the idea with the example in Figure 4a. Let C denote the constraints in this example, with α and β the interface variables, and σ, σ_1, and σ_2 the internal variables. The intersection of the solutions of all the pairs of constraints is: α is either $\bot$ or $\tau \to \bot$, and β is either $\bot$ or $\tau' \to \bot$ for some τ and τ'. However, the solutions of C require that if $\alpha = \tau \to \bot$ and $\beta = \tau' \to \bot$, and both τ and τ' are non-$\bot$, then $\tau = \tau'$, *i.e.*, $\alpha = \beta$. Thus the intersection of solutions of pairs of constraints contains more valuations than the solution set of the entire system. The reason is that when we consider the set $\{\sigma_1 \Rightarrow \sigma, \sigma_2 \Rightarrow \sigma\}$, the solutions w.r.t. $\{\alpha, \beta\}$ are all valuations. We lose the information that α and β need to be the same in their domain.

We would like to consider σ_1 and σ_2 as interface variables if $\sigma_1 \neq \bot \neq \sigma_2$. We introduce some constraints and new interface variables into the system to *close* it. The modified constraint system is shown in Figure 4b. To make explicit the relationship between α and β, two variables α_1 and β_1 (interface variables corresponding to σ_1 and σ_2, respectively) are created with the constraints $\alpha_1 \Rightarrow \sigma$ and $\beta_1 \Rightarrow \sigma$. With this modification, the intersection of solutions of pairs of constraints w.r.t. $\{\alpha, \beta, \alpha_1, \beta_1\}$ is the same as the solution of the modified system. Restricting this intersection w.r.t. $\{\alpha, \beta\}$ we get the solution of the original constraint system. We next show how to systematically close a constraint system.

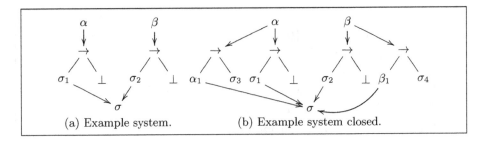

(a) Example system.   (b) Example system closed.

Fig. 4. An example constraint system and its closed system.

Definition 6 (TR). Consider a constraint $\alpha \Rightarrow \tau$ with the variable σ a *proper* subexpression of τ. We define a transformation TR on $\alpha \Rightarrow \tau$ over the structure of τ

- $\text{TR}(\sigma, \alpha \Rightarrow \sigma \rightarrow \tau') = \{\alpha \Rightarrow \alpha_1 \rightarrow \sigma_1\}$;
- $\text{TR}(\sigma, \alpha \Rightarrow \tau' \rightarrow \sigma) = \{\alpha \Rightarrow \sigma_2 \rightarrow \alpha_2\}$;
- $\text{TR}(\sigma, \alpha \Rightarrow \tau_1 \rightarrow \tau_2) =$
  $$\begin{cases} \{\alpha \Rightarrow \alpha_1 \rightarrow \sigma_1\} \cup \text{TR}(\sigma, \alpha_1 \Rightarrow \tau_1) & \text{if } \sigma \in \text{Var}(\tau_1) \\ \{\alpha \Rightarrow \sigma_2 \rightarrow \alpha_2\} \cup \text{TR}(\sigma, \alpha_2 \Rightarrow \tau_2) & \text{otherwise} \end{cases}$$
  Note if σ appears in both τ_1 and τ_2, TR is applied only to the occurrence of σ in τ_1.
- $\text{TR}(\sigma, \alpha = \tau) = \text{TR}(\sigma, \alpha \Rightarrow \tau)$.

The variables α_i's and σ_i's are fresh. The newly created α_i's are called *auxiliary variables*. The variables α_i in the first two cases are called the *matching variable for σ*. The variable α is called the *root* of α_i, and is denoted by $\text{ROOT}(\alpha_i)$. For each auxiliary variable α_i, we denote by $C_{\text{TR}}(\alpha_i)$ the TR constraints accumulated till α_i is created.

Putting this definition to use on the constraint system in Figure 4a, $\text{TR}(\sigma_1, \alpha \Rightarrow \sigma_1 \rightarrow \bot)$ yields the constraint $\alpha \Rightarrow \alpha_1 \rightarrow \sigma_3$ (shown in Figure 4b).

To understand the definition of $C_{\text{TR}}(\alpha_i)$, consider $\text{TR}(\sigma, \alpha \Rightarrow ((\sigma \rightarrow \bot) \rightarrow \bot)) = \{\alpha \Rightarrow \alpha_1 \rightarrow \sigma_1, \alpha_1 \Rightarrow \alpha_2 \rightarrow \sigma_2\}$, where α_1 and α_2 are the auxiliary variables. We have $C_{\text{TR}}(\alpha_1) = \{\alpha \Rightarrow \alpha_1 \rightarrow \sigma_1\}$ and $C_{\text{TR}}(\alpha_2) = \{\alpha \Rightarrow \alpha_1 \rightarrow \sigma_1, \alpha_1 \Rightarrow \alpha_2 \rightarrow \sigma_2\}$.

Definition 7 (Closed Systems). A system of conditional constraints C' is *closed* w.r.t. a set of variables E in C after the following steps:

1. Let $C' = \text{CONDRESOLVE}(C)$.
2. Set W to E.
3. For each variable $\alpha \in W$, if $\alpha \Rightarrow \tau$ is in C', where $\sigma \in \text{Var}(\tau)$, and $\sigma \Rightarrow \tau' \in C'$, add $\text{TR}(\sigma, \alpha \Rightarrow \tau)$ to C'. Let α' be the matching variable for σ and add $\alpha' \Rightarrow \tau'$ to C'.
4. Set W to the set of auxiliary variables created in Step 3 and repeat Step 3 until W is empty.

Step 3 of this definition warrants explanation. In the example $\mathrm{TR}(\sigma_1, \alpha \Rightarrow \sigma_1)$ we add the constraint $\alpha \Rightarrow \alpha_1 \to \sigma_3$ with α_1 as the matching variable for σ_1. We want to ensure that α_1 and σ_1 are actually the same, so we add the constraint $\alpha_1 \Rightarrow \sigma$. This process must be repeated to expose all such internal variables (such as σ_1 and σ_2).

Next we give the definition of a *forced variable*. Given a valuation ρ for the interface variables, if an internal variable σ is determined already by ρ, then σ is *forced by* ρ. For example, in Figure 4a, if α is non-$\perp$, then the value of σ_1 is forced by α.

Definition 8 (Forced Variables). We say that an internal variable σ is *forced* by a valuation ρ if any one of the following holds (A is the set of auxiliary variables)

- $\mathrm{ECR}(\sigma) = \perp$;
- $\mathrm{ECR}(\sigma) = \alpha$, where $\alpha \in E \cup A$;
- $\mathrm{ECR}(\sigma) = \tau_1 \to \tau_2$;
- $\rho(\alpha) \neq \perp$ and $\alpha \Rightarrow \tau$ is a constraint where $\sigma \in \mathrm{Var}(\tau)$ and $\alpha \in E \cup A$;
- σ' is forced by ρ to a non-$\perp$ value and $\sigma' \Rightarrow \tau$ is a constraint where $\sigma \in \mathrm{Var}(\tau)$.

Theorem 3. Let C be a closed system of constraints w.r.t. a set of interface variables E, and let A be the set of auxiliary variables of C. Let $C_=$ and $C_\Rightarrow$ be the systems of equality constraints and conditional constraints respectively. Then

$$S(C)|_{E \cup A} = \bigcap_{c_i, c_j \in C_\Rightarrow} S(C_= \cup \{c_i, c_j\})|_{E \cup A}.$$

In other words, it suffices to consider pairs of conditional constraints in determining the solutions of a closed constraint system.

Proof. Since C contains all the constraints in $C_= \cup \{c_i, c_j\}$ for all i and j, thus it follows that

$$S(C)|_{E \cup A} \subseteq \bigcap_{c_i, c_j \in C_\Rightarrow} S(C_= \cup \{c_i, c_j\})|_{E \cup A}.$$

It remains to show

$$S(C)|_{E \cup A} \supseteq \bigcap_{c_i, c_j \in C_\Rightarrow} S(C_= \cup \{c_i, c_j\})|_{E \cup A}.$$

Let ρ be a valuation in $\bigcap_{c_i, c_j \in C_\Rightarrow} S(C_= \cup \{c_i, c_j\})|_{E \cup A}$. It suffices to show that ρ can be extended to a satisfying valuation ρ' for C. To show this, it suffices to find an extension ρ' of ρ for C such that $\rho' \models C_= \cup \{c_i, c_j\}$ for all i and j.

Consider the valuation ρ' obtained from ρ by mapping all the internal variables not forced by ρ (in C) to $\perp$. The valuation ρ' can be uniquely extended to satisfy C if for any c_i and c_j, c_i' and c_j', if σ is forced by ρ in both $C_= \cup \{c_i, c_j\}$

and $C_= \cup \{c_i', c_j'\}$, then it is forced to the same value in both systems. The value that σ is forced to by ρ is denoted by $\rho^!(\sigma)$.

We prove by cases (cf. Definition 8) that if σ is forced by ρ, it is forced to the same value in pairs of constraints. Let $C_{i,j}$ denote $C_= \cup \{c_i, c_j\}$ and $C_{i',j'}$ denote $C_= \cup \{c_i', c_j'\}$.

- If $\text{ECR}(\sigma) = \bot$, then σ is forced to the same value, i.e., $\bot$, because $\sigma = \bot \in C_=$.
- If $\text{ECR}(\sigma) = \alpha$, with $\alpha \in E \cup A$, then σ is forced to $\rho(\alpha)$ in both systems, because $\sigma = \alpha \in C_=$.
- If $\text{ECR}(\sigma) = \tau_1 \to \tau_2$, one can show that ρ forces σ to the same value with an induction over the structure of $\text{ECR}(\sigma)$ (with the two cases above as base cases).
- Assume σ is forced in $C_{i,j}$ because $\alpha \Rightarrow \tau_1 \in C_{i,j}$ with $\rho(\alpha) \neq \bot$ and forced in $C_{i',j'}$ because $\beta \Rightarrow \tau_2 \in C_{i',j'}$ with $\rho(\beta) \neq \bot$. For each extension ρ_1 of ρ with $\rho_1 \vDash C_{i,j}$, and for each extension ρ_2 of ρ with $\rho_2 \vDash C_{i',j'}$, we have

$$\rho(\alpha) = \rho_1(\alpha) = \rho_1(\tau_1)$$
$$\rho(\beta) = \rho_2(\beta) = \rho_2(\tau_2)$$

  Consider the constraint system $C_= \cup \{\alpha \Rightarrow \tau_1, \beta \Rightarrow \tau_2\}$. The valuation ρ can be extended to ρ_3 with $\rho_3 \vDash C_= \cup \{\alpha \Rightarrow \tau_1, \beta \Rightarrow \tau_2\}$. Thus we have

$$\rho(\alpha) = \rho_3(\alpha) = \rho_3(\tau_1)$$
$$\rho(\beta) = \rho_3(\beta) = \rho_3(\tau_2)$$

  Therefore, $\rho_1(\tau_1) = \rho_3(\tau_1)$ and $\rho_2(\tau_2) = \rho_3(\tau_2)$. Hence, $\rho_1(\sigma) = \rho_3(\sigma)$ and $\rho_2(\sigma) = \rho_3(\sigma)$, which imply $\rho_1(\sigma) = \rho_2(\sigma)$. Thus σ is forced to the same value.
- Assume σ is forced in $C_{i,j}$ because σ_1 is forced to a non-$\bot$ value and $\sigma_1 \Rightarrow \tau_1 \in C_{i,j}$ and is forced in $C_{i',j'}$ because σ_2 is forced to a non-$\bot$ value and $\sigma_2 \Rightarrow \tau_2 \in C_{i',j'}$. Because C is a closed system, we must have two interface variables or auxiliary variables α and β with both $\alpha \Rightarrow \tau_1$ and $\beta \Rightarrow \tau_2$ appearing in C. Since σ_1 and σ_2 are forced, then we must have $\rho(\alpha) = \rho^!(\sigma_1)$ and $\rho(\beta) = \rho^!(\sigma_2)$, thus σ must be forced to the same value by the previous case.
- Assume σ is forced in $C_{i,j}$ because $\rho(\alpha) \neq \bot$ and $\alpha \Rightarrow \tau_1 \in C_{i,j}$ and forced in $C_{i',j'}$ because σ_2 is forced to a non-$\bot$ value and $\sigma_2 \Rightarrow \tau_2 \in C_{i',j'}$. This case is similar to the previous case.
- The remaining case, where σ is forced in $C_{i,j}$ because σ_1 is forced to a non-$\bot$ value and $\sigma_1 \Rightarrow \tau_1 \in C_{i,j}$ and is forced in $C_{i',j'}$ because $\rho(\alpha) \neq \bot$ and $\alpha \Rightarrow \tau_2 \in C_{i',j'}$, is symmetric to the above case.

$\square$

4.2   Entailment of Pair Constraints

In the previous subsection, we saw that a closed system can be decomposed into pairs of conditional constraints. In this section, we show how to efficiently determine entailment if the right-hand side consists of a pair of conditional constraints.

We first state a lemma (Lemma 2) which is important in finding a polynomial algorithm for entailment of pair constraints.

Lemma 2. Let C_1 be a system of conditional constraints and C_2 be a system of *equality* constraints with $E = \text{Var}(C_1) \cap \text{Var}(C_2)$. The decision problem $C_1 \vDash_E C_2$ is solvable in polynomial time.

Proof. Consider the following algorithm. We first solve C_1 using CONDRESOLVE, and add the terms appearing in C_2 to the resulting term graph for C_1. Then for any two terms appearing in the term graph, we decide, using the simple entailment algorithm in Figure 2, whether the two terms are the same. For terms which are equivalent we merge their equivalence classes. Next, for each of the constraints in C_2, we merge the left and right sides. For any two non-congruent classes that are unified, we require at least one of the representatives be a variable in $\text{Var}(C_2) \setminus E$. If this requirement is not met, the entailment does not hold. Otherwise, the entailment holds.

If the requirement is met, then it is routine to verify that the entailment holds. Suppose the requirement is not met, *i.e.*, there exist two non-congruent classes which are unified and none of whose ECRs is a variables in $\text{Var}(C_2) \setminus E$. Since the two classes are non-congruent, we can choose a satisfying valuation for C_1 which maps the two classes to different values (This is possible because, otherwise, we would have proven that they are the same with the simple entailment algorithm for conditional constraints.) The valuation $\rho \mid_E$ cannot be extended to a satisfying valuation for C_2 because, otherwise, this contradicts the fact that $C_1 \cup C_2$ entails the equivalence of the two non-congruent terms.

□

Theorem 4. Let C_1 be a system of conditional constraints. Let $C_=$ be a system of equality constraints. The following three decision problems can be solved in polynomial time:

1. $C_1 \vDash_E C_= \cup \{\alpha \Rightarrow \tau_1, \beta \Rightarrow \tau_2\}$, where $\alpha, \beta \in E$.
2. $C_1 \vDash_E C_= \cup \{\alpha \Rightarrow \tau_1, \mu \Rightarrow \tau_2\}$, where $\alpha \in E$ and $\mu \notin E$.
3. $C_1 \vDash_E C_= \cup \{\mu_1 \Rightarrow \tau_1, \mu_2 \Rightarrow \tau_2\}$, where $\mu_1, \mu_2 \notin E$.

Proof.

1. For the case $C_1 \vDash_E C_= \cup \{\alpha \Rightarrow \tau_1, \beta \Rightarrow \tau_2\}$, notice that $C_1 \vDash_E C_= \cup \{\alpha \Rightarrow \tau_1, \beta \Rightarrow \tau_2\}$ iff the following entailments hold
   - $C_1 \cup \{\alpha = \bot, \beta = \bot\} \vDash_E C_=$
   - $C_1 \cup \{\alpha = \bot, \beta = \nu_1 \rightarrow \nu_2\} \vDash_E C_= \cup \{\beta = \tau_2\}$
   - $C_1 \cup \{\alpha = \sigma_1 \rightarrow \sigma_2, \beta = \bot\} \vDash_E C_= \cup \{\alpha = \tau_1\}$
   - $C_1 \cup \{\alpha = \sigma_1 \rightarrow \sigma_2, \beta = \nu_1 \rightarrow \nu_2\} \vDash_E C_= \cup \{\alpha = \tau_1, \beta = \tau_2\}$
   where $\sigma_1, \sigma_2, \nu_1$, and ν_2 are fresh variables not in $\text{Var}(C_1) \cup \text{Var}(C_2)$. Notice that each of the above entailments reduces to entailment of equality constraints, which can be decided in polynomial time by Lemma 2.
2. For the case $C_1 \vDash_E C_= \cup \{\alpha \Rightarrow \tau_1, \mu \Rightarrow \tau_2\}$, we consider two cases:

  - $C_1 \cup \{\alpha = \bot\} \vDash_E C_= \cup \{\mu \Rightarrow \tau_2\}$;
  - $C_1 \cup \{\alpha = \sigma_1 \rightarrow \sigma_2\} \vDash_E C_= \cup \{\alpha = \tau_1, \mu \Rightarrow \tau_2\}$

where σ_1 and σ_2 are fresh variables not in $\mathrm{Var}(C_1) \cup \mathrm{Var}(C_2)$.
We have a few cases.

  - $\mathrm{ECR}(\mu) = \bot$
  - $\mathrm{ECR}(\mu) = \tau_1 \rightarrow \tau_2$
  - $\mathrm{ECR}(\mu) \in E$
  - $\mathrm{ECR}(\mu) \notin E$

Notice that the only interesting case is the last case ($\mathrm{ECR}(\mu) \notin E$) when there is a constraint $\beta = \tau$ in $C_=$ and μ appears in τ. For this case, we consider all the $\mathcal{O}(n)$ resulted entailments by setting β to some appropriate value according to the structure of τ, *i.e.*, we consider all the possible values for β. For example, if $\tau = (\mu \rightarrow \bot) \rightarrow \mu$, we consider the following cases:

  - $\beta = \bot$;
  - $\beta = \bot \rightarrow \nu_1$;
  - $\beta = (\bot \rightarrow \nu_2) \rightarrow \nu_1$;
  - $\beta = ((\nu_3 \rightarrow \nu_4) \rightarrow \nu_2) \rightarrow \nu_1$

where ν_1, ν_2, ν_3, and ν_4 are fresh variables.
Each of the entailments will have only equality constraints on the right-hand side. Thus, these can all be decided in polynomial time. Together, the entailment can be decided in polynomial time.

3. For the case $C_1 \vDash_E C_= \cup \{\mu_1 \Rightarrow \tau_1, \mu_2 \Rightarrow \tau_2\}$, the same idea as in the second case applies as well. The sub-case which is slightly different is when, for example, μ_2 appears in τ_1 only. In this case, for some β and τ, $\beta = \tau$ is in $C_=$ where μ_1 occurs in τ. Let $\tau' = \tau[\tau_1/\mu_1]$, where $\tau[\tau_1/\mu_1]$ denotes the type obtained from τ by replacing each occurrence of μ_1 by τ_1. Again, we consider $\mathcal{O}(n)$ entailments with right-side an equality constraint system by assigning β appropriate values according to the structure of τ'. Thus this form of entailment can also be decided in polynomial time.

$\square$

4.3   Reduction of Entailment to Closed Systems

We now reduce an entailment $C_1 \vDash_E C_2$ to entailment of closed systems, thus completing the construction of a polynomial time algorithm for restricted entailment over conditional constraints.

Unfortunately we cannot directly use the closed systems for C_1 and C_2 as demonstrated by the example in Figure 5. Figures 5a and 5c show two constraint systems C_1 and C_2. Suppose we want to decide $C_1 \vDash_{\{\alpha,\beta\}} C_2$. One can verify that the entailment does hold. Figures 5b and 5d show the closed systems for C_1 and C_2, which we name C_1' and C_2'. Note that we include the TR constraints of C_2 in C_1'. One can verify that the entailment $C_1' \vDash_{\{\alpha,\beta,\alpha_1,\beta_1\}} C_2'$ does not hold (take $\alpha = \beta = \bot$, $\alpha_1 = \bot \rightarrow \bot$, and $\beta_1 = \bot \rightarrow \top$, for example). The reason is that there is some information about α_1 and β_1 missing from C_1'. In particular, when both α_1 and β_1 are forced, we should have $\alpha_1 \Rightarrow \sigma'$ and $\beta_1 \Rightarrow \sigma'$ (actually in this case they satisfy the stronger relation that $\alpha_1 = \beta_1$). By replacing $\alpha \Rightarrow \alpha_1 \rightarrow \sigma_3$

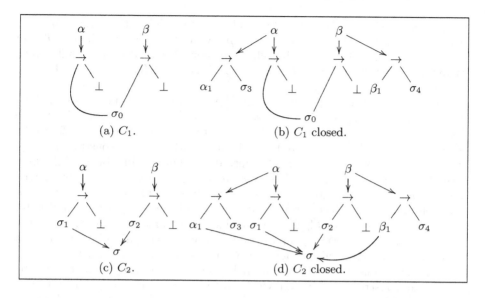

Fig. 5. Example entailment.

and $\beta \Rightarrow \beta_1 \rightarrow \sigma_4$ with $\alpha = \alpha_1 \rightarrow \sigma_3$ and $\beta = \beta_1 \rightarrow \sigma_4$ (because that is when both are forced), we can decide that $\alpha_1 = \beta_1$. The following definition of a *completion* does exactly what we have described.

Definition 9 (Completion). Let C be a closed constraint system of C_0 w.r.t. E. Let A be the set of auxiliary variables. For each pair of variables α_i and β_j in A, let $C(\alpha_i, \beta_j) = C_{TR}(\alpha_i) \cup C_{TR}(\beta_j)$ (see Definition 6) and $C^=(\alpha_i, \beta_j)$ be the equality constraints obtained by replacing $\Rightarrow$ with $=$ in $C(\alpha_i, \beta_j)$. Decide whether $C \cup C^=(\alpha_i, \beta_j) \vDash_{\{\alpha_i, \beta_j\}} \{\alpha_i \Rightarrow \sigma, \beta_j \Rightarrow \sigma\}$ (cf. Theorem 4). If the entailment holds, add the constraints $\alpha_i \Rightarrow \sigma_{(\alpha_i, \beta_j)}$ and $\beta_j \Rightarrow \sigma_{(\alpha_i, \beta_j)}$ to C, where $\sigma_{(\alpha_i, \beta_j)}$ is a fresh variable unique for α_i and β_j. The resulting constraint system is called the *completion* of C.

Theorem 5. Let C_1 and C_2 be two conditional constraint systems. Let C_2' be the closed system of C_2 w.r.t. to $E = \text{Var}(C_1) \cap \text{Var}(C_2)$ with A the set of auxiliary variables. Construct the closed system for C_1 w.r.t. E with A' the auxiliary variables, and add the TR constraints of closing C_2 to C_1 after closing C_1. Let C_1' be the completion of modified C_1. We have $C_1 \vDash_E C_2$ iff $C_1' \vDash_{E \cup A \cup A'} C_2'$.

Proof.

($\Leftarrow$): Assume $C_1' \vDash_{E \cup A \cup A'} C_2'$. Let $\rho \vDash C_1$. We can extend ρ to ρ' which satisfies C_1'. Since $C_1' \vDash_{E \cup A \cup A'} C_2'$, then there exists ρ'' such that $\rho'' \vDash C_2'$ with $\rho' \mid_{E \cup A \cup A'} = \rho'' \mid_{E \cup A \cup A'}$. Since $\rho'' \vDash C_2'$, we have $\rho'' \vDash C_2$. Also $\rho \mid_E = \rho' \mid_E = \rho'' \mid_E$. Therefore, $C_1 \vDash_E C_2$.

($\Rightarrow$): Assume $C_1 \vDash_E C_2$. Let $\rho \vDash C_1'$. Then $\rho \vDash C_1$. Thus there exists $\rho' \vDash C_2$ with $\rho \mid_E = \rho' \mid_E$. We extend $\rho' \mid_E$ to ρ'' with $\rho''(\alpha) = \rho'(\alpha)$ if $\alpha \in E$ and $\rho''(\alpha) = \rho(\alpha)$ if $\alpha \in (A \cup A')$. It suffices to show that ρ'' can be extended with mappings for variables in $\text{Var}(C_2') \setminus (E \cup A \cup A') = \text{Var}(C_2') \setminus (E \cup A)$, because $\rho'' \mid_{E \cup A \cup A'} = \rho \mid_{E \cup A \cup A'}$.

Notice that all the TR constraints in C_2' are satisfied by some extension of ρ'', because they also appear in C_1'. Also the constraints C_2 are satisfied by some extension of ρ''. It remains to show that the internal variables of C_2' are forced by ρ'' to the same value if they are forced by ρ'' in either the TR constraints or C_2. Suppose there is an internal variable σ forced to different values by ρ''. W.L.O.G., assume that σ is forced by ρ'' because $\rho''(\alpha_i) \neq \bot$ and $\alpha_i \Rightarrow \sigma$ and forced because $\rho''(\beta_j) \neq \bot$ and $\beta_j \Rightarrow \sigma$ for some interface or auxiliary variables α_i and β_j. Consider the interface variables $\text{ROOT}(\alpha_i)$ and $\text{ROOT}(\beta_j)$ (see Definition 6). Since the completion of C_1 does not include constraints $\{\alpha_i \Rightarrow \sigma', \beta_j \Rightarrow \sigma'\}$, thus we can assign $\text{ROOT}(\alpha_i)$ and $\text{ROOT}(\beta_j)$ appropriate values to force α_i and β_j to different non-$\bot$ values. However, C_2 requires α_i and β_j to have the same non-$\bot$ value. Thus, if there is an internal variable σ forced to different values by ρ'', we can construct a valuation which satisfies C_1, but the valuation restricted to E cannot be extended to a satisfying valuation for C_2. This contradicts the assumption that $C_1 \vDash_E C_2$. To finish the construction of a desired extension of ρ'' that satisfies C_2', we set the variables which are not forced to $\bot$.

One can easily verify that this valuation must satisfy C_2'. Hence $C_1' \vDash_{E \cup A \cup A'} C_2'$. $\qquad\square$

4.4   Putting Everything Together

Theorem 6. Restricted entailment for conditional constraints can be decided in polynomial time.

Proof. Consider the problem $C_1 \vDash_E C_2$. By Theorem 5, it is equivalent to testing $C_1' \vDash_{E \cup A \cup A'} C_2'$ (see Theorem 5 for the appropriate definitions of C_1', C_2', A, and A'). Notice that C_1' and C_2' are constructed in polynomial time in sizes of C_1 and C_2. Now by Theorem 3, this is equivalent to checking $\mathcal{O}(n^2)$ entailment problems of the form $C_1' \vDash_{E \cup A \cup A'} C_{2_=}' \cup \{c_i, c_j\}$, where $C_{2_=}'$ denote the equality constraints of C_2' and c_i and c_j are two conditional constraints of C_2'. And by Theorem 4, we can decide each of these entailments in polynomial time. Putting everything together, we have a polynomial time algorithm for restricted entailment over conditional constraints. $\qquad\square$

5   Extended Conditional Constraints

In this section, we show that restricted entailment for a natural extension of the standard conditional constraint language is coNP-complete. [2] This section

---

[2] Simple entailment for this extension is in P. See [26] for details.

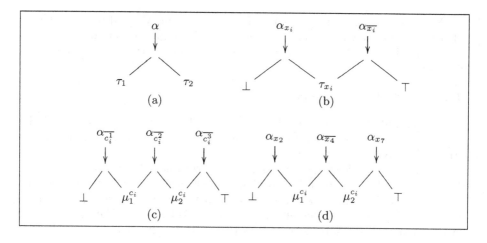

Fig. 6. Graph representations of constraints.

is helpful for a comparison between this constraint language with the standard conditional constraint language, which we consider in Section 3 and Section 4. The results in this section provide one natural boundary between tractable and intractable entailment problems.

We extend the constraint language with a new construct $\alpha \Rightarrow (\tau_1 = \tau_2)$, which holds iff either $\alpha = \bot$ or $\tau_1 = \tau_2$. We call this form of constraints *extended conditional equality constraints*. To see that this construct indeed extends $\alpha \Rightarrow \tau$, notice that $\alpha \Rightarrow \tau$ can be encoded in the new constraint language as $\alpha \Rightarrow (\alpha = \tau)$.

This extension is interesting because many equality based program analyses can be naturally expressed with this form of constraints. An example analysis that uses this form of constraints is the equality based flow analysis for higher order functional languages [19].

Note that satisfiability for this extension can still be decided in almost linear time with basically the same algorithm outlined for conditional equality constraints. We consider restricted entailment for this extended language.

5.1   Restricted Entailment

In this subsection, we consider the restricted entailment problem for extended conditional constraints. We show that the decision problem $C_1 \models_E C_2$ for extended conditional constraints is coNP-complete.

We define the decision problem NENT as the problem of deciding whether $C_1 \not\models_E C_2$, where C_1 and C_2 are systems of extended conditional equality constraints and $E = \text{Var}(C_1) \cap \text{Var}(C_2)$.

Theorem 7. The decision problem NENT for extended conditional constraints is in NP.

Next we show that the problem NENT is hard for NP, and thus an efficient algorithm is unlikely to exist for the problem. The reduction actually shows that with extended conditional constraints, even atomic restricted entailment [3] is coNP-hard.

Theorem 8. *The decision problem NENT is NP-hard.*

Proof. [Sketch] We reduce 3-CNFSAT to NENT. As mentioned, the reduction shows that even atomic restricted entailment over extended conditional constraints is coNP-complete.

Let ψ be a boolean formula in 3-CNF form and let $\{x_1, x_2, \ldots, x_n\}$ and $\{c_1, c_2, \ldots, c_m\}$ be the boolean variables and clauses in ψ respectively. For each boolean variable x_i in ψ, we create two term variables α_{x_i} and $\alpha_{\overline{x_i}}$, which we use to decide the truth value of x_i. The value $\perp$ is treated as the boolean value false and any non-$\perp$ value is treated as the boolean value true.

Note, in a graph, a constraint of the form $\alpha \Rightarrow (\tau_1 = \tau_2)$ is represented as shown in Figure 6a.

First we need to ensure that a boolean variable takes on at most one truth value. We associate with each x_i constraints C_{x_i}, graphically represented as shown in Figure 6b, where τ_{x_i} is some internal variable. These constraints guarantee that at least one of α_{x_i} and $\alpha_{\overline{x_i}}$ is $\perp$. These constraints still allow both α_{x_i} and $\alpha_{\overline{x_i}}$ to be $\perp$, which we deal with below.

In the following, let $\alpha_{\overline{\overline{x}}} = \alpha_x$. For each clause $c_i = c_i^1 \vee c_i^2 \vee c_i^3$ of ψ, we create constraints C_{c_i} that ensure every clause is satisfied by a truth assignment. A clause is satisfied if at least one of the literals is true, which is the same as saying that the negations of the literals cannot all be true simultaneously. The constraints are in Figure 6c, where $\mu_1^{c_i}$ and $\mu_2^{c_i}$ are internal variables associated with c_i. As an example consider $c_i = \overline{x_2} \vee x_4 \vee \overline{x_7}$. The constraints C_{c_i} are shown in Figure 6d.

We let C_1 be the union of all the constraints C_{x_i} and C_{c_j} for $1 \leq i \leq n$ and $1 \leq j \leq m$, i.e.,

$$C_1 = (\bigcup_{i=1}^{n} C_{x_i}) \cup (\bigcup_{j=1}^{m} C_{c_j})$$

There is one additional requirement that we want to enforce: not both α_{x_i} and $\alpha_{\overline{x_i}}$ are $\perp$. This cannot be enforced directly in C_1. We construct constraints for C_2 to enforce this requirement. The idea is that if for any x_i, the term variables α_{x_i} and $\alpha_{\overline{x_i}}$ are both $\perp$, then the entailment holds.

We now proceed to construct C_2. The constraints C_2 represented graphically are shown in Figure 7. In the constraints, all the variables except α_{x_i} and $\alpha_{\overline{x_i}}$ are internal variables. These constraints can be used to enforce the requirement that for all x_i at least one of α_{x_i} and $\alpha_{\overline{x_i}}$ is non-$\perp$. The intuition is that if α_{x_i} and $\alpha_{\overline{x_i}}$ are both $\perp$, the internal variable ν_i can be $\perp$, which breaks the chain of conditional dependencies along the bottom of Figure 7, allowing $\mu_1, \ldots, \mu_{i-1}$ to be set to $\perp$ and $\mu_i, \ldots, \mu_{n-1}$ to be set to $\top$.

---

[3] Only variables, $\perp$, and $\top$ are in the constraint system.

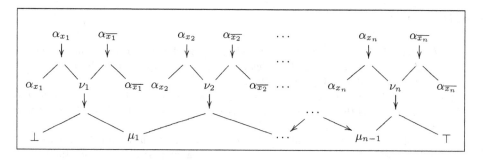

Fig. 7. Constructed constraint system C_2.

We let the set of interface variables $E = \{\alpha_{x_i}, \alpha_{\overline{x_i}} \mid 1 \leq i \leq n\}$. One can show that ψ is satisfiable iff $C_1 \nvDash_E C_2$. To prove the NP-hardness result, observe that the described reduction is a polynomial-time reduction. Thus, the decision problem NENT is NP-hard.

$\square$

We thus have shown that the entailment problem over extended conditional constraints is coNP-complete. The result holds even if all the constraints are restricted to be atomic.

Theorem 9. The decision problem $C_1 \vDash_E C_2$ over extended conditional constraints is coNP-complete.

6 Conclusions and Future Work

We have given a complete characterization of the complexities of deciding entailment for conditional equality constraints over finite types (finite trees). We believe the polynomial time algorithms in the paper are of practical use. There are a few related problems to be considered:

- What happens if we allow recursive types (*i.e.*, regular trees)?
- What is the relationship with strict constructors (*i.e.*, if $c(\bot) = \bot$)?
- What is the relationship with a type system equivalent to the equality-based flow systems [19]? In this type system, the only subtype relation is given by $\bot \leq t_1 \rightarrow t_2 \leq \top$, and there is no non-trivial subtyping between function types.

We believe the same or similar techniques can be used to address the above mentioned problems, and many of the results should carry over to these problem domains.

Acknowledgments. We thank Jeff Foster, Anders Møller, and the anonymous referees for their comments on an earlier version of this paper.

References

1. A. Aiken, E. Wimmers, and T.K. Lakshman. Soft Typing with Conditional Types. In *Twenty-First Annual ACM Symposium on Principles of Programming Languages*, pages 163–173, January 1994.
2. L. O. Andersen. *Program Analysis and Specialization for the C Programming Language*. PhD thesis, DIKU, University of Copenhagen, May 1994. DIKU report 94/19.
3. A. Colmerauer. Prolog and Infinite Trees. In K. L. Clark and S.-A. Tärnlund, editors, *Logic Programming*, pages 231–251. Academic Press, London, 1982.
4. A. Colmerauer. Equations and Inequations on Finite and Infinite Trees. In *2nd International Conference on Fifth Generation Computer Systems*, pages 85–99, 1984.
5. M. Fähndrich and A. Aiken. Making Set-Constraint Based Program Analyses Scale. In *First Workshop on Set Constraints at CP'96*, Cambridge, MA, August 1996. Available as Technical Report CSD-TR-96-917, University of California at Berkeley.
6. M. Fähndrich, J. Foster, Z. Su, and A. Aiken. Partial Online Cycle Elimination in Inclusion Constraint Graphs. In *Proceedings of the 1998 ACM SIGPLAN Conference on Programming Language Design and Implementation*, pages 85–96, Montreal, CA, June 1998.
7. C. Flanagan and M. Felleisen. Componential Set-Based Analysis. In *Proceedings of the 1997 ACM SIGPLAN Conference on Programming Language Design and Implementation*, pages 235–248, June 1997.
8. C. Flanagan, M. Flatt, S. Krishnamurthi, S. Weirich, and M. Felleisen. Catching Bugs in the Web of Program Invariants. In *Proceedings of the 1996 ACM SIGPLAN Conference on Programming Language Design and Implementation*, pages 23–32, May 1996.
9. J. Foster, M. Fähndrich, and A. Aiken. Monomorphic versus Polymorphic Flow-insensitive Points-to Analysis for C. In *Proceedings of the 7th International Static Analysis Symposium*, pages 175–198, 2000.
10. James Gosling, Bill Joy, and Guy Steele. *The Java Language Specification*. Addison Wesley, 1996.
11. N. Heintze. Set Based Analysis of ML Programs. In *Proceedings of the 1994 ACM Conference on LISP and Functional Programming*, pages 306–317, June 1994.
12. F. Henglein and J. Rehof. The Complexity of Subtype Entailment for Simple Types. In *Symposium on Logic in Computer Science*, pages 352–361, 1997.
13. F. Henglein and J. Rehof. Constraint Automata and the Complexity of Recursive Subtype Entailment. In *ICALP98*, pages 616–627, 1998.
14. Fritz Henglein. Global Tagging Optimization by Type Inference. In *1992 ACM Conference on Lisp and Functional Programming*, pages 205–215, June 1992.
15. Joxan Jaffar and Michael J. Maher. Constraint Logic Programming: A Survey. *The Journal of Logic Programming*, 19 & 20:503–582, May 1994.
16. N. D. Jones and S. S. Muchnick. Flow Analysis and Optimization of LISP-like Structures. In *Sixth Annual ACM Symposium on Principles of Programming Languages*, pages 244–256, January 1979.
17. S. Marlow and P. Wadler. A Practical Subtyping System For Erlang. In *Proceedings of the International Conference on Functional Programming (ICFP '97)*, pages 136–149, June 1997.

18. R Milner. A Theory of Type Polymorphism in Programming. *Journal of Computer and System Sciences*, 17(3):348–375, December 1978.

19. J. Palsberg. Equality-based Flow Analysis versus Recursive Types. *ACM Transactions on Programming Languages and Systems*, 20(6):1251–1264, 1998.

20. J. Palsberg and M. I. Schwartzbach. Object-Oriented Type Inference. In *Proceedings of the ACM Conference on Object-Oriented programming: Systems, Languages, and Applications*, pages 146–161, October 1991.

21. M.S. Paterson and M.N. Wegman. Linear Unification. *Journal of Computer and Systems Sciences*, 16(2):158–167, 1978.

22. J. C. Reynolds. *Automatic Computation of Data Set Definitions*, pages 456–461. Information Processing 68. North-Holland, 1969.

23. O. Shivers. Control Flow Analysis in Scheme. In *Proceedings of the ACM SIGPLAN '88 Conference on Programming Language Design and Implementation*, pages 164–174, June 1988.

24. G. Smolka and R. Treinen. Records for Logic Programming. *Journal of Logic Programming*, 18(3):229–258, 1994.

25. B. Steensgaard. Points-to Analysis in Almost Linear Time. In *Proceedings of the 23rd Annual ACM SIGPLAN-SIGACT Symposium on Principles of Programming Languages*, pages 32–41, January 1996.

26. Z. Su and A. Aiken. Entailment with Conditional Equality Constraints. Technical Report UCB//CSD-00-1113, University of California, Berkeley, October 2000.

27. Z. Su, M. Fähndrich, and A. Aiken. Projection Merging: Reducing Redundancies in Inclusion Constraint Graphs. In *Proceedings of the 27th Annual ACM SIGPLAN-SIGACT Symposium on Principles of Programming Languages*, pages 81–95, 2000.

28. R.E. Tarjan. Efficiency of a Good but Not Linear Set Union Algorithm. *JACM*, pages 215–225, 1975.

On the Complexity of Constant Propagation

Markus Müller-Olm and Oliver Rüthing

Universität Dortmund, FB Informatik, LS V,
D-44221 Dortmund, Germany
{mmo,ruething}@ls5.cs.uni-dortmund.de

Abstract. *Constant propagation* (*CP*) is one of the most widely used optimizations in practice (cf. [9]). Intuitively, it addresses the problem of statically detecting whether an expression always evaluates to a unique constant at run-time. Unfortunately, as proved by different authors [4, 16], CP is in general undecidable even if the interpretation of branches is completely ignored. On the other hand, it is certainly decidable in more restricted settings, like on loop-free programs (cf. [7]). In this paper, we explore the complexity of CP for a three-dimensional taxonomy. We present an almost complete complexity classification, leaving only two upper bounds open.

1 Motivation

Constant propagation (*CP*) is one of the most widely used optimizations in practice (cf. [1,4,9]). Intuitively, it aims at detecting expressions that always yield a unique constant value at run-time. Unfortunately, the constant propagation problem is undecidable even if the interpretation of branches is completely ignored, like in the common model of nondeterministic flow graphs where every program path is considered executable. Independent proofs of this important observation have been given by Hecht [4] and by Reif and Lewis [16]. We briefly recall the construction of Hecht, which is based on the Post correspondence problem. A Post correspondence system consists of a set of pairs $(u_1, v_1), \ldots, (u_k, v_k)$ with $u_i, v_i \in \{0, 1\}^*$. The correspondence system has a solution, iff there is a sequence $i_1, \ldots, i_n$ such that $u_{i_1} \cdot \ldots \cdot u_{i_n} = v_{i_1} \cdot \ldots \cdot v_{i_n}$. Figure 1 illustrates Hecht's reduction. The variables x and y are used as decimal numbers representing strings in $\{0, 1\}^*$. For each pair of the correspondence system a distinct branch of the loop appends the strings u_i and v_i to x and y, respectively.[1] It is easy to see that $x - y$ always evaluates to a value different from 0, if the Post correspondence problem has no solution.[2] In this case the expression $1 \operatorname{div} ((x-y)^2 + 1)$ always evaluates to 0. But if the Post correspondence system is solvable, this expression can evaluate to 1. Thus, r is constant (with value 0), if and only if the Post correspondence problem is not solvable. To exclude

---

[1] Technically, this is achieved by shifting the digits of x and y by $lg(u_i)$ and $lg(v_i)$ places first, where $lg(u_i)$ and $lg(v_i)$ are the length of the decimal representation of u_i and v_i, respectively.

[2] Note that the initialization of x and y with 1 avoids a problem with leading zeros.

D. Sands (Ed.): ESOP 2001, LNCS 2028, pp. 190–205, 2001.
© Springer-Verlag Berlin Heidelberg 2001

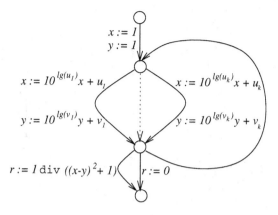

Fig. 1. Undecidability of CP: reduction of the Post correspondence problem.

r from being constantly 1 in the case that the Post correspondence system is universally solvable, r is set to 0 by a bypassing assignment statement.

On the other hand, constant propagation is certainly decidable for *acyclic*, i.e., loop-free, programs. But even in this setting the problem is intractable, as it has been shown to be co-NP-hard [7] recently . This result is based on a polynomial time reduction of the co-problem of 3-SAT, the *satisfiability* problem for clauses which are conjunctions consisting of three negated or unnegated Boolean variables (cf. [3]). An instance of 3-SAT is solvable if there is a variable assignment such that every clause is satisfied.

The reduction is illustrated in Figure 2 for a 3-SAT instance over the Boolean variables $\{b_1, \ldots, b_k\}$:

$$\underbrace{(b_3 \vee \overline{b_5} \vee b_6)}_{c_1} \wedge \ldots \wedge \underbrace{(b_2 \vee \overline{b_3} \vee b_5)}_{c_n} .$$

For each Boolean variable b_i two integer variables x_i and $\overline{x_i}$ are introduced that are initialized by 0. The idea underlying the reduction is the following: each path of the program chooses a witnessing literal in each clause by setting the corresponding variable to 1. If this can be done without setting both x_i and $\overline{x_i}$ for some i then we have found a satisfying truth assignment, and vice versa. On such a path $r1$ and consequently $r2$ evaluate to 0. On all other paths the value of $r1$ differs from 0 but stays in the range $\{1, \ldots, k\}$ enforcing that variable $r2$ is set to 1. Summarizing, $r2$ evaluates to 1 on every program path if and only if the underlying instance of 3-SAT has no solution. Similarly to the undecidability reduction of Figure 1 the assignment $r1 := 1$ avoids that $r1$ is constantly 0 in the case that all runs induce satisfying truth assignments.

Note that both reductions presented so far crucially depend on an operator like integer division (or modulo) which is capable of projecting many different values onto a single one.

Contributions. This paper aims at examining the borderline of intractability and undecidability more closely. To this end, we investigate the constant

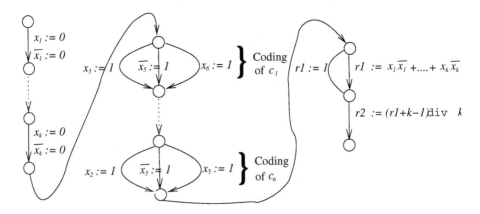

Fig. 2. Co-NP-hardness of CP for acyclic programs: reduction of co-3-SAT.

propagation problem for integers with respect to a three-dimensional taxonomy. The first dimension is given by the distinction between arbitrary and loop-free programs. We are currently also examining further extensions of this dimension towards interprocedural and explicitly parallel programs (for first results see [11]). However, this is beyond the scope of this paper whose focus is more directed towards examining the influences of the other two dimensions

The second dimension is concerned with the underlying signature. We consider signatures without operators (*copy-constants*), with linear expressions $x := ay + b$ (*linear constants*), with operators restricted to the set $\{+, -\}$ (Presburger constants), operators restricted to $\{+, -, *\}$ ($+, -, *$-constants), and the standard signature, i.e., the one with operators $+, -, *, \mathtt{div}, \mathtt{mod}$. Finally, in the third dimension we investigate the general nature of the constant propagation problem. Besides the standard *must-constancy* problem we also consider the less frequently addressed problem of *may-constancy* here. Essentially, this problem asks if a variable may evaluate to a given constant c on some program path. Inspired by the work of Muth and Debray [12] we further distinguish between a *single value* and a *multiple value* variant, where in the latter case the values of multiple variables might be checked simultaneously.[3]

While the most prominent application of must-CP is the *compile-time simplification* of expressions, the must- and may-variants are equally well suited for eliminating unnecessary branches in programs. Furthermore, the may-variant reveals some interesting insight in the complexity of (may-)aliasing of array elements.

In this paper, we present an almost complete complexity classification, providing all hardness results, i.e., lower bounds, leaving only two upper bounds open. In particular, we observe that detecting may-constants is significantly harder than detecting their must-counterparts. Furthermore, we demonstrate that Presburger must-constants are polynomial time detectable which is some-

---

[3] Muth and Debray introduced the single and multiple value variants as models for independent-attribute and relational-attribute data flow analyses [5].

how surprising, as non-distributivity in the standard setting already shows up for this class. Finally, as a by-product we obtain some interesting results on the decidability of may-aliasing of arrays.

2   The Setting

Flow Graphs. As usual in data-flow analysis and program optimization, we represent programs by *directed flow graphs* $G = (N, E, \mathbf{s}, \mathbf{e})$ with node set N, edge set E, a unique start node $\mathbf{s}$, and a unique end node $\mathbf{e}$, which are assumed to have no predecessors and successors, respectively. Each edge is associated with an assignment statement or with the statement "skip". Edges represent the branching structure and the statements of a program, while nodes represent program points. For readability the annotation "skip" is omitted in the figures.

By $pred(n)=_{df} \{ m \mid (m, n) \in E \}$ and $succ(n)=_{df} \{ m \mid (n, m) \in E \}$ we denote the set of immediate predecessors and successors of a node n. Additionally, by $source(e)$ and $dest(e)$, $e \in E$, we denote the *source node* and the *destination node* of edge e. A *finite path* in G is a sequence $(e_1, \ldots, e_q)$ of edges such that $dest(e_j) = source(e_{j+1})$ for $j \in \{1, \ldots, q-1\}$. It is called a path from m to n, if $source(e_1) = m$ and $dest(e_q) = n$. By $\mathbf{P}[m, n]$ we denote the set of all (finite) paths from m to n. Without loss of generality we assume that every node of a flow graph G lies on a path from $\mathbf{s}$ to $\mathbf{e}$.

Semantics of Terms. In this article we concentrate on integer expressions Exp which are inductively built from variables $v \in \mathbf{V}$, constants $c \in \mathbf{C}$, and binary integer operators $\mathbf{Op} = \{+, -, *, \mathrm{div}, \mathrm{mod}\}$. The *semantics* of integer expressions is induced by the *standard interpretation* $S = (\mathbb{Z}_\perp, S_0)$, where $\mathbb{Z}_\perp =_{df} \mathbb{Z} \cup \{\perp\}$ is the flat integer domain with least element $\perp$ and S_0 is a function mapping every integer constant $c \in \mathbf{C}$ to the corresponding datum $S_0(c) \in \mathbb{Z}$, and every integer operator $op \in \mathbf{Op}$ to the corresponding total and strict function $S_0(op) : (\mathbb{Z}_\perp)^2 \to \mathbb{Z}_\perp$. $\Sigma =_{df} \{ \sigma \mid \sigma : \mathbf{V} \to \mathbb{Z}_\perp \}$ denotes the set of *states*, and $\sigma_\perp$ the distinct *start state* assigning $\perp$ to all variables $v \in \mathbf{V}$. This choice reflects that we do not assume anything about the context of the analyzed program. The *semantics* of an expression $e \in$ Exp is then given by the evaluation function $\mathcal{E} :$ Exp $\to (\Sigma \to \mathbb{Z}_\perp)$ inductively defined by $\mathcal{E}(x)(\sigma)=_{df} \sigma(x)$ for $x \in \mathbf{V}$, $\mathcal{E}(c)(\sigma)=_{df} I_0(c)$ for $c \in \mathbf{C}$ and $\mathcal{E}(op(e_1, e_2))(\sigma)=_{df} I_0(op)(\mathcal{E}(e_1)(\sigma), \mathcal{E}(e_2)(\sigma))$ for composite expressions.

Each assignment statement $\iota \equiv x := e$ is associated with the *state transformation function* $\theta_\iota : \Sigma \to \Sigma$ which is defined by $\theta_\iota(\sigma)(y)=_{df} \mathcal{E}(e)(\sigma)$ if $y = x$ and $\theta_\iota(\sigma)(y)=_{df} \sigma(y)$ otherwise.

The statement $\iota \equiv skip$ is associated with the identity state transformer, $\theta_\iota(\sigma) = \sigma$. We obtain the set of states Σ_n, which are possible at a program point $n \in N$ as follows:[4] $\Sigma_n =_{df} \{ \theta_p(\sigma_\perp) \mid p \in \mathbf{P}[\mathbf{s}, n] \}$.

---

[4] In the definition of Σ_n, θ_p denotes the straightforward extension of the state transformation functions to paths.

Classes of Constants

In the following we briefly introduce some classes of constants that are of particular interest with respect to the taxonomy considered later on in the paper. We start by providing a distinction of constants into the more common class of must-constants and the less frequently considered class of may-constants. For both we provide their formal definitions as well as some application scenarios.

Must-Constants. Formally, an expression e is a must-constant at node n if and only if

$$\exists d \in \mathbb{Z} \ \forall \sigma \in \Sigma_n. \ \mathcal{E}(e)(\sigma) = d.$$

The problem of (must-)constancy propagation is to determine for a given expression e, whether e is a must-constant and if so what the value of the constant is. This information can be used in various ways. The most important application is the *compile-time simplification* of expressions. Furthermore, information on must-constancy can be exploited in order to eliminate conditional branches. For instance, if there is a condition $e \neq d$ situated at an edge leaving node n and e is determined a must-constant of value d at node n, then this branch can be classified unexecutable (cf. Figure 3(a)). Since (must-)constant propagation and the elimination of unexecutable branches mutually benefit from each other, approaches for *conditional constant propagation* where developed taking this effect into account [20,2].

May-Constants. Complementary to the must-constancy problem an expression e is a may-constant of value $d \in \mathbb{Z}$ at node n if and only if

$$\exists \sigma \in \Sigma_n. \ \mathcal{E}(e)(\sigma) = d.$$

Note that opposed to the must-constancy definition here the value of the constant is given as an additional input parameter. This naturally induces a *multiple value* extension of the notion of may-constancy. Given expressions $e_1, \dots, e_k$ and values $d_1, \dots, d_k \in \mathbb{Z}$ the corresponding multiple value may-constancy problem is defined by:

$$\exists \sigma \in \Sigma_n. \ \mathcal{E}(e_1)(\sigma) = d_1 \ \wedge \ \dots \ \wedge \mathcal{E}(e_k)(\sigma) = d_k.$$

While may-constancy information cannot be used for expression simplification, it has also some valuable applications. Most obvious is a complementary branch elimination transformation. If an expression e is not a may-constant of value d at node n then any branch being guarded by a condition $e = d$ is unexecutable (cf. Figure 3(b)).

May-constancy information is also valuable for reasoning about the aliasing of array elements. This can be used, for instance, for parallelization of code or for improving the precision of other analyses by excluding a worst-case treatment of assignments to elements in an array. Figure 4 gives such an example in the context of constant propagation. Here the assignment to x can be simplified towards

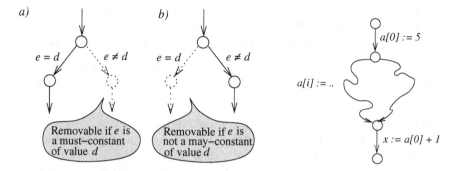

Fig. 3. Constancy information used for branch elimination.

Fig. 4. Using array alias information from may-constant propagation in the context of (must)-constant propagation.

$x := 6$, only if the assignment to $a[i]$ does not influence $a[0]$. This, however, can be guaranteed if i is not a may-constant of value 0 at the corresponding program node.

Next we formally introduce some classes of constants according to the form of expressions that are allowed on the right hand side of assignments. Except of linear constants these classes are induced by considering only a fragment of the standard signature. While the first two classes are well-known in the field of constant propagation and the class of Presburger constants is closely related to the class of affine constants investigated in [6][5], we are not aware of any work devoted to the fragment of $+, -, *$-constants.

Copy-Constants. If all expressions in the program are non-composite, then the resulting constants are denoted *copy-constants*. This is due to the fact that constants can only be produced by assignments $x := c$ and be propagated by assignments of the form $x := y$.

Linear Constants. If the expressions in the program are restricted to linear ones, which means that all assignments take the form $x := a\,z + b$ where a and b are integer constants and z is an integer variable,[6] then the resulting constants are denoted *linear constants*.

Presburger Constants. If the expressions of the program are restricted to ones built from the operator $+$ and $-$, then the resulting constants are denoted *Presburger constants*. We decided for this term according to Presburger arithmetics, where integer operations are also restricted to addition and subtraction. However, the complexity issues in deciding Presburger formulas and Presburger constants are of a completely different nature, since in the context of constant propagation the problem is mainly induced by path conditions and not by a given logical formula. As far as expressiveness is concerned Presburger expressions and

---

[5] Affine constants are linear ones generalized towards multiple variables, i.e., constants in programs where expressions take only the form $a_1 x_1 + \ldots + a_k x_k$.

[6] If $a = 0$ or $b = 0$ the corresponding summand may be omitted.

affine expressions coincide because multiplication with constants can be simulated by iterated addition. Affine expressions can, however, be more succinct. Nevertheless all results of this paper equally apply to both characterizations.

$+, -, *$**-Constants.** If the expressions of the program are restricted to ones built from the operator $+, -$ and $*$, then the resulting constants are called $+, -, *$-*Constants.*

It is for technical convenience and conceptual clarity that the classes of constants are introduced by means of a restriction to the form of all assignments in the considered programs. In practice, one uses a complete algorithm for either of the classes and extends it to programs with a more general kind of expressions in assignments by worst-case or approximating assumptions. The resulting algorithm can then still detect constants in the program completely that only depend on assignments of the given form. When judging the practical relevance of the results this should be kept in mind.

3   The Taxonomy and Complexity Results

3.1   Known Results

Table 1 summarizes the already known complexity results. Problems with a polynomial time algorithm are emphasized in a light shade of grey, those being decidable though intractable in a dark shade of grey, and the undecidable fields are filled black. White fields represent problems where the complexity and decidability is unknown or at least, to the best of our knowledge, undocumented.

In the following we briefly comment on these results. For an unrestricted signature we already presented Hecht's undecidability reduction for must-constants and the co-NP-hardness result for the acyclic counterpart.

It is also well-known that the must-constant propagation problem is distributive [4], if all right-hand side expressions are either constant or represent a one-to-one function in $\mathbb{Z} \to \mathbb{Z}$ depending on a single variable (see the remark on page 206 in [18]). Hence the class of linear constants defines a distributive data flow problem, which guarantees that the standard maximum fixed point iteration strategy over $\mathbb{Z} \cup \{\bot, \top\}$ computes the exact solution in polynomial time.[7]

On side of the may-constancy problem the class of copy-constant has recently been examined by Muth and Debray [12]. It is obvious, that the single value case can be dealt with efficiently. This is due to the fact that the number of constant values that a variable may posses at a program point (via copy-assignments) is bound to the number of assignments to constants in the program. Hence one can essentially keep track of any possible constant value at a program point by

---

[7] Sagiv, Reps and Horwitz [17] gave an alternative procedure for detecting linear constants by solving a graph reachability problem on the *exploded supergraph* of a program. They additionally showed that with this method linear constant propagation can be solved precisely even for interprocedural control flow.

Table 1. Complexity classification of a taxonomy of CP: the known results.

		Must-Constants	May-Constants	
			single value	multiple value
acyclic control flow	Copy Constants	**P**	**P**	**NP-complete** Muth & Debray [12]
	Linear Constants	**P** Sharir & Pnueli [18]		
	Pressburger Constants			
	+,-,* Constants			
	Full Constants	**Co-NP hard** Knoop & Rüthing [7]		
unrestricted control flow	Copy Constants	**P**	**P**	**PSPACE-compl.** Muth & Debray [12]
	Linear Constants	**P** Sharir & Pnueli [18]		
	Presburger Constants			
	+,-,* Constants			
	Full Constants	**undecidable** Hecht [4]		

collecting the set of possible values of variables. Formally, this can be achieved by computing the union-over-all-path solution in a union-distributive data flow framework over the lattice $\{\sigma | \sigma : \mathbf{V} \to \mathfrak{P}(\mathbb{Z}_G)\}$, where $\mathbb{Z}_G$ denotes the set of constant right-hand sides in the flow graph G under consideration.

The multiple value problem has been shown NP-complete in the acyclic case and PSPACE-complete in the presence of unrestricted control flow [12].

In the remainder of this section we aim at successively filling the white parts in Table 1. To this end, we start with providing new undecidability results, then give some new intractability results and finally indicate that constant propagation can be achieved efficiently for the class of Presburger constants.

3.2   New Undecidability Results

Fortunately, Hecht's construction that was sketched in the introduction can easily be adapted for proving undecidability of Presburger may-constants. The only modification necessary for this is to replace the two assignment to r in Figure 1 by a single assignment $x := x - y$. As argued before, x may equal y immediately after leaving the loop, if and only if the instance of the Post correspondence problem has a solution. Hence in this case $x - y$ may evaluate to 0. As the multiplications with the constants $10^{lg(u_i)}$ and $10^{lg(v_i)}$ can be expressed by iterated additions, we get:

Theorem 1. *Deciding single valued may-constancy at a program point is undecidable for the class of Presburger constants.*

This construction can be further modified to obtain an even stronger undecidability result for the class of multiple value may-constants. Here we have:

Theorem 2. *Deciding multiple valued may-constancy at a program point is undecidable for the class of linear constants. This even holds if only two values are questioned.*

The idea is to substitute the difference $x - y$ in the assignment to r by a loop which simultaneously decrements x and y. It is easy to see that $x = 0 \land y = 0$ may hold at the end of such a program fragment, if and only if x may equal y at the end of the main loop.

Complexity of Array Aliasing. The previous two undecidability results have an immediate impact on the problem of array aliasing, which complements similar results known in the field of pointer induced aliasing [8]. In fact as a consequence of Theorem 1 we have:

Corollary 1. *Deciding whether $a[i]$ may alias $a[c]$ for a one-dimensional array a, integer variable i and integer constant c is undecidable, even if i is computed only using the operators $+$ and $-$.*

In fact, Theorem 2 even provides some negative results for array accesses when using only linear index calculations.[8] We have:

Corollary 2. *Let c_1, c_2 be integer constants and i, j integer variables being computed only with linear assignments of the form $x := a\,y + b$. Then the following problems are undecidable:*

1. *Determining whether $a[i]$ may alias $a[j]$ for a one-dimensional array a.*
2. *Determining whether $a[i, j]$ may alias $a[c_1, c_2]$ for a two-dimensional array a.*

It should be noted that traditional work on array dependences like the omega test [14,15] is restricted to scenarios where array elements are addressed by affine functions depending on some index variables of possibly nested for-loops. In this setting the aliasing problem can be stated as an integer linear programming problem which can be solved effectively. In contrast, our results address the more fundamental issue of aliasing in the presence of arbitrary loops.

3.3 New Intractability Results

After having marked off the range of undecidability we prove in this section intractability of some of the uncovered fields.

We start by strengthening the result on the co-NP-hardness of must-constant propagation for acyclic control flow. Here the construction of Figure 2 can be modified such that the usage of integer division is no longer necessary. Basically, the trick is to use multiplication by 0 as the projective operation, i.e., as the

---

[8] The first part is not an immediate corollary, but relies on the same construction as Theorem 2.

operation with the power to map many different values onto a single one. In the construction of Figure 2 this requires the following modifications. All variables are now initialized by 1. The part reflecting the clauses then sets the corresponding variables to 0. Finally the assignments to r_1 and r_2 are substituted by a single assignment $r := (x_1 + \overline{x}_1) \cdot \ldots \cdot (x_k + \overline{x}_k)$ being bypassed by another assignment $r := 0$. It is easy to see that the instance of 3-SAT has no solution if and only if on every path both x_i and $\overline{x}_i$ are set to 0 for some $i \in \{1, \ldots, k\}$. This, however, guarantees that at least one factor of the right-hand side expression defining r is 0 which then ensures that r is a must-constant of value 0. Finally, the branch performing the assignment $r := 0$ assures that r cannot be a must-constant of any other value. Thus we have:

Theorem 3. *Must-constant propagation is co-NP hard even when restricted to acyclic control flow and to $+, -, *$-constants.*

On the other hand, we can show that the problem of must-constant propagation is in co-NP for acyclic control flow. To this end, one has to prove that the co-problem, i.e., checking non-constancy at a program point, is in NP, which is easy to see: a non-deterministic Turing machine can guess two paths through the program witnessing two different values. Since each path is of linear length in the program size and the integer operations can be performed in linear time with respect to the sum of the lengths of the decimal representation of their inputs, this can be done in polynomial time. Hence we have:

Theorem 4. *Must-constant propagation is in co-NP when restricted to acyclic control flow.*

Next we are going to show that the problem addressed by Theorem 3 gets presumably harder without the restriction to acyclic control flow.

Theorem 5. *Must-constant propagation is PSPACE-hard even when restricted to $+, -, *$-constants.*

Theorem 5 is proved by means of a polynomial time reduction from the language universality problem of nondeterministic finite automata (NDFA) (cf. remark to Problem AL1 in [3]). This is the question whether an NDFA $\mathcal{A}$ over an alphabet X accepts the universal language, i.e., $L(\mathcal{A}) = X^*$. W.l.o.g. let us thus consider an NDFA $\mathcal{A} = (X, S, \delta, s_1, F)$, where $X = \{0, 1\}$ is the underlying alphabet, $S = \{1, \ldots, k\}$ the set of states, $\delta \subseteq S \times X \times S$ the transition relation, s_1 the start state, and $F \subseteq S$ the set of accepting states. The polynomial time reduction to a constant propagation problem is depicted in Figure 5.

For every state $i \in \{1, \ldots, k\}$ a variable s_i is introduced. The idea of the construction is to guess an arbitrary input word letter by letter. While this is done, it is ensured by appropriate assignments that each variable s_i holds 0 if and only state i is reachable in the automaton under the word. $\prod_{i \in F} s_i$ is then 0 for all words if and only if $\mathcal{A}$ accepts the universal language.

Initially, only the start state variable s_1 is set to 0 as it is the only state which is reachable under the empty word. The central part of the program is

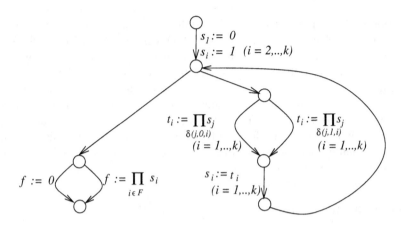

Fig. 5. PSPACE-hardness of must-constant propagation for $+, -, *$-constants.

a loop which guesses an alphabet symbol for the next transition. If we decide, for instance, for 0 then, for each i, an auxiliary state variable t_i is set to 0 by the assignment $t_i := \prod_{\delta(j,0,i)} s_j$, if and only if one of its 0-predecessors is recognized reachable.[9] After all variables t_i have been set in this way their values are copied to the variables s_i, respectively. The loop can be left at any time; then it is checked whether the guessed word is accepted. Like before, the direct assignment $f := 0$ has the purpose to ensure that constant values different from 0 are impossible. Therefore, f is a must-constant (of value 0) at the end of the program, if and only if the underlying automaton accepts the universal language $\{0,1\}^*$.

The final reduction in this section addresses the complexity of linear may-constants. Here we have:

Theorem 6. *May-constant propagation is NP-hard even when restricted to the class of linear constants.*

Again we employ a polynomial time reduction from 3-SAT which however differs from the ones seen before. The major idea here is to code a set of satisfied clauses by a number interpreted as a bit-string. For example, in an instance with four clauses the number 1100 would indicate that clause two and three are satisfied, while clause zero and one are not. To avoid problems with carry-over effects, we employ a $(k+1)$-adic number representation where k is the number of variables in the 3-SAT instance. With this coding we can use linear assignments to set the single "bits" corresponding to satisfied clauses.

---

[9] Auxiliary state variables are introduced in order to avoid overwriting state variables which are still used in consecutive assignments.

To illustrate our reduction let us assume an instance of 3-SAT with Boolean variables $\{b_1, \ldots, b_k\}$ and clauses $c_0, \ldots, c_{n-1}$, where the literal b_1 is contained in c_3 and c_5, and the negated literal $\neg b_1$ is contained in c_2 only. Then this is coded in a program as depicted in Figure 6. We have a non-deterministic choice part for each Boolean variable b_i. The left branch sets the bits for the clauses that contain b_i and the right branch those for the clauses that contain $\overline{b}_i$. Every assignment can be bypassed by an empty edge in case

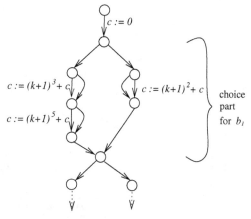

Fig. 6: NP-hardness of linear may-CP.

that the clause is also made true by another literal. It is now easy to see that r is a may-constant of value $\underbrace{1 \ldots 1}_{n \ times}$ (in $(k+1)$-adic number representation) if and only if the underlying instance of 3-SAT is satisfiable.

On the other hand, it is easy to see that detecting may-constancy is in NP for acyclic control flow, since a nondeterministic Turing machine can guess a witnessing path for a given constant in polynomial time. We have:

Theorem 7. *May-constant propagation is in NP when restricted to acyclic control flow.*

3.4   New Polynomial-Time Algorithm

In this section we fill the last field in our taxonomy by showing that all Presburger constants can be detected in polynomial time.

One way of showing this claim is by carefully investigating a polynomial-time algorithm proposed by Karr [6]. He employs a *forward* data flow analysis that establishes for each program point n an *affine vector space* (over $\mathbb{Q}$) that over-approximates Σ_n. This information can in turn be used to detect certain constants. It can be shown that the resulting algorithm is complete with respect to the detection of Presburger constants, a question that has not been explored by Karr, but this proof is beyond the scope of the current paper. In the following we sketch a new algorithm that leads to a more transparent proof of polynomial-time detectability of Presburger constants.

Figure 7 gives an impression on the problem dimension behind this class where the emphazised annotation will be explained later.

Part (a) of this Figure extends the classical non-distributivity pattern of constant propagation (cf. [4]). The point here is that z is a must-constant of value 14 at the end of the program. However, none of its operands is constant, although both are defined outside of any conditional branch. Part (b) shows a small loop example where z is a must-constant of value 0. However, also this

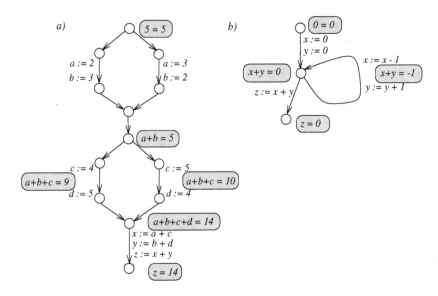

Fig. 7. Deciding Presburger constants by backward propagation of linear constraints.

example is outside of the scope of any standard algorithm except of Karr's, and even outside of the scope of Knoop's and Steffen's EXPTIME algorithm for detecting finite constants [19].

The algorithm at a glance. Our algorithm employs techniques known from linear algebra. In fact, we use a backward analysis propagating sets of *linear equational constraints* describing *affine vector spaces* (over $\mathbb{Q}$).

The Data Flow Framework. Given a set of program variables $\{x_1, \ldots, x_k\}$ a linear constraint is an equation of the form: $\sum_i a_i x_i = b$ where $a_i, b \in \mathbb{Q}$ ($i = 1, \ldots, k$). Since at most k of these linear constraints are linearly independent, an affine vector space can always be described by means of a linear equation system $\mathbf{A} x = b$ where $\mathbf{A}$ is a $k \times k$-matrix. The affine vector sub-spaces of $\mathbb{Q}^k$ can be partially ordered by set inclusion. This results in a (complete) lattice where the length of chains is bounded by k as any affine space strictly contained in another affine space has a smaller dimension.

The Meet Operation. The meet of two affine vector spaces represented by the equations $\mathbf{A}_1 x = b_1$ and $\mathbf{A}_2 x = b_2$ can be computed by normalizing the equation

$$\begin{pmatrix} \mathbf{A}_1 \\ \mathbf{A}_2 \end{pmatrix} x = \begin{pmatrix} b_1 \\ b_2 \end{pmatrix}$$

which can be done efficiently using Gauss-elimination [13].

Local Transfer Functions. The local transfer functions are realized by performing a backward substitution on the linear constraints. For instance, a constraint $3x + y = 10$ is backward-substituted along an assignment $x := 2u - 3v + 5$ towards

$3\,(2\,u - 3\,v + 5) + y = 10$ which then can be "normalized" towards $y + 6\,u - 9\,v = 5$. Clearly, this can be done in polynomial time. After this normalization, the resulting equation system is also simplified using Gauss-elimination.

The Overall Procedure. Our backward data flow analysis can be regarded as a demand-driven analysis which works separately for each variable x and program point n. Conceptually, it is organized in three stages:

Stage 1: Guess an arbitrary cycle-free path leading to n, for instance using depth-first search, and compute the value d of x on this path.

Stage 2: Solve the backward data flow analysis where initially the program point n is annotated by the affine vector space described by the linear constraint: $x = d$ and all other program points by the universal affine space, i.e., the one given by $\mathbf{0}\,x = 0$.

Stage 3: The guess generated in stage 1 is proved, if and only if the start node is still associated with the universal affine vector space.[10]

The completeness of the algorithm is a simple consequence of the distributivity of the analysis. Obviously, the guessed constraint is true iff the backward substitution along every path originating at the start node yields a universally valid constraint at the start node. Since this defines the meet-over-all-paths solution of our data flow framework the algorithmic solution is guaranteed to coincide if the transfer functions are distributive, which is immediate from the definition.

The algorithm can also be understood from a program verification point of view. By Stage 1, d is the only candidate value for x being constant at n. Stage 2 effectively computes the weakest (liberal) precondition of the assertion $x = d$ at program point n. Clearly, x is a constant at n if and only if the weakest liberal precondition of $x = d$ is universally valid.

As mentioned, the length of chains in the analysis is bound by the number of variables k. Any change at a node can trigger a reevaluation at its predecessor nodes. Therefore, we have at most $O(e \cdot k)$ Gauss-elimination steps, where e denotes the number of edges in the flow graph. Each Gauss-elimination step is of order $\mathcal{O}(k^3)$ [13]. Thus the complexity for the complete data flow analysis w.r.t. a single occurrence of a program variable is $\mathcal{O}(e\,k^4)$. For an exhaustive analysis that computes must-constancy information for any left-hand side occurrence of a variable the estimation becomes $\mathcal{O}(n\,e\,k^4)$, where n denotes the number of nodes in the flow graph. Summarizing, we have:

Theorem 8. *The class of Presburger must-constants can be detected in polynomial time.*

Finally, we are going to illustrate our algorithm by means of the example of Figure 7. The emphazised annotation of Figure 7 contains the constraints resulting from the initial guess $z = 14$ (in Figure 7(a)) and $z = 0$ (in Figure 7(b)), respectively. It should be noted that for the sake of presentation we did not

---

[10] In practice, one may already terminate with the result of non-constancy of x whenever a linear equation system encountered during the analysis renders unsolvable.

display the constraints for every program point. The particular power of this technique lies in the normalization performed on the linear constraints which provides a handle to cope with arithmetic properties like commutativity and associativity to a certain extent. For instance, the constraint $a + b = 5$ in Figure 7(a) has been the uniform result of two different intermediate constraints.

4   Summary and Conclusions

The decidability and complexity considerations of this paper are summarized in Table 2. In fact, we almost completely succeeded in filling the white fields of Table 1. As apparent, only two upper bounds are left open. At the moment we neither have an upper bound for the class of $+, -, *$-must-constants nor for the class of linear may-constants. Although we do not expect one of the problems to be undecidable, a solution might require some deeper number theoretical insights.

An interesting observation which is immediately obvious from inspecting the table is that the detection of may-constants is significantly harder than detecting their must-counterparts.

Future work will be concerned with answering the open upper bounds, with tuning the constraint based technique for Presburger constants into an algorithm that is usable in practice, and with extending the taxonomy by considering advanced settings, like interprocedural or parallel ones, too. In as yet unpublished work we show that in a setting with fork-join type parallelism the intraprocedural problem is PSPACE-complete already for may- and must-copy constants and becomes even undecidable for the corresponding interprocedural problems (see [11] for somewhat weaker results).

References

1. A. V. Aho, R. Sethi, and J. D. Ullman. *Compilers: Principles, Techniques and Tools*. Addison-Wesley, 1985.
2. C. Click and K. D. Cooper. Combining analyses, combining optimizations. *ACM Transactions on Programming Languages and Systems*, 17(2):181 – 196, 1995.
3. M. R. Garey and D. S. Johnson. *Computers and Intractability – A Guide to the Theory of NP-Completeness*. W.H. Freeman & Co, San Francisco, 1979.
4. M. S. Hecht. *Flow Analysis of Computer Programs*. Elsevier, North-Holland, 1977.
5. N. D. Jones and S. S Muchnick. Complexity of flow analysis, inductive assertion synthesis, and a language due to Dijkstra. In [10], chapter 12, pages 380–393.
6. M. Karr. Affine relationships among variables of a program. *Acta Informatica*, 6:133–151, 1976.
7. J. Knoop and O. Rüthing. Constant propagation on the value graph: simple constants and beyond. In *CC'2000*, LNCS 1781, pages 94–109, Berlin, Germany, 2000. Springer-Verlag.
8. W. Landi. Undecidability of static analysis. *ACM Letters on Programming Languages and Systems*, 1(4):323–337, 1992.

Table 2. Complexity classification of a taxonomy of CP: summarizing the results.

		Must-Constants	May-Constants	
			single value	multiple value
acyclic control flow	Copy Constants			
	Linear Constants			
	Pressburger Constants			
	+,-,* Constants	Co-NP compl.	NP complete	NP complete
	Full Constants			
unrestricted control flow	Copy Constants			PSPACE-compl.
	Linear Constants		NP-hard	
	Presburger Constants			
	+,-,* Constants	PSPACE-hard	undecidable	
	Full Constants			

9. S. S. Muchnick. *Advanced Compiler Design & Implementation*. Morgan Kaufmann, San Francisco, CA, 1997.
10. S. S. Muchnick and N. D. Jones, editors. *Program Flow Analysis: Theory and Applications*. Prentice Hall, Englewood Cliffs, NJ, 1981.
11. M. Müller-Olm. The complexity of copy constant detection in parallel programs. In *STACS'2001*, LNCS, 2001. Springer-Verlag. To appear.
12. R. Muth and S. Debray. On the complexity of flow-sensitive dataflow analysis. In *POPL'2000*, pages 67–81, ACM, Boston, MA, 2000.
13. C. H. Papadimitriou. *Computational Complexity*. Addison-Wesley, 1994.
14. W. Pugh. The Omega Test: a fast and practical integer programming algorithm for dependence analysis. In IEEE, editor, *Supercomputing '91*, Albuquerque, NM, pages 4–13. IEEE Computer Society Press, 1991.
15. W. Pugh and D. Wonnacott. Constraint-based array dependence analysis. *ACM Transactions on Programming Languages and Systems*, 20(3):635–678, 1998.
16. J. H. Reif and R. Lewis. Symbolic evaluation and the gobal value graph. *POPL'77*, pages 104–118, ACM, Los Angeles, CA, 1977.
17. M. Sagiv, T. Reps, and S. Horwitz. Precise interprocedural dataflow analysis with applications to constant propagation. *Theoretical Computer Science*, 167(1–2):131–170, 1996.
18. M. Sharir and A. Pnueli. Two approaches to interprocedural data flow analysis. In [10], chapter 7, pages 189–233.
19. B. Steffen and J. Knoop. Finite constants: Characterizations of a new decidable set of constants. *Theoretical Computer Science*, 80(2):303–318, 1991.
20. M. N. Wegman and F. K. Zadeck. Constant propagation with conditional branches. *ACM Transactions on Programming Languages and Systems*, 13(2), 1991.

What Are Polymorphically-Typed Ambients?

Torben Amtoft*, Assaf J. Kfoury**, and Santiago M. Pericas-Geertsen***

Boston University
{tamtoft,kfoury,santiago}@cs.bu.edu

Abstract. The Ambient Calculus was developed by Cardelli and Gordon as a formal framework to study issues of mobility and migrant code [6]. We consider an Ambient Calculus where ambients transport and exchange programs rather that just inert data. We propose different senses in which such a calculus can be said to be *polymorphically typed*, and design accordingly a *polymorphic* type system for it. Our type system assigns *types* to embedded programs and what we call *behaviors* to processes; a denotational semantics of behaviors is then proposed, here called *trace semantics*, underlying much of the remaining analysis. We state and prove a Subject Reduction property for our polymorphically-typed calculus. Based on techniques borrowed from finite automata theory, type-checking of fully type-annotated processes is shown to be decidable. Our polymorphically-typed calculus is a conservative extension of the typed Ambient Calculus originally proposed by Cardelli and Gordon [7].

1 Introduction

1.1 Background and Motivation

With the advent of the Internet a few years ago, considerable effort has gone into the study of *mobile computation* and programming languages that support it. On the theoretical side of this research, several concurrent and distributed calculi have been proposed, such as the Distributed Join Calculus [8], the Dπ Calculus [16], the Box-Pi Calculus [17], the Seal Calculus [20], among others. The *Ambient Calculus* (henceforth, **AC**) is a recent addition to this list and the starting point of our investigation.

Our long-term interest is the design and implementation of a strongly-typed programming language for mobile computation. Part of this effort is an examination of **AC** as a foundation for such a language. An important step in achieving a greater degree of modularity and a more natural style of programming, without sacrificing the benefits of strong typing, is to make ambients *polymorphically typed*. This is the focus of the present paper.

Early type systems for **AC** (see [7,5] among others) restrict ambients to be *monomorphic*: There can be only one "topic of conversation" (the type of exchanged data) in an ambient, initially and throughout its existence as a location

---

* http://www.cs.bu.edu/associates/tamtoft
** http://www.cs.bu.edu/~kfoury
*** http://cs-people.bu.edu/santiago

D. Sands (Ed.): ESOP 2001, LNCS 2028, pp. 206–220, 2001.
© Springer-Verlag Berlin Heidelberg 2001

of an enclosed process. Below, we identify 4 cases in which ambients can be said to be polymorphically typed. Very recent type systems for **AC** and for an object-oriented version of **AC**, in [23] and [3] respectively, include suitable forms of subtyping, one of the 4 cases below. But none of the other 3 cases has been yet integrated into a polymorphic type system for **AC** or for an extension of it. We illustrate each of the 4 cases with a very brief example, written in a syntax slightly more general than the original syntax of **AC**, as we allow processes to exchange arbitrary functional expressions (possibly unevaluated for now) rather than just inert data.

Case 1. Consider a process of the form:

$$p[\text{ in } r.\langle\text{even}, 3\rangle] \mid q[\text{ in } r.\langle\text{not}, \text{true}\rangle] \mid r[\ (f, x).\, n[\ \langle f\ x\rangle \mid P\ ]\ ] \mid \text{open } p \mid \text{open } q\ ]$$

Here, there are 3 ambients in parallel, named p, q and r, and one ambient named n inside r. Both p and q can move into r (expressed by the capability "in r") and, once inside r, both can be dissolved (expressed by the capabilities "open p" and "open q") in order to unleash their outputs. The type of the input pair (f, x) inside r can be (int $\rightarrow$ bool, int) or (bool $\rightarrow$ bool, bool), depending on whether output $\langle\text{even}, 3\rangle$ or output $\langle\text{not}, \text{true}\rangle$ is transmitted first, and in either case the type of the application $(f\ x)$ is bool. We assume the unspecified process P can be executed safely in parallel with the boolean output $\langle f\ x\rangle$. The polymorphism of r is basically the familiar *parametric polymorphism* of ML.

Case 2. A slight variation of the preceding process is:

$$p[\text{ in } r.\langle 3, 2\rangle] \mid q[\text{ in } r.\langle 3.6, 5.1\rangle] \mid r[\ (x, y).\, n[\ \langle\text{mult}(x, y)\rangle \mid P\ ]\ ] \mid \text{open } p \mid \text{open } q\ ]$$

where the operation mult : (real, real) $\rightarrow$ real multiplies two real numbers. Because the type of $\langle 3, 2\rangle$ is (int, int), which is a subtype of (real, real), it is safe to transmit the output $\langle 3, 2\rangle$ to the input variables (x, y). Both ambients p and q can enter the ambient r safely. The polymorphism of r is the familiar *subtype polymorphism* found in many other functional and object-oriented programming languages, and also incorporated in type systems for concurrent calculi, such as [14,15] for the π-calculus and [23] for **AC**.

Case 3. Consider now the following process:

$$n[\ \langle\text{true}, 5\rangle \mid \langle 5, 6, 3.6\rangle \mid (x, y).P \mid (x, y, z).Q\ ]$$

The outputs are transmitted depending on their arities, here 2 for the output $\langle\text{true}, 5\rangle$ and 3 for the output $\langle 5, 6, 3.6\rangle$. We assume that the unspecified processes $(x, y).P$ and $(x, y, z).Q$ can be executed safely if they input, respectively, (bool, int) pairs and (int, int, real) triples. There is no ambiguity as to which of the two outputs should be transmitted to which of these two processes, i.e., the arity is used as a "switch" to dispatch an output to its appropriate destination. Hence, the execution of the entire process enclosed in the ambient n can proceed safely, provided also that all other outputs of arity 2 and arity 3 in parallel with

$\langle$true, 5$\rangle$ and $\langle 5, 6, 3.6\rangle$ have types (bool, int) and (int, int, real), respectively. The polymorphism of n is appropriately called *arity polymorphism*[1].

Case 4. A more subtle sense in which the type of exchanged data can change over time, as the computation proceeds inside an ambient, is illustrated by:

$$m[\ \langle 7 \rangle\ |\ (x).\mathsf{open}\ n.\langle x = 42 \rangle\ |\ n[\ (y).P\ ]\ ]$$

where the type of the equality test "$x = 42$" is bool. Initially, the topic of conversation in the ambient m is int. After the output $\langle 7 \rangle$ is transmitted, the ambient n is opened and the topic of conversation now becomes bool. Assuming that the unspecified process $(y).P$ can be executed safely whenever it inputs a boolean value, the execution of the entire process enclosed in the ambient m can proceed safely. What takes place in the ambient m is a case of what we shall call *orderly communication*[2], and which raises entirely new problems not encountered before in the context of **AC**. The design of a type discipline enforcing it is a delicate matter, and the main focus of this paper.

Orderly communication bears a strong resemblance to what has been called "session types" in the π-calculus, originated with the work of Honda and his collaborators [18,10] whose approach is based on syntax, and more recently developed by Gay and Hole [9] where the session discipline is enforced by a type system for the π-calculus (also integrating subtyping and recursive types).

Of the four cases above, perhaps **3** and certainly **4** are arguably excluded from what "polymorphism" has usually meant. Nevertheless, these two cases allow the same ambient to hold different topics of conversation, either *simultaneously* (in **case 3**) or *consecutively* at different times (in **case 4**) — or both simultaneously and consecutively, as illustrated by more interesting examples. Hence, in a wider sense of the word which we here propose, it is appropriate to include **3** and **4** as cases of polymorphic ambients.

1.2   Scope and Contribution of Our Research

The core of our formal calculus is **AC**, augmented with a simply-typed functional language at the level of exchanged data; accordingly we call our calculus **AC+**. Although **AC+** is the result of combining **AC** and a functional language, the two are essentially kept separate in our framework, in the sense that communication between processes is limited to functional programs and cannot include other processes. This is a deliberate decision: We steer clear of a *higher-order* **AC+**, where processes can exchange other processes (in addition to programs), something that will certainly reproduce many of the challenges already encountered in higher-order versions of the π-calculus (as in the work of Hennessy and his collaborators [21,22] for example).

---

[1] The term "arity polymorphism" was used already by others, e.g. Moggi [12], to describe similar—though different in some respects—situations in functional programming languages.

[2] We thank Benjamin Pierce for suggesting the apt term "orderly communication".

In summary, our main accomplishments are (highlighted by bullet points):

- We design a type system for **AC+** where embedded programs are assigned *types* and processes are assigned what we call *behaviors*. Our type system smoothly integrates 3 of the 4 cases of polymorphism into a single framework: *subtype polymorphism*, *arity polymorphism* and *orderly communication*.

Our current type system does not include ML-style *parametric polymorphism*. Taking the cue from Turner's work [19], we expect its incorporation into our type system to proceed without major obstacles.

- We develop a perspicuous denotational semantics of behaviors, which we call their *trace semantics*. Behavior equivalence and behavior subsumption are defined relative to this trace semantics, which is further used to prove that our polymorphically-typed **AC+** satisfies a Subject Reduction property.
- Behavior subsumption and type subsumption are shown to be decidable relations, and this implies the decidability (at least exponential in the worse case) of *type-checking* for type-annotated **AC+** terms.

The proof of this result is of independent interest; it is a non-trivial adaptation of techniques from finite automata theory where, by contrast, decision procedures typically have low-degree polynomial time complexities. The more difficult problem of *type-inference* for (un-annotated) **AC+** terms is left for future work.

- Our polymorphically typed **AC+** is a conservative extension of the typed version of **AC** originally proposed by Cardelli and Gordon [7], in the sense that every process typable in the latter is typable in ours.

Further material and all missing proofs are included in the technical report [1], on which the current paper is based (this report can be downloaded from the Church Project web site at http://types.bu.edu/reports/).

1.3 Motivating Example

We now give an example, short but more interesting than the snippets in Sect. 1.1, to illustrate the expressive power and convenience of a polymorphically typed **AC+**, in particular the use of *orderly communication*. Aside from the embedded programs, the syntax of ambients is identical to that first proposed by Cardelli and Gordon [6] with the addition of a co-capability "coopen n" akin to a proposal already made by Levi and Sangiorgi [11]. For a process to open an ambient n, this ambient must contain a top-level process willing to exercise a coopen n (cf. (Red Open) in Fig. 2). We shall use $n\{P\}$ to abbreviate $n[P \mid \text{coopen } n]$.

Example 1 (Packet Routing). A packet enters a router and requests to be routed to a specific destination. A router reads the destination name (denoted by the string "bu") and then communicates a path (a sequence of in and out capabilities) back to the packet. The packet uses this path to route itself to the destination.

Expressions

$M \in \mathsf{Exp} ::= n \mid c \mid \lambda n : \sigma.M \mid M_1 M_2 \mid \times(M_1, \ldots, M_k) \mid$ if M_0 then M_1 else M_2
$\qquad \mid \epsilon \mid M_1.M_2 \mid$ in $M \mid$ out $M \mid$ open $M \mid$ coopen $M \qquad (k \geqslant 0)$

Processes

$P \in \mathsf{Proc} ::= \mathbf{0} \mid P_1 \mid P_2 \mid {!}P \mid (\nu n : \sigma).P \mid M.P \mid M[P] \mid (n_1 : \sigma_1, \ldots, n_k : \sigma_k).P$
$\qquad \mid \langle M \rangle \qquad\qquad\qquad\qquad\qquad\qquad\qquad\qquad (k \geqslant 0)$

When there is no ambiguity we write M for $M.0$.

Fig. 1. Syntax of **AC+**.

Orderly communication is needed since inside the packet there are *two* topics of conversation: first strings (the destination), and next capabilities (the path).

$$router\,[!route\{\text{in } packet.(dst).\text{open } hop.\langle\text{lookup-route}(dst)\rangle\}] \; \mid$$
$$packet\,[\text{in } router.\text{open } route.\langle\text{"bu"}\rangle \mid hop\{(x).x\}]$$

Notice that the packet reads and exercises the path by means of its subterm $(x).x$. Despite its simplicity, the term $(x).x$ is not typable in the Cardelli-Gordon type system for **AC** nor, to the best of our knowledge, in any of the type systems for **AC** available in the literature. In these systems, the only way to type a process that reads and exercises a capability is by using an extra ambient. Specifically, the process $(x).x$ must be written as $(x).n[x]$ for some ambient name n.   □

2   Types and Behaviors

Figure 1 depicts the syntax of our language **AC+**. A process $P \in \mathsf{Proc}$ is basically as in [7]: there are constructs for parallel composition ($P_1 \mid P_2$), replication (${!}P$), restriction (($\nu n : \sigma).P$); and there also are constructs for input and output. Note that communication is asynchronous, in that an outputting process has no "continuation"; a communication can thus (cf. the metaphor in [4]) be viewed as the placement, and subsequent removal, of a Post-It note on a message board that (unlike in [4]) has a section for each arity.

An expression $M \in \mathsf{Exp}$ denotes a computation over a domain that includes not only simple values (like integers) but also functions, tuples, ambient names, and (paths of) capabilities. Note that for all binding constructs in **AC+**, the name n being bound is annotated with a type σ (to be defined in Sect. 2.2).

2.1   Operational Semantics

The semantics of **AC+** is presented in Fig. 2. Before an expression M can be passed as an argument to a function or communicated to another process it must be evaluated to a value V, using the evaluation relation $M_1 \longrightarrow M_2$.

We write $P_1 \equiv P_2$ to denote that P_1 and P_2 are equivalent, modulo consistent renaming of bound names (which may be needed to apply (Red Beta) and (Red Comm)) and modulo "syntactic rearrangement" (we have, e.g., that $P \mid 0 \equiv P$ and $P \mid Q \equiv Q \mid P$). The definition is as in [7], except that we omit the rule $!P \equiv P \mid !P$ (in the presence of which we do not know whether it will be possible to establish Lemma 2) and instead allow this "unfolding" to take place via the rule (Red Repl).

We write $P_1 \overset{\ell}{\longrightarrow} P_2$ if P_1 reduces in one step to P_2 by performing "an action described by ℓ". Here $\ell = \text{comm}(\tau)$ if a value of type τ is communicated at top-level (Red Comm), and $\ell = \epsilon$ otherwise. We use a notion of "process evaluation contexts" to succinctly describe the place in a process where an expression (Red MctxtP) or subprocess (Red PctxtP) is reduced. Reducing inside an ambient is given a special treatment in (Red Amb), as the label "disappears" due to the fact that communications are invisible outside ambients. Note that $P \overset{\ell}{\longrightarrow} Q$ does not imply that $M.P \overset{\ell}{\longrightarrow} M.Q$ since M must evaluate to a capability which then is executed before P can be activated; similarly for other constructs.

2.2 Types and Behaviors

The syntax of types ($\tau, \sigma \in$ Typ) and the syntax of behaviors ($b \in$ Beh) are recursively defined in Fig. 3. The first five behavior constructs capture the intuition (cf. [2]) that we want to keep track of the relationship (sequential or parallel) between occurrences of input and output operations.

An ambient n has a type of the form $\text{amb}[b_0, b_1]$, where b_0 and b_1 can both be viewed as upper estimates of the behavior of a process "unleashed" by opening n. An example: for $n[\langle 7 \rangle \mid (x : \text{int}).\text{coopen } n.\langle x = 42 \rangle]$ we expect n to have the type $\text{amb}[\text{put(bool)}, \text{put(bool)}]$, reflecting that when n is opened the value 7 has already been communicated—something we would not know if we did not have the explicit occurrence of coopen n, which we keep track of using the behavior diss. The behaviors b_0 and b_1 will often be equal, in which case we may write $\text{amb}[b_0]$ for $\text{amb}[b_0, b_0]$; but as in [23] the possibility of them being distinct facilitates a smooth integration of subtyping.

A capability has a type of the form $\text{cap}[B]$ where B is a behavior context, that is a "behavior with a hole inside". To motivate this, consider a process $P = \text{open } n.P'$ where P' has behavior b' and n has type $\text{amb}[b]$. When P is executed, P' will run in parallel with a process of behavior b, so P should be assigned the behavior $b \mid b'$, which can be written as $(b \mid \square)\lfloor b' \rfloor$. This is why it makes sense to assign open n the capability type $\text{cap}[b \mid \square]$, cf. the rules (Exp Open) and (Proc Action) in Fig 4.

The first six behavior constructs in Fig. 3 alone, are sufficient to write a type system satisfying a subject reduction property (Sect. 4), but they do not enable the typing of processes performing (using replication) an unbounded number of input and output operations, and neither do they enable the typing of a conditional where one branch is a capability of type $\text{cap}[\text{put(int)} \mid \square]$ whereas the other branch is a capability of type $\text{cap}[\text{get(int)} \mid \square]$. Among many possible

Values $V ::= \cdots$ (omitted, as standard)

Evaluation Contexts for Expressions and Processes

$$\mathcal{E} ::= \square_e \mid \mathcal{E}M \mid V\mathcal{E} \mid \times(V_1, .., V_{i-1}, \mathcal{E}, M_{i+1}, .., M_k) \mid \text{if } \mathcal{E} \text{ then } M_1 \text{ else } M_2$$
$$\mid \mathcal{E}.M \mid V.\mathcal{E} \mid \text{in } \mathcal{E} \mid \text{out } \mathcal{E} \mid \text{open } \mathcal{E} \mid \text{coopen } \mathcal{E} \quad (k \geqslant 0)$$
$$\mathcal{P} ::= \square_p \mid \mathcal{E}.P \mid \mathcal{E}[P] \mid \langle \mathcal{E} \rangle \mid (\nu n : \sigma).\mathcal{P} \mid \mathcal{P} \mid P$$

$\mathcal{E}\lfloor M \rfloor$ is the expression resulting from replacing $\square_e$ with M in E.
$\mathcal{P}\lfloor M \rfloor_e$ is the process resulting from replacing $\square_e$ with M in $\mathcal{P}$.
$\mathcal{P}\lfloor P \rfloor_p$ is the process resulting from replacing $\square_p$ with P in $\mathcal{P}$.

Reduction Rules

Let ℓ be a label in $\{\epsilon\} \cup \{\text{comm}(\tau) \mid \tau \in \mathsf{Typ}\}$.
Let $\delta(c, V)$ be a partial function defined for every constant c.
In (Red Beta) and (Red Comm), we demand that there is no name capture.

$$(\lambda n : \sigma.M)V \longrightarrow M[n := V] \tag{Red Beta}$$
$$cV \longrightarrow V' \quad \text{where } V' = \delta(c, V) \tag{Red Delta}$$
$$\text{if true then } M_1 \text{ else } M_2 \longrightarrow M_1 \tag{Red IfTrue}$$
$$\text{if false then } M_1 \text{ else } M_2 \longrightarrow M_2 \tag{Red IfFalse}$$
$$\text{If } M_1 \longrightarrow M_2 \text{ then } \mathcal{E}\lfloor M_1 \rfloor \longrightarrow \mathcal{E}\lfloor M_2 \rfloor \tag{Red MctxtM}$$
$$n[\text{in } m.P \mid Q] \mid m[R] \xrightarrow{\epsilon} m[n[P \mid Q] \mid R] \tag{Red In}$$
$$m[n[\text{out } m.P \mid Q] \mid R] \xrightarrow{\epsilon} n[P \mid Q] \mid m[R] \tag{Red Out}$$
$$\text{open } n.P \mid n[\text{coopen } n.Q \mid R] \xrightarrow{\epsilon} P \mid Q \mid R \tag{Red Open}$$
$$(n_1 : \sigma_1, \dots, n_k : \sigma_k).P \mid \langle \times(V_1, \dots, V_k) \rangle \xrightarrow{\text{comm}(\tau)}$$
$$P[n_i := V_i] \quad \text{where } \tau = \times(\sigma_1, \dots, \sigma_k) \tag{Red Comm}$$
$$!P \xrightarrow{\epsilon} P \mid !P \tag{Red Repl}$$
$$\text{If } M_1 \longrightarrow M_2 \text{ then } \mathcal{P}\lfloor M_1 \rfloor_e \xrightarrow{\epsilon} \mathcal{P}\lfloor M_2 \rfloor_e \tag{Red MctxtP}$$
$$\text{If } P \xrightarrow{\ell} Q \text{ then } \mathcal{P}\lfloor P \rfloor_p \xrightarrow{\ell} \mathcal{P}\lfloor Q \rfloor_p \tag{Red PctxtP}$$
$$\text{If } P \xrightarrow{\ell} Q \text{ then } n[P] \xrightarrow{\epsilon} n[Q] \tag{Red Amb}$$
$$\text{If } P' \equiv P, P \xrightarrow{\ell} Q, Q \equiv Q' \text{ then } P' \xrightarrow{\ell} Q' \tag{Red $\equiv$}$$

Thus only tuples are communicated, and where there is no ambiguity we may write $\langle M_1, \dots, M_k \rangle$ for $\langle \times(M_1, \dots, M_k) \rangle$

Fig. 2. Operational semantics.

options for (approximating) constructs expressing recursion and choice, we in this paper settle for a simple one: the construct fromnow T with T the "topics of conversation", which can be thought of as the "union" of all behaviors composed of $\mathsf{put}(\tau)$ and $\mathsf{get}(\tau)$ with $\tau \in T$.

We shall use the notion of *level*: a type τ has level i if i is an upper bound of the depth of nested occurrences of $\mathsf{amb}[\_, \_]$ or $\mathsf{cap}[\_]$ within τ, similarly for T, b, and B. Example: $\tau_0 = \mathsf{int} \to \mathsf{int}$ has level zero, $b_1 = \mathsf{put}(\mathsf{cap}[\mathsf{put}(\tau_0) \mid \square])$ has level one, and $\tau_2 = \mathsf{amb}[b_1, b_1]$ has level two (as well as any higher level).

Types

$$\sigma, \tau \ \in \mathsf{Typ} \ ::= \ \mathsf{bool} \mid \mathsf{int} \mid \mathsf{real} \mid \mathsf{string} \mid \cdots \qquad \text{type constant}$$

$\mid \sigma \to \tau$	function type
$\mid \times(\sigma_1, \dots, \sigma_k)$	tuple with arity $k \geqslant 0$
$\mid \mathsf{amb}[b, b']$	type of ambient name
$\mid \mathsf{cap}[B]$	type of capability

$$T \in \mathsf{Topics} = \ \{\{\tau_1, \dots, \tau_m\} \mid m \geqslant 0 \text{ and } \mathsf{arity}(\tau_i) \neq \mathsf{arity}(\tau_j) \text{ for } i \neq j\}$$

When there is no ambiguity, we write σ for $\times(\sigma)$ and $(\sigma_1, \dots, \sigma_k)$ for $\times(\sigma_1, \dots, \sigma_k)$.

Behaviors

$$b \ \in \ \mathsf{Beh} \qquad ::= \ \varepsilon \qquad\qquad\qquad\qquad \text{no traceable action}$$

$\mid b_1.b_2$	first b_1 then b_2
$\mid b_1 \mid b_2$	parallel composition
$\mid \mathsf{put}(\sigma)$	output of type σ (a tuple)
$\mid \mathsf{get}(\sigma)$	input of type σ (a tuple)
$\mid \mathsf{diss}$	ambient dissolution
$\mid \mathsf{fromnow}\ T$	unordered communication
	of values with types in T

$$B \ \in \ \mathsf{BehCont} ::= \ \square \mid b.B \mid B.b \mid b \mid B \mid B \mid b \qquad \text{behavior context}$$

Notation: $B\lfloor b \rfloor$ is the behavior resulting from replacing $\square$ with b in B; similarly for the behavior context $B\lfloor B_1 \rfloor$.

Fig. 3. Syntax of types and behaviors.

2.3 Behavior Subsumption

We employ a relation $b_1 \leqslant b_2$, to be formally defined in Sect. 3, with the intuitive interpretation that b_2 is more "permissive" than b_1. For example, $\mathsf{put}(\mathsf{int}) \leqslant \mathsf{fromnow}\ \{\mathsf{int}, (\mathsf{int}, \mathsf{int})\}$, and if integers can be converted into real numbers then also $\mathsf{put}(\mathsf{int}) \leqslant \mathsf{put}(\mathsf{real})$, since a process that sends an integer thereby also sends a real number, and $\mathsf{get}(\mathsf{real}) \leqslant \mathsf{get}(\mathsf{int})$, since a process that accepts a real number also will accept an integer. Thus output is covariant and input is contravariant, while in other systems found in the literature it is the other way round—the reason for this discrepancy is that we take a *descriptive* rather than a *prescriptive* point of view. From a prescriptive point of view, a channel that allows the writing of real numbers also allows the writing of integers, and a channel that allows the reading of integers also allows the reading of real numbers.

The relation on behaviors induces a relation on behavior contexts:

Definition 1. $B_1 \leqslant B_2$ *holds iff for all level 0 behaviors b: $B_1\lfloor b \rfloor \leqslant B_2\lfloor b \rfloor$.*

2.4   Subtyping

We employ a relation $\tau_1 \leqslant \tau_2$, such that a value of type τ_1 also has type τ_2. On base types, we have int $\leqslant$ real. On composite types, the relation is defined using the following polarity rules (tuples with different arity are incompatible):

$$\ominus \to \oplus \quad (\oplus, \dots, \oplus) \quad \mathsf{amb}[\ominus, \oplus] \quad \mathsf{cap}[\oplus]$$

2.5   The Type System

Figure 4 defines judgements $E \vdash M : \tau$ and $E \vdash P : b$, where E is an environment mapping names into types. The function type() assigns types to constants.

The side condition in (Proc Repl) prevents us from assigning $!\langle 7 \rangle$ the incorrect behavior put(int) (but instead we can use (Proc Subsumption) and assign it the behavior fromnow {int}).

The side conditions for (Proc Amb) employ a couple of notions which will be formally defined in Sect. 3; below we shall convey the intuition by providing a few examples. First we address the notion of being *safe*.

- The behavior put(int) | get(bool) is not safe, since a process which expects a boolean may receive an integer.
- Referring back to "Case 4" from Sect. 1.1 (now with the appropriate type annotations, $n[\dots]$ replaced by $n\{\dots\}$ and P replaced by $\mathbf{0}$) the process enclosed within m has behavior

$$b = \mathsf{put(int)} \mid \mathsf{get(int).(get(bool)} \mid \mathsf{put(bool))} \tag{1}$$

  which *is* safe, since no matter how the parallel behaviors are interleaved in a "well-formed" way then *(i)* put(bool) cannot precede get(int); and *(ii)* put(int) cannot immediately precede get(bool).
- Perhaps surprisingly, the behavior diss.(put(int) | get(bool)) is considered safe, since nothing bad happens as long as no one attempts to open the enclosing ambient (a process doing that would not be safe).

Concerning the relation $b \rightsquigarrow b_0$, the idea is that b_0 denotes "what remains" of b after its first occurrence of diss. For example, with $b = \mathsf{get(int).diss} \mid \mathsf{put(int)}$ we have $b \rightsquigarrow \varepsilon$ (since we can infer that put(int) is performed before diss). And with $b = \mathsf{fromnow}\ T \mid \mathsf{diss}$, we have $b \rightsquigarrow \mathsf{fromnow}\ T$.

Example 2. With $b = \mathsf{get(string).(get(cap[\Box]).\varepsilon} \mid \mathsf{put(cap[\Box]))}$, we can construct a typing for Example 1 as follows: assign the behavior $\mathsf{get(cap[\Box]).\varepsilon} \mid \mathsf{diss}$ to the body of *hop* (which can then be given the type $\mathsf{amb[get(cap[\Box]).\varepsilon]}$), assign the (safe) behavior $b \mid \mathsf{diss}$ to the body of *route* (which can then be given the type $\mathsf{amb[b]}$), and assign $b \mid \mathsf{put(string)}$ (which is clearly safe) to the body of *packet*.   □

Non-structural Rules

(Proc Subsumption)

$$\frac{E \vdash P : b}{E \vdash P : b'} \quad (b \leqslant b')$$

(Exp Subsumption)

$$\frac{E \vdash M : \sigma}{E \vdash M : \sigma'} \quad (\sigma \leqslant \sigma')$$

Expressions (selected rules only)

(Exp App)

$$\frac{E \vdash M_1 : \sigma \to \tau \quad E \vdash M_2 : \sigma}{E \vdash M_1 M_2 : \tau}$$

(Exp Action)

$$\frac{E \vdash M_1 : \mathsf{cap}[B_1] \quad E \vdash M_2 : \mathsf{cap}[B_2]}{E \vdash M_1.M_2 : \mathsf{cap}[B_1 \lfloor B_2 \rfloor]}$$

(Exp ϵ)

$$\frac{}{E \vdash \epsilon : \mathsf{cap}[\square]}$$

(Exp In)

$$\frac{E \vdash M : \mathsf{amb}[b, b']}{E \vdash \mathsf{in}\ M : \mathsf{cap}[\square]}$$

(Exp Out)

$$\frac{E \vdash M : \mathsf{amb}[b, b']}{E \vdash \mathsf{out}\ M : \mathsf{cap}[\square]}$$

(Exp c)

$$\frac{\mathsf{type}(c) = \sigma}{E \vdash c : \sigma}$$

(Exp Open)

$$\frac{E \vdash M : \mathsf{amb}[b, b']}{E \vdash \mathsf{open}\ M : \mathsf{cap}[b' \mid \square]}$$

(Exp Coopen)

$$\frac{E \vdash M : \mathsf{amb}[b, b']}{E \vdash \mathsf{coopen}\ M : \mathsf{cap}[\mathsf{diss}.\square]}$$

Processes

(Proc Zero)

$$\frac{}{E \vdash \mathbf{0} : \varepsilon}$$

(Proc Par)

$$\frac{E \vdash P_1 : b_1 \quad E \vdash P_2 : b_2}{E \vdash P_1 \mid P_2 : b_1 \mid b_2}$$

(Proc Repl)

$$\frac{E \vdash P : b}{E \vdash\ !P : b} \quad (\text{if } (b \mid b) \leqslant b)$$

(Proc Action)

$$\frac{E \vdash M : \mathsf{cap}[B] \quad E \vdash P : b}{E \vdash M.P : B\lfloor b \rfloor}$$

(Proc Res)

$$\frac{E, n : \mathsf{amb}[b, b'] \vdash P : b_1}{E \vdash (\nu n : \mathsf{amb}[b, b']).P : b_1}$$

(Proc Amb)

$$\frac{E \vdash M : \mathsf{amb}[b, b'] \quad E \vdash P : b_1}{E \vdash M[P] : \varepsilon} \quad (\text{if } b_1 \text{ safe and } b_1 \rightsquigarrow b \text{ and } b \leqslant b')$$

(Proc Input)

$$\frac{E, n_1 : \tau_1, \cdots, n_k : \tau_k \vdash P : b}{E \vdash (n_1 : \tau_1, \ldots, n_k : \tau_k).P : \mathsf{get}(\tau_1, \cdots, \tau_k).b}$$

(Proc Output)

$$\frac{E \vdash M : \times(\tau_1, \ldots, \tau_k)}{E \vdash \langle M \rangle : \mathsf{put}(\tau_1, \cdots, \tau_k)}$$

Fig. 4. Typing rules.

3   Trace Semantics of Behaviors

In this section we shall define several relations on behaviors, in particular, an ordering relation. We have taken a semantic rather than an axiomatic approach, motivated by the observation that choosing the "right" set of axioms is often a somewhat ad-hoc exercise. An added advantage of the semantic approach is that in our case it considerably facilitates type checking.

Definition 2 (Traces). *A trace $tr \in$ Trace is a finite sequence of actions, where an action $a \in$ Act is a behavior that is either* $\mathsf{put}(\tau)$, $\mathsf{get}(\tau)$, *or* diss.

The semantics $[\![b]\!]$ of a behavior b belongs to the powerset $\mathcal{P}(\mathsf{Trace})$:

$$[\![\varepsilon]\!] = \{\bullet\} \qquad\qquad\qquad [\![\mathsf{diss}]\!] = \{\mathsf{diss}\}$$
$$[\![b_1.b_2]\!] = [\![b_1]\!] \diamond [\![b_2]\!] \qquad\qquad [\![b_1 \mid b_2]\!] = [\![b_1]\!] \parallel [\![b_2]\!]$$
$$[\![\mathsf{put}(\tau)]\!] = \{\mathsf{put}(\tau)\} \qquad\qquad [\![\mathsf{get}(\tau)]\!] = \{\mathsf{get}(\tau)\}$$
$$[\![\mathsf{fromnow}\ T]\!] = \{tr \mid \forall a \text{ occurring in } tr : \exists \tau \in T : a \in \{\mathsf{put}(\tau), \mathsf{get}(\tau)\}\}$$

Here $\bullet$ denotes the empty sequence, $tr_1 \diamond tr_2$ denotes the concatenation of tr_1 and tr_2 which trivially lifts to sets of traces (Tr ranges over such), and $Tr_1 \parallel Tr_2$ denotes all traces that can be formed by arbitrarily interleaving a trace in Tr_1 with a trace in Tr_2.

Consider the run-time behavior of a process not interacting with other processes. Each input must necessarily be preceded by an output with the same arity, and an error occurs if the type of the value being output is not a subtype of the type of the value being input. This motivates the following definition:

Definition 3 (Comm). *A trace tr belongs to* Comm *if $tr = \mathsf{put}(\tau)\,\mathsf{get}(\sigma)$ with* $\mathsf{arity}(\tau) = \mathsf{arity}(\sigma)$. *If in addition it holds that $\tau \leqslant \sigma$ we say that $tr \in$* WtComm, *the set of well-typed communications.*

Example 3. With b as in (1), it is easy to see that $[\![b]\!]$ is given by the 8 traces

put(int) get(int) put(bool) get(bool)	put(int) get(int) get(bool) put(bool)
get(int) put(int) put(bool) get(bool)	get(int) put(int) get(bool) put(bool)
get(int) put(bool) put(int) get(bool)	get(int) get(bool) put(int) put(bool)
get(int) put(bool) get(bool) put(int)	get(int) get(bool) put(bool) put(int)

Only the first of these traces belongs to Comm* (and even to WtComm*). The other traces, however, are still relevant if b is the behavior of a process placed in a non-empty context.   □

Definition 4 (Behavior subsumption). $b_1 \leqslant b_2$ *iff $[\![b_1]\!] \leqslant [\![b_2]\!]$, where the relations $\leqslant$ on* Act, Trace, *and* $\mathcal{P}(\mathsf{Trace})$ *are given by:*

- *on* Act, $\leqslant$ *is the least reflexive and transitive relation satisfying that if $\tau \leqslant \sigma$ then $\mathsf{put}(\tau) \leqslant \mathsf{put}(\sigma)$ and $\mathsf{get}(\sigma) \leqslant \mathsf{get}(\tau)$;*

- the relation $\leqslant$ on Act *extends pointwise to a relation* $\leqslant$ *on* Trace;
- $Tr_1 \leqslant Tr_2$ *iff for all* $tr_1 \in Tr_1$ *there exists* $tr_2 \in Tr_2$ *such that* $tr_1 \leqslant tr_2$.

Our definition of the relations $b_1 \leqslant b_2$ and $\tau \leqslant \sigma$ may seem circular, but is not: the development in this section shows how a relation on level i types gives rise to a relation on level i behaviors, whereas Sect. 2.4 shows how to define a relation on level 0 types, and how a relation on level i behaviors gives rise to a relation on level $i+1$ types (since, thanks to the restriction to level 0 behaviors in Def. 1, it induces a relation on level i behavior contexts).

The operators " $|$ " and " $.$ " on behaviors respect the relation $\leqslant$; thus the equivalence relation $\equiv$ induced by $\leqslant$ is a congruence on behaviors wrt. these operators. Modulo $\equiv$ it holds that " $|$ " is associative and commutative and that " $.$ " is associative, both with ε as neutral element. Note that $\varepsilon \equiv$ fromnow $\emptyset$.

The result below plays an important part in type checking:

Lemma 1. *Given* B_1 *and* B_2 *behavior contexts, we can construct a level zero behavior* test *such that the following conditions are equivalent:*

(a) $B_1 \leqslant B_2$
(b) $B_1 \lfloor b \rfloor \leqslant B_2 \lfloor b \rfloor$ *for all* b *(regardless of level)*
(c) $B_1 \lfloor \text{test.test} \rfloor \leqslant B_2 \lfloor \text{test.test} \rfloor$.

The following definition captures the intuition that if P can be assigned a *safe* behavior then all communications performed by P will be well-typed—at least until the ambient enclosing P is dissolved.

Definition 5 (Safety). *A behavior* b *is safe if no trace* $tr \in [\![b]\!]$ *can be written* $tr = tr_0 \diamond tr_1 \diamond tr_2$ *with* $tr_0 \in$ Comm* *and* $tr_1 \in$ Comm $\setminus$ WtComm.

Example 4. Referring back to Example 3, where the traces of a behavior b were listed, we can now demonstrate that b is in fact safe (as claimed in Sec. 2.5). For the first trace in b belongs to WtComm*; the second trace can be written as $tr_0 \diamond tr$ with $tr_0 \in$ WtComm and tr not of the form $tr_1 \diamond tr_2$ for any $tr_1 \in$ Comm; and none of the remaining traces are of the form $tr_1 \diamond tr_2$ with $tr_1 \in$ Comm. □

Definition 6 (Pruning). *The relation* $b \rightsquigarrow b'$, *read "b prunes to b'", amounts to the following property: whenever there exists* $tr_1 \in$ Comm* *and* tr *such that* $tr_1 \diamond$ diss $\diamond tr \in [\![b]\!]$, *then there exists* $tr' \in [\![b']\!]$ *with* $tr \leqslant tr'$.

4 Subject Reduction

In this section we shall show that our type system is semantically sound. This property is formulated as a subject reduction result (Theorem 1), intuitively stating that "well-typed processes communicate according to their behavior" and also stating that "well-typed safe processes never evolve into ill-typed processes". The latter "safety property" shows that the process $((n : \text{int}).\langle n + 7 \rangle) \mid \langle \text{true} \rangle$, though typeable, cannot be assigned a safe behavior since it evolves into the process $\langle \text{true} + 7 \rangle$, which clearly cannot be typed.

Lemma 2 (Subject congruence). *Suppose that $P \equiv Q$. Then $E \vdash P : b$ if and only if $E \vdash Q : b$.*

Assuming a suitable relationship between δ and type(), we have

Lemma 3 (Subject reduction for expressions). *Suppose $M_1 \longrightarrow M_2$. If $E \vdash M_1 : \tau$ then also $E \vdash M_2 : \tau$.*

The formulation of subject reduction for processes states that if a process having behavior b performs a step labeled ℓ then the resulting process can be assigned a behavior that denotes "what remains of b after ℓ". To formalize this, we employ a relation $\ell \sim b_0$ that is defined by stipulating that

$$\epsilon \sim \varepsilon$$
$$\mathsf{comm}(\tau) \sim \mathsf{put}(\tau^-).\mathsf{get}(\tau^+) \text{ if } \tau^- \leqslant \tau \leqslant \tau^+$$

Theorem 1 (Subject reduction for processes). *Suppose that $P \xrightarrow{\ell} Q$. If it holds that $E \vdash P : b$ with b safe, then there exists b_0 with $\ell \sim b_0$ and safe b' such that $E \vdash Q : b'$ and $b_0.b' \leqslant b$.*

5   Type Checking

In this section we show that given a complete type derivation for some process P, we can check its validity according to the rules from Fig. 4. For that purpose, we use techniques from the theory of finite non-deterministic automata. By induction we can show that for all b it is possible to construct an automaton G that *implements* b, i.e. an automaton G such that $[\![b]\!] = \{tr \mid G \text{ accepts } tr\}$.

Lemma 4. *Assume that for τ, σ of level i it is decidable whether $\tau \leqslant \sigma$. Let b_1, b_2 be of level i. Then it is decidable whether $b_1 \leqslant b_2$.*

The method is to first construct G_1 and G_2 implementing b_1 and b_2, then construct their "difference automaton" $G_1 \setminus G_2$, and finally to check whether the latter rejects all inputs.

Lemma 5. *Let τ, σ be of level i, and assume that for all b_1, b_2 of level j with $j < i$ it is decidable whether $b_1 \leqslant b_2$. Then it is decidable whether $\tau \leqslant \sigma$.*

The proof is by induction on the structure of τ and σ. Whenever $\tau = \mathsf{cap}[B]$ and $\sigma = \mathsf{cap}[B']$, we use Lemma 1 to test whether $B \leqslant B'$.

Theorem 2. *Given b_1 and b_2, it is decidable whether $b_1 \leqslant b_2$. Given τ and σ, it is decidable whether $\tau \leqslant \sigma$.*

This follows from Lemmas 4 and 5. We also have

Lemma 6. *Given behaviors b and b', it is decidable whether b is safe, and it is decidable whether $b \rightsquigarrow b'$.*

These results show that the side conditions for the rules (Proc Subsumption), (Exp Subsumption), (Proc Repl) and (Proc Amb) are decidable, yielding

Theorem 3 (Decidability of type checking). *Given a purported derivation of $E \vdash M : \tau$ or $E \vdash P : b$, we can effectively check its validity.*

6 Discussion

Our type system is a conservative extension of the type system for **AC** presented in [7, Sect. 3]. To see this, we employ a function *Plus* translating entities in the latter system into entities in the former; in particular "message types" W^C into types, and "exchange types" T^C into behaviors. *Plus* is defined recursively on the structure of its argument; most clauses are "homomorphisms" except for

$$Plus(M^C[P^C]) = Plus(M^C)[Plus(P^C) \mid \mathsf{coopen}\, Plus(M^C).0]$$
$$Plus(\mathsf{cap}[T^C]) = \mathsf{cap}[Plus(T^C) \mid \Box]$$
$$Plus(Shh) = \varepsilon$$
$$Plus(W_1^C \times \ldots \times W_n^C) = \mathsf{fromnow}\ \{\times(Plus(W_1^C), \ldots, Plus(W_n^C))\}$$

Theorem 4. *Suppose that* $E^C \vdash P^C : T^C$, *respectively* $E^C \vdash M^C : W^C$, *is derivable in the system of [7, Sect. 3]. Then* $Plus(E^C) \vdash Plus(P^C) : Plus(T^C)$, *respectively* $Plus(E^C) \vdash Plus(M^C) : Plus(W^C)$, *is derivable in our system.*

It is relatively straightforward to extend our system to record ambient movements: we augment Act with actions enter and exit, and augment Beh with behaviors that are suitable abstractions of sets of traces containing these actions[3]. As in [5] we can then express that an ambient is immobile. Thanks to diss and the relation $b \rightsquigarrow b_0$, we are able to declare ambients immobile even though they open packets that have moved, thus overcoming (as also [11] does) the problem faced in [5]. Another application might be to predict the shape of ambients, as done in [13] using tree grammars.

Besides the tasks mentioned in Sect. 1 (in particular type inference), future work includes investigating the relationship to the system proposed by Levi & Sangiorgi [11] which—using the notion of single-threadedness—made a first attempt to rule out so-called "grave" interferences (a notion that is not precisely defined in [11]). For that purpose we must extend our poly-typed **AC+** with coin and coout expressions, recorded also in the traces.

References

[1] Torben Amtoft, Assaf J. Kfoury, and Santiago Pericas-Geersten. What are polymorphically-typed ambients? Technical Report BUCS-TR-2000-021, Comp. Sci. Dept., Boston Univ., December 2000.

[2] Torben Amtoft, Flemming Nielson, and Hanne Riis Nielson. *Type and Effect Systems: Behaviours for Concurrency*. Imperial College Press, 1999.

[3] Michele Bugliesi, Giuseppe Castagna, and Silvia Crafa. Typed mobile objects. In *CONCUR 2000*, volume 1877 of *LNCS*, pages 504–520, 2000.

[4] Luca Cardelli. Abstractions for mobile computation. In Jan Vitek and Christian Jensen, editors, *Secure Internet Programming: Security Issues for Mobile and Distributed Objects*, volume 1603 of *LNCS*, pages 51–94. Springer-Verlag, 1999.

---

[3] In fact, the type system of [23] can be viewed as such an abstraction where, e.g., $[\![{}^\vee O \rightsquigarrow I]\!]$ is the set of traces containing actions $\mathsf{put}(\tau)$ with τ described by O, actions $\mathsf{get}(\tau)$ with τ described by I, but no enter or exit actions.

[5] Luca Cardelli, Giorgio Ghelli, and Andrew D. Gordon. Mobility types for mobile ambients. In Jiri Wiedermann, Peter van Emde Boas, and Mogens Nielsen, editors, *ICALP'99*, volume 1644 of *LNCS*, pages 230–239. Springer-Verlag, July 1999.

[6] Luca Cardelli and Andrew D. Gordon. Mobile ambients. In Maurice Nivat, editor, *FoSSaCS'98*, volume 1378 of *LNCS*, pages 140–155. Springer-Verlag, 1998.

[7] Luca Cardelli and Andrew D. Gordon. Types for mobile ambients. In *POPL'99, San Antonio, Texas*, pages 79–92. ACM Press, January 1999.

[8] Cedric Fournet, Georges Gonthier, Jean-Jacques Levy, Luc Maranget, and Didier Remy. A calculus of mobile agents. In *CONCUR 1996*, volume 1119 of *LNCS*, pages 406–421. Springer-Verlag, 1996.

[9] Simon Gay and Malcolm Hole. Types and subtypes for client-server interactions. In *Proc. European Symp. on Programming*, volume 1576 of *LNCS*, pages 74–90. Springer-Verlag, 1999.

[10] Kohei Honda, Vasco Vasconcelos, and Makoto Kubo. Language primitives and type discipline for structured communication-based programming. In *ESOP'98*, volume 1381 of *LNCS*, pages 122–138. Springer-Verlag, 1998.

[11] Francesca Levi and Davide Sangiorgi. Controlling interference in ambients. In *POPL'00, Boston, Massachusetts*, pages 352–364. ACM Press, January 2000.

[12] Eugenio Moggi. Arity polymorphism and dependent types. In *Subtyping & Dependent Types in Programming, Ponte de Lima, Portugal*, 2000. Proceedings online at http://www-sop.inria.fr/oasis/DTP00/Proceedings/proceedings.html.

[13] Hanne Riis Nielson and Flemming Nielson. Shape analysis for mobile ambients. In *POPL'00, Boston, Massachusetts*, pages 142–154. ACM Press, 2000.

[14] Benjamin C. Pierce and Davide Sangiorgi. Types and subtypes for mobile processes. *Mathematical Structures in Computer Science*, 6(5):409–454, 1996. A revised and extended version of a paper appearing at LICS'93.

[15] Benjamin C. Pierce and David N. Turner. Pict: A programming language based on the pi-calculus. Technical report, IU, 1997.

[16] James Riely and Matthew Hennessy. Trust and partial typing in open systems of mobile agents. In *POPL'99, San Antonio, Texas*, pages 93–104. ACM Press, 1999.

[17] Peter Sewell and Jan Vitek. Secure composition of insecure components. In *12th IEEE Computer Security Foundations Workshop (CSFW-12), Mordano, Italy*, June 1999.

[18] Kaku Takeuchi, Kohei Honda, and Makoto Kubo. An interaction-based language and its typing system. In *PARLE'94*, volume 817 of *LNCS*, pages 398–413. Springer-Verlag, 1994.

[19] David N. Turner. *The Polymorphic Pi-Calculus: Theory and Implementation*. PhD thesis, University of Edinburgh, 1995. Report no ECS-LFCS-96-345.

[20] Jan Vitek and Giuseppe Castagna. Seal: A framework for secure mobile computations. In *Internet Programming Languages*, volume 1686 of *LNCS*. Springer-Verlag, 1999.

[21] Nobuko Yoshida and Matthew Hennessy. Subtyping and locality in distributed higher order mobile processes. In *CONCUR 1999*, volume 1664 of *LNCS*, pages 557–573. Springer-Verlag, 1999.

[22] Nobuko Yoshida and Matthew Hennessy. Assigning types to processes. In *LICS 2000*, pages 334–345, 2000.

[23] Pascal Zimmer. Subtyping and typing algorithms for mobile ambients. In *FOSSACS 2000, Berlin*, volume 1784 of *LNCS*, pages 375–390. Springer-Verlag, 2000.

JOIN(X): Constraint-Based Type Inference for the Join-Calculus

Sylvain Conchon and François Pottier

INRIA Rocquencourt, {Sylvain.Conchon,Francois.Pottier}@inria.fr

Abstract. We present a generic constraint-based type system for the join-calculus. The key issue is type generalization, which, in the presence of concurrency, must be restricted. We first define a liberal generalization criterion, and prove it correct. Then, we find that it hinders type inference, and propose a cruder one, reminiscent of ML's *value restriction*. We establish type safety using a *semi-syntactic* technique, which we believe is of independent interest. It consists in interpreting typing judgements as (sets of) judgements in an underlying system, which itself is given a syntactic soundness proof.

1 Introduction

The join-calculus [3] is a name-passing process calculus related to the asynchronous π-calculus. The original motivation for its introduction was to define a process calculus amenable to a distributed implementation. In particular, the join-calculus merges reception, restriction and replication into a single syntactic form, the `def` construct, avoiding the need for distributed consensus. This design decision turns out to also have an important impact on typing. Indeed, because the behavior of a channel is fully known at definition time, its type can be safely generalized. Thus, `def` constructs become analogous to ML's `let` definitions. For instance, the following definition:

```
def apply(f,x) = f(x)
```

defines a channel `apply` which expects two arguments `f` and `x` and, upon receipt, sends the message `f(x)`. In Fournet *et al.*'s type system [4], `apply` receives the parametric type scheme $\forall \alpha.\langle\langle\alpha\rangle, \alpha\rangle$, where $\langle\cdot\rangle$ is the channel type constructor.

1.1 Motivation

Why develop a new type system for the join-calculus? The unification-based system proposed by Fournet *et al.* [4] shares many attractive features with ML's type system: it is simple, expressive, and easy to implement, as shown by the Jo-Caml experiment [1]. Like ML, it is *prescriptive*, i.e. intended to infer reasonably simple types and to enforce a programming discipline.

Type systems are often used as a nice formal basis for various program analyses, such as control flow analysis, strictness analysis, usage analysis, and so

D. Sands (Ed.): ESOP 2001, LNCS 2028, pp. 221–236, 2001.
© Springer-Verlag Berlin Heidelberg 2001

on. These systems, however, tend to be essentially *descriptive*, i.e. intended to infer accurate types and to reject as few programs as possible. To achieve this goal, it is common to describe the behavior of programs using a rich *constraint* language, possibly involving subtyping, set constraints, conditional constraints, etc. We wish to define such a descriptive type system for the join-calculus, as a vehicle for future type-based analyses.

Following Odersky *et al.* [6], we parameterize our type system with an arbitrary constraint logic X, making it more generic and more easily re-useable. Our work may be viewed as an attempt to adapt their constraint-based framework to the join-calculus, much as Fournet *et al.* adapted ML's type discipline.

1.2   Type Generalization Criteria

The def construct improves on let expressions by allowing synchronization between channels. Thus, we can define a variant of apply that receives the channel f and the argument x from different channels.

```
def apply(f) | args(x) = f(x)
```

This simultaneously defines the names apply and args. The message f(x) will be emitted whenever a message is received on both of these channels.

In a subtyping-constraint-based type system, one would expect apply and args to be given types $\langle\beta\rangle$ and $\langle\alpha\rangle$, respectively, *correlated* by the constraint $\beta \leq \langle\alpha\rangle$. The constraint requires the channels to be used in a *consistent* way: the type of x must match the expectations of f. Now, if we were to generalize these types separately, we would obtain apply : $\forall\alpha\beta[\beta \leq \langle\alpha\rangle].\langle\beta\rangle$ and args : $\forall\alpha\beta[\beta \leq \langle\alpha\rangle].\langle\alpha\rangle$, which are logically equivalent to apply : $\forall\alpha.\langle\langle\alpha\rangle\rangle$ and args : $\forall\alpha.\langle\alpha\rangle$. These types no longer reflect the consistency requirement!

To address this problem, Fournet *et al.* state that any type variable which is *shared* between two jointly defined names (here, apply and args), i.e. which occurs free in their types, must not be generalized. However, this criterion is based on the *syntax* of types, and makes little sense in the presence of an arbitrary constraint logic X. In the example above, apply and args have types $\langle\beta\rangle$ and $\langle\alpha\rangle$, so they share no type variables. The correlation is only apparent in the constraint $\beta \leq \langle\alpha\rangle$. When the constraint logic X is known, correlations can be detected by examining the (syntax of the) constraint, looking for *paths* connecting α and β. However, we want our type system to be parametric in X, so the syntax (and the meaning) of constraints is, in general, not available. This leads us to define a uniform, *logical* generalization criterion (Sect. 5.2), which we prove sound.

Unfortunately, and somewhat surprisingly, this criterion turns out to hinder type inference. As a result, we will propose a cruder one, reminiscent of ML's so-called *value restriction* [10].

$$P \mid Q \rightleftharpoons Q \mid P \qquad\qquad D_1, D_2 \rightleftharpoons D_2, D_1$$
$$P \mid 0 \rightleftharpoons P \qquad\qquad D, \epsilon \rightleftharpoons D$$
$$P \mid (Q \mid R) \rightleftharpoons (P \mid Q) \mid R \qquad\qquad D_1, (D_2, D_3) \rightleftharpoons (D_1, D_2), D_3$$

$$\begin{array}{ll}
(\mathtt{def}\ D\ \mathtt{in}\ P) \mid Q \rightleftharpoons \mathtt{def}\ D\ \mathtt{in}\ (P \mid Q) & \text{if } \mathrm{dn}(D) \cap \mathrm{fn}(Q) = \varnothing \\
\mathtt{def}\ D_1\ \mathtt{in}\ \mathtt{def}\ D_2\ \mathtt{in}\ P \rightleftharpoons \mathtt{def}\ D_1, D_2\ \mathtt{in}\ P & \text{if } \mathrm{fn}(D_1) \cap \mathrm{dn}(D_2) = \varnothing \\
\mathtt{def}\ D, J \triangleright P\ \mathtt{in}\ Q \mid \varphi J \to \mathtt{def}\ D, J \triangleright P\ \mathtt{in}\ Q \mid \varphi P & \text{if } \mathrm{dom}(\varphi) = \mathrm{ln}(J)
\end{array}$$

Fig. 1. Operational semantics

1.3   Overview

We first recall the syntax and semantics of the join-calculus, and introduce some useful notation. Then, we introduce a *ground* type system for the join-calculus, called B(T), and establish its correctness in a syntactic way (Sect. 4). Building on this foundation, Sect. 5 introduces JOIN(X) and proves it correct with respect to B(T). Sect. 6 studies type reconstruction, suggesting that a restricted generalization criterion must be adopted in order to obtain a complete algorithm.

By lack of space, we omit all proofs, except that of the main type soundness theorem (Theorem 5.9). The interested reader is referred to [2].

2   The Join-Calculus

We assume given a countable set of names $\mathcal{N}$, ranged over by $x, y, u, v, \ldots$ We write $\vec{u}$ for a tuple $(u_1, \ldots, u_n)$ and $\bar{u}$ for a set $\{u_1, \ldots, u_n\}$, where $n \geq 0$. The syntax of the join-calculus is as follows.

$$P ::= 0 \mid (P \mid P) \mid u\langle \vec{v} \rangle \mid \mathtt{def}\ D\ \mathtt{in}\ P$$
$$D ::= \epsilon \mid J \triangleright P \mid D, D$$
$$J ::= u\langle \vec{y} \rangle \mid (J \mid J)$$

The *defined names* $\mathrm{dn}(J)$ (resp. $\mathrm{dn}(D)$) of a join-pattern J (resp. of a definition D) are the channels defined by it. In a process $\mathtt{def}\ D\ \mathtt{in}\ P$, the defined names of D are bound within D and P. More details are given in [2].

Reduction $\to$ is defined as the smallest relation that satisfies the laws in Fig. 1. (α-conversion rules are omitted for brevity.) φ ranges over *renamings*, i.e. one-to-one maps from $\mathcal{N}$ into $\mathcal{N}$. $\rightleftharpoons$ stands for $\to \cap \leftarrow$. It is customary to distinguish structural equivalence and reduction, but this is unnecessary here.

3   Notation

Definition 3.1. *Given a set T, a T-environment, usually denoted Γ, is a partial mapping from $\mathcal{N}$ into T. If $N \subseteq \mathcal{N}$, $\Gamma|_N$ denotes the restriction of Γ to N. $\Gamma + \Gamma'$ is the environment which maps every $u \in \mathcal{N}$ to $\Gamma'(u)$, if it is defined, and to $\Gamma(u)$ otherwise. When Γ and Γ' agree on $\mathrm{dom}(\Gamma) \cap \mathrm{dom}(\Gamma')$, $\Gamma + \Gamma'$ is written $\Gamma \oplus \Gamma'$. If T is equipped with a partial order, it is extended point-wise to T-environments of identical domain.*

Definition 3.2. *Given a set T, ranged over by t, $\vec{t}$ denotes a tuple $(t_1, \ldots t_n)$, of length $n \geq 0$; we let $T^\star$ denote the set of such tuples. If T is equipped with a partial order, it is extended point-wise to tuples of identical length.*

Definition 3.3. *Given a set I, $(x_i : t_i)^{i \in I}$ denotes the partial mapping $x_i \mapsto t_i$ of domain $\bar{x} = \{x_i \, ; \, i \in I\}$. $(P_i)^{i \in I}$ denotes the parallel composition of the processes P_i. $(D_i)^{i \in I}$ denotes the conjunction of the definitions D_i.*

Definition 3.4. *The Cartesian product of a labelled tuple of sets $\mathcal{A} = (x_i : s_i)^{i \in I}$, written $\Pi \mathcal{A}$, is the set of tuples $\{(x_i : t_i)^{i \in I} \, ; \, \forall i \in I \quad t_i \in s_i\}$.*

Definition 3.5. *Given a partially ordered set T and a subset V of T, the* cone *generated by V within T, denoted by $\uparrow V$, is $\{t \in T \, ; \, \exists v \in V \quad v \leq t\}$. V is said to be* upward-closed *if and only if $V = \uparrow V$.*

4   The System B(T)

This section defines an intermediate type system for the join-calculus, called B(T). It is a *ground* type system: it does not have a notion of type variable. Instead, it has *monotypes*, taken to be elements of some set T, and *polytypes*, merely defined as certain subsets of T.

Assumptions. We assume given a set T, whose elements, usually denoted by t, are called *monotypes*. T must be equipped with a partial order $\leq$. We assume given a total function, denoted $\langle \cdot \rangle$, from $T^\star$ into T, such that $\langle \vec{t} \rangle \leq \langle \vec{t'} \rangle$ holds if and only if $\vec{t'} \leq \vec{t}$.

Definition 4.1. *A polytype, usually denoted by s, is a non-empty, upward-closed subset of T. Let S be the set of all polytypes. We order S by $\supseteq$, i.e. we write $s \leq s'$ if and only if $s \supseteq s'$.*

Note that $\leq$ and $\langle \cdot \rangle$ operate on T. Furthermore, S is defined on top of T; there is no way to inject S back into T. In other words, this presentation allows *rank-1* polymorphism only; impredicative polymorphism is ruled out. This is in keeping with the Hindley-Milner family of type systems [5,6].

Names

B-INST
$$\frac{\Gamma(u) = s \qquad t \in s}{\Gamma \vdash u : t}$$

B-SUB-NAME
$$\frac{\Gamma \vdash u : t' \qquad t' \leq t}{\Gamma \vdash u : t}$$

Definitions

B-EMPTY
$$\Gamma \vdash \epsilon :: \vec{0}$$

B-JOIN
$$\frac{\Gamma + (\vec{u}_i : \vec{t}_i)^{i \in I} \vdash P}{\Gamma \vdash (x_i \langle \vec{u}_i \rangle)^{i \in I} \triangleright P :: (x_i : \langle \vec{t}_i \rangle)^{i \in I}}$$

B-OR
$$\frac{\Gamma \vdash D_1 :: \mathcal{B}_1 \qquad \Gamma \vdash D_2 :: \mathcal{B}_2}{\Gamma \vdash D_1, D_2 :: \mathcal{B}_1 \oplus \mathcal{B}_2}$$

B-SUB-DEF
$$\frac{\Gamma \vdash D :: \mathcal{B} \qquad \mathcal{B} \leq \mathcal{B}'}{\Gamma \vdash D :: \mathcal{B}'}$$

B-GEN
$$\frac{\forall \mathcal{B} \in \Pi \mathcal{A} \qquad \Gamma \vdash D :: \mathcal{B}}{\Gamma \vdash D :: \mathcal{A}}$$

Processes

B-NULL
$$\Gamma \vdash 0$$

B-PAR
$$\frac{\Gamma \vdash P \qquad \Gamma \vdash Q}{\Gamma \vdash P \mid Q}$$

B-MSG
$$\frac{\Gamma \vdash u : \langle \vec{t} \rangle \qquad \Gamma \vdash \vec{v} : \vec{t}}{\Gamma \vdash u \langle \vec{v} \rangle}$$

B-DEF
$$\frac{\Gamma + \mathcal{A} \vdash D :: \mathcal{A} \qquad \Gamma + \mathcal{A} \vdash P}{\Gamma \vdash \mathbf{def}\ D\ \mathbf{in}\ P}$$

Fig. 2. The system B(T)

Definition 4.2. *A* monotype environment, *denoted by $\mathcal{B}$, is a T-environment. A* polytype environment, *denoted by Γ or $\mathcal{A}$, is an S-environment.*

Definition 4.3. *The type system B(T) is given in Fig. 2. By abuse of notation, in the first premise of rule B-JOIN, a monotype binding $(u : t)$ is implicitly viewed as the polytype binding $(u : \uparrow\{t\})$.*

Every typing judgement carries a polytype environment Γ on its left-hand side, representing a set of assumptions under which its right-hand side may be used. Right-hand sides come in four varieties. $u : t$ states that the name u has type t. $D :: \mathcal{B}$ (resp. $D :: \mathcal{A}$) states that the definition D gives rise to the environment fragment $\mathcal{B}$ (resp. $\mathcal{A}$). Then, dom($\mathcal{B}$) (resp. dom($\mathcal{A}$)) is, by construction, dn(D). Lastly, a right-hand side of the form P simply states that the process P is well-typed.

The most salient aspect of these rules is their treatment of polymorphism. Rule B-INST performs *instantiation* by allowing a polytype s to be specialized to any monotype $t \in s$. Conversely, rule B-GEN performs *generalization* by allowing the judgement $\Gamma \vdash D :: (x_i : s_i)^{i \in I}$ to be formed if $\Gamma \vdash D :: (x_i : t_i)^{i \in I}$ holds whenever $(x_i : t_i)^{i \in I} \in \Pi(x_i : s_i)^{i \in I}$, i.e. whenever $\forall i \in I \ \ t_i \in s_i$ holds. In other words, this system offers an *extensional* view of polymorphism: a polytype s is definitionally equal to the set of its monotype instances.

Rules other than B-GEN, B-INST and B-DEF are fairly straightforward; they involve monotypes only, and are similar to those found in common typed process calculi. The only non-syntax-directed rules are B-SUB-NAME and B-SUB-DEF; two canonical derivations lemmas show that their uses can in fact be eliminated. Rule B-GEN must (and can only) be applied once above every use of B-DEF, so it is not a source of non-determinism.

The following lemmas will be used in the proof of Theorem 5.9. The first one allows weakening type judgements by strengthening their environment. The second one is a corollary of the canonical derivations lemma (not shown).

Lemma 4.4. *If $\Gamma \vdash P$ and $\Gamma' \leq \Gamma$, then $\Gamma' \vdash P$.*

Lemma 4.5. *Assume $\Gamma \vdash (D, J \triangleright P) :: \mathcal{B}'$ and $\mathcal{B}'|_{dn(J)} \leq \mathcal{B}$. Then $\Gamma \vdash J \triangleright P :: \mathcal{B}$.*

We establish type soundness for $B(T)$ following the syntactic approach of Wright and Felleisen [11], i.e. by proving that $B(T)$ enjoys *subject reduction* and *progress* properties.

Theorem 4.6 (Subject reduction). *$\Gamma \vdash P$ and $P \rightarrow P'$ imply $\Gamma \vdash P'$.*

Definition 4.7. *A process of the form* def $D, J \triangleright P$ in $Q \mid u \langle \vec{v} \rangle$ *is faulty if J defines a message $u \langle \vec{y} \rangle$ where $\vec{v}$ and $\vec{y}$ have different arities.*

Theorem 4.8 (Progress). *No well-typed process is faulty.*

5   The System JOIN(X)

5.1   Presentation

Like $B(T)$, JOIN(X) is parameterized by a set of ground types T, equipped with a type constructor $\langle \cdot \rangle$ and a subtyping relation $\leq$. It is further parameterized by a first-order logic X, interpreted in T, whose variables and formulas are respectively called *type variables* and *constraints*. The logic allows describing subsets of T as constraints. Provided constraint satisfiability is decidable, this gives rise to a type system where type checking is decidable.

Our treatment is inspired by the framework HM(X) [6,9,8]. Our presentation differs, however, by explicitly viewing constraints as formulas interpreted in T, rather than as elements of an abstract cylindric constraint system. This presentation is more concise, and gives us the ability to explicitly manipulate *solutions* of constraints, an essential requirement in our formulation of type soundness (Theorem 5.9). Even though we lose some generality with respect to the cylindric-system approach, we claim the framework remains general enough.

Assumptions. We assume given $(T, \leq, \langle \cdot \rangle)$ as in Sect. 4. Furthermore, we assume given a constraint logic X whose syntax *includes* the following productions:

$$C ::= \mathbf{true} \mid \alpha = \langle \vec{\beta} \rangle \mid \alpha \leq \beta \mid C \wedge C \mid \exists \bar{\alpha}.C \mid \ldots$$

($\alpha, \beta, \ldots$ range over a denumerable set of type variables $\mathcal{V}$.) The syntax of constraints is only partially specified; this allows custom constraint forms, not known in this paper, to be later introduced.

The logic X must be equipped with an interpretation in T, i.e. a two-place predicate $\vdash$ whose first argument is an assignment, i.e. a total mapping ρ from $\mathcal{V}$ into T, and whose second argument is a constraint C. The interpretation must be standard, i.e. satisfy the following laws:

$$\rho \vdash \mathbf{true}$$

$$
\begin{array}{lll}
\rho \vdash \alpha_0 = \langle \vec{\alpha}_1 \rangle & \text{iff} & \rho(\alpha_0) = \langle \rho(\vec{\alpha}_1) \rangle \\
\rho \vdash \alpha_0 \leq \alpha_1 & \text{iff} & \rho(\alpha_0) \leq \rho(\alpha_1) \\
\rho \vdash C_0 \wedge C_1 & \text{iff} & \rho \vdash C_0 \wedge \rho \vdash C_1 \\
\rho \vdash \exists \bar{\alpha}.C & \text{iff} & \exists \rho' \; (\rho' \setminus \bar{\alpha} = \rho \setminus \bar{\alpha}) \wedge \rho' \vdash C
\end{array}
$$

($\rho \setminus \bar{\alpha}$ denotes the restriction of ρ to $\mathcal{V} \setminus \bar{\alpha}$.) The interpretation of any unknown constraint forms is left unspecified. We write $C \Vdash C'$ if and only if C entails C', i.e. if and only if every solution ρ of C satisfies C' as well.

JOIN(X) has *constrained type schemes*, where a number of type variables $\bar{\alpha}$ are universally quantified, subject to a constraint C.

Definition 5.1. *A type scheme is a triple of a set of quantifiers $\bar{\alpha}$, a constraint C, and a type variable α; we write $\sigma = \forall \bar{\alpha}[C].\alpha$. The type variables in $\bar{\alpha}$ are bound in σ; type schemes are considered equal modulo α-conversion. By abuse of notation, a type variable α may be viewed as a type scheme $\forall \varnothing[\mathbf{true}].\alpha$. The set of type schemes is written $\mathcal{S}$.*

Definition 5.2. *A polymorphic typing environment, denoted by Γ or A, is a $\mathcal{S}$-environment. A monomorphic typing environment, denoted by B, is a $\mathcal{V}$-environment.*

Definition 5.3. *JOIN(X) is defined by Fig. 3. Every judgement $C, \Gamma \vdash \mathcal{J}$ is implicitly accompanied by the side condition that C must be satisfiable.*

JOIN(X) differs from B(T) by replacing monotypes with type variables, polytypes with type schemes, and parameterizing every judgement with a constraint C, which represents an assumption about its free type variables. Rule WEAKEN allows strengthening this assumption, while $\exists$ INTRO allows hiding auxiliary type variables which appear nowhere but in the assumption itself. These rules, which are common to names, definitions, and processes, allow constraint simplification.

Because we do not have syntax for types, rules JOIN and MSG use constraints of the form $\beta = \langle \vec{\alpha} \rangle$ to encode type structure into constraints.

Our treatment of constrained polymorphism is standard. Whereas B(T) takes an extensional view of polymorphism, JOIN(X) offers the usual, *intensional* view. Type schemes are introduced by rule DEF, and eliminated by INST. Because implicit α-conversion is allowed, every instance of INST is able to rename the bound variables at will.

For the sake of readability, we have simplified rule DEF, omitting two features present in HM(X)'s $\forall$ INTRO rule [6]. First, we do not force the introduction of existential quantifiers in the judgement's conclusion. In the presence of WEAKEN and $\exists$ INTRO, doing so would not affect the set of valid typing judgements, so we prefer a simpler rule. Second, we move the whole constraint C into the type schemes $\forall \bar{\alpha}[C] \twoheadrightarrow B$, whereas it would be sufficient to copy only the part of C where $\bar{\alpha}$ actually occurs. This optimization can be easily added back in if desired.

5.2   A Look at the Generalization Condition

The most subtle (and, it turns out, questionable; see Sect. 6.1) aspect of this system is the generalization condition, i.e. the third premise of rule DEF, which determines which type variables may be safely generalized. We will now describe it in detail. To begin, let us introduce some notation.

Definition 5.4. *If* $B = (x_i : \beta_i)^{i \in I}$, *then* $\forall \bar{\alpha}[C] \twoheadrightarrow B$ *is the polymorphic environment* $(x_i : \forall \bar{\alpha}[C].\beta_i)^{i \in I}$. *This must not be confused with the notation* $\forall \bar{\alpha}[C].B$, *where the universal quantifier lies outside of the environment fragment* B.

The existence of these two notations, and the question of whether it is legal to confuse the two, is precisely at the heart of the generalization issue. Let us have a look at rule DEF. Its first premise associates a monomorphic environment fragment B to the definition $D = (J_i \rhd P_i)^{i \in I}$. If the type variables $\bar{\alpha}$ do not appear free in Γ, then it is surely correct to generalize the fragment as a whole, i.e. to assert that D has type $\forall \bar{\alpha}[C].B$. However, this is no longer a valid environment fragment, because the quantifier appears *in front of* the whole vector; so, we cannot typecheck P under $\Gamma + \forall \bar{\alpha}[C].B$. Instead, we must push the universal quantifier down into *each* binding, yielding $\forall \bar{\alpha}[C] \twoheadrightarrow B$, which is a well-formed environment fragment, and can be used to augment Γ.

However, $\forall \bar{\alpha}[C] \twoheadrightarrow B$ may be strictly more general than $\forall \bar{\alpha}[C].B$, because it binds $\bar{\alpha}$ separately in each entry, rather than once in common. We must avoid this situation, which would allow inconsistent uses of the defined names, by properly restricting $\bar{\alpha}$. (When $\bar{\alpha}$ is empty, the two notions coincide.)

To ensure that $\forall \bar{\alpha}[C] \twoheadrightarrow B$ and $\forall \bar{\alpha}[C].B$ coincide, previous works [4,7] propose syntactic criteria, which forbid generalization of a type variable if it appears free in two distinct bindings in B. In an arbitrary constraint logic, however, a syntactic occurrence of a type variable does not necessarily constrain its value. So, it seems preferable to define a logical, rather than syntactic, criterion. To do so, we first give logical meaning to the notations $\forall \bar{\alpha}[C] \twoheadrightarrow B$ and $\forall \bar{\alpha}[C].B$.

Names

$$\text{INST} \qquad \frac{\Gamma(u) = \forall\bar{\alpha}[C].\alpha}{C,\Gamma \vdash u : \alpha}$$

$$\text{SUB-NAME} \qquad \frac{C,\Gamma \vdash u : \alpha' \qquad C \Vdash \alpha' \leq \alpha}{C,\Gamma \vdash u : \alpha}$$

Definitions

$$\text{EMPTY} \qquad C,\Gamma \vdash \epsilon :: \vec{0}$$

$$\text{JOIN} \qquad \frac{C,\Gamma + (\vec{u}_i : \vec{\alpha}_i)^{i\in I} \vdash P \qquad \forall i \in I \quad C \Vdash \beta_i = \langle\vec{\alpha}_i\rangle}{C,\Gamma \vdash (x_i \langle \vec{u}_i \rangle)^{i\in I} \rhd P :: (x_i : \beta_i)^{i\in I}}$$

$$\text{OR} \qquad \frac{C,\Gamma \vdash D_1 : B_1 \qquad C,\Gamma \vdash D_2 : B_2}{C,\Gamma \vdash D_1, D_2 :: B_1 \oplus B_2}$$

$$\text{SUB-DEF} \qquad \frac{C,\Gamma \vdash D :: B' \qquad C \Vdash B' \leq B}{C,\Gamma \vdash D :: B}$$

Processes

$$\text{NULL} \qquad C,\Gamma \vdash 0$$

$$\text{PAR} \qquad \frac{C,\Gamma \vdash P \qquad C,\Gamma \vdash Q}{C,\Gamma \vdash P \mid Q}$$

$$\text{MSG} \qquad \frac{C,\Gamma \vdash u : \beta \qquad C,\Gamma \vdash \vec{v} : \vec{\alpha} \qquad C \Vdash \beta = \langle\vec{\alpha}\rangle}{C,\Gamma \vdash u \langle \vec{v} \rangle}$$

$$\text{DEF} \qquad \frac{\begin{array}{c} C,\Gamma + B \vdash (J_i \rhd P_i)^{i\in I} :: B \qquad \bar{\alpha} \cap \mathrm{fv}(\Gamma) = \varnothing \\ \forall i \in I \quad C \Vdash \forall\bar{\alpha}[C].B|_{\mathrm{dn}(J_i)} \leq \forall\bar{\alpha}[C]{\twoheadrightarrow}B|_{\mathrm{dn}(J_i)} \\ C',\Gamma + \forall\bar{\alpha}[C]{\twoheadrightarrow}B \vdash P \qquad C' \Vdash C \end{array}}{C',\Gamma \vdash \mathtt{def}\ (J_i \rhd P_i)^{i\in I}\ \mathtt{in}\ P}$$

Common

$$\text{WEAKEN} \qquad \frac{C',\Gamma \vdash \mathcal{J} \qquad C \Vdash C'}{C,\Gamma \vdash \mathcal{J}}$$

$$\exists\ \text{INTRO} \qquad \frac{C,\Gamma \vdash \mathcal{J} \qquad \bar{\alpha} \cap \mathrm{fv}(\Gamma,\mathcal{J}) = \varnothing}{\exists\bar{\alpha}.C,\Gamma \vdash \mathcal{J}}$$

Fig. 3. The system JOIN(X) (with a tentative DEF rule)

Definition 5.5. *The denotation of a type scheme $\sigma = \forall\bar{\alpha}[C].\alpha$ under an assignment ρ, written $[\![\sigma]\!]_\rho$, is defined as $\uparrow\{\rho'(\alpha)\,;\,(\rho' \setminus \bar{\alpha} = \rho \setminus \bar{\alpha}) \wedge \rho' \vdash C\}$ if this set is non-empty; it is undefined otherwise.*

This definition interprets a type scheme σ as the set of its instances in T, or, more precisely, as the upper cone which they generate. (Taking the cone accounts for the subtyping relationship ambient in T.) It is parameterized by an assignment ρ, which gives meaning to the free type variables of σ.

Definition 5.6. *The denotation of an environment fragment $A = (u_i : \sigma_i)^{i\in I}$ under an assignment ρ, written $(\!|A|\!)_\rho$, is defined as $\Pi[\![A]\!]_\rho = \Pi(u_i : [\![\sigma_i]\!]_\rho)^{i\in I}$. The denotation of $\forall\bar{\alpha}[C].B$ under an assignment ρ, written $(\!|\forall\bar{\alpha}[C].B|\!)_\rho$, is defined as $\uparrow\{\rho'(B)\,;\,(\rho' \setminus \bar{\alpha} = \rho \setminus \bar{\alpha}) \wedge \rho' \vdash C\}$.*

This definition interprets environment fragments as a whole, rather than point-wise. That is, $(\!|\cdot|\!)_\rho$ maps environment fragments to sets of tuples of mono-types. A polymorphic environment fragment A maps each name u_i to a type scheme σ_i. The fact that these type schemes are independent of one another is reflected in our interpretation of A as the Cartesian product of their interpretations. On the other hand, $\forall \bar\alpha[C].B$ is just a type scheme whose body happens to be a tuple, so we interpret it as (the upper cone generated by) the set of its instances, as in Definition 5.5.

Interpreting the notations $\forall \bar\alpha[C] \twoheadrightarrow B$ and $\forall \bar\alpha[C].B$ within the same mathematical space allows us to give a logical criterion under which they coincide.

Definition 5.7. *By definition, $C \Vdash \forall \bar\alpha[C].B \leq \forall \bar\alpha[C] \twoheadrightarrow B$ holds if and only if, under every assignment ρ such that $\rho \vdash C$, $(\!|\forall \bar\alpha[C].B|\!)_\rho \supseteq (\!|\forall \bar\alpha[C] \twoheadrightarrow B|\!)_\rho$ holds.*

The strength of this criterion is to be independent of the constraint logic X. This allows us to prove $\mathrm{JOIN}(X)$ correct in a pleasant generic way (see Sect. 5.3).

As a final remark, let us point out that, independently of how to *define* the generalization criterion, there is also a question of how to *apply* it. It would be correct for rule DEF to require $C \Vdash \forall \bar\alpha[C].B \leq \forall \bar\alpha[C] \twoheadrightarrow B$, as in [4]. However, when executing the program, only one clause of the definition at a time will be reduced, so it is sufficient to separately ensure that the messages which appear in each clause have consistent types. As a result, we successively apply the criterion to each clause $J_i \triangleright P_i$, by restricting B to the set of its defined names, yielding $B|_{\mathrm{dn}(J_i)}$. In this respect, we closely follow the JoCaml implementation [1] as well as Odersky *et al.* [7].

5.3   Type Soundness, Semi-syntactically

This section gives a type soundness proof for $\mathrm{JOIN}(X)$ by showing that it is safe with respect to $\mathrm{B}(T)$. That is, we show that every judgement $C, \Gamma \vdash \mathcal{J}$ describes the set of all $\mathrm{B}(T)$ judgements of the form $\rho(\Gamma \vdash \mathcal{J})$, where $\rho \vdash C$. Thus, we give logical (rather than syntactic) meaning to $\mathrm{JOIN}(X)$ judgements, yielding a concise and natural proof. As a whole, the approach is still semi-syntactic, because $\mathrm{B}(T)$ itself has been proven correct in a syntactic way.

Definition 5.8. *When defined (cf. Definition 5.5), $[\![\sigma]\!]_\rho$ is a polytype, i.e. an element of S. The denotation function $[\![\cdot]\!]_\rho$ is extended point-wise to typing environments. As a result, if Γ is an S-environment, then $[\![\Gamma]\!]_\rho$ is an S-environment.*

Theorem 5.9 (Soundness). *Let $\rho(u : \alpha)$, $\rho(D :: B)$, $\rho(P)$ stand for $u : \rho(\alpha)$, $D :: \rho(B)$, P, respectively. Then, $\rho \vdash C$ and $C, \Gamma \vdash \mathcal{J}$ imply $[\![\Gamma]\!]_\rho \vdash \rho(\mathcal{J})$.*

Proof. By structural induction on the derivation of the input judgement. We use exactly the notations of Fig. 3. In each case, we assume given some solution ρ of the constraint which appears in the judgement's conclusion.

Case INST. We have $[\![\Gamma]\!]_\rho(u) = [\![\forall \bar\alpha[C].\alpha]\!]_\rho \ni \rho(\alpha)$ because $\rho \vdash C$. The result follows by B-INST.

Case SUB-NAME. The induction hypothesis yields $[\![\Gamma]\!]_\rho \vdash u : \rho(\alpha')$. The second premise implies $\rho(\alpha') \leq \rho(\alpha)$. Apply B-SUB-NAME to conclude.

Case EMPTY. Immediate.

Case JOIN. Let $B = (x_i : \beta_i)^{i \in I}$. Applying the induction hypothesis to the first premise yields $[\![\Gamma]\!]_\rho + (\vec{u}_i : [\![\vec{\alpha}_i]\!]_\rho)^{i \in I} \vdash P$. Since $[\![\alpha]\!]_\rho$ is $\uparrow\{\rho(\alpha)\}$, this may be written $[\![\Gamma]\!]_\rho + (\vec{u}_i : \rho(\vec{\alpha}_i))^{i \in I} \vdash P$. (Recall the abuse of notation introduced in Definition 4.3.) The second premise implies $\forall i \in I \quad \rho(\beta_i) = \langle \rho(\vec{\alpha}_i) \rangle$. As a result, by B-JOIN, $[\![\Gamma]\!]_\rho \vdash D : \rho(B)$ holds.

Case OR. Then, D is $D_1 \wedge D_2$ and B is $B_1 \oplus B_2$. Applying the induction hypothesis to the premises yields $[\![\Gamma]\!]_\rho \vdash D_i : \rho(B_i)$. Apply B-OR to conclude.

Case SUB-DEF. The induction hypothesis yields $[\![\Gamma]\!]_\rho \vdash D : \rho(B')$. The second premise implies $\rho(B') \leq \rho(B)$. Apply B-SUB-DEF to conclude.

Cases NULL, PAR. Immediate.

Case MSG. Applying the induction hypothesis to the first two premises yields $[\![\Gamma]\!]_\rho \vdash u : \rho(\beta)$ and $[\![\Gamma]\!]_\rho \vdash \vec{v} : \rho(\vec{\alpha})$. The last premise entails $\rho(\beta) = \langle \rho(\vec{\alpha}) \rangle$. Apply B-MSG to conclude.

Case DEF. By hypothesis, $\rho \vdash C'$; according to the last premise, $\rho \vdash C$ also holds. Let $A = \forall \bar{\alpha}[C] \twoheadrightarrow B$. Take $\mathcal{B} \in (\!|A|\!)_\rho$. Take $i \in I$ and define $\mathcal{B}_i = \mathcal{B}|_{\mathrm{dn}(J_i)}$. Then, $\mathcal{B}_i$ is a member of $(\!|\forall \bar{\alpha}[C] \twoheadrightarrow B|_{\mathrm{dn}(J_i)}|\!)_\rho$, which, according to the third premise, is a subset of $(\!|\forall \bar{\alpha}[C].B|_{\mathrm{dn}(J_i)}|\!)_\rho$. Thus, there exists an assignment ρ' such that $(\rho' \setminus \bar{\alpha} = \rho \setminus \bar{\alpha}) \wedge \rho' \vdash C$ and $\rho'(B|_{\mathrm{dn}(J_i)}) \leq \mathcal{B}_i$. The induction hypothesis, applied to the first premise and to ρ', yields $[\![\Gamma + B]\!]_{\rho'} \vdash D :: \rho'(B)$. By Lemma 4.5, this implies $[\![\Gamma + B]\!]_{\rho'} \vdash J_i \triangleright P_i :: \mathcal{B}_i$.

Now, because $\bar{\alpha} \cap \mathrm{fv}(\Gamma) = \varnothing$, $[\![\Gamma]\!]_{\rho'}$ is $[\![\Gamma]\!]_\rho$. Furthermore, given the properties of ρ', we have $[\![B]\!]_{\rho'} \geq [\![\forall \bar{\alpha}[C] \twoheadrightarrow B]\!]_\rho = [\![A]\!]_\rho$. As a result, by Lemma 4.4, the judgement above implies $[\![\Gamma]\!]_\rho + [\![A]\!]_\rho \vdash J_i \triangleright P_i :: \mathcal{B}_i$.

Because this holds for any $i \in I$, repeated use of B-OR yields a derivation of $[\![\Gamma]\!]_\rho + [\![A]\!]_\rho \vdash D :: \mathcal{B}$. Lastly, because this holds for any $\mathcal{B} \in (\!|A|\!)_\rho$, B-GEN yields $[\![\Gamma]\!]_\rho + [\![A]\!]_\rho \vdash D :: [\![A]\!]_\rho$.

Applying the induction hypothesis to the fourth premise yields $[\![\Gamma]\!]_\rho + [\![A]\!]_\rho \vdash P$. Apply B-DEF to conclude.

Case WEAKEN. The second premise gives $\rho \vdash C'$. Thus, the induction hypothesis may be applied to the first premise, yielding the desired judgement.

Case $\exists$ INTRO. We have $\rho \vdash \exists \bar{\alpha}.C$. Then, there exists an assignment ρ' such that $(\rho' \setminus \bar{\alpha} = \rho \setminus \bar{\alpha}) \wedge \rho' \vdash C$. Considering the second premise, we have $[\![\Gamma]\!]_{\rho'} = [\![\Gamma]\!]_\rho$ and $\rho'(\mathcal{J}) = \rho(\mathcal{J})$. Thus, applying the induction hypothesis to the first premise and to ρ' yields the desired judgement.

This proof is, in our opinion, fairly readable. In fact, all cases except DEF are next to trivial.

In the DEF case, we must show that the definition D has type $[\![A]\!]_\rho$, where $A = \forall \bar{\alpha}[C] \twoheadrightarrow B$. Because B($T$) has extensional polymorphism (i.e. rule B-GEN), it suffices to show that it has every type $\mathcal{B} \in \Pi [\![A]\!]_\rho$. Notice how we must "cut $\mathcal{B}$ into pieces" $\mathcal{B}_i$, corresponding to each clause J_i, in order to make use of the per-clause generalization criterion. We use the induction hypothesis at the level of each clause, then recombine the resulting type derivations using B-OR. Notice how we use Lemma 4.4; proving an environment strengthening lemma at the level of JOIN(X) would be much more cumbersome.

The eight non-syntax-directed rules are easily proven correct. Indeed, their conclusion denotes fewer (SUB-NAME, SUB-DEF, WEAKEN) or exactly the same ($\exists$ INTRO) judgements in B(T) as their premise. In a syntactic proof, the presence of these rules would require several normalization lemmas.

Corollary 5.10. *No well-typed process gets faulty through reduction.*

Proof. Assume $C, \Gamma \vdash P$. Because C must be satisfiable, it must have at least one solution ρ. By Theorem 5.9, $[\![\Gamma]\!]_\rho \vdash P$ holds in B(T). The result follows by Theorems 4.6 and 4.8.

6   Type Inference

6.1   Trouble with Generalization

Two severe problems quickly arise when attempting to define a *complete* type inference procedure for JOIN(X). Both are caused by the *fragility* of the logical generalization criterion.

Non-determinism. To begin with, the criterion is non-deterministic. It states a sufficient condition for a given choice of $\bar{\alpha}$ to be correct. However, there seems to be, in general, no best choice.

Non-monotonicity. More subtly, *strengthening* the constraint C may, in some cases, cause apparent correlations to *disappear*. Consider the environment fragment $B = (a : \alpha; b : \beta)$ under the constraint $\gamma?\alpha = \beta$ (assuming the logic X offers such a constraint, to be read "if γ is non-$\bot$, then α must equal β"). There is a correlation between a and b, because, *in certain cases* (that is, when $\gamma \neq \bot$), α and β must coincide. However, let us now add the constraint $\gamma = \bot$. We obtain $\gamma?\alpha = \beta \wedge \gamma = \bot$, which is logically equivalent to $\gamma = \bot$. It is clear that, under the new constraint, a and b are no longer correlated. So, the set of generalizable type variables may *increase* as the constraint C is made more restrictive.

Given a definition D, a natural type inference algorithm will infer the weakest constraint C under which it is well-typed, then will use C to determine which type variables may be generalized. Because of non-monotonicity, the algorithm may find apparent correlations which would disappear if the constraint were deliberately strengthened. However, there is no way for the algorithm to guess if and how it should do so.

These remarks show that it is difficult to define a *complete* type inference algorithm, i.e. one which provably yields a single, most general typing.

Previous works [4,7] use a similar type-based criterion, yet report no difficulty with type inference. This leads us to conjecture that these problems do not arise when subtyping is interpreted as equality and no custom constraint forms are available. This may be true for other constraint logics as well. Thus, a partial

$$\text{DEF}$$
$$\dfrac{C, \Gamma + B \vdash (J_i \triangleright P_i)^{i \in I} :: B \qquad \bar{\alpha} \cap \mathrm{fv}(\Gamma) = \varnothing \\ (\exists i \in I \quad |\,\mathrm{dn}(J_i)\,| > 1) \Rightarrow \bar{\alpha} = \varnothing \\ C', \Gamma + \forall \bar{\alpha}[C] \twoheadrightarrow B \vdash P \qquad C' \Vdash C}{C', \Gamma \vdash \mathtt{def}\ (J_i \triangleright P_i)^{i \in I}\ \mathtt{in}\ P}$$

Fig. 4. Definitive DEF rule

solution would be to define a type inference procedure only for those logics, taking advantage of their particular structure to prove its completeness.

In the general case, i.e. under an arbitrary choice of X, we know of no solution other than to abandon the logical criterion. We suggest replacing it with a much more naïve one, based on the structure of the *definition* itself, rather than on type information. One possible such criterion is given in Fig. 4. It simply consists in refusing generalization entirely if the definition involves *any* synchronization, i.e. if any join-pattern defines more than one name. (It is possible to do slightly better, e.g. by generalizing all names not involved in a synchronization between two messages of non-zero arity.) It is clearly safe with respect to the previous criterion.

The new criterion is deterministic, and impervious to changes in C, since it depends solely on the structure of the definition D. It is the analogue of the so-called *value restriction*, suggested by Wright [10], now in use in most ML implementations. Experience with ML suggests that such a restriction is tolerable in practice; a quick experiment shows that all of the sample code bundled with JoCaml [1] is well-typed under it.

In the following, we adopt the restricted DEF rule of Fig. 4.

6.2 A Type Inference Algorithm

Fig. 5 gives a set of syntax-directed type inference rules. Again, in every judgement $C, \Gamma \vdash_I \mathcal{J}$, it is understood that C must be satisfiable. The rules implicitly describe an algorithm, whose inputs are an environment Γ and a sub-term u, D or P, and whose output, in case of success, is a judgement. Rule I-OR uses the following notation:

Definition 6.1. *The* least upper bound *of B_1 and B_2, written $B_1 \sqcup B_2$, is a pair of a monomorphic environment and a constraint. It is defined by:*

$$B_1 \sqcup B_2 = (u : \alpha_u)^{u \in U}, \qquad \bigwedge_{i \in \{1,2\}, u \in \mathrm{dom}(B_i)} B_i(u) \leq \alpha_u$$

where $U = \mathrm{dom}(B_1) \cup \mathrm{dom}(B_2)$ and the type variables $(\alpha_u)^{u \in U}$ are fresh.

Following [9], we have saturated every type inference judgement by existential quantification. Although slightly verbose, this style nicely shows which type variables are local to a sub-derivation, yielding the following invariant:

Names

I-INST
$$\frac{\Gamma(u) = \forall\bar{\alpha}[C].\alpha \qquad \beta \text{ fresh}}{\exists\bar{\alpha}.(C \wedge \alpha \leq \beta), \Gamma \vdash_I u : \beta}$$

Definitions

I-EMPTY
true, $\Gamma \vdash_I \epsilon :: \vec{0}$

I-JOIN
$$\frac{C, \Gamma + (\vec{u_i} : \vec{\alpha_i})^{i \in I} \vdash_I P \qquad (\vec{\alpha_i})^{i \in I}, (\beta_i)^{i \in I} \text{ fresh}}{\exists(\vec{\alpha_i})^{i \in I}.(C \wedge \bigwedge_{i \in I} \beta_i = \langle\vec{\alpha_i}\rangle), \Gamma \vdash_I (x_i \langle \vec{u_i} \rangle)^{i \in I} \triangleright P :: (x_i : \beta_i)^{i \in I}}$$

I-OR
$$\frac{C_1, \Gamma \vdash_I D_1 : B_1 \qquad C_2, \Gamma \vdash_I D_2 : B_2 \qquad B, C = B_1 \sqcup B_2 \qquad \bar{\beta} = \text{fv}(B_1, B_2)}{\exists\bar{\beta}.(C_1 \wedge C_2 \wedge C), \Gamma \vdash_I D_1, D_2 :: B}$$

Processes

I-NULL
true, $\Gamma \vdash_I 0$

I-PAR
$$\frac{C_1, \Gamma \vdash_I P \qquad C_2, \Gamma \vdash_I Q}{C_1 \wedge C_2, \Gamma \vdash_I P \mid Q}$$

I-MSG
$$\frac{C, \Gamma \vdash_I u : \beta \qquad \vec{C}, \Gamma \vdash_I \vec{v} : \vec{\alpha}}{\exists\beta\bar{\alpha}.(C \wedge \vec{C} \wedge \beta = \langle\vec{\alpha}\rangle), \Gamma \vdash_I u \langle \vec{v} \rangle}$$

I-DEF
$$\frac{\begin{array}{c} B \text{ fresh} \qquad \bar{\beta} = \text{fv}(B) \\ C_1, \Gamma + B \vdash_I (J_i \triangleright P_i)^{i \in I} :: B' \\ \bar{\beta}' = \text{fv}(B') \qquad C_2 = \exists\bar{\beta}'.(C_1 \wedge B' \leq B) \\ \text{if } \exists i \in I \quad |\text{dn}(J_i)| > 1 \text{ then } \bar{\alpha} = \varnothing \text{ else } \bar{\alpha} = \bar{\beta} \\ C_3, \Gamma + \forall\bar{\alpha}[C_2] \twoheadrightarrow B \vdash_I P \end{array}}{\exists\bar{\beta}.(C_2 \wedge C_3), \Gamma \vdash_I \textbf{def } (J_i \triangleright P_i)^{i \in I} \textbf{ in } P}$$

Fig. 5. Type inference

Lemma 6.2. *If* $C, \Gamma \vdash_I \mathcal{J}$ *holds, then* $\text{fv}(C) \subseteq \text{fv}(\Gamma, \mathcal{J})$ *and* $\text{fv}(\mathcal{J}) \cap \text{fv}(\Gamma) = \varnothing$.

We now prove the type inference rules correct and complete with respect to JOIN(X). For the sake of simplicity, we limit the statement to the case of processes (omitting that of names and definitions).

Theorem 6.3. $C, \Gamma \vdash_I P$ *implies* $C, \Gamma \vdash P$. *Conversely, if* $C, \Gamma \vdash P$ *holds, then there exists a constraint* C' *such that* $C', \Gamma \vdash_I P$ *and* $C \Vdash C'$.

7   Discussion

JOIN(X) is closely related to HM(X) [6,8], a similar type system aimed at purely functional languages. It also draws inspiration from previous type systems for the join-calculus [4,7], which were purely unification-based. JOIN(X) is an attempt to bring together these two orthogonal lines of research.

Our results are partly negative: under a natural generalization criterion, the existence of principal typings is problematic. This leads us, in the general case, to suggest a more drastic restriction. Nevertheless, the logical criterion may still be useful under certain specific constraint logics, where principal typings can still be achieved, or in situations where their existence is not essential (e.g. in program analysis).

To establish type safety, we interpret typing judgements as (sets of) judgements in an underlying system, which is given a syntactic soundness proof. The former step, by giving a logical view of polymorphism and constraints, aptly expresses our intuitions about these notions, yielding a concise proof. The latter is a matter of routine, because the low-level type system is simple. Thus, both logic and syntax are put to best use. We have baptized this approach *semi-syntactic*; we feel it is perhaps not publicized enough.

Acknowledgements. Alexandre Frey suggested the use of extensional polymorphism in the intermediate type system B(T). Martin Sulzmann kindly provided a proof of completeness of constraint-based type inference in HM(X), which was helpful in our own completeness proof. We would also like to acknowledge Martin Odersky and Didier Rémy for stimulating discussions.

References

[1] Sylvain Conchon and Fabrice Le Fessant. Jocaml: Mobile agents for Objective-Caml. In *First International Symposium on Agent Systems and Applications and Third International Symposium on Mobile Agents (ASA/MA'99)*, pages 22–29, Palm Springs, California, October 1999.
URL: http://para.inria.fr/~conchon/publis/asa99.ps.gz.

[2] Sylvain Conchon and François Pottier. JOIN(X): Constraint-based type inference for the join-calculus. Long version. URL: http://pauillac.inria.fr/ fpottier/publis/ conchon-fpottier-esop01-long.ps.gz, April 2001.

[3] Cédric Fournet and Georges Gonthier. The reflexive chemical abstract machine and the join-calculus. In *Proceedings of the 23rd ACM Symposium on Principles of Programming Languages*, pages 372–385, 1996.
URL: http://pauillac.inria.fr/~fournet/papers/popl-96.ps.gz.

[4] Cédric Fournet, Luc Maranget, Cosimo Laneve, and Didier Rémy. Implicit typing la ML for the join-calculus. In *8th International Conference on Concurrency Theory (CONCUR'97)*, volume 1243 of *Lecture Notes in Computer Science*, pages 196–212, Warsaw, Poland, 1997. Springer. URL: ftp://ftp.inria.fr/INRIA/ Projects/Didier.Remy/cristal/typing-join.ps.gz.

[5] Robin Milner. A theory of type polymorphism in programming. *Journal of Computer and System Sciences*, 17(3):348–375, December 1978.

[6] Martin Odersky, Martin Sulzmann, and Martin Wehr. Type inference with constrained types. *Theory and Practice of Object Systems*, 5(1):35–55, 1999. URL: http://www.cs.mu.oz.au/~sulzmann/publications/tapos.ps.

[7] Martin Odersky, Christoph Zenger, Matthias Zenger, and Gang Chen. A functional view of join. Technical Report ACRC-99-016, University of South Australia, 1999.
URL: http://lampwww.epfl.ch/~czenger/papers/tr-acrc-99-016.ps.gz.

[8] Martin Sulzmann. *A general framework for Hindley/Milner type systems with constraints.* PhD thesis, Yale University, Department of Computer Science, May 2000. URL: `http://www.cs.mu.oz.au/~sulzmann/publications/diss.ps.gz`.

[9] Martin Sulzmann, Martin Müller, and Christoph Zenger. Hindley/Milner style type systems in constraint form. Research Report ACRC–99–009, University of South Australia, School of Computer and Information Science, July 1999. URL: `http://www.ps.uni-sb.de/~mmueller/papers/hm-constraints.ps.gz`.

[10] Andrew K. Wright. Simple imperative polymorphism. *Lisp and Symbolic Computation*, 8(4):343–356, December 1995.

[11] Andrew K. Wright and Matthias Felleisen. A syntactic approach to type soundness. *Information and Computation*, 115(1):38–94, November 1994. URL: `http://www.cs.rice.edu/CS/PLT/Publications/ic94-wf.ps.gz`.

Modular Causality in a Synchronous Stream Language

Pascal Cuoq and Marc Pouzet

INRIA, LIP6*

Abstract. This article presents a causality analysis for a synchronous stream language with higher-order functions. This analysis takes the shape of a type system with rows. Rows were originally designed to add extensible records to the ML type system (Didier Rémy, Mitchell Wand). We also restate briefly the coiterative semantics for synchronous streams (Paul Caspi, Marc Pouzet), and prove the correctness of our analysis with respect to this semantics.

1 Introduction

1.1 History

This part gives a quick overview, in chronological order, of existing languages allowing the manipulation of infinite streams, and the position of LUCID SYNCHRONE[2] amongst them.

LUCID was the first language to propose the paradigm of streams as first-class citizens. Its purpose was to bring programming languages closer to logic languages in which properties can be expressed and proved. In LUCID, recursive equations on streams replaced imperative iteration.

Then appeared synchronous data-flow languages such as LUSTRE[8], SIGNAL[1], on the one hand, and lazy functional languages (*e.g.* HASKELL[9]) on the other hand. LUSTRE and SIGNAL are used in the fields of signal processing and automatic control. Lazy functional languages can handle infinite data structures in general, and streams in particular.

These two families evolved quite independently. LUSTRE and SIGNAL did not have higher-order functions, and the canonical representation of streams in a lazy functional language such as HASKELL did not have the reactivity nor the efficiency required by the kind of applications in which the former two are used. Wadler proposed a set of techniques for functional languages, "listlessness"[19], to avoid building intermediate lists which are de-constructed immediately. The resulting optimized programs are in some cases very similar to the ones that are generated by LUSTRE or SIGNAL.

LUCID SYNCHRONE is an attempt at filling the gap between these two families of languages, by proposing as many ML-style features as possible (and in particular modular compilation) while retaining an efficient representation of streams [3].

---

* This work has been partially supported by CNET-France Telecom

D. Sands (Ed.): ESOP 2001, LNCS 2028, pp. 237–251, 2001.

1.2 Plan

In section 2, we describe informally the core language which will be the subject
of this presentation. Section 3 describes the causality analysis which is the novel
part of this article. Section 4 gives a formal semantics to our core language, by
translating streams to their co-iterative representation. In section 5, we prove
that the analysis described in section 3 is correct with respect to the semantics
described in 4. Finally, our analysis is compared to other analyses in 6.

2 The Lucid Synchrone Core

2.1 Language Description

Here is the description of the subset of Lucid Synchrone which will be the
base of this presentation:

programs:

$$
\begin{array}{lll}
t ::= & (t_1, t_2) & \text{pair} \\
& |\ \textbf{fst}\ t\ |\ \textbf{snd}\ t & \text{projections} \\
& |\ x & \text{variable} \\
& |\ \lambda x.t & \lambda\text{-abstraction} \\
& |\ t_1\ t_2 & \text{application} \\
& |\ \textbf{let}\ x = t_1\ \textbf{in}\ t_2 & \text{non-recursive let} \\
& |\ \textbf{rec}\ x_1 = t_1\ \textbf{and}\ x_2 = t_2 & \text{recursive definition} \\
& |\ c & \text{constants} \\
& |\ p & \text{primitives} \\
& |\ \textbf{pre}\ c\ t & \text{a delay, initialized} \\
& & \text{with the constant } c
\end{array}
$$

The constants c are imported from an external scalar language, and lifted
into the corresponding constant stream. Likewise, primitive functions imported
from the scalar world are extended into pointwise functions on streams.

The abstraction, application, pair constructor, projections, and recursion
combinator behave exactly as in the λ-calculus.

Finally, $\textbf{pre}\ c\ u$ catenates the scalar value c in front of the stream u. In the
usual interpretation of streams as successive values of a node, $\textbf{pre}$ introduces a
delay of one instant.

u	$u_1\ u_2\ u_3\ u_4\ \ldots$
$\textbf{pre}\ c\ u$	$c\quad u_1\ u_2\ u_3\ \ldots$

Synchronous stream languages (Lustre, Signal, and Lucid Synchrone)
have in common another feature, which is not present here: a *clock* is associated
with each expression. A clock system allows to extract a sub-stream from a
stream by *sampling*. This feature is mostly orthogonal to the causality analysis,
and this is why we do not put it in our core language.

2.2 A Tutorial Example

The domain of application of synchronous languages is the design of reactive systems. The mathematical concept corresponding to a reactive system is a Mealy automaton, that is, a finite state automaton that, given one set of input values, compute a set of output values that are determined by the inputs and the state in which the previous inputs had left the system. For instance, a coffee machine will, given the input "Button pressed", react by beeping or delivering some coffee depending on whether the input "Coin inserted" has been seen recently.

Since the current outputs depend not only on the current inputs but on the state of the system, which in turn depends on the previous inputs, it is convenient to see a reactive program as a computation transforming the stream of inputs into a stream of outputs, being understood that the nth value of the output stream is allowed to depend only on the n first values of the input stream.

Not only does this point of view allow to program very straightforwardly a lot of common behaviors, but since the notion of state disappears completely from the programs, it also makes it easier to prove properties about them.

Here is how the mechanism of the simplistic coffee machine could be expressed in Lucid Synchrone:

```
let rec number_coins = prev_number_coins + inserted_coins -
                       (if deliver_coffee then 1 else 0)
and prev_number_coins = pre 0 number_coins
and deliver_coffee = button_pressed and (prev_number_coins >= 1)
```

`button_pressed` and `inserted_coins` are the input streams. `button_pressed` is a boolean stream, and `inserted_coins` is a stream of integers that indicates the number of coins inserted during instant t.

The output stream is `deliver_coffee`; the other streams are only defined as computation intermediaries. Output streams can be be used in the computation of other streams, as is the case here for `number_coins`.

`(if deliver_coffee then 1 else 0)` is an integer stream whose value is 1 at instant t if coffee is delivered at instant t, and 0 otherwise (we suppose that delivering one beverage is instantaneous).

Another aspect of reactive systems on which we have not insisted enough yet is that they usually must be able to propose an output in a bounded time after they have been provided with an input. This aspect is not emphasized much in synchronous languages, in which it is assumed (and can be checked *a posteriori* if necessary) that computations are always fast enough. Still, an important consequence is that instantaneous recursion is absent from the language; the provided recursion operator is only intended to define streams recursively, using the value from instant t-1 to compute the value at instant t (`number_coins` is a typical example). In the kind of application synchronous languages are used for, this apparent lack of expressiveness is rarely a problem, whereas bounded time computations are a prime necessity.

3   Causality Analysis of Lucid Synchrone Programs

In real life, causality forbids that information from the future be used in the present. Such interferences cannot happen in the context of a clock-less synchronous stream language, because there are no operators to express the future. However, since computations are supposed to be instantaneous, causality can still be broken by using the current value of a variable within its definition.

Recursive definitions such as `rec x=x` (which is valid as an equation, but does not define a stream) and `rec x=x+1` (which has no solution) must thus be detected and rejected statically. This is the purpose of the causality analysis.

On the other hand, thanks to the delay introduced by `pre`, the expression `1 + pre 0 x` no longer depends instantaneously on `x`; the recursive definition `rec x = 1 + pre 0 x` that denotes the stream of strictly positive integers, is valid, and must be accepted.

In the case of mutually recursive definitions, it would be too restrictive to require each right-hand-side expression to feature a `pre`. For instance, $rec\ x = y + 1$ and $y = $ `pre` $0\ x$ is a valid definition of two streams x and y.

Finally,   the   function   rewind   defined   by `let rewind = ` λf ` . (rec x = f x)` cannot be rejected *a priori*, since the recursion will be causal if it is applied to a function that contains a `pre`. On the other hand if it is applied to a strict function such as the identity, the recursion in the body of **rewind** is not causal.

The causality analysis about to be presented was designed to accept this kind of programs, and to be compatible with higher-order functions.

This analysis is in fact a type system. It features let-polymorphism similar to the type systems of ML and Haskell. The main change is that there is only one base type $\{\varphi\}$, and that it carries a dependency annotation φ, which is an association list mapping variables to their dependence information. A recursion variable x can be marked as "present" (notation $x{:}p$), meaning that the expression e having type $\{x : p, \varphi\}$ might depend instantaneously on x, or "absent" ($x{:}a$), meaning that e does not depend instantaneously on x.

The association lists between variables and dependence information are represented as rows ([20],[14]). Rows were originally designed to introduce extensible records in ML. Generally speaking, rows allow in some cases (and in ours in particular) to use polymorphism to replace subtyping.

The grammar of types is as follows:
types:

$$\tau ::= \quad \alpha \qquad \text{type variable}$$
$$| \ \{\varphi\} \qquad \text{dependency information (rows)}$$
$$| \ \tau_1 * \tau_2 \quad \text{pair}$$
$$| \ \tau_1 \rightarrow \tau_2 \ \text{arrow type}$$

rows:

$$\varphi ::= \quad \rho \qquad \text{row-variable}$$
$$| \ x{:}\pi, \varphi \qquad \text{one "field" concerning variable } x$$

presence information:
$$\pi ::=\quad a \text{ absent}$$
$$| \ p \text{ present}$$
$$| \ \delta \text{ presence variable}$$

type schemes:
$$\sigma ::= \quad \tau \ | \ \forall \alpha, \sigma \ | \ \forall \rho, \sigma \ | \ \forall \delta, \sigma$$

Our equational theory on rows is the same as the one used in the context of extensible records:
$$x : \pi, y : \pi', \varphi = y : \pi', x : \pi, \varphi$$

Likewise, our notion of sorts is the same as the one for extensible records: the sort of a row φ is a set of labels (in our case, recursion variables) which intuitively are the fields which can not appear in φ, because they are already present on the left-hand side of a larger row of which φ is the tail. One can check easily that all the rules listed in this section are well-sorted. For all these reasons general theorems about rows([13,14]) apply and our system has the principal typing property.

The binder $\forall$ plays its usual role in type schemes. There is also the classic relation "to be an instance of" between types and types schemes, noted $\tau < \sigma$, and inductively defined by:

$\tau < \tau$

If $\tau < \sigma$, then for any τ' and α, $\tau[^{\tau'}/_\alpha] < \forall \alpha, \sigma$

If $\tau < \sigma$, then for any row φ and row-variable ρ of the same sort, $\tau[^\varphi/_\rho] < \forall \rho, \sigma$

If $\tau < \sigma$, then for any π and δ, $\tau[^\pi/_\delta] < \forall \delta, \sigma$

We will assume that all the bound variables of the program being analyzed are distinct. If we had used a notion of reduction to define the semantics of streams programs, this assumption would be a cause of technical complications since it would not remain true after a reduction; but since the co-iterative semantics of stream programs is given by translation to a functional language instead it is a reasonable assumption to make.

Typing judgments are of the form $\Gamma \vdash t : \tau$.
Γ is a typing environment, associating type schemes to program variables.

The originality of this system resides in the types given to the operators **rec** and **pre**. This should not be surprising since **rec** is the construction that makes this analysis necessary, and **pre**, on the other hand, is the one that allows recursive definitions to be well-founded.

pre c is given the type scheme $\forall \rho, \rho', \{\rho\} \rightarrow \{\rho'\}$:

$$\frac{\Gamma \vdash t : \{\varphi\}}{\Gamma \vdash \textbf{pre } c \ t : \{\varphi'\}}$$

In this rule, whatever variables t has been found to depend on (the variables marked p in φ), the row $\{\varphi'\}$ of pre $c\,t$ is unconstrained. This may seem counter-intuitive: one would expect this rule to say in essence "pre $c\,t$ does not depend on anything", whereas its actual meaning is more like "The dependencies of pre $c\,t$ can be anything you like". But note that if you choose $\{\varphi'\}$ to be for instance $\{x{:}a, y{:}p, \rho\}$, you have only (correctly) lost the information that pre $c\,t$ does not depend on y.

This allows us to accept a term such as plus x (pre $0\,x$) where the pointwise addition on streams plus has the type $\forall \rho, \{\rho\} \rightarrow \{\rho\} \rightarrow \{\rho\}$. In this case the rule for pre is instantiated with identical rows for $\{\varphi\}$ and $\{\varphi'\}$. The result is found to have the same dependencies as x.

The rule for unary recursion is as follows:

$$\frac{\Gamma, x : \{x{:}p, \varphi\} \vdash t : \{x{:}a, \varphi\}}{\Gamma \vdash \text{rec } x = t : \{x{:}\pi, \varphi\}}$$

The recursion variable x is put in the environment, associated with the row $\{x : p, \varphi\}$. This way, any expression t depending on x (such as x itself, or plus x (pre $0\,x$)) will have in its row a field x associated to p. This row won't be unifiable with the expected one of the form $\{x{:}a, \varphi\}$, and rec $x = t$ will be rejected.

Another, perhaps more intuitive conclusion for this rule would be $\Gamma \vdash$ rec $x = t : \{\varphi\}$. Unfortunately, this would break the sorting rules on rows: φ should only be used with some $x : \pi$ on its left-hand side.

Leaving the instance of π open can help to accept contrived examples with nested recursions, such as rec $z = (\text{rec } x = \text{pre } 0\ (x + z))$.

Mutual recursion involves one row for each of the recursion variables:

$$\frac{\Gamma, x : \{x{:}p, y{:}\pi_1, \varphi_1\}, y : \{x{:}\pi_2, y{:}p, \varphi_2\} \vdash t_1 : \{x{:}a, y{:}\pi_1, \varphi_1\} \quad \Gamma, x : \{x{:}p, y{:}\pi_1, \varphi_1\}, y : \{x{:}\pi_2, y{:}p, \varphi_2\} \vdash t_2 : \{x{:}\pi_2, y{:}a, \varphi_2\}}{\Gamma \vdash \text{rec } x = t_1 \text{ and } y = t_2 : \{x{:}\pi_3, y{:}\pi_4, \varphi_1\} * \{x{:}\pi_5, y{:}\pi_6, \varphi_2\}}$$

This rule is a generalization of the one for unary recursion. x (resp. y) is associated in the environment to a row which carries the information "depends on x(resp. y)".

Of course there is nothing wrong with t_1 depending on y, as in the example rec $x = y$ and $y = \text{pre } 0\ y$. Just instantiate π_1 with p.

We've seen that, if t_1 depends on y, we want to prevent t_2 from depending on x. Here is how this is achieved: if t_1 depends on y, t_2 is analyzed in an environment in which x is associated to $\{x{:}p, y{:}p, \rho\}$. In these circumstances, if t_2 depends on x, it too has $y{:}p$ in its dependencies, and the second premise can not be satisfied. Indeed, one can check that there is no derivation for the term rec $x = y$ and $y = x$.

The key is that π_1 and π_2 are shared between both premises.

Constants are given the type scheme $\forall \rho, \{\rho\}$:

$$\overline{\Gamma \vdash c : \{\varphi\}}$$

All the remaining rules are identical to those of the Hindley-Milner type system:

$$\frac{\Gamma \vdash t : \tau_1 * \tau_2}{\Gamma \vdash \mathbf{fst}\ t : \tau_1} \qquad \frac{\Gamma \vdash t : \tau_1 * \tau_2}{\Gamma \vdash \mathbf{snd}\ t : \tau_2} \qquad \frac{\Gamma \vdash t_1 : \tau_1 \quad \Gamma \vdash t_2 : \tau_2}{\Gamma \vdash (t_1, t_2) : \tau_1 * \tau_2}$$

$$\frac{\tau < \sigma}{\Gamma, x : \sigma \vdash x : \tau} \qquad \frac{\Gamma, x : \tau \vdash t : \tau'}{\Gamma \vdash \lambda x.t : \tau \to \tau'} \qquad \frac{\Gamma \vdash t_1 : \tau \to \tau' \quad \Gamma \vdash t_2 : \tau}{\Gamma \vdash t_1\ t_2 : \tau'}$$

$$\frac{\Gamma \vdash t : \tau \quad \Gamma, x : \forall(\mathcal{FV}(\tau) - \mathcal{FV}(\Gamma)), \tau \vdash t' : \tau'}{\Gamma \vdash \mathbf{let}\ x = t\ \mathbf{in}\ t' : \tau'}$$

The typing rules for **pre** and **rec** use row types instead of general types: the second argument of the **pre** operator can therefore only be a stream, and the only possible recursive definitions are definitions of streams. Being unable to recursively define a pair, we need the **rec** operator to explicitly handle mutual recursion, instead of encoding it as a recursion on a pair, as it is done in a traditional functional system.

These restrictions are not as arbitrary as it may at first seem. Firstly, we do not know how to give a semantics to (**pre** $c\ e$) where e is a function. Secondly, assuming for the sake of the argument that we knew how to define such a semantics, and assuming that (**pre** c) had the type $\forall \alpha \forall \alpha', \alpha \to \alpha'$ instead of $\forall \rho \forall \rho', \{\rho\} \to \{\rho'\}$, the type system would allow to infer that (**pre** ($\lambda x.$**pre** $0\ x$) ($\lambda x.x$)) y does not depend on y, whereas it would (again, if this program meant anything at all) after the first instant.

Recursively defined functions are a different problem. For higher-order recursion, the well-foundedness of the recursion depends on semantic conditions and can not be checked by this causality analysis. Although recursive functions are not allowed by this system, it is still possible, in an actual implementation, to have a different operator for functional recursion, and a compiler flag for either authorize the programmer to use it or to forbid its use (and guarantee reactiveness).

Examples:

- Constant streams
  Constant streams didn't really need to be integrated in the language, as the constant stream c can be defined as **rec** $z = $ **pre** $c\ z$. The type scheme given to this expression, $\forall \rho, \delta, \{z : \delta, \rho\}$, is equivalent to the type scheme of constant streams $\forall \rho, \{\rho\}$ under the hypothesis we made that all the variables bound in a program are distinct.
- The "rewind" combinator $\lambda\mathbf{f}.\mathbf{rec}\ \mathbf{x} = \mathbf{f(x)}$ is causal, of type scheme
  $\forall \rho, \delta, (\{x : p, \rho\} \to \{x : a, \rho\}) \to \{x : \delta, \rho\}$.

- Mutual recursion: the example `rec x = y and y = pre 0 x` is accepted. In the rule for the mutual recursion, π_1 (presence information of `y` in the row associated to x in the environment) is instantiated with p, and π_2, presence information of x in the row of y, is instantiated with a.
- Higher-order mutual recursion: the function
  $$F \equiv \lambda f.\lambda g.\mathtt{rec}\ x = g(y)\ \mathtt{and}\ y = f(x)$$
  is well-typed, and has the type scheme:
  $$\forall \rho_1, \rho_2, \delta_1, \delta_2, \delta_3, \delta_4, \delta_5, \delta_6, (\{x:\delta_2, y:p, \rho_2\} \to \{x:a, y:\delta_1, \rho_1\}) \to$$
  $$(\{x:p, y:\delta_1, \rho_1\} \to \{x:\delta_2, y:p, \rho_2\}) \to (\{x:\delta_3, y:\delta_4, \rho_1\} * \{x:\delta_5, y:\delta_6, \rho_2\})$$
  Moreover, the partial application of F to a strict function such as the identity gives a function which can be applied to $\lambda x.\mathtt{pre}\ c\ x$ but not to a strict function, whereas the partial application of F to $\lambda x.\mathtt{pre}\ c\ x$ gives a function which can be applied to a strict function.
- The use of unification instead of polymorphism makes the computation of dependencies "bidirectional": for instance the example `rec x = pre 0 (x+y) and y = x` is rejected. What happens is that the rows for `x` and `y` become unified when `x` and `y` are added together, and these variables become interdependent. This is probably the biggest drawback of the system; Fortunately the types of variables and functions bound by a `let` construct can usually be generalized, which breaks this bidirectionality.

4   Co-iteration

In [3], synchronous streams are given a concrete representation made of an initial state and a transition function returning a value and a new state when applied to a state.

In this section, we will re-state the co-iterative representation of streams. The target language is a functional language, and it is best to think of it as lazily evaluated for now.

We choose to represent streams in the target language by the triple $(\llbracket t \rrbracket_i, \llbracket t \rrbracket_v, \llbracket t \rrbracket_s)$, where:

- $\llbracket t \rrbracket_i$ is the initial state.
- $\llbracket t \rrbracket_v$ is a function returning a value when applied to the current state.
- $\llbracket t \rrbracket_s$ is a function returning the new state when applied to the current state.

Comparing this representation to the one of [3], we split the transition function into two separate ones, one returning the value and the other returning the new state. Of course, the two representations are equivalent, but this one allows for a simpler expression of the causality of programs.

The translations of constant streams, `pre`, pairs and projections are relatively straightforward. More details are available in the extended version of this article [5] and in [3].

A constant stream needs no memory, so its state is `Nil`.

$$\llbracket c \rrbracket_i = \texttt{Nil}$$
$$\llbracket c \rrbracket_v = \lambda\texttt{Nil}.c$$
$$\llbracket c \rrbracket_s = \lambda\texttt{Nil}.\texttt{Nil}$$

– **pre c t:**

$$\llbracket \texttt{pre } c\ t \rrbracket_i = (c, \llbracket t \rrbracket_i)$$
$$\llbracket \texttt{pre } c\ t \rrbracket_v = \lambda(v, s).v$$
$$\llbracket \texttt{pre } c\ t \rrbracket_s = \lambda(v, s).(\llbracket t \rrbracket_v\ s, \llbracket t \rrbracket_s\ s)$$

– (t_1, t_2):

$$\llbracket (t_1, t_2) \rrbracket_i = (\llbracket t_1 \rrbracket_i, \llbracket t_2 \rrbracket_i)$$
$$\llbracket (t_1, t_2) \rrbracket_v = \lambda(s_1, s_2).(\llbracket t_1 \rrbracket_v\ s_1, \llbracket t_2 \rrbracket_v\ s_2)$$
$$\llbracket (t_1, t_2) \rrbracket_s = \lambda(s_1, s_2).(\llbracket t_1 \rrbracket_s\ s_1, \llbracket t_2 \rrbracket_s\ s_2)$$

– **fst t:**

$$\left(\llbracket \texttt{fst } t \rrbracket_i, \llbracket \texttt{fst } t \rrbracket_v, \llbracket \texttt{fst } t \rrbracket_s\right) = \left(\llbracket t \rrbracket_i, \lambda s.\texttt{fst}\ (\llbracket t \rrbracket_v\ s), \llbracket t \rrbracket_s\right)$$

– Recursion:

The definitions of $\llbracket t \rrbracket_i$, $\llbracket t \rrbracket_v$ and $\llbracket t \rrbracket_s$ use inductively the translations of the sub-terms of t. In the case of the translation of $\texttt{rec}\ x = t_1\ \texttt{and}\ y = t_2$, x and y are free variables in t_1 and t_2, and we need something to substitute $\llbracket x \rrbracket_i$, $\llbracket x \rrbracket_v, \ldots$ with in $\llbracket t_1 \rrbracket$ and $\llbracket t_2 \rrbracket$. In particular, in $\llbracket \texttt{rec}\ x = t_1\ \texttt{and}\ y = t_2 \rrbracket_v$ we replace $\llbracket x \rrbracket_v$ by the function returning the value being recursively computed, and in $\llbracket \texttt{rec}\ x = t_1\ \texttt{and}\ y = t_2 \rrbracket_s$ we replace it by the function returning the value computed by $\llbracket \texttt{rec}\ x = t_1\ \texttt{and}\ y = t_2 \rrbracket_v$.

$$\llbracket \texttt{rec}\ x = t_1\ \texttt{and}\ y = t_2 \rrbracket_i = (\llbracket t_1 \rrbracket_i, \llbracket t_2 \rrbracket_i)[^{\texttt{Nil}}/_{\llbracket x \rrbracket_i}][^{\texttt{Nil}}/_{\llbracket y \rrbracket_i}]$$

$$\llbracket \texttt{rec}\ x = t_1\ \texttt{and}\ y = t_2 \rrbracket_v = \lambda(s_1, s_2).$$
$$\qquad \texttt{let rec}\ (x_v, y_v) =$$
$$\qquad\qquad \left((\llbracket t_1 \rrbracket_v\ s_1, \llbracket t_2 \rrbracket_v\ s_2)[^{\lambda\texttt{Nil}.x_v, \lambda\texttt{Nil}.y_v}/_{\llbracket x \rrbracket_v, \llbracket y \rrbracket_v}]\right)$$
$$\qquad \texttt{in}\ (x_v, y_v)$$

$$\llbracket \texttt{rec}\ x = t_1\ \texttt{and}\ y = t_2 \rrbracket_s = \lambda(s_1, s_2).$$
$$\qquad \texttt{let rec}\ (x_v, y_v) =$$
$$\qquad\qquad \left((\llbracket t_1 \rrbracket_v\ s_1, \llbracket t_2 \rrbracket_v\ s_2)[^{\lambda\texttt{Nil}.x_v, \lambda\texttt{Nil}.y_v}/_{\llbracket x \rrbracket_v, \llbracket y \rrbracket_v}]\right)\ \texttt{in}$$
$$\qquad (\llbracket t_1 \rrbracket_s\ s_1, \llbracket t_2 \rrbracket_s\ s_2)[^{\lambda\texttt{Nil}.x_v, \lambda\texttt{Nil}.y_v, \lambda\texttt{Nil}.\texttt{Nil}, \lambda\texttt{Nil}.\texttt{Nil}}/_{\llbracket x \rrbracket_v, \llbracket y \rrbracket_v, \llbracket x \rrbracket_s, \llbracket y \rrbracket_s}]$$

5 Correctness Proof

In this section, we give the correctness proof for the system presented in section 3.

Here, we consider the target language as a λ-calculus equipped with strong β-reduction. We will in particular make heavy use of the Church-Rosser property. The recursion construct is just syntactic sugar above the Y fixpoint combinator.

We will also use the property that terms of the target language that do not use the recursion operator have a normal form for strong β-reduction. This is due to the fact that all the terms we are dealing with can be typed.

The property that we intend to prove is essentially that if the term t has type $\{x\!:\!a,\ldots\}$, then t "does not depend" on x.

For a stream t, "not to depend" on x means that the instantaneous value $[\![t]\!]_v\ s$ of t can be computed without requiring the instantaneous value of x. Or, still more concretely, x does not occur in the normal form of $[\![t]\!]_v\ s$ [1].

Still informally, we will define the set of terms t that do not depend on x as the *interpretation* of the type $\{x\!:\!a,\ldots\}$. Obviously, with our definition of "not depending on", the membership of a term t to this interpretation only depends on the normal form of $[\![t]\!]_v\ s$.

The presence of polymorphism in the system requires us to define a notion of "candidate", as in [7]. A candidate is a set of terms that has the correct shape to be the interpretation of a type. Quite naturally, our notion of candidate will be "any set to which the membership of a term t only depends on a property of the normal form of $[\![t]\!]_v\ s$".

Definitions:

- A candidate C is a set of terms such that the property "$t \in C$" can be expressed under the form "$[\![t]\!]_v$ and $[\![t]\!]_s$ do not use recursion and, for all states s, t_1 being the normal form of $[\![t]\!]_v\ s$, $\mathcal{R}(t_1)$", for some arbitrary predicate $\mathcal{R}$.
- A row-candidate Q is a set of terms such that the property "$t \in Q$" can be expressed under the form:

  "$[\![t]\!]_v$ and $[\![t]\!]_s$ do not use recursion and
  For all states s, if t_1 is the normal form of $[\![t]\!]_v\ s$, then $\mathcal{R}(t_1)$"

where $\mathcal{R}$ is a predicate that can be expressed under the form:

$$\mathcal{R}(t) \equiv \bigwedge_{x \in X} (x \text{ does not occur in } t)$$

These preliminary definitions deserve a couple of remarks:

- This definition is simpler that the one of a candidate in, for instance, the strong normalisation proof of the System F[7]. This is due to the fact that the property we want to prove is itself simpler.
- On the other hand, our system features rows, which need their own notion of candidate. This was to be expected, in the light of the fact that, as we pointed out previously, rules for **pre** and **rec** can only be instantiated with rows, and would become incorrect if instantiated with arbitrary types.

---

[1] In this informal explanation, we refer to "the" normal form of $[\![t]\!]_v\ s$ (for strong β-reduction). In fact, the existence of the normal form will be proved at the same time as the correctness of the dependency analysis. This will be done by proving that causal recursion on streams can be translated without recursion in the target language.

- Note that the definition of the interpretation on rows is compatible with the equational theory. That is, whichever particular syntactic representation of a given row yields the same interpretation.
- A row-candidate is a candidate. In fact, the last sentence is the image in the world of interpretations of the sentence "a row is a type".

We will now consider mappings from type variables to candidates, and row-variables and presence variables to row-candidates. Such a mapping is called a valuation and will be denoted V. Given a valuation V, we write $V \sqcup \alpha \mapsto C$ the valuation that maps α to C, and any other variable β to $V(\beta)$.

When referring to a valuation V, we will take for implicit the fact that the sets of terms associated to type variables (resp. row-variables and presence variables) are candidates (resp. row-candidates).

Definition of the interpretation $\mathcal{P}_V$ of a type (relative to a valuation V):

- $t \in \mathcal{P}_V(\{x:a, \varphi\})$ if $[\![t]\!]_v$ and $[\![t]\!]_s$ do not use recursion, and the normal form of its application to a state[2] does not contain x, and if $t \in \mathcal{P}_V(\{\varphi\})$.
- $\mathcal{P}_V(\{x:p, \varphi\}) = \mathcal{P}_V(\{\varphi\})$.
- $t \in \mathcal{P}_V(\{x:\delta, \varphi\})$ if $t \in V(\delta)$ and $t \in \mathcal{P}_V(\{\varphi\})$
- $\mathcal{P}_V(\rho) = V(\rho)$
- $\mathcal{P}_V(\tau_1 * \tau_2)$ is defined as the set of terms t such that fst $t \in \mathcal{P}_V(\tau_1)$, and snd $t \in \mathcal{P}_V(\tau_2)$
- $\mathcal{P}_V(\tau_1 \to \tau_2)$: the set of terms t such that $[\![t]\!]_v$ and $[\![t]\!]_s$ do not use recursion, and such that for all $t_1 \in \mathcal{P}_V(\tau_1)$, $(t\ t_1) \in \mathcal{P}_V(\tau_2)$
- $\mathcal{P}_V(\alpha) = V(\alpha)$

We need to generalize our interpretation to non-empty environments. Classically, this is done by requiring the term to satisfy the interpretation property under all possible substitutions of terms (satisfying the interpretation of the type they are assigned in the environment) to free variables.

More formally, we first extend the interpretation to type schemes:

$t \in \mathcal{P}_V(\forall \alpha, \sigma)$ if for all candidate C, $t \in \mathcal{P}_{V \sqcup \alpha \mapsto C}(\sigma)$.

$t \in \mathcal{P}_V(\forall \rho, \sigma)$ if for all row-candidate Q, $t \in \mathcal{P}_{V \sqcup \rho \mapsto Q}(\sigma)$.

$t \in \mathcal{P}_V(\forall \delta, \sigma)$ if for all row-candidate Q, $t \in \mathcal{P}_{V \sqcup \delta \mapsto Q}(\sigma)$.

Let us now list a few properties relative to interpretations and candidates:

Property 1. For any valuation V, $\mathcal{P}_V(\{\varphi\})$ is a row-candidate.

Proof: by induction on φ.

Property 2. For any valuation V, $\mathcal{P}_V(\tau)$ is a candidate.

Proof: by induction on τ.

---

[2] All successive states are normalizable because $[\![t]\!]_s$ does not use recursion. For this reason and because $[\![t]\!]_v$ does not use recursion "the" normal form of the application of $[\![t]\!]_v$ to a state exists

As expected, the interpretations of type schemes are included in the interpretations of their instances. This can be stated as:

Property 3. For all valuations V, if $t \in \mathcal{P}_V(\sigma)$ then for all $\tau < \sigma$, $t \in \mathcal{P}_V(\tau)$.

The proof is by induction on σ.

Theorem 1. *If $\Gamma \vdash t : \tau$, then for all V, for any substitution S adapted to Γ (under V)* [3], *$S(t) \in \mathcal{P}_V(\tau)$.*

The bulk of the proof is an induction on the inference tree of the causality analysis. We'll only present some interesting cases.

1. The case of **pre** is an interesting one, even though it is simple: $\mathcal{P}_V(\{\varphi'\})$ is a row-candidate. Since $[\![\text{pre } c \ t]\!]_v = \lambda(v, s).v$, obviously **pre** $c \ t$ is in this set.
2. The rule for **rec**:
    Take some fixed V and S.
    The interpretation $\mathcal{P}_V(\{y : \pi_1, \varphi_1\})$ is a row-candidate. Therefore, there exists X a set of variables such that t belongs to $\mathcal{P}_V(\{y : \pi_1, \varphi_1\})$ if and only if t does not depend on any variable of X.
    Let us distinguish two cases:
    a) $y \in X$
        In this case, the induction hypothesis for the first premise yields that neither x not y occur in the normal form of $[\![(S \sqcup x \mapsto x \sqcup y \mapsto y)(t_1)]\!]_v \ s$ (i.e. $[\![S(t_1)]\!]_v \ s$).
        That means that the code for the "value" transition function $[\![\text{rec } x = t_1 \text{ and } y = t_2]\!]_v$ could simply have been implemented as [4]:

$$
\begin{aligned}
&\lambda(s_1, s_2). \\
&\quad \text{let } x_v = [\![t_1]\!]_v \ s_1 \text{ in} \\
&\quad \text{let } y_v = [\![t_2]\!]_v \ s_2 \text{ in} \\
&\quad (x_v, y_v)
\end{aligned}
$$

    b) $y \notin X$
        Claim: For all s, x does not appear in the normal form of $[\![t_2]\!]_v \ s$.
        Let us suppose it was otherwise, and build a contradiction: The idea is to substitute x with a term that depends on y (for instance, y itself) since it satisfies the interpretation of $\{x : p, \varphi_1\}$.
        Applying the induction hypothesis for the second premise with $(S \sqcup x \mapsto y \sqcup y \mapsto y)(t_2)$ shows that if x appeared in $[\![t_2]\!]_v \ s$, then t_2 could not have the type $\{y : a, \varphi_2\}$.

---

[3] That is, for any substitution S associating to each variable x of Γ a term t such that $t \in \mathcal{P}_V(\Gamma(x))$

[4] In fact, we are using this notation to lead the reader to believe that there is no recursive definition of values any longer, and that a strict functional language would be enough to implement this recursion. We are cheating: we only proved that x and y did not occur *in the normal form* of $[\![t_1]\!]_v \ s_1$, not that they didn't occur in $[\![t_1]\!]_v \ s_1$. Thanks for bearing our bad faith.

Therefore, the "value" transition function for rec $x = t_1$ and $y = t_2$ is equivalent to:

$$\lambda(s_1, s_2).$$
$$\texttt{let } y_v = [\![t_2]\!]_v \; s_2 \texttt{ in}$$
$$\texttt{let } x_v = [\![t_1]\!]_v \; s_1 \texttt{ in}$$
$$(x_v, y_v)$$

In both cases, the LUCID SYNCHRONE rec could be represented without recursion in the target language, and the alternative representation clearly satisfies the induction invariant.

However, note that when, for instance, producing the code for the function $\lambda f.\lambda g.\texttt{rec } x = f(y)$ and $y = g(x)$, it is not yet possible to know which case will apply. Since the type scheme is polymorphic and the produced code is not, both versions of the code can be required, if this function is later applied several times.

6   Related Work

There are quite a few systems whose purpose is to verify the productivity of recursive definitions. The closest to the one presented in this article is described in [18]: it is a causality analysis for an extension of Signal with higher-order functions. To the best of our understanding, although the rules for pre in both systems are very similar, the rule for recursion in [18] seems to be the classical one (if supposing $x : \tau$ one can prove $e : \tau, \dots$), which would imply that non-causal programs have to be ruled out by side-conditions external to the system. In this sense, the novelty in the system presented here would be that these conditions are expressed inside the type system. Benefits of the absence of external side-conditions are that it allows us to have principal types, and that types, and typing errors, are easier to print.

Explicit handling of dependency graphs (as is done in LUSTRE, or in [15]) is more expressive than our system, but it isn't modular. Some information is lost when graphs are encoded in types (even with the expressivity granted by rows) but each piece of program can be rejected, or accepted and given a type, independently of the context in which it is used.

Most of other causality analyses are designed for languages in which streams can be de-constructed. This of course complicates the problem: the dependency on x in pre 0 x (or Cons 0 x) is only temporarily hidden, it can reappear if the stream is de-constructed.

In consequence, it is necessary to count how many Cons have been produced in each expression. This in turn makes subtyping almost unavoidable, if one wants to accept programs such as x + (Cons 0 x) (+ being the pointwise operator on streams). An instance of such a system is [6].

The system proposed by J.Hughes, L.Pareto and A.Sabry in [10] is much more expressive, but also much more complex. Their system makes use of subtyping. It allows to express linear relations between stream sizes, thus verifying at the same time causality and what would correspond to well-clockedness in a synchronous language.

In the case of *hardware* design, this analysis can be considered too restrictive. Circuits with cycles can be causal, as shown in [11]. The Esterel compiler has a causality analysis[16] aimed at accepting such cyclic programs. Other languages for hardware design, this time using Haskell streams, are LAVA[17] and HAWK[4]). It should be noted that their use of streams conforms to the synchronous hypothesis, and that, on the other hand, compilation to hardware has a different set of requirements than compilation to software. Compilation to hardware is usually not modular so it is less annoying if an analysis isn't either.

Analogous analyses are used in general programming languages to obtain information about the strictness of functions, or the information flow of programs. In general, in these analyses there is no special treatment of recursion, whereas in our case the recursion construct is the end, and expressing the relationships between functions arguments and results are only a mean to this end.

7   Conclusion and Future Work

We presented a causality analysis for a language of synchronous streams. Good properties such as principal typing and ease of implementation are inherited from the use of rows instead of subtyping. Although the correctness proof is specific to Lucid Synchrone's co-iterative semantics, the analysis itself should be generalizable to mutually recursive definitions where there is no operation (such as `tail`) to transform a guarded expression into a non-guarded one.

A fine-grained causality analysis imposes a different approach to code generation than is usually done in synchronous stream languages. We moreover expect that results from the causality analysis can be used for type-directed optimization of this code.

Acknowledgements. We are grateful to Michel Mauny and Didier Rémy for their help with early versions of this article. François Pessaux had used a type system with rows to statically detect uncaught exceptions[12], and his explanations were very beneficial. We would also like to thank the referees for their constructive suggestions.

References

1. A. Benveniste, P. LeGuernic, and C. Jacquemot. Synchronous programming with events and relations: the SIGNAL language and its semantics. *Science of Computer Programming*, 16:103–149, 1991.
2. P. Caspi and M. Pouzet. The Lucid Synchrone distribution.
   http://www-spi.lip6.fr/~pouzet/lucid-synchrone/.

3. P. Caspi and M. Pouzet. A co-iterative characterisation of synchronous stream functions. Technical Report 07, VERIMAG, October 1997. Workshop on Coalgebraic Methods in Computer Science (CMCS'98), Electronic Lecture Notes in Theoretical Computer Science, Portugal, Lisbon (28-29 March 1998).
4. B. Cook, J. Launchbury, and J. Matthews. Specifying superscalar microprocessors in Hawk. In *1998 Workshop on Formal Techniques for Hardware*, 1998.
5. P. Cuoq and M. Pouzet. Modular causality in a stream language. http://pauillac.inria.fr/~cuoq/streams/pl.dvi.
6. E. Giménez. Structural recursive definitions in type theory. In *ICALP'98*, LNCS series no. 1443, July 1998.
7. J.-Y. Girard, Y. Lafont, and P. Taylor. *Proofs and Types*, volume 7 of *Cambridge Tracts in Theoretical Computer Science*. Cambridge University Press, 1989.
8. N. Halbwachs, P. Caspi, P. Raymond, and D. Pilaud. The synchronous dataflow programming language lustre. *Proceedings of the IEEE*, 79(9):1305–1320, September 1991.
9. P. Hudak, S. Peyton Jones, and P. Wadler. Report on the programming language Haskell, a non strict purely functional language (version 1.2). *ACM SIGPLAN Notices*, 27(5), 1990.
10. J. Hughes, L. Pareto, and A. Sabry. Proving the Correctness of Reactive Systems Using Sized Types. In *ACM Principles of Programming Languages*, St Petersburg, Florida, January 1996.
11. S. Malik. Analysis of cyclic combinational circuits. *IEEE Transactions on Computer Aided Design*, 13(7):950–956, July 1994.
12. F. Pessaux and X. Leroy. Type-based analysis of uncaught exceptions. *ACM Trans. Prog. Lang. Syst.*, 22(2):340–377, 2000.
13. D. Rémy. Extending ML type system with a sorted equational theory. Research Report 1766, Institut National de Recherche en Informatique et Automatique, Rocquencourt, BP 105, 78 153 Le Chesnay Cedex, France, 1992. ftp://ftp.inria.fr/INRIA/Projects/cristal/Didier.Remy/eq-theory-on-types.ps.gz.
14. D. Rémy. Type inference for records in a natural extension of ML. In C. A. Gunter and J. C. Mitchell, editors, *Theoretical Aspects Of Object-Oriented Programming. Types, Semantics and Language Design*. MIT Press, 1993. ftp://ftp.inria.fr/INRIA/Projects/cristal/Didier.Remy/taoop1.ps.gz.
15. J. Saraiva, D. Swiersrta, M. Kuiper, and M. Pennings. Strictification of lazy functions. Technical report, 1996. http://www.cs.ruu.nl/docs/research/publication/TechList2.html.
16. T. R. Shiple, G. Berry, and H. Touati. Constructive analysis of cyclic circuits. In *Proc. International Design and Testing Conference*, Paris, 1996.
17. S. Singh and M. Sheeran. Designing FPGA circuits in Lava. Technical report. http://www.dcs.gla.ac.uk/~satnam/lava/lava_intro.ps.
18. J.-P. Talpin and D. Nowak. A synchronous semantics of higher-order processes for modeling reconfigurable reactive systems. *Conference on Foundations of Software Technology and Theoretical Computer Science*, 1998.
19. P. Wadler. Deforestation: transforming programs to eliminate trees. *Theoretical Computer Science, (Special issue of selected papers from 2'nd European Symposium on Programming)*, 73:231–248, 1990.
20. M. Wand. Type inference for record concatenation and multiple inheritance. *Information and Computation*, 93:1–15, 1991.

Control-Flow Analysis in Cubic Time

Flemming Nielson[1] and Helmut Seidl[2]

[1] Computer Science Department, Aarhus University (Bldg. 540), Ny Munkegade,
DK-8000 Aarhus C, Denmark, `fn@daimi.au.dk`
[2] FB IV – Informatik, Universität Trier, D-54286 Trier, Germany,
`seidl@uni-trier.de`

Abstract. It is well-known that context-independent control flow analysis can be performed in cubic time for functional and object-oriented languages. Yet recent applications of control flow analysis to calculi of computation (like the π-calculus and the ambient calculus) have reported considerably higher complexities. In this paper we introduce two general techniques, the use of *Horn clauses with sharing* and the use of *tiling of Horn clauses*, for reducing the worst-case complexity of analyses. Applying these techniques to the π-calculus and the ambient calculus we reduce the complexity from $\mathcal{O}(n^5)$ to $\mathcal{O}(n^3)$ in both cases.

Keywords: Program analysis, Horn clauses with sharing, tiling of Horn clauses, π-calculus, ambient calculus, 0-CFA.

1 Introduction

Program analyses often can be separated into two phases. In the first phase, the program to be analyzed is translated into a suitable constraint system describing *safe* information about the program, and where the unknowns represent the desired information. In the second phase, a solution for the unknowns (typically the least) is produced by an appropriate constraint solver. Accordingly, there are also two common sources of inefficiency for a program analyzer constructed in this way. Clearly, efficiency cannot be hoped for if already the presentation of the system itself is extremely large. Therefore, a constraint formalism should be chosen which is expressive enough to represent the generated constraints succinctly. Even so, efficiency might be lost when the constraint formalism is "stronger than necessary", meaning that the solving procedure for the selected class of constraints incurs a large though otherwise unnecessary overhead.

As an example, consider the analysis of the π-calculus as presented in [2]. For a program of size n this analysis succeeds in generating a constraint system of size $\mathcal{O}(n^3)$ using set inclusion constraints. Thus from a practical point of view, even if a cubic worst case behavior is inevitable, such an extensive constraint system is unsatisfactory as it prohibits simpler programs to be analyzed faster. Actually, the presentation of the analysis used in [2] is even less likely to scale to larger programs as the generated constraint system, when fed into an off-the-shelf solver, would consume $\mathcal{O}(n^5)$ steps of solving time in the worst case. In a similar way, the analysis of the ambient calculus as presented in [10] generates a

D. Sands (Ed.): ESOP 2001, LNCS 2028, pp. 252–268, 2001.
© Springer-Verlag Berlin Heidelberg 2001

constraint system of size $\mathcal{O}(n^4)$ using set membership constraints and the same $\mathcal{O}(n^5)$ worst case constraint solving time.

The goal of this paper is to improve on these methods. As a general framework within which these problems can be addressed, we propose the concept of *Horn clauses with sharing* (HCS's for short). While being much more succinct than classical Horn clauses, they still admit rather efficient constraint solving techniques. We demonstrate the usefulness of this concept in several ways. By using Horn clauses with sharing instead of ordinary ones we are able to generate linear size constraint systems for analyses of the π-calculus and for the ambient calculus as they have been published in the literature. By using state-of-the-art solvers for Horn clauses with sharing, we bring down the complexity of the 0-CFA analysis of the π-calculus as presented in [2] from $\mathcal{O}(n^5)$ to $\mathcal{O}(n^3)$. It turns out that these methods still do not suffice to get a similar improvement for the ambient calculus. Therefore, we develop *tiling* as a source-to-source transformation of Horn clauses; indeed, tiling may be of independent interest also for other applications. In our application it allows us to reduce the complexity for the ambient calculus from $\mathcal{O}(n^5)$ to $\mathcal{O}(n^3)$ as well. In practical terms, $\mathcal{O}(n^3)$ is likely to be sufficiently good that it will be possible to analyse medium-sized programs whereas lower complexities are called for to analyse large programs.

2   Horn Clauses with Sharing

There are several formalisms around in which to specify constraints for program analyses; two of the more widely used ones are conditional set constraints (see e.g. [1]) and Horn clauses (see e.g. [7]). We base our work on Horn clauses in order to build on the techniques for complexity estimation presented in [7].

A system of *Horn clauses* (abbreviated: HC's) usually is a set of implications where the conclusion is a single relation, and the antecedent is a conjunction of relations. In order to facilitate the introduction of sharing we shall represent a system of Horn clauses as a formula derived by the nonterminal clause' in the grammar below:

$$
\begin{array}{lcl}
\mathsf{pre'} & ::= & R\,(x_1,\cdots,x_k) \quad | \quad \mathsf{pre}'_1 \wedge \mathsf{pre}'_2 \\
\mathsf{clause'} & ::= & R\,(x_1,\cdots,x_k) \quad | \quad \mathbf{1} \quad | \quad \mathsf{clause}'_1 \wedge \mathsf{clause}'_2 \\
& & | \quad \mathsf{pre'} \Rightarrow R\,(x_1,\cdots,x_k) \quad | \quad \forall x : \mathsf{clause'}
\end{array}
$$

Here we assume that we are given a fixed countable set $X = \{x, x_1, \cdots\}$ of variables and a finite ranked alphabet $\mathcal{R} = \{R, R_1, \cdots\}$ of relation symbols of predicates. In this notation we are explicit about the otherwise implicit universal quantification in Horn clauses, and $\mathbf{1}$ is the always true clause.

To obtain *Horn clauses with sharing* (abbreviated: HCS's) we extend this formalism by allowing

- disjunctions and existential quantification in pre-conditions, and
- conjunctions of clauses in conclusions.

Disjunctions have been added merely for technical convenience. Existential quantification in pre-conditions, however, allows us to limit the scopes of variables, whereas conjunctions of clauses in conclusions allow us to merge multiple conclusions without the technical inconvenience of introducing auxiliary predicates. The set of HCS's are defined by the nonterminal clause in the grammar below:

$$\begin{array}{lll} \text{pre} & ::= & R\,(x_1,\cdots,x_k) \quad | \quad \text{pre}_1 \wedge \text{pre}_2 \quad | \quad \text{pre}_1 \vee \text{pre}_2 \quad | \quad \exists x : \text{pre} \\ \text{clause} & ::= & R\,(x_1,\cdots,x_k) \quad | \quad 1 \quad | \quad \text{clause}_1 \wedge \text{clause}_2 \\ & & | \quad \text{pre} \Rightarrow \text{clause} \quad | \quad \forall x : \text{clause} \end{array}$$

Occurrences of $R(\cdots)$ in pre-conditions are also called *queries*, whereas the others are called *assertions* of predicate R.

Given a universe $\mathcal{U}$ of atomic values (or atoms) together with interpretations ρ and σ for relation symbols and free variables, respectively, we define the satisfaction relations $(\rho,\sigma) \models \text{pre}$ and $(\rho,\sigma) \models \text{clause}$ as follows (where t is a pre-condition or clause):

$$\begin{array}{llll} (\rho,\sigma) \models 1 & \text{iff} & \text{true} \\ (\rho,\sigma) \models R\,(x_1,\cdots,x_k) & \text{iff} & (\sigma\, x_1,\cdots,\sigma\, x_k) \in \rho\, R \\ (\rho,\sigma) \models \text{pre}_1 \vee \text{pre}_2 & \text{iff} & (\rho,\sigma) \models \text{pre}_1 \quad \text{or} \quad (\rho,\sigma) \models \text{pre}_2 \\ (\rho,\sigma) \models t_1 \wedge t_2 & \text{iff} & (\rho,\sigma) \models t_1 \quad \text{and} \quad (\rho,\sigma) \models t_2 \\ (\rho,\sigma) \models \text{pre} \Rightarrow \text{clause} & \text{iff} & (\rho,\sigma) \models \text{clause} \quad \text{whenever} \quad (\rho,\sigma) \models \text{pre} \\ (\rho,\sigma) \models \forall x : \text{clause} & \text{iff} & (\rho,\sigma \oplus \{x \mapsto a\}) \models \text{clause} \quad \text{for all } a \in \mathcal{U} \\ (\rho,\sigma) \models \exists x : \text{pre} & \text{iff} & (\rho,\sigma \oplus \{x \mapsto a\}) \models \text{pre} \quad \text{for some } a \in \mathcal{U} \end{array}$$

In the sequel, we will view the free variables occurring in a HCS (or HC) as *constant* symbols or *atoms* from the *finite* universe $\mathcal{U}$. Thus, given an interpretation σ of the constant symbols in clause, we call an interpretation ρ of the relational symbols $\mathcal{R}$ a *solution* provided $(\rho,\sigma) \models \text{clause}$.

Let $\Delta_\sigma = \{\rho \mid (\rho,\sigma) \models \text{clause}\}$ denote the set of solutions of clause (given a fixed σ). Then Δ_σ is partially ordered in the natural way by the componentwise ordering $\sqsubseteq$. It is standard (see e.g. [9, Subsection 3.2.3]) that Δ_σ is a Moore family, i.e. closed under greatest lower bounds $\sqcap$, and we conclude that Δ_σ has a least element which we call the *least solution* of clause. It is well-known [7,5] that in the case of HC's this solution can be computed efficiently. The following result establishes a similar result[1] for HCS's.

Proposition 1. *Given an interpretation of the constant symbols, the least solution of a HCS formula $c_1 \wedge \cdots \wedge c_m$ can be computed in time*

$$\mathcal{O}(N^{r_1} \cdot n_1 + \cdots + N^{r_m} \cdot n_m)$$

where N is the number of atoms in $\mathcal{U}$, n_i is the size of c_i, and r_i is the maximal nesting depth of quantifiers in c_i.

Proof. See Appendix A for an algorithm whose worst case complexity is as stated. We are currently experimenting with a solver having the same worst case complexity but a potentially much lower best case complexity.

---

[1] All our complexity bounds refer to the RAM model with a uniform cost measure.

3   The Virtues of Sharing

We now show how sharing facilitates developing a cubic time algorithm for performing control flow analysis [3,2] for the π-calculus [8].

3.1   Example: The π-Calculus

Introduction to the π-calculus. Let $\mathcal{N}$ be an infinite set of *names* ranged over by $a, b, \cdots, x, y, \cdots$ and let τ be a distinguished element not in $\mathcal{N}$. Then *processes* $P \in \mathcal{P}$ are built from names according to the following syntax:

$$P ::= \mathbf{0} \mid \mu.P \mid P + P \mid P|P \mid (\nu x^{\chi})P \mid [x = y]P \mid \,!P$$
$$\mu ::= x(y^{\beta}) \mid \overline{x}y \mid \tau$$

The prefix μ is the first atomic action that the process $\mu.P$ can perform. The input prefix $x(y^{\beta})$ binds the name y in the prefixed process and corresponds to a name y that is received along the link named x. The superscript β is a "variable type"; we write $\mathcal{B}$ for the set of variable types. The output prefix $\overline{x}y$ does not bind the name y and corresponds to the name y that is sent along x. The silent prefix τ denotes an action which is invisible to an external observer of the system.

Turning to the processes, $P + Q$ behaves either as P or as Q whereas $P|Q$ performs P and Q simultaneously and also allows them to communicate with each other (as when one performs an input and the other an output on the same common link). The restriction operator $(\nu x^{\chi})P$ binds the name x in the process P that it prefixes, in such a way that x is a unique name in P that is different from all external names. The agent $(\nu x^{\chi})P$ behaves as P except that sending along $\overline{x}$ and receiving along x is blocked. The superscript χ is a "channel type" in the manner of the "variable type" discussed above; we write $\mathcal{C}$ for the set of channel types. Matching $[x = y]P$ is an if-then operator: process P is activated if $x = y$. Finally, replication $!P$ behaves as $P|P|\cdots$ as many times as needed.

Flow Logic specification of 0-CFA. The result of control flow analyzing a process P is a pair (R, K) (called (ρ, κ) in [3,2]). The first component, $R : \mathcal{B} \to \wp(\mathcal{C})$, is an abstract environment which gives information about the set of channels to which names can be bound. The second component, $K : \mathcal{C} \to \wp(\mathcal{C})$, is an abstract channel environment which gives information about the set of channels that can flow over given channels. The correctness of a proposed solution (R, K) is validated by a set of clauses operating upon judgments of the form, $(R, K) \models_{me} P$, where the functionality of $R : \mathcal{B} \to \wp(\mathcal{C})$ is extended[2] to $R : (\mathcal{B} \cup \mathcal{C}) \to \wp(\mathcal{C})$ by stipulating that $\forall \chi \in \mathcal{C} : R(\chi) = \{\chi\}$. As in [3,2] the control flow analysis is developed relative to a "marker environment" $me : \mathcal{N} \to (\mathcal{B} \cup \mathcal{C})$ that maps names to their variable type (in $\mathcal{B}$) or channel type (in $\mathcal{C}$) as appropriate; in the interest of simplicity we sometimes simplify explanation by pretending that me is the identity.

---

[2] This seemingly ad-hoc definition is made because the π-calculus does not make a syntactic distinction between "variables" and "channels".

Table 1. Flow Logic for the π-calculus (taken from [2]).

$(R, K) \models_{me} \mathbf{0}$	iff *true*
$(R, K) \models_{me} \tau.P$	iff $(R, K) \models_{me} P$
$(R, K) \models_{me} \overline{x}y.P$	iff $(R, K) \models_{me} P \wedge$
	$\forall \chi \in R(me(x)) : R(me(y)) \subseteq K(\chi)$
$(R, K) \models_{me} x(y^\beta).P$	iff $(R, K) \models_{me[y \mapsto \beta]} P \wedge$
	$\forall \chi \in R(me(x)) : K(\chi) \subseteq R(\beta)$
$(R, K) \models_{me} P_1 + P_2$	iff $(R, K) \models_{me} P_1 \wedge (R, K) \models_{me} P_2$
$(R, K) \models_{me} P_1|P_2$	iff $(R, K) \models_{me} P_1 \wedge (R, K) \models_{me} P_2$
$(R, K) \models_{me} (\nu x^\chi)P$	iff $(R, K) \models_{me[x \mapsto \chi]} P$
$(R, K) \models_{me} [x = y]P$	iff $(R(me(x)) \cap R(me(y)) \neq \emptyset$
	$\Rightarrow (R, K) \models_{me} P$
$(R, K) \models_{me} !P$	iff $(R, K) \models_{me} P$

The Control Flow Analysis is given by the Flow Logic in Table 1. All the rules dealing with a compound process require that the components are validated, apart from the one for matching. Moreover, the second conjunct of the rule for output requires that the set of channels that can be communicated along each element of $R(x)$ (pretending here that *me* is the identity) includes the channels to which y can evaluate. Symmetrically, the rule for input demands that the set of channels that can pass along x is included in the set of channels to which y can evaluate. The condition for matching says that the continuation P needs to be validated if there is at least one channel to which both x and y can evaluate. Similar "reachability" considerations can be performed also for input and output without invalidating Theorem 1 below. We refer to [2] for further explanation of the analysis and for proofs of its semantic correctness.

An algorithm for obtaining the least solution in[3] time $\mathcal{O}(n^5)$ in the size n of processes is given in [2].

Horn Clauses with Sharing for 0-CFA. To generate HCS's corresponding to the Flow Logic specification in Table 1 we shall perform the following systematic transformations in order to adhere to the format of Horn clauses with sharing:

- A set inclusion of the form $X \subseteq Y$ is expressed using set memberships of the form $\forall u : u \in X \Rightarrow u \in Y$.
- A set membership of the form $u \in R(v)$ is written using a binary predicate of the form $R(u, v)$.

---

[3] In [3] it is conjectured that the constraints can be solved in $\mathcal{O}(n^3)$ bit-vector operations which corresponds to overall time $\mathcal{O}(n^4)$ but no algorithm is given.

Table 2. Horn Clauses with Sharing for the π-calculus.

$$\mathcal{G}[\![0]\!]_{me} = 1$$

$$\mathcal{G}[\![\tau.P]\!]_{me} = \mathcal{G}[\![P]\!]_{me}$$

$$\mathcal{G}[\![\overline{x}y.P]\!]_{me} = \mathcal{G}[\![P]\!]_{me} \land$$
$$\forall u : \forall v : (R(u, me(x)) \land R(v, me(y)))) \Rightarrow K(v, u)$$

$$\mathcal{G}[\![x(y^{\beta}).P]\!]_{me} = \mathcal{G}[\![P]\!]_{me[y \mapsto \beta]} \land$$
$$\forall u : \forall v : (R(u, me(x)) \land K(v, u)) \Rightarrow R(v, \beta)$$

$$\mathcal{G}[\![P_1 + P_2]\!]_{me} = \mathcal{G}[\![P_1]\!]_{me} \land \mathcal{G}[\![P_2]\!]_{me}$$

$$\mathcal{G}[\![P_1 | P_2]\!]_{me} = \mathcal{G}[\![P_1]\!]_{me} \land \mathcal{G}[\![P_2]\!]_{me}$$

$$\mathcal{G}[\![(\nu x^{\chi})P]\!]_{me} = \mathcal{G}[\![P]\!]_{me[x \mapsto \chi]} \land R(\chi, \chi)$$

$$\mathcal{G}[\![[x = y]P]\!]_{me} = (\exists u : R(u, me(x)) \land R(u, me(y)))) \Rightarrow \mathcal{G}[\![P]\!]_{me}$$

$$\mathcal{G}[\![!P]\!]_{me} = \mathcal{G}[\![P]\!]_{me}$$

To obtain a finite algorithm we shall restrict our attention to a finite universe, $\mathcal{C}_{\star}$, containing all the relevant channels; this corresponds to the set $\mathcal{U}_{\star} \cap \mathcal{C}$ considered in [2]. The constraint generation in Table 2 differs from the one in [2] because Horn clauses with sharing facilitate a more succinct representation of constraints. In particular, in the clause $[x = y]P$ we directly generate the condition $(\exists u : R(u, x) \land R(u, y))$ (once more pretending that me is the identity) shared for all of P without the need to duplicate it for each individual constraint (as would be needed to generate constraints in the form of Horn clauses). Also we "enforce" the convention that $R(\chi) = \{\chi\}$ by generating the constraint $R(\chi, \chi)$ when appropriate and by only considering the least solution.

We state without proof that the two formulations of the analysis are equivalent (using the notational conventions explained above):

Lemma 1. $(R, K) \models_{me} P$ *holds if and only if* $\mathcal{G}[\![P]\!]_{me}$.

For a universe of size $\mathcal{O}(n)$ we prove in Theorem 1 below that the resulting constraints can be solved in cubic time.

3.2 The Complexity of Constraint Specifications

The complexity of the control flow analysis can be established by applying Proposition 1 to the constraints generated for a program but it is more convenient to argue directly in terms of the constraint generation function itself. As will become clear in the next section it is convenient to define a *constraint specification* to be a triple $(\mathcal{T}, \alpha, c)$ where $\mathcal{T}$ is a compositionally defined constraint generation function (like $\mathcal{G}$ in Table 2), c is a global constraint (absent above, hence could be taken to be 1), and α is an initial context for the constraint generation function. Here, contexts are supposed to consist of a bounded number of atoms from the universe together with a bounded number of functions to extract atoms from pieces of syntax (like me above). Given a program P the constraint generated then is $\mathcal{T}[\![P]\!]_\alpha \wedge c$.

A constraint specification $(\mathcal{T}, \alpha, c)$ is said to be *linear HCS* if each defining equation of $\mathcal{T}$ takes the form

$$\mathcal{T}[\![\phi'(P_1, \cdots, P_{m'})]\!]_{\alpha'} = c' \wedge \bigwedge_{i \in I} p'_i \Rightarrow \mathcal{T}[\![P_i]\!]_{\alpha'_i}$$

where $I \subseteq \{1, \cdots, m'\}$, the P_i are distinct and non-overlapping components of the program $\phi'(P_1, \cdots, P_{m'})$ and α'_i is computed from α' and ϕ'; the formulae c' and p'_i chosen for ϕ' may contain free variables $\tilde{z}$ occurring in α' or extracted from ϕ' (using the extraction functions in α'). Since a universally true pre-condition can be written $T()$ for a fresh relation symbol defined by the clause $T()$ we do not consider the possibility of having no pre-condition. The constraint specification is *linear HC* when additionally all clauses (c', p'_i and c) are formulae of HC.

A constraint specification $(\mathcal{T}, \alpha, c)$ is said to have *cost coefficient* r if r is minimal such that each defining equation of $\mathcal{T}$ have quantifiers nested at most to depth $r - 1$ and if the global constraint c has quantifiers nested at most to depth r; note that r will always be greater than zero.

Proposition 2. *Given a linear HCS constraint specification $(\mathcal{T}, \alpha, c)$ of cost coefficient r, a program P of size $\mathcal{O}(n)$ and a universe of size $\mathcal{O}(n)$; the constraint $\mathcal{T}[\![P]\!]_\alpha \wedge c$ has size $\mathcal{O}(n)$ and its least solution can be found in time $\mathcal{O}(n^r)$.*   □

Proof. Clearly $\mathcal{T}[\![P]\!]_\alpha$ has size $\mathcal{O}(n)$ with quantifiers nested at most to depth $r - 1$ and c has size $\mathcal{O}(1)$ with quantifiers nested at most to depth r. The result then follows from Proposition 1.   □

Theorem 1. *Control Flow Analysis for the π-calculus (as in [2]) can be done in cubic time.*   □

Proof. Clearly $(\mathcal{G}, me, 1)$ is a linear HCS constraint specification with cost coefficient 3. Also the universe has size linear in the program. The result then follows from Proposition 2.   □

4   The Virtues of Tiling

We now show how tiling facilitates developing a cubic time algorithm for performing control flow analysis [10] for the ambient calculus [4].

4.1   Example: The Ambient Calculus

Introduction to mobile ambients. The syntax of processes $P \in \mathbf{Proc}$, capabilities $M \in \mathbf{Cap}$ and namings $N \in \mathbf{Nam}$ is given by:

$$P ::= (\nu\, n^\mu)P \quad\quad \text{restriction} \quad\quad M ::= \text{in}^t N \quad\quad \text{enter } N$$
$$\mid\; \mathbf{0} \quad\quad\quad \text{inactivity} \quad\quad\quad \mid\; \text{out}^t N \quad\quad \text{exit } N$$
$$\mid\; P \mid P' \quad\quad\; \text{composition} \quad\quad \mid\; \text{open}^t N \quad\quad \text{open } N$$
$$\mid\; !P \quad\quad\quad\; \text{replication}$$
$$\mid\; N^l[P] \quad\quad\; \text{ambient} \quad\quad\quad N ::= n \quad\quad\quad\quad \text{name}$$
$$\mid\; M.\,P \quad\quad\; \text{movement}$$

Processes contain a number of constructs known from the π-calculus; an example is the restriction operator where $\mu \in \mathbf{SNam}$ is the "ambient type" (in the manner of the "variable type" and "channel type" considered above) called "stable name" in [10]. The final two constructs are unique to the ambient calculus. An ambient is a process operating inside a named border. Movement of ambients is governed by capabilities. The in-capability directs the enclosing ambient to enter a sibling named N. The out-capability directs the enclosing ambient to move out of its parent named N. The open-capability dissolves the border around a sibling ambient named N. Finally, namings are names. Much as in [10] we have placed labels $l \in \mathbf{ALab}$ on ambients and labels $t \in \mathbf{TLab}$ on capabilities (or transitions) in order to have explicit notation for the various subterms.

Flow Logic specification. An ambient will be identified by its label $l \in \mathbf{ALab}$ and a transition by its associated *capability type* $\tilde{m} \in \mathbf{SCap}$ called "stable capability" in [10]; capability types are given by

$$\tilde{m} ::= \text{in}^t \mu \mid \text{out}^t \mu \mid \text{open}^t \mu$$

and correspond to capabilities except that names have been replaced by ambient types. The analysis records which ambients and transitions occur inside what ambients in the component $I : \mathbf{ALab} \to \wp(\mathbf{ALab} \cup \mathbf{SCap})$. We also use the "inverse" mapping $I^{-1} : (\mathbf{ALab} \cup \mathbf{SCap}) \to \wp(\mathbf{ALab})$ that returns the set of ambients in which the given ambient or transition might occur; formally $z \in I(l)$ if and only if $l \in I^{-1}(z)$.

Each occurrence of an ambient has an ambient type and to keep track of this information the analysis also contains the component $H : \mathbf{ALab} \to \wp(\mathbf{SNam})$. As above we use the "inverse mapping" $H^{-1} : \mathbf{SNam} \to \wp(\mathbf{ALab})$ that returns the set of ambients that might have the given ambient type.

The acceptability of the analysis is defined by the following four predicates defined by the Flow Logic in Table 3:

$(I, H) \models^l_{me} P$ for checking a process $P \in \mathbf{Proc}$;

$(I, H) \rhd_{me} M : \tilde{M}$ for translating a capability $M \in \mathbf{Cap}$ into a set $\tilde{M} \in \wp(\mathbf{SCap})$ of capability types;

$(I, H) \Vmodels_{me} N : \tilde{N}$ for decoding a naming $N \in \mathbf{Nam}$ into a set $\tilde{N} \in \wp(\mathbf{SNam})$ of ambient types;

$(I, H) \models^l \tilde{m}$ for checking a capability type. $\tilde{m} \in \mathbf{SCap}$.

Much as before a marker environment $me : \mathbf{Nam} \to_{\text{fin}} \mathbf{SNam}$ is used for mapping names to ambient types. We refer to [10] for further explanation of the analysis and for proofs of its semantic correctness.

Table 3. Flow Logic for the ambient calculus (taken from [10]).

$(I, H) \models^l_{me} (\nu n^\mu) P$ iff $(I, H) \models^l_{me[n \mapsto \mu]} P$

$(I, H) \models^l_{me} \mathbf{0}$ iff true

$(I, H) \models^l_{me} P \mid P'$ iff $(I, H) \models^l_{me} P \wedge (I, H) \models^l_{me} P'$

$(I, H) \models^l_{me} {!}P$ iff $(I, H) \models^l_{me} P$

$(I, H) \models^l_{me} N^{l'}[P]$ iff $(I, H) \models^{l'}_{me} P \wedge l' \in I(l) \wedge$
$\qquad\qquad (I, H) \Vdash_{me} N : \tilde{N} \wedge \tilde{N} \subseteq H(l')$

$(I, H) \models^l_{me} M.P$ iff $(I, H) \models^l_{me} P \wedge$
$\qquad\qquad (I, H) \rhd_{me} M : \tilde{M} \wedge \forall \tilde{m} \in \tilde{M} : (I, H) \models^l \tilde{m}$

$(I, H) \rhd_{me} \mathsf{in}^t N : \tilde{M}$ iff $(I, H) \Vdash_{me} N : \tilde{N} \wedge \tilde{M} \supseteq \{\mathsf{in}^t \mu \mid \mu \in \tilde{N}\}$

$(I, H) \rhd_{me} \mathsf{out}^t N : \tilde{M}$ iff $(I, H) \Vdash_{me} N : \tilde{N} \wedge \tilde{M} \supseteq \{\mathsf{out}^t \mu \mid \mu \in \tilde{N}\}$

$(I, H) \rhd_{me} \mathsf{open}^t N : \tilde{M}$ iff $(I, H) \Vdash_{me} N : \tilde{N} \wedge \tilde{M} \supseteq \{\mathsf{open}^t \mu \mid \mu \in \tilde{N}\}$

$(I, H) \Vdash_{me} n : \tilde{N}$ iff $\tilde{N} \supseteq \{me(n)\}$

$(I, H) \models^l \mathsf{in}^t \mu$ iff $\mathsf{in}^t \mu \in I(l) \wedge$
$\qquad\qquad \forall l^a \in I^{-1}(\mathsf{in}^t \mu) : \forall l'^a \in I^{-1}(l^a) :$
$\qquad\qquad\qquad \forall l''^a \in I(l'^a) \cap H^{-1}(\mu) : l^a \in I(l''^a)$

$(I, H) \models^l \mathsf{out}^t \mu$ iff $\mathsf{out}^t \mu \in I(l) \wedge$
$\qquad\qquad \forall l^a \in I^{-1}(\mathsf{out}^t \mu) : \forall l'^a \in I^{-1}(l^a) \cap H^{-1}(\mu) :$
$\qquad\qquad\qquad \forall l''^a \in I^{-1}(l'^a) : l^a \in I(l''^a)$

$(I, H) \models^l \mathsf{open}^t \mu$ iff $\mathsf{open}^t \mu \in I(l) \wedge$
$\qquad\qquad \forall l^a \in I^{-1}(\mathsf{open}^t \mu) : \forall l'^a \in I(l^a) \cap H^{-1}(\mu) :$
$\qquad\qquad\qquad \forall l' \in I(l'^a) : l' \in I(l^a)$

An algorithm for obtaining the least solution in[4] time $\mathcal{O}(n^5)$ is given in [10].

Constraint generation. To generate the constraints as simply as possible we note that in the communication-free fragment of the mobile ambients studied here the only possible naming (N) is a name (n). Thus namings can be replaced by names everywhere and this makes the judgement $(I, H) \Vdash_{me} n : \tilde{N}$ dispensable (essentially by always choosing for $\tilde{N}$ the least choice $\{me(n)\}$).

In a similar way we can dispense with the judgement $(I, H) \rhd_{me} M : \tilde{M}$ if we arrange that the translation from names to ambient types also becomes the duty of the judgement $(I, H) \models^l \tilde{m}$ that thus takes the form $(I, H) \models^l_{me} M$.

This leaves us with the judgements $(I, H) \models^l_{me} P$ and $(I, H) \models^l_{me} M$ and they give rise to constraint generation functions $\mathcal{G}[\![P]\!]^l_{me}$ and $\mathcal{G}'[\![M]\!]^l_{me}$, respectively. To satisfy the Horn clause format we perform the following systematic transformations:

---

[4] In [10] it is conjectured that a more sophisticated implementation will be able to achieve $\mathcal{O}(n^4)$ but no details are provided.

Table 4. Horn Clauses for the ambient calculus.

$$\mathcal{G}[\![(\nu\, n^\mu)P]\!]^l_{me} = \mathcal{G}[\![P]\!]^l_{me[n \mapsto \mu]}$$

$$\mathcal{G}[\![0]\!]^l_{me} = 1$$

$$\mathcal{G}[\![P \mid P']\!]^l_{me} = \mathcal{G}[\![P]\!]^l_{me} \;\wedge\; \mathcal{G}[\![P']\!]^l_{me}$$

$$\mathcal{G}[\![!P]\!]^l_{me} = \mathcal{G}[\![P]\!]^l_{me}$$

$$\mathcal{G}[\![n^{l'}[P]]\!]^l_{me} = \mathcal{G}[\![P]\!]^{l'}_{me} \;\wedge\; I(l',l) \;\wedge\; H(me(n),l')$$

$$\mathcal{G}[\![M.P]\!]^l_{me} = \mathcal{G}[\![P]\!]^l_{me} \;\wedge\; \mathcal{G}'[\![M]\!]^l_{me}$$

$$\mathcal{G}'[\![\mathsf{in}^t n]\!]^l_{me} = I(\mathsf{in}^t me(n),l) \;\wedge$$
$$\forall l^a : \forall l'^a : \forall l''^a : (I(\mathsf{in}^t me(n),l^a) \;\wedge\; I(l^a,l'^a) \;\wedge$$
$$I(l''^a,l'^a) \;\wedge\; H(me(n),l''^a)) \Rightarrow I(l^a,l''^a)$$

$$\mathcal{G}'[\![\mathsf{out}^t n]\!]^l_{me} = I(\mathsf{out}^t me(n),l) \;\wedge$$
$$\forall l^a : \forall l'^a : \forall l''^a : (I(\mathsf{out}^t me(n),l^a) \;\wedge\; I(l^a,l'^a) \;\wedge$$
$$H(me(n),l'^a) \;\wedge\; I(l'^a,l''^a)) \Rightarrow I(l^a,l''^a)$$

$$\mathcal{G}'[\![\mathsf{open}^t n]\!]^l_{me} = I(\mathsf{open}^t me(n),l) \;\wedge$$
$$\forall l^a : \forall l'^a : \forall l' : (I(\mathsf{open}^t me(n),l^a) \;\wedge\; I(l'^a,l^a) \;\wedge$$
$$H(me(n),l'^a) \;\wedge\; I(l',l'^a)) \Rightarrow I(l',l^a)$$

- A set membership involving an "inverse" relation of the form $u \in R^{-1}(v)$ is rewritten to the form $v \in R(u)$ thus avoiding "inverse" relations.
- As in Subsection 3.1 a set membership of the form $u \in R(v)$ is written using a binary predicate of the form $R(u,v)$.

Using the notational conventions explained above we state without proof that the formulations of Tables 3 and 4 are equivalent:

Lemma 2. $(I,H) \models^l_{me} P$ *holds if and only if* $\mathcal{G}[\![P]\!]^l_{me}$.

Clearly $(\mathcal{G},(l,me),1)$ is a linear HCS constraint specification with cost coefficient 4 that operates over a universe of size linear in the size of the program so that by Proposition 2 the constraints can be solved in time $\mathcal{O}(n^4)$; we now develop the notion of tiling in order to obtain a cubic bound.

4.2   Tiling of Constraint Specifications

Tiling applies to a linear HC constraint specification and systematically rewrites it into another with the aim of eventually reducing the cost coefficient. There are two main tricks to be played when tiling a constraint specification $(\mathcal{T},\alpha,c)$:

- to remove quantifiers in c or in the defining equations of $\mathcal{T}$, and
- to transfer sub-formulae from a defining equation of $\mathcal{T}$ into the global constraint c.

We first apply the techniques to the analysis of the mobile ambients and then show how to perform it in general.

Theorem 2. *Control Flow Analysis for the mobile ambients (as in [10]) can be done in cubic time.*

Proof. The constraint specification $(\mathcal{H}, (l, me), c_{\mathcal{H}})$ of Table 5 has cost coefficient 3 and so by Proposition 2 we can solve $\mathcal{H}[\![P]\!]^l_{me} \wedge c_{\mathcal{H}}$ in cubic time.

It remains to show that the least solution to $\mathcal{H}[\![P]\!]^l_{me} \wedge c_{\mathcal{H}}$ equals the least solution to $\mathcal{G}[\![P]\!]^l_{me}$ (ignoring the auxiliary relations). The key idea to reducing the complexity is to ensure that the formulae generated are "tiled" such that subformulae with three nested quantifiers are only generated a constant number of times whereas subformulae with two nested quantifiers may be generated a linear number of times.

Concentrating on the clause for in-capabilities we note that it establishes that l^a and l''^a are siblings because they have the same parent (namely l'^a). Imagine that we have a relation S for expressing the sibling relation: $S(l^a, l''^a)$ if and only if $\exists l'^a : I(l^a, l'^a) \wedge I(l''^a, l'^a)$. Then the clause for $\mathcal{G}'[\![\mathsf{in}^t n]\!]^l_{me}$ is equivalent to the formula:

$$I(\mathsf{in}^t me(n), l) \wedge$$
$$\forall l^a : \forall l''^a : (I(\mathsf{in}^t me(n), l^a) \wedge S(l^a, l''^a) \wedge H(me(n), l''^a)) \Rightarrow I(l^a, l''^a)$$

Indeed the relation S can be obtained by generating the Horn clause

$$\forall l^a : \forall l'^a : \forall l''^a : (I(l^a, l'^a) \wedge I(l''^a, l'^a)) \Rightarrow S(l^a, l''^a)$$

and taking the least solution (assuming that this is the only clause defining S).

The clause for out-capabilities has a slightly different structure so here we make use of a predicate $O(l^a, l'^a)$ for indicating when l^a may be a candidate for moving out of l'^a. Similarly in the clause for open-capabilities we make use of a predicate $P(l'^a, l^a)$ for indicating when l'^a may be a candidate for being opened inside l^a. This concludes the proof. □

In fact it is not necessary to have any deep insights in the analysis in order to perform tiling. To make this clear we now develop a purely mechanical notion of tiling, $\longmapsto$, such that Theorem 2 follows from merely noting that, except for a few additional simplifications,

$$(\mathcal{G}, (l, me), 1) \longmapsto^* (\mathcal{H}, (l, me), c_{\mathcal{H}})$$

and then relying on Proposition 3 below.

Tiling individual constraints. We begin by considering a tiling transformation on certain individual constraints. It takes the form $c \overset{o}{\mapsto} c_1 \& c_2$ where the idea is that c should be replaced by c_1 and that c_2 should be moved out to the global constraint; the superscript o will be 0 when the constraint c occurs in the global constraint and 1 when it occurs in a defining equation for the constraint specification.

The intention is to reduce the quantifier depth of c by possibly generating additional "cheap" clauses; in intuitive terms, reduction of quantifier depth means reducing the number of variables that are "simultaneously active" when expressing the analysis. The general form of a formula c to be tiled is

$$c = \forall y_1 : \cdots \forall y_k : \mathsf{pre}' \Rightarrow R(\tilde{w})$$

Table 5. Tiled Horn Clauses for the ambient calculus.

$$\mathcal{H}[\![(\nu\,n^{\mu})P]\!]^l_{me} = \mathcal{H}[\![P]\!]^l_{me[n\mapsto\mu]}$$

$$\mathcal{H}[\![\mathbf{0}]\!]^l_{me} = 1$$

$$\mathcal{H}[\![P\mid P']\!]^l_{me} = \mathcal{H}[\![P]\!]^l_{me}\ \wedge\ \mathcal{H}[\![P']\!]^l_{me}$$

$$\mathcal{H}[\![!P]\!]^l_{me} = \mathcal{H}[\![P]\!]^l_{me}$$

$$\mathcal{H}[\![n^{l'}[P]]\!]^l_{me} = \mathcal{H}[\![P]\!]^{l'}_{me}\ \wedge\ I(l',l)\ \wedge\ H(me(n),l')$$

$$\mathcal{H}[\![M.P]\!]^l_{me} = \mathcal{H}[\![P]\!]^l_{me}\ \wedge\ \mathcal{H}'[\![M]\!]^l_{me}$$

$$\mathcal{H}'[\![\mathsf{in}^t n]\!]^l_{me} = I(\mathsf{in}^t me(n),l)\ \wedge$$
$$\forall l^a:\forall l''^a:(I(\mathsf{in}^t me(n),l^a)\ \wedge\ S(l^a,l''^a)\ \wedge$$
$$H(me(n),l''^a))\Rightarrow I(l^a,l''^a)$$

$$\mathcal{H}'[\![\mathsf{out}^t n]\!]^l_{me} = I(\mathsf{out}^t me(n),l)\ \wedge$$
$$\forall l^a:\forall l'^a:(I(\mathsf{out}^t me(n),l^a)\ \wedge\ I(l^a,l'^a)\ \wedge$$
$$H(me(n),l'^a))\Rightarrow O(l^a,l'^a)$$

$$\mathcal{H}'[\![\mathsf{open}^t n]\!]^l_{me} = I(\mathsf{open}^t me(n),l)\ \wedge$$
$$\forall l^a:\forall l'^a:(I(\mathsf{open}^t me(n),l^a)\ \wedge\ I(l'^a,l^a)\ \wedge$$
$$H(me(n),l'^a))\Rightarrow P(l'^a,l^a)$$

$$c_{\mathcal{H}} = \forall l^a:\forall l'^a:\forall l''^a:(I(l^a,l'^a)\ \wedge\ I(l''^a,l'^a))\Rightarrow S(l^a,l''^a)\ \wedge$$
$$\forall l^a:\forall l'^a:\forall l''^a:(O(l^a,l'^a)\ \wedge\ I(l'^a,l''^a))\Rightarrow I(l^a,l''^a)\ \wedge$$
$$\forall l^a:\forall l'^a:\forall l':(P(l'^a,l^a)\ \wedge\ I(l',l'^a))\Rightarrow I(l',l^a)$$

where $\tilde{w}$ may contain bound variables from $y_1,\cdots,y_k$ as well as variables occurring in the program; we shall write $\tilde{z}$ for the latter. To define the transformation we first introduce two auxiliary concepts. We shall say that a bound variable y_i is a *candidate* in case it does not occur in $\tilde{w}$; similarly, we shall say that the special symbol $\square$ is a *candidate* in case no symbol from $\tilde{z}$ occurs in $\tilde{w}$. Furthermore, we say that two distinct bound variables y_i and y_j are *neighbours* in case there is a query $R'(\cdots)$ in pre' that mentions both y_i and y_j; similarly, we shall say that a bound variable y_i and the special symbol $\square$ are *neighbours* in case there is a query $R'(\cdots)$ in pre' that mentions both y_i and some variable from $\tilde{z}$.

There are three rules defining $c \overset{o}{\mapsto} c_1\&c_2$, each one removing a candidate having at most 2 neighbours. The first rule removes a bound variable that is a neighbour of $\square$:

$$\forall y_1:\cdots\forall y_k:\mathsf{pre}'\Rightarrow R(\tilde{w})$$
$$\overset{o}{\mapsto}\ (\forall y'_1:\cdots\forall y'_{k-1}:A_{\mathrm{fresh}}(x_1,\cdots,x_d,\tilde{z})\wedge\mathsf{pre}'_2\Rightarrow R(\tilde{w}))\wedge$$
$$(\forall y:\forall x_1:\cdots\forall x_d:\mathsf{pre}'_1\Rightarrow A_{\mathrm{fresh}}(x_1,\cdots,x_d,\tilde{z}))$$
$$\&\ 1$$

if y is a candidate with neighbour list $x_1,\cdots,x_d,\square$ and $o+k\geq 4, d\leq 1$

Here y is a bound variable and $y'_1,\ldots,y'_{k-1}$ is an enumeration of the remaining bound variables. Furthermore, pre'_1 denotes the conjunction of all queries from pre$'$ containing y, pre$'_2$ denotes the conjunction of the remaining ones, and $\tilde{z}$ is an enumeration of the program variables occurring in pre$'_1$. The auxiliary relation A_{fresh} is chosen fresh for each use of the rule.

The next rule removes a bound variable that is not a neighbour of $\square$:

$$\forall y_1 : \cdots \forall y_k : \text{pre}' \Rightarrow R(\tilde{w})$$
$$\overset{o}{\mapsto} \forall y'_1 : \cdots \forall y'_{k-1} : A_{\text{fresh}}(x_1, \cdots, x_d) \wedge \text{pre}'_2 \Rightarrow R(\tilde{w})$$
$$\&\ \forall y : \forall x_1 : \cdots \forall x_d : \text{pre}'_1 \Rightarrow A_{\text{fresh}}(x_1, \cdots, x_d)$$
if y is a candidate with neighbour list $x_1, \cdots, x_d$ and $o + k \geq 4, d \leq 2$

As before, y is a bound variable and $y'_1, \ldots, y'_{k-1}$ is an enumeration of the remaining bound variables. Also pre$'_1$ denotes the conjunction of all queries from pre$'$ containing y, pre$'_2$ denotes the conjunction of the remaining ones, and the auxiliary relation A_{fresh} is chosen fresh for each use of the rule.

The final rule could perhaps be said to remove $\square$ by transferring the program independent parts of the clause into the global constraint:

$$\forall y_1 : \cdots \forall y_k : \text{pre}' \Rightarrow R(\tilde{w})$$
$$\overset{o}{\mapsto} \forall x_1 : \cdots \forall x_d : \text{pre}'_1 \Rightarrow A_{\text{fresh}}(x_1, \cdots, x_d)$$
$$\&\ \forall y_1 : \cdots \forall y_k : A_{\text{fresh}}(x_1, \cdots, x_d) \wedge \text{pre}'_2 \Rightarrow R(\tilde{w})$$
if $\square$ is a candidate with neighbour list $x_1, \cdots, x_d$ and $o = 1, d \leq 2$

As before pre$'_1$ denotes the conjunction of all queries from pre$'$ containing some program variable (from $\tilde{z}$), pre$'_2$ denotes the conjunction of the remaining ones, and the auxiliary relation A_{fresh} is chosen fresh for each use of the rule. (The condition $o = 1$ merely says that the rule cannot be applied to the global constraint.)

Tiling constraint specifications. The tiling transformation $(\mathcal{T}, \alpha, c) \longmapsto (\mathcal{T}', \alpha', c')$ on constraint specifications is defined by the following rules:

$$(\mathcal{T}, \alpha, \cdots \wedge c \wedge \cdots) \longmapsto (\mathcal{T}, \alpha, \cdots \wedge c_1 \wedge c_2 \wedge \cdots)$$
if $c \overset{1}{\mapsto} c_1 \& c_2$

$$(\mathcal{T}, \alpha, c) \longmapsto (\mathcal{T}', \alpha, c \wedge c_2)$$
if $c' \overset{0}{\mapsto} c_1 \& c_2$ and $\mathcal{T}'$ is as $\mathcal{T}$ except that
$$\mathcal{T}[\![\phi'(P_1, \cdots, P_m)]\!]_{\alpha'} = \cdots \wedge c' \wedge \cdots \wedge \bigwedge_{i=1}^{m''} \text{pre}'_i \Rightarrow \mathcal{T}[\![P_i]\!]_{\alpha'_i}$$
$$\mathcal{T}'[\![\phi'(P_1, \cdots, P_m)]\!]_{\alpha'} = \cdots \wedge c_1 \wedge \cdots \wedge \bigwedge_{i=1}^{m''} \text{pre}'_i \Rightarrow \mathcal{T}'[\![P_i]\!]_{\alpha'_i}$$

The following result establishes the correctness of the tiling transformation; since tiling is not able always to reduce the complexity to cubic it is important also to show that the non-determinism is purely benign:

Proposition 3. *Let $(\mathcal{T}, \alpha, c)$ be a linear CH constraint specification of cost coefficient r. If $(\mathcal{T}, \alpha, c) \longmapsto (\mathcal{T}', \alpha', c')$ then*

- *$(\mathcal{T}', \alpha', c')$ is a linear CH constraint specification of cost coefficient $r' \leq r$.*
- *For all programs P the least solution to $\mathcal{T}'[\![P]\!]_{\alpha'} \wedge c'$ equals the least solution to $\mathcal{T}[\![P]\!]_\alpha \wedge c$ (ignoring the auxiliary relations introduced).*

The $\longmapsto$ rewrite relation is terminating and if some maximal reduction sequence leads to cost coefficient r' then so do all.

Proof. See Appendix B.

5   Conclusion

The search for the techniques reported here was partly stimulated by the Theorem of Robertson and Seymour (see e.g. [6]) that says that for a large class of properties of graphs (essentially those that are closed under taking subgraphs) it can be decided in cubic time whether or not a graph has the property. While not immediately applicable to the problem of control flow analysis for calculi of computation it nonetheless motivates careful scrutiny of those instances where more than cubic time seems to be needed. Indeed we managed to reduce two previously published bounds from a higher polynomial to cubic and we are currently working on extending the techniques to deal also with the full ambient calculus where communication is admitted.

References

1. A. Aiken. Introduction to set constraint-based program analysis. *Science of Computer Programming*, 35:79–111, 1999.
2. C. Bodei, P. Degano, F. Nielson, and H. Riis Nielson. Static analysis for the π-calculus with applications to security. *Information and Computation*, (to appear), 2001.
3. C. Bodei, P. Degano, F. Nielson, and H. Riis Nielson. Control flow analysis for the π-calculus. In *Proceedings of CONCUR'98*, volume 1466 of *LNCS*, pages 84–98. Springer-Verlag, 1998.
4. L. Cardelli and A. D. Gordon. Mobile ambients. In *Proceedings of FoSSaCS'98*, volume 1378 of *LNCS*, pages 140–155. Springer-Verlag, 1998.
5. W. F. Dowling and J. H. Gallier. Linear-time algorithms for testing the satisfiability of propositional Horn formulae. *Journal of Logic Programming*, 3:267–284, 1984.
6. J. van Leeuwen. Graph Algorithms. *Handbook of Theoretical Computer Science*, A:525–631, 1990.
7. D. McAllester. On the complexity analysis of static analyses. In *6th Static Analysis Symposium (SAS)*, pages 312–329. LNCS 1694, Springer Verlag, 1999.
8. R. Milner, J. Parrow, and D. Walker. A calculus of mobile processes (I and II). *Information and Computation*, 100(1):1–77, 1992.
9. F. Nielson, H. Riis Nielson, and C. L. Hankin. *Principles of Program Analysis*. Springer, 1999.
10. F. Nielson, H. Riis Nielson, R. R. Hansen, and J. G. Jensen. Validating firewalls in mobile ambients. In *Proceedings of CONCUR'99*, volume 1664 of *LNCS*, pages 463–477, 1999.
11. J. Rehof and T. Mogensen. Tractable constraints in finite semilattices. *Science of Computer Programming (SCP)*, 35(1):191–221, 1999.
12. M. Yannakakis. Graph-theoretic concepts in database theory. In *9th ACM Symp. on Principles of Database Systems (PODS)*, pages 230–242, 1990.

A   Proof of Proposition 1

The proof proceeds in three phases. First we transform $c = c_1 \wedge \cdots \wedge c_n$ to $\tilde{c}$ by replacing every universal quantification $\forall x :$ clause by the conjunction of all N possible instantiations of clause and every existential quantification $\exists x :$ pre by the disjunction of all N possible instantiations of pre. The resulting clause $\tilde{c}$ is logically equivalent to c, has size

$$\mathcal{O}(N^{r_1} \cdot n_1 + \cdots + N^{r_m} \cdot n_m) \tag{1}$$

and is *boolean*; the latter just means that there are no variables or quantifications and all literals are viewed as nullary predicates.

For the second phase we now describe a transformation $F \longmapsto F_1, \ldots, F_l$ that for each boolean HCS formula F, produces a sequence of boolean "almost-HC" formulae $F_1, \ldots, F_l$. The transformation first replaces all top-level conjunctions in F with ",". Then it proceeds by successively replacing clauses occurring in the sequence with sequences of simpler ones.

$$\begin{aligned}
\text{pre} \Rightarrow \text{clause}_1 \wedge \text{clause}_2 &\longmapsto \text{pre} \Rightarrow A_{\text{fresh}}, \\
&\qquad A_{\text{fresh}} \Rightarrow \text{clause}_1, \ A_{\text{fresh}} \Rightarrow \text{clause}_2 \\
\text{pre}_1 \Rightarrow \text{pre}_2 \Rightarrow \text{clause} &\longmapsto \text{pre}_1 \wedge \text{pre}_2 \Rightarrow \text{clause} \\
\text{pre} \Rightarrow \mathbf{1} &\longmapsto \mathbf{1}
\end{aligned}$$

Here A_{fresh} is a new fresh nullary predicate generated for each application of the relevant transformation. The transformation is completed, with result $\tilde{F}$, as soon as none of these rewrite rules can be applied. Clearly the conjunction of the resulting formulae $\tilde{F}$ is logically equivalent to F (ignoring the fresh predicates).

To show that this process terminates and that the size of $\tilde{F}$ is at most a constant times the size of the input formula F, we assign a cost to the formulae. Let us define the *cost* of a sequence of clauses as the sum of costs of all occurrences of predicate symbols and operators (excluding ",") and $\mathbf{1}$. In general, the cost of a symbol or operator is 1 — except implications "$\Rightarrow$" which count 2, and conjunctions in conclusions which count 8. Then the first rule decreases the cost from $k + 10$ to $k + 9$, the second rule decreases the cost from $k + 4$ to $k + 3$, whereas the third rule decreases the cost from $k + 3$ to 1 (for suitable values of k). Since the cost of the initial sequence is at most 8 times the size of F, only a linear number of rewrite steps can be performed. Since each step increases the size at most by a constant, we conclude that the $\tilde{F}$ has increased just by a constant factor. Consequently, when applying this transformation to $\tilde{c}$, we obtain a boolean formula without sharing of size as in (1).

Finally, the third phase consists in solving the resulting system of boolean Horn clauses (possibly with disjunctions). This can be done in linear time using the techniques in e.g. [11]. Alternatively one can remove also the disjunctions, by replacing each $\text{pre}_1 \vee \text{pre}_2$ by A_{fresh} and two new clauses $\text{pre}_1 \Rightarrow A_{\text{fresh}}$ and $\text{pre}_2 \Rightarrow A_{\text{fresh}}$. Assigning all symbols a cost of 1 — except disjunction that counts 6 — suffices for showing that the size does not increase by more than a constant factor here as well. The resulting system can then be solved in linear time by the classical techniques of e.g. [5].

B   Proof of Proposition 3

It is straightforward to prove that $(\mathcal{T}', \alpha', c')$ is a linear CH constraint specification of cost coefficient $r' \leq r$ and that the least solution to $\mathcal{T}'[\![P]\!]_{\alpha'} \wedge c'$ equals the least solution to $\mathcal{T}[\![P]\!]_{\alpha} \wedge c$ (ignoring the auxiliary relations introduced).

The key ingredient in showing that $\longmapsto$ is terminating is to note that $\stackrel{o}{\mapsto}$ is only applied to formulae whose cost coefficient is at least 4, that the cost coefficient is reduced by 1, and that all auxiliary clauses generated have cost coefficient at most 3.

The key ingredient in showing that all maximal transformation sequences of $\longmapsto$ lead to the same cost coefficient is to note that $\stackrel{o}{\mapsto}$ is confluent. To show this we develop a simple graph model and then prove a diamond property. The undirected graph g_c associated with a clause

$$c = \forall y_1 : \cdots \forall y_k : \mathsf{pre}' \Rightarrow R(\tilde{w})$$

has nodes $\{y_1, \cdots, y_k, \Box\}$ and edges between any two nodes that are neighbours (in the sense of Subsection 4.2). We now present three reduction rules on undirected graphs which allow the removal of candidate nodes (in the sense of Subsection 4.2).

Formally, let $g_i = (V_i, E_i)$, $i = 1, 2$, denote two undirected finite graphs and let Y be the complement of the set of candidate nodes. We say that g_1 can be reduced to g_2 (by removal of vertex v), i.e., $g_1 \rightarrow_v g_2$, provided that $v \in V_1 \backslash Y$ and $V_2 = V_1 \backslash \{v\}$, and one of the following conditions are satisfied:

- $\deg v = 0$ and $E_2 = E_1$; or
- $\deg v = 1$ and $E_2 = E_1 \backslash \{e\}$ where e is the unique edge incident with v; or
- $\deg v = 2$ and $E_2 = (E_1 \backslash \{e_1, e_2\}) \cup \{e\}$ where $e_i = \{u_i, v\}$, $i = 1, 2$ are the two unique edges incident with v, and $e = \{u_1, u_2\}$.

Whenever one of the rules of Subsection 4.2 is applied the effect on the undirected graph is recorded by one of the rules above (ignoring the clauses with cost coefficient at most 3) and vice versa. In particular, this graph formalization reveals that our tiling technique can be seen as a generalization of the reduction of "chain queries" in Datalog as considered in [12].

Let g denote a finite undirected graph with n nodes. Since every reduction step decreases the number of vertices by 1, we conclude that every maximal sequence of reduction steps has length at most $n - |Y|$. Since the reduction is terminating, Proposition 3 follows from the following 1-step diamond property:

Lemma 3. *Assume that for finite undirected graphs g_0, g_1, g_2, and vertices $v_1 \neq v_2$, we have $g_0 \rightarrow_{v_1} g_1$ and $g_0 \rightarrow_{v_2} g_2$. Then there is a finite undirected graph g_3 such that also $g_1 \rightarrow_{v_2} g_3$ and $g_2 \rightarrow_{v_1} g_3$:*

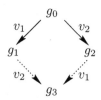

Proof. Lemma 3 is proved by case distinction on the various possibilities of relative positions of v_1 and v_2 in g_0. In case, v_1 and v_2 are not neighbours in g_0, the property holds, since their reductions do not interfere. Therefore assume that v_1 and v_2 are neighbours in g_0, i.e., $\{v_1, v_2\}$ is an edge in g_0. Then either both have degree 2, or, one of them has degree 2 whereas the other has degree 1, or both have degree 1. Assume for example that v_1 and v_2 have degrees 2 and 1, respectively. Then there must be an edge $\{u, v_1\}$ in g_0 for some $u \neq v_2$:

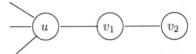

Reduction of v_1 results in a graph g_1 where v_1 has been removed and the two edges $\{u, v_1\}$ and $\{v_1, v_2\}$ have been replaced with an edge $\{u, v_2\}$:

In particular, the degree of v_2 is still 1. Accordingly, reduction of v_2 results in a graph g_2 where v_1 has been removed together with the edge $\{v_1, v_2\}$:

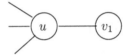

In particular, the degree of v_1 has decreased to 1. Thus, reduction of v_2 in g_1 as well as reduction of v_1 in g_2 results in the same graph g_3 which can be obtained from g_1 by removing both v_1 and v_2 together with the edges $\{v_1, v_2\}$ and $\{u, v_1\}$:

The cases where v_1 and v_2 are neighbours and both have degree 2 or 1 is similar. This concludes the proof of Lemma 3.   □

The Recursive Record Semantics of Objects Revisited

(Extended Abstract)*

Gérard Boudol

INRIA Sophia Antipolis
BP 93 – 06902   Sophia Antipolis Cedex, France

Abstract. In a call-by-value language, representing objects as recursive
records requires using an unsafe fixpoint. We design, for a core language including extensible records, a type system which rules out unsafe
recursion and still supports the reconstruction of a principal type. We
illustrate by means of various examples the expressive power of this language with respect to object-oriented programming constructs.

1   Introduction

During the past fifteen years there has been very active research about the formalization of object-oriented programming concepts. One of the main purposes
of this research was to design operational models of objects supporting rich type
systems, so that one could benefit both from the flexibility of the object-oriented
style, and from the safety properties guaranteed by typing. Let us be more precise here: our goal is to have an expressive language – as far as object-oriented
constructs are concerned – with a type discipline à la ML [12,24], i.e. implicit
typing with reconstruction of a principal type, ruling out run-time errors. This
goal has proven difficult to achieve, and most of the many proposals that were
put forward fall short of achieving it – with the exception of OCAML [21,27],
that we will discuss later.

While the meaning of "typing à la ML" should be clear, it is perhaps less easy
to see what is meant by "object-oriented". We do not claim to answer to this
question here. Let us just say that, in our view, objects encapsulate a state and
react to messages, i.e. method invocations, by udating their state and sending
messages, possibly to themselves. Moreover, in our view, object-orientation also
involves inheritance, which includes – but should not be limited to, as we shall
see – the ability to add and redefine methods. With this informal notion of
object-orientation in mind, let us review some of the proposals we alluded to.

An elegant proposal was made by Wand [31], based on his *row variables* [30],
consisting of a class-based model, where classes are functions from instance variables and a self parameter to extensible records of methods, and objects are

---

* Work partially supported by the RNRT Project MARVEL, and by the CTI "Objets
Migrants: Modélisation et Vérification", France Télécom R&D.

D. Sands (Ed.): ESOP 2001, LNCS 2028, pp. 269–283, 2001.

fixpoints of instantiated classes, that is, recursive records. In this model invoking the method of an object amounts to selecting the corresponding component of the record representing the object. An operation of record extension is used to provide a simple model of inheritance, à la SMALLTALK. Unfortunately, although its elegance and simplicity make it very appealing, Wand's model is not expressive enough. More specifically, it does not support state changes in objects: one may override a method in an inherited class, but one apparently cannot modify the state of the object during its life-time (see for instance [1] Section 6.7.2). This is because in creating the object, the self parameter is bound too early.

Wand's model is an instance of what is known as the *recursive record semantics* for objects (see [16]), initiated by Cardelli [8]. Based on this idea that an object is the fixpoint of an instantiated class, Cook proposed a more elaborate model [11], where updating the state of an object is possible, by creating new objects, instances of the same class. This model is operationally quite expressive, but the type theory that it uses is also quite elaborate, and does not fulfil our desires, of reconstruction of a principal type. The same remark actually applies to all the object models that use higher-order types, e.g. [1,6,13,15,25].

In another approach, due to Kamin [20] and known as the *self-application semantics*, an object is a record of pre-methods, that are functions of the object itself. The object is bound to self only when a method is invoked, by applying the pre-method to the object. In this way, the state of the object may dynamically be updated. In this model, which looks indeed operationally satisfactory, an object is not quite a record, since from a typing point of view, we must know that the first parameters (that is, self) of all its pre-methods have the same type. In other words, one must have in this approach specific constructs for objects and object types, depending on the type of self, thus different from record types. This has been developed in *object calculi*, most notably by Fisher and Mitchell [14,15,16] (who call it "the axiomatic approach") and Abadi and Cardelli [1], but as we already noticed, in calculi that support a rich form of inheritance, and in particular object extension, like [15], the type theory which is used is quite elaborate, and does not support implicit typing.

Object calculi claim to fix the principles for objects, thus providing simple formal models, but they actually take design decisions, about inheritance in particular – a concept which is still a matter of debate in the object-oriented programming community (see [29] for example). As a matter of fact, many of the proposals for an object model, including OCAML, follow this approach of designing a specific calculus, e.g. [1,3,6,15,27]. However, there could be some benefits from deriving object-oriented concepts from more basic principles: first, their typing could be derived within simple, unquestionable typing systems. Second, they could be better integrated in a standard computational model, in which one could formalize and compare various approaches to objects, and get more flexible object models. Furthermore, we would not have to develop specific theories for reasoning about them.

In this paper we pursue Wand's approach, aiming at encoding object-oriented concepts by means of extensible records. One may observe that the update operation of object calculi [1,15] is actually overloaded: it serves both in inheritance, to override methods, and in the dynamic behaviour of an object, to update the state. As we have seen, the first usage is not problematic in Wand's model, whereas the second is. Then an obvious idea is to abandon the "functional update" approach in favor of a rather more natural *imperative update* approach, as in [1, 3,13,27]. This means that we are in a language with *references* (following ML's terminology), where a call-by-value strategy is assumed for evaluation. Now a new problem arises: to build objects as recursive records one must have the ability to build recursive non-functional values, and this, in principle, is not supported in a typed call-by-value language. More specifically, we would like to use (let rec $x = N$ in M), where N may be of a record type. This is evaluated by first computing a value for N, returning a cyclic binding to this value for x, and then computing M. Notice that side effects and creation of new references arising from the evaluation of N are completed before a cyclic binding is returned. This is what we need to install the state of an object before returning its (recursive) record of methods. The resulting object model is similar to what is known as the "cyclic record" encoding, see [1], Sections 18.2.4 and 18.3.4.

As remarked by Rémy [26], a recursive record semantics of objects works fine with the let rec construct, except that this construct is *unsafe*. Indeed, some langages, like SCHEME or OCAML, provide us with this feature, but, except for defining recursive functions, its semantics is implementation-dependent. More precisely, in computing (let rec $x = N$ in M), it could happen that evaluating N we have to call the value of x, which is not yet computed, thus getting stuck at this point. One must then have means to prevent such a run-time error in order to design a "safe" object model from recursive records. We must point out that, although this problem of determining restrictions on recursive definitions to ensure that they define something is not at all a new one, no obvious solution to our specific problem emerges from the literature, since (let rec $x = (Gx)$ in M) must sometimes be accepted, where G reduces to a "generator" $\lambda \text{self} M$ [10].

The main contribution of this paper is a solution to this problem: first, we extend the core "Reference ML" language, as considered by Wright and Felleisen [32], with operations on records, similar to the ones of Cardelli and Mitchell [9]. We then provide a type system for this language, refining the simple types by assigning a boolean "degree of harmlessness" to the argument of a function, considering types of the form $\theta^d \to \tau$, and to variables in the typing context. Typically, a variable occurring within a value is harmless, hence may have degree 1, and applying a function of type $\theta^0 \to \tau$ means that the argument might be put in a dangerous position. The "harmlessness degree" is used to determine whether a variable may or may not be safely recursively bound. We show that the evaluation of a typable term either diverges or returns a value, thus avoiding to get stuck in run-time errors, and, adapting a result by Jategaonkar and Mitchell [19], we show that a principal type may be computed for any typable expression. Although our goal here is not to design and encode an object-oriented layer in the language, we examine various examples, to assess the usefulness of the approach, and to illustrate the expressive power of the model.

Note. The proofs of the technical results are not included in this extended abstract. They are to be found in the full version of the paper, at the author's web page (`http://www-sop.inria/mimosa/personnel/Gerard.Boudol.html`).

$$
\begin{array}{lll}
M, N \ldots \; ::= & & \textit{expressions} \\
& V \mid (MN) \mid (\text{let } D \text{ in } M) & \textit{core constructs} \\
& \mid \; \langle M, \ell = N \rangle \mid (M.\ell) \mid (M\backslash\ell) & \textit{record operations} \\
V, W \ldots \; ::= & x \mid \text{ref} \mid \, ! \mid \text{set} \mid (\text{set } V) & \textit{values} \\
& \mid \; \lambda x M \mid () \mid R & \\
R \; ::= & x \mid \Diamond \mid \langle R, \ell = V \rangle & \textit{record values} \\
D \; ::= & x = N \mid \text{rec } x = N & \textit{declarations}
\end{array}
$$

Fig. 1. Syntax

2   The Calculus

Assuming that a set $\mathcal{X}$ of variables, ranged over by x, y, $z \ldots$, and a set $\mathcal{L}$ of labels are given, the syntax of our core language is given in Figure 1, where $x \in \mathcal{X}$ and $\ell \in \mathcal{L}$. It contains the "Reference ML" calculus of [32] – defining the call-by-value fixpoint combinator Y as $(\text{let rec } y = \lambda f. f(\lambda x.(yf)x) \text{ in } y)$, and denoting $:=$ by set. Free (fv) and bound (bv) variables are defined as usual, and we denote by $\{x \mapsto N\}M$ the capture-free substitution.

Regarding records, we use the operations of [9], denoting by $\langle M, \ell = N \rangle$ the record M extended with a new field, labelled ℓ, with value N. As in [9], this will only be well-typed if M does not exhibit an ℓ field, whereas the restriction operation, still denoted $(M\backslash\ell)$ and consisting of removing the ℓ field from M, will only be well-typed here if M does contain an ℓ field. The overriding operation is denoted $\langle M, \ell \leftarrow N \rangle$; this is an abbreviation for $\langle (M\backslash\ell), \ell = N \rangle$. We shall write $\langle \ell_1 = M_1, \ldots, \ell_n = M_n \rangle$ for the record $\langle \cdots \langle \Diamond, \ell_1 = M_1 \rangle \ldots, \ell_n = M_n \rangle$.

Now we specify the semantics of our language, defining an *evaluation relation* $M \to M'$, that we also call *local* (or *functional*) *reduction*, which can be performed in *evaluation contexts*. The axioms and rules are given in Figure 3. To describe the semantics of the imperative constructs, given by the rules for *global reduction* in Figure 4, we enrich the language with a denumerable set $\mathcal{N}$ of *names*, or *locations* u, v, $w \ldots$, distinct from the variables and the labels. These names are also values. A *configuration* is a pair $(S \mid M)$ of an expression M and a *store*, that is a mapping from locations to values. We use the following syntax for stores:

$$
S \; ::= \; \varepsilon \mid u := V; S
$$

$$\mathbf{E} ::= [] \mid (\mathbf{E}N) \mid (V\mathbf{E}) \mid (\text{let } x = \mathbf{E} \text{ in } M) \mid (\text{let rec } x = \mathbf{E} \text{ in } M)$$
$$\mid \langle \mathbf{E}, \ell = N \rangle \mid \langle R, \ell = \mathbf{E} \rangle \mid (\mathbf{E}.\ell) \mid (\mathbf{E} \backslash \ell)$$

Fig. 2. Evaluation Contexts

$$(\lambda x M V) \rightarrow \{x \mapsto V\} M$$
$$(\text{let } x = V \text{ in } M) \rightarrow \{x \mapsto V\} M$$
$$(\text{let rec } x = V \text{ in } M) \rightarrow \{x \mapsto (\text{let rec } x = V \text{ in } V)\} M$$
$$(\langle R, \ell = V \rangle.\ell) \rightarrow V$$
$$(\langle R, \ell = V \rangle.\ell') \rightarrow (R.\ell') \qquad\qquad \ell' \neq \ell$$
$$(\langle R, \ell = V \rangle \backslash \ell) \rightarrow R$$
$$(\langle R, \ell = V \rangle \backslash \ell') \rightarrow \langle (R \backslash \ell'), \ell = V \rangle \qquad\qquad \ell' \neq \ell$$
$$M \rightarrow M' \;\Rightarrow\; \mathbf{E}[M] \rightarrow \mathbf{E}[M']$$

Fig. 3. Local Reduction

$$M \rightarrow M' \Rightarrow (S \mid M) \rightarrow (S \mid M')$$
$$(S \mid \mathbf{E}[(\text{ref } V)]) \rightarrow (u := V; S \mid \mathbf{E}[u]) \qquad u \notin \text{dom}(S)$$
$$(S \mid \mathbf{E}[(!u)]) \rightarrow (S \mid \mathbf{E}[V]) \qquad\qquad S(u) = V$$
$$(S \mid \mathbf{E}[((\text{set } u)V)]) \rightarrow ([u := V]S \mid \mathbf{E}[()])$$

Fig. 4. Global Reduction

The value $S(u)$ of a name in the store, and the partial operation $[u := V]S$ of updating the store, are defined in the obvious way. In the rules for global reduction, we have omitted the side condition that $\text{fv}(V) \cap \text{capt}(\mathbf{E}) = \emptyset$, where $\text{capt}(\mathbf{E})$ is the set of variables that are bound in $\mathbf{E}$ by a let rec binder introducing a sub-context. Let us see an example – which will be the standard object-oriented example of a "point". Assuming that some arithmetical operations are given, we define a "class" of unidimensional points as follows:

$$\text{let point} = \lambda x \lambda \text{self} \langle \text{pos} = \text{ref } x,$$
$$\text{move} = \lambda y((\text{set self.pos})(!\text{self.pos} + y)) \rangle \text{ in} \dots$$

Within the scope of this definition, we may define a point object, instance of that class, by intantiating the position parameter x to some initial value, and building a recursive record of methods. Let us define the fixpoint operator fix as follows:

$$\text{fix} =_{\text{def}} \lambda f(\text{let rec } x = fx \text{ in } x)$$

Then we have for instance, if we let $V = \lambda y((\text{set } x.\text{pos})(!x.\text{pos} + y))$ and $R = \langle \text{pos} = u, \text{move} = V \rangle$:

$$(\varepsilon \mid \text{fix}(\text{point } 0)) \overset{*}{\to} (\varepsilon \mid (\text{let rec } x = \langle \text{pos} = \text{ref } 0, \text{move} = V \rangle \text{ in } x))$$

$$\to (u := 0; \varepsilon \mid (\text{let rec } x = R \text{ in } x))$$

$$\overset{*}{\to} (u := 0; \varepsilon \mid \langle \text{pos} = u, \text{move} = \{x \mapsto O\}V \rangle$$

where $O = (\text{let rec } x = R \text{ in } R)$. One can see that there are two parts in this evaluated object: a state part, which records the (mutable) position of the object, and the (recursive, immutable) record of methods. Moreover, the state can only be accessed using the methods. Now imagine that we want to enhance the point class with a clear method that resets the position to the origin. Then we introduce a new class inheriting from point:

$$\text{let point}' = \lambda x \lambda \text{self} \langle (\text{point } x)\text{self}, \text{clear} = ((\text{set self.pos})0) \rangle \text{ in} \dots$$

However, we cannot create an object instance of that class. More precisely, the type system will reject an expression like $\text{fix}(\text{point}' 0)$, and rightly so. Indeed, if we try to compute this expression, we get stuck in $(u := 0; \varepsilon \mid (\text{let rec } x = \mathbf{E}[x] \text{ in } x)$ where $\mathbf{E} = \langle \text{pos} = u, \text{move} = V, \text{clear} = ((\text{set } [].\text{pos})0) \rangle$. In the clear method, the self parameter ought to be protected from being evaluated, by defining this method as a "thunk" $\text{clear} = \lambda y((\text{set self.pos})0)$. This is the main technical point of the paper: to create objects instance of some class, we must be able to sometimes accept, sometimes reject terms of the form $(\text{let rec } x = (Gx) \text{ in } N)$, in particular when $G \overset{*}{\to} \lambda \text{self} M$, depending on whether the function (with side effects) G is "protective" towards its argument or not.

In order to establish a type safety result, we need to analyse the possible behaviour of expressions under evaluation: computing an expression may end on a value, or may go forever, but there are other possibilities – in particular an expression may "go wrong" [24] (or "be faulty", following the terminology of [32]). Our analysis is slightly non-standard here, since we have to deal with open terms. Besides the faulty expressions, we distinguish what we call "global redexes" and "head expressions", where a variable appears in a position where it has to be evaluated, and where something has to be done with its value.

DEFINITION 0.1. *A term M is a global redex if M is $\mathbf{E}[(\text{ref } V)]$, or $\mathbf{E}[(!u)]$, or else $\mathbf{E}[((\text{set } u)V)]$ for some value V and location u, with $\text{fv}(V) \cap \text{capt}(\mathbf{E}) = \emptyset$.*

DEFINITION 0.2. *A term M is a head expression if $M = \mathbf{H}[x]$ with $x \notin \text{capt}(\mathbf{H})$, where the $\mathbf{H}$ contexts are given as follows:*

$$\mathbf{H} ::= \mathbf{E}[([]V)] \mid \mathbf{E}[(![])] \mid \mathbf{E}[(\text{set } [])] \mid \mathbf{E}[([].\ell)] \mid \mathbf{E}[([]\backslash\ell)]$$

DEFINITION 0.3. *A term M is faulty if it contains a sub-expression of one of the following forms:*
(i) (VN), where V is either a location, or $()$, or a record value;
(ii) $(\text{let rec } x = \mathbf{H}[x] \text{ in } M)$ with $x \notin \text{capt}(\mathbf{H})$
(iii) $(\text{let rec } x = \mathbf{E}[N] \text{ in } M)$ where N is either $(\text{ref } V)$ or $((\text{set } u)V)$ with $x \in \text{fv}(V)$;

(iv) $(!V)$ or $(\mathsf{set}\ V)$ where V is neither a variable nor a location;

(v) $\langle V, \ell = N \rangle$ where V is not a record value;

(vi) $(V.\ell)$ or $(V \backslash \ell)$, where V is neither a variable, nor a non-empty record-value.

Then our first result is:

PROPOSITION 0.4. *For any expression M, either M reduces, i.e. $M \to M'$ for some M', or M is a head expression, or a faulty expression, or a global redex, or a value.*

COROLLARY 0.5. *For any closed configuration $(S \mid M)$ such that any location occurring in M is in $\mathsf{dom}(S)$, either its evaluation does not terminate, or it ends with $(S' \mid N)$ where N is either faulty or a value.*

3 The Type System

The aim in using a type system is to prevent run-time errors – and also to provide some interesting information about expressions. Then we have to design such a system in a way that rules out faulty expressions. The only case which is non-standard is the one of let rec expressions, that is (ii) and (iii) of Definition 0.3. To exclude unsafe recursion, we will use "decorated types", where the decorations, also called "harmlessness degrees" are boolean values 0 or 1 (with $0 \leqslant 1$), to which we must add, in order to obtain principal types, degree variables p, $q \ldots$ We denote by d, $e \ldots \in \mathcal{D}$ these *degrees*, either constant or variable.

Following Milner [24], we use a polymorphic let construct. This is crucial for defining classes that may be inherited in various ways, and instantiated into objects. Then we will use *type schemes*. As in [19], we do not allow the same label to occur several times in a given record type – but our treatment of row variables is quite different from the one of [19]. Therefore, in quantifying on a row variable, we must take into account the context in which it occurs, by means of the set L of labels that it must not contain. We call such a finite set of labels an *annotation*[1], and we have a simple "annotating" system to ensure that (record) types are well-formed. Given a set $\mathcal{T}y\mathcal{V}ar$ of type variables, the syntax of types and type schemes is:

$$\tau, \theta \ldots \ ::= \ \mathsf{unit} \ \mid \ t \ \mid \ (\theta^d \to \tau) \ \mid \ \tau\ \mathsf{ref} \ \mid \ \rho$$
$$\rho \ ::= \ t \ \mid \ \Diamond \ \mid \ \langle \rho, \ell : \tau \rangle$$
$$\sigma, \varsigma \ldots \ ::= \ \tau \ \mid \ (\forall C.\sigma)$$

where t is any type variable, d is any degree, and $C = t_1 :: L_1, \ldots, t_n :: L_n$. The annotation of type variables is not the only constraint we have to take into account in the type system: we also have to deal with constraints on degrees, that take the form of a set of inequalities $p \leqslant a$ where p is a degree variable and a is a *degree expression*, built from degrees by using the meet operation $\sqcap$. We denote by a, b, $c \ldots \in \mathcal{DE}xp$ these expressions. In order to give a simple form

---

[1] we borrow this terminology from Fisher's thesis [14].

to typing rules, we group the two kinds of constraints into a single component, called a *constraint*, still denoted by C. Notice that the constraints on degrees are obviously satisfiable, e.g. assigning uniformly 0 to the degree variables. For lack of space, we omit the constraint system, by which one can prove that a type is well-formed and does not posses some given labels, in notation $C \vdash \sigma :: L$, and that a degree inequality is a consequence of the given constraint, denoted $C \vdash a \leqslant b$ (the corresponding inference systems are quite trivial).

As usual, we need the notion of an instance of a type scheme, obtained by substituting not only types for type variables, but also degrees for degree variables. Then a type and degree substitution S is a mapping from type variables to types, and from degree variables to degrees (not degree expressions), which is the identity, except for a finite set $\mathsf{dom}(S)$ of variables. Moreover, we need to ensure that applying a substitution to a type scheme, which we denote $S(\sigma)$, results in a well-formed type. Given two constraints C_0 and C_1, we then define $\mathit{Sub}(C_0, C_1)$ as follows:

$$S \in \mathit{Sub}(C_0, C_1) \quad \Leftrightarrow_{\mathrm{def}} \quad \mathsf{dom}(S) \subseteq \mathsf{dom}(C_0) \ \& \ C_1 \vdash S(C_0)$$

where $S(C) = \{\, S(t) :: L \mid t :: L \in C \,\} \cup \{\, S(p) \leqslant S(a) \mid p \leqslant a \in C \,\}$. Then for instance the standard relation of being a *generic instance* (see [12]) is relative to some constraint, and is written $C \vdash \sigma \preceq \varsigma$.

The typing judgements have the form $C \,; \Gamma \vdash M : \tau$, where C is a constraint, τ is a type[2], and Γ is a *typing context*. This maps a finite set $\mathsf{dom}(\Gamma)$ of variables not only to type schemes, but also to degree expressions. The idea is that with a variable x we associate an assumption about the fact that it will or will not occur in a dangerous position, typically $\mathbf{H}[x]$ (some other cases are mentionned in the point (iii) of Definition 0.3). This assumption is the *harmlessness degree*, or simply the degree of the variable in the context – 0 standing for "dangerous". We also need to type locations, and therefore a context is a mapping from a finite set of variables to pairs (σ, a), written σ^a, and from a finite set of locations to types. We shall write $\Gamma_{\mathsf{typ}}(x) = \sigma$ and $\Gamma_{\mathsf{deg}}(x) = a$ if $\Gamma(x) = \sigma^a$, and similarly $\Gamma_{\mathsf{typ}}(u) = \Gamma(u)$. To simplify the presentation of the system, we omit the obvious side conditions by which the types and contexts introduced in the axioms are well-formed with respect to the constraint C. We use the following predicate and operations on the typing contexts:

(i) $C \vdash \Delta \leqslant \Gamma$ if and only if $\Gamma_{\mathsf{typ}} = \Delta_{\mathsf{typ}}$ and $C \vdash \Gamma_{\mathsf{deg}}(x) \leqslant \Delta_{\mathsf{deg}}(x)$ for all x;

(ii) let δ be a mapping from variables to degrees. Then we define the context Γ^δ as follows: $(\Gamma^\delta)_{\mathsf{typ}} = \Gamma_{\mathsf{typ}}$ and $(\Gamma^\delta)_{\mathsf{deg}}(x) = \delta(x)$. We let $\Gamma^{\lceil \delta \rceil}$ denote $\Gamma^{\gamma \sqcap \delta}$, where $\gamma = \Gamma_{\mathsf{deg}}$.

We mainly use these last notations when δ is $\lambda x(\text{if } x \in \mathsf{fv}(M) \text{ then } a \text{ else } 1)$, which is abbreviated into a_M. We also abusively write 1 for $\lambda x.1$, and similarly for 0.

Now let us comment on some of the rules that are presented in Figure 5. The first one is a "degree weakening" rule, stating that "optimistic" assumptions,

---

[2] to simplify the presentation we do not include the usual rules of instantiation and generalization (see [12]), but they would easily be shown to be admissible if judgements $C \,; \Gamma \vdash M : \sigma$ were allowed, and therefore we will use them in the examples.

$$\frac{C\,;\Gamma \vdash M : \tau\ ,\ C \vdash \Delta \leqslant \Gamma}{C\,;\Delta \vdash M : \tau} \qquad \frac{C \vdash \sigma \succeq \tau}{C\,;x : \sigma^1 , \Gamma \vdash x : \tau} \qquad C\,;u : \tau , \Gamma \vdash u : \tau\,\mathsf{ref}$$

$$\frac{C\,;x : \theta^d , \Gamma \vdash M : \tau}{C\,;\Gamma^1 \vdash \lambda x M : (\theta^d \to \tau)} \qquad \frac{C\,;\Gamma \vdash M : \theta^d \to \tau\ ,\ C\,;\Gamma \vdash N : \theta}{C\,;\Gamma^{\lceil 0_M \sqcap d_N \rceil} \vdash (MN) : \tau}$$

$$\frac{C' , C\,;\Gamma \vdash N : \theta\ ,\ C\,;x : (\forall C'.\theta)^a , \Gamma \vdash M : \tau}{C\,;\Gamma^{\lceil a_N \rceil} \vdash (\mathsf{let}\ x = N\ \mathsf{in}\ M) : \tau} \quad (*)$$

$$\frac{C' , C\,;x : \theta^1 , \Gamma \vdash N : \theta\ ,\ C\,;x : (\forall C'.\theta)^a , \Gamma \vdash M : \tau}{C\,;\Gamma^{\lceil a_N \rceil} \vdash (\mathsf{let\,rec}\ x = N\ \mathsf{in}\ M) : \tau} \quad (*)$$

$$C\,;\Gamma \vdash \mathsf{ref} : \tau^0 \to \tau\,\mathsf{ref} \qquad C\,;\Gamma \vdash\, ! : (\tau\,\mathsf{ref})^0 \to \tau$$

$$C\,;\Gamma \vdash \mathsf{set} : (\tau\,\mathsf{ref})^0 \to \tau^0 \to \mathsf{unit} \qquad C\,;\Gamma \vdash () : \mathsf{unit}$$

$$C\,;\Gamma \vdash \Diamond : \Diamond \qquad \frac{C\,;\Gamma \vdash M : \rho\ ,\ C\,;\Gamma \vdash N : \tau\ ,\ C \vdash \rho :: \{\ell\}}{C\,;\Gamma \vdash \langle M , \ell = N \rangle : \langle \rho , \ell : \tau \rangle}$$

$$\frac{C\,;\Gamma \vdash M : \langle \rho , \ell : \tau \rangle}{C\,;\Gamma^{0_M} \vdash (M.\ell) : \tau} \qquad \frac{C\,;\Gamma \vdash M : \langle \rho , \ell : \tau \rangle}{C\,;\Gamma^{0_M} \vdash (M\backslash \ell) : \rho}$$

$$C\,;\Gamma \vdash \varepsilon \qquad \frac{C\,;u : \tau , \Gamma \vdash V : \tau\ ,\ C\,;u : \tau , \Gamma \vdash S}{C\,;u : \tau , \Gamma \vdash u := V;S} \qquad \frac{C\,;\Gamma \vdash S\ ,\ C\,;\Gamma \vdash M : \tau}{C\,;\Gamma \vdash (S \mid M) : \tau}$$

$(*)$ where $t \in \mathsf{dom}(C') \;\Rightarrow\; t \notin C , \Gamma$ and C' is empty if N is neither a value nor (let rec $x = V$ in V).

Fig. 5. The Type System

assigning for instance degree 1 to some variables, can always be safely downgraded. Notice that a variable in isolation is harmless: indeed the evaluation of (let rec $x = x$ in x) diverges, hence does not result in a run-time error. In the rule for abstraction of x, we assume that the degree of x does not contain the $\sqcap$ operation, but this is not a restriction, since we may always add a fresh constraint $p \leqslant a$ and use the weakening rule. The rule for abstraction promotes the typing context to a definitely harmless one (Γ^1), since all the variables occurring in the abstraction value are protected from being evaluated by the λ (notice that this holds for record values too). Conversely, the variables occurring in the function part of an application are potentially dangerous, like for instance x in $(\lambda y.xy)V$. Then they are all downgraded to having the degree 0. Regarding the argument, we must be more careful: applying a function of type $\theta^1 \to \tau$ that does not put its argument in danger, like λxx for instance, we may keep the degree of its free variable as it is. More generally, applying a function of type $\theta^d \to \tau$ places the argument in a position where the variables have a degree which is, at best, d or the degree they have in the argument. This is where we use the $\sqcap$ operation. For instance, we have, if $C = t :: \emptyset, t' : :: \emptyset, p \leqslant 0, q \leqslant r$:

$$\vdots$$

$$\frac{C \,;\, f : (t^r \to t')^0 \,,\, x : t^{r \sqcap 1} \vdash fx : t'}{C \,;\, f : (t^r \to t')^p \,,\, x : t^r \vdash fx : t'} \quad p \leqslant 0,\ q \leqslant r \sqcap 1$$

$$C \,;\, \vdash \lambda fx.fx : (t^r \to t')^p \to t^q \to t'$$

To see why we need the meet operation, the reader may try to type $f(gx)$, where the degree of x depends on the nature of both f and g. The rule for the let rec construct is the only one involving a real – i.e. possibly unsatisfiable – constraint on degrees, namely $1 \leqslant a$. It is exemplified by the following typing of the fixpoint combinator, where $\Gamma = f : (t^1 \to t)^1, x : t^1$ and $\Delta = f : (t^1 \to t)^0, x : t^1$:

$$\frac{\dfrac{t :: \emptyset \,;\, \Gamma \vdash f : (t^1 \to t) \qquad t :: \emptyset \,;\, \Gamma \vdash x : t}{t :: \emptyset \,;\, \Delta \vdash fx : t} \qquad \dfrac{t :: \emptyset \,;\, \Gamma \vdash x : t}{t :: \emptyset \,;\, \Delta \vdash x : t}}{\dfrac{t :: \emptyset \,;\, f : (t^1 \to t)^0 \vdash (\text{let rec } x = fx \text{ in } x) : t}{t :: \emptyset;\, \vdash \text{fix} : (t^1 \to t)^0 \to t}}$$

Notice that, as in ML, (let rec $f = \lambda xN$ in M) is always allowed, provided that M and N have appropriate typings. The functional core of the language concentrates all the subtelties of the use of degrees – the rest of the type system is quite trivial, and in particular there is not much choice in the typing of the record constructs.

There is a general rule governing typing, which is that all the variables that occur in an expression placed in a head position, that is in the hole in an **H** context, are regarded as potentially dangerous, as we have seen with the application construct. This explains the resulting downgraded typing context in the rules for selection and restriction. The clauses (ii) and (iii) of Definition 0.3 also indicate that referencing, de-referencing and assignment are not protective operations. Considering these explanations, one should not be surprised that the following holds:

LEMMA 0.6. *The faulty expressions are not typable.*

Then we have the standard "type preservation" property, which relies, as usual, on a property relating typing and substitution:

PROPOSITION (TYPE PRESERVATION) 0.7. *If C ; $\Gamma \vdash M : \tau$ and $M \overset{*}{\to} N$ then C ; $\Gamma \vdash N : \tau$.*

Proving a similar property for global reduction, and then combining these results with the Corollary 0.5 and the Lemma 0.6, we get:

THEOREM (TYPE SAFETY) 0.8. *For any typable closed configuration $(S \mid M)$ of type τ such that any location occurring in M is in $\mathsf{dom}(S)$, either its evaluation does not terminate, or it ends with $(S' \mid V)$ where V is a value of type τ.*

This is our first main result. The second one is that if an expression M is typable, then it has a computable principal type, of which any other type of M is an instance:

THEOREM (PRINCIPAL TYPE) 0.9. *There is an algorithm that, given Γ_{typ} and M, fails if M is not typable in the context Γ^γ for some γ, and otherwise returns a type τ, a degree assignment δ and a constraint C such that C ; $\Gamma^\delta \vdash M : \tau$, and if C' ; $\Gamma^\gamma \vdash M : \tau'$ then $\tau' = \mathsf{S}(\tau)$ and $C' \vdash \Gamma^\gamma \leqslant \mathsf{S}(\Gamma^\delta)$ for some substitution $\mathsf{S} \in \mathcal{S}ub(C, C')$.*

To perform type reconstruction we have, as usual, to solve equations on types, by means of unification. Using a "strict" record extension operation (and similarly a "strict" restriction), rather than the one originally used by Wand [30], which combines extension with overriding, allows one to solve these equations, up to annotation constraints, in a simple way, as shown by Jategaonkar and Mitchell [19]. As a matter of fact, we also have to solve some degree equalities $d = e$ arising from $\theta_0^d \to \tau_0 = \theta_1^e \to \tau_1$, but these are quite trivial (if d and e are both constants, then the equality is trivially true or false, and if one is a variable, the equality can be treated as a substitution). To construct a type for the let rec construct, we have to solve equations $a = 1$ (or $1 \leqslant a$), but these are also easy to solve, since $(a \sqcap b) = 1$ is equivalent to $a = 1$ and $b = 1$. The only case of failure arising from degrees is when we have to solve $0 = 1$, that is when a potentially dangerous recursion is detected.

4 Some Examples

In this section we illustrate the expressive power of our calculus, as regards object-orientation, both from an operational and from a typing point of view. Let us first see how to type the "point class" previously defined – assuming that $+$ is of type $\mathsf{int}^0 \to \mathsf{int}^0 \to \mathsf{int}$. We recall that this class is given by

$$\mathsf{point} = \lambda x \lambda \mathsf{self} \langle \mathsf{pos} = \mathsf{ref}\, x,$$
$$\mathsf{move} = \lambda y((\mathsf{set}\ \mathsf{self.pos})(!\mathsf{self.pos} + y)))$$

In the record of methods of the point class, the x parameter may have any type, but it is placed in a dangerous position, being an argument of ref. Then it has type t^0, where t is a type variable. Regarding the self parameter, we see from its use in the move method that it must have a record type, containing a field pos, of type int ref. Moreover, self only occurs within a value, and therefore it has type $\langle s, \mathsf{pos} : \mathsf{int}\,\mathsf{ref} \rangle^p$, with no constraint on p, where the row variable s must not contain the pos field. Then, abbreviating $(\forall t :: \emptyset.\sigma)$ into $(\forall t.\sigma)$, the (polymorphic) type of point is:

point: $\forall t.\forall s :: \{\text{pos}\}.t^0 \rightarrow \langle s, \text{pos}: \text{int ref}\rangle^p \rightarrow \langle \text{pos}: t \text{ ref}, \text{move}: \text{int}^0 \rightarrow \text{unit}\rangle$

This type may be used in (let point $= P$ in $\cdots$) since the class P is a value, being a function. Following Wand [31], for a class $A = \lambda x_1 \ldots x_n \lambda z.M$ with instance variables $x_1, \ldots, x_n$ and self parameter z, where M is a record expression, we may denote by new $A(N_1, \ldots, N_n)$ the expression fix$(AN_1 \cdots N_n)$, which creates an object instance of the class A. Notice that in typing A, the type of the self parameter z has a priori no relation with the type of the body M of the class: we only have to arrange that z has appropriate type with respect to its uses in M (see the point example). Now to create an object of class A, we have to solve some constraints on the type of the self parameter, since, as we have seen, the fixpoint fix has (principal) type fix: $\forall t.(t^1 \rightarrow t)^0 \rightarrow t$. Then for instance, assuming that 0 has type int, to type the expression new point(0) we have to solve the equation $\langle s, \text{pos}: \text{int ref}\rangle = \langle \text{pos}: t \text{ ref}, \text{move}: \text{int}^0 \rightarrow \text{unit}\rangle$, and the equation $p = 1$. In particular, we have to instantiate s into $\langle \text{move}: \text{int}^0 \rightarrow \text{unit}\rangle$ (which obviously satisfies the constraint of not containing a pos field). In the context of previous declarations for fix and point, this gives us the expected type for a point object, that is new point(0): Point where

Point $= \langle \text{pos}: \text{int ref}, \text{move}: \text{int}^0 \rightarrow \text{unit}\rangle$

As one can see, one can create an object instance of a class only if that class is "protective" towards its self argument. That is, once instantiated with initial values for the instance variables, it must have a type of the form $\theta^1 \rightarrow \tau$ (moreover θ – the type of self – and τ – the type of the record of methods – should be unifiable). This is not possible with a clear method with body ((set self.pos)0), for instance, since here self is doomed to have degree 0. One might have the discipline that, if the self parameter occurs free in the body of a method of a class, then this body is a value, but as we shall see, there are other uses of self.

Now let us see how to type a simple inheritance situation, again following Wand's model [31]: to inherit from a class A, a class B is defined as $B = \lambda y_1 \ldots y_k \lambda z \langle (AN_1 \cdots N_n)z \cdots \rangle$ where $\langle (AN_1 \cdots N_n)z \cdots \rangle$ typically consists in extending and modifying the record of methods of class A. This may also be defined using a super variable, representing the current object as a member of the superclass, as in $B = \lambda y_1 \ldots y_k \lambda z (\text{let super} = (AN_1 \cdots N_n)z \text{ in } \langle \text{super} \cdots \rangle)$. For example, we define a class of "resetable" points, inheriting from point, as follows

rPoint $= \lambda x \lambda \text{self} \langle (\text{point } x)\text{self}, \text{reset} = \lambda y((\text{set self.pos})y)\rangle$

The x and self parameters have the same type here as in point, and the type of the reset method is $\text{int}^0 \rightarrow \text{unit}$. Now, as usual, we want more "flashy" points, exhibiting a color, that we can change by painting the object. Since we want this extension to be applicable to a variety of points – or other objects –, it is natural to define a function, taking as argument a class, or more accurately an instantiated class g – that is, a generator [10], which is a function of self only –, and returning an extended class:

coloring $= \lambda g \lambda c \lambda \text{self} \langle (g \text{ self}), \text{color} = \text{ref } c, \text{paint} = \lambda y((\text{set self.color})y)\rangle$

The reader will easily check that to type the body of this function, the best is to assume that self has type $\langle s, \text{color}: t' \text{ ref}\rangle^p$ where p depends on the function g. Then g must be applicable to any record that contains, or may be extended to contain a color field of type τ ref. We let the reader check how to type coloring, with g of type $\langle s, \text{color}: t' \text{ ref}\rangle^p \rightarrow t''$, as well as the derived classes

$$\text{cPoint} = \lambda x(\text{coloring}(\text{point } x))$$
$$\text{cRPoint} = \lambda x(\text{coloring}(\text{rPoint } x))$$

Notice that since coloring requires that self has a color field, the point and rPoint classes are used here with an instantiated type for self, namely replacing s by $\langle s', \text{color}: t' \text{ ref}\rangle$. The polymorphism offered by Wand's row variables is crucial here for the inheritance mechanism to work properly, where one usually employs some form of subtyping (see [7,16]). The coloring function may be regarded as an example of what has been called a *mixin*, that is a class definition parameterized over its superclass (see [5]), which bears some similarity with the parameterized classes of EIFFEL [23] and the "virtual classes" of BETA [22]. This notion of a mixin has recently received some attention, see for instance [2,4,17].

Continuing with the same example, one may have wished, in defining a colored "resetable" point, to modify the reset method so that not only the position, but also the color may be reset. Then we may define this by means of a "wrapper" [10], that is a function of super and self parameters:

$$W = \lambda \text{super}\lambda \text{self}\langle \text{super}, \text{reset} \leftarrow \lambda y\lambda d(\text{super.reset } y) ; (\text{super.paint } d)\rangle$$
$$\text{CRPoint} = \lambda x\lambda c\lambda \text{self}(\text{let super} = ((\text{cRPoint } xc) \text{ self}) \text{ in } (W \text{ super})\text{self})$$

It is interesting to notice that here the reset method is redefined to have a type which is unrelated to the one it has in the superclass. This is a kind of inheritance which is usually not supported in object-oriented calculi and languages (except, obviously, untyped languages like SMALLTALK). This is not problematic here since no other method of the superclass was using reset.

The fact that classes and objects are "first class citizens" in our core language allows one not only to pass them as arguments and return them as results, as in the "mixin" or "wrapper" facilities, but also to imagine new schemes of "inheritance" – or more generally code reuse, which in our calculus manifests itself through the use of the let construct. For instance, one may build a class as an instance of another class, by fixing the initial value of some instance parameters, like in the specialization of the point class into the class oPoint $= \lambda \text{self}.(\text{point } 0)\text{self}$ of the points initially at the origin. One may also decide to dynamically introduce a class of unicolored points, by disallowing the use of the paint method:

$$\text{uCPoint} = \lambda x\lambda c\lambda \text{self}((\text{cPoint } xc)\text{self}\backslash \text{paint})$$

We can create an object of that class, since the type of self in $(\text{cPoint } xc)\text{self}$ is not required to contain the paint method. Similarly, one can restrict a method to be private to an object; for instance, if we let $o = \text{new point}(0)\backslash \text{pos}$ then this object behaves as a point, except that it does not accept pos messages. We could even do that with a method hidePos $= \lambda y(\text{self}\backslash \text{pos}\backslash \text{hidePos})$. Such a facility does not seem to be supported by the self-application semantics of objects. Some similar examples of excluding methods, like for instance building a class of stacks from a class of dequeues, were given long ago by Snyder [28]. Clearly, introducing such reuse mechanisms would reinforce the fact that "inheritance is not subtyping" [11]. In the full version of the paper we give some further examples, and discuss related work.

5 Conclusion

In this paper we have adapted and extended Wand's typed model of classes and objects [31] to an imperative setting, where the state of an object is a set of mutable values. Our main achievement is the design of a type system which only accepts safe let rec declarations, while retaining the ability to construct a principal type for a typable term. We believe that our type system does not impose any new restriction on the underlying language, where recursion is limited to (let rec $x = N$ in M) where N is a value: it should not be difficult to show that a term of this language is typable, without using degrees, if and only if it is typable, with the "same" type, in our system, thus showing that our typing is a conservative extension of the usual one, if we forget about degrees. Type reconstruction in our system is based upon solving very simple equations on degree expressions, as we have indicated, and therefore this should not complicate the standard algorithm. This issue has to be investigated from a pragmatic point of view, to see whether our solution is practically useful. This is left for further work, but we hope we have at least suggested that our calculus is very expressive, especially regarding object-oriented programming constructs. We could then use it as a guideline to design a type safe object-oriented layer.

References

[1] M. ABADI, L. CARDELLI, *A Theory of Objects*, Springer-Verlag (1996).
[2] D. ANCONA, E. ZUCCA, *A theory of mixin modules: basic and derived operators*, Math. Struct. in Comput. Sci. Vol. 8 (1998) 401-446.
[3] V. BONO, A. PATEL, V. SHMATIKOV, J. MITCHELL, *A core calculus of classes and objects*, MFPS'99, Electronic Notes in Comput. Sci. Vol. 20 (1999).
[4] V. BONO, A. PATEL, V. SHMATIKOV, J. MITCHELL, *A core calculus of classes and mixins*, ECOOP'99, Lecture Notes in Comput. Sci. 1628 (1999) 43-66.
[5] G. BRACHA, W. COOK, *Mixin-based inheritance*, ECOOP/OOPSLA'90 (1990) 303-311.
[6] K. BRUCE, *Safe type checking in a statically-typed object-oriented programming language*, POPL'93 (1993) 285-298.
[7] K. BRUCE, L. PETERSEN, A. FIECH, *Subtyping is not a good "match" for object-oriented languages*, ECOOP'97, Lecture Notes in Comput. Sci. 1241 (1997) 104-127.
[8] L. CARDELLI, *A semantics of multiple inheritance*, Semantics of Data Types, Lecture Notes in Comput. Sci. 173 (1984) 51-67. Also published in Information and Computation, Vol. 76 (1988).
[9] L. CARDELLI, J.C. MITCHELL, *Operations on records*, in [18], 295-350.

[10] W. COOK, J. PALSBERG, *A denotational semantics of inheritance and its correctness*, OOPSLA'89, ACM SIGPLAN Notices Vol. 24 No. 10 (1989) 433-443.

[11] W. COOK, W. HILL, P. CANNING, *Inheritance is not subtyping*, in [18], 497-517.

[12] L. DAMAS, R. MILNER, *Principal type-schemes for functional programs*, POPL'82 (1982) 207-212.

[13] J. EIFRIG, S. SMITH, V. TRIFONOV, A. ZWARICO, *An interpretation of typed OOP in a langage with state*, LISP and Symbolic Computation Vol. 8 (1995) 357-397.

[14] K. FISHER, *Types Systems for Object-Oriented Programming Languages*, PhD Thesis, Stanford University (1996).

[15] K. FISHER, F. HONSELL, J. MITCHELL, *A lambda calculus of objects and method specialization*, LICS'93 (1993) 26-38.

[16] K. FISHER, J. MITCHELL, *The development of type systems for object-oriented languages*, Theory and Practice of Object Systems Vol. 1, No. 3 (1996) 189-220.

[17] M. FLATT, S. KRISHNAMURTHI, M. FELLEISEN, *Classes and Mixins*, POPL'98 (1998) 171-183.

[18] C. GUNTER, J. MITCHELL (Eds.), *Theoretical Aspects of Object-Oriented Programming*, The MIT Press (1994).

[19] L. A. JATEGAONKAR, J. MITCHELL, *Type inference with extended pattern matching and subtypes*, Fundamenta Informaticae Vol. 19 (1993) 127-166.

[20] S. KAMIN, *Inheritance in SMALLTALK-80: a denotational definition*, POPL'88 (1988) 80-87.

[21] X. LEROY, D. DOLIGEZ, J. GARRIGUE, D. RÉMY, J. VOUILLON, *The Objective Caml System*, release 3.00, Documentation and user's manual, available at http://caml.inria.fr (2000).

[22] O. L. MADSEN, B. MØLLER PEDERSEN, *Virtual Classes: A powerful mechanism in object-oriented programming*, OOPSLA'89, ACM SIGPLAN Notices Vol. 24 No. 10 (1989) 397-406.

[23] B. MEYER, *Genericity versus inheritance*, OOPSLA'86, ACM SIGPLAN Notices Vol. 21 No. 11 (1986) 391-405.

[24] R. MILNER, *A theory of type polymorphism in programming*, J. of Computer and System Sciences Vol. 17 (1978) 348-375.

[25] B. C. PIERCE, D. TURNER, *Simple type-theoretic foundations for object-oriented programming*, J. of Functional Programming Vol. 4 No. 2 (1994) 207-247.

[26] D. RÉMY, *Programming with ML-ART: an extension to ML with abstract and record types*, TACS'94, Lecture Notes in Comput. Sci. 789 (1994) 321-346.

[27] D. RÉMY, J. VOUILLON, *Objective ML: an effective object-oriented extension of ML*, Theory and practice of Objects Systems, Vol. 4, No. 1 (1998) 27-50.

[28] A. SNYDER, *Encapsulation and inheritance in object-oriented programming languages*, OOPSLA'86, ACM SIGPLAN Notices Vol. 21 No. 11 (1986) 38-45.

[29] A. TAIVALSAARI, *On the notion of inheritance*, ACM Computing Surveys Vol. 28 No. 3 (1996) 438-479.

[30] M. WAND, *Complete type inference for simple objects*, LICS'87 (1987) 37-44.

[31] M. WAND, *Type inference for objects with instance variables and inheritance*, in [18], 97-120.

[32] A. WRIGHT, M. FELLEISEN, *A syntactic approach to type soundness*, Information and Computation Vol. 115 No. 1 (1994) 38-94.

A Formalisation of
Java's Exception Mechanism

Bart Jacobs

Dep. Comp. Sci., Univ. Nijmegen,
P.O. Box 9010, 6500 GL Nijmegen, The Netherlands.
bart@cs.kun.nl   http://www.cs.kun.nl/~bart

Abstract. This paper examines Java's exception mechanism, and formalises its main operations (`throw`, `try-catch` and `try-catch-finally`)
in a type-theoretic setting. This formalisation uses so-called coalgebras
for modeling Java statements and expressions, thus providing a convenient setting for handling the various termination options that may arise
in exception handling (closely following the Java Language Specification). This semantics of exceptions is used within the LOOP project on
Java program verification. It is illustrated in two example verifications
in PVS.

1 Introduction

The LOOP project [27] at the University of Nijmegen aims at Java program
verification using proof tools (such as PVS [23] and Isabelle [24]) and a special
purpose front-end compiler (the so-called LOOP tool, see [3]) for translating Java
classes into the logic of the back-end proof tools. Incorporated in this LOOP
tool is a semantics of (sequential) Java in the higher order logic of PVS and
Isabelle. A distinguishing feature of this semantics is its mathematical basis
given by so-called coalgebras. Several aspects of this semantics have already
been described elsewhere (see [15,2,10,9,8]), but the semantics of exceptions has
not been published yet. It will be the topic of the present paper. The aim of the
formalisation is to (1) clarify the existing informal specification, and (2) provide
a semantical basis for (tool-assisted) verification of Java programs. Currently,
the main application area is JavaCard [25,26].

As in earlier publications we shall not describe Java semantics in the language
of PVS or of Isabelle/HOL, but in a type-theoretic common abstraction of these,
which incorporates the essentials of higher order logic. It is described briefly in
Section 2 below. The main type constructors are labeled product and coproduct,
function space and list. For more information, see *e.g.* [8]. Higher order logic is
too much for what we need in this paper, but since it exists both in PVS and
Isabelle/HOL, we take it for granted.

Exceptions form an integrated aspect of the Java programming language,
which can contribute to the reliability and robustness of programs written in
Java—if the semantics of the exception mechanism is clear. Exceptions occur in

D. Sands (Ed.): ESOP 2001, LNCS 2028, pp. 284–301, 2001.

programs when certain constraints are violated, *e.g.* a division by zero, an array access out of the arrays bounds, an object creation when there is no unused memory left, or a situation which is seen as unexpected or inappropriate by the programmer. The occurrence of an exception in a program leads to what is called abrupt termination[1]. It means that all subsequent statements are skipped (and locks are released), until (possibly) an exception handler is reached. One says that an exception "is thrown" at the point where it occurs, and "is caught" at the point where it is handled. As we shall see, exception handling is based on the exceptions type. It will restore normal operation[2], when the exception is handled properly. The Java exception mechanism is integrated with the synchronisation model, but that will not be relevant here: we only consider what it means when exceptions are thrown or caught, and not how this affects the flow of control in a multi-threaded scenario.

We describe a part of Java's pre-defined exception hierarchy, with superclasses sitting above subclasses.

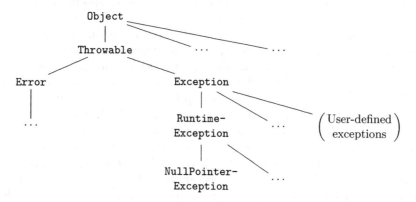

The class `Throwable` is a direct subclass of the root class `Object`. It has two subclasses, `Error` and `Exception`. Errors (instances of `Error`) are exceptions from which programs are not ordinarily expected to recover [7, §§11.5]. Instances of `Error` and `RuntimeException` are special because they are the only so-called unchecked exceptions. For all other, checked, exceptions the Java compiler makes sure that each method either handles this exception (via a `catch` statement) or declares it in its method header, as in: `void m() throws IOException {...}`. This `throws` clause may be understood as a contract between the implementor and the user (in the style of Design-by-Contract [20]), see [7, §§11.2]. An overriding method in a subclass must respect the `throws` clause of the method that is being overridden in the superclass, *i.e.* cannot throw more exceptions. Whether or not an exception is checked does not play a rôle for the Java semantics within the LOOP project.

---

[1] A `return`, `break` or `continue` statement in Java also leads to abrupt termination.

[2] Normal termination is not restored at the point where the exception arises: Java has a so-called termination model for exceptions, and not a resumption model, see [4, §16.4].

The semantics of programming languages with exceptions forms a good illustration of the appropriateness of using coalgebras to organise the relevant structure (via different termination modes, distinguished via coproduct types). In general, a coalgebra is a "transition" function of the form $S \longrightarrow \boxed{\cdots S \cdots}$ with a structured result type that captures a certain kind of computation, where S is a set of states. See [14] for an introduction. Such a semantics can also be described in terms of monads [13]. The monadic view emphasises the input-output relation, whereas the coalgebraic view emphasises the state-based aspect of the computations—and thus leads to notions like invariant and bisimilarity (which will not be used here), but also to a logic with appropriate modalities, which we shall briefly describe here as a Hoare logic (like in [10,12]). The advantage of this coalgebraic approach—and the reason why we emphasise it—is that the type system forces one to explicitly handle all possible termination options (in the box above). See for instance the many cases in the definitions of TRY-CATCH and TRY-CATCH-FINALLY in Section 5 below, closely corresponding to the cases that are distinguished in the Java Language Specification [7]. A very different alternative is to incorporate exceptions into one's state space, like in the continuation-based approach of [1] or the operational and axiomatic approaches of [22,21]. This simplifies the type of state transformers, at the expense of complicating the state space (certainly when the other forms of abrupt termination are taken into account), and makes the handling of the various cases less transparent. The axiomatic semantics of exceptions is studied in for example [5, 18,17] (mostly via a weakest precondition calculus), involving a single possible exception, and not many forms of abrupt termination (like in Java).

This paper starts with two introductory sections. First there is a brief account of the simple type theory that will be used, concentrating on labeled (co)products. Next, the (coalgebraic) representation of Java statements and expressions is explained, together with an associated Hoare logic dealing with the different termination modes. This forms the basis for the formalisations of exception throwing in Section 4 and exception handling in Section 5. The latter section has two parts, one for try-catch and one for try-catch-finally. Each part contains an extensive quote from the Java Language Specification [7], containing the informal explanations of exception handling. Subsequently, Section 6 describes two example programs involving some tricky aspects of exception handling. Appropriate specifications are provided in the language JML [16], and proved (after translation by the LOOP tool) in PVS.

2   A Brief Look at the Type Theory

The type theory that we use is the same as in [2,10,9,8]. It has some basic types like bool, string and unit (for a singleton type), plus function types, labeled products and coproducts, list *etc.* as type constructors. We assume that these are more or less familiar, and only wish to mention the notation we use for labeled (co)product and function types.

Given types $\sigma_1, \ldots, \sigma_n$, we can form a product (or record) type $[\,\mathsf{lab}_1 : \sigma_1, \ldots,$ $\mathsf{lab}_n : \sigma_n\,]$ and a labeled coproduct (or variant) type $\{\,\mathsf{lab}_1 : \sigma_1 \mid \ldots \mid \mathsf{lab}_n : \sigma_n\,\}$, where all labels lab_i are assumed to be different. An example is the well-known lift type constructor $\mathsf{lift}[\alpha] = \{\,\mathsf{bot} : \mathsf{unit} \mid \mathsf{up} : \alpha\,\}$ which adds a bottom element to an arbitrary type α. For terms $M_i : \sigma_i$, there is a labeled tuple $(\,\mathsf{lab}_1 = M_1, \ldots, \mathsf{lab}_n = M_n\,)$ inhabiting the corresponding product type $[\,\mathsf{lab}_1 : \sigma_1, \ldots, \mathsf{lab}_n : \sigma_n\,]$. For a term $N : [\,\mathsf{lab}_1 : \sigma_1, \ldots, \mathsf{lab}_n : \sigma_n\,]$ in this product type, we write $N.\mathsf{lab}_i$ for the selection term of type σ_i. Similarly, for a term $M : \sigma_i$ there is a labeled or tagged term $\mathsf{lab}_i\, M$ in the coproduct type $\{\,\mathsf{lab}_1 : \sigma_1 \mid \ldots \mid \mathsf{lab}_n : \sigma_n\,\}$. And for a term $N : \{\,\mathsf{lab}_1 : \sigma_1 \mid \ldots \mid \mathsf{lab}_n : \sigma_n\,\}$ in this coproduct type, together with n terms $L_i : \tau$ containing a free variable $x_i : \sigma_i$ there is a case term $\mathsf{CASES}\ N\ \mathsf{OF}\ \{\,\mathsf{lab}_1\, x_1 \mapsto L_1 \mid \ldots \mid \mathsf{lab}_n\, x_n \mapsto L_n\,\}$ of type τ which binds the x_i. For function types we shall use the standard notation $\lambda x : \sigma.\, M$ for lambda abstraction and $N \cdot L$ for application.

3   Basics of Java Semantics

As described earlier, the LOOP tool provides a semantics for (sequential) Java by translating Java classes into the higher order logic of PVS or Isabelle. This section will introduce the basic aspects of the semantics and provide the setting for the description of exception handling in the remainder of the paper. It will concentrate on some special types, on the (coalgebraic) representation of statements and expressions, and on some basic language constructs.

A memory model is constructed as a specific type OM, for object memory. It consists of a heap, a stack, and static memory, each consisting of an infinite series of memory cells. These memory cells can store the contents of objects and arrays. The type OM comes with various put and get operations for reading and writing in the object memory. Its precise structure is not so relevant for what follows, and the interested reader is referred to [2] for more information. Elements of OM will often be called states.

References will be values of the following type.

─ TYPE THEORY ─────────────────────────────────

$$\mathsf{RefType} : \mathsf{TYPE} \overset{\mathrm{def}}{=}$$
$$\{\,\mathsf{null} : \mathsf{unit} \mid \mathsf{ref} : \mathsf{MemLoc}\,\}$$

───

Thus a reference is either a null-reference, or a non-null-reference consisting of a memory location (inhabiting an appropriate type MemLoc) pointing to a memory cell on the heap. In [2] we have included type information in references, but here we shall assume it to be part of memory cells. Therefore, there is a function

─ TYPE THEORY ─────────────────────────────────

$$\mathsf{gettype} : \mathsf{MemLoc} \to \mathsf{OM} \to \mathsf{ClassName} \qquad \text{where} \qquad \mathsf{ClassName} \overset{\mathrm{def}}{=} \mathsf{string}$$

───

which gives for a specific memory location p the type of the object stored at p on the heap. This type is represented as a string. There is also a special predicate

--- TYPE THEORY ---

$$\mathsf{SubClass?: ClassName \to ClassName \to bool} \qquad (1)$$

incorporating the subtype relationship between classes, given as strings.

Statements and expressions in Java may have different termination modes: they can hang (*e.g.* because of an infinite loop), terminate normally, or terminate abruptly (typically because of an exception, but (statements) also because of a `return`, `break` or `continue`). All these options are captured in appropriate datatypes. First, abnormal termination leads to the following two types, one for statements and one for expressions.

--- TYPE THEORY ---

$\mathsf{StatAbn : TYPE} \overset{\mathrm{def}}{=}$
$\quad \{\, \mathsf{excp: [es: OM, ex: RefType]}$
$\quad |\ \mathsf{rtrn: OM}$
$\quad |\ \mathsf{break: [bs: OM, blab: lift[string]\,]}$
$\quad |\ \mathsf{cont: [cs: OM, clab: lift[string]\,]\,}\}$

$\mathsf{ExprAbn : TYPE} \overset{\mathrm{def}}{=}$
$\quad \mathsf{[es: OM, ex: RefType]}$

These types are used to define the result types of statements and expressions:

--- TYPE THEORY ---

$\mathsf{StatResult : TYPE} \overset{\mathrm{def}}{=}$
$\quad \{\, \mathsf{hang: unit}$
$\quad |\ \mathsf{norm: OM}$
$\quad |\ \mathsf{abnorm: StatAbn}\,\}$

$\mathsf{ExprResult[\alpha] : TYPE} \overset{\mathrm{def}}{=}$
$\quad \{\, \mathsf{hang: unit}$
$\quad |\ \mathsf{norm: [ns: OM, res: \alpha\,]}$
$\quad |\ \mathsf{abnorm: ExprAbn}\,\}$

A Java statement is then translated as a state transformer function $\mathsf{OM} \to$ $\mathsf{StatResult}$, and a Java expression of type $\mathtt{Out}$ as a function $\mathsf{OM} \to$ $\mathsf{ExprResult[Out]}$. Thus both statements and expressions are coalgebras. The result of such functions applied to a state $x: \mathsf{OM}$ yields either hang, norm, or abnorm (with appropriate parameters), indicating the sort of outcome.

On the basis of this representation of statements and expressions all language constructs from (sequential) Java are translated. For instance, the composition of two statements is defined as:

─ TYPE THEORY ─────────────────────────────────

$$s, t \colon \mathsf{OM} \to \mathsf{StatResult} \ \vdash$$

$$(s\,;t) \colon \ \mathsf{OM} \to \mathsf{StatResult} \ \stackrel{\mathrm{def}}{=}$$

$$\lambda x \colon \mathsf{OM}.\ \mathsf{CASES}\ s \cdot x\ \mathsf{OF}\ \{$$
$$\mid \mathsf{hang} \mapsto \mathsf{hang}$$
$$\mid \mathsf{norm}\ y \mapsto t \cdot y$$
$$\mid \mathsf{abnorm}\ a \mapsto \mathsf{abnorm}\ a\ \}$$

───

What is important to note is that if s hangs or terminates abruptly, then so does the composition $s\,;t$. In particular, if an exception is thrown, subsequent statements are not executed.

Recall that `Throwable` is the root class of all exceptions. Its constructors call a native method for creating an exception object. In the LOOP semantics there is a corresponding function, called MAKE-EXCEPTION. It takes a string as argument, for the exceptions message, and performs some basic memory operations: allocating an appropriate new memory cell on the heap, and storing the message[3]. We skip the details of MAKE-EXCEPTION and only mention its type:

─ TYPE THEORY ─────────────────────────────────

$$\mathsf{MAKE\text{-}EXCEPTION} \colon \mathsf{string} \to \mathsf{OM} \to [\,\mathsf{es} \colon \mathsf{OM}, \mathsf{ex} \colon \mathsf{RefType}\,]$$

───

It takes a string and a state, and produces an appropriately adapted return state together with a (non-null) reference to the exception object that it created in the return state.

Exception classes in the Java API typically call the constructors from `Throwable` to create new instances. Therefore we can also use MAKE-EXCEPTION for these classes directly.

3.1   Specifications with Exceptions

The coalgebraic representation of statements and expressions formalises the different termination modes that can occur. It naturally gives rise to a Hoare logic with different, corresponding modes for reasoning about "normal" and "abnormal" states, see [10]. For example, there is a partial Hoare triple:

$$\{\mathsf{pre}\}\ \mathsf{stat}\ \{\mathsf{exception}(E, \mathsf{post})\}$$

Informally, it says that if the precondition pre holds and the statement stat terminates abruptly by throwing a non-null exception (see (2) below), this exception belongs to class E and the postcondition post holds. More formally,

───────────────

[3] Our semantics does not take the `backtrace` field in `Throwable` into account.

── TYPE THEORY ─────────────────────────────────────

pre: OM → bool, post: OM → RefType → bool,
           stat: OM → StatResult, E: ClassName ⊢

$\{$pre$\}$ stat $\{$exception$(E,$ post$)\}$: bool $\overset{\text{def}}{=}$

$\forall x:$ OM. pre $\cdot x \Rightarrow$ CASES stat $\cdot x$ OF $\{$
                          | hang $\mapsto$ true
                          | norm $y \mapsto$ true
                          | abnorm $a \mapsto$
                                CASES a OF $\{$
                                   | excp $e \mapsto$
                                        CASES $e.$ex OF$\{$
                                           | null $\mapsto$ true
                                           | ref $p \mapsto$
                                                SubClass? $\cdot$ (gettype $\cdot p \cdot (e.$es$)) \cdot E$
                                                $\wedge$ post $\cdot (e.$es$) \cdot (e.$ex$) \}$
                                   | rtrn $z \mapsto$ true
                                   | break $b \mapsto$ true
                                   | cont $c \mapsto$ true $\} \}$

──

Notice that the postcondition has type OM → RefType → bool and can thus also say something about the exception object (like in the example in Subsection 6.2). Similar such Hoare triples can be defined for the other termination modes. They are essential for reasoning about Java programs, for example for proving a suitable postcondition for a program which involves an exception inside a while loop, see *e.g.* [11].

These different termination modes also occur in the behavioural interface specification language JML [16] that will be used in Section 6. JML has pre- and post-conditions which can be used to describe "normal" and "exceptional" behaviour. The LOOP tool translates these JML specifications into suitable Hoare formulas, combining several termination options, see [12] for details.

4   Throwing Exceptions

A programmer in Java can explicitly throw an exception via the command throw *Expression*, where *Expression* should belong to Throwable, or one of its subclasses. This statement will immediately lead to abrupt termination. The Java Language Specification [7, §§14.17] says:

> A throw statement first evaluates the *Expression*. If the evaluation of the *Expression* completes abruptly for some reason, then the throw completes abruptly for that reason. If evaluation of *Expression* completes normally, producing a non-null value V, then the throw statement completes abruptly, the reason being a throw with value V. If evaluation of the *Expression* completes

normally, producing a `null` value, then an instance V' of class `NullPointer-Exception` is created and thrown instead of `null`. The `throw` statement then completes abruptly, the reason being a `throw` with value V'.

The LOOP tool uses the following translation of throw statements.

$$[\![\, \texttt{throw}\ Expression\,]\!] \overset{\text{def}}{=} \mathsf{THROW} \cdot [\![\, Expression\,]\!]$$

The function THROW captures the above explanation in ordinary language in a type-theoretic formulation.

─ TYPE THEORY ──

$e\colon \mathsf{OM} \to \mathsf{ExprResult[RefType]} \vdash$

$\quad \mathsf{THROW} \cdot e\ :\ \mathsf{OM} \to \mathsf{StatResult} \overset{\text{def}}{=}$

$\qquad \lambda x\colon \mathsf{OM}.\ \mathsf{CASES}\ e \cdot x\ \mathsf{OF}\ \{$
$\qquad\qquad |\ \mathsf{hang} \mapsto \mathsf{hang}$
$\qquad\qquad |\ \mathsf{norm}\ y \mapsto$
$\qquad\qquad\qquad \mathsf{CASES}\ y.\mathsf{res}\ \mathsf{OF}\{$
$\qquad\qquad\qquad |\ \mathsf{null} \mapsto$
$\qquad\qquad\qquad\qquad \mathsf{LET}\ d = \mathsf{MAKE\text{-}EXCEPTION} \cdot$
$\qquad\qquad\qquad\qquad\qquad (\text{``NullPointerException''}) \cdot (y.\mathsf{ns})$
$\qquad\qquad\qquad\qquad \mathsf{IN}\ \mathsf{abnorm}(\mathsf{excp}(\mathsf{es} = d.\mathsf{es}, \mathsf{ex} = d.\mathsf{ex}))$
$\qquad\qquad\qquad |\ \mathsf{ref}\ p \mapsto \mathsf{abnorm}(\mathsf{excp}(\mathsf{es} = y.\mathsf{ns}, \mathsf{ex} = \mathsf{ref}\ p))\ \}$
$\qquad\qquad |\ \mathsf{abnorm}\ a \mapsto \mathsf{abnorm}\ a\ \}$

──

Interestingly, the formalisations within the LOOP project and the Bali project (see [22, p. 123]) revealed an omission in the first edition of the Java Language Specification [6, §§14.16]: the case where *Expression* evaluates to a null-reference was not covered. Following a subsequent suggestion for improvement, this was repaired in the second edition [7] (as described in the quote above).

There is an important implicit assumption about Java related to this, namely:

$$\boxed{\text{A thrown exception is never a null-reference.}} \qquad (2)$$

This "invariant" holds clearly for exceptions thrown by users (as can be seen from the definition of THROW, or the explanation of `throw`), but also holds for exceptions that are thrown by the Java Virtual Machine (both for synchronous and asynchronous exceptions), see [19]. It seems that this assumption has not been made explicit before (but it is hard-wired into the Bali semantics [22,21]: there it automatically holds because of a syntactic distinction between valid locations and Null; exceptions can only return valid locations). It will play a rôle in the way we formalise the catching mechanism.

5   Catching Exceptions

For neatly handling possible exceptional cases in a statement S, Java uses `try` S followed by a series of `catch` blocks for different exceptions, possibly followed by a `finally` block. When S terminates normally, no `catch` block is executed, but the `finally` block is (if any). If S results in an exception, say belonging to class E, the first `catch` block in the series that handles E-exceptions is executed, followed by the `finally` block (if any).

The list of catches in a `try` statement will be translated into a list (in type theory) consisting of pairs of strings (with label exc) and functions (with label handler) from RefType to statements for the corresponding handler code. The possible input of these functions is a reference to the exception thrown by the `try` statement. The parameter exceptions are treated as local variables. These are initialised to the RefType input of the handler function. The interpretations used by the LOOP tool look as follows.

$$\llbracket \texttt{try\{tb\}catch(E1 e1)\{h1\}} \ldots \texttt{catch(En en)\{hn\}} \rrbracket$$
$$\overset{\text{def}}{=} \textsf{TRY-CATCH} \cdot \llbracket \texttt{tb} \rrbracket \cdot$$
$$[\,(\,\textsf{exc} = \text{``E1''},$$
$$\quad \textsf{handler} = \lambda v_1 \colon \textsf{RefType}. \llbracket \texttt{E1 e1 = } v_1 \texttt{; h1} \rrbracket\,),$$
$$\vdots$$
$$(\,\textsf{exc} = \text{``En''},$$
$$\quad \textsf{handler} = \lambda v_n \colon \textsf{RefType}. \llbracket \texttt{En en = } v_n \texttt{; hn} \rrbracket\,)\,]$$

$$\llbracket \texttt{try\{tb\}catch(E1 e1)\{h1\}} \ldots \texttt{catch(En en)\{hn\}finally\{fb\}} \rrbracket$$
$$\overset{\text{def}}{=} \textsf{TRY-CATCH-FINALLY} \cdot \llbracket \texttt{tb} \rrbracket \cdot$$
$$[\,(\,\textsf{exc} = \text{``E1''},$$
$$\quad \textsf{handler} = \lambda v_1 \colon \textsf{RefType}. \llbracket \texttt{E1 e1 = } v_1 \texttt{; h1} \rrbracket\,),$$
$$\vdots$$
$$(\,\textsf{exc} = \text{``En''},$$
$$\quad \textsf{handler} = \lambda v_n \colon \textsf{RefType}. \llbracket \texttt{En en = } v_n \texttt{; hn} \rrbracket\,)\,] \cdot$$
$$\llbracket \texttt{fb} \rrbracket$$

The two type-theoretic functions TRY-CATCH and TRY-CATCH-FINALLY used for these interpretations will be described separately. They involve many subtle case distinctions, which are not easy to understand without direct access to the relevant descriptions of the Java Language Specification. Therefore, these are included.

5.1   Try-Catch

The Java Language Specification [7, §§14.19.1] says:

> A `try` statement without a `finally` block is executed by first executing the `try` block. Then there is a choice:

- If execution of the **try** block completes normally, then no further action is taken and the **try** statement completes normally.
- If execution of the **try** block completes abruptly because of a throw of a value V, then there is a choice:
  - ◆ If the run-time type of V is assignable (§5.2) to the *Parameter* of any **catch** clause of the **try** statement, then the first (leftmost) such **catch** clause is selected. The value V is assigned to the parameter of the selected **catch** clause, and the Block of that **catch** clause is executed. If that block completes normally, then the **try** statement completes normally; if that block completes abruptly for any reason, then the **try** statement completes abruptly for the same reason.
  - ◆ If the run-time type of V is not assignable to the parameter of any **catch** clause of the **try** statement, then the **try** statement completes abruptly because of a **throw** of the value V.
- If execution of the **try** block completes abruptly for any other reason, then the **try** statement completes abruptly for the same reason.

This behaviour will be realised by the TRY-CATCH function below. It first executes its first argument s (the meaning of the try block), and then, when an exception occurs, it calls a recursive function TRY-LOOP; otherwise it does nothing else. By the earlier mentioned invariant (2), this exception can be assumed to be a non-null reference. Therefore we can choose an arbitrary outcome (hang) when the null reference case is distinguished.

── TYPE THEORY ──

s : OM $\rightarrow$ StatResult,
ℓ : list[[exc : ClassName, handler : RefType $\rightarrow$ OM $\rightarrow$ StatResult]] $\vdash$

> TRY-CATCH $\cdot\, s \cdot \ell$: OM $\rightarrow$ StatResult $\overset{\text{def}}{=}$
>
> > λx : OM. CASES $s \cdot x$ OF {
> > > | hang $\mapsto$ hang
> > > | norm $y \mapsto$ norm y
> > > | abnorm $a \mapsto$
> > > > CASES a OF {
> > > > > | excp $e \mapsto$
> > > > > > CASES e.ex OF {
> > > > > > > | null $\mapsto$ hang   // don't care, see (2)
> > > > > > > | ref $r \mapsto$ TRY-LOOP $\cdot\, r \cdot \ell \cdot (e$.es$)$ }
> > > > > | rtrn $z \mapsto$ rtrn z
> > > > > | break $b \mapsto$ break b
> > > > > | cont $c \mapsto$ cont c } }

───

The TRY-LOOP function recursively goes through the list of exception class names and corresponding handler functions, checking whether an exception is assignable to a parameter. It uses the SubClass? predicate from (1). If the end of the list is reached and the exception is still not handled, it is returned.

─ TYPE THEORY ───

p: MemLoc, ℓ: list[[exc: ClassName, handler: RefType $\to$ OM $\to$ StatResult]] $\vdash$

   TRY-LOOP $\cdot p \cdot \ell$: OM $\to$ StatResult $\overset{\text{def}}{=}$

      λx: OM. CASES ℓ OF {
            | nil $\mapsto$ abnorm(excp(es $= x$, ex $=$ ref p))
            | cons(h, t) $\mapsto$ IF SubClass? $\cdot$ (gettype $\cdot p \cdot x$) $\cdot$ (h.exc)
                           THEN (h.handler) $\cdot$ (ref p) $\cdot x$
                           ELSE TRY-LOOP $\cdot p \cdot t \cdot x$
                           ENDIF }

───

5.2 Try-Catch-Finally

Again, our starting point is the Java Language Specification [7, §§14.19.2]. Now there are many more cases to be distinguished.

> A **try** statement with a **finally** block is executed by first executing the **try** block. Then there is a choice:
> - If execution of the **try** block completes normally, then the **finally** block is executed, and then there is a choice:
>   - If the **finally** block completes normally, then the **try** statement completes normally.
>   - If the **finally** block completes abruptly for reason S, then the **try** statement completes abruptly for reason S.
> - If execution of the **try** block completes abruptly because of a **throw** of a value V, then there is a choice:
>   - If the run-time type of V is assignable to the parameter of any **catch** clause of the **try** statement, then the first (leftmost) such **catch** clause is selected. The value V is assigned to the parameter of the selected **catch** clause, and the Block of that **catch** clause is executed. Then there is a choice:
>   - If the **catch** block completes normally, then the **finally** block is executed. Then there is a choice:
>   - If the **finally** block completes normally, then the **try** statement completes normally.
>   - If the **finally** block completes abruptly for any reason, then the **try** statement completes abruptly for the same reason.
>   - If the **catch** block completes abruptly for reason R, then the finally block is executed. Then there is a choice:
>   - If the **finally** block completes normally, then the **try** statement completes abruptly for reason R.
>   - If the **finally** block completes abruptly for reason S, then the **try** statement completes abruptly for reason S (and reason R is discarded).
>   - If the run-time type of V is not assignable to the parameter of any **catch** clause of the **try** statement, then the **finally** block is executed. Then there is a choice:

- If the **finally** block completes normally, then the **try** statement completes abruptly because of a **throw** of the value V.
- If the **finally** block completes abruptly for reason S, then the **try** statement completes abruptly for reason S (and the **throw** of value V is discarded and forgotten).
- If execution of the **try** block completes abruptly for any other reason R, then the **finally** block is executed. Then there is a choice:
  - If the **finally** block completes normally, then the **try** statement completes abruptly for reason R.
  - If the **finally** block completes abruptly for reason S, then the **try** statement completes abruptly for reason S (and reason R is discarded).

─ TYPE THEORY ───

s, f: OM → StatResult,
ℓ: list[[exc: ClassName, handler: RefType → OM → StatResult]] ⊢

TRY-CATCH-FINALLY $\cdot\ s \cdot \ell \cdot f$: OM → StatResult $\overset{\text{def}}{=}$

λx: OM. CASES $s \cdot x$ OF {
    | hang ↦ hang
    | norm y ↦ $f \cdot y$
    | abnorm a ↦
        CASES a OF {
          | excp e ↦
              CASES e.ex OF {
                | null ↦ hang   // don't care, see (2)
                | ref r ↦ TRY-LOOP-FINALLY $\cdot\ r \cdot \ell \cdot f \cdot (e.\text{es})$ }
          | rtrn z ↦
              CASES $f \cdot z$ OF {
                | hang ↦ hang
                | norm y' ↦ abnorm(rtrn y')
                | abnorm a' ↦ abnorm a' }
          | break b ↦
              CASES $f \cdot (b.\text{bs})$ OF {
                | hang ↦ hang
                | norm y' ↦ abnorm(break(bs = y', blab = b.blab))
                | abnorm a' ↦ abnorm a' }
          | cont c ↦
              CASES $f \cdot (c.\text{cs})$ OF {
                | hang ↦ hang
                | norm y' ↦ abnorm(cont(cs = y', clab = c.clab))
                | abnorm a' ↦ abnorm a' } } }

───

Fig. 1. Formalisation of Java's **try-catch-finally**

As before, this is formalised in two steps, see Figures 1 and 2. The main difference with the TRY-CATCH function is in the occurrence of the additional "finally" statement f, which is executed after each possible outcome of the "try" statement s, and the catch statements. The most subtle point is that in case the statement s terminates abruptly because of a **return**, **break** or **continue**, and the finally clause f terminates normally, the side-effect of f is passed on in the eventual result (via the state y'). This is not so explicitly stated in (the above quote from) [7, §§14.19.2], but made explicit in our type-theoretic formalisation. It will be illustrated in an example in the next section.

The function TRY-LOOP-FINALLY in Figure 2 handles the actual catching much like before, except that the "finally" statement needs to be executed after every possibility. This involves appropriate handling of side-effects, like for TRY-CATCH-FINALLY above. The following results are then as expected.

Lemma 1. *Let* skip: OM $\rightarrow$ StatResult *be the function* $\lambda x: OM.$ norm x *which directly terminates normally. For all locations* p: MemLoc, *statements* s: $OM \rightarrow$ StatResult *and lists* ℓ: list[[exc: ClassName, handler: RefType $\rightarrow$ OM $\rightarrow$ StatResult]],

1. TRY-LOOP-FINALLY $\cdot p \cdot \ell \cdot$ skip $=$ TRY-LOOP $\cdot p \cdot \ell$
2. TRY-CATCH-FINALLY $\cdot p \cdot \ell \cdot$ skip $=$ TRY-CATCH $\cdot p \cdot \ell$.

Proof. The first statement follows by induction on ℓ. The second one by unpacking the definitions, distinguishing many cases, and using 1.   □

6   Examples

In order to illustrate the rôle of our formalisation of Java's exception mechanism we shall discuss two examples. These are two artificial Java programs, concentrating on exception handling. The relevant properties of these programs are stated as annotations, written in the behavioural specification language JML [16]. We shall not describe this language in detail, and hope that the annotations are largely self-explanatory. The two examples have been translated into PVS [23], using the LOOP tool. The JML annotations become predicates, on class implementations. The actual Java code is translated into a specific implementation. Thus it becomes possible to prove in PVS that the given implementation satisfies the JML specification. This has been done for both the examples. The proofs proceed almost entirely by automatic rewriting—unfolding in particular the type-theoretic functions for exception handling from the previous section—and do not require real user interaction. Hence there is not much to say about these proofs. But we hope that the reader appreciates the organisational and semantical complications that are involved.

6.1   Side Effects in Finally Clauses

In the previous section the formalisations TRY-CATCH-FINALLY and TRY-LOOP-FINALLY showed the handling of side effects of the finally clause f (via the state y'). Here we shall see that these effects indeed take place in Java. For this purpose we use the following Java program.

─ TYPE THEORY ──────────────────────────────────

p: MemLoc, f: OM → StatResult
ℓ: list[[exc: ClassName, handler: RefType → OM → StatResult]] ⊢

TRY-LOOP-FINALLY $\cdot p \cdot \ell \cdot f$: OM → StatResult $\stackrel{\text{def}}{=}$

λx: OM. CASES ℓ OF {
    | nil ↦
        CASES $f \cdot x$ OF {
          | hang ↦ hang
          | norm y ↦ abnorm(excp(es = y, ex = ref p))
          | abnorm a ↦ abnorm a }
    | cons(h, t) ↦
        IF SubClass? $\cdot$ (gettype $\cdot p \cdot x$) $\cdot$ (h.exc)
        THEN
          CASES (h.handler) $\cdot$ (ref p) $\cdot x$ OF {
           | hang ↦ hang
           | norm y ↦ $f \cdot y$
           | abnorm a ↦
             CASES a OF {
               | excp e ↦
                 CASES $f \cdot (e.\text{es})$ OF {
                   | hang ↦ hang
                   | norm y' ↦ abnorm(excp(es = y',
                                    ex = e.ex))
                   | abnorm a' ↦ abnorm a' }
               | rtrn z ↦
                 CASES $f \cdot z$ OF {
                   | hang ↦ hang
                   | norm y' ↦ abnorm(rtrn y')
                   | abnorm a' ↦ abnorm a' }
               | break b ↦
                 CASES $f \cdot (b.\text{bs})$ OF {
                   | hang ↦ hang
                   | norm y' ↦ abnorm(break(bs = y',
                                    blab = b.blab))
                   | abnorm a' ↦ abnorm a' }
               | cont c ↦
                 CASES $f \cdot (c.\text{cs})$ OF {
                   | hang ↦ hang
                   | norm y' ↦ abnorm(cont(cs = y',
                                    clab = c.clab))
                   | abnorm a' ↦ abnorm a' } } }
        ELSE TRY-LOOP-FINALLY $\cdot p \cdot t \cdot f \cdot x$
        ENDIF }

──────────────────────────────────

Fig. 2. Formalisation of the auxiliary function TRY-LOOP-FINALLY used in Figure 1

```
─ JAVA ─────────────────────────────────────────────────────
   class SideEffectFinally {
       int i, j;
       int aux_test() { try { return i; }
                        finally { i += 10; j += 100; } }
       /*@ normal_behavior
         @    requires: true;
         @ modifiable: i, j;
         @    ensures: \result == \old(i) + \old(j) + 100
         @               && i == \old(i) + 10 && j == \old(j) + 100;
         @*/
       int test() { return aux_test() + j; }
   }

   class SideEffectFinallyPrint {
       public static void main (String[] args) {
           SideEffectFinally a = new SideEffectFinally();
           System.out.println(a.test());   }
   }
───────────────────────────────────────────────────────────
```

This example contains two classes, namely `SideEffectFinally` and `SideEffectFinallyPrint`. The latter is only used for printing one specific result, namely the outcome of the `test` method after both i and j from `SideEffectFinally` have been initialised to the default value 0. The `main` method will then print 100. There are actually two subtle points here. First, of course that the `finally` clause does have an effect after the `return` statement (which leads to abrupt termination). Secondly, the result of the `aux_test` method only shows the effect on j because the value of i has already been bound to the result of the method before the `finally` clause, so that the increment statement i += 10 does not have an influence on the outcome.

The JML specification for the `test` method involves a higher degree of generality, because it is not restricted to the case where both i and j are 0. It states that the `test` method always terminates normally and that its result equals the sum of the values of i and j *before* the method call, plus 100. It also states that this method may modify both i and j—which it actually does, but the modification of i is not shown via the result of the method. As said, this specification holds for the method implementation. The proof in PVS relies on the `try-catch-finally` formalisation from Subsection 5.2.

6.2 Exception Selection

The second example concentrates on the selection of the appropriate `catch` clause, for a thrown exception. It requires several auxiliary exception classes, with suitable inheritance relations between them, namely:

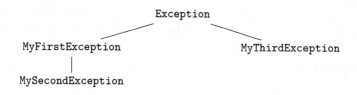

```
Exception
```

```
           MyFirstException                          MyThirdException

           MySecondException
```

— JAVA ———

```java
class MyFirstException extends Exception {
    public MyFirstException(String s) { super(s); }
}
class MySecondException extends MyFirstException {
    public MySecondException(String s) { super(s); }
}
class MyThirdException extends Exception {
    public MyThirdException(String s) { super(s); }
}
class MyExceptions {
    int i;
    void throwSecond() throws Exception {
        throw new MySecondException("oops"); }
    /*@ exceptional_behavior
      @   requires: true;
      @ modifiable: i;
      @   signals: (MyFirstException e) i == \old(i) + 1010 &&
      @                     e.getMessage().equals("oops");
      @*/
    void test() throws Exception {
        String s = "";
        try { throwSecond(); }
        catch (MyThirdException e) { i += 1; }
        catch (MyFirstException e) {
            i += 10;
            s = e.getMessage();
            throw new MyThirdException("bla"); }
        catch (Exception e) { i += 100; }
        finally { i += 1000; throw new MyFirstException(s); } }
}
```

——

The exception that is thrown by the method `throwSecond` is handled by the second `catch`, because `MySecondException` is a subclass of `MyFirstException`. Subsequently, the third `catch` clause is not executed, but, of course, the `finally` clause is. Thus `i` is incremented by 10 + 1000 = 1010. The exception thrown in the `finally` clause is the one that eventually appears.

The JML specification of the method `test` tells that this method will terminate abruptly because of a `MyFirstException`. Further, that in the resulting "abnormal" state the value of i is 1010 more than in the original state (before the method call), and the message of the exception is "oops". The verification in PVS proceeds entirely automatic, and involves almost 5000 small rewrite steps.

7   Conclusion

Java's exception handling mechanism can be a powerful technique for increasing the reliability and robustness of programs written in Java. Proper use of it requires proper understanding of its behaviour. The type-theoretic semantics presented in this paper helps to clarify the different termination possibilities that may occur, by describing them via coalgebras in a precise formal language. It also allows us to precisely formalise the throw and catch behaviour, following the informal language specification. This semantics forms the basis for Java program verification with an appropriate Hoare logic, using proof tools. This has been illustrated with two Java programs involving non-trivial exception handling, whose specifications in JML were verified in PVS.

Acknowledgements. Thanks to Gilad Bracha, Tobias Nipkow and David von Oheimb for discussing (and confirming) the exception invariant (2). Joachim van den Berg, Marieke Huisman, Hans Meijer and Erik Poll provided useful feedback on a first draft.

References

1. J. Alves-Foss and F. S. Lam. Dynamic denotational semantics of Java. In J. Alves-Foss, editor, *Formal Syntax and Semantics of Java*, number 1523 in Lect. Notes Comp. Sci., pages 201–240. Springer, Berlin, 1998.
2. J. van den Berg, M. Huisman, B. Jacobs, and E. Poll. A type-theoretic memory model for verification of sequential Java programs. In D. Bert, C. Choppy, and P. Mosses, editors, *Recent Trends in Algebraic Development Techniques*, number 1827 in Lect. Notes Comp. Sci., pages 1–21. Springer, Berlin, 2000.
3. J. van den Berg and B. Jacobs. The LOOP compiler for Java and JML. Techn. Rep. CSI-R0019, Comput. Sci. Inst., Univ. of Nijmegen. To appear at TACAS'01., 2000.
4. T. Budd. *Understanding Object-Oriented Programming with Java*. Addison-Wesley, 2000. Updated Edition.
5. F. Christian. Correct and robust programs. *IEEE Trans. on Software Eng.*, 10(2):163–174, 1984.
6. J. Gosling, B. Joy, and G. Steele. *The Java Language Specification*. The Java Series. Addison-Wesley, 1996.
7. J. Gosling, B. Joy, G. Steele, and G. Bracha. *The Java Language Specification Second Edition*. The Java Series. Addison-Wesley, 2000.
8. M. Huisman. *Reasoning about JAVA Programs in higher order logic with PVS and Isabelle*. PhD thesis, Univ. Nijmegen, 2001.
9. M. Huisman and B. Jacobs. Inheritance in higher order logic: Modeling and reasoning. In M. Aagaard and J. Harrison, editors, *Theorem Proving in Higher Order Logics*, number 1869 in Lect. Notes Comp. Sci., pages 301–319. Springer, Berlin, 2000.

10. M. Huisman and B. Jacobs. Java program verification via a Hoare logic with abrupt termination. In T. Maibaum, editor, *Fundamental Approaches to Software Engineering*, number 1783 in Lect. Notes Comp. Sci., pages 284–303. Springer, Berlin, 2000.

11. M. Huisman, B. Jacobs, and J. van den Berg. A case study in class library verification: Java's Vector class. Techn. Rep. CSI-R0007, Comput. Sci. Inst., Univ. of Nijmegen. To appear in *Software Tools for Technology Transfer*, 2001.

12. B. Jacobs and E. Poll. A logic for the Java Modeling Language JML. Techn. Rep. CSI-R0018, Comput. Sci. Inst., Univ. of Nijmegen. To appear at FASE'01., 2000.

13. B. Jacobs and E. Poll. A monad for basic Java semantics. In T. Rus, editor, *Algebraic Methodology and Software Technology*, number 1816 in Lect. Notes Comp. Sci., pages 150–164. Springer, Berlin, 2000.

14. B. Jacobs and J. Rutten. A tutorial on (co)algebras and (co)induction. *EATCS Bulletin*, 62:222–259, 1997.

15. B. Jacobs, J. van den Berg, M. Huisman, M. van Berkum, U. Hensel, and H. Tews. Reasoning about classes in Java (preliminary report). In *Object-Oriented Programming, Systems, Languages and Applications (OOPSLA)*, pages 329–340. ACM Press, 1998.

16. G.T. Leavens, A.L. Baker, and C. Ruby. JML: A notation for detailed design. In H. Kilov and B. Rumpe, editors, *Behavioral Specifications of Business and Systems*, pages 175–188. Kluwer, 1999.

17. K.R.M. Leino. *Toward Reliable Modular Programs*. PhD thesis, California Inst. of Techn., 1995.

18. K.R.M. Leino and J.L.A. van de Snepscheut. Semantics of exceptions. In E.-R. Olderog, editor, *Programming Concepts, Methods and Calculi*, pages 447–466. North-Holland, 1994.

19. T. Lindholm and F. Yellin. *The Java Virtual Machine Specification Second Edition*. The Java Series. Addison-Wesley, 1999.

20. B. Meyer. *Object-Oriented Software Construction*. Prentice Hall, 2nd rev. edition, 1997.

21. D. von Oheimb. *Analyzing Java in Isabelle/HOL: Formalization, Type Safety and Hoare Logic*. PhD thesis, Techn. Univ. München, 2000.

22. D. von Oheimb and T. Nipkow. Machine-checking the Java specification: Proving type-safety. In J. Alves-Foss, editor, *Formal Syntax and Semantics of Java*, number 1523 in Lect. Notes Comp. Sci., pages 119–156. Springer, Berlin, 1998.

23. S. Owre, J.M. Rushby, N. Shankar, and F. von Henke. Formal verification for fault-tolerant architectures: Prolegomena to the design of PVS. *IEEE Trans. on Softw. Eng.*, 21(2):107–125, 1995.

24. L.C. Paulson. Isabelle: The next 700 theorem provers. In P. Odifreddi, editor, *Logic and computer science*, pages 361–386. Academic Press, London, 1990. The APIC series, vol. 31.

25. E. Poll, J. van den Berg, and B. Jacobs. Specification of the JavaCard API in JML. In J. Domingo-Ferrer, D. Chan, and A. Watson, editors, *Smart Card Research and Advanced Application*, pages 135–154. Kluwer Acad. Publ., 2000.

26. E. Poll, J. van den Berg, and B. Jacobs. Formal specification of the JavaCard API in JML: the APDU class. *Comp. Networks Mag.*, 2001. To appear.

27. Loop Project. http://www.cs.kun.nl/~bart/LOOP/.

A Formal Executable Semantics
of the JavaCard Platform

Gilles Barthe[1], Guillaume Dufay[1], Line Jakubiec[1,2],
Bernard Serpette[1], and Simão Melo de Sousa[1,3]

[1] INRIA Sophia-Antipolis, France
{Gilles.Barthe,Guillaume.Dufay,Bernard.Serpette,Simao.Desousa}@inria.fr
[2] Université de Provence, Marseille, France jakubiec@lim.univ-mrs.fr
[3] Universidade da Beira Interior, Covilhã, Portugal

Abstract. We present a formal executable specification of two crucial
JavaCard platform components, namely the Java Card Virtual Machine
(JCVM) and the ByteCode Verifier (BCV). Moreover, we relate both
components by giving a proof of correctness of the ByteCode Verifier.
Both formalisations and proofs have been machined-checked using the
proof assistant Coq.

1 Introduction

1.1 Background

JavaCard [17] is a popular programming language for multiple application smart
cards. According to the JavaCard Forum [16], which involves key players in
the field of smart cards, including smart card manufacturers and banks, the
JavaCard language has two important features that make it the ideal choice for
smart cards:

- JavaCard programs are written in a subset of Java, using the JavaCard APIs
  (Application Programming Interfaces). JavaCard developers can therefore
  benefit from the well-established Java technology;
- the JavaCard security model enables multiple applications to coexist on the
  same card and communicate securely, and in principle, enables new applications to be loaded on the card after its issuance.

Yet recent research has unveiled several problems in the JavaCard security
model, most notably with object sharing. This has emphasised the necessity
to develop environments for verifying the security of the JavaCard platform and
of JavaCard programs. Thus far JavaCard security (and also Java security) has
been studied mainly at two levels:

- platform level: here the goal is to prove safety properties of the language, in
  particular type safety and properties related to memory management;
- application level: here the goal is to prove that a specific program obeys
  a given property, and in particular that it satisfies a security policy, for
  example based on information flow.

D. Sands (Ed.): ESOP 2001, LNCS 2028, pp. 302–319, 2001.
© Springer-Verlag Berlin Heidelberg 2001

Over the last few years, both fields have been the subject of intensive investigations, see Subsection 6.1. Despite impressive progress, much work remains to be done. In particular, there is no complete formalisation of the JavaCard platform as yet nor widely used tools to verify applets' properties. Besides, we do not know of any environment that supports verification both at platform and application levels.

1.2 Our Work

The main contributions reported here are (1) a formal executable specification of two crucial JavaCard 2.1. platform components, namely the Java Card Virtual Machine JCVM and the ByteCode Verifier BCV; (2) a machine-checked proof of correctness of the ByteCode Verifier. Both formalisations and proofs have been carried out in the proof assistant Coq [4]. The salient features of our formal specification are:

- *executability.* Our formal semantics (both of the virtual machine and of the verifier) may be executed on any JavaCard program (given a Coq implementation of the native methods used by the program) and its behaviour can be checked against reference implementations, in this case Sun's implementation of the JavaCard Virtual Machine. We view executability as a crucial asset for reliability and, in our opinion, a formal operational semantics for a (realistic) programming language must be executable;
- *completeness.* Our virtual machine is complete in the sense that it treats the whole set of JavaCard instructions and it considers all the important aspects of the platform, including the firewall mechanism around which JavaCard security is organised. Our ByteCode Verifier handles the whole set of instructions but (1) it does not treat object initialisation; (2) subroutines are treated in a somewhat restrictive way.
- *suitability for reasoning.* Our formalisation may be used to reason about the JavaCard platform itself, as shown here, but also to prove properties of JavaCard programs. In particular, our formalisation is well-suited to reason about security properties formulated as temporal-logic properties over execution traces [28].

Thus our development offers the most comprehensive to-date machine-checked account of the JavaCard platform and compares well to similar efforts carried out in the context of Java, see 6.1.

1.3 JavaCard vs. Java

JavaCard is an ideal language for formal verification, since it is a reasonably-sized language with industrial applications. As compared to Java, the JavaCard Virtual Machine (in its current version) lacks garbage collection, dynamic class loading and multi-threading. In contrast, the firewall mechanism is a complex feature that is proper to JavaCard.

1.4   Organisation of the Paper

The remaining of this paper is organised as follows: in Section 2, we describe our formalisation of JavaCard programs (after linking). In Section 3, we describe a small-step operational semantics of the JavaCard Virtual Machine, where each instruction is modelled as a state transformer. In Section 4, we derive from the virtual machine an abstract virtual machine that operates on types (instead of values) and prove its correctness. In Section 5, we use the abstract virtual machine to build a ByteCode Verifier and prove it correct. In Section 6, we conclude with related and future work.

1.5   A Primer on Coq

Coq [4] is a proof assistant based on the Calculus of Inductive Constructions. It combines a specification language (featuring inductive and record types) and a higher-order predicate logic (via the Curry-Howard isomorphism). All functions in Coq are required to be terminating. In order to enforce termination, recursive functions must be defined by structural recursion. Besides, all functions are required to be total. To handle partial functions, we use the lift monad which is introduced through the inductive type:

```
Inductive Exc[A:Set]:Set := value: A->(Exc A) | error: (Exc A)
```

Our specifications only make a limited use of dependent types—a salient feature of Coq. This design choice was motivated by portability; by not using dependent types in an essential way, our formalisations can be transposed easily to other proof assistants, including PVS and Isabelle.

We close this primer with some notation. We use * to denote cartesian product of two types, (a,b) to denote pairs, [x:A] b to denote a λ-abstraction, (x:A) B to denote a dependent function space. Finally, a record type R is represented as an inductive type with a single constructor Build_R. Selectors are functions (defined by case-analysis) so we write l a instead of the more standard a.l.

2   Representation of JavaCard Programs

JavaCard programs are nothing but Java programs satisfying additional constraints. They can be compiled on a class by class basis by a standard compiler, yielding a class file for each class being compiled. For the purpose of JavaCard, compilation is followed by a further transformation phase where a converter transforms the set of class files corresponding to a package into a single CAP file, provided the former are JavaCard compliant. Finally, CAP files are linked before execution (recall JavaCard does not support dynamic class loading); during this last phase, constant pools are resolved and eliminated. Our representation of programs is based on this last format.

2.1 Representation of Data Structures

The JavaCard Virtual Machine distinguishes between primitive types and reference types (for instances of arrays, classes and interfaces). We use a mutual inductive type to enforce the distinction. Formally, the type of primitive types is defined (in Coq) by:

```
Inductive type_prim : Set :=
   Byte          : type_prim |
   Short         : type_prim |
   Int           : type_prim |
   Boolean       : type_prim |
   Void          : type_prim |
   ReturnAddress : type_prim.
```

while the type of (JavaCard) types is defined by:

```
Mutual Inductive type : Set :=
   Prim : type_prim -> type |
   Ref  : type_ref -> type
with type_ref : Set :=
   Ref_array     : type -> type_ref |
   Ref_instance  : nat -> type_ref  |
   Ref_interface : nat -> type_ref .
```

In principle our representation of types allows to form arrays of arrays, which is not permitted in JavaCard. However our formalisation, in particular the implementation of anewarray, does not allow to form such a type. (It is also straightforward to modify our formalisation not to allow such types to be formed.)

2.2 Representation of Programs

A JavaCard program is simply represented by its interfaces, classes and methods:

```
Record jcprogram : Set := {
   interfaces : (list Interface);
   classes    : (list Class);
   methods    : (list Method)
}.
```

Note that, by default, interfaces and classes of the java.lang package and instances of these classes are an integral part of our program. This includes in particular the class Object, the interface Shareable, and Exception classes.

The types Interface, Class and Method are themselves defined as record types. We briefly describe the structure of classes and methods below. Interfaces are described in the full version of this paper.

Classes. A class is described by its superclasses[1] (if any), its methods (including constructors and distinguishing between public methods and package methods), the interfaces it implements, its class variables and, in the case of Java Card, its owning package. For execution purposes, we also need to keep track of the index of the class. Formally, we use the following structure to represent classes:

```
Record Class : Set := {
            (* List of all super classes of this class *)
    super          : (list class_idx);
            (* List of public methods *)
    public_methods : (list Method);
            (* List of package methods *)
    package_methods : (list Method);
            (* List of implemented interfaces *)
            (* For each interface we provide the list of methods *)
            (*   implementing the  interface's methods. Methods   *)
            (*   are tagged with their visibility.                *)
    int_methods    : (list interf_idx*(list vis_method_idx)));
            (* List of types of class variables *)
    class_var      : (list type);
            (* Identification of the owner package*)
    package        : Package;
            (* Index of class *)
    class_id       : class_idx
}.
```

where `class_idx` and `interf_idx` are the types of indexes for classes and interfaces respectively and `vis_method_idx` is the inductive (sum) type:

```
Inductive vis_method_idx : Set :=
            pub_method_idx: method_idx -> vis_method_idx
        |   pac_method_idx: method_idx -> vis_method_idx.
```

where `method_idx` is the type of method indexes (the constructors are used to flag methods' visibility).

Our representation does not take into account the maximum depth of the operand stack during execution of the method. It is a simple matter to include this information but, during execution, we would need to perform many checks.

Methods. A method is characterised by its status (whether it is static or not), its signature (against which one can type-check its arguments upon invocation),

---

[1] Our description of a class c refers to all the classes from which c inherits, i.e. to which c is related by the transitive closure of the superclass relation. For execution purposes, these classes are gathered into a list. Our convention is that the immediate superclass of c appears first in the list. This encoding is chosen to avoid defining functions by well-founded recursion over the subclass relation.

its number of local variables (for initialising its execution context), its exception handlers, its list of instructions to be executed and finally the indexes of the method and of its owning class. Formally, we use the following structure to represent methods:

```
Record Method : Set := {
  (* Indicates whether a method is static or not *)
  is_static : bool;
  (* Signature of the method, pair of domain / codomain *)
  signature   : ((list type)*type);
  (* Number of local variables. *)
  local       : nat;
  (* List of exception handlers *)
  handler_list : (list handler_type);
  (* List of all instructions to be executed. *)
  bytecode    : (list Instruction);
  (* Index of the method in program*)
  method_id   : method_idx;
  (* Index of the owning class *)
  owner       : class_idx
}.
```

where the type `handler_type` collects the information required to define the best handler for a given program counter and exception. Formally, we use the following structure to represent handler types:

```
Definition handler_type :=
              (bytecode_idx*bytecode_idx*class_idx*bytecode_idx).
```

The first two elements define the range at which the exception handler is active. The third element defines the class of exceptions that the handler is meant to catch, whereas the last element points to the first bytecode to execute if this handler is chosen.

A remark on correctness. The above representation makes some implicit assumptions about the program. For example, the index of a method should be less or equal to the number of methods contained in the program. These assumptions are formalised as predicates on `jcprogram`. This is the (mild) price to pay for not using dependent types to represent programs.

2.3 The JCVM Tools

The transformation of JavaCard programs into cap files may be performed by standard tools, namely any Java compiler and JavaCard converter. In order to translate JavaCard programs into our format, we have developed a toolset, called the JCVM Tools (over 4,000 lines of Java code). The JCVM Tools transform a set of CAP files into a Coq expression of type `jcprogram`. In addition, the JCVM

Tools provide a graphical user interface to browse through programs and allow to modify compiled JavaCard programs (so as to check the behaviour of our formal semantics on incorrect programs). We have used the JCVM Tools to debug our formalisation.

3   The Virtual Machine

The Virtual Machine is described by a small-step semantics; more precisely, each instruction is formalised as a state transformer, i.e. a function that takes as input a state (before the instruction is executed) and returns a new state (after the instruction has been executed).

3.1   Values

In order to formalise the virtual machine, we first need to represent, for each JavaCard type, its possible values. These can either be arithmetic values or non-computational values such as memory addresses. Both can be represented as integers; for the latter, we use an implicit coercion from non-computational values to integers. As in [27], we tag values with their types. Formally, we set:[2]

```
Definition valu := type*Z.
```

Here Z is the (inductive) type of binary integers provided by the Coq library. While the inductive representation is suitable for reasoning (each integer has a unique representation in Z), it is less suited for computing and functions such as division are not part of the standard library. Besides, existing operations are not suitable to model overflows. In order to provide an accurate treatment of arithmetic, we therefore proceed as follows:

1. we introduce an alternative representation Z_bits of integers as lists of bits;
2. we define all arithmetic operations as functions over Z_bits. These functions abide to Sun's specifications for overflows;
3. we define bi-directional coercions between Z and Z_bits to switch between the two representations.

3.2   The Memory Model

States are formalised as triples consisting of the heap (containing the objects created during execution), the static heap (containing static fields of classes) and a stack of frames (environments for executing methods). Formally, states are defined by:

```
Definition jcvm_state := static_heap*heap*stack.
```

---

[2] The expression value is already used for the lift monad so we use valu instead.

The static heap is defined as a list of values, whereas the heap is defined as a list of objects. These can either be class instances or arrays, as formalized by the inductive (sum) type:

```
Inductive obj : Set :=
          Instance : type_instance -> obj |
          Array    : type_array -> obj.
```

Both `type_instance` and `type_array` are record types that contain all the relevant information for describing instances and arrays respectively. For example, a class instance is described by the index of the class from which the object is an instance, the instance variables (as a list of `valu`), the reference to the owning package and a flag to indicate whether the object is an entry point and whether it is a permanent or temporary entry point (entry points are used in the JavaCard security model for access control). Formally, we set:

```
Record type_instance : Set := {
  reference              : class_idx;
  contents_i             : (list valu);
  owner_i                : Package;
  is_entry_point         : bool;
  is_permanent_entry_point : bool;
}.
```

Arrays are formalised in a similar fashion.

As to the stack, it is a list of frames that are created upon execution of a method and destroyed upon completion of the method's execution. Formally, we set:

```
Definition stack := (list frame).
```

Each frame has its own array of local variables and its own operand stack which is used to store a method's parameters and results. A frame also has a counter pointing to the next instruction to be executed, a reference to the current method, and a reference to the context of the current method (this context plays a fundamental role in the firewall mechanism). Formally, a frame is described by:

```
Record frame : Set := {
  locvars         : (list valu);       (* Local Variables *)
  opstack         : (list valu);       (* Operand stack *)
  p_count         : bytecode_idx       (* Program counter *)
  method_loc      : method_idx;        (* Location of the method *)
  context_ref     : Package;           (* Context Information *)
  analyzed_method : bool
}.
```

The `analyzed_method` is only used in Section 5 to define the abstraction function that maps each state to an abstract state; the abstraction function is itself used to express the correctness of the ByteCode Verifier.

3.3   Instructions

The semantics of each instruction is formalised using a function of type:

$$\texttt{jcvm\_state * operands} \rightarrow \texttt{returned\_state}$$

The type operands is not a Coq expression but a type determined by the instruction to be executed. In order to handle abrupt termination (that may arise because of uncaught exceptions), the codomain of the function is an inductive (sum) type:

```
Inductive returned_state: Set :=
  Normal   :        jcvm_state->returned_state |
  Abnormal : xcpt->jcvm_state->returned_state.
```

In case of normal execution, the returned state is the one obtained after execution of the instruction (tagged with Normal), whereas in the case of abrupt termination, the returned state is that of the virtual machine when the uncaught exception was raised (tagged with Abnormal and the nature of the uncaught exception). In order to execute the virtual machine, we collect the semantics of each instruction in a one-step execution function exec_instr of type:

$$\texttt{instruction*state*program} \rightarrow \texttt{returned\_state}$$

where instruction is the sum type of instructions. The function takes as inputs an instruction i, a state s and a program p and returns sem_i s o where sem_i is the semantics of i (of type state*operands → returned_state) and o is the list of operands required to execute the instruction (extracted from state).

Note that one cannot use exec_instr to build a function that takes as input a program and returns as output its result because Coq only supports terminating functions. However, we have used Coq's extraction mechanism successfully to derive a one-step execution function in CAML and wrapped it up with a while-loop to produce a certified JavaCard Virtual Machine.

3.4   Exception Management

JavaCard exceptions can either be raised by the program, via the instruction athrow, or by the virtual machine. In addition, execution may simply fail in case of an incoherence due to a memory problem, e.g. if a reference is not found in heap, or an execution problem, e.g. an empty stack for a pop. Our formalisation collects these three kinds of exceptions in an inductive (sum) type. Beware that exceptions in the virtual machine are represented as instances of exception classes, and not as inhabitants of the type xpct. In fact, we use the latter to give the semantics of exception handling.

We now turn to exception handling. Two situations may occur:

- the machine aborts. In the case of a JCVMError, the virtual machine is unable to continue the execution and, by calling an abort function, an abnormal state labelled by the error is returned;
- the exception handling mechanism is launched. In order to catch an exception, one searches for an adequate handler through the stack. This procedure is recursive (it is one of the few places where our formalisation uses recursion), see the full version of this paper.

3.5   Semantics of Invokevirtual

Most instructions have a similar execution pattern: (1) the initial state is decomposed; (2) fragments F of the state are retrieved; (3) observations O are made to determine the new state; (4) the final state is built on the basis of O and F. In this subsection we describe the semantics of invokevirtual. Because of space restrictions, we only consider the main function new_frame_invokevirtual. The function decomposes a state and creates a new frame for the method being invoked.

```
Definition new_frame_invokevirtual :=
[nargs:nat][m:Method][nhp:obj][state:jcvm_state][cap:jcprogram]
Cases state of
(sh, (hp, nil)) => (AbortCode state_error state) |
(sh, (hp, ((cons h lf) as s))) =>

  (* extraction of the list of arguments *)
  Cases (l_take nargs (opstack h)) (l_drop nargs (opstack h)) of
  (value l) (value l') =>

    (* security checking *)
    (if (violation_security_invokevirtual h nhp)
    then (ThrowException Security state cap)
    else

      (* then a signature check is performed *)
      (if (sig_ok l (signature m) cap)
        (* in case of success, the stack of frames is updated *)
      then (Normal (sh, (hp, (cons (Build_frame (nil valu)
                                                (make_locvars l (local m))
                                                (method_id m)
                                                (get_owner_context nhp)
                                                false
                                                (0))
                                   (cons (Build_frame l'
                                                      (locvars h)
                                                      (method_loc h)
                                                      (context_ref h)
                                                      (analyzed h)
                                                      (p_count h))
                                         (tail s))))))
        else (AbortCode signature_error state)
      )
    ) |
    _ _ => (AbortCode opstack_error state)
  end
end.
```

The function performs various security checks, including those imposed by JavaCard firewalls. E.g. the function violation_security_invokevirtual will verify, in case the object nhp is an instance, whether (1) the active context is the JavaCard Runtime Environment context[3] or; (2) the active context is also the context of the instance's owner or; (3) the instance is an entry point. If not, the function returns `true` to flag a security violation.

4   Abstract Virtual Machine

When reasoning about the virtual machine and/or applications, it is convenient to omit some of its intricacies and consider simplified virtual machines instead. In this section, we develop such an abstract virtual machine that manipulates types instead of values. This abstract virtual machine represents, in some sense, a type-checking algorithm for the concrete virtual machine and indeed, in the next section, we show how to derive a ByteCode Verifier from this abstraction.

4.1   Abstract Memory Model

As a first approximation, we would like our abstract values to be the set of (JavaCard) types. However, return addresses needs a special treatment. In the semantics of the instruction `ret`, it is required that the first operand is a value `val` of type `Return_Address` and the integer part of `val` is used to indicate the next value of the program counter. If we simply forget about the integer part of `val`, we are simply unable to indicate the program point where execution is to be continued. We therefore adapt the definition of (abstract, JavaCard) types to store the value to which the program counter needs to be updated. Formally, abstract values (identified with) abstract types are defined as a mutual inductive type, together with abstract primitive types:

```
Inductive abs_type_prim : Set :=
                abs_ReturnAddress : nat -> abs_type_prim | ...
```

The memory model is simplified likewise:

- the heap disappears. Indeed, the type of objects created during execution is always stored in the stack so the heap is not needed any longer.
- the stack disappears and is replaced by a frame. Indeed, execution may be performed on a method by method basis so that only the return type is required for executing a method's invocation (we return to the abstract semantics of invokevirtual in the next subsection). Hence we only need to consider one abstract frame instead of the stack.

We still need to maintain the static heap, abstracted as a list of types. The static heap is used for example in the semantics of `get_static`. Formally, we set:

```
Definition abs_jcvm_state := abs_static_heap*abs_frame.
```

We now turn to the execution model. Execution becomes non-deterministic because some branching instructions may return to different program points depending upon the value on top of the operand stack (and we do not have access to

---

[3] The JavaCard Runtime Environment is privileged and may access all objects.

the value). In order to handle this non-determinism, the corresponding abstract instructions are required to return a list of possible returned states. Formally, instructions are formalised as functions of type:

```
abs_jcvm_state * operands → (list abs_returned_state)
```

As for the concrete virtual machine, one defines a one-step abstract execution function abs_exec_instruction of type:

```
instruction*abs_state*program → abs_returned_state
```

4.2   Exception Management

The abstract virtual machine cannot handle standard JavaCard exceptions such as NullPointer or Arithmetic exceptions because they depend on values forgotten during the abstraction. In fact, the only exceptions handled by the abstract virtual machine are those caused by an incorrect program.

4.3   Semantics of the Abstract Invokevirtual

The abstract semantics for new_frame_invokevirtual does not create a new frame nor perform a check for security exceptions. Moreover the resulting state becomes:

```
(abs_Normal (sh, (Build_abs_frame
                    (app_return_type l' (Snd (signature m)))
                    (abs_locvars h)
                    (abs_method_loc h)
                    (abs_context_ref h)
                    (S (abs_p_count h)))))
```

The return type of the method called (if different from Void) is added to the operand stack of the current frame by calling the function app_return_type and the program counter is incremented.

4.4   Correctness

In order to state the correctness of the abstraction, we want to define a function that maps states to abstract states. As a first step, we define a function alpha_val mapping values to abstract values. Formally, we set:

```
Definition alpha_val [v:valu] : abs_valu :=
Cases (Fst v) of
 (Prim ReturnAddress) =>
                  (abs_Prim (abs_ReturnAddress (absolu (Snd v))))
|    _                 => (type_to_abs_type (Fst v))
end.
```

where `absolu` coerces an integer to its absolute value and `type_to_abs_type` coerces a type to its corresponding abstract type.

Now we need to extend the function `alpha_val` to a function `alpha` that maps every state to an abstract state. It is a simple matter to extract an abstract static heap from a state, but some care is needed to extract an abstract frame from a stack. Indeed, we cannot map a stack to the abstraction of its top frame, because of the invokevirtual function (concrete execution creates a new frame whereas abstract execution does not). In order to cope with this situation, we use the flag of the current analysed frame `m`. If `m` is on the top of the stack then it is abstracted. If there are other frames above, the return type of the frame just above the analysed frame is added to the operand stack of `m` and `m` is then abstracted.

Finally, we extend the function `alpha` to a function `alpha_ret` that maps every returned state to an abstract returned state. The correctness of the abstraction is then stated as a "commuting diagram" relating concrete and abstract execution (up to subtyping), see Figure 1. The hooked vertical arrow on the right-hand side of the diagram and the $\leq$ sign at the bottom-right corner mean that the abstraction of the concrete returned state is, up to subtyping, a member of the list of abstract returned states.

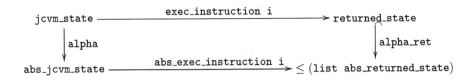

Fig. 1. Commutative diagram of concrete and abstract execution

We have shown[4] in Coq that the diagram commutes (up to subtyping), provided concrete execution does not raise any exception except by calling `AbortCode` (as discussed above, other exceptions cannot be handled by the abstract virtual machine). It follows that every call to `AbortCode` at the concrete level is matched at the abstract level. This is the key to proving the correctness of the ByteCode Verifier.

5   Application: A Certified ByteCode Verifier

The ByteCode Verifier is a key component of JavaCard's security. Below we present a certified ByteCode Verifier derived from the abstract virtual machine described in the previous section. Our ByteCode Verifier ensures that, at every

---

[4] Our proof assumes that the virtual machine verifies some basic properties w.r.t. memory management.

program point, the local variables and the operand stack are appropriately typed for the instruction to be executed. It also ensures that, if a program point is reached several times, the size and type of the operand stack must remain equal. Our ByteCode Verifier treats the whole set of instructions but is not complete: it does not treat subroutines in their full generality nor object initialisation.

5.1   The Verification Algorithm

All the properties suggested above, except the last one, can be verified by executing the abstract Virtual Machine. For the last property, we also have to record the (abstract) state of the (abstract) virtual machine after each step of execution. More precisely, we store an uninitialised returned state for each program point of the analysed method. After each step of execution, we check if the instruction has been performed before and if so, unify in a suitable way the returned state with the state that was stored for this instruction. In case of success, the resulting state after unification state is saved again. If, after unification, the saved state has not changed, the execution can stop for this particular execution path.

Some instructions require some extra care, e.g. (1) for instructions that can lead to two different program points, the execution must continue from both branching points; (2) for exception handlers, the catch block must be executed from the beginning with the appropriate arguments, and at the return point of the exception handler, an unification must occur.

5.2   Correctness of the ByteCode Verifier

The correctness of the ByteCode Verifier comprises two parts:

- a proof of termination. It requires to define a well-founded relation on types and to prove that each unification step produces a state that is strictly smaller than the state that was previously stored. The proof is highly non trivial and is used to define by well-founded recursion the ByteCode Verifier as a function bcv:jcprogram → bool;
- a proof of correctness. One needs to prove that, if bytecode verification is successful, then the function AbortCode will not be called. The proof, which uses the correctness of the abstraction, ensures that the ByteCode Verifier enforces the expected properties.

6   Conclusion

We have presented an executable formal semantics of the JavaCard Virtual Machine and ByteCode Verifier. With 15,000 lines of Coq scripts, our formalisation constitutes the most in-depth machine-checked account of the JavaCard platform to date.

6.1   Related Work

Applications of formal methods and programming language theory to Java and JavaCard are flourishing. Due to space constraints, we only comment on works that emphasise machine-checked verification of the Java or JavaCard platforms, either at platform or application level. Other works that do not emphasise machine-checked verification are discussed in the full version of this paper.

Platform-oriented projects. One of the most impressive achievements to date is that of the Bali project [2], which has formalised in Isabelle/HOL a large body of the Java platform, including (1) the type system and the operational semantics of both the source language and the bytecode, with a proof of type-safety at both levels; (2) the compiler, an abstract ByteCode Verifier and an abstract lightweight ByteCode Verifier, with a proof of their correctness; (3) a sound and complete axiomatic semantics to reason about Java programs. This work is comprehensive in that it treats all components of the Java platform, both at source and bytecode level, but does not take all aspects of Java (let alone JavaCard) into account. For example, Pusch's account [27] of the Java Virtual Machine does not handle arithmetic, exceptions, interfaces and initialisation and Nipkow's [24] and Klein and Nipkow's [19] accounts of the ByteCode Verifier focus on an even smaller fragment of the JVM. Thus, we see our work as complementary to theirs and as further evidence that, as suggested in [25], "machine-checking the design of a non-trivial programming language has become a reality".

Other partial formalisations of the Java and JavaCard platforms are reported by Y. Bertot [5] (object initialisation in Coq after [13]), by R. Cohen [10] (defensive JVM in ACL2), by T. Jensen and co-authors [29] (converter in Coq), by J.-L. Lanet and A. Requet [20] (JCVM in B), by Z. Qian and co-workers [9] (JVM and BCV in Specware) and by D. Syme [31] (operational semantics, type system and type soundness of source Java in DECLARE).

Application-oriented projects. Application-oriented projects may be further classified on the basis of the verification techniques used. These can either be mostly logical or mostly algorithmic.

Logical approaches. The LOOP tool [22], which allows to reason about (source) Java programs via a front-end to PVS and Isabelle, has been applied successfully to the verification of some standard Java class libraries and more recently to the JavaCard APIs. The key ingredients underlying the LOOP's approach are (1) a type-theoretical semantics of Java programs and of the Java memory model; (2) an axiomatic logic to reason about Java programs and Java features, including exceptions, abrupt termination and inheritance; (3) a tool to compile Java classes into PVS or Isabelle theories that form the basis for actual verifications. The main differences with our work are that their semantics works at source level and that it is not directly executable.

Rather similar techniques have been developed independently by A. Poetsch-Heffter and co-workers [23,26], while in [7], P. Brisset combines logical and algorithmic techniques to verify the correctness of Java's security manager. Further uses of logical techniques for the verification of Java programs are reported in [1,11,14].

Algorithmic approaches. The Bandera project [3] has developed a toolset to verify automatically properties of (source) Java programs via a back-end to model-checkers such as SMV and Spin. The toolset has been successfully applied to verify properties of multi-threaded Java programs. The key ingredients underlying the Bandera's approach are (1) a (temporal logic like) specification language to describe program properties; (2) a toolset[5] that extracts from Java source code compact finite-state models; (3) an abstraction specification language and an abstraction engine that derives the abstract program for a given program and abstraction.

Further uses of algorithmic techniques to verify Java programs have been reported e.g. by P. Bieber and co-authors [6] (abstraction and model-checking to detect transitive flows in JavaCard), T. Jensen and co-workers [18] (abstraction and finite-state verification to verify control-flow security properties of Java programs), K. Havelund [15] (Java Path Finder, model-checking of concurrent Java programs), K. R. M. Leino and co-authors [21] (Extended Static Checking, with a back-end to the theorem-prover Simplify). In addition, numerous program analyses and type systems have been designed to verify properties of Java programs.

6.2   Future Work

Our primary objective is to complete our work into a full formalisation of the JavaCard platform (at the bytecode level) that may be used as a basis for reasoning about JavaCard programs. Clearly, much work remains to be done. Below we only outline the most immediate problems we intend to tackle.

Platform level. First and foremost, one needs to complete the formalisation of the ByteCode Verifier. The key challenge is of course to handle subroutines. We see two complementary options here: the first one is to provide a full account of subroutines along the lines of [13,30]. An alternative, first suggested by S. Freund in [12] and recently implemented in the KVM [8], would be to consider a program transformation that translates away subroutines and prove its correctness. Second, it would be interesting to extend our semantics with some features of Java, such as garbage collection, multi-threading and remote method invocation (RMI).

Application level. Many security properties can be expressed as temporal logic formulae over a program's execution trace and can in principle be verified by suitable algorithmic techniques. For these algorithmic verifications to be effective, they should be preceded by abstraction techniques that help reduce the state space. In this paper, we focused on the type abstraction which, in many

---

[5] The toolset combines several program analyses/program transformation techniques, including slicing and partial evaluation.

respects, underlies the ByteCode Verifier. We are currently trying to develop a method to generate automatically an abstract virtual machine and a proof of its correctness for any abstraction function mapping states to a suitably chosen notion of abstract states.

Acknowledgements. The authors would like to thank to Yves Bertot, Marieke Huisman, Jean-Louis Lanet, Shen-Wei Yu and the referees for their comments on this work. Simão Sousa is partially supported by a grant from the Portuguese Fundação para a Ciencia e a Technologia under grant SFRH/BD/790/2000.

References

1. W. Ahrendt, T. Baar, B. Beckert, M. Giese, E. Habermalz, R. Hähnle, W. Menzel, and P. H. Schmitt. The Key approach: integrating design and formal verification of Java Card programs. In *Proceedings of the Java Card Workshop, co-located with the Java Card Forum, Cannes, France*, 2000.
2. BALI project. http://www4.informatik.tu-muenchen.de/~isabelle/bali
3. Bandera project. http://www.cis.ksu.edu/santos/bandera
4. B. Barras, S. Boutin, C. Cornes, J. Courant, Y. Coscoy, D. Delahaye, D. de Rauglaudre, J.-C. Filliâtre, E. Giménez, H. Herbelin, G. Huet, H. Laulhère, P. Loiseleur, C. Muñoz, C. Murthy, C. Parent-Vigouroux, C. Paulin-Mohring, A. Saïbi, and B. Werner. *The Coq Proof Assistant User's Guide. Version 6.3.1*, December 1999.
5. Y. Bertot. Formalizing in Coq a type system for object initialization in the Java bytecode language. Manuscript, 2000.
6. P. Bieber, J. Cazin, V. Wiels, G. Zanon, P. Girard, and J.-L. Lanet. Electronic purse applet certification: extended abstract. In S. Schneider and P. Ryan, editors, *Proceedings of the workshop on secure architectures and information flow*, volume 32 of *Electronic Notes in Theoretical Computer Science*. Elsevier Publishing, 2000.
7. P. Brisset. A Case Study In Java Software Verification: SecurityManager.checkConnect(). In S. Drossopoulou, S. Eisenbach, B. Jacobs, G. T. Leavens, P. Müller, and A. Poetzsch-Heffter, editors, *Formal Techniques for Java Programs*. Technical Report 269, 5/2000, Fernuniversität Hagen, Fernuniversität Hagen, 2000.
8. CLDC and the K Virtual Machine (KVM). http://java.sun.com/products/cldc
9. A. Coglio, A. Goldberg, and Z. Qian. Towards a Provably-Correct Implementation of the JVM Bytecode Verifier. In *Formal Underpinnings of Java Workshop at OOPSLA*, 1998.
10. R. M. Cohen. Defensive Java Virtual Machine Specification Version 0.5. Manuscript, 1997.
11. M. Dam and P. Giambiagi. Confidentiality for mobile code: The case of a simple payment protocol. In *Proceedings of CSFW'00*. IEEE Press, 2000.
12. S. N. Freund. The Costs and Benefits of Java Bytecode Subroutines. In *Formal Underpinnings of Java Workshop at OOPSLA*, 1998.
13. S. N. Freund and J. C. Mitchell. A type system for object initialization in the Java bytecode language. In *Proceedings of OOPSLA '98*, volume 33(10) of *ACM SIGPLAN Notices*, pages 310–328. ACM Press, October 1998.
14. R. Goré and L. Nguyen. CardKt: Automated Logical Deduction on Java Cards. In *Proceedings of the Java Card Workshop, co-located with the Java Card Forum, Cannes, France*, 2000.

15. K. Havelund. Java PathFinder—A Translator from Java to Promela. In D. Dams, R. Gerth, S. Leue, and M. Massink, editors, *Proceedings of 5th and 6th International SPIN Workshops*, volume 1680 of *Lecture Notes in Computer Science*, page 152. Springer-Verlag, 1999.
16. JavaCard Forum. http://www.javacardforum.org
17. JavaCard Technology. http://java.sun.com/products/javacard
18. T. Jensen, D. Le Métayer, and T. Thorn. Verification of control flow based security policies. In *Proceedings of the IEEE Symposium on Research in Security and Privacy*, pages 89–103. IEEE Computer Society Press, 1999.
19. G. Klein and T. Nipkow. Lightweight bytecode verification. In S. Drossopoulou, S. Eisenbach, B. Jacobs, G. T. Leavens, P. Müller, and A. Poetzsch-Heffter, editors, *Formal Techniques for Java Programs*. Technical Report 269, 5/2000, Fernuniversität Hagen, Fernuniversität Hagen, 2000.
20. J.-L. Lanet and A. Requet. Formal Proof of Smart Card Applets Correctness. In *Proceedings of CARDIS'98*, 1998.
21. K. R. M. Leino, J. B. Saxe, and R. Stata. Checking Java programs via guarded commands. In B. Jacobs, G. T. Leavens, P. Müller, and A. Poetzsch-Heffter, editors, *Formal Techniques for Java Programs*. Technical Report 251, 1999, Fernuniversität Hagen, Fernuniversität Hagen, 1999.
22. LOOP project. http://www.cs.kun.nl/~bart/LOOP
23. J. Meyer and A. Poetzsch-Heffter. An architecture for interactive program provers. In S. Graf and M. Schwartzbach, editors, *Proceedings of TACAS'2000*, volume 1785 of *Lecture Notes in Computer Science*, pages 63–77. Springer-Verlag, 2000.
24. T. Nipkow. Verified Bytecode Verifiers. In F. Honsell, editor, *Proceedings of FOSSACS'01*, volume xxxx of *Lecture Notes in Computer Science*. Springer-Verlag, 2001. To appear.
25. T. Nipkow and D. von Oheimb. Java$_{light}$ is type-safe—definitely. In *Proceedings of POPL'98*, pages 161–170. ACM Press, 1998.
26. A. Poetzsch-Heffter and P. Müller. A Programming Logic for Sequential Java. In D. Swiestra, editor, *Proceedings of ESOP'99*, volume 1576 of *Lecture Notes in Computer Science*, pages 162–176. Springer-Verlag, 1999.
27. C. Pusch. Proving the soundness of a Java bytecode verifier specification in Isabelle/HOL. In W. R. Cleaveland, editor, *Proceedings of TACAS'99*, volume 1579 of *Lecture Notes in Computer Science*, pages 89–103. Springer-Verlag, 1999.
28. F. B. Schneider. Enforceable security policies. Technical Report TR99-1759, Cornell University, October 1999.
29. G. Ségouat. Preuve en Coq d'une mise en oeuvre de Java Card. Master's thesis, University of Rennes 1, 1999.
30. R. Stata and M. Abadi. A type system for Java bytecode subroutines. In *Proceedings of POPL'98*, pages 149–160. ACM Press, 1998.
31. D. Syme. Proving Java type soundness. In J. Alves-Foss, editor, *Formal Syntax and Semantics of Java*, volume 1523 of *Lecture Notes in Computer Science*, pages 83–118. Springer-Verlag, 1999.

Modeling an Algebraic Stepper

John Clements, Matthew Flatt*, and Matthias Felleisen**

Department of Computer Science
Rice University
6100 Main St.
Houston, TX 77005-1892

Abstract. Programmers rely on the correctness of the tools in their programming environments. In the past, semanticists have studied the correctness of compilers and compiler analyses, which are the most important tools. In this paper, we make the case that other tools, such as debuggers and steppers, deserve semantic models, too, and that using these models can help in developing these tools.

Our concrete starting point is the algebraic stepper in DrScheme, our Scheme programming environment. The algebraic stepper explains a Scheme computation in terms of an algebraic rewriting of the program text. A program is rewritten until it is in a canonical form (if it has one). The canonical form is the final result.

The stepper operates within the existing evaluator, by placing breakpoints and by reconstructing source expressions from source information placed on the stack. This approach raises two questions. First, do the run-time breakpoints correspond to the steps of the reduction semantics? Second, does the debugging mechanism insert enough information to reconstruct source expressions?

To answer these questions, we develop a high-level semantic model of the extended compiler and run-time machinery. Rather than modeling the evaluation as a low-level machine, we model the relevant low-level features of the stepper's implementation in a high-level reduction semantics. We expect the approach to apply to other semantics-based tools.

1 The Correctness of Programming Environment Tools

Programming environments provide many tools that process programs semantically. The most common ones are compilers, program analysis tools, debuggers, and profilers. Our DrScheme programming environment [9,8] also provides an algebraic stepper for Scheme. It explains a program's execution as a sequence of reduction steps based on the ordinary laws of algebra for the functional core [2,

* Current Address: School of Computing, 50 S. Central Campus Dr., Rm. 3190, University of Utah, SLC, UT 84112-9205

** Work partially supported by National Science Foundation grants CCR-9619756, CDA-9713032, and CCR-9708957, and a state of Texas ATP grant.

D. Sands (Ed.): ESOP 2001, LNCS 2028, pp. 320–334, 2001.
© Springer-Verlag Berlin Heidelberg 2001

21] and more general algebraic laws for the rest of the language [6]. An algebraic stepper is particularly helpful for teaching; selective uses can also provide excellent information for complex debugging situations.

Traditionally researchers have used semantic models to verify and to develop compilation processes, analyses, and compiler optimizations. Other semantics-based programming environment tools, especially debuggers, profilers, or steppers, have received much less attention. Based on our development of DrScheme, however, we believe that these tools deserve the same attention as compilers or analyses. For example, a debugging compiler and run-time environment should have the same *extensional* semantics as the standard compiler and run-time system. Otherwise a programmer cannot hope to find bugs with these tools.

The implementation of an algebraic stepper as part of the compiler and run-time environment is even more complex than that of a debugger. A stepper must be able to display all atomic reduction steps as rewriting actions on program text. More specifically, an embedded stepper must be guaranteed

1. to stop for every reduction step in the algebraic semantics; and
2. to have enough data to reconstruct the execution state in textual form.

To prove that an algebraic stepper has these properties, we must model it at a reasonably high level so that the proof details do not become overwhelming.

In this paper, we present a semantic model of our stepper's basic operations *at the level of a reduction semantics*. Then we show in two stages that the stepper satisfies the two criteria. More precisely, in the following section we briefly demonstrate our stepper. The third section introduces the reduction model of the stepper's run-time infrastructure and presents the elaboration theorem, which proves that the stepper infrastructure can keep track of the necessary information. The fourth section presents the theory behind the algebraic stepper and the stepper theorem, which proves that the inserted breakpoints stop execution once per reduction step in the source language. Together, the two theorems prove that our stepper is correct modulo elaboration into a low-level implementation. The paper concludes with a brief discussion of related and future work.

2   An Algebraic Stepper for Scheme

Most functional language programmers are familiar with the characterization of an evaluation as a series of reduction steps. As a toy example, consider the first few steps in the evaluation of a simple factorial function in Scheme:

$$
\begin{aligned}
&\boxed{(\text{fact } 3)} \\
&= (\text{if } \boxed{(=\ 3\ 1)}\ 1\ (* (\text{fact } (-\ 3\ 1))\ 3)) \\
&= \boxed{(\text{if false } 1\ (* (\text{fact } (-\ 3\ 1))\ 3))} \\
&= (* (\text{fact } \boxed{(-\ 3\ 1)})\ 3) \\
&\ \cdots
\end{aligned}
$$

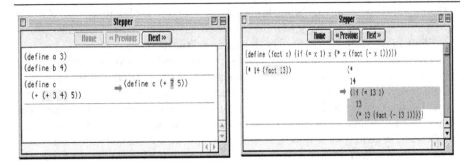

An arithmetic reduction   A procedure application

Fig. 1. The stepper in action

Each step represents the entire program. The boxed subexpression is the standard redex. The sequence illustrates the reduction of function applications (β_v), primitive applications (δ_v), and **if** expressions.

DrScheme implements a more sophisticated version of the same idea. The two screen dumps of fig. 1 show the visual layout of the stepper window. The window is separated into three parts. The top shows evaluated forms. Each expression or definition moves to the upper pane when it has been reduced to a canonical form. The second pane shows the redex and the contractum of the current reduction step. The redex is highlighted in green, while the contractum—the result of the reduction—is highlighted in purple. The fourth pane is reserved for expressions that are yet to be evaluated; it is needed to deal with lexical scope and effects.

The two screen dumps of fig. 1 illustrate the reduction of an arithmetic expression and a procedure call. The call to the procedure is replaced by the body of the procedure, with the argument values substituted for the formal parameters. Other reduction steps are modeled in a similar manner. Those of the imperative part of Scheme are based on Felleisen and Hieb's work on a reduction semantics for Scheme [6]; they require no changes to the infrastructure itself. For that reason, we ignore the imperative parts of Scheme in this paper and focus on the functional core.

3   Marking Continuations

The implementation of our stepper requires the extension of the existing compiler and its run-time machinery. The compiler must be enriched so that it emits instructions that maintain connections between the machine state and the original program text. The run-time system includes code for decoding this additional information into textual form.

To model this situation, we can either design a semantics that reflects the details of a low-level machine, or we can enrich an algebraic reduction framework with constructs that reflect how the compiler and the run-time system keep track of the state of the evaluation. We choose the latter strategy for two reasons.

1. The reduction model is smaller and easier to manage than a machine model that contains explicit environments, stacks, heaps, etc. The research community understands how compilers manage associations between variables and values. Modeling this particular aspect would only pollute the theorems and proofs, without making any contribution.
2. Furthermore, it is possible to derive all kinds of low-level machines from a high-level semantics [5,13]. These derivations work for our extended framework, which means the proof carries over to several implementations of the low-level mechanism.

The goal of this section is to introduce the source-level constructs that model the necessary continuation-based information management and to show that they can keep track of the necessary information. The model is extended in the next section to a model of a stepper for the core of a functional language.

Section 3.1 presents *continuation marks*, the central idea of our model. Section 3.2 formalizes this description as an extension of the functional reduction semantics of Scheme. Section 3.3 introduces an elaboration function that inserts these forms into programs and states a theorem concerning the equivalence of a program, its elaborated form, and the annotations in the reduction semantics.

3.1   Introduction to Continuation Marks

It is natural to regard a program's continuation as a series of frames. In this context, a *continuation mark* is a distinct frame that contains a single value.

Continuation-mark frames are transparent to the evaluation. When control returns to such a frame, the mark frame is removed. When a program adds a mark to a continuation that is already marked (that is, when two marks appear in succession), the new mark replaces the old one. This provision preserves tail-optimizations for all derived implementations. Not all machines are tail-optimizing, e.g., the original SECD machine [17], but due to this provision our framework works for both classes of machines.

In addition to the usual constructs of a functional language, our model contains two new continuation operations:

(with-continuation-mark *mark-expr expr*) : *mark-expr* and *expr* are arbitrary expressions. The first evaluates to a mark-value, which is then placed in a marked frame on top of the continuation. If the current top frame is already marked, the new frame replaces it. Finally, *expr* is evaluated. Its value becomes the result of the entire **with-continuation-mark** expression.

(current-continuation-marks) : The result of this expression is the list of values in the mark frames of the current continuation.

The two programs in fig. 2 illustrate how an elaborator may instrument a factorial function with these constructs.[1] Both definitions implement a factorial

---

[1] For space reasons, **with-continuation-mark** and current-continuation-marks are abbreviated as **w-c-m** and **c-c-m** from now on.

```
(define (fact n)                      (define (fact-tr n)
   (letrec                               (letrec
      ([! (lambda (n)                        ([! (lambda (n a)
            (if (= n 0)                            (if (= n 0)
               (begin                                (begin
                  (display (c-c-m))                      (display (c-c-m))
                  (newline)                              (newline)
                  1)                                     a)
               (w-c-m n                              (w-c-m n
                  (* n (! (- n 1)))))))])               (! (- n 1) (* a n)))))))])
      (! n)))                                 (! n 1)))

> (fact 4)                            > (fact 4)

(1 2 3 4) ; displayed output           (1) ; displayed output

24                                    24
```

Fig. 2. The relationship between continuation-marks and tail-recursion

function that marks its continuation at the recursive call site and reports the continuation-mark list before returning. The one in the left column is properly recursive, the one on the right is tail-recursive. The boxed texts are the outputs that applications of their respective functions produce. For the properly recursive program on the left, the box shows that the continuation contains four mark frames. For the tail-recursive variant, only one continuation mark remains; the others have been overwritten during the evaluation.[2]

3.2   Breakpoints and Continuation Marks

To formulate the semantics of our new language constructs and to illustrate their use in the implementation of a stepper, we present a small model and study its properties. The model consists of a source language, a target language, and a mapping from the former to the latter.

The source and target language share a high-level core syntax, based on the λ-calculus. The source represents the surface syntax, while the target is a representation of the intermediate compiler language. The source language of this section supports a primitive inspection facility in the form of a **(breakpoint)** expression. The target language has instead a continuation mark mechanism.

---

[2] This elision of continuation marks is the principal difference between our device and that of Moreau's dynamic bindings [19]. If we were to use dynamic bindings to preserve runtime information, the resulting programs would lose tail-call optimizations, which are critical in a functional world.

$$L, M, N = n \mid \text{'}x \mid \textbf{true} \mid \textbf{false} \mid (\textbf{if } M\ M\ M) \mid (\textbf{cons } M\ M) \mid (\textbf{car } M) \mid$$
$$(\textbf{cdr } M) \mid \textbf{null} \mid (M\ M) \mid (P\ M\ M) \mid (\textbf{lambda } (x)\ M) \mid$$
$$x \mid (\textbf{breakpoint})$$
$$P = + \mid eq\textit{?}$$
$$V, W = n \mid \textbf{true} \mid \textbf{false} \mid \text{'}x \mid (\textbf{cons } V\ V) \mid x \mid \textbf{null} \mid (\textbf{lambda } (x)\ M)$$
$$E = (\textbf{cons } E\ M) \mid (\textbf{cons } V\ E) \mid (\textbf{if } E\ M\ M) \mid (\textbf{car } E) \mid (\textbf{cdr } E) \mid$$
$$(E\ M) \mid (V\ E) \mid (P\ E\ M) \mid (P\ V\ E) \mid []$$
$$\mathcal{L} = E \cup \{\tau\}$$

final states $= V \cup \{\textbf{error}\}$ $\qquad x \in$ variables $\qquad n \in$ numbers

$$E[(V\ W)] \xmapsto{\tau} \begin{cases} E[[W/x]M] \text{ if } V = (\textbf{lambda } (x)\ M) \\ \textbf{error} \qquad \text{otherwise} \end{cases}$$

$$E[(+\ V\ W)] \xmapsto{\tau} \begin{cases} E[V + W] \text{ if } V \text{ and } W \text{ are numbers} \\ \textbf{error} \qquad \text{otherwise} \end{cases}$$

$$E[(eq\textit{?}\ V\ W)] \xmapsto{\tau} \begin{cases} E[\textbf{true}] \text{ if } V \text{ and } W \text{ are the same symbol} \\ E[\textbf{false}] \text{ if } V \text{ and } W \text{ are different symbols} \\ \textbf{error} \qquad \text{otherwise} \end{cases}$$

$$E[(\textbf{car }\ V)] \xmapsto{\tau} \begin{cases} E[W] \text{ if } V = (\textbf{cons } W\ Z) \\ \textbf{error} \text{ otherwise} \end{cases}$$

$$E[(\textbf{cdr }\ V)] \xmapsto{\tau} \begin{cases} E[Z] \text{ if } V = (\textbf{cons } W\ Z) \\ \textbf{error} \text{ otherwise} \end{cases}$$

$$E[(\textbf{if }\ V\ M\ N)] \xmapsto{\tau} \begin{cases} E[M] \text{ if } V = \textbf{true} \\ E[N] \text{ if } V = \textbf{false} \\ \textbf{error} \text{ otherwise} \end{cases}$$

$$E[(\textbf{breakpoint})] \xmapsto{E} E[13]$$

Fig. 3. Grammar and Reduction rules for the source language

The translation from the source to the target demonstrates how the continuation mark mechanism can explain the desired breakpoint mechanism.

The syntax and semantics of the source language are shown in fig. 3. The set of program expressions is the closed subset of M. The primitives are the set P. The set of values is described by V. The semantics of the language is defined using a rewriting semantics [6].[3] E denotes the set of evaluation contexts. Briefly, a program is reduced by separating it into an evaluation context and an

---

[3] Following Barendregt [2], we assume syntactic α-equivalence to sidestep the problem of capture in substitution. We further use this equivalence to guarantee that no two lexically bound identifiers share a name.

$$M_t = n \mid {}'x \mid \textbf{true} \mid \textbf{false} \mid (\textbf{if } M_t \ M_t \ M_t) \mid \textbf{cons } M_t \ M_t) \mid (\textbf{car } M_t) \mid$$
$$(\textbf{cdr } M_t) \mid \textbf{null} \mid (M_t \ M_t) \mid (P \ M_t \ M_t) \mid (\textbf{lambda } (x) \ M_t) \mid$$
$$x \mid (\textbf{w-c-m } M_t \ M_t) \mid (\textbf{c-c-m}) \mid (\textbf{output } M_t)$$
$$E_t = (\textbf{w-c-m } V \ F_t) \mid F_t$$
$$F_t = (\textbf{cons } E_t \ M_t) \mid (\textbf{cons } V \ E_t) \mid (\textbf{if } E_t \ M_t \ M_t) \mid (\textbf{car } E_t) \mid (\textbf{cdr } E_t) \mid$$
$$(E_t \ M_t) \mid (V \ E_t) \mid (P \ E_t \ M_t) \mid (P \ V \ E_t) \mid (\textbf{output } E_t) \mid []$$
$$\mathcal{L}_t = V \cup \{\tau\}$$
$$\text{final states} = V \cup \{\textbf{error}\}$$

The function '$\mapsto_t$' extends '$\mapsto$' with the following rules:

$$E_t[(\textbf{w-c-m } V \ (\textbf{w-c-m } W \ M))] \xrightarrow{\tau}_t E_t[(\textbf{w-c-m } W \ M)] \ (\text{where } E_t \neq E_t'[(\textbf{w-c-m } Z \ [])])$$
$$E_t[(\textbf{w-c-m } V \ W)] \xrightarrow{\tau}_t E_t[W] \ (\text{where } E_t \neq E_t'[(\textbf{w-c-m } V \ [])])$$
$$E_t[(\textbf{c-c-m})] \xrightarrow{\tau}_t E_t[X[\![E_t]\!]]$$
$$E_t[(\textbf{output } V)] \xrightarrow{V}_t E_t[13]$$

where

$$X[\![(\textbf{w-c-m } V \ E_t)]\!] = (\textbf{cons } V \ X[\![E_t]\!])$$

$$X[\![E_t]\!] = X[\![E_t']\!] \text{ where } E_t = \begin{cases} (\textbf{cons } E_t' \ M) \\ (\textbf{cons } V \ E_t') \\ (\textbf{if } E_t' \ M \ M) \\ \dots \end{cases}$$

$$X[\![[]]\!] = \textbf{null}$$

Fig. 4. Extension of the source language M to the target language M_t

instruction—the set of instructions is defined implicitly by the left-hand-sides of the reductions—then applying one of the reduction rules. This is repeated until the process halts with a value or an error.

To model output, our reduction semantics uses a Labeled Transition System [18], where $\mathcal{L}$ denotes the set of labels. $\mathcal{L}$ includes the evaluation contexts along with τ, which denotes the transition without output. The only expression that generates output is the **(breakpoint)** expression. It displays the current evaluation context. Since the instruction at the breakpoint must in fact be **(breakpoint)**, this is equivalent to displaying the current program expression. The expression reduces to 13, an arbitrarily chosen value. When we write $\mapsto$ with no superscript, it indicates not that there is no output, but rather that the output is not pertinent.

The relation $\mapsto$ is a function. That is, an expression reduces to at most one other expression. This follows from the chain of observations that:

1. the set of values and the set of instructions are disjoint,
2. the set of values and the set of reducible expressions are therefore disjoint,

3. the instructions may not be decomposed except into the empty context and the instruction itself, and therefore that

4. an expression has at most one decomposition.

Multi-step evaluation $\mapsto\!\!\!\!\rightarrow$ is defined as the transitive, reflexive closure of the relation $\mapsto$. That is, we say that $M_0 \overset{O}{\mapsto\!\!\!\!\rightarrow} M_n$ if there exist $M_0, \ldots, M_n$ such that $M_i \overset{l_i}{\mapsto\!\!\!\!\rightarrow} M_{i+1}$ and $O \in \mathcal{L}^* = l_0 l_1 \ldots l_{n-1}$.

The evaluation function eval(M) is defined in the standard way:

$$\text{eval}(M) = \begin{cases} V & \text{if } M \mapsto\!\!\!\!\rightarrow V \\ \text{error} & \text{if } M \mapsto\!\!\!\!\rightarrow \text{error} \end{cases}$$

For a reduction sequence $S = (M_0 \mapsto M_1 \mapsto \cdots \mapsto M_n)$, we define trace$(S)$ to be the sequence of non-empty outputs:

$$\text{trace}(S) = \begin{cases} () & \text{if } S = (M) \\ \text{trace}(M_1 \mapsto \cdots \mapsto M_n) & \text{if } S = (M_0 \overset{\tau}{\mapsto} M_1 \mapsto \cdots \mapsto M_n) \\ (E \, . \, \text{trace}(M_1 \mapsto \cdots \mapsto M_n)) & \text{if } S = (M_0 \overset{E}{\mapsto} M_1 \mapsto \cdots \mapsto M_n) \end{cases}$$

The target language of our model is similar to the source language, except that it contains **w-c-m** and **c-c-m**, and an **output** instruction that simply displays a given value. The grammar and reduction rules for this language are an adaptation of that of the source language. They appear in fig. 4.

The evaluation of the target language is designed to concatenate neighboring **w-c-m**'s, which is critical for the preservation of tail-call optimizations in the source semantics. Frame overwriting is enforced by defining the set of evaluation contexts to prohibit immediately nested occurrences of **w-c-m**-expressions. In particular, the set E_t may include any kind of continuation, but its **w-c-m** variant F_t requires a subexpression that is not a **w-c-m** expression.

Note also the restriction on the **w-c-m** reductions that the enclosing context must not end with a **w-c-m**. This avoids two ambiguities: one that arises when two nested **w-c-m** expressions occur with a value inside the second, another that occurs when three or more **w-c-m** expressions appear in sequence.

For the target language, the set of labels is the set of values plus τ. The **output** instruction is the only instruction that generates output.

The standard reduction relation $\mapsto_t$ is a function. This follows from an argument similar to that for the source language. Multiple-step reduction is defined as in the source language by the transitive, reflexive closure of $\mapsto_t$, written as $\mapsto\!\!\!\!\rightarrow_t$. The target language's evaluation function eval$_t$ and trace function trace$_t$ are adapted mutatis mutandis from their source language counterparts, with $\mapsto$ and $\mapsto\!\!\!\!\rightarrow$ replaced by $\mapsto_t$ and $\mapsto\!\!\!\!\rightarrow_t$.

Roughly speaking, (**breakpoint**) is a primitive breakpoint facility that displays the program's execution state. The purpose of our model is to show that we can construct an elaboration function $\mathcal{A}$ from the source language to the target language that creates the same effect via a combination of continuation marks and a simple **output** expression.

$$\mathcal{A}[\![V]\!] = \begin{cases} (\textbf{cons } \mathcal{A}[\![V]\!] \ \mathcal{A}[\![W]\!]) & \text{if } V = (\textbf{cons } V \ W) \\ (\textbf{lambda } (x) \ \mathcal{A}[\![M]\!]) & \text{if } V = (\textbf{lambda } (x) \ M) \\ V & \text{otherwise} \end{cases}$$

$$\mathcal{A}[\![(\textbf{breakpoint})]\!] = (\textbf{w-c-m } (\textbf{list } \text{'break}) \ (\textbf{output } (\textbf{c-c-m})))$$

$$\mathcal{A}[\![(V \ M)]\!] = (\textbf{w-c-m } (\textbf{list } \text{'appB } \mathcal{A}[\![V]\!]) \ (\mathcal{A}[\![V]\!] \ \mathcal{A}[\![M]\!]))$$

$$\mathcal{A}[\![(M \ N)]\!] = (\textbf{w-c-m } (\textbf{list } \text{'appA } \mathcal{Q}[\![N]\!])$$
$$((\textbf{lambda } (\mathcal{F}) \ (\textbf{w-c-m } (\textbf{list } \text{'appB } \mathcal{F}) \ (\mathcal{F} \ \mathcal{A}[\![N]\!]))) \ \mathcal{A}[\![M]\!]))$$

$$\mathcal{A}[\![(\textbf{if } L \ M \ N)]\!] = (\textbf{w-c-m } (\textbf{list } \text{'if } \mathcal{Q}[\![M]\!] \ \mathcal{Q}[\![N]\!]) \ (\textbf{if } \mathcal{A}[\![L]\!] \ \mathcal{A}[\![M]\!] \ \mathcal{A}[\![N]\!]))$$

$$\mathcal{A}[\![(\textbf{cons } V \ M)]\!] = (\textbf{w-c-m } (\textbf{list } \text{'consB } \mathcal{A}[\![V]\!]) \ (\textbf{cons } \mathcal{A}[\![V]\!] \ \mathcal{A}[\![M]\!]))$$

$$\mathcal{A}[\![(\textbf{cons } M \ N)]\!] = (\textbf{w-c-m } (\textbf{list } \text{'consA } \mathcal{Q}[\![N]\!])$$
$$((\textbf{lambda } (\mathcal{F}) \ (\textbf{w-c-m } (\textbf{list } \text{'consB } \mathcal{F}) \ (\textbf{cons } \mathcal{F} \ \mathcal{A}[\![N]\!])))$$
$$\mathcal{A}[\![M]\!]))$$

$$\mathcal{A}[\![(\textbf{car } M)]\!] = (\textbf{w-c-m } (\textbf{list } \text{'car}) \ (\textbf{car } \mathcal{A}[\![M]\!]))$$

$$\mathcal{A}[\![(\textbf{cdr } M)]\!] = (\textbf{w-c-m } (\textbf{list } \text{'cdr}) \ (\textbf{cdr } \mathcal{A}[\![M]\!]))$$

$$\mathcal{A}[\![(P \ V \ M)]\!] = (\textbf{w-c-m } (\textbf{list } \text{'primB } P \ V) \ (P \ V \ \mathcal{A}[\![M]\!]))$$

$$\mathcal{A}[\![(P \ M \ N)]\!] = (\textbf{w-c-m } (\textbf{list } \text{'primA } P \ \mathcal{Q}[\![N]\!])$$
$$((\textbf{lambda } (\mathcal{F}) \ (\textbf{w-c-m } (\textbf{list } \text{'primB } P \ \mathcal{F}) \ (P \ \mathcal{F} \ \mathcal{A}[\![N]\!]))) \ \mathcal{A}[\![M]\!]))$$

where

$$\mathcal{Q}[\![x]\!] = (\textbf{list } \text{'val } x)$$
$$\mathcal{Q}[\![\text{'x}]\!] = (\textbf{list } \text{'quote } \text{'x})$$
$$\mathcal{Q}[\![M]\!] = \begin{cases} (\textbf{list } \text{'app } \mathcal{Q}[\![M_1]\!] \ \mathcal{Q}[\![M_2]\!]) & \text{if } M = (M_1 \ M_2) \\ (\textbf{list } \text{'if } \mathcal{Q}[\![M_1]\!] \ \mathcal{Q}[\![M_2]\!] \ \mathcal{Q}[\![M_3]\!]) & \text{if } M = (\textbf{if } M_1 \ M_2 \ M_3) \\ \dots \end{cases}$$

Fig. 5. The annotating function, $\mathcal{A} : M \to M_t$

The elaboration function is defined in fig. 5.[4] It assumes that the identifier $\mathcal{F}$ does not appear in the source program. It also relies upon a quoting function, $\mathcal{Q}$, which translates source terms to values representing them, except for the unusual treatment of variable names. These are not quoted, so that substitution occurs even within marks.

3.3   Properties of the Model

The translation from the breakpoint language to the language with continuation marks preserves the behavior of all programs. In particular, terminating programs in the source model are elaborated into terminating programs in the target language. Programs that fail to converge are elaborated into programs that also fail to converge. Finally, there is a function $\mathcal{T}$, shown in fig. 6, mapping the values produced by **output** in the target program to the corresponding

---

[4] The **list** constructor is used in the remainder of the paper as a syntactic abbreviation for a series of **cons**es.

$$\mathcal{T}[\![(\textbf{cons } (\textbf{list } \text{'appA } N) \ M)]\!] = (\mathcal{T}[\![M]\!] \ \overline{\mathcal{Q}}[\![N]\!])$$
$$\mathcal{T}[\![(\textbf{cons } (\textbf{list } \text{'appB } V) \ M)]\!] = (V \ \mathcal{T}[\![M]\!])$$
$$\mathcal{T}[\![(\textbf{cons } (\textbf{list } \text{'if } N \ L) \ M)]\!] = (\textbf{if } \mathcal{T}[\![M]\!] \ \overline{\mathcal{Q}}[\![N]\!] \ \overline{\mathcal{Q}}[\![L]\!])$$
$$\mathcal{T}[\![(\textbf{cons } (\textbf{list } \text{'consA } N) \ M)]\!] = (\textbf{cons } \mathcal{T}[\![M]\!] \ \overline{\mathcal{Q}}[\![N]\!])$$
$$\mathcal{T}[\![(\textbf{cons } (\textbf{list } \text{'consB } V) \ M)]\!] = (\textbf{cons } V \ \mathcal{T}[\![M]\!])$$
$$\mathcal{T}[\![(\textbf{cons } (\textbf{list } \text{'car}) \ M)]\!] = (\textbf{car } \mathcal{T}[\![M]\!])$$
$$\mathcal{T}[\![(\textbf{cons } (\textbf{list } \text{'cdr}) \ M)]\!] = (\textbf{cdr } \mathcal{T}[\![M]\!])$$
$$\mathcal{T}[\![(\textbf{cons } (\textbf{list } \text{'primA } P \ N) \ M)]\!] = (P \ \mathcal{T}[\![M]\!] \ \overline{\mathcal{Q}}[\![N]\!])$$
$$\mathcal{T}[\![(\textbf{cons } (\textbf{list } \text{'primB } P \ V) \ M)]\!] = (P \ V \ \mathcal{T}[\![M]\!])$$
$$\mathcal{T}[\![(\textbf{cons } \text{'break null})]\!] = [\,]$$

where

$$\overline{\mathcal{Q}}[\![(\textbf{list } \text{'val } \mathcal{A}[\![V]\!])]\!] = V$$
$$\overline{\mathcal{Q}}[\![(\textbf{list } \text{'quote } \text{'x}]\!] = \text{'x}$$
$$\overline{\mathcal{Q}}[\![M]\!] = \begin{cases} (M_1 \ M_2) & \text{if } M = (\textbf{list } \text{'app } \overline{\mathcal{Q}}[\![M_1]\!] \ \overline{\mathcal{Q}}[\![M_2]\!]) \\ (\textbf{if } M_1 \ M_2 \ M_3) & \text{if } M = (\textbf{list } \text{'if } \overline{\mathcal{Q}}[\![M_1]\!] \ \overline{\mathcal{Q}}[\![M_2]\!] \ \overline{\mathcal{Q}}[\![M_3]\!]) \\ \dots \end{cases}$$

Fig. 6. The Translation function, $\mathcal{T} : V \to E$

evaluation contexts produced by **(breakpoint)** expressions. We extend $\mathcal{T}$ to sequences of values in a pointwise fashion.

Theorem 1 (Elaboration Theorem). *For any program in the source language M, the following statements hold for the program M_0 and the elaborated program $N_0 = \mathcal{A}[\![M]\!]_0$:*

1. *$eval(M_0) = V$ iff $eval_t(N_0) = \mathcal{A}[\![V]\!]$.*
2. *$eval(M_0) = error$ iff $eval_t(N_0) = error$.*
3. *if $S = (M_0 \mapsto \cdots \mapsto M_n)$, there exists $S_t = (N_0 \mapsto_t \cdots \mapsto_t N_k)$ s.t. $trace[\![S]\!] = \mathcal{T}(trace[\![S_t]\!])$.*

Proof Sketch: The relevant invariant of the elaboration is that every non-value is wrapped in exactly one **w-c-m**, and values are not wrapped at all. The **w-c-m** wrapping of an expression indicates what kind of expression it is, what stage of evaluation it is in, and all subexpressions and values needed to reconstruct the program expression.

The proof of the theorem is basically a simulation argument upon the two program evaluations. It is complicated by the fact that one step in the source program corresponds to either one, two, or four steps in the elaborated program. The additional steps in the elaborated program are **w-c-m** reductions, which patch up the invariant that the source program and the elaborated program are related by $\mathcal{A}$. ∎

4   Stepping with Continuation Marks

The full stepper is built on top of the framework of section 3, and also comprises an elaborator and reconstructor. The elaborator transforms the user's program into one containing **breakpoints** that correspond to the reduction steps of the source program. At runtime, the reconstructor translates the state of the evaluation into an expression from the information in the continuation marks.

In this section we develop the model of our stepper implementation and its correctness proof. Subsection 4.1 describes the elaborator and the reconstructor, and formalizes them. Subsection 4.2 presents the stepper theorem, which shows that the elaborator and reconstructor simulate algebraic reduction.

4.1   Elaboration and Reconstruction

The stepper's elaborator extends the elaborator from section 3.2. Specifically, the full elaborator is the composition of a "front end" and a "back end." In fact, the back end is simply the function $\mathcal{A}$ of section 3.

The front end, $\mathcal{B}$, translates a plain functional language into the source language of section 3. More specifically, it accepts expressions in M_s, which is the language M without the **(breakpoint)** expression. Its purpose is to insert as many breakpoints as necessary so that the target program stops once for each reduction step according to the language's semantics. Fig. 7 shows the definition of $\mathcal{B}$. The translation is syntax-directed according to the expression language. Since some expressions have subexpressions in non-tail positions, $\mathcal{B}$ must elaborate these expressions so that a breakpoint is inserted to stop the execution after the evaluation of the subexpressions and before the evaluation of the expression itself. We use $\mathcal{I}_0$, $\mathcal{I}_1$, and $\mathcal{I}_2$ as temporary variables that do not appear in the source program. In this and later figures we use the **let*** expression as syntactic shorthand.[5]

The full elaborator is the composition of $\mathcal{B}$ and $\mathcal{A}$. It takes terms in M_s to terms in M_t, via a detour through M.

Like the elaborator, the reconstructor is based on the infrastructure of section 3. The execution of the target program produces a stream of output values. The function $\mathcal{T}$ of fig. 6 maps these values back to evaluation contexts of the intermediate language, that is, the source language of section 3. Since the instruction filling these contexts must be **breakpoint**, the reconstruction function $\mathcal{R}$ is defined simply as the inversion of the annotation applied to the context filled with **breakpoint**. In other words, $\mathcal{R}[\![E]\!] = \mathcal{B}^{-1}[\![E[(\textbf{breakpoint})]]\!]$. [6] Like $\mathcal{T}$, $\mathcal{R}$ is extended pointwise to sequences of expressions.

The full reconstructor is the composition of $\mathcal{R}$ and $\mathcal{T}$. It takes terms in E_t to terms in M_s.

---

[5] The **let*** expression is roughly equivalent to the sequential **let** of ML. It is used as syntactic shorthand for a corresponding set of applications like those in fig. 5.

[6] Inspection of the definition of $\mathcal{B}$ demonstrates that it is invertible.

$$\mathcal{B}[\![V]\!] = \begin{cases} (\textbf{lambda } (x) \ \mathcal{B}[\![M]\!]) \\ \quad \text{if } V = (\textbf{lambda } (x) \ M) \\ (\textbf{cons } \mathcal{B}[\![M]\!] \ \mathcal{B}[\![N]\!]) \\ \quad \text{if } V = (\textbf{cons } M \ N) \\ V \text{ otherwise} \end{cases}$$

$$\mathcal{B}[\![(M \ N)]\!] = (\textbf{let}* \ ([\mathcal{I}_0 \ \mathcal{B}[\![M]\!]] \\ [\mathcal{I}_1 \ \mathcal{B}[\![N]\!]] \\ [\mathcal{I}_2 \ (\textbf{breakpoint})]) \\ (\mathcal{I}_0 \ \mathcal{I}_1))$$

$$\mathcal{B}[\![(V \ N)]\!] = (\textbf{let}* \ ([\mathcal{I}_1 \ \mathcal{B}[\![N]\!]] \\ [\mathcal{I}_2 \ (\textbf{breakpoint})]) \\ (V \ \mathcal{I}_1))$$

$$\mathcal{B}[\![(V \ U)]\!] = (\textbf{let}* \ ([\mathcal{I}_2 \ (\textbf{breakpoint})]) \\ (V \ U))$$

$$\mathcal{B}[\![(\textbf{if } M \ N \ L)]\!] = (\textbf{let}* \ ([\mathcal{I}_0 \ \mathcal{B}[\![M]\!]] \\ [\mathcal{I}_1 \ (\textbf{breakpoint})]) \\ (\textbf{if } \mathcal{I}_0 \ \mathcal{B}[\![N]\!] \ \mathcal{B}[\![L]\!]))$$

$$\mathcal{B}[\![(\textbf{if } V \ N \ L)]\!] = (\textbf{let}* \ ([\mathcal{I}_0 \ (\textbf{breakpoint})]) \\ (\textbf{if } V \ \mathcal{B}[\![N]\!] \ \mathcal{B}[\![L]\!]))$$

$$\mathcal{B}[\![(\textbf{car } M)]\!] = (\textbf{let}* \ ([\mathcal{I}_0 \ \mathcal{B}[\![M]\!]] \\ [\mathcal{I}_1 \ (\textbf{breakpoint})]) \\ (\textbf{car } \mathcal{I}_0))$$

$$\mathcal{B}[\![(\textbf{car } V)]\!] = (\textbf{let}* \ ([\mathcal{I}_2 \ (\textbf{breakpoint})]) \\ (\textbf{car } V))$$

$$\mathcal{B}[\![(\textbf{cdr } M)]\!] = (\textbf{let}* \ ([\mathcal{I}_0 \ \mathcal{B}[\![M]\!]] \\ [\mathcal{I}_1 \ (\textbf{breakpoint})]) \\ (\textbf{cdr } \mathcal{I}_0))$$

$$\mathcal{B}[\![(\textbf{cdr } V)]\!] = (\textbf{let}* \ ([\mathcal{I}_2 \ (\textbf{breakpoint})]) \\ (\textbf{cdr } V))$$

$$\mathcal{B}[\![(P \ M \ N)]\!] = (\textbf{let}* \ ([\mathcal{I}_0 \ \mathcal{B}[\![M]\!]] \\ [\mathcal{I}_1 \ \mathcal{B}[\![N]\!]] \\ [\mathcal{I}_2 \ (\textbf{breakpoint})]) \\ (P \ \mathcal{I}_0 \ \mathcal{I}_1))$$

$$\mathcal{B}[\![(P \ V \ N)]\!] = (\textbf{let}* \ ([\mathcal{I}_1 \ \mathcal{B}[\![N]\!]] \\ [\mathcal{I}_2 \ (\textbf{breakpoint})]) \\ (P \ V \ \mathcal{I}_1))$$

$$\mathcal{B}[\![(P \ V \ U)]\!] = (\textbf{let}* \ ([\mathcal{I}_2 \ (\textbf{breakpoint})]) \\ (P \ V \ U))$$

Fig. 7. The stepper's breakpoint-inserting function, $\mathcal{B} : M_s \to M$

4.2 Properties of the Stepper

To prove that the stepper works correctly, we must show that the elaborated program produces one piece of output per reduction step in the source semantics and that the output represents the entire program.

Theorem 2 (Stepping Theorem). *For an evaluation sequence $S = (M_0 \mapsto \cdots \mapsto M_n)$, there exists an evaluation sequence $S_t = (\mathcal{A}[\![\mathcal{B}[\![M_0]\!]]\!] \mapsto_t \cdots \mapsto_t N_k)$ such that $S = \mathcal{R}[\![\mathcal{T}[\![trace[\![S_t]\!]]\!]]\!]$.*

Proof Sketch: By the Elaboration theorem, it suffices to prove that, given a sequence S as in the theorem statement, there exists $S_a = (\mathcal{B}[\![M_0]\!] \mapsto \cdots \mapsto N_{k'})$ such that $S = \mathcal{R}[\![trace_t[\![S_a]\!]]\!]$.

The proof again uses a simulation argument. Evaluation of the source program for one step and evaluation of the target program for either one or two steps maintains the invariant that the source program and the target program are related by $\mathcal{B}$. ∎

4.3 From Model to Implementation

From an implementation perspective, the key idea in our theorems is that the stepper's operation is independent of the intermediate state in the evaluation of the elaborated program. Instead, the elaborated program contains information in the marked continuations that suffices to reconstruct the source program from the *output*. The correctness theorem holds for any evaluator that properly implements the continuation-mark framework. That is, the stepper's correct operation is entirely orthogonal to the implementation strategy and optimizations of the evaluator; as long as that evaluator correctly implements the language with continuation marks, the stepper will work properly.

5   Related Work

The idea of elaborating a program in order to observe its behavior is a familiar one. Early systems included BUGTRAN [7] and EXDAMS [1] for FORTRAN. More recent applications of this technique to higher-order languages include Tolmach's smld [24], Kellomaki's PSD [14], and several projects in the lazy FP community [12,20,22,23]. None of these, however, addressed the correctness of the tool — not only that the transformation preserves the meaning of the program, but also that the information divulged by the elaborated program matches the intended purpose.

Indeed, work on modeling the action of programming environment tools is sparse. Bernstein and Stark [3] put forward the idea of specifying the semantics of a debugger. That is, they specify the actions of the debugger with respect to a low-level machine. We extend this work to show that the tool preserves the semantics and also performs the expected computation.

Kishon, Hudak, and Consel [15] study a more general idea than Bernstein and Stark. They describe a theoretical framework for extending the semantics of a language to include execution monitors. Their work guarantees the preservation of the source language's semantics. Our work extends this (albeit with a loss of generality) with a proof that the information output by the tool is sufficient to reconstruct a source expression.

Bertot [4] describes a semantic framework for relating an intermediate state in a reduction sequence to the original program. Put differently, he describes the semantic foundation for source tracking. In contrast, we exploit a practical implementation of source tracking by Shriram Krishnamurthi [16] for our implementation of the stepper. Bertot's work does not verify a stepper but simply assumes that the language evaluator *is* a stepper.

6   Conclusion

Our paper presents a high-level model of an algebraic stepper for a functional language. Roughly speaking, the model extends a conventional reduction semantics with a high-level form of weak continuation manipulations. The new constructs represent the essence of the stepper's compiler and run-time actions. They allow programs to mark continuations with values and to observe the mark values, without any observable effect on the evaluation. Using the model, we can prove that the stepper adds enough information to the program so that it can stop for every reduction step. At each stop, furthermore, the source information in the continuation suffices for a translation of the execution state into source syntax—no matter how the back end represents code and continuations.

Because the model is formulated at a high level of abstraction, the model and the proofs are robust. First, the model should accommodate programming environment tools such as debuggers and profilers that need to associate information about the program with the continuation. After all, marking continuations and observing marks are two actions that are used in the run-time environment of monitoring tools; otherwise, these tools are simply aware of the representations of values, environments, heaps, and other run-time structures. Indeed, we are experimenting at this moment with an implementation of a conventional debugger directly based on the continuation mark mechanism. Performance penalties for the debugger prototype run to a factor of about four.

Second, the proof applies to all implementations of steppers. Using conventional machine derivation techniques from the literature [5,6], one can translate the model to stack and heap machines, conventional machines (such as Landin's SECD [17] machine) or tail-optimizing machines (such as Felleisen's CE(S)K machine). In each case, minor modifications of the adequacy proofs for the transformations show that the refined stepper is still correct.

The model of this paper covers only the functional kernel of Scheme. Using the extended reduction semantics of Felleisen and Hieb [6], the model scales to full Scheme without much ado. We also believe that we could build an algebraic stepper for Java-like languages, using the model of Flatt et al. [11]. In contrast, it is an open question how to accommodate the GUI (callback) and concurrency facilities of our Scheme implementation [10], both in practice and in theory. We leave this topic for future research.

References

1. Balzer, R. M. EXDAMS — EXtendable Debugging And Monitoring System. In *AFIPS 1969 Spring Joint Computer Conference*, volume 34, pages 567–580. AFIPS Press, May 1969.

2. Barendregt, H. P. *The Lambda Calculus: Its Syntax and Semantics*, volume 103 of *Studies in Logic and the Foundations of Mathematics*. North-Holland, revised edition, 1984.

3. Bernstein, K. L. and E. W. Stark. Operational semantics of a focusing debugger. In *Eleventh Conference on the Mathematical Foundations of Programming Semantics, Volume 1 of Electronic Notes in Computer Science*. Elsevier, March 1995.

4. Bertot, Y. Occurrences in debugger specifications. In *ACM SIGPLAN Conference on Programming Language Design and Implementation*, 1991.

5. Felleisen, M. Programming languages and their calculi. Unpublished Manuscript. http://www.cs.rice.edu/~matthias/411/mono.ps.

6. Felleisen, M. and R. Hieb. The revised report on the syntactic theories of sequential control and state. *Theoretical Computer Science*, 102:235–271, 1992.

7. Ferguson, H. E. and E. Berner. Debugging systems at the source language level. *Communications of the ACM*, 6(8):430–432, August 1963.

8. Findler, R. B., J. Clements, C. Flanagan, M. Flatt, S. Krishnamurthi, P. Steckler and M. Felleisen. Drscheme: A programming environment for Scheme. *Journal of Functional Programming*, 2001.

9. Findler, R. B., C. Flanagan, M. Flatt, S. Krishnamurthi and M. Felleisen. DrScheme: A pedagogic programming environment for Scheme. In *International Symposium on Programming Languages: Implementations, Logics, and Programs*, number 1292 in Lecture Notes in Computer Science, pages 369–388, 1997.

10. Flatt, M. PLT MzScheme: Language manual. Technical Report TR97-280, Rice University, 1997.

11. Flatt, M., S. Krishnamurthi and M. Felleisen. Classes and mixins. In *ACM SIGPLAN-SIGACT Symposium on Principles of Programming Languages*, pages 171–183, January 1998.

12. Hall, C. and J. O'Donnell. Debugging in a side effect free programming environment. In *ACM SIGPLAN symposium on Language issues in programming environments*, 1985.

13. Hannan, J. and D. Miller. From operational semantics to abstract machines. *Journal of Mathematical Structures in Computer Science*, 2(4):415–459, 1992.

14. Kellomaki, P. Psd — a portable scheme debugger, Feburary 1995.

15. Kishon, A., P. Hudak and C. Consel. Monitoring semantics: a formal framework for specifying, implementing and reasoning about execution monitors. In *ACM SIGPLAN Conference on Programming Language Design and Implementation*, pages 338–352, June 1991.

16. Krishnamurthi, S. PLT McMicMac: Elaborator manual. Technical Report 99-334, Rice University, Houston, TX, USA, 1999.

17. Landin, P. J. The mechanical evaluation of expressions. *Comput. J.*, 6(4):308–320, 1964.

18. Milner, R. *Communication and Concurrency*. Prentice Hall, 1989.

19. Moreau, L. A syntactic theory of dynamic binding. *Higher-Order and Symbolic Computation*, 11(3):233–279, 1998.

20. Naish, L. and T. Barbour. Towards a portable lazy functional declarative debugger. In *19th Australasian Computer Science Conference*, 1996.

21. Plotkin, G. D. Call-by-name, call-by-value and the λ-calculus. *Theoretical Computer Science*, pages 125–159, 1975.

22. Sansom, P. and S. Peyton-Jones. Formally-based profiling for higher-order functional languages. *ACM Transactions on Programming Languages and Systems*, 19(1), January 1997.

23. Sparud, J. and C. Runciman. Tracing lazy functional computations using redex trails. In *Symposium on Programming Language Implementation and Logic Programming*, 1997.

24. Tolmach, A. *Debugging Standard ML*. PhD thesis, Department of Computer Science, Princeton University, October 1992.

Typestate Checking of Machine Code

Zhichen Xu[1], Thomas Reps[2], and Barton P. Miller[2]

[1] Hewlett-Packard Laboratories, Palo Alto
[2] University of Wisconsin at Madison
zhichen@hpl.hp.com, {reps,bart}@cs.wisc.edu

Abstract. We check statically whether it is safe for untrusted foreign machine code to be loaded into a trusted host system. Our technique works on ordinary machine code, and mechanically synthesizes (and verifies) a safety proof. Our earlier work along these lines was based on a C-like type system, which does not suffice for machine code whose origin is C++ source code. In the present paper, we address this limitation with an improved typestate system and introduce several new techniques, including: summarizing the effects of function calls so that our analysis can stop at trusted boundaries, inferring information about the sizes and types of stack-allocated arrays, and a symbolic range analysis for propagating information about array bounds. These techniques make our approach to safety checking more precise, more efficient, and able to handle a larger collection of real-life code sequences than was previously the case.

1 Introduction

Our goal is to check statically whether it is safe for a piece of untrusted foreign machine code to be loaded into a trusted host system. (Here "safety" means that the program abides by a memory-access policy that is supplied on the host side.) We start with ordinary machine code and mechanically synthesize (and verify) a safety proof. In an earlier paper [24], we reported on initial results from our approach, the chief advantage of which is that it opens up the possibility of being able to certify code produced by a general-purpose off-the-shelf compiler from programs written in languages such as C, C++, and Fortran. Furthermore, in our work we do not limit the safety policy to just a fixed set of memory-access conditions that must be avoided; instead, we perform safety checking with respect to a safety policy that is supplied on the host side.

Our earlier work was based on a C-like type system, which does not suffice for machine code whose origin is C++ source code. In the present paper, we address this limitation and also introduce several other techniques that make our safety-checking analysis more precise and scalable. These techniques include:

1. An improved typestate-checking system that allows us to perform safety-checking on untrusted machine code that implements inheritance polymorphism via physical subtyping [15]. This work introduces a new method for coping with subtyping in the presence of mutable pointers (Section 3).

2. A mechanism for summarizing the effects of function calls via safety pre- and postconditions. These summaries allow our analysis to stop at trusted boundaries. They form a first step toward checking untrusted code in a modular fashion, which makes the safety-checking technique more scalable (Section 4).

3. A technique to infer the sizes and types of stack-allocated arrays (local arrays). This was left as an open problem in our previous paper [24] (Section 5).

D. Sands (Ed.): ESOP 2001, LNCS 2028, pp. 335–351, 2001.
© Springer-Verlag Berlin Heidelberg 2001

4. A symbolic range analysis for propagating information about array bounds. This analysis makes the safety-checking algorithm less dependent upon expensive program-verification techniques (Section 6).

Section 2 provides a brief review of the safety-checking technique from our earlier work [24]. Section 7 illustrates the benefits of our techniques via a few case studies. Section 8 compares our techniques with related work.

As a result of these improvements, we can handle a broader class of real-life code sequences with better precision and efficiency. For example, allowing subtyping among structures and pointers allows us to analyze code originating from object-oriented source code. The use of symbolic range analysis eliminated 55% of the total attempts to synthesize loop invariants in the 11 programs of our test suite that have array accesses. In 4 of these programs, it eliminated the need to synthesize loop invariants altogether. The resulting speedup for global verification ranges from -4% to 53% (with a median of 29%). Together with improvements that we made to our global-verification phase, range analysis allows us to verify untrusted code that we were not able to handle previously.

2   Safety Checking of Machine Code

We briefly review the safety-checking technique from our earlier work [24]. The safety-checking analysis enforces a default collection of safety conditions to prevent type violations, array out-of-bounds violations, address-alignment violations, uses of uninitialized variables, null-pointer dereferences. In addition, the host side can specify a precise and flexible *access policy*. This access policy specifies the host data that can be accessed by the untrusted code, and the host functions (methods) that can be called. It provides a means for the host to specify the "least privilege" the untrusted code needs to accomplish its task.

Our approach is based on annotating the global data in the host. The type information in the untrusted code is inferred. Our analysis starts with information about the initial memory state at the entry of the untrusted code. It abstractly interprets the untrusted code to produce a safe approximation of the memory state at each program point. It then annotates each instruction with the safety conditions each instruction must obey and checks these conditions.

The memory states at the entry, and other program points of the untrusted code, are described in terms of an *abstract storage model*. An *abstract store* is a total map from *abstract locations* to *typestates*. An abstract location summarizes one or more physical locations so that our analysis has a finite domain to work over. A typestate describes the type, state, and access permissions of the values stored in an abstract location.

The initial memory state at the entry of the untrusted code is given by a *host-typestate specification*, and an *invocation specification*. The host typestate specification describes the type and the state of the host data before the invocation of the untrusted code, as well as safety pre- and post-conditions for calling host functions (methods). The invocation specification provides the binding information from host resources to registers and memory locations that represent initial inputs to the untrusted code.

The safety-checking analysis consists of five phases. The first phase, *preparation,* combines the information that is provided by the host-typestate specification, the invocation specification, and the access policy to produce an abstract store for the program's entry point. It also produces an interprocedural control-flow graph for the untrusted code. The second phase, *typestate-propagation,* takes the control-flow graph and the abstract store for the program's entry point as inputs. It abstractly interprets [6] the untrusted code to produce a safe approximation of the memory contents (i.e., a typestate for each abstract location) at each program point. The third phase, *annotation,* takes as input the typestate information discovered in the typestate-propagation phase, and annotates each instruction with *local* and *global safety conditions* and *assertions*: the local safety preconditions are conditions that can be checked using typestate information alone; the assertions are restatements (as logical formulas) of facts that are implicit in the typestate information. The fourth phase, *local verification,* checks the local safety conditions. The fifth phase, *global verification,* checks for array out-of-bounds violations, null-pointer dereferences, and misaligned loads and stores.

At present, our implementation handles only non-recursive programs.

3   An Improved Typestate System

In our past work, our analysis made the assumption that a register or memory location stored values of a single type at any given program point (although a register/memory location could store different types of values at different program points). However, this approach had some drawbacks for programs written in languages that support subtyping and inheritance, and also for programs written in languages like C in which programmers have the ability to simulate subtyping and inheritance.

In this section, we describe how we have extended the typestate system [24] to incorporate a notion of subtyping among pointers. With this approach, each use of a register or memory location at a given occurrence of an instruction is resolved to a polymorphic type (i.e., a super type of the acceptable values). In the rest of this section, we describe the improved type component of our typestate system.

3.1   Type Expressions

Figure 1 shows the language of type expressions used in the typestate system. Compared with our previous work, the typestate system now additionally includes (i) bit-level representations of integer types, and (ii) top and bottom types that are parameterized with a size parameter. The type $int(g{:}s{:}v)$ represents a signed integer that has $g+s+v$ bits, of which the highest g bits are ignored, the middle s bits represent the sign or are the result of a sign extension, and the lowest v bits represent the value. For example, a 32-bit signed integer is represented as $int(0{:}1{:}31)$, and an 8-bit signed integer (e.g., a C/C++ char) with a 24-bit sign extension is represented as $int(0{:}25{:}7)$. The type $uint(g{:}s{:}v)$ represents an unsigned integer, whose middle s bits are zeros. The type $t(n]$ denotes a pointer that points somewhere into the middle of an array of type t of size n.

The bit-level representation of integers allows us to express the effect of instructions that load (or store) partial words. For example, the following code fragment (in

t :: ground		*Ground types*
	t [*n*]	*Pointer to the base of an array of type t of size n*
	t (*n*)	*Pointer into the middle of an array of type t of size n*
	t ptr	*Pointer to t*
	s {m$_1$, ..., m$_k$}	*struct*
	u {m$_1$, ..., m$_k$}	*union*
	(*t*$_1$, ..., *t*$_k$) → *t*	*Function*
	T(n)	*Top type of n bits*
	⊥(n)	*Bottom type of n bits (Type "any" of n bits)*
m:: (*l*, *t*, *i*)		*Member labeled l of type t at offset i*
ground:: int(*g:s:v*) | uint(*g:s:v*) | ...		

Figure 1 *A Simple Language of Type Expressions. t stands for type, and m stands for a struct or union member. Although the language in which we have chosen to express the type system looks a bit like C, we do not assume that the untrusted code was necessarily written in C or C++*

SPARC machine language) copies a character pointed to by register %o1 to the location that is pointed to by register %o0:

```
ldub [%o1],%g2

stb %g2,[%o0]
```

If %o1 points to a signed character and a C-like type system is used (i.e., as in [24]), typestate checking will lose precision when checking the above code fragment. There is a loss of precision because the instruction "ldub [%o1],%g2" loads register %g2 with a byte from memory and zero-fills the highest 24 bits, and thus the type system of [24] treats the value in %g2 as an unsigned integer. In contrast, with the bit-level integer types of Figure 1, we can assign the type int(24:1:7) to %g2 after the execution of the load instruction. This preserves the fact that the lowest 8 bits of %g2 store a signed character (i.e., an int(0:1:7)).

3.2   A Subtyping Relation

We now introduce a notion of subtyping on type expressions, adopted from the *physical-subtyping* system of [15], which takes into account the layout of aggregate fields in memory. Figure 2 lists the rules that define when a type *t* is a *physical subtype* of *t'* (denoted by *t* <: *t'*).[1] (In Figure 2, the rules [*Top*], [*Bottom*], [*Ground*], [*Pointer*], and [*Array*] are our additions to the physical-subtyping system given in [15].) An integer type *t* is a subtype of type *t'* if the range represented by *t* is a subrange of the range represented by *t'*, and *t* has at least as many sign-extension bits as *t'*. Rule [*First Member*] states that a structure is a subtype of type *t'* if the type of the first member of the structure is a subtype of *t'*. The consequence of this rule is that it is valid for a program to pass a

---

1. Note that the subtype ordering is conventional. However, during typestate checking the ordering is flipped: t$_1$ ≤ t$_2$ in the type lattice iff t$_2$ <: t$_1$.

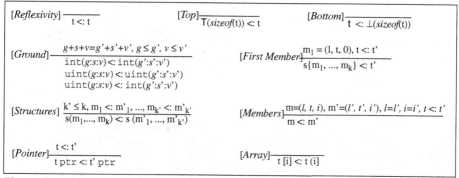

Figure 2 *Inference Rules that Define the Subtyping Relation*

structure in a place where a supertype of its first member is expected. The rules [*Structures*] and [*Members*] state that a structure *s* is a subtype of *s'* if *s'* is a prefix of *s*, and each member of *s'* is a supertype of the corresponding member of *s*. The rule [*Pointer*] states if *t* is a subtype of *t'*, than *t* ptr is a subtype of *t'* ptr. *Rule* [*Array*] states that a pointer to the base of an array is a subtype of a pointer into the middle of an array.

In our system, an assignment is legal *only if* the type of the right-hand-side expression is a physical subtype of the type of the receiving location, and the receiving location has enough space. The Rule [*Array*] is valid because t (i) describes a larger set of states than t [i]. (The global-verification phase of the analysis will check that all array references are within bounds.)

Allowing subtyping among integer types, structures, and pointers allows the analysis to handle code that implements inheritance polymorphism via physical subtyping. Figure 3 shows an example that involves subtyping among structures and pointers. According to the subtyping inference rules for structures and pointers, type Color-Point* is a subtype of Point*. Function f is polymorphic because it is legal to pass an actual parameter that is of type ColorPoint* to function f.

struct Point {	struct ColorPoint {	void f(Point* p) {
int(0:1:31) x;	int(0:1:31) x;	p->x++;
int(0:1:31) y;	int(0:1:31) y;	p->y--;
};	uint(24:0:8) color;	}
	};	

Figure 3 *Subtyping Among Pointer Types*

For object-oriented languages such as C++, there is an additional complication that arises from the use of virtual functions, where a virtual function could be implemented by any of the subclasses. As long as we have full information about the class hierarchy, we can simply assume that the callee of a call to a virtual function can be any of the functions that implement the virtual function and check all of them.

3.3   The State and Access Component of our Typestate system

We briefly review the state and access components of the typestate system. The state lattice contains a bottom element $\perp_s$ that denotes an undefined value of any type. For a scalar type *t*, its state can be *u* or *i*, which denote uninitialized and initialized values, re-

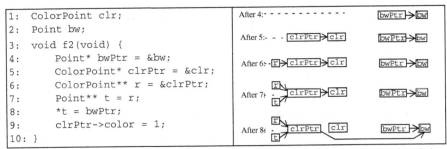

```
1:   ColorPoint clr;
2:   Point bw;
3:   void f2(void) {
4:        Point* bwPtr = &bw;
5:        ColorPoint* clrPtr = &clr;
6:        ColorPoint** r = &clrPtr;
7:        Point** t = r;
8:        *t = bwPtr;
9:        clrPtr->color = 1;
10: }
```

Figure 4 *Rule [Pointer] is unsound for flow-insensitive type checking in the absence of alias-ing information. (Assume the same type declarations as shown in Figure 3.)*

spectively. We define $u \leq i$ in the state lattice. For a pointer type p, its state can be either u or P (a non-empty set of abstract locations referenced); we define $u \leq P$. One of the elements of P can be null. For sets P_1 and P_2, we define $P_1 \leq P_2$ *iff* $P_2 \subseteq P_1$. For an aggregate type G, its state is given by the states of its fields.

   An access permission is either a subset of $\{f, x, o\}$, or a tuple of access permissions. The access permission f is introduced for pointer-typed values to indicate whether the pointer can be dereferenced. The access permission x applies to values that hold the address of a function to indicate whether the function pointed to can be called by the untrusted code. The access permission o includes the rights to "examine", "copy", and perform other operations not covered by x and f. The meet of two access-permission sets is their intersection. The meet of two tuples of access permissions is given by the meet of their respective elements.

3.4   Typestate Checking with Subtyping

Readers who are familiar with the problems encountered with subtyping in the presence of mutable pointers may be suspicious of rule [*Pointer*]. In fact, rule [*Pointer*] is unsound for traditional flow-insensitive type systems in the absence of alias information. This is because a flow-insensitive analysis that does not account for aliasing is unable to determine whether there are any indirect modifications to a shared data structure, and some indirect modifications can have disastrous effects. Figure 4 provides a concrete example of this. The statement at line 8 changes `clrPtr` to point to an object of the type `Point` indirectly via the variable `t`, so that `clrPtr` can no longer fulfill the obligation to supply the `color` field at line 9.

   A static technique to handle this problem has to be able to detect whether such disastrous indirect modifications could happen. There are several approaches to this problem found in the literature. For example, the linear type system given in [22] avoids aliases altogether (and hence any indirect modifications) by "consuming" a pointer as soon as it is used once. Smith *et al* [18] use singleton types to track pointers, and alias constraints to model the shape of the store. (Their goal is to tracks non-aliasing to facilitate memory reuse and safe deallocation of objects.)

   Another approach involves introducing the notions of immutable fields and objects [1]. The idea is that if t is a subtype of type t', type t `ptr` is a subtype of t' `ptr` only if any field of t that is a subtype of the corresponding field of t' is immutable. Moreover, if a field of t is a pointer, then the object pointed by it must also be immutable. This rule applies transitively. For this approach to work correctly, a mechanism is needed to enforce these immutability restrictions.

Our work represents yet a fourth technique. Our system performs typestate checking, which is a flow-sensitive analysis that tracks aliasing relationships among abstract locations. (These state descriptors resemble the storage-shape graphs of Chase *et al* [4], and are similar to the diagrams shown in the right-hand column of Figure 4.) By inspecting the storage-shape graphs at program points that access heap-allocated storage, we can (safely) detect whether an illegal field access can occur. For instance, from the shape graph that arises after statement 8 in Figure 4, the analysis can determine that the access to `color` in statement 9 represents a possible memory-access error. Programs with such accesses are rejected by our safety checker.

4   Summarizing Function Calls

By summarizing function calls, the safety-checking analysis can stop at the boundaries of trusted code. Instead of tracing into the body of a trusted callee, the analysis can check that a call obeys a safety pre-condition, and then use the post-condition in the rest of the analysis. We describe a method for summarizing trusted calls with safety pre- and post-conditions in terms of abstract locations, typestates, and linear constraints. The safety pre-conditions describe the obligations that the actual parameters must meet, whereas the post-conditions provide a guarantee on the resulting state.

Currently, we produce the safety pre- and post-conditions by hand. This process is error-prone, and it would be desirable to automate the generation of function summaries. Recent work on interprocedural pointer analysis has shown that pointer analysis can be performed in a modular fashion [5]. These techniques analyze each function assuming unknown initial values for parameters (and globals) at a function's entry point to obtain a *summary function* for the dataflow effect of the function. In future work, we will investigate how to use such techniques to create safety pre- and post- conditions automatically.

We represent the obligation that must be provided by an actual parameter as a *placeholder* abstract location (placeholder) whose size, access permissions, and typestate provide the detailed requirements that the actual parameter must satisfy. When a formal parameter is a pointer, its state descriptor can include references to other placeholders that represent the obligations that must be provided by the locations that may be pointed to by the actual parameter. In our model, the state descriptor of a pointer-typed placeholder can refer to `null`, to a placeholder, or to a placeholder and `null`. If it refers to just `null`, then the actual parameter must point to `null`. If it refers to a placeholder, then all locations that are pointed to by the actual parameter must satisfy the obligation denoted by the placeholder. If the state descriptor refers to both `null` and a placeholder, then the actual parameter must either point to `null`, or to locations that satisfy the obligation. We represent the pre-conditions as a list of the form "*placeholder : typestate*".

The safety post-conditions provide a way for the safety-checking analysis to compute the resulting state of a call to a summarized function. They are represented by a list of post-conditions of the form [*alias context, placeholder : typestate*]. An *alias context*

```
int gettimeofday (struct timeval *tp);
    Safety Pre-condition:
        %o0: <struct timeval ptr, {null, t}, fo>
        t: <struct timeval, u, wo>
    Safety Post-condition:
        [(), t: <struct timeval, [0:<int(0:1:31), i, o>, 32:<int(0:1:31), i, o>], o>]
        [(), %o0 : <int(0:1:31), i, o>]
        [(), %o1-%o5, %g1-%g7: <⊥(32), ⊥, o>]
```

Figure 5 *Safety Pre- and Post- Conditions. The typestate of an aggregate is given by the typestates of its components (enclosed in "[" and "]"). Each component is labeled by its offset (in bits) in its closest enclosing aggregate*

[5] is a set of potential aliases (l eq l') (or potential non-aliases (l neq l')), where l and l' are placeholders. The alias contexts capture how aliasing among the actual parameters can affect the resulting state.

The safety pre- and post-conditions can also include linear constraints. When they appear in the safety pre-conditions, they represent additional safety requirements. When they appear in the post-conditions, they provide additional information about the resulting memory state after the call.

To make this idea concrete, Figure 5 shows an example that summarizes the C library function gettimeofday. It specifies that for the call to be safe, %o0 must either be (i) null or (ii) be the address of a writable location of size sufficient for storing a value of the type struct timeval.The safety post-conditions specify that after the execution of the call, the two fields of the location will be initialized, and %o0 will be an initialized integer. (On SPARC, the actual parameters will be passed through the registers %o0, %o1, ..., %o5, and the return value of the function will be stored in the register %o0.)

In the example in Figure 5, the alias contexts are empty because there is no ambiguity about aliasing. Having alias contexts allows us to summarize function calls with better precision (as opposed to having to make fixed assumptions about aliasing). Now consider the example in Figure 6, which shows how alias contexts can provide better precision. Function g returns either null or the object that is pointed to by the first parameter, depending on whether *p1 and *p2 are aliases.

Checking a call to a trusted function involves a *binding* process and an *update* process. The binding process matches the placeholders with actual abstract locations, and checks whether they meet the obligation. The update process updates the typestates of

`PointPtr`
 	
`g(PointPtr *p1, PointPtr* p2){`
 	
`    *p2 = null;`
 	
`    return *p1`
 	
`}`
	Safety Pre-condition:
	    %o0: <PointPtr ptr, {q1}, fo>
	    %o1: <PointPtr ptr, {q2}, fo>
	    q1: <PointPtr, {r1}, fo>
	Safety Post-condition:
	    [(q1 neq q2), %o0 : <PointPtr, {r1}, ...>]
	    [(q1 eq q2), %o0 : <PointPtr, {null}, ...>]

Figure 6 *An example of safety pre- and post-conditions with alias contexts.*

all actual locations that are represented by the placeholders according to the safety post-conditions.

Our goal is to summarize library functions, which generally do not do very complicated things with pointers. Thus, at present we have focused only on obligations that can be represented as a tree of placeholders. When obligations cannot be represented in this way, we fall back on letting the typestate-propagation phase trace into the body of the function. Tree-shaped placeholders allow the binding process to be carried out with a simple algorithm: The binding algorithm iterates over all formal parameters, and obtains the respective actual parameters from the typestate descriptors at the call site. It then traverses the obligation tree, checks whether the actual parameter meets the obligation, and establishes a mapping between the placeholders and the set of abstract locations they may represent in the store at the callsite.

The binding process distinguishes between may information and must information. Intuitively, a placeholder must represent a location if the binding algorithm can establish that it can only represent a unique concrete location. The algorithm for the updating process interprets each post-condition. It distinguishes a strong update from a weak update depending on whether a placeholder must represent a unique location or may represent multiple locations, and whether the alias context evaluates to true or false. A strong update happens when the placeholder represents a unique location and the alias context evaluates to true. A weak update happens if the placeholder may represent multiple locations or the alias context cannot be determined to be either definitely true or definitely false; in this case, the typestate of the location receives the meet of its typestate before the call and the typestate specified in the post-condition. When the alias context cannot be determined to be either definitely true or definitely false, the update specified by the post-condition may or may not take place. We make the safest assumption via a weak update.

5   Inferring Information about Stack-Allocated Arrays

Determining information about arrays that reside on the stack is difficult because we need to figure out both their types and their bounds. Our previous work [24] required manual annotations of procedures that made use of local arrays. In this section, we describe a method for inferring that a subrange of a stack frame holds an array, and illustrate the method with a simple example.

Figure 7 shows a C program that updates a local array; the second column shows the SPARC machine code that is produced by compiling the program with "gcc -O" (version 2.7.2.3). To infer that a local array is present, we examine all live pointers each time the typestate-propagation algorithm reaches the entry of a loop. In the following discussion, the abstract location SF denotes the stack frame that is allocated by the add instruction at line 2; $SF[n]$ denotes the point in SF at offset n; and $SF[s,t]$ denotes the subrange of SF that starts at offset s and ends at offset t-1.

By abstractly interpreting the add instructions at lines 3 and 5, we find that %g3 points to $SF[96]$ and %g2 points to $SF[176]$. The first time the typestate-checking algorithm visits the loop entry, %g2 and %o1 both point to $SF[176]$ (see the third column of Figure 7). Abstractly interpreting the instructions from line 10 to line 14 reveals that

C program	SPARC Machine Language	First Time	Second Time

`typedef struct {`
`  int f;`
`  int g;`
`} s;`
`int main() {`
`  s a[10];`
`  s *p = &a[0];`
`  int i=0;`
`  while (p<a+10) {`
`    (p++)->f = i++;`
`  }`
`}`
	`1:   main:`
	`2:       add %sp,-192,%sp`
	`3:       add %sp,96,%g3`
	`4:       mov 0,%o0`
	`5:       add %sp,176,%g2`
	`6:       cmp %g3,%g2`
	`7:       bgeu .LL3`
	`8:       mov %g2,%o1`
	`9:   .LL4:`
	`10:      st %o0,[%g3]`
	`11:      add %g3,8,%g3`
	`12:      cmp %g3,%o1`
	`13:      blu .LL4`
	`14:      add %o0,1,%o0`
	`15:  .LL3:`
	`16:      retl`
	`17:      sub %sp,-192,%sp`		

Figure 7 *Inferring the Type and Size of a Local Array. The label* .LL4 *represents the entry of the while loop.*

$SF[96,100]$ stores an integer. The second time the typestate-checking algorithm visits the loop entry, %g3 points to either $SF[96]$ or $SF[104]$. We now have a candidate for a local array. The reasoning runs as follows: if we create two fictitious components A and B of SF (as shown in the right-most column in Figure 7), then %g3 can point to either A or B (where B is a component of A). However, an instruction can have only one (polymorphic) usage at a particular program point; therefore, a pointer to A and a pointer to B must have compatible types. The only choice (in our type system) is a pointer into an array. Letting τ denote the type of the array element, we compute a most general type for τ by the following steps:

1. Compute the size of τ. We compute the greatest common divisor (GCD) of the sizes of the slots that are delimited by the pointer under consideration. In this example, there is only one slot: $SF[96, 104]$, whose size is 8. Therefore, the size of τ is 8.

2. Compute the possible limits of the array. We assume that the array ends at the location just before the closest live pointer into the stack (other than the pointer under consideration).

3. Compute the type of τ. Assuming that the size of τ we have computed is n, we create a fictitious location e of size n, and give it an initial type $\mathsf{T}(n)$. We then slide e over the area that we have identified in the second step, n bytes at a time—e.g., $SF[96,176]$, 8 bytes at a time—and perform a meet operation with whatever is covered by e. If an area covered by e (or a sub-area of it) does not have a type associated with it, we assume that its type is T. In this example, the τ that we find is

```
struct {
    int m1;
    T(32) m2;
}
```

No more refinement is needed for this example. In general, we may need to make refinements to our findings in later iterations of the typestate-checking algorithm. Each refinement will bring the element type of the array down in the type lattice. In this example, the address under consideration is the value of a register; in general it could be of the form "r_1+r_2" or "r_1+n", where r_1 and r_2 are registers and n is an integer.

This method uses some heuristics to compute the possible limits of the array. This does not affect the soundness of this approach for the following two reasons: (i) The typestate-propagation algorithm will make sure that the program is type correct. This will ensure that the element type inferred is correct. (ii) The global-verification phase will verify later that all references to the local array are within the inferred bounds.

Note that it does not matter to the analysis whether the original program was written in terms of an n-dimensional array or in terms of a 1-dimensional array; the analysis treats all arrays as 1-dimensional arrays. This approach works even when the original code was written in terms of an n-dimensional array because the layout scheme that compilers use for an n-dimensional array involves a linear indexing scheme, which is reflected in linear relationships that the analysis infers for the values of registers.

6   Range Analysis

The technique we have used for array bounds checking in our earlier work [24], and techniques such as those described by Cousot and Halbwachs [7,19] are precise, but have a high cost. We describe a simple range analysis that determines safe estimates of the range of values each register can take on at each program point [21].This information can be used for determining whether accesses on arrays are within bounds. We take advantage of the synergy of an efficient range analysis and an expensive but powerful technique that can be applied on demand. We apply the program-verification technique only for the conditions that cannot be proven by the range analysis.

The range-analysis algorithm that we use is a standard worklist-based forward data-flow algorithm. It finds a symbolic range for each register at each program point. In our analysis, a range is denoted by $[l, u]$, where l and u are lower and upper bounds of the form $ax+by+c$ (a, b, and c are integer constants, and x and y are symbolic names that serve as placeholders for either the base address or the length of an array). The reason that we restrict the bounds to the form of $ax+by+c$ is because that array-bounds checks usually involves checking either that the range of an array index is a subrange of [0, $length$-1], or that the range of a pointer that points into an array is a subrange of [$base$, $base+length$-1], where $base$ and $length$ are the base address and length of the array, respectively. In the analysis, symbolic names such as x and y stand for (unknown) values of quantities like $base$ and $length$. Symbolic information about bases and lengths of the arrays are initially given in the host-typestate specification, and are then propagated to the various program points during range analysis.

Ranges form a meet semi-lattice with respect to the following meet operation: for ranges $r=[l, u]$, $r'=[l', u']$, the meet of r and r' is defined as $[min(l, l'), max(u, u')]$; the top element is the empty range; the bottom element is the largest range $[-\infty, \infty]$. The function $min(l, l')$ returns the smaller of l and l'. If l and l' are not *comparable* (i.e., we cannot determine the relative order of l and l' because, for instance, $l=ax+by+c$, $l'=a'x'+b'y'+c'$, $x\neq x'$, and $y\neq y'$), min returns $-\infty$. The function max is defined similarly except that it returns the greater of its two parameters, and ∞ if its two parameters are not comparable.

Operation		$x=x', y=y'$	$x=x', y\neq y'$	$x\neq x', y=y'$	$x\neq x', y\neq y'$
$+_+$	$(a+a')x+(b+b')y+c+c'$	if $(a+a')=0$, $by+b'y'+c+c'$ otherwise, ∞	if $(b+b')=0$, $ax+a'x'+c+c'$ otherwise, ∞	∞
$+_-$		if $(a+a')=0$, $by+b'y'+c+c'$ otherwise, $-\infty$	if $(b+b')=0$, $ax+a'x'+c+c'$ otherwise, $-\infty$	$-\infty$
$-_+$	$(a-a')x+(b-b')y+c-c'$	if $(a-a')=0$, $by-b'y'+c-c'$ otherwise, ∞	if $(b-b')=0$, $ax-a'x'+c-c'$ otherwise, ∞	∞
$-_-$		if $(a-a')=0$, $by-b'y'+c-c'$ otherwise, $-\infty$	if $(b-b')=0$, $ax-a'x'+c-c'$ otherwise, $-\infty$	$-\infty$

Figure 8 *Binary Operations over Symbolic Expressions*

We give a dataflow transfer function for each machine instruction, and define data-flow transfer functions to be strict with respect to the top element. We introduce four basic abstract operations, $+$, $-$, $\times$, and $\div$, for describing the dataflow transfer functions. The abstract operations are summarized below, where n is an integer:

$$[l, u] + [l', u'] = [l +_- l', u +_+ u']$$
$$[l, u] - [l', u'] = [l -_- u', u -_+ l']$$
$$[l, u] \times n = [l \times n, u \times n]$$
$$[l, u] \div n = [l \div n, u \div n]$$

The arithmetic operations $+_+$, $+_-$, $-_+$, $-_-$ over bounds $ax+by+c$ and $a'x' + b'y'+c'$ are given in Figure 8, where a, b, a', and b' are non-zero integers. These arithmetic operations ensure that the bounds are always of the form $ax+by+c$.

Comparison instructions are a major source of bounds information. Because our analysis works on machine code, we need only consider tests of two forms: $w \leq v$ and $w = v$ (where w and v are program variables). Figure 9 summarizes the dataflow transfer functions for these two forms. We assume that the ranges of w and v are $[l_w, u_w]$ and $[l_v, u_v]$ before the tests. The function $min_1(l, l')$ and $max_1(l, l')$ are defined as follows:

$$min_1(l, l') = \begin{cases} min(l, l') & \text{if comparable}(l,l') \\ l & \text{otherwise} \end{cases} \quad \text{and} \quad max_1(l, l') = \begin{cases} max(l, l') & \text{if comparable}(l,l') \\ l & \text{otherwise} \end{cases}$$

If a upper bound of a range is smaller than its lower bound, the range is equivalent to the empty range. For the dataflow functions for variables w and v along the false branch of the test $w=v$, we could improve precision slightly by returning the empty range when l_w, u_w, l_v, and u_v are all equal.

To ensure the convergence of the range-analysis algorithm in the presence of loops, we perform a widening operation [7] at a node in the loop that dominates the source of the loop backedge. Let $r=[l, u]$ be the range of an arbitrary variable x at the previous

Test		w	v
$w = v$	True Branch	$[max_1(l_w, l_v), min_1(u_w, u_v)]$	$[max_1(l_v, l_w), min_1(u_v, u_w)]$
	False Branch	$[l_w, u_w]$	$[l_v, u_v]$
$w \leq v$	True Branch	$[l_w, min_1(u_w, u_v)]$	$[max_1(l_v, l_w), u_v]$
	False Branch	$[max_1(l_w, l_v+1), u_w]$	$[l_v, min_1(u_v, u_w-1)]$

Figure 9 *Dataflow Functions for Tests*

iteration and r'=[l', u'] be the dataflow value of x at the current iteration. The resulting range will be r''= r ∇ r' where ∇ is the widening operator defined as follows:

$$[l,u]\nabla \, [l', u'] = [l'', u''], \text{ where } l'' = \begin{cases} -\infty & \text{if } (l'<l) \\ l & \text{otherwise} \end{cases} \text{ and } u'' = \begin{cases} \infty & \text{if } (u'>u) \\ u & \text{otherwise} \end{cases}$$

We sharpen the basic range analysis with two enhancements. The first enhancement deals with selecting the most suitable spot in a loop to perform widening. The key observation is that for a "do-while" loop (which is the kind that dominates in binary code[1]), it is more effective to perform widening right before the test to exit the loop. In the case of a loop that iterates over an array (e.g., where the loop test is "$i < length$") this strategy minimizes the imprecision of our relatively crude widening operation: the range for i is widened to [0, +∞] just before the loop test, but is then immediately sharpened by the transfer function for the loop test, so that the range propagated along the loop's backedge is [0, $length$-1]. Consequently, the analysis quiesces after two iterations. The second enhancement is to utilize correlations between register values. For example, if the test under consideration is $r < n$ and we can establish that $r = r'+c$ at that program point, where c is a constant, we can incorporate this information into the range analysis by assuming that the branch also tests $r' < n\text{-}c$.

7   Case Studies

All of the techniques described above, except for the technique to infer sizes of local arrays (Section 5), have been implemented in our safety-checker for SPARC machine programs [24]. We illustrate the benefits of these improvements on a few example programs. These examples include array sum, start-timer and stop-timer code taken from Paradyn's performance-instrumentation suite [11], two versions of Btree traversal (one version compares keys via a function call), hash-table lookup, a kernel extension that implements a page-replacement policy [17], bubble sort, two versions of heap sort (one manually inlined version and one interprocedural version), stack-smashing (example 9.b described in [16]), MD5Update of the MD5 Message-Digest Algorithm [13], several functions from jPVM [9] (two cases, where one case includes more functions), and a module in the device driver /dev/kerninst [20] that reads the kernel symbol table.

In our experiments, we were able to find a safety violation in the example that implements a page-replacement policy—it attempts to dereference a pointer that could be null—and we identified all array out-of-bounds violations in the stack-smashing example, and all array out-of-bounds violations in the /dev/kerninst example. Figure 10 summarizes the time needed to verify each of the examples on a 440MHz Sun Ultra 10 machine. The times are divided into the times to perform typestate propagation, create

---

1. Although "while" and "for" loops are more common in source code, compilers typically transform them to an "if" with a "do-while" in the "then-part" of the "if". After this transformation has been done, the compiler can exploit the fact that the code in the body of the "do-while" will always be executed at least once if the loop executes. Thus, it is possible to perform code-motion without the fear of ever slowing down the execution of the program. In particular, the compiler can hoist expressions from within the body of the loop to the point in the "then-part" just before the loop, where they are still guarded by the "if".

	SUM	PAGING POLICY	START TIMER	HASH	BUBBLE SORT	STOP TIMER	BTREE	BTREE2	HEAP SORT 2	HEAP SORT	JPVM	STACK-SMASHING	JPVM 2	/DEV /KERNINST	MD5
INSTRUCTIONS	13	20	22	25	25	36	41	51	71	95	157	309	315	339	883
BRANCHES	2	5	1	4	5	3	11	11	9	16	12	89	16	45	11
LOOPS (INNER)	1	2 (1)	0	1	2 (1)	0	2 (1)	2 (1)	4 (2)	4 (2)	3	7(1)	3	6(4)	5(2)
PROCEDURAL CALLS (TRUSTED)	0	0	1 (1)	1 (1)	0	2 (2)	0	4 (4)	3	0	21 (21)	2	40 (40)	36 (25)	6
GLOBAL CONDITIONS (BOUNDS CHECKS)	4 (2)	9	13	15 (2)	16 (8)	17	35 (14)	39 (14)	56 (26)	84 (42)	49 (18)	100 (74)	99 (18)	116 (42)	121 (30)
SOURCE LANGUAGE	C	C	C	C	C	C	C	C	C	C	C	C	C	C++	C
TYPESTATE PROPAGATION	0.02	0.05	0.02	0.04	0.04	0.03	0.09	0.11	0.17	0.15	0.63	0.69	3.05	4.88	5.92
ANNOTATION	0.003	0.005	0.005	0.006	0.005	0.007	0.008	0.01	0.015	0.015	0.034	0.03	0.069	0.068	0.082
RANGE ANALYSIS	0.01	0	0	0.01	0.03	0	0.03	0.04	0.08	0.12	0.13	0.54	0.24	0.68	1.24
GLOBAL VERIFICATION	0.08	0.18	0.13	0.40	0.18	0.14	0.40	0.35	1.15	2.46	0.78	12.74	1.55	8.60	3.41
TOTAL (SECONDS)	0.1	0.23	0.16	0.46	0.26	0.18	0.53	0.51	1.42	2.75	1.57	14.0	4.91	14.2	10.65

Figure 10   *Characteristics of the Examples and Performance Results*

annotations and perform local verification, perform range analysis, and perform global verification. Figure 10 also characterizes the examples in terms of the number of machine instructions, number of branches, number of loops (total versus number of inner loops), number of calls (total versus number of calls to trusted functions), number of global safety conditions (number of bounds checks), and the source language in which each test case is written. Note that the checking of the lower and upper bounds are regarded as two separate safety conditions. The times to verify these examples range from 0.1 seconds to 14 seconds.

The extensions to the typestate system allow us to handle a broader class of real-life examples. Having bit-level representations of integers allow the analysis to deal with instructions that load/store a partial word in the Md5Update and stack-smashing examples. The technique to summarize trusted functions allows the analysis to use summaries of several host and library functions in hash, start- and stop-timer, Btree2, the two jPVM examples, and /dev/kerninst. Subtyping among structures and pointers allows summaries to be given for JNI [8] methods that are polymorphic. For example, the JNI function "jsize GetArrayLength(JNIEnv* env, jarray array)" takes the type jarray as the second parameter, and it is also applicable to the types jintArray and jobjectArray, both of which are subtypes of jarray. Because all Java objects have to be manipulated via the JNI interface, we model the types jintArray and jobjectArray as physical subtypes of jarray when summarizing the JNI interface functions.

Symbolic range analysis allows the system to identify the boundaries of an array that is one field of a structure in the MD5 example. When the typestate-propagation algorithm needs information about the range of a register value, we run an intraprocedural version of the range analysis on demand, and the intraprocedural range analysis is run at most once for each function. In the 11 of our test cases that have array accesses, range

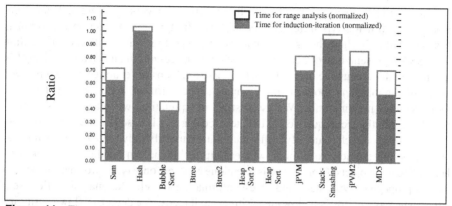

Figure 11   *Times to perform global verification with range analysis normalized with respect to times to perform global verification without range analysis.*

analysis eliminated 55% of the total attempts to synthesize loop invariants. In 4 of the 11 test cases, it eliminated the need to synthesize loop invariants altogether. The resulting speedup for global verification ranges from -4% to 53% (with a median of 29%). Furthermore, in conjunction with improvements that we made to our global-verification phase, range analysis allows us to verify the /dev/kerninst example, which we were not able to handle previously. Figure 11 shows the times for performing global verification, together with the times for performing range analysis (normalized with respect to the times for performing global verification without range analysis). The reason that the analysis of the stack-smashing example is not speeded up is because most array accesses in that example are out of bounds. When the array accesses are, in fact, out of bounds, range analysis will not speed up the overall analysis because the analysis still needs to apply the program-verification technique before it can conclude that there are array out-of-bounds violations. Similarly, the reason that hash is slowed down is because only 2 of the 14 conditions are array-bounds checks, and the range analysis cannot prove that the array accesses are within bounds.

Note that range analysis has eliminated the need to synthesize loop invariants for array bounds checks in about 55% of the cases. Two of the reasons why range analysis has not been able to do better are: (i) lost precision due to widening, and (ii) the inability of the range-analysis algorithm to recognize certain correlations among registers. In our implementation, we perform a widening operation just before the test to exit a loop for better precision. However, with nested loops, a widening operation in an inner loop could cause information in its outer loop to lose precision. A potential improvement to range analysis would be to not perform widening for variables that are invariants in the loop that contains the widening point. Another potential improvement is to identify correlations among loop induction variables and to include a pass after range analysis to make use of these correlations.

8   Related Work

There are several papers that have investigated topics related to the typestate-checking system and symbolic range analysis that we use.

Mycroft [10] described a technique that reverse engineers C programs from target machine code using type-inference techniques. His type-reconstruction algorithm is based on Milner's algorithm W [12]; it associates type constraints with each instruction in an SSA representation of a program; type reconstruction is via unification. Mycroft's technique infers recursive data-types when there are loops or recursive procedures. We start from annotations about the initial inputs to the untrusted code, whereas his technique requires no annotation. We use abstract interpretation, whereas he uses unification. Note that the technique we use to detect local arrays is based on the same principle as his unification technique. Mycroft's technique currently only recovers types for registers (and not memory locations), whereas our technique can handle both stack- and heap-allocated objects. Moreover, his technique recovers only type information, whereas ours propagates type, state, and access information as well. Our analysis is flow-sensitive, whereas Mycroft's is flow-insensitive, but it recovers a degree of flow sensitivity by using SSA form so that different variables are associated with different live ranges.

Several people have described techniques that can be used to statically check for out-of-bounds array accesses. Cousot and Halbwachs [7] described a method that is based on abstract interpretation using convex hulls of polyhedra. Their technique is precise in that it does not simply try to verify assertions, but instead tries to discover assertions that can be deduced from the semantics of the program. Our range analysis can be regarded as a simple form of Cousot and Halbwachs' analysis with an eye towards efficiency. Our goal is to take advantage of the synergy of an efficient range analysis and an expensive but powerful program-verification technique [24] that can be applied on demand. We apply the program-verification technique only for conditions that cannot be proven by the range analysis.

Verbrugge *et al* [21] described a range-analysis technique called Generalized Constant Propagation (GCP). Our symbolic range analysis differs from GCP in the following respects: GCP uses a domain of intervals of scalars, whereas we use symbolic ranges. GCP attempts to balance convergence and precision of analysis by "stepping up" ranges for variables that have failed to converge after some fixed number of iterations. We perform a widening operation right away for quicker convergence, but sharpen our analysis by selecting suitable spots in loops for performing the widening operation, and also by incorporating correlations among register values. Both GCP and our technique use points-to information discovered in an earlier analysis phase. Our current implementation of range analysis is context-insensitive, whereas GCP is context-sensitive.

Rugina and Rinard [14] also use symbolic bounds analysis. Their analysis gains context sensitivity by representing the symbolic bounds for each variable as functions (polynomials with rational coefficients) of the initial values of formal parameters. Their analysis proceeds as follows: For each basic block, it generates the bounds for each variable at the entry; it then abstractly interprets the statements in the block to compute the bounds for each variable at each program point inside and at the exit of the basic block. Based on these bounds, they build a symbolic constraint system, and solve the constraints by reducing it to a linear program over the coefficient variables from the symbolic bound polynomials. They solve the symbolic constraint system with the goal of minimizing the upper bounds and maximizing the lower bounds.

Other techniques for eliminating array bounds checks include the work described by Bodik *et al* [2] and Wegner *at al* [23].

References

1. M. Abadi, and L. Cardelli. **A Theory of Objects**. Monographs in Computer Science, D. Gries, and F. B. Schneider (Ed.). Springer-Verlag New York (1996).
2. R. Bodik, R. Gupta, and V. Sarkar. ABCD: Eliminating Array Bounds Checks on Demand. *SIGPLAN Conference on Programming Language Design and Implementation*. Vancouver B.C., Canada (June 2000).
3. S. Chandra, and T. Reps. Physical Type Checking for C. *PASTE '99: SIGPLAN-SIGSOFT Workshop on Program Analysis for Software Tools and Engineering*. Toulouse, France (September 1999).
4. D. R. Chase, M. Wegman, and F. Zadeck. Analysis of Pointers and Structures. *SIGPLAN Conference on Programming Language Design and Implementation*. New York, NY (1990).
5. B. Chatterjee, B. G. Ryder, and W. A. Landi. Relevant Context Inference. *ACM Symposium on Principles of Programming Languages*. San Antonio, TX (January 1999).
6. P. Cousot, R. Cousot: Abstract Interpretation: A Unified Lattice Model for Static Analysis of Programs by Construction or Approximation of Fixpoints. *The 4th ACM Symposium on Principles of Programming Languages*. Los Angeles, California (January 1977).
7. P. Cousot, and N. Halbwachs. Automatic Discovery of Linear Restraints Among Variables of a Program. *Fifth Annual ACM Symposium on Principles of Programming Languages*. Tucson, AZ (January 1978).
8. JavaSoft. **Java Native Interface Specification**. Release 1.1 (May 1997).
9. jPVM: A Native Methods Interface to PVM for the Java Platform. http://www.chmsr.gatech.edu/jPVM (2000).
10. A. Mycroft. Type-Based Decompilation (or Program Reconstruction via Type Reconstruction). *8th European Symposium on Programming, ESOP'99*. Amsterdam, The Netherlands (March 1999).
11. B. P. Miller, M. D. Callaghan, J. M. Cargille, J. K. Hollingsworth, R. B. Irvin, K. L. Karavanic, K. Kunchithapadam, and T. Newhall.The Paradyn Parallel Performance Measurement Tools. *IEEE Computer* **28**, 11 (November 1995).
12. R. Milner. A Theory of Type Polymorphism in Programming. *Journal of Computer and System Sciences* **17**, 3 (1978).
13. R. Rivest. The MD5 Message-Digest Algorithm. **Request for Comments: 1321**. MIT Laboratory for Computer Science and RSA Data Security, Inc (April 1992).
14. R. Rugina and M. Rinard. Symbolic Bounds Analysis of Pointers, Array Indices, and Accessed Memory Regions. *SIGPLAN Conference on Programming Language Design and Implementation*. Vancouver B.C., Canada (June 2000).
15. M. Siff, S. Chandra, T. Ball, K. Kunchithapadam, and T. Reps. Coping with type casts in C. *Seventh European Software Engineering Conference and Seventh ACM SIGSOFT Symposium on the Foundations of Software Engineering*. Toulouse, France (September 1999).
16. N. P. Smith. Stack Smashing Vulnerabilities in the UNIX Operating System. http://www.destroy.net/machines/security (2000).
17. C. Small, and M. A. Seltzer. Comparison of OS Extension Technologies. *USENIX 1996 Annual Technical Conference*. San Diego, CA (January 1996).
18. F. Smith, D. Walker, and G. Morrisett. Alias Types. *European Symposium on Programming*. Berlin, Germany (March 2000).
19. N. Susuki, and K. Ishihata. Implementation of an Array Bound Checker. *4th ACM Symposium on Principles of Programming Languages*. Los Angeles, CA (January 1977).
20. A. Tamches, and B. P. Miller. Fine-Grained Dynamic Instrumentation of Commodity Operating System Kernels. *Third Symposium on Operating System Design and Implementation*. New Orleans, LA (February 1999).
21. C. Verbrugge, P. Co, and L. Hendren. Generalized Constant Propagation A Study in C. *6th International Conference on Compiler Construction*. Linköping, Sweden (April 1996).
22. P. Wadler. A taste of linear logic. Mathematical Foundations of Computer Science, Lecture Notes in Computer Science **711**. Springer-Verlag. Gdansk, Poland (August 1993).
23. D. Wegner, J. Foster, E. Brewer, and A. Aiken. A First Step Towards Automated Detection of Buffer Overrun Vulnerabilities. *The 2000 Network and Distributed Systems Security Conference*. San Diego, CA (February 2000).
24. Z. Xu, B. P. Miller, and T. W. Reps. Safety Checking of Machine Code. *SIGPLAN Conference on Programming Language Design and Implementation*. Vancouver B.C., Canada (June 2000).

Proof-Directed De-compilation of Low-Level Code*

Shin-ya Katsumata[1]** and Atsushi Ohori[2]***

[1] Laboratory for Foundations of Computer Science, University of Edinburgh,
Edinburgh EH9 3JZ, UK; sxk@dcs.ed.ac.uk
[2] School of Information Science,
Japan Advanced Institute of Science and Technology,
Tatsunokuchi, Ishikawa 923-1292, JAPAN; ohori@jaist.ac.jp

Abstract. We present a proof theoretical method for de-compiling low-level code to the typed lambda calculus. We first define a proof system for a low-level code language based on the idea of Curry-Howard isomorphism. This allows us to regard an executable code as a proof in intuitionistic propositional logic. As being a proof of intuitionistic logic, it can be translated to an equivalent proof of natural deduction proof system. This property yields an algorithm to translate a given code into a lambda term. Moreover, the resulting lambda term is not a trivial encoding of a sequence of primitive instructions, but reflects the behavior of the given program. This process therefore serves as *proof-directed de-compilation* of a low-level code language to a high-level language. We carry out this development for a subset of Java Virtual Machine instructions including most of its features such as jumps, object creation and method invocation. The proof-directed de-compilation algorithm has been implemented, which demonstrates the feasibility of our approach.

1 Introduction

The ability to analyze compiled code before its execution is becoming increasingly important due to recently emerging network computing, where pieces of executable code are dynamically exchanged over the Internet and used under the user's own privileges. In such circumstances, it is a legitimate desire to verify that a foreign code satisfies some desired properties before it is executed. This problem has recently attracted the attention of programming language researchers. One notable approach toward verification of properties of compiled code is to construct a formal proof of certain desired properties of a code using a theorem prover, and to package the code with its proof to form a *proof-carrying code* [8]. The user of the code can then check the attached proof against the code

---

* A part of this work was done while both authors were at RIMS, Kyoto University.
** Shin-ya Katsumata's research was supported in part by a scholarship provided by the Laboratory for Foundations of Computer Science, University of Edinburgh.
*** Atsushi Ohori's work was partially supported by the Japanese Ministry of Education Grant-in-Aid for Scientific Research No. 12680345.

D. Sands (Ed.): ESOP 2001, LNCS 2028, pp. 352–366, 2001.

to ensure that the code satisfies the properties. Another approach is to develop a static type system for compiled code [1,6,7,13]. By checking the type consistency of a code, the user can ensure that the code does not cause any run-time type errors.

Both of these are effective in verifying certain predetermined safety properties. In many cases, however, the user would like to know the actual behavior of a foreign code for ensuring that the code correctly realizes its expected functionality. Moreover, analysis of the exact behavior of a code would open up a new possibility of network computing, where foreign code can be dynamically analyzed and adapted or optimized to suit the user's environment.

An executable code is a large sequence of instructions, which can be rather hard for humans to understand. However this does not mean, at least in principle, that a code is incomprehensible. A properly compiled code of a correct program is a consistent syntactic object that can be interpreted by a machine to perform the function denoted by the original program. This fact suggests that it should be possible to develop a systematic method to extract the logical structure of a code and present it in a high-level language.

The key to developing a code analysis system is the Curry-Howard isomorphism for machine code presented in [11]. In this paradigm, a code language corresponds to a variant of the sequent calculus of intuitionistic propositional logic, called the *sequential sequent calculus*. Being a proof system of the logic, it can be translated to and from other languages corresponding to proof systems of intuitionistic logic. Compilation is one instance, which translates natural deduction to the sequential sequent calculus. It is shown that the converse is also possible, leading to the proof-directed *de-compilation* of machine code. In the next section, we outline our approach based on the Curry-Howard isomorphism.

The purpose of the present paper is to show that this general idea can be used to develop a de-compiler for a low-level code language. Our de-compilation method is most naturally applicable to lambda calculus. We also believe that the general principle of the method can be applicable to a wide range of low-level code languages. To demonstrate the practical feasibility of our method we carry out the development for the Java bytecode language [4], which is the target language of the Java programming language [3]. This language provides several practically useful features such as objects and methods at the bytecode level, for which there is no obvious Curry-Howard isomorphism. The language with these features is a good touchstone for the scalability of our approach to practical extra-logical structures.

We first give, in Section 3, a term language called JAL^0 for a subset of Java Virtual Machine (JVM) assembly language including basic instructions and develop a de-compilation from JAL^0 to a PCF-like language. We show that this de-compilation algorithm preserves both the typing and the semantics of a given bytecode program. We then give an extention, called JAL, of JAL^0 with objects and methods in Section 4. Based on these results, we have implemented a proof-directed de-compiler for the Java bytecode language supporting most of its features. Figure 1 shows an actual output of our decompiler. The input JVM bytecode is the result of compiling the following Java program.

An input to the de-compiler.

```
.method public           istore_1
    static fact(I)I       iinc 0 -1
  iconst_1               L12:
  istore_1                iload_0
  goto L12                iconst_1
L5:                       if_icmpgt L5
  iload_1                 iload_1
  iload_0                 ireturn
  imul                  .end method
```

Output of the de-compiler.

```
fact(e0) =
  L12(e0, 1)

L12(e0, e1) =
  if(1 < e0) then
    L12(e0 - 1, e1 * e0)
  else
    return e1
```

Fig. 1. An example of the proof-directed de-compilation

```
public static int fact (int n) { int m;
  for(m = 1; n > 1; --n)
    m = m * n;
  return m; }
```

As seen in this example, our de-compiler correctly recovers the factorial program as a tail recursive function without using any knowledge other than the given bytecode. Section 5 describes our prototype de-compiler. Section 6 compares our approach with related work, and Section 7 concludes the paper.

Limitations of space make it difficult to cover the de-compilation method fully; the authors intend to present a more detailed description in another paper.

Conventions and Notations: We count the elements of a list from the left starting with 0. We write $|l|$ for the length of the list l, and write l, e for the list obtained from l by adding the element e at the end of l. We write $\{d_1 : e_1, \cdots, d_n : e_n\}$ for the function which maps d_j to e_j $(1 \leq j \leq n)$, and write $f\{d : e\}$ for the function f' such that $\mathrm{dom}(f') = \mathrm{dom}(f) \cup \{d\}$, $f'(d) = e$ and $f'(x) = f(x)$ for any $x \neq d$.

2 Logical Approach to Code Analysis

In this section, we describe Curry-Howard isomorphism for machine code presented in [11] and outline the proof-directed de-compilation.

We let Δ range over lists of formula representing an assumption set of a logical sequent. The basic observation underlying the logical interpretation of machine code is to consider each instruction I as a logical inference step of the form $\dfrac{\Delta' \triangleright B : \tau}{\Delta \triangleright I; B : \tau}$ similar to a left rule in Gentzen's sequent calculus. Regarding the assumption set as a description of machine memory (stack), an inference rule of this form represents a primitive machine instruction that transforms a memory state Δ to that of Δ'. The conclusion τ of the judgement $\Delta \triangleright B : \tau$ is the type of the value returned by the code B.

A bytecode language corresponds to a proof system consisting of this form of rules, called a sequential sequent calculus, which has the same deducibility as intuitionistic propositional logic. One important implication of this result is that

$$\frac{}{\Delta, \tau \rhd \mathsf{return} : \tau} \qquad \frac{\Delta, \Delta_i \rhd B : \tau \quad 0 \le i < |\Delta|}{\Delta \rhd \mathsf{acc}\ i; B : \tau} \qquad \frac{\Delta, \mathsf{int} \rhd B : \tau}{\Delta \rhd \mathsf{iconst}\ n; B : \tau}$$

$$\frac{\Delta, \tau' \times \tau'' \rhd B : \tau}{\Delta, \tau', \tau'' \rhd \mathsf{pair}; B : \tau} \qquad \frac{\Delta, \tau' \rhd B : \tau}{\Delta, \tau' \times \tau'' \rhd \mathsf{fst}; B : \tau} \qquad \frac{\Delta, \tau'' \rhd B : \tau}{\Delta, \tau' \times \tau'' \rhd \mathsf{snd}; B : \tau}$$

$$\frac{\Delta, (\Delta_0 \Rightarrow \tau') \rhd B : \tau}{\Delta \rhd \mathsf{code}\ B_0; B : \tau}\ (\text{if } \Delta_0 \rhd B_0 : \tau') \qquad \frac{\Delta, \tau' \rhd B : \tau}{\Delta, (\Delta_0 \Rightarrow \tau'), \Delta_0 \rhd \mathsf{call}\ n; B : \tau}\ (|\Delta_0| = n)$$

Fig. 2. A sequential sequent calculus for a simple bytecode language

a bytecode language can be translated to and from other proof systems of intuitionistic propositional logic. Compilation of lambda terms can be regarded as a proof transformation from natural deduction (i.e. typed lambda calculus) into this proof system. Moreover, it is shown that the converse is also possible. The lambda term obtained through the inverse transformation exhibits the logical structure of the code. This process can therefore be regarded as *de-compilation*. Below, we outline this process using a simple bytecode language.

The set of types (ranged over by τ), *instructions* (ranged over by I) and *code blocks* (ranged over by B) of the bytecode language are given below.

$$\tau ::= \mathsf{int} \mid \tau \times \tau \mid \tau, \cdots, \tau \Rightarrow \tau$$
$$B ::= \mathsf{return} \mid I; B$$
$$I ::= \mathsf{iconst}\ n \mid \mathsf{acc}\ i \mid \mathsf{pair} \mid \mathsf{fst} \mid \mathsf{snd} \mid \mathsf{code}\ B \mid \mathsf{call}\ n$$

The type $\tau_1, \cdots, \tau_n \Rightarrow \tau$ is the type of functions which map lists of values of type $\tau_1, \cdots, \tau_n$ to values of type τ. Instructions $\mathsf{iconst}\ n$, $\mathsf{acc}\ i$, and $\mathsf{code}\ B$ push onto the stack the integer value n, the ith element of the stack, and the pointer to the code block B, respectively. pair constructs a pair on the stack, and fst and snd take the first and second element of a pair on the stack. $\mathsf{call}\ n$ pops n elements and a code pointer off the stack, and calls the code with the n arguments.

We consider a list Δ of types as a type of a machine stack with the convention that the right-most formula in a list corresponds to the top of the stack, and interpret a block of this bytecode language as a proof of the sequential sequent calculus. The term assignment system for the sequential sequent calculus is given in Figure 2.

The intended semantics of each instruction should be understood by reading the corresponding proof rule "backward". For example, pair changes the stack state from Δ, τ, τ' to $\Delta, \tau \times \tau'$ indicating the operation that replaces the top-most 2 elements with their product.

We consider the following typed lambda calculus as the target of de-compilation.

$$\tau ::= \mathsf{int} \mid \tau \times \tau \mid \tau \to \tau$$
$$M ::= n \mid x \mid (M, M) \mid \mathsf{fst}(M) \mid \mathsf{snd}(M) \mid \lambda x.M \mid M\ M$$

$$[\![\Delta, \tau \rhd \text{return} : \tau]\!] = s_{|\Delta|}$$
$$[\![\Delta \rhd \text{acc } i; B : \tau]\!] = [s_i/s_{|\Delta|}][\![\Delta, \Delta_i \rhd B : \tau]\!]$$
$$[\![\Delta \rhd \text{iconst } n; B : \tau]\!] = [n/s_{|\Delta|}][\![\Delta, \text{int} \rhd B : \tau]\!]$$
$$[\![\Delta, \tau', \tau'' \rhd \text{pair}; B : \tau]\!] = [(s_{|\Delta|}, s_{|\Delta|+1})/s_{|\Delta|}][\![\Delta, \tau' \times \tau'' \rhd B : \tau]\!]$$
$$[\![\Delta, \tau' \times \tau'' \rhd \text{fst}; B : \tau]\!] = [\text{fst}(s_{|\Delta|})/s_{|\Delta|}][\![\Delta, \tau' \rhd B : \tau]\!]$$
$$[\![\Delta, \tau' \times \tau'' \rhd \text{snd}; B : \tau]\!] = [\text{snd}(s_{|\Delta|})/s_{|\Delta|}][\![\Delta, \tau'' \rhd B : \tau]\!]$$
$$[\![\Delta \rhd \text{code } B_0; B : \tau]\!] =$$
$$[\lambda s_0 \cdots s_{|\Delta'|-1}.[\![\Delta' \rhd B' : \tau']\!]/s_{|\Delta|}][\![\Delta, (\Delta' \Rightarrow \tau') \rhd B : \tau]\!]$$
$$[\![\Delta, (\Delta' \Rightarrow \tau'), \Delta' \rhd \text{call } n; B : \tau]\!] =$$
$$[(s_{|\Delta|} \, s_{|\Delta|+1} \cdots s_{|\Delta|+n})/s_{|\Delta|}][\![\Delta, \tau' \rhd B : \tau]\!] \quad (n = |\Delta'|)$$

Fig. 3. De-compilation algorithm for a simple bytecode language

Its type system is the standard one. We write $[M/x]N$ for the term obtained from N by substituting M for x (with necessary bound-variable renaming.)

We write $[\![\Delta \rhd B : \tau]\!]$ for the lambda term obtained by transforming the derivation $\Delta \rhd B : \tau$. The general idea behind the transformation is to assign a variable s_i to each element Δ_i in the assumption list Δ, and to proceed by induction on the derivation of the code. The algorithm translates an initial sequent to the variable corresponding to the top of the stack. For a compound proof, the algorithm first obtains the term corresponding to its sub-proof. It then applies the transformation corresponding to the first instruction to obtain the desired lambda term. The set of equations in Figure 3 defines the transformation.

3 JAL⁰ : The JVM Assembly Language without Objects

Compared to the simple bytecode language considered above, Java bytecode has the following additional features.

1. *Restricted stack access and local variable support.* JVM does not include an instruction to access an arbitrary stack element. This restriction is compensated by JVM's support for directly accessible mutable local variables.
2. *Labels and jumps.* As in most existing computer architectures, JVM uses labels and jumps to realize control flow.
3. *Classes, objects and methods.* JVM has types and instructions to support object-oriented features.

Since the third feature requires significantly new machinery, we divide our development into two stages. In this section, we define a JVM assembly language without objects, denoted by JAL⁰, supporting the first two features, and present its proof system and the proof-directed de-compilation algorithm for JAL⁰. Then we state the semantic correctness of the de-compilation algorithm. Later, in Section 4, we describe the necessary extensions to objects and methods.

3.1   Syntax of JAL⁰

With the introduction of labels and jumps, an executable program unit is no longer a sequence of instructions, but a collection of labelled blocks, mutually referenced through labels. We let l range over a given countably infinite set of *labels*, and i range over a given countably infinite set of *local variables*. We assume a fixed linear order on the set of local variables, and that any sequence of local variables mentioned in the following development is ordered by this relation.

The syntax of *program units* (ranged over by K), *blocks* (ranged over by B) and *instructions* (ranged over by I) of JAL⁰ are given below.

$$K ::= \{l : B, \cdots, l : B\}$$
$$B ::= \mathsf{ireturn} \mid \mathsf{goto}\ l \mid I;B$$
$$I ::= \mathsf{iconst}\ n \mid \mathsf{pop} \mid \mathsf{dup} \mid \mathsf{swap} \mid \mathsf{iload}\ i \mid \mathsf{istore}\ i \mid \mathsf{iadd} \mid \mathsf{ifzero}\ l$$

ireturn is for returning an integer value. goto l transfers control to the block labelled l. iconst n is the same as before. pop, dup, swap are the stack operations for popping the stack, for duplicating the top element, and for swapping the top two elements, respectively. iload i pushes the contents of the local variable i onto the stack. istore i pops the top value off the stack and stores it in the local variable i. iadd pops two integers off the stack and pushes back the sum of the two. ifzero l pops the top element off the stack, and transfers control to the code block labelled l if it is 0. A *JAL⁰ program* is a program unit K with a distinguished *entry label* l, written $K.l$.

The following example is a JAL⁰ program, which takes an integer input through local variable i_0 and returns 1 if it is 0, otherwise returns 0.

$$K_0.l \equiv \left\{ \begin{array}{l} l : \quad \mathsf{iload}\ i_0; \mathsf{ifzero}\ l'; \mathsf{iconst}\ 0; \mathsf{goto}\ l'' \\ l' : \quad \mathsf{iconst}\ 1; \mathsf{goto}\ l'' \\ l'' : \mathsf{ireturn} \end{array} \right\}.l$$

3.2   The Type System for JAL⁰

Each JAL⁰ instruction operates on the stack and the local variables, and is represented as an inference rule of the form $\dfrac{\Gamma; \Delta \rhd B : \tau}{\Gamma'; \Delta' \rhd I;B : \tau}$ where Γ is a *local variable context* which maps local variables to value types, Δ is a *stack context* which is a finite sequence of value types, and τ is the value type of the block B. In JAL⁰ considered in this section, the only possible value type is "int" of integers. In Section 4, we extend JAL⁰ to include object types.

Since blocks in general refer to other blocks through labels, the typing of a block is determined relative to an assumption on the types of blocks assigned to the labels. We define a *block type* to be a logical sequent of the form $\Gamma; \Delta \rhd \tau$ denoting possible blocks B such that $\Gamma; \Delta \rhd B : \tau$. We let Λ range over *label contexts*, which maps labels to block types.

Judgement forms and typing rules of JAL⁰ are given in Figure 4. The definition of typing $\Lambda \rhd K$ of a program unit K is essentially the same as the typing

Judgements:

$\Lambda \mid \Gamma; \Delta \triangleright B : \tau$ block B has block type $\Gamma; \Delta \triangleright \tau$ under Λ

$\Lambda \triangleright K$ program unit K is well-typed with Λ

$\Lambda \mid \Gamma; \Delta \triangleright K.l : \tau$ the entry point l of a program $K.l$ has block type $\Gamma; \Delta \triangleright \tau$ under Λ

Typing rules for blocks:

$$\frac{}{\Lambda \mid \Gamma; \Delta, \text{int} \triangleright \text{ireturn} : \text{int}} \quad \frac{\Lambda(l) = \Gamma; \Delta \triangleright \tau}{\Lambda \mid \Gamma; \Delta \triangleright \text{goto } l : \tau} \quad \frac{\Lambda \mid \Gamma; \Delta \triangleright B : \tau'}{\Lambda \mid \Gamma; \Delta, \tau \triangleright \text{pop}; B : \tau'}$$

$$\frac{\Lambda \mid \Gamma; \Delta, \tau, \tau \triangleright B : \tau'}{\Lambda \mid \Gamma; \Delta, \tau \triangleright \text{dup}; B : \tau'} \quad \frac{\Lambda \mid \Gamma; \Delta, \tau', \tau \triangleright B : \tau''}{\Lambda \mid \Gamma; \Delta, \tau, \tau' \triangleright \text{swap}; B : \tau''} \quad \frac{\Lambda \mid \Gamma; \Delta, \text{int} \triangleright B : \tau}{\Lambda \mid \Gamma; \Delta \triangleright \text{iconst } n; B : \tau}$$

$$\frac{\Lambda \mid \Gamma; \Delta, \text{int} \triangleright B : \tau \quad \Gamma(i) = \text{int}}{\Lambda \mid \Gamma; \Delta \triangleright \text{iload } i; B : \tau} \quad \frac{\Gamma\{i : \text{int}\}; \Delta \triangleright B : \tau}{\Lambda \mid \Gamma; \Delta, \text{int} \triangleright \text{istore } i; B : \tau}$$

$$\frac{\Lambda \mid \Gamma; \Delta, \text{int} \triangleright B : \tau}{\Lambda \mid \Gamma; \Delta, \text{int}, \text{int} \triangleright \text{iadd}; B : \tau} \quad \frac{\Lambda \mid \Gamma; \Delta \triangleright B : \tau \quad \Lambda(l) = \Gamma; \Delta \triangleright \tau}{\Lambda \mid \Gamma; \Delta, \text{int} \triangleright \text{ifzero } l; B : \tau}$$

Typing of program units: Typing of programs:

$$\frac{\forall l \in \text{dom}(\Lambda). \Lambda \mid \Gamma; \Delta \triangleright K(l) : \tau \quad \Lambda(l) = \Gamma; \Delta \triangleright \tau}{\Lambda \triangleright K} \quad \frac{\Lambda \triangleright K \quad \Lambda(l) = \Gamma; \Delta \triangleright \tau}{\Lambda \mid \Gamma; \Delta \triangleright K.l : \tau}$$

Fig. 4. Type system of JAL^0

rule for recursive definitions in a functional language. The rules for pop, dup and swap correspond to logical rules for weakening, contraction and exchange, respectively. The rules for iload i and istore i can also be understood as structural rules across two assumptions Γ and Δ. Conditional branch and jump instructions are, as already mentioned, considered as rules referring to other blocks in a program unit. These rules require that the type of the referenced block has the same local variable context, stack context and return type as those of the reference point.

As an example, let Λ_0 be a label context

$$\Lambda_0 = \{l : \{i_0 : \text{int}\}; \emptyset \triangleright \text{int}, l' : \{i_0 : \text{int}\}; \emptyset \triangleright \text{int}, l'' : \{i_0 : \text{int}\}; \text{int} \triangleright \text{int}\}.$$

Then the program unit K_0 given in the previous subsection has the typing $\Lambda_0 \triangleright K_0$ and therefore $\Lambda_0 \mid \{i_0 : \text{int}\}; \emptyset \triangleright K_0.l : \text{int}$.

3.3 Operational Semantics of JAL^0 and the Type Soundness

The language JAL^0 is intended to model a subset of JVM bytecode. As such, we define its operational semantics by specifying the effect of each instruction on a machine state. A machine state is described by a triple $(E; S; B)$ of a *local variable environment* E which maps local variables to run-time values, a *stack* S which is a sequence of run-time values, and a *current block* B where the left-most instruction is the next one to be executed. For JAL^0, the possible run-time values (ranged over by v) are integers.

We write $(E; S; (I; B)) \longrightarrow_K (E'; S'; B')$ if the state $(E; S; (I; B))$ is changed to $(E'; S'; B')$ by the execution of I. Figure 5 gives the set of transition

$$
\begin{array}{ll}
(E;\ S;\ \mathsf{iload}\ i;\ B) & \longrightarrow_K (E;\ S, E(i);\ B) \quad (E;\ S, v;\ \mathsf{pop};\ B) \quad \longrightarrow_K (E;\ S;\ B) \\
(E;\ S, v;\ \mathsf{dup};\ B) & \longrightarrow_K (E;\ S, v, v;\ B) \quad (E;\ S;\ \mathsf{iconst}\ n;\ B) \longrightarrow_K (E;\ S, n;\ B) \\
(E;\ S, v_1, v_2\ \mathsf{swap};\ B) & \longrightarrow_K (E;\ S, v_2, v_1;\ B) \quad (E;\ S, v;\ \mathsf{ireturn}) \quad \longrightarrow_K (\emptyset;\ v;\ \emptyset) \\
(E;\ S, v;\ \mathsf{istore}\ i;\ B) & \longrightarrow_K (E\{i:v\};\ S;\ B) \quad (E;\ S;\ \mathsf{goto}\ l;\ B) \quad \longrightarrow_K (E;\ S;\ K(l)) \\
(E;\ S, n, m;\ \mathsf{iadd};\ B) & \longrightarrow_K (E;\ S, n+m;\ B) \quad (E;\ S, 0;\ \mathsf{ifzero}\ l;\ B) \longrightarrow_K (E;\ S;\ K(l)) \\
(E;\ S, n;\ \mathsf{ifzero}\ l;\ B) & \longrightarrow_K (E;\ S;\ B) \quad (n \neq 0)
\end{array}
$$

Fig. 5. Operational semantics of JAL^0

rules. The reflexive transitive closure of $\longrightarrow_K$ is denoted by $\overset{*}{\longrightarrow}_K$. A program $K.l$ computes a value v from an initial local variable environment E and a stack S, written $(E;\ S;\ K.l) \overset{*}{\longrightarrow} v$, if $(E;\ S;\ K(l)) \overset{*}{\longrightarrow}_K (\emptyset;\ v;\ \emptyset)$.

We show that the type system of JAL^0 is sound with respect to this operational semantics. We write $\models v : \tau$ if v has type τ, and define the typing relations for local variable environments and stacks as follows.

$$
E \models \Gamma \iff \mathrm{dom}(E) = \mathrm{dom}(\Gamma) \text{ and } \forall i \in \mathrm{dom}(E).\ \models E(i) : \Gamma(i)
$$
$$
S \models \Delta \iff |S| = |\Delta| \text{ and } \forall 0 \leq i < |S|.\ \models S_i : \Delta_i
$$

Since JAL^0 only contains integers, the typing relation for values is the trivial relation between integers and int, but can easily be extended to other primitive types. We can then show the following.

Theorem 1. *If* $E \models \Gamma, S \models \Delta$ *and* $\Lambda \mid \Gamma; \Delta \rhd K.l : \tau$ *then either* $(E;\ S;\ K.l) \overset{*}{\longrightarrow} v$ *such that* $\models v : \tau$ *or the computation of a program* $K.l$ *under* E, S *does not terminate.*

3.4   Proof-Directed De-compilation of JAL^0

To develop a proof-directed de-compilation algorithm for JAL^0, we need to account for jump instructions and local variables. Our strategy is to translate a labelled block to a function from its contexts to its return type, and to translate a jump to a label as a tail call of the function corresponding to the label. Since basic blocks in a program may have jumps mutually calling the other blocks, we assume that the target language supports mutual recursion.

As we mentioned earlier, manipulation of local variables can be modelled by structural rules across a local variable context and a stack context. Their mutability is reduced to introducing a new binding each time a value is stored to a variable, and therefore no additional mechanism is required.

Our target language is the following PCF-like language, which we call λ^{rec}:

$$
\tau ::= \mathsf{int} \mid \tau \to \tau
$$
$$
M ::= n \mid x \mid \lambda x.M \mid M\ M
$$
$$
\mid \mathsf{ifzero}\ M\ \mathsf{then}\ M\ \mathsf{else}\ M \mid \mathsf{iadd}\ (M, N) \mid \mathsf{rec}\ \{x = M, \cdots, x = M\}\ \mathsf{in}\ x
$$

$$[\![\Gamma; \Delta, \mathsf{int} \triangleright \mathsf{ireturn} : \mathsf{int}]\!] = s_{|\Delta|}$$

$$[\![\Gamma; \Delta, \tau \triangleright \mathsf{pop}; B : \tau]\!] = [\![\Gamma; \Delta \triangleright B : \tau]\!]$$

$$[\![\Gamma; \Delta, \tau \triangleright \mathsf{dup}; B : \tau]\!] = [s_{|\Delta|}/s_{|\Delta|+1}][\![\Gamma; \Delta, \tau, \tau \triangleright B : \tau]\!]$$

$$[\![\Gamma; \Delta, \tau, \tau' \triangleright \mathsf{swap}; B : \tau]\!] = [s_{|\Delta|+1}/s_{|\Delta|}, s_{|\Delta|}/s_{|\Delta|+1}][\![\Gamma; \Delta, \tau', \tau \triangleright B : \tau]\!]$$

$$[\![\Gamma; \Delta \triangleright \mathsf{iconst}\ n; B : \tau]\!] = [n/s_{|\Delta|}][\![\Gamma; \Delta, \mathsf{int} \triangleright B : \tau]\!]$$

$$[\![\Gamma; \Delta \triangleright \mathsf{iload}\ i; B : \tau]\!] = [i/s_{|\Delta|}][\![\Gamma; \Delta, \mathsf{int} \triangleright B : \tau]\!]$$

$$[\![\Gamma; \Delta, \mathsf{int} \triangleright \mathsf{istore}\ i; B : \tau]\!] = [s_{|\Delta|}/i][\![\Gamma\{i : \mathsf{int}\}; \Delta \triangleright B : \tau]\!]$$

$$[\![\Gamma; \Delta, \mathsf{int} \triangleright \mathsf{ifzero}\ l; B : \tau]\!] = \mathsf{ifzero}(s_{|\Delta|}, \mathsf{apply}(l, \Gamma, \Delta), [\![\Gamma; \Delta \triangleright B : \tau]\!])$$

$$[\![\Gamma; \Delta, \mathsf{int}, \mathsf{int} \triangleright \mathsf{iadd}; B : \tau]\!] = [\mathsf{iadd}\ (s_{|\Delta|}, s_{|\Delta|+1})/s_{|\Delta|}][\![\Gamma; \Delta, \mathsf{int} \triangleright B : \tau]\!]$$

$$[\![\Gamma; \Delta \triangleright \mathsf{goto}\ l : \tau]\!] = \mathsf{apply}(l, \Gamma, \Delta)$$

Fig. 6. De-compilation algorithm for JAL^0 blocks

rec $\{x_1 = M_1, \cdots, x_n = M_n\}$ in x_j denotes the term M_j with mutually recursive definitions, where $x_1, \ldots, x_n$ may appear in $M_1, \ldots, M_n$. The type system of λ^{rec} is standard. We write $\Gamma \triangleright M : \tau$ if M has type τ under context Γ.

To present our de-compilation algorithm, we introduce some definitions and notations. We assume that the set of variables of λ^{rec} is the disjoint union of the set of labels, the set of local variables, and a given countably infinite set of *stack variables* indexed with natural numbers. We write s_i for the stack variable of index i. We define the application of all variables in the context $\Gamma; \Delta$ to the label l, written $\mathsf{apply}(l, \Gamma, \Delta)$, as the term $l\ i_0 \cdots i_n\ s_0 \cdots s_{|\Delta|-1}$ for which $\mathrm{dom}(\Gamma) = \{i_0, \cdots, i_n\}$. The de-compilation algorithm for blocks is given by the equations in Figure 6.

We turn to de-compilation of JAL^0 programs. First we define a *closure* of a basic block, written $Cls(\Gamma; \Delta \triangleright B : \tau)$, as the λ^{rec} term $\lambda i_0 \cdots i_n s_0 \cdots s_{|\Delta|-1}.[\![\Gamma; \Delta \triangleright B : \tau]\!]$. Let $\Lambda = \{l_1 : \Gamma_1; \Delta_1 \triangleright \tau_1, \ldots, l_n : \Gamma_n; \Delta_n \triangleright \tau_n\}$ and K be a JAL^0 program unit such that $\Lambda \triangleright K$. The transformation of a program $\Lambda \mid \Gamma_j; \Delta_j \triangleright K.l_j : \tau_j$ is given as follows:

$$[\![\Lambda \mid \Gamma_j; \Delta_j \triangleright K.l_j : \tau_j]\!] = \mathrm{rec}\ \{l_1 = Cls(\Gamma_1; \Delta_1 \triangleright K(l_1) : \tau_1), \cdots,$$
$$l_n = Cls(\Gamma_n; \Delta_n \triangleright K(l_n) : \tau_n)\}\ \mathrm{in}\ l_j.$$

The above de-compilation algorithm is a proof transformation and as such it preserves types. We establish this statement via the following translation of block types in JAL^0 to types in λ^{rec}.

$$\overline{\Gamma; \Delta \triangleright \tau} = \Gamma(i_0) \to \cdots \to \Gamma(i_n) \to \Delta_0 \to \cdots \to \Delta_{|\Delta|-1} \to \tau$$

Theorem 2. *If $\Lambda \mid \Gamma; \Delta \triangleright K.l : \tau$ then the judgement $\emptyset \triangleright [\![\Lambda \mid \Gamma; \Delta \triangleright K.l : \tau]\!] : \overline{\Gamma; \Delta \triangleright \tau}$ is derivable in λ^{rec}.*

We apply the above transformation to the example $K_0.l$:

$$[\![\Lambda_0 \mid \{i_0 : \text{int}\}; \emptyset \triangleright K_0.l : \text{int}]\!] = \text{rec} \left\{ \begin{array}{l} l = \lambda i_0.\text{ifzero } (i_0, \ l' \ i_0, \ l'' \ i_0 \ 0) \\ l' = \lambda i_0.l'' \ i_0 \ 1 \\ l'' = \lambda i_0 s_0.s_0 \end{array} \right\} \text{ in } l.$$

3.5   Correctness of the De-compilation

From Theorem 2, one can see that our de-compilation algorithm is a proof transformation preserving typing. We provide further evidence of the correctness of our de-compilation algorithm by establishing that the algorithm also preserves semantics of JAL^0 programs.

An operational semantics of λ^{rec} is defined in the same way as the standard semantics of call-by-value PCF language. The semantics is determined by the evaluation relation $M \Downarrow W$ which says that the term M evaluates to the value W. A value W is either a natural number n or a term of the form $\lambda x.M$ (i.e. closure). Here we only show the evaluation rule for the mutual recursion operator:

$$\frac{[\cdots \text{rec } \{x_1 = M_1, \cdots, x_n = M_n\} \text{ in } x_i/x_i \cdots]M_j \Downarrow W}{\text{rec } \{x_1 = M_1, \cdots, x_n = M_n\} \text{ in } x_j \Downarrow W}.$$

The other evaluation rules are standard.

We establish the preservation of semantics via the following interpretation of virtual machine states as term substitutions in λ^{rec}. Let Λ be a label context, K be a program unit, E be a local variable environment and S be a stack. The interpretation $\overline{\Lambda \triangleright K; E; S}$ of a machine state $\Lambda \triangleright K; E; S$ is the term substitution defined by the following partial function from variables to λ^{rec} terms.

$$\overline{\Lambda \triangleright K; E; S}(x) = \left\{ \begin{array}{ll} [\![\Lambda \mid \Gamma; \Delta \triangleright K.x : \tau]\!] & x \in \text{dom}(K) \wedge \Lambda(x) = \Gamma; \Delta \triangleright \tau \\ E(x) & x \in \text{dom}(E) \\ S_j & x \equiv s_j \wedge 0 \leq j < |S| \end{array} \right.$$

Then the preservation of semantics is stated as the following theorem.

Theorem 3. *If* $\Lambda \triangleright K$, $\Lambda \mid \Gamma; \Delta \triangleright B : \tau$, $E \models \Gamma$, $S \models \Delta$ *and* $(E; S; B) \xrightarrow{*}_K$ $(\emptyset; V; \emptyset)$, *then* $\overline{\Lambda \triangleright K; E; S}([\![\Lambda \mid \Gamma; \Delta \triangleright B : \tau]\!]) \Downarrow V.$

4   Bytecode with Objects and Methods

This section develops the framework for proof-directed de-compilation with object oriented features. We concentrate on the basic mechanism for creating objects and invoking their methods, and leave the other object-oriented features to future research. This development requires us to extend both JAL^0 and the target language λ^{rec}. We extend both of them by adding primitives having the same functionality for object manipulation. In this approach the de-compiler just sends these primitives from the source to the target language. Another approach is to extend the target language with rich types so that the de-compiler can give an encoding of objects. However, we do not adopt this approach, because giving such an encoding is usually associated with compilation process, which is the inverse of de-compilation.

There still remains one complication in this basic model, which is related to object initialization. As observed by Freund and Mitchell [1], a straightforward formulation of a type system for Java bytecode language is unsound due to the possibility of accessing uninitialized objects. Their solution is to distinguish types of initialized objects from those of uninitialized ones by indexing the type of an uninitialized object with the invocation of the corresponding object creation method. Although their type system is based on the one by Stata and Abadi, this mechanism has sufficient generality that it can be adopted to our framework.

4.1   JAL: JAL^0 with Objects and Classes

We give an extention, called JAL, of JAL^0 with object-oriented features. We assume there is a countably infinite set of *class identifiers*(ranged over by c) and a countably infinite set of *object indexes*(ranged over by u). An object index indicates the invocation point of the object creation method. The syntax of types is extended with class identifiers as follows.

$$\kappa ::= c \mid c_u \qquad \tau ::= \text{int} \mid \kappa$$

The type c_u is for a reference to an uninitialized object created at the point u.

We let f and m range over the set of *field names* and the set of *method names*, respectively. We define a *class structure* as a pair of the form $(\{f_1 : \tau_1, \cdots, f_n : \tau_n\}, \{m_1 : \Gamma_1; \emptyset \triangleright \tau_1, \cdots m_n : \Gamma_n; \emptyset \triangleright \tau_n\})$. A class structure specifies the types of fields and methods in a class. We regard class structures as overloaded functions for field names and method names. We define a *class context*, ranged over by $\mathcal{C}$, as a map from class identifiers to class structures.

The set of instructions are extended with the following new instructions.

areturn   aload i astore i new c init c invoke c, m getfield c, f putfield c, f

areturn, aload and astore have analogous behavior on object references as the corresponding ones on integers. new c creates an uninitialized object instance of class c and pushes its reference onto the stack. init c pops an uninitialized object reference off the stack and initializes it by replacing each c with c_u. Practically, this instruction corresponds to invoking initialization method of uninitialized object. We omit its arguments for simplicity. invoke c, m invokes a method m on an object of class c by popping m arguments and an object off the stack and transferring control to the method code m of the object. The return value of the method is pushed onto the stack. getfield c, f and setfield c, f reads and writes field f of instance objects of class c respectively. invoke, getfield and setfield instructions fail if they operate on uninitialized object instances.

Judgement forms and typing rules of JAL are given in Figure 7. Typing rules for instructions not included in the figure are the same as those in JAL^0. In the rule for init, $[c/c_u]\Gamma$ or $[c/c_u]\Delta$ is obtained from Γ or Δ by substituting c for each occurrence of c_u respectively. The mechanism for type safe object initialization realized by the rules for new and init is the adaptation of that of [1].

Judgements:

$\mathcal{C}; \Lambda \mid \Gamma; \Delta \rhd B : \tau$ block B has block type $\Gamma; \Delta \rhd \tau$ under $\mathcal{C}$ and Λ

$\mathcal{C}; \Lambda \rhd K$ program unit K is well-typed under $\mathcal{C}$ and Λ

$\mathcal{C}; \Lambda \mid \Gamma; \Delta \rhd K.l : \tau$ the entry point l of the program $K.l$ has block type $\Gamma; \Delta \rhd \tau$
          under $\mathcal{C}$ and Λ

Typing rules for blocks involving objects:

$$\frac{}{\mathcal{C}; \Lambda \mid \Gamma; \Delta, c \rhd \mathsf{areturn} : c} \qquad \frac{\mathcal{C}; \Lambda \mid \Gamma; \Delta, \kappa \rhd B : \tau \quad \Gamma(i) = \kappa}{\mathcal{C}; \Lambda \mid \Gamma; \Delta \rhd \mathsf{aload}\ i; B : \tau} \qquad \frac{\mathcal{C}; \Lambda \mid \Gamma\{i : \kappa\}; \Delta \rhd B : \tau}{\mathcal{C}; \Lambda \mid \Gamma; \Delta, \kappa \rhd \mathsf{astore}\ i; B : \tau}$$

$$\frac{\mathcal{C}; \Lambda \mid \Gamma; \Delta, c_u \rhd B : \tau \quad c \in \mathrm{dom}(\mathcal{C}) \quad u\ \text{fresh}}{\mathcal{C}; \Lambda \mid \Gamma; \Delta \rhd \mathsf{new}\ c; B : \tau} \qquad \frac{\mathcal{C}; \Lambda \mid [c/c_u]\Gamma; [c/c_u]\Delta \rhd B : \tau}{\mathcal{C}; \Lambda \mid \Gamma; \Delta, c_u \rhd \mathsf{init}\ c; B : \tau}$$

$$\frac{\mathcal{C}; \Lambda \mid \Gamma; \Delta, \mathcal{C}(c)(f) \rhd B : \tau}{\mathcal{C}; \Lambda \mid \Gamma; \Delta, c \rhd \mathsf{getfield}\ c, f; B : \tau} \qquad \frac{\mathcal{C}; \Lambda \mid \Gamma; \Delta \rhd B : \tau}{\mathcal{C}; \Lambda \mid \Gamma; \Delta, c, \mathcal{C}(c)(f) \rhd \mathsf{putfield}\ c, f; B : \tau}$$

$$\frac{\mathcal{C}; \Lambda \mid \Gamma; \Delta, \tau \rhd B : \tau' \quad \mathcal{C}(c)(m) = \{i_0 : c,\ i_1 : \tau_1, \cdots, i_n : \tau_n\}; \emptyset \rhd \tau}{\mathcal{C}; \Lambda \mid \Gamma; \Delta, c, \tau_1, \cdots, \tau_n \rhd \mathsf{invoke}\ c, m; B : \tau'}$$

Typing of program units: Typing of programs:

$$\frac{\forall l \in \mathrm{dom}(\Lambda).\mathcal{C}; \Lambda \mid \Gamma; \Delta \rhd K(l) : \tau \quad \Lambda(l) = \Gamma; \Delta \rhd \tau}{\mathcal{C}; \Lambda \rhd K} \qquad \frac{\mathcal{C}; \Lambda \rhd K \quad \Lambda(l) = \Gamma; \Delta \rhd \tau}{\mathcal{C}; \Lambda \mid \Gamma; \Delta \rhd K.l : \tau}$$

Fig. 7. Type system of JAL

4.2   De-compilation Algorithm

The target language of the de-compilation is an extention of λ^{rec} with primitives for object manipulation corresponding to those in JAL. We call it λ^{obj}. The set of types and terms of λ^{obj} is the following:

$$\tau ::= c \mid \mathsf{int} \mid \tau \to \tau$$
$$M ::= \cdots \mid \mathsf{let}\ x = \mathsf{new}\ c\ \mathsf{in}\ M \mid x.\mathsf{init}\ c; M \mid \mathsf{let}\ x = x.m(M, \cdots, M)\ \mathsf{in}\ M$$
$$\mid \mathsf{let}\ x = x.f\ \mathsf{in}\ M \mid x.f := M; M$$

The last five terms are those for object creation, object initialization, method invocation, object field extraction and object field update. The typing rules for these additional terms to λ^{rec} are shown in Figure 8. The type system for λ^{obj} is defined relative to a fixed class context $\mathcal{C}$. We should note that this type system does not take into account of uninitialized object types. Because of the higher-order feature, the Freund and Mitchell's technique does not easily extend to the lambda calculus. In this type system, uninitialized object types of the form c_u are identified with c. As a result, we can only show the type preservation up to this identification.

The de-compilation algorithm is obtained by extending the one for JAL^0 presented in the previous section with the equations for object manipulation instructions. Figure 9 shows the additional equations required for this extension. The transformation of JAL programs is given in the same way as the one for JAL^0 using the mutual recursion operator.

$$\frac{\mathcal{C}\,|\,\Gamma\{x:c\}\,\triangleright\,M:\tau \quad c\in\mathrm{dom}(\mathcal{C})}{\mathcal{C}\,|\,\Gamma\,\triangleright\,\mathsf{let}\;x=\mathsf{new}\;c\;\mathsf{in}\;M:\tau}\qquad \frac{\mathcal{C}\,|\,\Gamma\,\triangleright\,M:\tau \quad \Gamma(x)=c}{\mathcal{C}\,|\,\Gamma\,\triangleright\,x.\mathsf{init}\;c;\,M:\tau}$$

$$\frac{\mathcal{C}\,|\,\Gamma\,\triangleright\,L_i:\tau_i\ (1\le i\le n) \quad \mathcal{C}\,|\,\Gamma\{y:\tau\}\,\triangleright\,M:\tau' \quad \Gamma(x)=c \quad \mathcal{C}(c)(m)=\{i_0:c,\,i_1:\tau_1,\dots,i_n:\tau_n\};\emptyset\,\triangleright\,\tau}{\mathcal{C}\,|\,\Gamma\,\triangleright\,\mathsf{let}\;y=x.m(L_1,\dots,L_n)\;\mathsf{in}\;M:\tau'}$$

$$\frac{\mathcal{C}\,|\,\Gamma\{y:\tau\}\,\triangleright\,M:\tau' \quad \Gamma(x)=c \quad \mathcal{C}(c)(f)=\tau}{\mathcal{C}\,|\,\Gamma\,\triangleright\,\mathsf{let}\;y=x.f\;\mathsf{in}\;M:\tau'}\qquad \frac{\mathcal{C}\,|\,\Gamma\,\triangleright\,M:\tau \quad \mathcal{C}\,|\,\Gamma\,\triangleright\,N:\tau' \quad \Gamma(x)=c \quad \mathcal{C}(c)(f)=\tau}{\mathcal{C}\,|\,\Gamma\,\triangleright\,x.f:=M;\,N:\tau'}$$

Fig. 8. Additional typing rules for objects

$$[\![\Gamma;\Delta,\tau\,\triangleright\,\mathsf{areturn}:\tau]\!]_c=s_{|\Delta|}$$

$$[\![\Gamma;\Delta\,\triangleright\,\mathsf{aload}\;i;B:\tau]\!]_c=[i/s_{|\Delta|}][\![\Gamma;\Delta,\Gamma(i)\,\triangleright\,B:\tau]\!]_c$$

$$[\![\Gamma;\Delta,\kappa\,\triangleright\,\mathsf{astore}\;i;B:\tau]\!]_c=[s_{|\Delta|}/i][\![\Gamma\{i:\kappa\};\Delta\,\triangleright\,B:\tau]\!]_c$$

$$[\![\Gamma;\Delta\,\triangleright\,\mathsf{new}\;c;B:\tau]\!]_c=\mathsf{let}\;s_{|\Delta|}=\mathsf{new}\;c\;\mathsf{in}\;[\![\Gamma;\Delta,c_u\,\triangleright\,B:\tau]\!]_c$$

$$[\![\Gamma;\Delta,c_u\,\triangleright\,\mathsf{init}\;c;B:\tau]\!]_c=s_{|\Delta|}.\mathsf{init}\;c;\,[\![[c/c_u]\Gamma;[c/c_u]\Delta\,\triangleright\,B:\tau]\!]_c$$

$$[\![\Gamma;\Delta,c,\tau_1,\cdots,\tau_n\,\triangleright\,\mathsf{invoke}\;c,m;B:\tau']\!]_c=\mathsf{let}\;s_{|\Delta|}=s_{|\Delta|}.m(s_{|\Delta|+1},\cdots,s_{|\Delta|+n})$$
$$\mathsf{in}\;[\![\Gamma;\Delta,\tau\,\triangleright\,B:\tau']\!]_c$$
$$\mathsf{where}\;\mathcal{C}(c)(m)=\{i_0:c,i_1:\tau_1,\cdots,i_n:\tau_n\};\emptyset\,\triangleright\,\tau$$

$$[\![\Gamma;\Delta,c\,\triangleright\,\mathsf{getfield}\;c,f;B:\tau]\!]_c=\mathsf{let}\;s_{|\Delta|}=s_{|\Delta|}.f\;\mathsf{in}\;[\![\Gamma;\Delta,\mathcal{C}(c)(f)\,\triangleright\,B:\tau]\!]_c$$

$$[\![\Gamma;\Delta,c,\mathcal{C}(c)(f)\,\triangleright\,\mathsf{setfield}\;c\;f;B:\tau]\!]_c=s_{|\Delta|}.f:=s_{|\Delta|+1};\,[\![\Gamma;\Delta\,\triangleright\,B:\tau]\!]_c$$

Fig. 9. De-compilation algorithm for object primitives in JAL

As in the case for the de-compilation algorithm for JAL^0, this algorithm is a type-preserving proof transformation from a sequential sequent calculus to (an extension of) natural deduction. The following theorem formally establishes this property.

Theorem 4. *If* $\mathcal{C};\Lambda\,|\,\Gamma;\Delta\,\triangleright\,K.l:\tau$ *then the judgement* $\mathcal{C}\,|\,\emptyset\,\triangleright\,[\![\Lambda\,|\,\Gamma;\Delta\,\triangleright\,K.l:$ $\tau]\!]_c:\overline{\Gamma;\Delta\,\triangleright\,\tau}$ *is derivable in* λ^{obj} *up to the identification of* c_u *with* c.

5   A Prototype Implementation of a De-compiler

We have implemented a prototype de-compiler, JD, based on the transformation algorithm presented in this paper. Input to JD is an JVM assembly language source file in the format of Jasmin described in [5], which can be mechanically constructed from a JVM class file. JD first parses a given source file to obtain an internal representation of a set of sequences of JVM instructions, each of which corresponds to one method. JD then converts each sequence of instructions into a program unit consisting of blocks. In doing this, JD considers a cascaded block as a collection of blocks connected by implicit jumps, and inserts jumps to make the block structure explicit. This insertion does not change the semantics of the program. Finally, JD de-compiles each program unit by applying the algorithm presented in this paper to generate a term in the lambda calculus with objects.

JD supports more instructions and types than those we have considered in the formal framework, including those for arithmetics, arrays, double-word types. In addition, JD performs more jobs than we presented in the previous sections. One is removing intermediate labels and temporary variables. Since most Java bytecode programs consist of many small blocks, without this processing, the resulting lambda term would contain many redundant labels and variables. JD achieves this removal by applying a code manipulation which corresponds to some β reductions in the target language. In Figure 1, the block corresponding to label L5 is eliminated by this process.

6   Related Work

The work most relevant to ours is perhaps Stata and Abadi [13] on a type system for Java bytecode subroutines. This work is further refined in [9,1]. In these approaches, a type system is used to check the consistency of an array of instructions. The result of typechecking is success or failure indicating whether the array of instruction is type consistent or not. In contrast, our approach is to interpret a given code as a constructive proof representing its computation. This allows us to de-compile a code to a lambda term.

Our work is also related to the typed assembly language (TAL) of Morrisett et. al. [6,7]. Their type system is designed to check the type consistency of a sequence of instruction, and is not intended to serve as a logic. Nonetheless, some of our proof rules are similar to the corresponding ones in their type system. In our proof theory, for example, a jump instruction is interpreted as a rule to refer to an existing proof, which has some similarity to the TAL's treatment of jumps.

Our de-compilation performs proof transformation from a variant of the sequent calculus to natural deduction. Raffalli [12] considers compilation as proof transformation. The TAL approach emphasizes the benefit of compilation as type-preserving transformation, which can be regarded as proof transformation. In the general perspective, our approach shares the same spirit with these approaches. However, the problem of the converse of compilation has not been investigated. From a logical perspective, the relationship between Gentzen's intuitionistic sequent calculus and natural deduction has been extensively studied. (See [2] for a survey.) Our proof system for bytecode languages is similar to the Gentzen's sequent calculus, and therefore some of the cases in de-compilation algorithm have the similar structure to the corresponding cases in proof transformation from the Gentzen's sequent calculus to the natural deduction.

There are a number of works for "reverse engineering" machine code. (See for example [14].) There are also several working de-compilers for Java bytecode language. However, little has been known about the foundation of de-compilation. The major technical contribution of our work is to provide a logical foundation for systematic development of a de-compilation algorithm, for reasoning about the de-compilation process, and for establishing its correctness.

7   Conclusions

We have developed a framework for proof-directed de-compilation of low-level code based on the Curry-Howard isomorphism for machine code, and have presented a proof-directed de-compilation algorithm for a subset of Java bytecode language including integer primitives, stack operations, local variable manipulation, conditional and unconditional jumps. A prototype de-compiler for Java bytecode has been implemented, which demonstrates the feasibility of the proof-directed de-compilation approach presented in this paper. We believe that by combining the existing strategies and heuristic techniques, the method presented in this paper will contribute to developing a practical and robust de-compiler.

Acknowledgements. We thank some of anonymous referees for thorough and careful reading of the paper and for providing many helpful comments, which have been very useful for improving the presentation of the paper.

References

1. S. Freund and J. Mitchell. A type system for object initialization in the Java byte code language. In *Proc. OOPSLA'98*, pages 310–328, 1998.
2. J. Gallier. Constructive logics part I: A tutorial on proof systems and typed λ-calculi. *Theoretical Computer Science 110*, pages 249–339, 1993.
3. J. Gosling, B. Joy, and G. Steele. *The Java Language Specification*. Addison-Wesley, 1996.
4. T. Lindholm and F. Yellin. *The Java virtual machine specification*. Addison Wesley, 2nd edition, 1999.
5. J. Meyer and T. Downing. *Java Virtual Machine*. O'Reilly, 1997.
6. G. Morrisett, K. Crary, N. Glew, and D. Walker. Stack-based typed assembly language. In *Proc. Types in Compilation, LNCS 1473*, pages 28-52, 1998.
7. G. Morrisett, D. Walker, K. Crary, and N. Glew. From system F to typed assembly language. In *Proc. POPL'98*, pages 85-97, 1998.
8. G. Necula. Proof-carrying code. In *Proc. POPL'98*, pages 106–119, 1998.
9. R. O'Callahan. A simple, comprehensive type system for Java bytecode subroutines. In *Proc. POPL'99*, pages 70–78, 1999.
10. A. Ohori. A Curry-Howard isomorphism for compilation and program execution. In *Proc. TLCA'99, LNCS 1581*, pages 280–294, 1999.
11. A. Ohori. The logical abstract machine: a Curry-Howard isomorphism for machine code. In *Proc. FLOPS'99, LNCS 1722*, pages 300-318,1999.
12. C. Raffalli. Machine deduction. In *Proc. Types for Proofs and Program, LNCS 806*, pages 333–351, 1994.
13. R. Stata and M. Abadi. A type system for Java bytecode subroutines. In *Proc. POPL'98*, pages 149–160, 1998.
14. *Proceedings of Working Conference on Reverse Engineering*. IEEE Computer Society Press, 1993–.

Backwards Abstract Interpretation of Probabilistic Programs

David Monniaux

LIENS, 45 rue d'Ulm
75230 Paris cedex 5, France
http://www.di.ens.fr/~monniaux

1 Introduction

In industrial contexts, safety regulations often mandate upper bounds on the probabilities of failure. Now that embedded computers are part of many industrial environments, it is often needed to analyze programs with non-deterministic and probabilistic behavior. We propose a general abstract interpretation based method for the static analysis of programs using random generators or random inputs. Our method also allows "ordinary" non-deterministic inputs, not necessarily following a random distribution.

1.1 Our Approach

Our method is set in the general framework of abstract interpretation. We first introduce an adjoint semantics for probabilistic programs using "weight functions", basing ourselves on the standard semantics of probabilistic programs as linear operators on measures [8,9,12] (see §1.4 for an explanation on measures). Similarly as it has been done for the standard semantics [12], we introduce a notion of abstract interpretation on weight functions. We then propose a highly generic construction of abstract lattices, lifting an "ordinary" abstract lattice used for the analysis of non-probabilistic programs to one suitable for probabilistic programs.

As salient point of this method is that it starts from the description of an output event (for instance, an anomalous condition) and computes back a description of areas in the input domain describing their probability of making the behavior happen. This allows finding what parts of the input domain are more likely to elicit anomalous behavior, as an extension to probabilistic programs of ordinary backwards analysis.

We shall give all our examples using a simple imperative language extended with nondeterministic and probabilistic inputs, for the sake of simplicity. This by no means indicates our method is restricted to imperative languages. There has been much work done, for instance, on the analysis of complex imperative languages [1], and our method can be applied to lift it to probabilistic cases as well.

D. Sands (Ed.): ESOP 2001, LNCS 2028, pp. 367–382, 2001.

1.2   Comparison with Other Approaches

There has been several propositions of weakest precondition semantics and associated sets of rules, similar to Dijkstra's for non-probabilistic programs [7,11,14, 15]. However, these methods, while adequate for computer-aided program design or verification, cannot be automated easily.

Abstract interpretation has already been applied to probabilistic semantics [12]. However, the method that we describe here, while similar, considers different semantics, hence leads to different informations about the programs. In [12], following the standard semantics proposed by Kozen [8,9] and used in most analysis schemes, the semantics of a program is a function mapping an input probability measure onto an output probability measure, taking into account the random generators and random inputs happening in the meantime. The goal is to derive knowledge on the output from knowledge of the input. Here, we derive weights on the input from an area in the output. Another notion of forward probabilistic abstract interpretation has been proposed by Di Pierro and Wiklicky [4], but it is unclear how it can handle problems except in simple, discrete cases; furthermore, their model does not support nondeterminism.

Statistical sampling methods are already used to test software, and they were improved to allow for both nondeterministic and probabilistic behavior [13] in a mathematically sound fashion. However, when dealing with rare behavior, these methods are greatly improved using additional knowledge on the system allowing for stratified sampling or importance sampling [16, chap. 4]. The analysis we describe in this paper could be used to supply data for importance sampling, improving the speed of precision of the Monte-Carlo method of [13].

1.3   Nondeterminism and Probabilities

We shall make clear what we call "nondeterministic" and "probabilistic". A nondeterministic choice allows for several independent outcomes of the choice. A probabilistic choice also allows for several outcomes, but constrains the frequency of those outcomes. For instance, let us consider an input $x \in [0, 1]$ to the program. If it is nondeterministic, then the only thing we know is that it is in $[0, 1]$. Simply supposing it is probabilistic, without any additional knowledge, already establishes that this variable has numerous properties such as an average and a standard deviate, and implies statistical properties on successive uses of this input.

With respect to program semantics, purely probabilistic programs are to be treated much like nondeterministic nonprobabilistic ones [7], except that the values that are manipulated are (sub)probability measures on the set of program environments instead of program environments. A notion of nondeterministic, probabilistic programs arises when nondeterministic choice between several measures is allowed. Our analysis takes care of that most complex case.

1.4   Notations, Measures, and Integrals

Standard probability theory is based on **measures** [17,5]. A probability measure μ on a set X is a function that assigns to each event (subset of X) its probability.

For instance, the **uniform** probability measure on the segment $[0,1]$ assigns to each segment $[a,b]$ the probability $b - a$. The **Dirac** measure δ_{x_0} assigns 1 to any event containing x_0 and 0 otherwise; it modelizes a value that is "known for sure" to be x_0. For technical reasons, not all subsets are necessarily measurable — this is not a problem in our case. A **measurable space** is the couple of a set and an associated set of events (measurable subsets).

A function f is said to be **measurable** if and only if for any measurable set X, $f^{-1}(X)$ is measurable; we shall often use the vector space $M(X, \mathbb{R})$ of measurable functions from a measurable space to $\mathbb{R}$ (the real field).

For technical reasons, we shall also use **signed measures** in this paper. Signed measures over a measurable set X, using the norm of the total variation [5] $\| \cdot \|$, constitute a vector space $\mathcal{M}(X)$. $\mathcal{M}_+(X)$ will denote the positive measures. We shall consider continuous linear operators [10] over such spaces. As an extension to the usual notion of the **adjoint** of a linear operator with respect to a hermitian form [10, VIII, §4], we use adjoints of linear operators with respect to a bilinear form.

We shall often use **integrals**, in the sense of Lebesgue integration [17]. $\int f \, d\mu$ denotes the integral of the function f with respect to the measure μ. For instance, if the integration set is $\mathbb{R}$ and μ is the usual Lebesgue measure on the segment $[a,b]$ (the measure that assigns to each segment its length), $\int f \, d\mu$ is the usual integral $\int_a^b f(x) \, dx$; if the measure μ is the Dirac measure at x_0, then $\int f \, d\mu$ is $f(x_0)$.

We shall often use the vector space $\mathcal{B}(X, \mathbb{R})$ of bounded measurable functions from X to $\mathbb{R}$, with the norm $\|f\|_\infty = \sup_{x \in X} |f(x)|$.

$\mathcal{L}(X, Y)$ is the vector space of **linear functions** from X to Y. The phrase "linear function" shall always be taken in its linear algebra sense.

2   Adjoint Semantics

In his seminal papers, Kozen proposed semantics of probabilistic programs as continuous linear operators on measure spaces. We shall see that operators representing the semantics of probabilistic programs have adjoints, in a certain sense that we shall define (§2.3). These adjoints are the basis of our analysis techniques; furthermore, their existence yields a proof of a theorem of Kozen's.

2.1   Intuition

Let us consider a very simple C program (Fig. 1) where `centered_uniform()` is a random generator returning a `double` uniformly distributed in $[-1,1]$, independent of previous calls. We are interested in the relationship between the probability of executing B depending on the probability distribution generated in x by A. What we would therefore like is a (linear) function f mapping the probability measure μ generated at A onto the probability $f(\mu)$ that program point B is executed. It will be proved that there exists a "weight function" g such that $f(\mu) = \int g \, d\mu$. We shall see how to compute such a g.

A plotting of g is featured in figure 2. Let us give a few examples of the use of this function:

```
double x, y;
... /* A */
y = centered_uniform()+centered_uniform();
x += y/2;

...

if (fabs(x) <= 1)
{
    ... /* B */
}
```

Fig. 1. A simple probabilistic program.

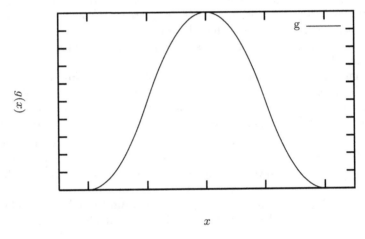

Fig. 2. Weight function g such that the probability of outcome of step B (see Fig. 1) given the probability measure μ at step A is $\int g \, d\mu$. x is the value of variable x.

- The probability that B will happen if A drives x according to some uniform distribution in $[a, b]$ is $\displaystyle\int_a^b g(x) \, dx$.
- The probability that B will happen if A sets x to a constant C is $g(C)$.

The set $g^{-1}(0)$ is the set of values at step A that have no chance of starting a program trace reaching step B. Please note that this is slightly different from the set of values that cannot start a program trace reaching step B. This is the difference between "impossible" and "happening with 0 probability". For instance, if in the program of Fig 1 we put x=2; as statement A, then statement B is reachable; however $g(2) = 0$ thus there is zero probability that statement B is reached.

2.2   Summary of Semantics According to Kozen

The semantics of a probabilistic program c can be seen as a linear operator $[\![c]\!]_p$ mapping the input probability distribution (measure μ) onto an output

```
double x, y;
... /* A */
if (x+y >= -1)
{
  x += 2;
}
y = centered_uniform()+centered_uniform();
x += y/2;
...
if (fabs(x) <= 1)
{
  ... /* B */
}
```

Fig. 3. Another probabilistic program.

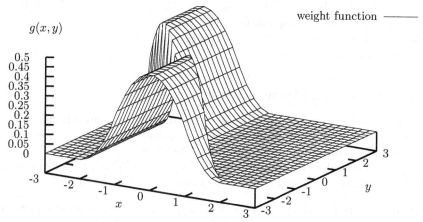

Fig. 4. Weight function g such that the probability of outcome of step B (see Fig. 3) given the probability measure μ at step A is $\int g \, d\mu$. x and y are the respective values of variables x and y.

measure $[\![c]\!]_p.\mu$. Values given by random number generators can either be seen as successive reads from streams given as inputs or are handled internally in the semantics [8,9]; here we shall use the second approach, though both approaches are equivalent. We shall not discuss here the technical details necessary to ensure continuity of operators, convergences etc ... and we shall refer the reader to [12][extended version].

The semantics of a program c whose initial environment lies in the measurable set X and whose final environment lies in the measurable set Y shall be given as a linear operator (of norm less than 1 for the norm of total variation [5] on measures). If c contains no calls to random number generators, $[\![c]\!]$ is just a measurable function.

We shall base ourselves on an ordinary denotational semantics: $[\![c]\!]$ is a function from set X to set Y if c has type $X \to Y$. For the sake of simplicity, we shall not deal with nontermination here so no $\bot$ value is needed. To make meaningful probabilities, X and Y are measurable sets (for instance, countable sets) and $[\![c]\!]$ is assumed to be a measurable function. These restrictions are of a technical nature and do not actually restrict the scope of the analysis in any way; the reader shall refer to [12] for more details.

Let us summarize the probabilistic semantics $[\![c]\!]_p : \mathcal{L}(\mathcal{M}_+(X), \mathcal{M}_+(Y))$:

Elementary constructs (assignments etc...) get simple semantics: $[\![c]\!]_p.\mu = \lambda X.\mu([\![c]\!]^{-1}(X))$.

Random number generation. Let us suppose each invocation of `random` yields a value following distribution μ_R, each invocation being independent from another, and stores the value into a fresh variable. Then $[\![c]\!]_p.\mu = \mu \otimes \mu_R$ where $\otimes$ is the product on measures.

Tests. Let us define $\phi_W(\mu) = \lambda X.\mu(X \cap W)$.
Then $[\![\text{if } c \text{ then } e_1 \text{ else } e_2]\!]_p(\mu) = [\![e_1]\!]_p \circ \phi_{[\![c]\!]}(\mu) + [\![e_2]\!]_p \circ \phi_{[\![c]\!]^C}(\mu)$ where X^C denotes the complement of the subset X.

Loops $[\![\text{while } c \text{ do } e]\!]_p(\mu) = \sum_{n=0}^{\infty} \phi_{[\![c]\!]^C} \circ ([\![e]\!]_p \circ \phi_{[\![c]\!]})^n(\mu)$, the limit being taken set-wise [5, §III.10].

2.3   Adjoints and Pseudo-Adjoints

In this section, we shall recall the usual definition of an adjoint of a linear operator and give a definition of a pseudo-adjoint. We shall also give some easy properties, without proofs for the sake of brevity.

Let us consider two measurable sets (X, σ_X) and (Y, σ_Y). Let us first define, for f a measurable function and μ a measure, $\langle f, \mu \rangle = \int f \, d\mu$.

Proposition 1. *Taking $f \in \mathcal{B}(X, \mathbb{R})$ and $\mu \in \mathcal{M}(X)$, this defines a continuous bilinear scalar form. Moreover, this form has the following properties:*

- *for all f and μ, $|\langle f, \mu \rangle| \leq \|f\|_\infty . \|\mu\|$;*
- *$\langle f, \cdot \rangle = \mu \mapsto \langle f, \mu \rangle$ has norm $\|f\|_\infty$;*
- *$\langle \cdot, \mu \rangle = f \mapsto \langle f, \mu \rangle$ has norm $\|\mu\|$.*

Corollary 1. *If $\langle f, \cdot \rangle = 0$ then $f = 0$. If $\langle \cdot, \mu \rangle = 0$ then $\mu = 0$.*

Let us consider a linear operator H from the signed measures on X to the signed measures on Y, and we can consider whether it admits an **adjoint operator** R:

$$\int (R.f) \, d\mu = \int f \, d(H.\mu) \tag{1}$$

or $\langle R.f, \mu \rangle = \langle f, H.\mu \rangle$.

Proposition 2. *If an operator has an adjoint, then this adjoint is unique.*

Proof. Follows from corollary 1.

Lemma 1. *If R is the adjoint of H:*

- *R is continuous if and only H is continuous;*
- *$\|R\| = \|H\|$.*

Corollary 2. *The operator mapping an operator onto its adjoint is therefore a linear isometry.*

The reason why we consider such adjoints is the following lemma:

Lemma 2. *If $H \in \mathcal{L}(\mathcal{M}(X), \mathcal{M}(Y))$ has an adjoint operator $R \in \mathcal{L}(\mathcal{B}(Y, \mathbb{R}), \mathcal{B}(X, \mathbb{R}))$ and H is zero on all the Dirac measures, then H is zero.*

The implications of this lemma on probabilistic program semantics is that if we can prove, which we shall do later, that linear operators representing program semantics have adjoints, then the semantics of two programs will be identical on all input measures if and only if they are identical on discrete measures.

Proposition 3. *In general, not all positive continuous linear operators on measures have adjoints in the above sense.*

For technical reasons, we shall also have to use a notion of pseudo-adjoint. Let H be a function from $\mathcal{M}(X)$ to $\mathcal{M}(Y)$. Let us suppose there exists a function R such that for any measurable function $f : Y \to [0, \infty]$ $R(f) : X \to [0, \infty]$, $\langle f, H.\mu \rangle = \langle R.f, \mu \rangle$. We shall then call R the **pseudo-adjoint** of H. As previously, we have:

Proposition 4. *An operator has a unique pseudo-adjoint.*

Adjoints and pseudo-adjoints are identical notions in well-behaved cases. A continuity condition ensures that we do not get undefined cases, e.g. $\infty - \infty$.

Lemma 3. *If H is a continuous positive linear operator on measures (positive meaning that $\mu \geq 0 \Rightarrow H.\mu \geq 0$) and R is a positive linear operator that is the pseudo-adjoint of H, then R is the adjoint of H and $\|R\| = \|H\|$.*

2.4   Program Semantics Have Adjoints

A few facts are easily proved:

Proposition 5. *Operators on measures that are lifted from functions (e.g. f_p where $f_p.\mu$ is the measure $X \mapsto \mu(f^{-1}(X))$) have (pseudo-)adjoints: the (pseudo-)adjoint of f_p is $g \mapsto g \circ f$.*

Proposition 6. *If H_1 and H_2 have (pseudo-)adjoints R_1 and R_2, then $R_2 \circ R_1$ is the adjoint of $H_1 \circ H_2$.*

Proposition 7. ϕ_W *has (pseudo-)adjoint* $R_W = f \mapsto f.\chi_W$ *where* χ_W *is the characteristic function of* W.

Proposition 8. *If* H_1 *and* H_2 *have respective (pseudo-)adjoint* R_1 *and* R_2*, then* $H_1 + H_2$ *has (pseudo-)adjoint* $R_1 + R_2$.

Proposition 9. *If* μ_R *is a* σ-*finite positive measure,* $\mu \mapsto \mu \otimes \mu_R$ *has pseudo-adjoint* $f \mapsto \left(x \mapsto \int f(x,\cdot) \, d\mu_R\right)$.

This is an application of the Fubini-Tonelli theorem [5, VI.10].

Lemma 4. *If* $f : X \to [0; \infty]$ *is a positive measurable function and* $(\mu_n)_{n \in \mathbb{N}}$ *is a sequence of positive measures, then*

$$\int f \, d\left(\sum_{n=0}^{\infty} \mu_n\right) = \sum_{n=0}^{\infty} \int f \, d\mu_n. \tag{2}$$

The sum of measures is taken set-wise.

Corollary 3. *If* $(H_n)_{n \in \mathbb{N}}$ *are operators on measures with respective pseudo-adjoints* $(R_n)_{n \in \mathbb{N}}$*, then* $\sum_{n=0}^{\infty} H_n$ *has pseudo-adjoint* $\sum_{n=0}^{\infty} R_n$ *(these sum being taken as simple convergences).*

Theorem 1. *Let* c *be a probabilistic program. Then the linear operator* $[\![c]\!]_p$ *has a pseudo-adjoint.*

Corollary 4. *Since program semantics operators are continuous, of norm less than 1, they have adjoints of norm less than 1.*

Kozen proved [8,9] the following theorem:

Theorem 2. *Semantics of probabilistic programs differ if and only if they differ on point masses.*

Proof. This theorem follows naturally from the preceding corollary and lemma 2.

We shall often note T^* the adjoint of T. We therefore have defined an adjoint semantics for programs: $[\![c]\!]_p^* \in L(M(Y, \mathbb{R}_+), M(X, \mathbb{R}_+))$.

3   Abstract Interpretation of Backwards Probabilistic Semantics

We wish to apply the usual framework of abstract interpretation to the above semantics; that is, for any program c, whose type (not considering probabilistic and nondeterministic effects) is $X \to Y$, we want:

- abstract domains $X_w^\sharp$ and $Y_w^\sharp$, representing sets of weight functions respectively on X and Y;
- a computable abstraction $[\![c]\!]_p^{*\sharp}$ of $[\![c]\!]_p^*$.

The construction of the abstract shall be made compositionnally. We shall first see briefly what we call "abstraction". The reader shall refer to the standard texts on abstract interpretation for more information [3].

3.1   Abstract Interpretation

Taking nondeterminism into consideration, our program semantics is defined as a function $[\![c]\!]^{*^{\flat}}$ from the set $Y_w = \mathcal{P}(M(X, \mathbb{R}_+))$ of sets of weight functions on X to the set $X_w = \mathcal{P}(M(Y, \mathbb{R}_+))$ of sets of weight functions on Y. To simplify the treatment of such sets of weight functions and make operations effectively computable, we choose to over-approximate them by sets of a "simpler" form. Those sets are characterized by elements $x_w^{\sharp}$ of a preordered **abstract domain** $X_w^{\sharp}$ (resp. $Y_w^{\sharp}$). We also consider a $\gamma : X_w^{\sharp} \rightarrow X_w$ function, which maps an element of the abstract domain to what it represents: if $A \subseteq \gamma(A^{\sharp})$, then $A^{\sharp}$ is said to be an **abstraction** of A and A a **concretization** of $A^{\sharp}$.

A function $H_w^{\sharp} : Y_w^{\sharp} \rightarrow X_w^{\sharp}$ is said to be an **abstraction** of an operator $H_w : Y_w \rightarrow X_w$ if for any weight function f_w in Y_w and any abstraction $f_w^{\sharp}$ of f_w, then $H_w^{\sharp}(y_w^{\sharp})$ is an abstraction of $H_w(y_w)$.

Our idea is the following: as seen earlier, our objective is to give bounds on integrals of the form $V = \langle [\![c]\!]^{*}.\chi_P, \mu \rangle$ where P is a subset of Y; we take an abstraction $\chi_P^{\sharp}$ of its characteristic function, then compute $f_w^{\sharp} = [\![c]\!]^{*^{\sharp}}(\chi_P^{\sharp})$. We then compute a bound V' such that for any weight function f_w and any concretization f_w of $f_w^{\sharp}$, $\langle f_w, \mu \rangle \leq V'$; then $V \leq V'$. Of course, we choose the abstract domain so that computing such a V' from $f_w^{\sharp}$ is easy.

For technical reasons, we shall also require the concretizations to be topologically closed with respect to the topology of simple convergence on the weight functions. More precisely, we require that for any abstract element $f^{\sharp}$ and ascending sequence $(f_n)_{n \in \mathbb{N}}$ of concretizations of $f^{\sharp}$, then the point-wise limit $x \mapsto \lim_{n \to \infty} f_n(x)$ is also a concretization of $f^{\sharp}$.

3.2   Ordinary Backwards Abstract Interpretation

We shall suppose we have an abstraction of the normal, non-probabilistic, semantics, suitable for backwards analysis: for any elementary construct (assignments, arithmetic operations...) c such that $[\![c]\!] : X \rightarrow Y$, we must have a monotonic function $[\![c]\!]^{-1^{\sharp}} : Y^{\sharp} \rightarrow X^{\sharp}$ such that for all $A^{\sharp}$, $[\![c]\!]^{-1}(\gamma_Y(A^{\sharp})) \subseteq \gamma_X([\![c]\!]^{-1^{\sharp}}(A))$. We also must have abstractions for the $\phi_{[\![c]\!]}$ functions.

Let us note the following interesting property of the "usual" assignment operator: $[\![x := e]\!]^{-1} = \bar{\pi}_x \circ \phi_{[\![x = e]\!]}$ where $\bar{\pi}_x$ is the "projection parallel to x": $\bar{\pi}_x(W) = \{ v \mid \exists v' \; \forall x' \; x' \neq x \Rightarrow v_{x'} = v_x \}$. It is therefore quite easy to build reverse abstractions for the elementary constructs.

3.3   General Form of Abstract Computations

Let us now suppose we have an abstract domain with appropriate abstract operators for the elementary constructs of the language (we shall give an example of construction of such domains in the next section). We shall see in this section how to deal with the flow-control constructs: the sequence, the test and the loop. The abstract domain shall therefore also supply abstract operators $R_{[\![c]\!]}^{\sharp}$ and $+^{\sharp}$.

Sequence. Since $[\![e_1;e_2]\!]_p^* = [\![e_1]\!]_p^* \circ [\![e_2]\!]_p^*$ then $[\![e_1;e_2]\!]_p^{*\sharp} = [\![e_1]\!]_p^{*\sharp} \circ [\![e_2]\!]_p^{*\sharp}$.

Tests. Let us recall the reverse semantics of the `if` construct:

$$[\![\text{if } c \text{ then } e_1 \text{ else } e_2]\!]_p^* = R_{[\![c]\!]} \circ [\![e_1]\!]_p^* + R_{[\![c]\!]^C} \circ [\![e_2]\!]_p^* \tag{3}$$

This equation gets straightforwardly lifted to the abstract domain:

$$[\![\text{if } c \text{ then } e_1 \text{ else } e_2]\!]_p^{*\sharp} = R_{[\![c]\!]}^\sharp \circ [\![e_1]\!]_p^{*\sharp} +^\sharp R_{[\![c]\!]^C}^\sharp \circ [\![e_2]\!]_p^{*\sharp} \tag{4}$$

is a valid abstraction.

Loops. Let us recall the reverse semantics of the `while` construct:

$$[\![\text{while } c \text{ do } e]\!]_p^* = \sum_{n=0}^{\infty} \left(R_{[\![c]\!]} \circ [\![e]\!]_p^* \right)^n \circ R_{[\![c]\!]^C} \tag{5}$$

Defining f_n recursively, as follows: $f_0 = \lambda x.0$ and $f_{n+1} = \psi f_n$, with

$$\psi(g) = R_{[\![c]\!]^C}.f + R_{[\![c]\!]} \circ [\![e]\!]_p^*.g,$$

we can rewrite equation 5 as $[\![\text{while } c \text{ do } e]\!]_p^*.f = \lim_{n\to\infty} f_n$. We wish to approximate this limit in the measure space by an abstract element.
ψ gets lifted straightforwardly to an abstract operator:

$$\psi^\sharp(g^\sharp) = R_{[\![c]\!]^C}^\sharp.f^\sharp +^\sharp R_{[\![c]\!]}^\sharp \circ [\![e]\!]_p^{*\sharp}.g^\sharp. \tag{6}$$

Let us define $f_0^\sharp$ to be an abstraction of the set $\{f_0\}$ and $f_{n+1}^\sharp = \psi^\sharp(f_n^\sharp)$. Obviously, for all n, $f_n \in \gamma(f_n^\sharp)$. If there exists an N such that $\forall n \geq N$, $f_n \in \gamma(f_N^\sharp)$ then $\lim_{n\to\infty} f_n \in \gamma(f_N^\sharp)$ since $\gamma(f_N^\sharp)$ is topologically closed. We have therefore found an abstraction of $[\![\text{while } c \text{ do } e]\!]_p^*.f$.

If the lattice $T^\sharp$ is such that all ascending sequences are stationary, then such a N will necessarily exist. In general, such a N does not exist and we are forced to use so-called **widening operators** [3, §4.3], as follows: we replace the sequence f_n by the sequence defined by $\hat{f}_0^\sharp = f_0^\sharp$ and $\hat{f}_{n+1}^\sharp = \hat{f}_n^\sharp \nabla_n \psi^\sharp(\hat{f}_n^\sharp)$ where ∇_n are widening operators:

- for all a and b, $a \sqsubseteq a\nabla b$ and $b \sqsubseteq a\nabla b$;
- for all sequence $(u_n)_{n\in\mathbb{N}}$ and any sequence $(v_n)_{n\in\mathbb{N}}$ defined recursively as $v_{n+1} = v_n \nabla u_n$, then (v_n) is stationary.

Obviously, for all n, $f_n \sqsubseteq \gamma(\hat{f}_n^\sharp)$. Since $(\hat{f}_n^\sharp)_{n\in\mathbb{N}}$ is stationary after rank N, and $\gamma(\hat{f}_N^\sharp)$ is topologically closed, this implies that $\lim_{n\to\infty} f_n \in \gamma(\hat{f}_N^\sharp)$ as above.
    This proof extends to the cases where the body of the loop contains nondeterministic constructs in addition to probabilistic ones — we then consider a set of ascending sequences, each having a limit in $\gamma(\hat{f}_N^\sharp)$.

4   A Generic Construction of Abstract Domains

Our goal now is to have an efficient way of representing sets of weight functions. In this section we propose an abstract lattice based on **step functions**. As usual in Lebesgue integration theory, a step function is a finite linear combination of characteristic functions of (measurable) subsets of the domain (see Fig. 5); this generalizes the usual definition when the domain is $\mathbb{R}$. χ_M will denote the characteristic function of subset M — that is, the function mapping x onto 1 if $x \in M$ and 0 elsewhere.

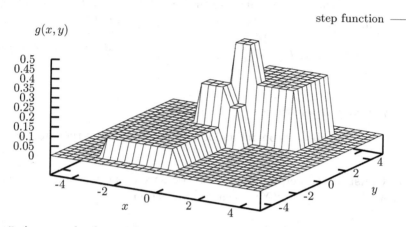

Fig. 5. An example of a step function: $0.2\chi_{[-1,1] \times [0,2]} + 0.3\chi_{[0,3] \times [1,4]} + 0.1\chi_{[-3,0] \times [-4,1]}$. The nonvertical slopes are of course an artefact from the plotting software.

4.1   Representation

Let us take an "ordinary" abstract interpretation lattice $X^\sharp$ for the domain X. This means we have a nondecreasing function $\gamma : (X^\sharp, \sqsubseteq) \to (\mathcal{P}(X), \subseteq)$. We shall only consider the set $X^\sharp_w$ of step functions of the form $\sum_k \alpha_k \cdot \chi_{\gamma A^\sharp_k}$ where $A^\sharp_k \in X^\sharp$. This function can be represented in machine by a finite list of couples $(A^\sharp_k, \alpha_k)_{1 \le k \le n}$.

The set $X^\sharp_w$ is pre-ordered by the usual pointwise ordering: $(A^\sharp_k, \alpha_k) \sqsubseteq (B^\sharp_k, \beta_k)$ if and only if for all $x \in X$ then $\sum_k \alpha_k \cdot \chi_{\gamma A^\sharp_k}(x) \le \sum_k \beta_k \cdot \chi_{\gamma B^\sharp_k}(x)$. Please note that while the pointwise ordering $\le$ on step function is indeed antisymmetric, $\sqsubseteq$ is only a preorder since representation is not unique: $(([0,1],1), (]1,2],1))$ and $(([0,2],1))$ both represent $\chi_{[0,2]}$. Let us define

$$\gamma_w : \begin{vmatrix} (X^\sharp_w, \sqsubseteq) \to (\mathcal{P}(M(X, \mathbb{R}_+)), \subseteq) \\ (A^\sharp_k, \alpha_k) \mapsto \{f \in M(X, \mathbb{R}_+) \mid f \le \sum_k \alpha_k \cdot \chi_{\gamma A^\sharp_k}\} \end{vmatrix} \tag{7}$$

$(X^\sharp_w, \sqsubseteq)$ is therefore a suitable abstract domain for weight functions.

4.2 Comparison

Our abstract lattice does not have unicity of representation, as noted above. Yet comparisons and equivalence testings are easily computable, provided the underlying abstract domain provides an intersection test — a computable function

$$(A^\sharp, B^\sharp) \mapsto \begin{cases} 1 & \text{if } \gamma(A) \cap \gamma(B) \neq \emptyset \\ 0 & \text{otherwise.} \end{cases}$$

Let us take two abstract values $A_w^\sharp = ((A_i^\sharp, \alpha_i)_{1 \leq i \leq m})$ and $B_w^\sharp = ((B_j^\sharp, \alpha_j)_{1 \leq j \leq n})$. Let us consider the set C of nonempty intersections $\bigcap \gamma(A_i^\sharp)_{i \in I} \cap \bigcap \gamma(B_j^\sharp)_{j \in J} \neq \emptyset$ where I is a subset of the indices $1..m$ and J is a subset of the indices $1..n$: each element of C is denoted by a couple (I, J).

Let us define $w : \begin{vmatrix} C & \to \mathbb{R} \\ (I, J) \mapsto \sum_{i \in I} \alpha_i - \sum_{j \in J} \beta_i. \end{vmatrix}$ Then $A_w^\sharp \sqsubseteq B_w^\sharp \iff \forall c \in C\ w(c) \leq 0.$

4.3 Abstract Operations

We must provide abstract operators for each construction of the language.

Basic Constructs. Let us now suppose we have an abstraction $[\![c]\!]^{-1^\sharp}$ of the function $[\![c]\!]^{-1} : \mathcal{P}(Y) \to \mathcal{P}(X)$. Then an abstraction of $[\![c]\!]_p^*$ is

$$[\![c]\!]_p^{*\sharp} = (X_\lambda^\sharp, \alpha_\lambda)_{\lambda \in \Lambda} \mapsto ([\![c]\!]^{-1^\sharp}(X_\lambda^\sharp), \alpha_\lambda)_{\lambda \in \Lambda} \tag{8}$$

Random Number Generation. We shall obtain here an abstraction of `r:=random` where `r` is a new variable and `random` follows probability measure μ_R. Let us suppose the random variable lies in a set R. $[\![\texttt{r:=random}]\!]^*$ is therefore a linear operator from $M(X \times R, \mathbb{R}_+)$ to $M(X, \mathbb{R}_+)$.

Let us suppose that $\mu_R = \sum_{k=1}^n \mu_k$ where each μ_k is concentrated on a subset M_k or R. For instance, taking $R = \mathbb{R}$, the uniform probability measure on $[0, 1]$ can be split into n measures μ_k, the Lebesgue measure on $[k/n, (k+1)/n]$. Let us call π_X and π_R the projections of $X \times R$ onto X and R respectively.

Using prop. 9,

$$[\![\texttt{r:=random}]\!]^*.\chi_A = x \mapsto \sum_{k=1}^n \int \chi_A(x, y)\, \mathrm{d}\mu_k(y). \tag{9}$$

But $\int \chi_A(x, y)\, \mathrm{d}\mu_k(y) \leq \mu_k(\pi_R(A))$, and $\int \chi_A(x, y)\, \mathrm{d}\mu_k(y) = 0$ if $x \notin \pi_X(A)$. Therefore

$$[\![\texttt{r:=random}]\!]^*.\chi_A \leq \mu_k(\pi_R(A)).\chi_{\pi_X(A)}. \tag{10}$$

Lifting to abstract semantics is then easy: $[\![\texttt{r:=random}]\!]^{*\sharp}(A_i^\sharp, \alpha_i)_{1 \leq i \leq m}$ maps to $(A_{i,k}^\sharp, \alpha_i.\beta_{i,k})_{1 \leq i \leq m, 1 \leq k \leq n}$ where $A_{i,k}^\sharp$ is an abstraction of $\pi_X(\gamma(A_i^\sharp) \cap (X \times$

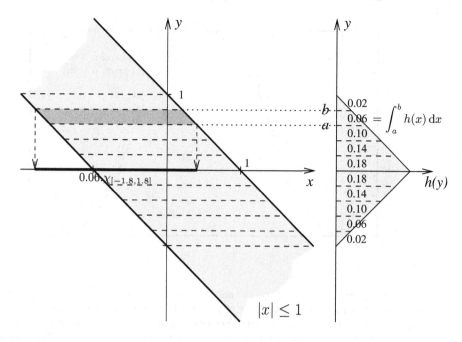

Fig. 6. Construction of the output value of Fig. 7 for $n = 10$. The $|x + y| \leq 1$ abstract area is sliced along divisions on the y axis. Each slice S_k is projected onto the y axis and the integral of the distribution function h of `(centered_uniform()+centered_uniform())/2` is taken on this projection, yielding a coefficient α_k. The slice is then projected on the x axis and this projection B_k, with the α_k coefficient is an element of the abstract value $\sum_{k=i}^{n} \alpha_k \cdot \chi_{B_k}$. The approximations plotted in Fig. 7 are those sums, with various numbers of slices.

M_k)) and $\beta_{i,k} \geq \mu_k(\pi_R(A))$ (Fig. 6 explains how we built the approximations in Fig. 7). Both the $A_{i,k}^{\sharp}$ and the $\beta_{i,k}$ can be computed easily for many underlying abstract domains, such as the nondependent product of intervals [2].

Of course, there is some amount of choice in the choice of how to cut μ into μ_k. We suggest to cut into measures of equal weights. Of course, the higher the number of μ_k's, the better the immediate results (Fig. 7), nevertheless a high number of elements in abstract values may necessitate an early use of widenings (see 4.3). We hope the forthcoming implementation will help adjust such heuristic parameters.

Tests. The semantics for tests gets straightforwardly lifted to abstract semantics, provided we have abstract operators for R_W and $+$:

$$[\![\text{if } b \text{ then } c_1 \text{ else } c_2]\!]_p^{*\sharp} . f^{\sharp} = R_{[\![b]\!]}^{\sharp} \circ [\![c_1]\!]_p^{*\sharp} . f^{\sharp} +^{\sharp} R_{[\![b]\!]^C}^{\sharp} \circ [\![c_2]\!]_p^{*\sharp} . f^{\sharp} \qquad (11)$$

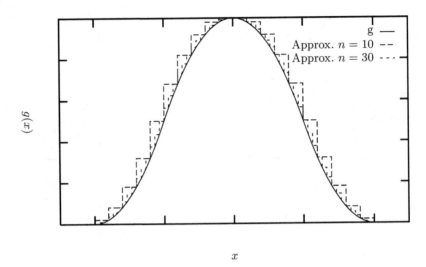

Fig. 7. Two approximations of the actual distribution of Fig. 2, resulting from the abstract interpretation of the program of Fig. 1. Our generic lattice is parameterized by the product lattice of intervals. Different discretizations of the probability measure $h(x)\,dx$ of (centered_uniform()+centered_uniform())/2 yield more or less precise abstractions. Here, the interval $[-1, 1]$ where h is nonzero is divided into n segments of equal size, yielding n elements in the output abstract value.

Abstracting $+$ is easy: $+^\sharp$ is the concatenation operator on sequences (or families); as for R_W:

$$R_{W^\sharp}^\sharp = (X_\lambda^\sharp, \alpha_\lambda)_{\lambda \in \Lambda} \mapsto (X_\lambda^\sharp \cap^\sharp W^\sharp, \alpha_\lambda)_{\lambda \in \Lambda} \tag{12}$$

Widening Operators. Using the above abstractions for R_W and $+^\sharp$, it is easy (3.3) to find an approximation of the semantics of the loop, provided we have suitable widening operators. We shall here propose a few heuristics for widenings. Widenings are also useful since they provide a way to "simplify" abstract elements, to save memory, even if such a simplification loses precision.

Let us suppose we have a widening sequence ∇_k on $X^\sharp$. We shall now give heuristics for computing $x\nabla_k y$ where $x = (X_i^\sharp, \alpha_i)_{1 \leq i \leq a}$ and $y = (Y_j^\sharp, \beta_j)_{1 \leq j \leq b}$. For the sake of simplicity, we shall suppose we aim at keeping Λ index sets less than n elements for a certain fixed n. We shall suppose that $a \leq n$.

The main idea is that of coalescing. For each element $(X_i^\sharp)$, find "close" elements $(Y_{j_{i,1}}^\sharp), \ldots, (Y_{j_{i,m}}^\sharp)$, the closeness criterion being largely heuristic and dependent on the chosen lattice; this criterion does not influence the correctness of the method, only its precision and efficiency. We then pose

$$x\nabla_k y = (X_i^\sharp \nabla_k \left(Y_{j_{i,1}}^\sharp \cup \cdots \cup Y_{j_{i,m}}^\sharp\right), \max(\alpha_i, \beta_{j_{i,1}} + \ldots + \beta_{j_{i,m}})). \tag{13}$$

Let us now take a sequence $(x^{(k)})_{k \in \mathbb{N}}$ such that $x^{(}k+1) = x^{(k)} \nabla y^{(}k)$. Then for all $1 \leq i \leq n$, $X^{(}k+1)_i = X_i^{(k)} \nabla v_i^{(k)}$ for some $v_i^{(k)}$, so the sequence $(X_i^{(k)})_{k \in \mathbb{N}}$ is stationary. Since this holds for all i, this means that $(x^{(k)})$ is stationary.

The design of widenings is an inherently heuristic process, and we thus expect to have better widenings as implementation progresses and experiments are possible.

5   Comparison with Other Methods

Let us first remark that our method is a natural extension of conventional backwards abstract interpretation. Indeed, let us consider only programs containing no **random**-like operations; any program, even including **random**-like operations, can be transformed into a program containing none by moving the streams of random numbers into the environment of the program (this corresponds to the first semantics proposed by Kozen [8,9]).

With such programs, our framework is equivalent to computing reverse images of sets: $[\![c]\!]_p^* . \mu . \chi_W = \mu([\![c]\!]^{-1}(W))$ and our proposed abstract domain just expresses that $[\![c]\!]_p^* . \mu . \chi_W \leq \mu \circ \gamma \circ [\![c]\!]^{-1^\sharp}(W^\sharp)$. There are nevertheless two differences that makes our abstract domain more interesting:

- in the presence of streams of random numbers, our abstract domain just makes use of an ordinary abstract domain, while computing approximate reverse images in the presence of infinite streams requires an abstract domain capable of abstracting infinite sequences so that the results remain interesting;
- we can "simplify" abstract values representing weight functions heuristically so that we do not waste time giving too much precision to negligible parts of the domain.

6   Conclusions

We have proposed a general scheme for the backwards abstract interpretation of nondeterministic, probabilistic programs. This scheme allows the effective computation of upper bounds on the probability of outcomes of the program. It is based on abstract interpretation, which it extends to an adequate "adjoint semantics" of probabilistic programs. We propose a parametric abstract domain for this analysis; this domain is based on an underlying "ordinary" abstract domain, which can be any domain proposed for abstract interpretation of nonprobabilistic programs.

References

1. François Bourdoncle. Interprocedural abstract interpretation of block structured languages with nested procedures, aliasing and recursivity. In *PLILP '90*, volume 456 of *LNCS*, pages 307–323. Springer-Verlag, 1990.

2. P. Cousot and R. Cousot. Static determination of dynamic properties of programs. In *Proceedings of the Second International Symposium on Programming*, pages 106–130. Dunod, Paris, France, 1976.

3. Patrick Cousot and Radhia Cousot. Abstract interpretation and application to logic programs. *J. Logic Prog.*, 2-3(13):103–179, 1992.

4. Alessandra Di Pierro and Herbert Wiklicky. Concurrent constraint programming: Towards probabilistic abstract interpretation. In *2nd International Conference on Principles and Practice of Declarative Programming (PPDP 2000)*, 2000.

5. J.L. Doob. *Measure Theory*, volume 143 of *Graduate Texts in Mathematics*. Springer-Verlag, 1994.

6. Paul R. Halmos. *Measure theory*. The University series in higher mathematics. Van Nostrand, 1950.

7. Jifeng He, K. Seidel, and A. McIver. Probabilistic models for the guarded command language. *Science of Computer Programming*, 28(2–3):171–192, April 1997. Formal specifications: foundations, methods, tools and applications (Konstancin, 1995).

8. D. Kozen. Semantics of probabilistic programs. In *20th Annual Symposium on Foundations of Computer Science*, pages 101–114, Long Beach, Ca., USA, October 1979. IEEE Computer Society Press.

9. D. Kozen. Semantics of probabilistic programs. *Journal of Computer and System Sciences*, 22(3):328–350, 1981.

10. Serge Lang. *Linear algebra*. Springer-Verlag, New York, 1989.

11. Gavin Lowe. Representing nondeterminism and probabilistic behaviour in reactive processes. Technical Report TR-11-93, Oxford University, 1993.

12. David Monniaux. Abstract interpretation of probabilistic semantics. In *Seventh International Static Analysis Symposium (SAS'00)*, number 1824 in Lecture Notes in Computer Science. Springer-Verlag, 2000. © Springer-Verlag.

13. David Monniaux. An abstract Monte-Carlo method for the analysis of probabilistic programs (extended abstract). In *28th Symposium on Principles of Programming Languages (POPL '01)*. Association for Computer Machinery, 2001. To appear.

14. Carroll Morgan, Annabelle McIver, Karen Seidel, and J. W. Sanders. Probabilistic predicate transformers. Technical Report TR-4-95, Oxford University, February 1995.

15. Carroll Morgan, Annabelle McIver, Karen Seidel, and J. W. Sanders. Refinement-oriented probability for CSP. *Formal Aspects of Computing*, 8(6):617–647, 1996.

16. Reuven Y. Rubinstein. *Simulation and the Monte-Carlo Method*. Wiley series in probabilities and statistics. John Wiley & Sons, 1981.

17. Walter Rudin. *Real and Complex Analysis*. McGraw-Hill, 1966.

Tool Demonstration: Finding Duplicated Code Using Program Dependences

Raghavan Komondoor and Susan Horwitz

Computer Sciences Department, University of Wisconsin-Madison {raghavan, horwitz}@cs.wisc.edu

1 Introduction

The results of several studies [1,7,8] indicate that 7–23% of the source code for large programs is duplicated code. Duplication makes programs harder to maintain because when enhancements or bug fixes are made in one instance of the duplicated code, it is necessary to search for the other instances in order to perform the corresponding modification.

A tool that finds clones (instances of duplicated code) can help to alleviate this problem. When code is modified, the tool can be used to find the other copies that also need modification. Alternatively, the clones identified by the tool can be extracted into a new procedure, and the clones themselves replaced by calls to that procedure. In that case, there is only one copy to maintain (the new procedure), and the fact that the procedure can be reused may cut down on future duplication.

We have designed and implemented a tool for C programs that finds clones and displays them to the programmer. To find clones in a program, we represent each procedure using its program dependence graph (PDG) [6]. In the PDG, nodes represent program statements and predicates, and edges represent data and control dependences. To find a pair of clones we use a variation on *backward slicing* [11,10]. We start with two matching nodes (nodes that represent statements or predicates with matching syntactic structure, ignoring variable names and literal values), and we then slice backwards from those nodes in lock step, including a predecessor (and the connecting edge) in one slice iff there is a corresponding, matching predecessor in the other slice. Thus, when the process finishes, we will have identified two isomorphic subgraphs (two partial backward slices), that represent two clones. Pairs of clones are then combined into groups using a kind of transitive closure. For example, clone pairs $(S1, S2)$, $(S1, S3)$, and $(S2, S3)$ would be combined into the clone group $(S1, S2, S3)$.

The key benefits of a slicing-based approach, compared with previous approaches to clone detection such as [1,2,7,4,9,3,5], is that our tool can find non-contiguous clones (i.e., clones whose statements do not occur as contiguous text in the program), clones in which matching statements have been reordered, and clones that are intertwined with each other. (Our tool can also find clones in which variables have been renamed, and different literal values have been used; however, this is also true of some previous clone-detection algorithms.) Furthermore, the clones found using slicing are likely to be meaningful computations,

D. Sands (Ed.): ESOP 2001, LNCS 2028, pp. 383–386, 2001.

and thus good candidates for procedural extraction. These benefits arise mainly because slicing is based on the PDG, which provides an abstraction that ignores arbitrary sequencing choices made by the programmer, and instead captures the important dependences among program components. In contrast, most previous approaches to clone detection use the program text, its control-flow graph, or its abstract-syntax tree, all of which are more closely tied to the (sometimes irrelevant) lexical structure.

2   Example Clones Found by Our Tool

Non-contiguous clones: Shown below are three fragments of code from the Unix utility *bison* that contain a group of three clones identified by our tool. The clones (which were found by slicing back from the statement "`*p++ = c;`") are indicated by "`++`" signs. The function of the clones is to grow the buffer pointed to by p if needed, append the current character c to the buffer and then read the next character. The clone in Fragment 3 is contiguous, but the corresponding clones in Fragments 1 and 2 are non-contiguous.

```
   Fragment 1:                              Fragment 3:

       while (isalpha(c) ||                     while (c != '>') {
            c == '_' || c == '-') {                  if (c == EOF) fatal();
++         if (p == token_buffer + maxtoken)        if (c == '\n') {
++             p = grow_token_buffer(p);                warn("unterminated type name");
           if (c == '-') c = '_';                        ungetc(c, finput);
++         *p++ = c;                                     break;
++         c = getc(finput);                         }
           }                              ++         if (p == token_buffer + maxtoken)
                                          ++             p = grow_token_buffer(p);
                                          ++         *p++ = c;
   Fragment 2:                            ++         c = getc(finput);
                                                     }
   while (isdigit(c)) {
++     if (p == token_buffer + maxtoken)
++         p = grow_token_buffer(p);
       numval = numval*20 + c - '0';
++     *p++ = c;
++     c = getc(finput);
       }
```

Although two of the three clones are non-contiguous, they can still be extracted into a procedure: in both cases the statement in the middle of the clone can be moved out of the way without affecting semantics. We have observed that non-contiguous clones that are good candidates for extraction (as in the example above) occur frequently in real programs. Therefore, the fact that our approach can find such clones is a significant advantage over most previous approaches to clone detection.

Reordered clones: Non-contiguous clones are a kind of *near* duplication. Another kind of near duplication occurs when the ordering of matching nodes is different in the different clones, as illustrated below by two code fragments from *bison*. Both clones modify a portion of a bit array (`lookaheadset` / `base`) by performing a bit-wise *or* with the contents of another array (LA / F). The clones are identified by slicing back from the statement inside the while loop. Fragment 2 differs from Fragment 1 in two ways: the variables have been renamed (including renaming fp1 to fp2 and vice versa), and the order of the first and second lines has been reversed. Since this renaming and reordering does not affect the data or control dependences, the first and second statements of Fragment 1 are matched with the second and first statements of Fragment 2 by our approach (and the two while loops are matched with each other).

```
Fragment 1:                              Fragment 2:
++ fp1 = LA + i * tokensetsize;          ++ fp1 = base;
++ fp2 = lookaheadset;                   ++ fp2 = F + j * tokensetsize;
++ while (fp2 < fp3)                      ++ while (fp1 < fp3)
++     *fp2++ |= *fp1++;                  ++     *fp1++ |= *fp2++;
```

Intertwined clones: The use of backward slicing is also effective in finding intertwined clones. An example from the Unix utility *sort* is given below. In this example, one clone is indicated by "++" signs while the other clone is indicated by "xx" signs. The clones take a character pointer (a/b) and advance the pointer past all blank characters, also setting a temporary variable (tmp1/tmpb) to point to the first non-blank character. The final component of each clone is an if predicate that uses the temporary. Those predicates were the roots of the slices used to find the two clones (the second one – the last line shown below – occurs 43 lines further down in the code).

```
++ tmpa = UCHAR(*a),
xx tmpb = UCHAR(*b);
++ while (blanks[tmpa])
++     tmpa = UCHAR(*++a);
xx while (blanks[tmpb])
xx     tmpb = UCHAR(*++b);
++ if (tmpa == '-')
    ...
xx else if (tmpb == '-') ...
```

3   Experimental Results

We have performed several studies in which we compared the output of our tool to the clone groups identified by a programmer. We found that the tool is quite effective at identifying interesting clones; in particular, it found at least one clone group for every human-identified group of clones. Furthermore, many of the clones were non-contiguous and involved variable renaming; some also involved reordering and intertwining; this is an indication that our approach is capable of finding interesting clones that would be missed by other approaches.

A limitation of the tool is that the clones that it finds are often not "ideal", i.e., are not exactly those that a human would have identified. Instead, they contain some extra statements, or fail to contain some statements that should be part of the clones. Because of this, the tool often identifies several overlapping groups of clones that are variants of each other rather than identifying a single group of ideal clones (i.e., the clones in each group found by the tool have many statements in common with the clones in the other groups, but are not exactly the same). For example, in one study the programmer identified 4 ideal clone groups in one file, while the tool identified 17 clone groups that were variations on the 4 ideal groups. Future work includes finding heuristics that will help the tool to identify clones that are as close as possible to ideal.

Acknowledgements. This work was supported in part by the National Science Foundation under grants CCR-9970707 and CCR-9987435, and by IBM.

References

1. B. Baker. On finding duplication and near-duplication in large software systems. In *Proc. IEEE Working Conf. on Reverse Eng.*, pages 86–95, July 1995.
2. B. Baker. Parameterized duplication in strings: Algorithms and an application to software maint. *SIAM Jrnl. of Computing*, 26(5):1343–1362, Oct. 1997.
3. I. Baxter, A. Yahin, L. Moura, M. Sant'Anna, and L. Bier. Clone detection using abstract syntax trees. In *Int. Conf. on Software Maint.*, pages 368–378, 1998.
4. N. Davey, P. Barson, S. Field, R. Frank, and D. Tansley. The development of a software clone detector. *Int. Jrnl. of Applied Software Tech.*, 1(3-4):219–36, 1995.
5. S. Debray, W. Evans, R. Muth, and B. D. Sutter. Compiler techniques for code compaction. *ACM Trans. on Prog. Lang. and Sys.*, 22(2):378–415, Mar. 2000.
6. J. Ferrante, K. Ottenstein, and J. Warren. The program dependence graph and its use in optimization. *ACM Trans. on Prog. Lang. and Sys.*, 9(3):319–349, July 1987.
7. K. Kontogiannis, R. Demori, E. Merlo, M. Galler, and M. Bernstein. Pattern matching for clone and concept detection. *Automated Software Eng.*, 3(1–2):77–108, 1996.
8. B. Lague, D. Proulx, J. Mayrand, E. Merlo, and J. Hudepohl. Assessing the benefits of incorporating function clone detection in a development process. In *Int. Conf. on Software Maint.*, pages 314–321, 1997.
9. J. Mayrand, C. Leblanc, and E. Merlo. Experiment on the automatic detection of function clones in a software system using metrics. In *Proc. of the Int. Conf. on Software Maint.*, pages 244–254, 1996.
10. K. Ottenstein and L. Ottenstein. The program dependence graph in a software development environment. In *Proc. ACM SIGSOFT/SIGPLAN Software Eng. Symp. on Practical Software Development Environments*, pages 177–184, 1984.
11. M. Weiser. Program slicing. *IEEE Trans. on Software Eng.*, SE-10(4):352–357, July 1984.

Compiling Problem Specifications into SAT

Marco Cadoli[1] and Andrea Schaerf[2]

[1] Dipartimento di Informatica e Sistemistica
Università di Roma "La Sapienza", Via Salaria 113, I-00198 Roma, Italy
cadoli@dis.uniroma1.it   http://www.dis.uniroma1.it/~cadoli
[2] Dipartimento di Ingegneria Elettrica, Gestionale e Meccanica
Università di Udine, Via delle Scienze 208, I-33100 Udine, Italy
schaerf@uniud.it   http://www.diegm.uniud.it/schaerf

Abstract. We present a compiler that translates a problem specification into a propositional satisfiability test (SAT). Problems are specified in a logic-based language, called NP-SPEC, which allows the definition of complex problems in a highly declarative way, and whose expressive power is such to capture exactly all problems which belong to the complexity class NP. The target SAT instance is solved using any of the various state-of-the-art solvers available from the community. The system obtained is an executable specification language for all NP problems which shows interesting computational properties. The performances of the system have been tested on a few classical problems, namely graph coloring, Hamiltonian cycle, and job-shop scheduling.

1 Introduction

We present a system for writing and executing specifications for search problems, which makes use of NP-SPEC, a highly declarative specification language. NP-SPEC has a DATALOG-like, i.e., PROLOG with no function symbols, syntax; its semantics is based on the notion of *model minimality*, an extension of the well-known least-fixed-point semantics of the Horn fragment of first-order logic [26]. NP-SPEC allows the user to express every problem belonging to the complexity class NP [12], which notoriously includes many problems interesting for real-world applications. Restriction of expressiveness to NP guarantees termination and helps to obtain efficient executions.

The core of our system is the compiler, called SPEC2SAT, that translates problem specifications written in NP-SPEC into instances of the *propositional satisfiability* problem (SAT). An instance π of the original problem is translated into a formula T of propositional logic in conjunctive normal form, in such a way that T is satisfiable if and only if π has a solution. Moreover, from the variable assignments that satisfy T the system reconstructs the solution of π.

A specification S of π is a set of metarules defining the search space, plus a set of rules defining the admissibility function. Both metarules and rules are transformed into a set of clauses of T encoding their semantics. The translation of rules is based on their ground instantiation over the *Herbrand universe*. Our

D. Sands (Ed.): ESOP 2001, LNCS 2028, pp. 387–401, 2001.

algorithm for instantiation uses complex auxiliary data structures so as to try as much as possible to avoid the generation of useless clauses.

The approach of translation into SAT is motivated by the huge amount of research devoted to such a problem in last years (see, e.g., [15]), and the number of fast solvers available from the research community. Such solvers, both complete and incomplete ones, are able to solve in a few seconds instances of hundreds of thousands of clauses; and this result was unconceivable only a few years ago. In addition, the community working on SAT is still very active, and even better SAT solvers can be expected to come up in the future.

SAT is the prototypical NP-complete problem, and every instance π of a problem in NP can be translated into an instance of SAT of polynomial size in the size of π. In practice, this idea has been exploited since several years for various problems such as planning [17,16], scheduling [7], theorem proving in finite algebra [11], generation of test patterns for combinatorial circuits [18], and cryptography [21]. Those papers showed that translating a problem into SAT can give good performance of the resulting system, when compared with state-of-the-art dedicated solvers.

The shortcoming of those previous works is that the translation had to be done completely by hand for each problem. Conversely, we aim at a system that automatically translates any NP problem into SAT using the simple and declarative language NP-SPEC.

In terms of performances NP-SPEC cannot compete with state-of-the-art solvers of well-studied problems, anyway we believe that it is a valuable tool for developing fast prototypes for new problems, or variations of known ones, for which no specific solver is available. Nevertheless, experimental results show that our system is able to solve in reasonable time medium-size instances of various classical problems. In addition, it works much faster that the original engine of NP-SPEC [5,3] which is based on a translation of the input specification in the logic programming language PROLOG.

2   Preliminaries

2.1   Overview of the NP-SPEC Language

An NP-SPEC program consists of a DATABASE section and a SPECIFICATION section. The former section includes the definition of extensional relations, and of integer intervals and constants. The latter section consists of two parts: a *search space* declaration, and a stratified DATALOG program [2], which can include the six predefined relational operators and negative literals.

As a first example, we show an NP-SPEC program for the *Hamiltonian path* NP-complete problem, i.e., the problem where the input is a graph and the question is whether there is a traversal that touches each node exactly once.

```
DATABASE
     NODES = 6;
     EDGE = {(1,2),(3,1),(2,3),(6,2),(5,6),(4,5),(3,5),(1,4),(4,1)};
```

```
SPECIFICATION
      Permutation({1..NODES},path).                          // H1
      fail <-- path(X,P), path(Y,P+1), NOT edge(X,Y).        // H2
```

The following comments are in order:

- The input graph is defined in the DATABASE section.
- In the search space declaration (metarule H1) the user declares the predicate symbol path to be a "guessed" one of arity 2. All other predicate symbols are, by default, not guessed. Being guessed means that we admit all extensions for the predicate, subject to the other constraints.
- path is declared to be a permutation of the finite domain {1..NODES}. This means that its extension must represent a permutation of order 6. As an example, $\{(1,5),(2,3),(3,6),(4,2),(5,1),(6,4)\}$ is a valid extension.
- Comments can be inserted using the symbol "//".
- Rule H2 is the constraint permutations must obey in order to be Hamiltonian paths: a permutation fails, i.e., it is not valid, if two nodes X and Y which are adjacent in the permutation are not connected by an edge. X and Y are adjacent because they occupy places P and P+1 of the permutation, respectively.

Running this program on the NP-SPEC compiler produces the following output:

```
path: (1, 1) (2, 5) (3, 6) (4, 2) (5, 3) (6, 4)
```

which means "1 is the first node in the path, 4 is the second node in the path, ..., 3 is the sixth node in the path", and is indeed an Hamiltonian path.

As another example, in the *graph coloring* NP-complete problem the input are a graph G and a positive integer k representing the number of available colors, and the question is whether it is possible to give each node of G a color in such a way that adjacent nodes are never colored the same way. The intuitive structure of the search space in this case is a *partition* of the nodes of G into k distinct subsets, since an assignment of nodes to colors must be guessed. The NP-SPEC program for checking colorability is:

```
DATABASE
      K = 3;
      N = 6;
      EDGE = {(1,2),(3,1),(2,3),(6,2),(5,6),(4,5),(3,5)};
SPECIFICATION
      Partition({1..N},coloring,K).                          // GC1
      fail <-- edge(X,Y), coloring(X,C), coloring(Y,C).      // GC2
```

Another typical structure of the search space is the *integer function*, i.e., the assignment of a value in a specified domain to a set of variables. As an example, in the quadratic Diophantine equations NP-complete problem the input are three positive integers a, b, c, and the question is whether there is an integer solution to the equation $ax^2 + by = c$. In NP-SPEC the program is the following (we declare that we are considering assignments to x and y in the range 10..100):

```
DATABASE
      a = 5; b = 3; c = 1874;
SPECIFICATION
      IntFunc({x,y},assign,10..100).
      fail <-- assign(x,Xval), assign(y,Yval), c != a*Xval^2 + b*Yval.
```

Finally, we present the specification for the SAT problem (cf. Subsection 2.4). In this case, we just want to guess a *subset* of the variables, and assign them the value *true*; other variables are assigned the value *false*.

```
DATABASE
      N = 100;        // number of propositional variables
      IN_CLAUSE = { // IN_CLAUSE(X,Y) <--> literal X is in clause Y
                  (12,1),(25,1),(71,2),(-23,2), ... };
SPECIFICATION
      Subset({1..N},true).
      good_clause(Y) <-- in_clause(X,Y), X > 0, true(X).
      good_clause(Y) <-- in_clause(X,Y), X < 0, NOT true(-X).
      fail <-- NOT good_clause(Y).
```

We note that predicate good_clause is defined, i.e., is in the head of auxiliary rules. A guessed assignment fails if it produces a clause which is not good; a clause is good if it contains at least a literal which is assigned a truth value that makes it true.

We remark that the declarative style of programming in NP-SPEC is very similar to that of DATALOG, and it is therefore easy to extend programs for incorporating further constraints. As an example, the program for the Hamiltonian path can be extended to the Hamiltonian cycle problem by adding the following rule

```
      fail <-- path(X,NODES), path(Y,1), NOT edge(X,Y).          // H3
```

Moreover, undirected graphs can be handled by including a further literal NOT edge(Y,X) in the body of both rules H2 and H3.

2.2   Formal Properties of NP-SPEC

The formal properties of NP-SPEC are explained in detail in [3]. Concerning syntax, we remark that NP-SPEC offers also useful aggregates, such as SUM, COUNT, MIN, and MAX.

The semantics of NP-SPEC is based on a generalization of the *minimal model* semantics of [26], called (P, Q)-*minimal* model semantics [20]. The formal definition can be found in [4], here we just recall some elementary notions. The *Herbrand universe* U of an NP-SPEC program S is the set of all constant symbols occurring in S. The *Herbrand base* of S is the set $\{p(e_1, \ldots, e_n) \mid p$ is a predicate symbol of arity n of S and $e_1, \ldots, e_n \in U\}$. A model of S is a subset of its Herbrand base which satisfies its rules and assigns *false* to fail.

As for its computational properties, the *data complexity* of NP-SPEC, i.e., the complexity of query answering measured in the size of the input extensional database only, is NP-complete. The *expressiveness* of NP-SPEC is such that the language captures NP. This has been proven showing that, for each problem A in NP, there is a *fixed* database-free NP-SPEC program SP such that for each instance db of A encoded as an input database DB, it holds that $SP \cup DB$ returns a solution iff db is a "yes" instance of A. This means that NP-SPEC is capable of specifying exactly all problems belonging to NP. We remind that, conversely, DATALOG is capable of expressing only a strict subset of the polynomial-time problems. As an example, it cannot express the "even" query, which input is a domain C of objects, and which question is: "Is the cardinality of C even?".

2.3 Prolog-Based Compilation

The first implementation of NP-SPEC has been in ECL^iPS^e [1], a PROLOG engine integrated with several extensions.

The compiler takes two files, one containing the specification section, and another containing the database section of a NP-SPEC program, and merges them with a program-independent header to form an ECL^iPS^e target program file.

The ECL^iPS^e runtime system evaluates the target program file and produces the results. The prototype implements a simple guess-and-check evaluation strategy. This is obtained by defining the search space using ECL^iPS^e constraint declaration mechanisms, and then instantiating all domain variables before proceeding with constraint checking.

This approach allowed us to obtain a fast implementation, because it relies on the mechanisms of unification typical of PROLOG. As for the efficiency, we were able to solve just toy-size instances of NP-complete problems.

2.4 SAT Technology

A propositional formula in *conjunctive normal form* (CNF) is a set of *clauses*, and a clause is a set of *literals*. A literal is either a propositional variable or the negation of a propositional variable. Sometimes a formula in CNF is referred to as a *conjunction* of clauses, and a clause as a *disjunction* of literals. The *vocabulary* $V(T)$ of T is the set of propositional variables occurring in T. An interpretation of T is an assignment of a Boolean value, i.e., either *true* or *false*, to each variable in $V(T)$. A *model* of T is an interpretation that assigns *true* to T, using the usual semantic rules for the interpretation of negation, disjunction, and conjunction. The SAT problem has as input a formula T in CNF and the question is whether T is *satisfiable*, i.e., if it has a model, or not.

Algorithms for the SAT problem are either *complete*, i.e., if there is a model, they are guaranteed to find one, or *incomplete*, i.e., they may fail to find a model if there is one.

The main complete algorithms for SAT are based on the famous DPLL procedure [9,8], and may differ quite a lot on the heuristics for the variable selection.

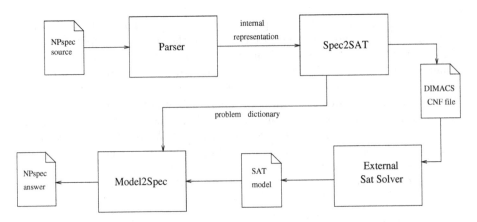

Fig. 1. Architecture of the NP-SPEC compilation and execution environment

We have performed preliminary tests with various solvers. The relatively simple mechanism of constraint propagation of DPLL can be implemented in a quite efficient way, and gives surprisingly good results. Complete algorithms are able to solve SAT instances of several hundreds of variables and several thousands of clauses in the worst conditions, i.e., at the so-called *crossover point* [25]. Such point refers to a particular random generation of CNFs, and is determined experimentally as the point in which the probability of a formula to be satisfiable equals the probability of being unsatisfiable. As for instances of SAT which are not randomly generated, the size of formulae that can be dealt with is quite larger. Generally, incomplete algorithms are much faster than complete ones. Most popular algorithms such as GSAT and WALKSAT [24] are based on randomized local search.

Many solvers are publicly available on the WWW, cf. e.g., [23], and use the DIMACS [15] input format, i.e., a text file containing one clause per line, where each line contains an integer for each literal, and is terminated by 0.

In the experiments presented in Section 4 we used the DPLL-based complete system SATZ, described in [19].

3   Compilation into SAT

Our system is written in C++, and its general architecture is shown in Figure 1.

The module PARSER receives a text file containing the specification S in NP-SPEC, parses it, and builds its internal representation. The module SPEC2SAT compiles S into a CNF formula T in DIMACS format, and builds an object representing a dictionary which makes a 1-1 correspondence between ground atoms of the Herbrand base of S and variables of the vocabulary $V(T)$. The file in DIMACS format is given as an input to the SAT solver, which delivers either a text file containing a model of T, if satisfiable, or the indication that it is unsatisfiable. At this point, the MODEL2SPEC module performs, using the dictionary, a backward translation of the model (if found) in the original language of the specification.

In the current version we do not allow aggregates, recursion and negative occurrences of defined predicates in NP-SPEC. It is important to note that such syntactic restrictions do not limit the expressive power of NP-SPEC [4].

3.1   Basic Algorithm of SPEC2SAT

From this point on we focus on the SPEC2SAT module, the most important of the system. Formally, the module receives as input an NP-SPEC specification $S = \langle DB, SP \rangle$, and outputs a propositional formula T in CNF such that T is satisfiable if and only if the answer to S is "yes"; moreover, if T is satisfiable, then each model of T corresponds to a solution of S.

As an example, Figure 2 shows an instance of graph 3-coloring (a), the corresponding dictionary (b) and the DIMACS file generated (c).

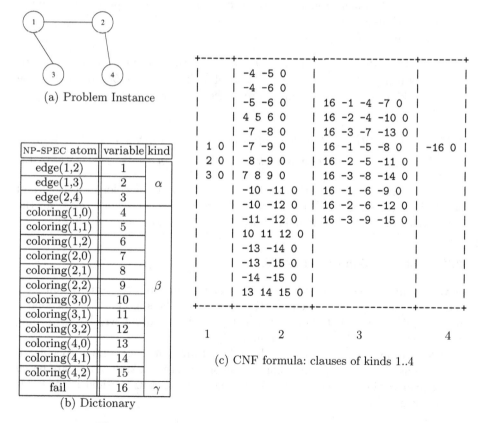

(a) Problem Instance

NP-SPEC atom	variable	kind
edge(1,2)	1	
edge(1,3)	2	α
edge(2,4)	3	
coloring(1,0)	4	
coloring(1,1)	5	
coloring(1,2)	6	
coloring(2,0)	7	
coloring(2,1)	8	
coloring(2,2)	9	β
coloring(3,0)	10	
coloring(3,1)	11	
coloring(3,2)	12	
coloring(4,0)	13	
coloring(4,1)	14	
coloring(4,2)	15	
fail	16	γ

(b) Dictionary

```
+-----+---------------+------------------+-------+
|     |    -4 -5 0    |                  |       |
|     |    -4 -6 0    |                  |       |
|     |    -5 -6 0    | 16 -1 -4 -7 0    |       |
|     |    4 5 6 0    | 16 -2 -4 -10 0   |       |
|     |    -7 -8 0    | 16 -3 -7 -13 0   |       |
| 1 0 |    -7 -9 0    | 16 -1 -5 -8 0    | -16 0 |
| 2 0 |    -8 -9 0    | 16 -2 -5 -11 0   |       |
| 3 0 |    7 8 9 0    | 16 -3 -8 -14 0   |       |
|     |    -10 -11 0  | 16 -1 -6 -9 0    |       |
|     |    -10 -12 0  | 16 -2 -6 -12 0   |       |
|     |    -11 -12 0  | 16 -3 -9 -15 0   |       |
|     |    10 11 12 0 |                  |       |
|     |    -13 -14 0  |                  |       |
|     |    -13 -15 0  |                  |       |
|     |    -14 -15 0  |                  |       |
|     |    13 14 15 0 |                  |       |
+-----+---------------+------------------+-------+
   1            2                3           4
```

(c) CNF formula: clauses of kinds 1..4

Fig. 2. Example of the results of the SPEC2SAT module

In order to understand how the given dictionary and file are obtained, we first notice that only a subset of the Herbrand base of S is really meaningful for the compilation process. For example, ground instantiations of a predicate in DB which are not facts in the database can be neglected when building the vocabulary $V(T)$. More precisely, $V(T)$ is made of variables of three kinds:

α. one variable for every fact in DB;
β. one variable for every ground instantiation of a guessed predicate on elements of the relevant domain;
γ. one variable for every ground instantiation of other predicates.

Figure 2(b) shows the three kinds of variables for the graph coloring problem. In particular, for the *coloring* predicate we have $N \cdot K$ atoms of the kind β.

The set of clauses of T is made of clauses of four kinds:

1. A clause $\{c\}$ for each variable c of the kind α.
2. Clauses using variables of the kind β encoding the meaning of the corresponding metarule.
3. Clauses using variables of the kind α, β, and γ encoding the meaning of the rules of SP. Each ground instantiation of a rule can in principle originate several clauses.
4. The clause $\{\neg fail\}$.

Figure 2(c) shows the four sets of clauses for the current example. In particular, metarule GC1 originates the clauses of kind 2 and rule GC2 originates the clauses of kind 3. Clauses of kind 2 are of the following two subkinds:

$$\neg coloring(r, c_1) \vee \neg coloring(r, c_2) \quad \forall r \in \{1..n\} \;\; \forall c_1, c_2 \in \{0..k-1\} \; (1)$$
$$coloring(r, 0) \vee \cdots \vee coloring(r, k-1) \quad \forall r \in \{1..n\} \tag{2}$$

Set of clauses (1) states that each node has at most one color in $0..k-1$ and set (2) that each node has at least one color. Similar sets of clauses exist for the other kinds of metapredicates, i.e., for Permutation, IntFunc, and Subset.

3.2   Optimization of SPEC2SAT

Several simplifications of T are possible, some simple and some more complex. The simple ones consist in eliminating the unary clauses, i.e., those of kind 1 and 4. This implies that clauses in which such literals occur will be –according to the sign– either shortened or eliminated.

More complex optimizations –which do not apply for very simple specifications such as the one for graph coloring– involve clauses of kind 3, and are based on the elimination of useless variables of the kind γ. Let us consider for example the following rule:

$$\texttt{p(X,Y,Z) <-- q(X,Y), s(Y,Z,W), r(Z,W).} \tag{3}$$

In principle, a clause of T is generated for each of the $|U|^4$ ground instantiations of the rule (one for each possible value assignment to the four variables occurring in it). This can be obviously unpractical when the Herbrand universe U is sufficiently large, e.g., $|U| > 100$.

Our goal is to avoid most of those instantiations, by using information on the plausible extensions of the predicates. In order to do that, first of all we build the *precedence graph* G of SP. The nodes of G are the predicates of SP, and there is an edge from q to p iff there is a rule with p in the head and q in the body in SP. Predicates of SP are naturally partitioned in two subsets:

- "primitive", i.e., sources in G; they are either predicates of DB, or guessed predicates;
- "defined", i.e., they occur in the head of some rule.

Note that the special predicate `fail` is defined, and it is actually the only sink of G. Note also that G is a DAG, since recursion is not allowed.

Basically, predicates are processed in the order given by the topological sort of G, i.e., no node is visited before all of its predecessors are visited, and each predicate contributes to T with a set of clauses. In particular, primitive predicates are quite straightforward to deal with, and they are taken into account by the clauses of kinds 1 and 2.

As for a defined predicate p, using the assumption that it is considered only after all predicates occurring in the body of rules with p in the head have been considered, in some important cases we can discard several instantiations of such rules. As an example, in rule (3) if q is a DB predicate we have to consider only value assignments to X and Y which correspond to facts in DB, instead of all $|U|^2$ assignments.

Generalizing this idea, we introduce the notion of "alive" for ground instantiations of predicates. In particular, the set $alive(p)$ (a subset of the Herbrand base) of ground instances of p is defined in the following way:

- if p is a primitive predicate, $alive(p)$ is the set of the ground instantiations corresponding to variables of the kinds α and β;
- if p is a defined predicate, $alive(p)$ is recursively defined as the set of atoms occurring in the head of ground instances of rules with p in the head, such that all positive literals in the body are alive.

Our algorithm traverses G following its topological sort. When a predicate p is under analysis, the set $alive(p)$ is built, and clauses (kind 3) corresponding to instantiations of rules with p in the head are generated. Referring to the above example, in rule (3) we must consider only value assignments to the four variables according to $alive(q)$, $alive(s)$, and $alive(r)$.

Another key point of the algorithm concerns the way assignments to the variables are generated. As we already mentioned the number n of variables in a rule is a crucial parameter, because in the worst case $|U|^n$ variable assignments must be taken into account. In very simple specifications, n can be as large as 10 (cf. Section 4.3), and $|U|$ as large as 100, therefore it is very important to avoid a simple-minded enumeration of all variable assignments.

To this aim we use a backtracking-based algorithm that for each rule explores a tree of depth n (one level for each variable) and uses sets *alive* for pruning the search. The algorithm considers *partial* assignments, i.e., assignments to a subset of m variables, with $m < n$. As an example, referring to rule (3), if Z and W have already been assigned to, e.g., 2 and 7, and $r(2,7) \notin alive(r)$, then it is useless to consider assignments to the other variables X and Y.

4   Considerations on Performance

In this section we discuss the effectiveness of the system for the solution of NP-complete problems. It is quite obvious that, in terms of performances, our system cannot compete with state-of-the-art solvers of the original problems. In fact, our system is meant mainly for developing executable specifications, rather than for effective program development. The main emphasis of our work is on obtaining simple and readable specifications, an activity that in NP-SPEC typically takes hours or even minutes; on the other hand implementing a very efficient solver for a new problem in NP may take weeks or even months. Nevertheless, we want to show that the system is able to solve medium-size instances of various classical hard problems.

Conversely, the enumerative algorithm of the original PROLOG engine of NP-SPEC is able to solve only small instances. We believe that the ability to solve non-toy cases helps the user to get a better understanding of her/his application and to capture aspects of the problem that might fail to appear in very small instances.

In the following subsections, we analyze the performances of our system on three problems: graph coloring, Hamiltonian cycle, and job shop scheduling. Experiments use the solver SATZ and run on a Pentium II PC at 300 MHz. Times are expressed in seconds of CPU use, and the symbol "–" means that SATZ did not terminate within half an hour.

The total time for finding a solution is the sum of the compilation time t_1 and the time t_2 needed by SATZ. We remark that, asymptotically, t_1 is polynomial in the size of the input, while t_2 can be exponential in the worst case. Nevertheless, in some cases $t_1 > t_2$, as an example when the generated CNF is quite large and has many models.

4.1   Graph Coloring

The specification of the graph coloring problem has been provided in Section 2.1.

Given a graph G with n nodes, e edges, and k colors, the compilation of the metarule GC1 generates a formula with $n \cdot k$ variables, one for each pair $(\langle node \rangle, \langle color \rangle)$. The formula contains $O(n \cdot k^2)$ clauses which state that each node has exactly one color. The rule GC2 adds $e \cdot k$ clauses that forbid two adjacent nodes to have the same color (cf. Figure 2(c)).

For the experimentation of the system, we use a set of instances taken from the DIMACS benchmark repository. In particular, we select the family DSJC of randomly-generated graphs proposed in [14]. Table 1 reports our results.

Table 1. Performances on the graph coloring problem

graph	nodes	edges	colors (min)	colorable	compile time	SAT time	variables	clauses
125.1	125	736	4	NO	3.19	0.33	500	3,819
125.1	125	736	5 (5)	YES	3.27	0.20	625	5,055
125.5	125	7,782	21 (16)	YES	26.62	54.10	2,625	108,086
250.1	250	3,218	9 (9)	YES	30.53	4.12	2,250	38,212
250.5	250	31,336	40 (27)	YES	234.1	215.6	10,000	821,970
500.1	500	12,456	16 (14)	YES	243.52	63.91	8,000	259,828

The table shows that the system has been able to solve some large instances. In one case, i.e., the instance DSJC.125.1, it has been able also to prove the minimality of k. Such a result has been obtained by proving the unsatisfiability of the formula generated with $k - 1$ colors. Conversely, for some instances it found a solution only for a less constrained instance with a number of colors larger than the minimum (provided in parenthesis).

4.2   Hamiltonian Cycle

The specification of the Hamiltonian cycle problem has also been provided in Section 2.1.

Given a graph G with n nodes and e edges, the resulting SAT formula has n^2 variables and $O(n^3)$ clauses. In fact, the compilation generates a variable for each fact of the form path(i,j), with i and j ranging from 1 to n. The number of clauses generated by the metapredicate Permutation is $O(n^3)$. The number of clauses generated by the rules H2 and H3 depends on e. In the two extreme cases of complete and empty graph, no clauses and exactly n^3 clauses, respectively, are generated.

We experiment our system on random instances. It is known [6] that the hardest random instances are obtained for a number of edges e equal to $p = n \log n / 2$, i.e., p is the crossover point. We consider graphs such that $e = p$, taking into account both solvable and unsolvable instances. In addition, we consider graphs far from that point: solvable instances with $e = 3p/2$, and unsolvable ones with $e = p/2$.

Table 2 shows our average results of 5 instances for $n = 15$, 17, and 20 ($p = 60$, 70, and 86, respectively). We note that compilation is quite fast, while the SAT solver is very slow. In fact, the solver is able to handle easily only satisfiable instances with $n = 15$ and 17. Unsatisfiable instances are solved very slowly by SATZ, even for "easy" instances for the original problem. For larger instances, the solver is quite inefficient for the satisfiable cases, and ineffective for unsatisfiable ones.

Experiments with other SAT solvers provide similar results, whereas current solvers of the Hamiltonian cycle problem are able to solve instances with thousands of nodes quite easily.

Table 2. Performances on the Hamiltonian cycle problem

nodes	edges	cycle	compile time	avg. SAT time	variables	clauses
15	30	NO	1.00	478.47	225	6,570
15	60	NO	1.00	1,577.00	225	6,090
15	60	YES	1.00	0.53	225	6,090
15	90	YES	1.00	0.39	225	5,190
17	35	NO	1.33	1,342.87	289	8,976
17	70	NO	1.33	–	289	8,364
17	70	YES	1.33	4.03	289	8,364
17	105	YES	1.33	1.09	289	7,752
20	43	NO	2.73	–	400	14,780
20	86	NO	2.73	–	400	13,900
20	86	YES	2.73	704.61	400	13,900
20	130	YES	2.73	324.41	400	13,020

4.3   Job Shop Scheduling

Job shop scheduling [12, Prob. SS18, p. 242] is a very popular NP-complete
scheduling problem. In job shop scheduling, there are n jobs, m tasks, and p
processors. Jobs are ordered collections of tasks and each task has a length
and the processor that performs it. Each processor can perform a task at the
time, and the tasks belonging to the same job must be performed in their order.
Finally, there is a global deadline D that has to be met by all jobs. In NP-SPEC
the problem is specified as follows.

```
DATABASE
    TASKS = 36;   D = 55;
        // task(T,J,Po,Pr,L): the task T belongs to job J in position Po,
        // it runs on processor Pr with length L
    task = {(1,1,1,2,1), (2,1,2,6,3), (3,1,3,1,6), ..., (36,6,6,2,1)};
SPECIFICATION
        // start_time(T,S): task T starts at time S
    IntFunc({1..TASKS},start_time,0..D-1).
        // tasks T1 and T2 of job J are ordered correctly
    fail <-- start_time(T1, S1), task(T1, J, Po, _, L1),
             start_time(T2, S2), task(T2, J, Po + 1, _, _),
             S2 < S1 + L1.
        // no overlap of tasks in the same processor
    fail <-- start_time(T1, S1), task(T1, _, _, Pr, L1),
             start_time(T2, S2), task(T2, _, _, Pr, L2),
             T1 != T2,  S1 <= S2,  S2 < S1 + L1.
    fail <-- start_time(T1, S1), task(T1, _, _, Pr, L1),
             start_time(T2, S2), task(T2, _, _, Pr, L2),
             T1 != T2,  S2 <= S1,  S1 < S2 + L2.
        // meet the deadline
    fail <-- start_time(T1, S1), task(T1, _, _, _, L1),
             L1 + S1 > D.
```

The compilation of this NP-SPEC file generates a SAT instance with $m \cdot D$ variables. Regarding the number of clauses, for each quadruple $\langle t_1, t_2, i, j \rangle$ formed by two tasks t_1 and t_2 and two time points i and j, there is a clause if and only if one of the rules prohibits t_1 to start at i and t_2 to start at j jointly. This number of clauses is $O(m^2 \cdot D^2)$, and its actual value depends on the relative length of the tasks which belong to either the same job or the same processor.

Many benchmark instances are available for this problem, whose sizes range from 36 to 1,000 tasks. We consider two relatively small instances, known as FT06 (36 tasks, 6 jobs, 6 processors, solvable with deadline 55), and LA02 (50 tasks, 10 jobs, 5 processors, solvable with deadline 655).

As shown in Table 3 the first instance is solved easily, and the proof of the optimality of the deadline (i.e., no solution with deadline 54) is quite fast as well. Unfortunately, for the second instance, the SAT instance generated has more than a billion clauses, and it is too big to be solved by the current solvers. In order to find at least an approximate solution, we create a new instance called LA02r in which all lengths are divided by 20 and rounded up. This corresponds to reducing the granularity of the problem, and allowing only starting times divisible by 20. The smallest deadline found for LA02r is $D = 46$, which corresponds to $920 (= 46 \cdot 20)$ in LA02. If we give a looser deadline of 1,000, the problem is solved much faster. We remark that the minimum value of the deadline for this instance is 655, and all state-of-the art solvers find solutions below 700.

Table 3. Performances on the job shop scheduling problem

instance	tasks	deadline	solvable	compile time	SAT time	variables	clauses
FT06	36	54	NO	215.07	53.07	1,944	355,871
FT06	36	55	YES	220.17	20.140	1,980	365,333
LA02	50	920	YES	335.830	364.74	2,300	392,816
LA02	50	1,000	YES	426.71	19.390	2,500	440,628

Summing up, these results show that for job shop scheduling, the critical factors are the compilation times and the size of the SAT formula obtained. Conversely, the solution of such formula is relatively fast compared with its size.

We remark that, without the optimizations described in Section 3.2, none of the instances of Table 3 was compiled by SPEC2SAT in less than one day.

5   Conclusions, Related, and Future Work

We have presented a novel approach for the execution of specifications of problems in NP, based on the translation into SAT. The performance of the resulting system is very good, compared to the previous, PROLOG-based, engine underlying NP-SPEC. As an example, we were able to solve benchmarks of graph coloring problems with 500 nodes, while the previous approach was able to deal with graph of just 14 nodes. As another example, we were able to increase the size of the chessboard in the n-queens problem –in which the goal is to place n non-attacking queens on a $n \times n$ chessboard– from 12 to 60. The reason for such an increase in performance is that we exploit the best SAT solvers, developed by third parties. Further improvements of SAT solvers will reflect in an improvement of our system.

Moreover, our system can be used as a tool for the generation of new benchmark instances of SAT. In fact, SAT solvers are currently tested on encodings of a variety of problems, such as graph coloring, planning, Latin square, blocks world, Towers of Hanoi, circuit fault analysis, and others [23]. For example, the encoding used for graph coloring is the same as the one generated by SPEC2SAT with our specification of Section 2.

As for related research, we have listed in the introduction several approaches to the solution of problems, ranging from planning to cryptography, based on translation into SAT.

Other researchers [10,22] propose DATALOG-like languages for problem specification. The main difference between NP-SPEC and the other languages relies in its semantics, which is based on the notion of model minimality. Alloy Analyzer, a system for reasoning in an extension of first-order logic based on a translation to SAT, has been proposed in [13]. The main difference wrt NP-SPEC is that in Alloy Analyzer in general decidability is not guaranteed, and consequently the user must supply a bound on the number of atoms in the universe.

In the future, first we plan to include aspects of NP-SPEC that have been neglected in this version, such as aggregates and recursion. Furthermore, we plan to introduce some form of program transformation for improving compilation in terms of both the size and the hardness of the generated formula. Finally, we want to equip the system with a learning mechanism for automatic selection of the best SAT solver for the instance at hand. In particular, fast incomplete algorithms could be used for instances that are known to be satisfiable.

Acknowledgements. The authors are grateful to Giovambattista Ianni, Luigi Palopoli, and Domenico Vasile for useful discussion and for providing some examples.

References

1. A. Aggoun *et al. ECL^{i}PS^e User Manual (Version 4.0)*. IC-Parc, London (UK), July 1998.
2. K. R. Apt, H. A. Blair, and A. Walker. Towards a theory of declarative knowledge. In J. Minker, editor, *Foundations of Deductive Databases and Logic Programming*, pages 89–142. Morgan Kaufmann, Los Altos, 1988.
3. M. Cadoli, G. Ianni, L. Palopoli, A. Schaerf, and D. Vasile. NP-SPEC: An executable specification language for solving all problems in NP. Technical Report 00-13, Dip. di Inf. e Sist., Univ. di Roma "La Sapienza", 2000.
4. M. Cadoli and L. Palopoli. Circumscribing DATALOG: expressive power and complexity. *Theor. Comp. Sci.*, 193:215–244, 1998.

5. M. Cadoli, L. Palopoli, A. Schaerf, and D. Vasile. NP-SPEC: An executable specification language for solving all problems in NP. In *Proc. of PADL'99*, number 1551 in LNAI, pages 16–30. Springer-Verlag, 1999.

6. P. Cheeseman, B. Kanefski, and W. M. Taylor. Where the really hard problem are. In *Proc. of IJCAI'91*, pages 163–169, 1991.

7. J. M. Crawford and A. B. Baker. Experimental results on the application of satisfiability algorithms to scheduling problems. In *Proc. of AAAI'94*, pages 1092–1097, 1994.

8. M. Davis, G. Logemann, and D. W. Loveland. A machine program for theorem proving. *Comm. of the ACM*, 5(7):394–397, 1962.

9. M. Davis and H. Putnam. A computing procedure for quantification theory. *J. of the ACM*, 7:201–215, 1960.

10. T. Eiter, N. Leone, C. Mateis, G. Pfeifer, and F. Scarcello. The KR system dlv: Progress report, Comparisons and Benchmarks. In *Proc. of KR'98*, pages 406–417, 1998.

11. M. Fujita, J. Slaney, and F. Bennett. Automatic generation of some results in finite algebra. In *Proc. of IJCAI'93*, pages 52–57, 1993.

12. M. R. Garey and D. S. Johnson. *Computers and Intractability—A guide to NP-completeness*. W.H. Freeman and Company, San Francisco, 1979.

13. D. Jackson. Automating first-order relational logic. In *Proc. of ACM SIGSOFT'00: 8th SIGSOFT Symposium on Foundation of Software Engineering*, 2000.

14. D. S. Johnson, C. R. Aragon, L. A. McGeoch, and C. Schevon. Optimization by simulated annealing: an experimental evaluation; part II, graph coloring and number partitioning. *Operations Research*, 39(3):378–406, 1991.

15. D. S. Johnson and M. A. Trick, eds. *Cliques, Coloring, and Satisfiability. Second DIMACS Implementation Challenge*, volume 26 of *DIMACS Series in Discrete Mathematics and Theoretical Computer Science*. American Math. Soc., 1996.

16. H. A. Kautz, D. McAllester, and B. Selman. Encoding plans in propositional logic. In *Proc. of KR'96*, pages 374–384, 1996.

17. H. A. Kautz and B. Selman. Planning as satisfiability. In *Proc. of ECAI'92*, pages 359–363, 1992.

18. T. Larrabee. Test pattern generation using Boolean satisfiability. *IEEE Trans. on Computer-Aided Design*, pages 4–15, 1992.

19. C. Li and Anbulagan. Heuristics based on unit propagation for satisfiability problems. In *Proc. of IJCAI'97*, pages 366–371, 1997.

20. V. Lifschitz. Computing circumscription. In *Proc. of IJCAI'85*, pages 121–127, 1985.

21. F. Massacci and L. Marraro. Logical cryptanalysis as a SAT-problem: Encoding and analysis of the U.S. Data Encryption Standard. *J. of Automated Reasoning*, 24(1-2):165–203, 2000.

22. I. Niemelä. Logic programs with stable model semantics as a constraint programming paradigm. *Ann. of Mathematics and Artif. Intell.*, 25(3,4):241–273, 1999.

23. SATLIB - The Satisfiability Library.
http://www.informatik.tu-darmstadt.de/AI/SATLIB.

24. B. Selman, H. Kautz, and B. Cohen. Noise strategies for improving local search. In *Proc. of AAAI'94*, pages 337–343, 1994.

25. B. Selman, D. Mitchell, and H. Levesque. Generating Hard Satisfiability Problems. *Artificial Intelligence*, 81:17–29, 1996.

26. M. H. van Emden and R. A. Kowalski. The semantics of predicate logic as a programming language. *J. of the ACM*, 23(4):733–742, 1976.

Semantics and Termination of Simply-Moded Logic Programs with Dynamic Scheduling

Annalisa Bossi[1], Sandro Etalle[2,3], Sabina Rossi[1], and Jan-Georg Smaus[3]

[1] Università di Venezia, {bossi,srossi}@dsi.unive.it
[2] Universiteit Maastricht, etalle@cs.unimaas.nl
[3] CWI, Amsterdam, jan.smaus@cwi.nl

Abstract. In logic programming, *dynamic scheduling* refers to a situation where the selection of the atom in each resolution (computation) step is determined at runtime, as opposed to a fixed selection rule such as the left-to-right one of Prolog. This has applications e.g. in parallel programming. A mechanism to control dynamic scheduling is provided in existing languages in the form of *delay declarations*.

Input-consuming derivations were introduced to describe dynamic scheduling while abstracting from the technical details. In this paper, we first formalise the relationship between delay declarations and input-consuming derivations, showing in many cases a one-to-one correspondence. Then, we define a model-theoretic semantics for input-consuming derivations of simply-moded programs. Finally, for this class of programs, we provide a necessary and sufficient criterion for termination.

1 Introduction

Background. Logic programming is based on giving a computational interpretation to a fragment of first order logic. Kowalski [14] advocates the separation of the *logic* and *control* aspects of a logic program and has coined the famous formula

$$\text{Algorithm} = \text{Logic} + \text{Control}.$$

The programmer should be responsible for the logic part. The control should be taken care of by the logic programming system.

In reality, logic programming is far from this ideal. Without the programmer being aware of the control and writing programs accordingly, logic programs would usually be hopelessly inefficient or even non-terminating.

One aspect of control in logic programs is the *selection rule*, stating which atom in a query is selected in each derivation step. The standard selection rule in logic programming languages is the fixed left-to-right rule of Prolog. While this rule provides appropriate control for many applications, there are situations, e.g. in the context of parallel execution or the test-and-generate paradigm, that require a more flexible control mechanism, namely, *dynamic scheduling*, where the selectable atoms are determined at runtime. Such a mechanism is provided in modern logic programming languages in the form of *delay declarations* [16].

D. Sands (Ed.): ESOP 2001, LNCS 2028, pp. 402–416, 2001.
© Springer-Verlag Berlin Heidelberg 2001

To demonstrate that on the one hand, the left-to-right selection rule is sometimes inappropriate, but that on the other hand, the selection mechanism must be controlled in some way, consider the following programs APPEND and IN_ORDER

```
%   append(Xs,Ys,Zs)  ← Zs is the result of concatenating the lists Xs and Ys
    append([H|Xs],Ys,[H|Zs])  ← append(Xs,Ys,Zs).
    append([],Ys,Ys).
```

```
%   in_order(Tree,List)  ← List is an ordered list of the nodes of Tree
    in_order(tree(Label,Left,Right),Xs)  ← in_order(Left,Ls),
        in_order(Right,Rs), append(Ls,[Label|Rs],Xs).
    in_order(void,[]).
```

together with the query (read_tree and write_list are defined elsewhere)

$$q : \text{read\_tree(Tree)}, \text{in\_order(Tree,List)}, \text{write\_list(List)}.$$

If read_tree cannot read the whole tree at once – say, it receives the input from a stream – it would be nice to be able to run the "processes" in_order and write_list on the available input. This can only be done if one uses a dynamic selection rule (Prolog's rule would call in_order only after read_tree has finished, while other fixed rules would immediately diverge). In order to avoid nontermination one should adopt appropriate delay declarations, namely

```
delay in_order(T,_) until nonvar(T).
delay append(Ls,_,_) until nonvar(Ls).
delay write_list(Ls,_) until nonvar(Ls).
```

These declarations avoid that in_order, append and write_list are selected "too early", i.e. when their arguments are not "sufficiently instantiated". Note that instead of having interleaving "processes", one can also select several atoms in *parallel*, as long as the delay declarations are respected. This approach to parallelism has been first proposed in [17] and "has an important advantage over the ones proposed in the literature in that it allows us to parallelise programs written in a large subset of Prolog by merely adding to them delay declarations, so *without modifying* the original program" [4].

Compared to other mechanisms for user-defined control, e.g., using the cut operator in connection with built-in predicates that test for the instantiation of a variable (var or ground), delay declarations are more compatible with the declarative character of logic programming. Nevertheless, many important declarative properties that have been proven for logic programs do not apply to programs with delay declarations. The problem is mainly related to *deadlock*.

In the first place, for such programs the well-known equivalence between model-theoretic and operational semantics does not hold. For example, the query append(X,Y,Z) does not succeed (it *deadlocks*) and this is in contrast with the fact that (infinitely many) instances of append(X,Y,Z) are contained in the least Herbrand model of APPEND. This shows that a model-theoretic semantics in the classical sense is not achievable, in fact the problem of finding a suitable declarative semantics is still open. Moreover, while for the left-to-right selection rule there are results that allow us to characterise when a program is terminating, these results do not apply any longer in presence of dynamic scheduling.

Contributions. This paper contains essentially four contributions tackling the above problems.

In order to provide a characterisation of dynamic scheduling that is reasonably abstract and hence amenable to semantic analysis, we consider *input-consuming derivations* [18], a formalism similar to *Moded GHC* [20]. In an input-consuming derivation, only atoms whose input arguments are not instantiated through the unification step may be selected. Moreover, we restrict our attention to the class of *simply-moded* programs, which are programs that are, in a well-defined sense, consistent wrt. the modes. As also shown by the benchmarks in Sec. 6, most practical programs are simply-moded. We analyse the relations between input-consuming derivations and programs with delay declarations. We demonstrate that under some statically verifiable conditions, input-consuming derivations are exactly the ones satisfying the (natural) delay declarations of programs.

We define a denotational semantics which enjoys a model-theoretical reading and has a bottom-up constructive definition. We show that it is compositional, correct and fully abstract wrt. the computed answer substitutions of successful derivations. E.g., it captures the fact that the query `append(X,Y,Z)` does not succeed.

Since dynamic scheduling also allows for parallelism, it is sometimes important to model the result of *partial* (i.e., incomplete) derivations. For instance, one might have queries (processes) that never terminate, which by definition may never reach the state of *success*, i.e. of successful completion of the computation. Therefore, we define a second semantics which enjoys the same properties as the one above. We demonstrate that it is correct, fully abstract and compositional wrt. the computed substitutions of partial derivations. We then have a uniform (in our opinion elegant) framework allowing us to model both successful and partial computations.

Finally, we study the problem of termination of input-consuming programs. We present a result which fully characterises termination of simply-moded input-consuming programs. This result is based on the semantics mentioned in the previous paragraph.

The rest of this paper is organised as follows. The next section introduces some preliminaries. Section 3 defines input-consuming derivations and delay declarations, and formally compares the two notions. Section 4 provides a result on denotational semantics for input-consuming derivations, first for complete derivations, then for incomplete (input-consuming) derivations. Section 5 provides a sufficient and necessary criterion for termination of programs using input-consuming derivations. Section 6 surveys some benchmark programs. Section 7 concludes. The proofs have been omitted and can be found in [8].

2   Preliminaries

The reader is assumed to be familiar with the terminology and the basic results of the semantics of logic programs [1,2,15]. Following [2], we use boldface characters to denote sequences of objects: $\mathbf{t}$ denotes a sequence of terms, $\mathbf{B}$ is a query (i.e., a possibly empty sequence of atoms). The empty query is denoted by $\Box$. The relation symbol of an atom A is denoted $Rel(A)$. The set of variables occurring in a syntactic object o is denoted $Var(o)$. We say that o is *linear* if every variable occurs in it at most once. Given a *substitution* $\sigma = \{x_1/t_1, \ldots, x_n/t_n\}$, we say that $\{x_1, \ldots, x_n\}$ is its *domain* (denoted by $Dom(\sigma)$), and $Var(\{t_1, \ldots, t_n\})$ is its *range* (denoted by $Ran(\sigma)$). Note that $Var(\sigma) = Dom(\sigma) \cup Ran(\sigma)$. If $t_1, \ldots, t_n$ is a permutation of $x_1, \ldots, x_n$ then we say that σ is a *renaming*. The *composition* of substitutions is denoted by juxtaposition $(x\theta\sigma = (x\theta)\sigma)$. We say that a term t is an *instance* of t' iff for some σ, $t = t'\sigma$; further, t is a *variant* of t', written $t \approx t'$, iff t and t' are instances of each other. A substitution θ is a *unifier* of terms t and t' iff $t\theta = t'\theta$. We denote by $mgu(t, t')$ any *most general unifier* (*mgu*, in short) of t and t'. A query $Q : \mathbf{A}, B, \mathbf{C}$ and a clause $c : H \leftarrow \mathbf{B}$ (variable disjoint with Q) yield the resolvent $(\mathbf{A}, \mathbf{B}, \mathbf{C})\theta$ with $\theta = mgu(B, H)$. We say that $\mathbf{A}, B, \mathbf{C} \stackrel{\theta}{\Longrightarrow} (\mathbf{A}, \mathbf{B}, \mathbf{C})\theta$ is a *derivation step (using c)*, and call B the *selected atom*. A *derivation* of $P \cup \{Q\}$ is a sequence of derivation steps $Q \stackrel{\theta_1}{\Longrightarrow} Q_1 \stackrel{\theta_2}{\Longrightarrow} \cdots$ using (variants of) clauses in the program P. A finite derivation $Q \stackrel{\theta_1}{\Longrightarrow} \cdots \stackrel{\theta_n}{\Longrightarrow} Q_n$ is also denoted $Q \stackrel{\vartheta}{\longrightarrow}_P Q_n$, where $\vartheta = \theta_1 \ldots \theta_n$. The restriction of ϑ to Q is a *computed answer substitution* (*c.a.s.*). If $Q_n = \Box$, the derivation is *successful*.

Delay Declarations. Logic programs with delay declarations consist of two parts: a set of clauses and a set of delay declarations, one for each of its predicate symbols. A *delay declaration* associated with an n-ary predicate symbol p has the form

$$\texttt{delay}\ \ p(t_1, \ldots, t_n)\ \ \texttt{until}\ \ Cond(t_1, \ldots, t_n)$$

where $Cond(t_1, \ldots, t_n)$ is a formula in some assertion language [12]. A derivation is *delay-respecting* if an atom $\mathbf{p}(t_1, \ldots, t_n)$ is selected only if $Cond(t_1, \ldots, t_n)$ is satisfied. In particular, we consider delay declarations of the form

$$\texttt{delay}\ \ \texttt{p}(\texttt{X}_1, \ldots, \texttt{X}_n)\ \ \texttt{until}\ \ \texttt{nonvar}(\texttt{X}_{i_1}) \wedge \ldots \wedge \texttt{nonvar}(\texttt{X}_{i_k}).$$

where $1 \leq i_1 < \ldots < i_k \leq n$.[1] The condition $\texttt{nonvar}(t_{i_1}) \wedge \ldots \wedge \texttt{nonvar}(t_{i_k})$ is satisfied if and only if $t_{i_1}, \ldots, t_{i_k}$ are non-variable terms. Such delay declarations are equivalent to the $\texttt{block}$ declarations of SICStus Prolog [13].

Moded Programs. A *mode* indicates how a predicate should be used.

---

[1] For the case that $k = 0$, the empty conjunction might be denoted as $\texttt{true}$, or the delay declaration might simply be omitted.

Definition 2.1. A *mode* for a predicate symbol p of arity n, is a function m_p from $\{1, \ldots, n\}$ to $\{In, Out\}$. □

If $m_p(i) = In$ (resp. *Out*), we say that i is an *input* (resp. *output*) *position* of p. We denote by $In(Q)$ (resp. $Out(Q)$) the sequence of terms filling in the input (resp. output) positions of predicates in Q. Moreover, when writing an atom as $p(\mathbf{s}, \mathbf{t})$, we are indicating that $\mathbf{s}$ is the sequence of terms filling in its input positions and $\mathbf{t}$ is the sequence of terms filling in its output positions.

The notion of simply-moded program is due to Apt and Etalle [3].

Definition 2.2. A clause $p(\mathbf{t}_0, \mathbf{s}_{n+1}) \leftarrow p_1(\mathbf{s}_1, \mathbf{t}_1), \ldots, p_n(\mathbf{s}_n, \mathbf{t}_n)$ is *simply-moded* iff $\mathbf{t}_1, \ldots, \mathbf{t}_n$ is a linear vector of variables and for all $i \in [1, n]$

$$Var(\mathbf{t}_i) \cap Var(\mathbf{t}_0) = \emptyset \quad \text{and} \quad Var(\mathbf{t}_i) \cap \bigcup_{j=1}^{i} Var(\mathbf{s}_j) = \emptyset.$$

A query $\mathbf{B}$ is *simply-moded* iff the clause $q \leftarrow \mathbf{B}$ is simply-moded, where q is any variable-free atom. A program is simply-moded iff all of its clauses are. □

Thus, a clause is simply-moded if the output positions of body atoms are filled in by distinct variables, and every variable occurring in an output position of a body atom does not occur in an earlier input position. In particular, every unit clause is simply-moded. Notice also that programs APPEND and IN_ORDER are simply-moded wrt. the modes append(In,In,Out) and in_order(In,Out).

3   Input-Consuming Programs

Input-consuming derivations are a formalism for describing dynamic scheduling in an abstract way [18].

Definition 3.1. A derivation step $\mathbf{A}, B, \mathbf{C} \overset{\theta}{\Longrightarrow} (\mathbf{A}, \mathbf{B}, \mathbf{C})\theta$ is *input-consuming* iff $In(B)\theta = In(B)$. A derivation is *input-consuming* iff all its derivation steps are input-consuming. □

Thus, allowing only input-consuming derivations is a form of dynamic scheduling, since selectability depends on the degree of instantiation at runtime. If no atom is resolvable via an input-consuming derivation step, the query *deadlocks*.[2]

It has been shown that the input-consuming resolvent of a simply-moded query using a simply-moded clause is simply-moded [4].

Example 3.2.   Consider again the delay declaration

```
delay append(Ls, _, _) until nonvar(Ls).
```

---

[2] Notice that there is a difference between this notion of deadlock and the one used for programs with delay declarations; see [6] for a detailed discussion.

It is easy to check that *every* derivation starting in a query `append(t,s,X)`, where X is a variable disjoint from s and t, is input-consuming wrt. `append(In,In,Out)` *iff* it respects the delay declaration. □

To show the correspondence between delay declarations and input-consuming derivations suggested by Ex. 3.2, we need some further definitions. We call a term t *flat* if t has the form $f(x_1, \ldots, x_n)$ where the x_i are distinct variables. Note that constants are flat terms. The significance of flat term arises from the following observation: if s and t are unifiable, s is non-variable and t is flat, then s is an instance of t. Think here of s being a term in an input position of a selected atom, and t being the term in that position of a clause head.

Definition 3.3. A program P is *input-consistent* iff for each clause $H \leftarrow \mathbf{B}$ of it, the family of terms filling in the input positions of H is linear, and consists of variables and flat terms. □

We also consider here delay declarations of a restricted type.

Definition 3.4. A program with delay declarations is *simple* if every delay declaration is of the form

$$\texttt{delay } p(\mathtt{X}_1, \ldots, \mathtt{X}_n) \texttt{ until } \texttt{nonvar}(\mathtt{X}_{i_1}) \wedge \ldots \wedge \texttt{nonvar}(\mathtt{X}_{i_k}).$$

where $i_1, \ldots, i_k$ are input positions of p.

Moreover, we say that the positions $i_1, \ldots, i_k$ of p are *controlled*, while the other input positions of p are *free*. □

Thus the controlled positions are those "guarded" by a delay declaration. The main result of this section shows that, under some circumstances, using delay declarations is equivalent to restricting to input-consuming derivations.

Lemma 3.5. Let P be simply-moded, input-consistent and simple. Let Q be a simply-moded query.

- If for every clause $H \leftarrow \mathbf{B}$ of P, H contains variables in its free positions, then every derivation of $P \cup \{Q\}$ respecting the delay declarations is input-consuming (modulo renaming).
- If in addition for every clause $H \leftarrow \mathbf{B}$ of P, the head H contains flat terms in its controlled positions, then every input-consuming derivation of $P \cup \{Q\}$ respects the delay declarations. □

In order to assess how realistic these conditions are, we have checked them against a number of programs from various collections. (The results can be found in Sec. 6). Concerning the statement that all delay-respecting derivations are input-consuming, we are convinced that this is the case in the overwhelming majority of practical cases. Concerning the converse, that is, that all input-consuming derivations are delay-respecting, we could find different examples in which this was not the case. In many of them this could be fixed by a simple transformation of the programs[3], in other cases it could not (e.g., `flatten`, [19]). Nevertheless, we strongly believe that the latter form a small minority.

The delay declarations for the considered programs were either given or derived based on the presumed mode. Note that delay declarations as in Def. 3.4 can be more efficiently implemented than, e.g., delay declarations testing for groundness. Usually, the derivations permitted by the latter delay declarations are a strict subset of the input-consuming derivations.

4   A Denotational Semantics

Previous declarative semantics for logic programs cannot correctly model dynamic scheduling. E.g., none of them reflects the fact that `append(X,Y,Z)` deadlocks. We define a model-theoretic semantics that models computed answer substitutions of input-consuming derivations of simply-moded programs and queries.

We now define *simply-local* substitutions, which reflect the way clauses become instantiated in input-consuming derivations. A simply-local substitution can be decomposed into several substitutions, corresponding to the instantiation of the *output* of each *body atom*, as well as the *input* of the *head*.

Definition 4.1. Let θ be a substitution. We say that θ is *simply-local* wrt. the clause $c : p(\mathbf{t}_0, \mathbf{s}_{n+1}) \leftarrow p_1(\mathbf{s}_1, \mathbf{t}_1), \dots, p_n(\mathbf{s}_n, \mathbf{t}_n)$ iff there exist substitutions $\sigma_0, \sigma_1 \dots, \sigma_n$ and disjoint sets of fresh (wrt. c) variables $v_0, v_1, \dots, v_n$ such that $\theta = \sigma_0 \sigma_1 \cdots \sigma_n$ where for $i \in \{0, \dots, n\}$,

- $Dom(\sigma_i) \subseteq Var(\mathbf{t}_i)$,
- $Ran(\sigma_i) \subseteq Var(\mathbf{s}_i \sigma_0 \sigma_1 \cdots \sigma_{i-1}) \cup v_i.$[4]

θ is *simply-local* wrt. a query $\mathbf{B}$ iff θ is simply-local wrt. the clause $q \leftarrow \mathbf{B}$ where q is any variable-free atom. $\square$

Note that if $\mathbf{A}, B, \mathbf{C} \stackrel{\theta}{\Longrightarrow} (\mathbf{A}, \mathbf{B}, \mathbf{C})\theta$ is an input-consuming derivation step using clause $c : H \leftarrow \mathbf{B}, $, then $\theta_{|H}$ is simply-local wrt. the clause $H \leftarrow$ and $\theta_{|B}$ is simply-local wrt. the query B.

Example 4.2. Consider `APPEND` in mode `append(In,In,Out)`, and its recursive clause $c : \mathtt{append([H|Xs], Ys, [H|Zs])} \leftarrow \mathtt{append(Xs, Ys, Zs)}$. The substitution $\theta = \{\mathtt{H/V, Xs/[], Ys/[W], Zs/[W]}\}$ is simply-local wrt. c: let $\sigma_0 = \{\mathtt{H/V, Xs/[], Ys/[W]}\}$ and $\sigma_1 = \{\mathtt{Zs/[W]}\}$; then $Dom(\sigma_0) \subseteq \{\mathtt{H, Xs, Ys}\}$, and $Ran(\sigma_0) \subseteq v_0$ where $v_0 = \{\mathtt{V,W}\}$, and $Dom(\sigma_1) \subseteq \{\mathtt{Zs}\}$, and $Ran(\sigma_1) \subseteq Var((\mathtt{Xs, Ys})\sigma_0)$.

---

[3] To give an intuitive idea, the transformation would, e.g., replace the clause `even(s(s(X))):- even(X).` with `even(s(Y)):- s_decomp(Y,X), even(X).`, where we define `s_decomp(s(X),X).` and the mode is `s_decomp(In,Out)`.

[4] Note that $\mathbf{s}_0$ is undefined. By abuse of notation, $Var(\mathbf{s}_0 \dots) = \emptyset$.

4.1 Modelling Complete Derivations

In predicate logic, an interpretation states which formulas are true and which ones are not. For our purposes, it is convenient to formalise this by defining an interpretation I as a set of atoms closed under variance. Based on this notion and simply-local substitutions, we now define a restricted notion of model.

Definition 4.3. Let M be an interpretation. We say that M is a *simply-local model* of $c : H \leftarrow B_1, \ldots, B_n$ iff for every substitution θ simply-local wrt. c,

$$\text{if } B_1\theta, \ldots, B_n\theta \in M \text{ then } H\theta \in M. \tag{1}$$

M is a *simply-local model* of a program P iff it is a simply-local model of each clause of it. □

Note that a simply-local model is not necessarily a model in the classical sense, since the substitution in (1) is required to be simply-local. For example, given the program $\{q(1), p(X) \leftarrow q(X)\}$ with modes $q(\text{In}), p(\text{Out})$, a model must contain the atom $p(1)$, whereas a simply-local model does not necessarily contain $p(1)$, since $\{X/1\}$ is not simply-local wrt. $p(X) \leftarrow q(X)$.

We now show that there exists a minimal simply-local model and that it is bottom-up computable. For this we need the following operator T_P^{SL} on interpretations: Given a program P and an interpretation I, define

$$T_P^{SL}(I) = \{H\theta \mid \exists\, c : H \leftarrow B_1, \ldots, B_n \in P$$
$$\exists\, \theta \text{ simply-local wrt.} c$$
$$B_1, \ldots, B_n\theta \in I \qquad \}.$$

Operator's powers are defined in the standard way: $T_P^{SL} \uparrow 0(I) = I$, $T_P^{SL} \uparrow (i+1)(I) = T_P^{SL}(T_P^{SL} \uparrow i(I))$, and $T_P^{SL} \uparrow \omega(I) = \bigcup_{i=0}^{\infty} T_P^{SL} \uparrow i(I)$. It is easy to show that T_P^{SL} is continuous on the lattice where interpretations are ordered by set inclusion. Hence, by well-known results, $T_P^{SL} \uparrow \omega$ exists and is the least fixpoint of T_P^{SL}. We can now state our main result.

Theorem 4.4. Let P be simply-moded. Then $T_P^{SL} \uparrow \omega(\emptyset)$ is the least simply-local model of P. □

We now prove correctness, fully abstractness and compositionality of the semantics. We denote the least simply-local model of P by M_P^{SL}.

Theorem 4.5. Let the program P and the query $\mathbf{A}$ be simply-moded. The following statements are equivalent:

(i) there exists an input-consuming successful derivation $\mathbf{A} \xrightarrow{\vartheta}_P \square$,
(ii) there exists a substitution θ, simply-local wrt. $\mathbf{A}$, such that $\mathbf{A}\theta \in M_P^{SL}$,

where $\mathbf{A}\theta$ is a variant of $\mathbf{A}\vartheta$. □

Example 4.6. Considering again APPEND, we have that

$$M_{\text{APPEND}}^{SL} = \bigcup_{n=0}^{\infty} \{\text{append}([t_1, \ldots, t_n], s, [t_1, \ldots, t_n | s]) \mid t_1, \ldots, t_n, s \text{ are any terms }\}.$$

Using Thm. 4.5, we can conclude that the query append([a,b],X,Y) succeeds with computed answer $\theta = \{Y/[a,b|X]\}$. In fact, append([a,b],X,[a,b|X]) $\in M_{\text{APPEND}}^{SL}$, and θ is simply-local wrt. the query above.

On the other hand, we can also say that the query append(X,[a,b],Y) has *no successful input-consuming derivations.* In fact, for every $A \in M_{\text{APPEND}}^{SL}$ we have that the first input position of A is filled in by a non-variable term. Therefore there is no simply-local θ such that append(X,[a,b],Y)$\theta \in M_{\text{APPEND}}^{SL}$. This shows that this semantics allows us to model correctly deadlocking derivations.

However, append(X,[a,b],Y) has instances in M_{APPEND}^{SL}, and successful derivations, if the requirement of simply-local substitutions, resp. input-consuming derivations, is ignored.

4.2   Modelling Partial Derivations

Dynamic scheduling also allows for parallelism. In this context it is important to be able to model the result of partial derivations. That is to say, instead of considering computed answer substitutions for complete derivations, we now consider computed answer substitutions for partial derivations. As we will see, this will be essential in order to prove termination of the programs.

Let SM_P be the set of all simply-moded atoms of the extended Herbrand universe of P. In analogy to Theorem 4.4, we have the following theorem.

Theorem 4.7. Let P be simply-moded. Then $T_P^{SL} \uparrow \omega(SM_P)$ is the least simply-local model of P containing SM_P.   □

We denote the least simply-local model of P containing SM_P by PM_P^{SL}, for *partial model.* We now show correctness, fully abstractness and compositionality of this semantics for partial derivations.

Theorem 4.8. Let the program P and the query $\mathbf{A}$ be simply-moded. The following statements are equivalent:

(i) there exists an input-consuming derivation $\mathbf{A} \xrightarrow{\vartheta}_P \mathbf{A}'$,
(ii) there exists a substitution θ, simply-local wrt. $\mathbf{A}$, such that $\mathbf{A}\theta \in PM_P^{SL}$,

where $\mathbf{A}\theta$ is a variant of $\mathbf{A}\vartheta$.   □

Note that the derivation in point (i) ends in $\mathbf{A}'$, which might be non-empty.

Example 4.9. Consider again APPEND. First, PM_{APPEND}^{SL} contains M_{APPEND}^{SL} as a subset (see Ex. 4.6). Note that M_{APPEND}^{SL} is obtained by starting from the fact clause append([],Ys,Ys) and repeatedly applying the T_P^{SL} operator using the recursive clause of APPEND. Now to obtain the remaining atoms in PM_{APPEND}^{SL}, we must repeatedly apply the T_P^{SL} operator, starting from any simply moded atom, i.e., an atom of the form $\texttt{append}(s, t, x)$ where s and t are arbitrary terms but x does not occur in s or t. It is easy to see that we thus have to add SM_P together with

$$\{\texttt{append}([t_1, \ldots, t_n | s], t, [t_1, \ldots, t_n | x]) \mid t_1, \ldots, t_n, s, t \text{ are arbitrary terms,}$$
$$x \text{ is a fresh variable}\}.$$

Using Thm. 4.8, we can conclude that the query $\texttt{append}(\texttt{[a,b|X]},\texttt{Y},\texttt{Z})$ has a partial derivation with computed answer $\theta = \{\texttt{Z}/[\texttt{a}, \texttt{b}|\texttt{Z}']\}$, and indeed, $\texttt{append}([\texttt{a}, \texttt{b}|\texttt{X}], \texttt{Y}, [\texttt{a}, \texttt{b}|\texttt{Z}']) \in PM_{\texttt{APPEND}}^{SL}$, and θ is simply-local wrt. the query above. Notice that, following the same reasoning, one can also conclude that the query also has a partial derivation with computed answer $\theta = \{\texttt{Z}/[\texttt{a}|\texttt{Z}']\}$.

5   Termination

Input-consuming derivations were originally conceived as an abstract and "reasonably strong" assumption about the selection rule in order to prove termination [18]. The first result in this area was a sufficient criterion applicable to well- and nicely-moded programs. This was improved upon by dropping the requirement of well-modedness, which means that one also captures termination by deadlock [6]. In this section, we only consider *simply* moded programs and queries (simply-moded and well-moded programs form two largely overlapping, but distinct classes), and we provide a criterion for termination which is sufficient and *necessary*, and hence an exact characterisation of termination. We first define our notion of termination.

Definition 5.1. A program is *input terminating* iff all its input-consuming derivations started in a simply-moded query are finite.   □

   In order to prove that a program is input terminating we need the concept of moded level mapping [10].

Definition 5.2. A function $|\ |$ is a *moded level mapping* iff it maps atoms into $\mathbb{N}$ and such that for any $\mathbf{s}, \mathbf{t}$ and $\mathbf{u}$, $|p(\mathbf{s}, \mathbf{t})| = |p(\mathbf{s}, \mathbf{u})|$.   □

   The condition $|p(\mathbf{s}, \mathbf{t})| = |p(\mathbf{s}, \mathbf{u})|$ states that the *level* of an atom is independent from the terms in its output positions.

   Note that programs without recursion terminate trivially. In this context, we need the following standard definitions [2].

Definition 5.3. Let P be a program, p and q be relations. We say that

 - p *refers to* q iff there is a clause in P with p in the head and q in the body.
 - p *depends on* q iff (p, q) is in the reflexive and transitive closure of the relation *refers to*.
 - p and q are *mutually recursive*, written $p \simeq q$, iff p and q depend on each other.   □

We now define *simply-acceptability*, which is in analogy to acceptability [5], but defined to deal with simply-moded and input-consuming programs.

Definition 5.4. Let P be a program and M a simply-local model of P containing SM_P. A clause $H \leftarrow \mathbf{A}, B, \mathbf{C}$ is *simply-acceptable wrt. the moded level mapping* $| \ |$ *and* M iff for every substitution θ simply-local wrt. it,

$$\text{if } \mathbf{A}\theta \in M \text{ and } Rel(H) \simeq Rel(B) \text{ then } |H\theta| > |B\theta|.$$

The program P is *simply-acceptable wrt.* M iff there exists a moded level mapping $| \ |$ such that each clause of P is simply-acceptable wrt. $| \ |$ and M.

We also say that P is *simply-acceptable* if it is simply acceptable wrt. some M. We can now show that this concept allows to characterize the class of input terminating programs.

Theorem 5.5. A simply-moded program P is simply-acceptable iff it is input terminating. In particular, if P is input terminating, then it is simply-acceptable wrt. PM_P^{SL}. $\qquad\qquad\qquad\Box$

Let us compare simply-acceptability to acceptability, used to prove left-termination [5]. Acceptability is based on a (classical) model M of the program, and for a clause $H \leftarrow A_1, \ldots, A_n$, one requires $|H\theta| > |A_i\theta|$ only if $M \models (A_1, \ldots, A_{i-1})\theta$. The reason is that for LD-derivations, $A_1, \ldots, A_{i-1}$ must be completely resolved before A_i is selected. By the correctness of LD resolution [2], it turns out that the c.a.s. θ, just before A_i is selected, is such that $M \models (A_1, \ldots, A_{i-1})\theta$. It has been argued previously that it is difficult to use a similar argument for input-consuming derivations [18]. Using the results of the previous section, we have overcome this problem. We exploited that provided that programs and queries are simply-moded, we know that even though $A_1, \ldots, A_{i-1}$ may not be resolved completely, $A_1, \ldots, A_{i-1}\theta$ will be in any "partial model" of the program.

Example 5.6. Figure 1 shows program 15.3 from [19]: `quicksort` using a form of difference lists (we permuted two body atoms for the sake of clarity). This program is simply-moded, and when used in combination with dynamic scheduling, the standard delay declarations for it are the following:

```
delay quicksort(Xs, _) until nonvar(Xs)
delay quicksort_dl(Xs, _, _) until nonvar(Xs)
delay partition(Xs, _, _, _) until nonvar(Xs)
delay =<(X,Y) until ground(X) and ground(Y)
delay >(X,Y) until ground(X) and ground(Y)
```

The last two declarations fall out of the scope of Lemma 3.5. Nevertheless, if we think of the built-ins > and =< as being conceptually defined by a program containing infinitely many ground facts of the form $>(n,m)$, with n and m being two appropriate integers, the derivations respecting the above delay declarations

```
% quicksort(Xs, Ys) ← Ys is an ordered permutation of Xs.

quicksort(Xs,Ys) ← quicksort_dl(Xs,Ys,[]).

quicksort_dl([X|Xs],Ys,Zs) ← partition(Xs,X,Littles,Bigs),
    quicksort_dl(Bigs,Ys1,Zs).
    quicksort_dl(Littles,Ys,[X|Ys1]),
quicksort_dl([],Xs,Xs).

partition([X|Xs],Y,[X|Ls],Bs) ← X =< Y, partition(Xs,Y,Ls,Bs).
partition([X|Xs],Y,Ls,[X|Bs]) ← X > Y, partition(Xs,Y,Ls,Bs).
partition([],Y,[],[]).

mode quicksort(In,Out).
mode quicksort_dl(In,Out,In).
mode partition(In,In,Out,Out).
mode =<(In,In).
mode >(In,In).
```

Fig. 1. The quicksort program

are exactly the input-consuming ones. We can prove that the program is input terminating. Define *len* as

$$len([h|t]) = 1 + len(t),$$
$$len(a) = 0 \qquad \text{if } a \text{ is not of the form } [h|t].$$

We use the following moded level mapping (positions with _ are irrelevant)

$$|\text{quicksort\_dl}(l,\_,\_)| = len(l),$$
$$|\text{partition}(l,\_,\_,\_)| = len(l).$$

The level mapping of all other atoms can be set to 0. Concerning the model, the simplest solution is to use the model that expresses the dependency between the list lengths of the arguments of partition, i.e., M should contain all atoms of the form partition(l_1, x, l_2, l_3) where $len(l_1) > len(l_2)$ and $len(l_1) > len(l_3)$.

6   Benchmarks

In order to assess how realistic the conditions of Lemma 3.5 are, we have looked into three collections of logic programs, and we have checked whether those programs were simply moded (**SM**), input-consistent (**IC**) and whether they satisfied both sides of Lemma 3.5 (**L**). Notice that programs which are not input-consistent do not satisfy the conditions of Lemma 3.5. For this reason, some **L** columns are left blank. The results, reported in Tables 1 to 3, show that our results apply to the majority of the programs considered. We considered in Table 1 the programs from Apt's collection [2,5], in Table 2 those of the DPPD's collection, (http://dsse.ecs.soton.ac.uk/~mal/systems/dppd.html), and in Table 3 some programs of Lindenstrauss's collection (http://www.cs.huji.ac.il/~naomil).

Table 1. Programs from Apt's Collection

	SM	IC	L		SM	IC	L
append(In,In,Out)	yes	yes	yes	mergesort(In,Out)	yes	no	
append(Out,Out,In)	yes	yes	no	mergesort(Out,In)	no		
append3(In,In,In,Out)	yes	yes	yes	mergesort_variant(In,Out,In)	yes	yes	no
color_map(In,Out)	yes	no		ordered(In)	yes	no	
color_map(Out,In)	yes	yes	yes	overlap(In,In)	yes	no	
dcsolve(In,_)	yes	yes	yes	overlap(In,Out)	yes	yes	yes
even(In)	yes	no		overlap(Out,In)	yes	yes	yes
fold(In,In,Out)	yes	yes	yes	perm_select(In,Out)	yes	yes	no
list(In)	yes	yes	yes	perm_select(Out,In)	yes	yes	no
lte(In,In)	yes	yes	no	qsort(In,Out)	yes	yes	yes
lte(In,Out)	yes	yes	yes	qsort(Out,In)	no		
lte(Out,In)	yes	yes	no	reverse(In,Out)	yes	yes	yes
map(In,In)	yes	yes	yes	reverse(Out,In)	yes	yes	yes
map(In,Out)	yes	yes	yes	select(In,In,Out)	yes	no	
map(Out,In)	yes	yes	yes	select(Out,In,Out)	yes	yes	yes
member(In,In)	yes	no		subset(In,In)	yes	no	
member(In,Out)	yes	yes	yes	subset (Out,In)	yes	yes	yes
member(Out,In)	yes	yes	yes	sum(In,In,Out)	yes	yes	yes
type(In,In,Out)	no			sum(Out,Out,In)	yes	yes	yes

7   Conclusion

In this paper, we have proven a result that *demonstrates* – for a large class of programs – the equivalence between delay declarations and input-consuming derivations. This was only speculated in [6,7]. In fact, even though the class of programs we are considering here (simply-moded programs) is only slightly smaller than the one of nicely-moded programs considered in [6,7], for the latter a result such as Lemma 3.5 does not hold.

We have provided a denotational semantics for input-consuming derivations using a variant of the well-known T_P-operator. Our semantics follows the s-semantics approach [9] and thus enjoys the typical properties of semantics in this class. This semantics improves on the one introduced in [7] in two respects: The semantics of this paper models (within a uniform framework) both complete and incomplete derivations, and there is no requirement that the program must be well-moded.

Falaschi *et al.* [11] have defined a denotational semantics for CLP programs with dynamic scheduling of a somewhat different kind: the semantics of a query is given by a set of closure operators; each operator is a function modelling a possible effect of resolving the query on a program state (i.e., constraint on the program variables). However, we believe that our approach is more suited to termination proofs.

Table 2. Programs from DPPD's Collection

	SM	IC	L		SM	IC	L
applast(In,In,Out)	yes	yes	yes	relative (In,Out)	yes	yes	yes
depth(In,Out)	yes	no		relative (Out,In)	yes	yes	yes
flipflip(In,Out)	yes	yes	yes	rev_acc(In,In,Out)	yes	yes	yes
flipflip(Out,In)	yes	yes	yes	rotate(In,Out)	yes	yes	yes
generate(In,In,Out)	yes	no		rotate(Out,In)	yes	yes	yes
liftsolve(In,In)	yes	yes	yes	solve(In,In,Out))	yes	no	
liftsolve(In,Out)	yes	yes	yes	square_square(In,Out)	yes	yes	yes
match(In,In)	yes	no		squretr(In,Out)	yes	yes	yes
match_app(In,In)	yes	yes	no	ssupply(In,In,Out)	yes	yes	yes
match_app(In,Out)	yes	yes	no	trace(In,In,Out)	yes	no	
max_lenth(In,Out,Out)	yes	yes	yes	trace(In,Out,Out)	no		
memo_solve(In,Out)	yes	no		transpose(In,Out)	yes	no	
prune(In,Out)	yes	no		transpose(Out,In)	yes	yes	yes
prune(Out,In)	yes	no		unify(In,In,Out)	yes	no	

Table 3. Programs from Lindenstrauss's Collection

	SM	IC	L		SM	IC	L
ack(In,In,_)	yes	yes	no	huffman(In,Out)	no		
concatenate(In,In,Out)	yes	yes	yes	huffman(In,Out)	no		
credit(In,Out)	yes	yes	yes	normal_form(_,In)	yes	no	
deep(In,Out)	yes	yes	yes	queens(In,Out)	yes	yes	yes
deep(Out,In)	no			queens(Out,In)	yes	yes	no
descendant(In,Out)	yes	yes	yes	rewrite(In,Out)	yes	no	
descendant(Out,In)	yes	yes	yes	transform(In,In,In,Out)	yes	yes	yes
holds(In,Out)	yes	yes	yes	twoleast(In,Out)	no		

As mentioned in Sec. 4.2, in the context of parallelism and concurrency [17], one can have derivations that never *succeed*, and yet compute substitutions. Moreover, input-consuming derivations essentially correspond to the execution mechanism of (Moded) FGHC [20]. Thus we have provided a model-theoretic semantics for such programs/programming languages, which go beyond the usual success-based SLD resolution mechanism of logic programming.

On a more practical level, our semantics for partial derivations is used in order to prove termination. We have provided a necessary and sufficient criterion for termination, applicable to a wide class of programs, namely the class of simply-moded programs. For instance, we can now prove the termination of QUICKSORT, which is not possible with the tools of [18,6] (which provided only a sufficient condition). In the termination proofs, we exploit that any selected atom in an input-consuming derivation is in a model for partial derivations, in a similar way as this is done for proving left-termination. It is only on the basis of the semantics that we could present a characterisation of input-consuming termination for simply-moded programs.

References

1. K. R. Apt. Introduction to Logic Programming. In J. van Leeuwen, editor, *Handbook of Theoretical Computer Science*, volume B: Formal Models and Semantics, pages 495–574. Elsevier, Amsterdam and The MIT Press, Cambridge, 1990.
2. K. R. Apt. *From Logic Programming to Prolog*. Prentice Hall, 1997.
3. K. R. Apt and S. Etalle. On the unification free Prolog programs. In A. Borzyszkowski and S. Sokolowski, editors, *Proceedings of MFCS '93*, LNCS, pages 1–19. Springer-Verlag, 1993.
4. K. R. Apt and I. Luitjes. Verification of logic programs with delay declarations. In V. S. Alagar and M. Nivat, editors, *Proceedings of AMAST'95*, LNCS, pages 66–90. Springer-Verlag, 1995. Invited Lecture.
5. K. R. Apt and D. Pedreschi. Modular termination proofs for logic and pure Prolog programs. In G. Levi, editor, *Advances in Logic Programming Theory*, pages 183–229. Oxford University Press, 1994.
6. A. Bossi, S. Etalle, and S. Rossi. Properties of input-consuming derivations. *ENTCS*, 30(1), 1999. http://www.elsevier.nl/locate/entcs.
7. A. Bossi, S. Etalle, and S. Rossi. Semantics of input-consuming programs. In J. Lloyd, editor, *CL 2000*. Springer-Verlag, 2000.
8. A. Bossi, S. Etalle, S. Rossi, and J.-G. Smaus. Semantics and termination of simply-moded logic programs with dynamic scheduling. Available via CoRR: http://arXiv.org/archive/cs/intro.html, 2001.
9. A. Bossi, M. Gabbrielli, G. Levi, and M. Martelli. The *s*-semantics approach: theory and applications. *Journal of Logic Programming*, 19/20:149–197, 1994.
10. S. Etalle, A. Bossi, and N. Cocco. Termination of well-moded programs. *Journal of Logic Programming*, 38(2):243–257, 1999.
11. M. Falaschi, M. Gabbrielli, K. Marriott, and C. Palamidessi. Constraint logic programming with dynamic scheduling: A semantics based on closure operators. *Information and Computation*, 137:41–67, 1997.
12. P. M. Hill and J. W. Lloyd. *The Gödel Programming Language*. The MIT Press, 1994.
13. Intelligent Systems Laboratory, Swedish Institute of Computer Science, PO Box 1263, S-164 29 Kista, Sweden. *SICStus Prolog User's Manual*, 1998. http://www.sics.se/sicstus/docs/3.7.1/html/sicstus_toc.html.
14. R. A. Kowalski. Algorithm = Logic + Control. *Communications of the ACM*, 22(7):424–436, 1979.
15. J. W. Lloyd. *Foundations of Logic Programming*. Symbolic Computation – Artificial Intelligence. Springer-Verlag, 1987.
16. L. Naish. *Negation and Control in Prolog*, volume 238 of *LNCS*. Springer-Verlag, 1986.
17. L. Naish. Parallelizing NU-Prolog. In R. A. Kowalski and K. A. Bowen, editors, *Proceedings of ICLP/SLP '88*, pages 1546–1564. MIT Press, 1988.
18. J.-G. Smaus. Proving termination of input-consuming logic programs. In D. De Schreye, editor, *Proceedings of ICLP'99*, pages 335–349. MIT Press, 1999.
19. L. Sterling and E. Shapiro. *The Art of Prolog*. MIT Press, 1986.
20. K. Ueda and M. Morita. Moded Flat GHC and its message-oriented implementation technique. *New Generation Computing*, 13(1):3–43, 1994.

The **Def**-inite Approach to Dependency Analysis

Samir Genaim and Michael Codish

The Department of Computer Science
Ben-Gurion University of the Negev
Beer-Sheva, Israel
{genaim,mcodish}@cs.bgu.ac.il

Abstract. We propose a new representation for the domain of Definite Boolean functions. The key idea is to view the set of models of a Boolean function as an incidence relation between variables and models. This enables two dual representations: the usual one, in terms of models, specifying which variables they contain; and the other in terms of variables, specifying which models contain them. We adopt the dual representation which provides a clean theoretical basis for the definition of efficient operations on **Def** in terms of classic ACI1 unification theory. Our approach illustrates in an interesting way the relation of **Def** to the well-known set-**Sharing** domain which can also be represented in terms of sets of models and ACI1 unification. From the practical side, a prototype implementation provides promising results which indicate that this representation supports efficient groundness analysis using **Def** formula. Moreover, widening on this representation is easily defined.

1   Introduction

Boolean functions play an important role in various formal methods for specification, verification and analysis of software systems. In program analysis, Boolean functions are often used to approximate properties of the set of states encountered at a given program point. For example, a conjunction $x \wedge y$ could specify that variables x and y satisfy some property whenever control reaches a given program point. A Boolean function $\varphi_1 \to \varphi_2$ could specify that if φ_1 is satisfied at a program point (perhaps depending on the unknown inputs to the program) then also φ_2 is satisfied. A disjunction $\varphi_1 \vee \varphi_2$ could arise as a consequence of a branch in the control where φ_1 and φ_2 approximate properties of the **then** and **else** branches respectively.

For program analysis, we often consider the *positive* Boolean functions, **Pos**. Namely, those for which $f(true,\ldots,true) = true$. This restriction is natural as, due to the element of approximation, the result of an analysis is not a *"yes/no"* answer, but rather a *"yes/maybe not"* answer. In this case there is no "negative" information. Sophisticated **Pos**-based analyzers implemented using binary decision diagrams (BDD's) [4] have been shown [12] to give good experimental results both with regards to precision as well as with regards for the efficiency of the analyzers. However, scalability is a problem and inputs (programs) for which

D. Sands (Ed.): ESOP 2001, LNCS 2028, pp. 417–431, 2001.

the analysis requires an exponential number of iterations or exponentially large data structures are encountered [6].

In general, scalability problems with program analyses are often tackled by introducing widening operations [14]. Widening techniques can be applied to restrict the number of iterations as well as to limit the size of data-structures. A disadvantage of the use of binary decision diagrams for Pos-based groundness analyses is the lack of suitable widening techniques which maintain reasonable precision on the one hand and guarantee scalability on the other.

The domain, Def, of definite Boolean functions is a subdomain of Pos. These are the positive functions whose sets of models are closed under intersection. The domain Def is less expressive than Pos. For example, the formula $x \vee y$ is not in Def. However, Def-based analyzers can be implemented using less complex data structures and can be faster than Pos-based analyzers. As for precision, Def has been shown to provide a reasonable tradeoff between efficiency and precision for goal dependent groundness analyses (where a description of the inputs to the program being analyzed is given) [20,19]. Our present work indicates that in practice, for a large set of benchmark programs, goal independent Def analysis is just as precise as goal dependent analysis with respect to the groundness information derived. However, scalability remains a problem for Def. In [17], the authors demonstrate a series of inputs (programs) for which Def-based groundness analysis involves $2^{\sqrt{n}}$ iterations (where n is the size of the input). An advantage of basing analyses on Def is the fact that widening operations are not difficult to define and implement.

This paper investigates a new representation for Def functions. The key idea is to abstract the terms to the set of variables they contain, then dependencies between the terms are represented by set expressions. This turns out to be equivalent to viewing the models of a Boolean function (the dependencies) as an incidence relation between the variables of the function and its models which are sets of variables. This leads to two dual views of the structure. The usual view looks at the sets and specifies which are their elements. The dual view looks at the variables and specifies which are their sets. We take the dual view and show that Def is isomorphic to the domain of tuples of sets of variables modulo ACI1 equivalence.

The approach and the design of our domain build on two previous results, presented in [8] and in [9,10]. The work presented in [8] illustrates the application of logic programming with sets (of variables) to support an isomorphic representation for set sharing analysis. This approach is theoretically pleasing as the operations for sharing analysis are based on a classic ACI1 equality theory. In [9,10], the authors present an isomorphism between Sharing and Pos which leads to a better understanding of the similarities between groundness and sharing analyses. In particular Def analyses in the two domains are shown to coincide exactly extending an important result by Cortesi et al. [11]. From the practical point of view, the consequence is that the operations in a Sharing analysis are simplified when the focus is restricted to Def information.

This result is applied by King *et al.* in [20] where the authors quotient the Sharing domain to perform groundness analysis in Def. Their analyzer is reported to perform well in comparison to a Pos analysis using BDD's. In a sequel to [20] described in [19], the authors obtain a much faster analysis by factoring the representation into three components: G (ground arguments), E (equivalent arguments) and P (a propositional Horn clause component). The G and the E components can be represented as an atom containing only variables and the constant *true*. For example, the atom $p(A, true, A, B, true)$ represents the Def function $(x_1 \leftrightarrow x_3) \wedge x_2 \wedge x_5$ on five variables. The approach is similar to the GER representation for Pos described in [3].

This paper, supports the view that groundness dependencies in Def can be obtained efficiently by quotienting a Sharing analysis. We are motivated by the preliminary results described in [20] and challenged by the speed of the analyzer described in [19]. We argue that when adopting the set logic programming approach of [8] we obtain "for free" a factoring of the domain to consider separately ground arguments and equivalence between arguments. Moreover, we obtain a representation which is easy to implement and to widen.

From the technical point of view, the set logic programming approach is attractive because we prove that the quotient of Sharing for Def in our representation is the well-studied and classic notion of ACI1 equivalence. Namely, two atoms with sets of variables as terms, representing corresponding Sharing elements are equivalent in Def if and only if they are ACI1 equivalent. All of the operations for Def analysis in Sharing are shown to be classic operations for ACI1 terms which are in our special case known to be efficient to maintain. This is in contrast to the use of ACI1 theory in the context of sharing analysis which requires a specialized notion of ACI1 unification (which chooses the most general unifier according to a non-standard ordering).

So, the quotient of Sharing for Def in our representation sums up to applying the standard ACI1 ordering on tuples of sets instead of the specialized ordering used in [8].

2   A Motivating Example

Groundness dependencies, as expressed using Boolean functions, capture information about the sets of variables that can occur in the terms the arguments of a predicate are bound to during the execution of a program. For example, the dependency $p(x_1, x_2) \leftarrow (x_1 \rightarrow x_2)$ specifies that if x_1 and x_2 are bound (during program execution) to the terms t_1 and t_2 respectively, then for any substitution θ, if θ grounds t_1 then it also grounds t_2. Essentially all this means is that the variables in t_2 are a subset of those in t_1. Viewing x_1 and x_2 as denoting sets of variables (instead of terms) we can represent this dependency as $p(x_1, x_2) \leftarrow (x_1 \supseteq x_2)$ or alternatively using *"set expressions"* as $p(x_1, x_2) \leftarrow (x_1 = a \cup b) \wedge (x_2 = b)$ where a and b are existentially quantified (names for) sets. This paper illustrates that representing groundness dependencies in terms of set expressions has practical implications.

Table 1 illustrates these two representations for positive Boolean functions and some relations between them. Each row in the first and second columns depicts a (positive) Boolean function φ on n variables V and its set of models $[\![\varphi]\!]$. Each model is represented as a set of variables indicating that the function assumes the value true under the assignment of these variables to *true* and all other variables to *false*. The model $\{x, y\}$ (for example, in the first row) is written xy for short and $\bot$ (for example, in the third row) denotes the empty model. Note that a positive function always contains V as one of its models. Throughout the example we take $n = 2$. In the third column the models of φ are

Table 1. Representations of Positive Boolean functions on $\{x, y\}$.

φ	$[\![\varphi]\!]$	$[\![coneg(\varphi)]\!]$	Tuple_n	$\varphi\!\downarrow$
$x \wedge y$	$\{xy\}$	$\{\bot\}$	$\langle \bot, \bot \rangle$	$(x \leftrightarrow true) \wedge (y \leftrightarrow true)$
x	$\{x, xy\}$	$\{y, \bot\}$	$\langle \bot, a \rangle$	$\exists_a.((x \leftrightarrow true) \wedge (y \leftrightarrow a))$
$x \leftrightarrow y$	$\{\bot, xy\}$	$\{xy, \bot\}$	$\langle a, a \rangle$	$\exists_a.((x \leftrightarrow a) \wedge (y \leftrightarrow a))$
$x \rightarrow y$	$\{\bot, y, xy\}$	$\{xy, x, \bot\}$	$\langle ab, a \rangle$	$\exists_{a,b}.((x \leftrightarrow a \wedge b) \wedge (y \leftrightarrow a))$
$y \rightarrow x$	$\{\bot, x, xy\}$	$\{xy, y, \bot\}$	$\langle a, ab \rangle$	$\exists_{a,b}.((x \leftrightarrow a) \wedge (y \leftrightarrow a \wedge b))$
$x \vee y$	$\{x, y, xy\}$	$\{y, x, \bot\}$	$\langle a, b \rangle$	$\exists_{a,b}.((x \leftrightarrow b) \wedge (y \leftrightarrow a))$
$true$	$\{\bot, x, y, xy\}$	$\{xy, y, x, \bot\}$	$\langle ac, ab \rangle$	$\exists_{a,b,c}.((x \leftrightarrow a \wedge c) \wedge (y \leftrightarrow a \wedge b))$

pointwise complemented with respect to V. These are the models of the "dual negation" of φ which is denoted $coneg(\varphi)$. Some readers may observe that the elements of this column correspond to elements of the Sharing domain (which always contain $\bot$ as a model). Dual negation is discussed in [10] and shown to provide an isomorphism between Sharing and Pos. The forth column represents φ in terms of set expressions. The set-expression $a \cup b$ is written ab for short and the notation is thus an n-tuple of sets ("Tuple_n") of variables disjoint from V. To obtain this representation, the models of $coneg(\varphi)$ are first given arbitrary names $(a, b, c, \ldots)$. The ith set in a tuple then specifies which models of $coneg(\varphi)$ contain the ith variable of V. For example, if we name the models in

$$[\![coneg(x \rightarrow y)]\!] = \{xy, x, \bot\}$$

by a, b and c respectively, then the Tuple_n representation of $x \rightarrow y$ is $\langle ab, a \rangle$: ab in the first position because x occurs in both a and b; and a in the second position because y occurs only in a. This is the representation used in [8] which is shown to be isomorphic to the Sharing domain when viewed modulo an appropriate notion of equivalence. It is also the representation we work with in this paper where we make the observation that looking at the elements of this column modulo standard ACI1 equivalence gives precisely Def.

The fifth column in Table 1 illustrates the relation between the tuples of sets representation of a positive Boolean function φ and its strongest logical consequence which is in Def (denoted $\varphi\downarrow$). All of the functions in the example, except for $x \vee y$, satisfy $\varphi\downarrow= \varphi$ because they are already in Def. For $x \vee y$ we have $(x \vee y)\downarrow= true$. In the sequel (1)we will observe that the tuples $\langle a, b \rangle$ and $\langle ac, ab \rangle$ corresponding to $x \vee y$ and $true$ are ACI1 equivalent.

The class of definite Boolean functions is a complete lattice ordered by implication. The meet of two functions is their conjunction (Def is closed under conjunction) and the join is obtained by closing their disjunction under intersection of models (Def is not closed under disjunction).

Adopting the tuples of sets notation for Def, the join operation is defined as pointwise union. For example, the joins of x and $x \leftrightarrow y$ and of x and y are obtained as: $\langle \perp, b \rangle \sqcup \langle a, a \rangle = \langle a, ab \rangle$ and $\langle \perp, b \rangle \sqcup \langle a, \perp \rangle = \langle a, b \rangle$ which correspond to $y \rightarrow x$ and $true$ respectively. The meet is defined in terms of ACI1 unification. For example the meet of $x \rightarrow y$ and $y \rightarrow x$ is obtained as the ACI1 unification of the corresponding (renamed apart) tuples $\langle ab, a \rangle$ and $\langle c, cd \rangle$. The unification involves solving the system of ACI1 equations $\{ab = c, a = cd\}$ and applying the result on the given tuples. The result is $\langle a', a' \rangle$ which corresponds to the formula $x \leftrightarrow y$. In the sequel we formalize these definitions.

3   Preliminaries

Boolean Functions

Let $B = \{true, false\}$. A Boolean function on $V = \{x_1, \ldots, x_n\}$ is a function $\varphi : B^n \rightarrow B$. An *interpretation* $\mu : V \rightarrow B$ is an assignment of truth values to the variables in V. An interpretation μ is a *model* for φ, denoted $\mu \models \varphi$, if $\varphi(\mu(x_1), \ldots, \mu(x_n)) = true$. We write an interpretation as the set of variables which are assigned to the value $true$. The set of models of φ is thus viewed as a set of sets of variables defined by $[\![\varphi]\!]_V = \{ \ \{x \in V \mid \mu(x) = true\} \mid \mu \models \varphi \ \}$. Much of the time we will omit the subscript V as it will be clear from the context.

Let φ be a Boolean function on V. We say that φ is *positive* if $V \in [\![\varphi]\!]$, that is, $\varphi(true, \ldots, true) = true$. We say that φ is *down-closed* if $[\![\varphi]\!]$ is closed under intersection. We denote by $\varphi\downarrow$ the strongest logical consequence of φ which is down-closed. In other words, $[\![\varphi\downarrow]\!] = [\![\varphi]\!]\downarrow$ is the smallest set that contains $[\![\varphi]\!]$ and is closed under intersection.

The class of positive Boolean functions ordered by logical consequence is a complete lattice denoted as Pos (sometimes we write Pos_V). An element of Pos is *definite* if it is down-closed. The definite Boolean functions form a sub-lattice of Pos denoted by Def (sometimes we write Def_V).

The *dual* of a Boolean function is the function that results when the roles of *false* and *true* are interchanged. For any Boolean function φ we denote by $coneg(\varphi)$ the dual of the negation of φ (or, equivalently, the negation of its dual). In terms of the models of a function φ we have the following *pointwise complementation principle* [10] which states that to move from $[\![\varphi]\!] = \{m_1, \ldots, m_n\}$ to its dual negated counterpart, we should replace each element m_i by its complement:

$$[\![coneg(\varphi)]\!]_V = \{V \setminus m \mid m \in [\![\varphi]\!]\}.$$

ACI1 Equivalence and Tuples of Sets

We assume a denumerable set of variables $\mathcal{V}$ and an alphabet $\Sigma = \{\oplus, \bot\}$ consisting of a binary function symbol $\oplus$ and a constant symbol $\bot$. Sets of variables from $\mathcal{V}$ are represented as elements of the term algebra $T(\Sigma, \mathcal{V})$ modulo an equality theory consisting of the following axioms:

$$
\begin{aligned}
(x \oplus y) \oplus z &= x \oplus (y \oplus z) \quad &(associativity) \\
x \oplus y &= y \oplus x \quad &(commutativity) \\
x \oplus x &= x \quad &(idempotence) \\
x \oplus \bot &= x \quad &(unit\ element)
\end{aligned}
$$

The corresponding equivalence relation on terms is denoted $\approx_{aci1}$. This notion of equivalence suggests that set expressions can be viewed as flat sets of variables. For example, the terms $x_1 \oplus x_2 \oplus x_3$, $x_1 \oplus x_2 \oplus x_3 \oplus \bot$, and $x_1 \oplus x_2 \oplus x_3 \oplus x_2$ can each be viewed as representing the set $\{x_1, x_2, x_3\}$ of three variables. The set of n-tuples of set expressions is denoted $\mathsf{Tuple}_n(\Sigma, \mathcal{V})$. Set atoms are entities of the form $p(\bar{\tau})$ where p/n is an n-ary predicate symbol and $\bar{\tau}$ is an n-tuple of set expressions.

Set substitutions are substitutions which map variables of $\mathcal{V}$ to set expressions from $T(\Sigma, \mathcal{V})$. The application of a set substitution μ to a syntactic object τ is defined as usual by replacing occurrences of each variable x in τ by the set expression $\mu(x)$. The standard operations on set substitutions such as projection and composition are also defined just as for usual substitutions.

A preorder $\preceq_{aci1}$ on tuples of set expressions (and other syntactic objects) is defined as usual so that $\tau_1 \preceq_{aci1} \tau_2$ if there exists a set substitution μ such that $\tau_1 =_{aci1} \mu(\tau_2)$. In this case we say that τ_1 is less instantiated (modulo ACI1) than τ_2. This preorder induces a corresponding equivalence relation $\approx_{aci1}$ on tuples and a partial order $\preceq_{aci1}$ on the equivalence classes. For each natural n, $\mathsf{Tuple}_n = (\mathsf{Tuple}_n(\Sigma, \mathcal{V})/_{\approx_{aci1}}, \preceq_{aci1})$ is a complete lattice. The join is defined by

$$
\langle \tau_1, \ldots, \tau_n \rangle \sqcup \langle \tau_1', \ldots, \tau_n' \rangle = \langle (\tau_1 \oplus \tau_1'), \ldots, (\tau_n \oplus \tau_n') \rangle
$$

and the meet is defined through ACI1 unification [2]. An ACI1 unifier for two tuples τ_1 and τ_2 is a set substitution μ such that $\mu(\tau_1) =_{aci1} \mu(\tau_2)$.

Example 1. Consider the tuples $\bar{\tau}_1 = \langle a \oplus c, a \oplus b \rangle$ and $\bar{\tau}_2 = \langle a', b' \rangle$. Their ACI1 equivalence is illustrated by the substitutions $\mu_1 = \{a \mapsto \bot, b \mapsto b', c \mapsto a'\}$ and $\mu_2 = \{a' \mapsto a \oplus c, b' \mapsto a \oplus b\}$.

In our case, the underlying alphabet contains only the two (interpreted) function symbols $\{\oplus, \bot\}$. In this case the unification problem is classified as *elementary* [2]. The elementary unification problem is trivial (there always exists a unifier which binds all variables to $\bot$), the problem is unitary (there always exists a unique most general unifier) and the unification algorithm is efficient. The unique most general unifier for two set expressions (in our special case) τ and τ' is a substitution μ which maps variables to sets of variables as follows:

$$
\mu(X) = \left\{ Z_{ab} \ \middle| \ \begin{array}{c} (a, b) \in vars(\tau) \times vars(\tau') \\ and \ \ X \in \{a, b\} \end{array} \right\}
$$

where a fresh variable Z_{ab} from $\mathcal{V}$ is introduced for each pair (a, b).

Example 2. Let $\tau = w \oplus u$ and $\tau' = x \oplus y$. The most general ACI1 unifier of τ and τ' is obtained as:

$$\mu = \begin{cases} w \mapsto Z_{wx} \oplus Z_{wy}, \; u \mapsto Z_{ux} \oplus Z_{uy}, \\ x \mapsto Z_{ux} \oplus Z_{wx}, \; y \mapsto Z_{uy} \oplus Z_{wy} \end{cases}.$$

4   Boolean Functions as Tuples of Sets

Let $V \subseteq \mathcal{V}$ be a finite set of variables. A set $M = \{m_1, \dots, m_k\}$ of subsets of V can be represented as an incidence structure $S = (V, \mathcal{M}, \rho)$ where $\mathcal{M} \subseteq \mathcal{V}$ is a set of variables, disjoint from V, corresponding to the (names of the) sets in M and $\rho \subseteq V \times \mathcal{M}$ is a relation which specifies which elements from V belong to which sets from M. If $(x, m) \in \rho$ then we say that x and m are *incident*. For $m \in \mathcal{M}$ and $x \in V$ we denote the elements of m by $(m) = \{y \in V \mid (y, m) \in \rho\}$ and the sets containing x by $(x) = \{q \in \mathcal{M} \mid (x, q) \in \rho\}$. For $V = \{x_1, \dots, x_n\}$, we denote the n-tuple $\langle (x_1), \dots, (x_n) \rangle$ by $\mathcal{T}(M)$.

Example 3. Consider the set $M = \{\bot, x, y, xy\}$ over $V = \{x, y\}$. Its representation as an incidence structure is illustrated in Figure 1.

$$
\begin{array}{ll}
(a) = \{x\} & (x) = \{a, b\} \\
(b) = \{x, y\} & (y) = \{b, c\} \\
(c) = \{y\} & \\
(d) = \emptyset & \langle (x), (y) \rangle = \langle \{a, b\}, \{b, c\} \rangle
\end{array}
$$

Fig. 1. Incidence structure for $\{\bot, x, y, xy\}$.

Viewing a set of sets of variables M over $V = \{x_1, \dots, x_n\}$ as an incidence structure $(V, \mathcal{M}, \rho)$ provides two alternative representations. The original set M is obtained as $\{(m) \mid m \in \mathcal{M}\}$. A dual representation is obtained as $\mathcal{T}(M) = \langle (x_1), \dots, (x_n) \rangle$. Note that the number of symbols in the two representations is always the same. Note also that the dual representation is ambiguous concerning the presence of the empty set. Luckily, in our application the empty set will always be present and hence there will be no ambiguity. This is because $\varphi \in \mathsf{Pos}$ if and only if $[\![coneg(\varphi)]\!]$ contains the empty set.

In the remainder of this section we prove that for $V = \{x_1, \dots, x_n\}$, Def_V is isomorphic to Tuple_n.

Definition 1.   *Let* $V = \{x_1, \dots, x_n\}$. *We define the mapping* iff : $\mathsf{Tuple}_n \to \mathsf{Def}_V$ *such that for* $\bar{\tau} = \langle \tau_1, \dots, \tau_n \rangle \in \mathsf{Tuple}_n$:

$$\textit{iff}(\bar{\tau}) = \exists_{vars(\bar{\tau})} . \bigwedge_i (x_i \leftrightarrow \wedge \tau_i)$$

where $vars(\bar{\tau})$ denotes the set of variables in $\bar{\tau}$ and $\wedge\tau_i$ is the conjunction of the variables in the ith argument τ_i of $\bar{\tau}$. Note that $iff(\bar{\tau}) \in$ Def because Def is closed under existential quantification and $x_i \leftrightarrow (a_1 \wedge \cdots \wedge a_n)$ is equivalent to $[(a_1 \wedge \cdots \wedge a_n) \rightarrow x_i] \wedge [(x_i \rightarrow a_1) \wedge \cdots \wedge (x_i \rightarrow a_n)]$ which is in propositional definite form.

Example 4. Consider $\bar{\tau} = \langle a \oplus b, b \rangle$. We have $iff(\bar{\tau}) = \exists_{a,b}.(x_1 \leftrightarrow a \wedge b) \wedge (x_2 \leftrightarrow b)$ which is equivalent to $x_1 \rightarrow x_2$.

Theorem 1. *Let $V = \{x_1, \ldots, x_n\}$ then Tuple_n and Def_V are isomorphic domains.*

The results follows from Definition 1, and the following two lemmas which state that $\mathcal{T}$ is 1-1 and onto. The full proofs appear in [16].

Lemma 1. *Let $\tau_1, \tau_2 \in \mathsf{Tuple}_n$ then: $\tau_1 \leq_{aci1} \tau_2 \Leftrightarrow (iff(\tau_1) \rightarrow iff(\tau_2))$.*

Lemma 2. *Let $\varphi \in \mathsf{Pos}$ and $\bar{\tau} = \mathcal{T}([\![coneg(\varphi)]\!])$ then $iff(\bar{\tau}) = \varphi\!\downarrow$*

5   Groundness Analysis Using Tuple_n

The specification of a program analysis within the framework of abstract interpretation [13] requires: (1) a concrete semantics, (2) an abstract domain, and (3) abstract operations. Our abstract domain is Tuple_n and is isomorphic to Def. This section focuses on the abstract operations required to support groundness analyses as determined by the standard choices of a concrete semantics. In addition, we suggest two widening techniques which can be applied to improve the scalability properties of the analysis.

Representation and Abstract Operations

We adopt a non-ground representation. The sets of variables in a tuple are represented as lists of (Prolog) variables. In this way we benefit from the underlying renaming mechanism of Prolog. For example, the Def object $p(x_1, x_2) \leftarrow (x_1 \rightarrow x_2)$ is represented by $p([A, B], [A])$.

The isomorphism between Def and Tuple establishes the formal correspondence between the domain elements and operations (join and meet). The complexity of the join operator is linear in the number of the arguments (pointwise union). The complexity of the meet operator (ACI1 unification) is quadratic in the size of the atoms being unified (because ACI1 unification introduces a quadratic number of fresh variables). Projection is also straightforward to define (it is the same as the standard operation on atoms).

There is one additional operation that we must consider. Given two elements from Tuple_n (which are representatives of equivalence classes), we need to determine if they are ACI1 equivalent. To this end we introduce a *normal form*

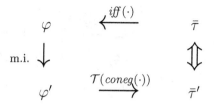

Fig. 2. Normal form representation in Tuple.

representation and hence an operation which given a tuple of sets computes its normal form.

Figure 2 illustrates the definition of the normal form operation which is more easily described through Def. We have a tuple of sets of variables $\bar{\tau}$ (on the top right side of the figure) with $\mathit{iff}(\bar{\tau}) = \varphi$ (on the top left). We take as φ' (bottom left) the conjunction of all of the Boolean functions $\psi \in$ Pos such that $\psi{\downarrow} = \varphi$. Stated alternatively: $[\![\varphi]\!]'$ is the meet irreducible subset of $[\![\varphi]\!]$. Namely we remove from $[\![\varphi]\!]$ any model obtained as the intersection of other models. The existence and uniqueness of φ' is justified by Proposition 1 (below). Our normal form is the tuple (on the bottom right side of the figure) $\bar{\tau}' = \mathcal{T}(coneg(\varphi'))$.

Proposition 1. *Let $\varphi_1, \varphi_2 \in$ Pos and $\varphi_1{\downarrow} = \varphi_2{\downarrow}$ then $(\varphi_1 \wedge \varphi_2){\downarrow} = \varphi_1{\downarrow} = \varphi_2{\downarrow}$.*

In the implementation, the normal form is computed directly on the tuple representation. Whereas in Def we removed sets obtained as the intersection of others, for tuples (which encode the *coneg* of the formula) we remove variables that correspond to models obtained as the union of others. The operation is described viewing the n-tuple in terms of the incidence structure it represents. We demonstrate the computation of the normal form of the tuple

$$\langle \underbrace{abce}_{x}, \underbrace{acd}_{y}, \underbrace{ae}_{z} \rangle$$

which represents the *coneg* models $\{a = \{x, y, z\}, b = \{x\}, c = \{x, y\}, d = \{y\}, e = \{z, x\}, f = \bot\}$. The corresponding incidence structure is illustrated in Figure 3 (on the left).

We should eliminate a (obtained as the union of e and d) and c (obtained as the union of d and b). We refer to the points on the left of the incidence structure (x, y, z) as *variables* and to those on the right (a, b, c, d, e) as *models*. The algorithm considers each model m to determine if can be obtained as the union of other models as follows:

1. color the variables connected to m;
2. color the models, except m, which are connected only to colored variables;
3. if each of the colored variables is connected to at least one colored model then remove m.

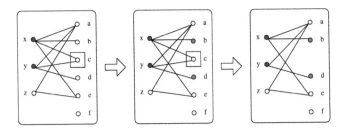

Fig. 3. Computing a normal form: eliminating c.

Figure 3 depicts the process of eliminating the model c in our example. First the variables x and y (connected to c) are colored and then the models b and d (connected only to colored variables) are colored. The colored variables are each connected to at least one colored model, so c is removed. Repeating this operation for all models gives the normal form $\langle be, d, de \rangle$.

The complexity of the algorithm is $O(|V| * |E|)$, where $|V|$ and $|E|$ are the number of vertices and edges in the incidence structure (note that $|V|$ and $|E|$ might be exponential in the number of arguments).

Widening the Tuples

The size of a (normal form) representation of a tuple of sets is potentially exponential in the number of sets. This can be problematic because the operations for meet and for computing a normal form (as implemented) are quadratic in the size of their inputs. As an illustration, consider the n-ary Boolean function whose set of models consist of the empty set together with the $\binom{n}{n/2}$ sets with $\frac{n}{2}$ variables. This set of models is meet irreducible and of exponential size. Hence so is the normal form of its dual representation as a tuple of sets.

In addition to the potential size problem, we also know from [17] that the number of iterations in a Def analysis has a worst case of at least $2^{\sqrt{n}}$. To guarantee a robust analysis we introduce two possible widening operations [14] on our tuple representation. Note that widening operations are usually used to avoid infinite chains during an analysis. In our case, the domain is of finite height. Widening is applied to avoid generating tuples with large sets as well as to reduce the number of iterations needed to reach a fixed point.

Restricting the size of sets: A simple widening operation is obtained by restricting the size of the sets which occur in a (normalized) tuple to contain at most k variables. Similar to a depth-k abstraction on terms [21], a tuple which violates the restriction is replaced by a more general tuple which contains smaller sets and captures less dependencies between arguments. In contrast to a depth-k abstraction on terms the operation on tuples of sets cannot be described as an abstraction in the adjoint framework [13] because there is no *"best approximation"*.

Restricting the size of the sets in a tuple limits the types of dependencies that we can express. For example, with $k = 1$ we can express groundness information and equivalences between arguments as in $p([A], [\ ], [A], [B], [\ ])$ which corresponds in Def to $p(x_1, x_2, x_3, x_4, x_5) \leftarrow (x_1 \leftrightarrow x_3) \wedge x_2 \wedge x_5$. With $k = 2$ we can express simple dependencies such as in $p([A, B], [A])$ which corresponds in Def to $p(x_1, x_2) \leftarrow (x_1 \rightarrow x_2)$ and as $append([A], [B], [A, B])$ which corresponds in Def to $append(x_1, x_2, x_3) \leftarrow ((x_1 \wedge x_2) \leftrightarrow x_3)$.

The widening algorithm should generalize a given tuple $\bar{\tau}$ (which contains sets larger than k) to provide a tuple $\bar{\tau}'$ in which the sets have no more than k elements. It is always possible to find such a generalization because the most general tuple $\langle [\_], [\_], \ldots, [\_] \rangle$ contains sets of size 1 consisting of distinct variables.

A naive widening algorithm simply "drops" sets with more than k elements (replacing them by fresh singletons) hence maintaining the dependencies between the smaller sets.

Example 5 (Naive widening). Consider $\pi = p([A, B, C, D], [A, B, C], [A, B], [A])$, which corresponds in Def to $p(x_1, x_2, x_3, x_4) \leftarrow (x_1 \rightarrow x_2) \wedge (x_2 \rightarrow x_3) \wedge (x_3 \rightarrow x_4)$, and $k = 2$. The naive widening of π with $k = 2$ results in $p([X], [Y], [A, B], [A])$ which corresponds in Def to $p(x_1, x_2, x_3, x_4) \leftarrow (x_3 \rightarrow x_4)$. The dependencies (in π) that involve sets with more than 2 elements, i.e $(x_1 \rightarrow x_2)$ and $(x_2 \rightarrow x_3)$, are lost.

A less naive widening algorithm might capture some of the dependencies between the large sets. A simple approach is to rename the variables in the large sets and apply normalization. For instance, applying this technique to the tuple $p([A, B, C, D], [A, B, C], [A, B], [A])$ from Example 5 gives $p([X, W, Z, Y], [X, W, Z], [A, B], [A])$ which is normalized to $p([X, Y], [X], [A, B], [A])$. This approach may be applied iteratively until no sets are larger than k, or until normalization does not further reduce the size of the sets in the tuple (in which case we can apply the naive approach).

It is interesting to note that widening with $k = 1$ results in an analysis over the domain $EPos$ described in [18] which is a polynomial analysis that captures groundness information and equivalences between pairs of variables. The reader familiar with that work will note that where $EPos$ analysis is inefficient due to the use of non-deterministic iff/2 atoms, our approach applies deterministic ACI1 unifications. In [18] the authors avoided the non-determinism of $EPos$ by application of local iteration with some loss of precision. Our approach with $k = 1$ is both efficient and precise.

Restricting the size of unifications: An alternative approach to avoid generating large sets in tuples is to restrict the application of operations which generate complex dependencies. Given a sequence of ACI1 unifications that need to be solved (for example unifications of the atoms of a clause body with the current approximations for these atoms) we can obtain a more general solution is obtained by "dropping" unifications between large sets. Recall that the unification between sets containing n and m variables respectively generates $n * m$ fresh variables. If n and m are large this introduces an even larger number of fresh variables, many of which are redundant and eliminated by a subsequent but costly application of the normalization algorithm. Strictly speaking this operation could be described as a less precise unification algorithm. But to formalize it that way we would have to normalize before each application of unification.

With this approach we drop equations such that both m and n (the number of variables in each side) are greater than a constant u. For example, with $u = 1$ we drop any unification for which both m and n are larger than 1. Note that the ACI1 unification for $u = 1$ is very efficient because: (1) Solving equations of the form $\bot = [A_1, \ldots, A_n]$ results in the bindings $\{A_1 \mapsto \bot, \ldots, A_n \mapsto \bot\}$; and (2) Solving equations of the form $[B] = [A_1, \ldots, A_n]$ gives $\{B \mapsto [A_1, \ldots, A_n]\}$. In both cases no fresh variables are introduced.

6   Experimentation

We have implemented a prototype analyzers based on the Tuple domain isomorphic to Def for groundness analysis. The implementation is based on a simple bottom-up meta-interpreter enhanced by ACI1 unification. The implementation was coded in SICStus Prolog (version 3, release 7), and the experiments where performed on a Pentium III (300 MHz) and 64MB memory that run Linux Redhat 6.2 (kernel 2.2.4-15). The implementation effort itself involved a small effort given the analyzers described in [8] and in [7]. The main difference is in the simplifications made in the unification and in the normal form algorithms.

For goal-dependent analyses we use an interpreter which applies induced magic-sets [5] and eager evaluation [22]. This is basically the same analysis engine used in [20] and [19]. We have performed 4 experiments for goal-dependent analysis, on a set of 60 benchmarks programs from the benchmark suit used in [19]. Analysis times are described in Table 2. The first two columns in the table ($Def_{k=1}$ and $Def_{k=2}$) correspond to Def analysis widened (using the less naive approach described above) to restrict the size of sets to $k = 1$ and $k = 2$. The third column ($Def_{u=1}$) corresponds to a Def analysis restricting the size of unifications to $u = 1$. The last column corresponds to a Def analysis without widening. The entries of the first three columns represent the time (in seconds) required to perform the analysis. Programs from the benchmark suit, the Def analysis of which requires less than 0.1 seconds and which exhibit no loss of precision for the widenings, are not shown (the full table is available in [16]). In the first three columns the notation $(\frac{n_1}{n_2})$ indicates a loss of precision of n_1 ground arguments with respect to the n_2 ground arguments found in the corresponding Def analysis.

For Def analyses the analyzer exhibits better timings than those described in [20] (for Def and widenings of Def). It *"times out"* only on the aqua_c benchmark, while the analyzer of [20] *"times out"* also on reducer.pl and ili.pl. For $Def_{k=1}$ the analyzer looses some precision on 6 out of the 60 programs. This analysis is equivalent to groundness analysis over the $EPos$ domain that described in [18]. Our analyzer is faster than the non-deterministic version of [18]. For $Def_{k=2}$ the analysis looses some precision for three benchmark programs. For $Def_{u=1}$ the analysis gives no lose of precision Comparing to the timing results of our analyzer to those of [19] show that their analyzer is 2 to 5 times faster than

Table 2. Benchmarks : Times (in seconds) and loss of precision.

Program	$Def_{k=1}$	$Def_{k=2}$	$Def_{u=1}$	Def
aircraft	0.75	0.73	0.70	0.69
ann	0.33	0.49	0.41	0.52
asm	0.15	0.15	0.15	0.15
bryant	0.27	0.49	0.39	0.89
chat_80	2.30 $\left(\frac{3}{855}\right)$	2.86 $\left(\frac{3}{855}\right)$	2.85	3.38
chat_parser	0.96 $\left(\frac{1}{505}\right)$	0.99 $\left(\frac{1}{505}\right)$	1.16	1.18
essln	0.39 $\left(\frac{4}{162}\right)$	0.39	0.39	0.40
flatten	0.13	0.16	0.17	0.22
ili	0.40	0.57	0.54	1.15
ime_v2-2-1	0.12 $\left(\frac{1}{101}\right)$	0.16	0.17	0.17
lnprolog	0.21 $\left(\frac{33}{145}\right)$	0.18	0.17	0.17
map	0.34	0.34	0.33	0.32
music	0.07	0.10	0.11	1.34
nandc	0.05 $\left(\frac{3}{37}\right)$	0.05	0.04	0.05
nbody	0.14	0.16	0.16	0.16
peep	0.15	0.18	0.19	0.18
peval	0.36	0.42	0.44	0.59
press	0.28 $\left(\frac{1}{53}\right)$	0.42	0.36	4.59
reducer	0.22	0.29	0.31	3.77
rotate	0.00 $\left(\frac{1}{3}\right)$	0.01	0.00	0.01
rubik	0.26	0.24	0.24	0.23
scc1	0.25	0.26	0.24	0.25
sdda	0.14	0.16	0.17	0.18
semi	0.14	0.16	0.16	0.15
sim	0.64	0.93	0.87	0.99
sim_v5-2	0.15	0.15	0.14	0.33
simple_ana	0.54	0.66	0.74	1.70
trs	0.47	0.72	0.63	0.78
unify	0.16	0.19	0.23	0.24
aqua_c	14.55 $\left(\frac{63}{1285}\right)$	86.41 $\left(\frac{33}{1285}\right)$	21.16	time out

our analyzer and in particular it does not *"times out"* on the aqua_c benchmark. This is mainly because of the technique they apply for *"entailment checking"* (checking if a new atom descreption is already entailed by an old one without applying join and projection). Experiments show that in our analyzer more than 80% of the attempts to add new tuples to the database fails. Namely, more that 80% of the calls to join and normal form could be avoided if we had *"entailment checking"*.

We also implemented a goal-independent analyzer based on a semi-naive interpreter optimized for strongly connected components. For this analyses, it is interesting to note that although Def is known not to be a condensing domain, the amount of groundness obtained when applying a goal independent analysis is precisely the same as with the goal dependent analysis for the set of benchmarks chosen. However, for goal independent analyses, extreme widening such as $k = 2$ and $u = 1$ are not realistic with regards to the loss of precision. A table with run times for this analysis available in [16].

7   Conclusion

The study of the relationships between Pos, Sharing and Def has been the topic of many research papers in the last 10 years. Analyses using Def were defined early on in the work of Dart [15] and an evaluation of various representations for Def can be found in [1]. However, the use of BDD's for Pos analysis is more popular. Due to the difficulty in widening BDD representations, it is a recent trend to look for weaker domains which support analyses that are fast and do not exhibit (or can be widened so as not to exhibit) the underlying worst case complexity for the occasional hard example. Recent results described in [20] and [19] indicate that Def is a promising candidate for the groundness analysis of (constraint) logic programs.

We provide a new representation for Def based on n-tuples of sets of variables as proposed in [8] for representing set Sharing. Our main result states that the quotient of Sharing to Def is precisely the quotient of our n-tuples representation with respect to ACI1 equivalence. From the practical point of view this provides the basis to implement program analysis over Def using the classic and well-studied ACI1 unification algorithms. For the special case where the only constant symbol is the unit element this is efficient and simple to implement. An advantage of basing Def analyses on tuples representation is the simplicity of which the widening can be defined and implemented.

The absence of an *"entailment checking"* for tuples is the main reason why the analysis of [19] is faster than ours. Filling this gap is the topic of ongoing reaserch.

References

1. T. Armstrong, K. Marriott, P. Schachte, and H. Søndergaard. Two classes of Boolean functions for dependency analysis. *Science of Computer Programming*, 31(1):3–45, 1998.
2. F. Baader and J. Siekmann. Unification theory. In D. Gabbay, C. Hogger, and J. Robinson, editors, *Handbook of Logic in Artificial Intelligence and Logic Programming*, volume 2, pages 41–126. Oxford Science Publications, 1994.
3. R. Bagnara and P. Schachte. Factorizing equivalent variable pairs in ROBDD-based implementations of *Pos*. In A. M. Haeberer, editor, *AMAST'98*, volume 1548 of *LNCS*, pages 471–485, Amazonia, Brazil, 1999. Springer-Verlag, Berlin.
4. R. Bryant. Symbolic Boolean manipulation with ordered binary-decision diagrams. *ACM Computing Surveys*, 24(3):293–318, 1992.
5. M. Codish. Efficient goal directed bottom-up evaluation of logic programs. *Journal of Logic Programming*, 38(3):354–370, 1999.
6. M. Codish. Worst-case groundness analysis using positive Boolean functions. *Journal of Logic Programming*, 41(1):125–128, 1999.
7. M. Codish and V. Lagoon. Type dependencies for logic programs using aci-unification. *Theoretical Computer Science*, 2000.
8. M. Codish, V. Lagoon, and Bueno F. An algebraic approach to sharing analysis of logic programs. *Journal of Logic Programming*, 41(2):110–149, 2000.
9. M. Codish and H. Søndergaard. The Boolean logic of set sharing analysis. In C. Palamidessi, H. Glaser, and K. Meinke, editors, *Principles of Declarative Programming*, volume 1490 of *LNCS*, pages 89–101, Berlin, 1998. Springer.

10. M. Codish, H. Søndergaard, and P. J. Stuckey. Sharing and groundness dependencies in logic programs. *ACM Transactions on Programming Languages and Systems*, 21(5):948–976, 1999.

11. A. Cortesi, G. Filé, and W. Winsborough. The quotient of an abstract interpretation. *Theoretical Computer Science*, 202(1–2):163–192, 1998.

12. A. Cortesi, B. Le Charlier, and P. Van Hentenryck. Evaluation of the domain Prop. *Journal of Logic Programming*, 23(3):237–278, 1995.

13. P. Cousot and R. Cousot. Abstract interpretation: A unified lattice model for static analysis of programs by construction or approximation of fixpoints. In *Proceedings of the Fourth ACM Symposium on Principles of Programming Languages*, pages 238–252, January 1977.

14. P. Cousot and R. Cousot. Comparing the Galois connection and widening/narrowing approaches to abstract interpretation. Number 631 in LNCS, pages 269–295, Leuven, Belgium, 1992. Springer-Verlag, Berlin.

15. P. W. Dart. On derived dependencies and connected databases. *The Journal of Logic Programming*, 11(1 & 2):163–188, July 1991.

16. S. Genaim and M. Codish. The Def-inite Approach to Dependency Analysis. Technical report, Computer Science, Ben-Gurion University, 2000. http://www.cs.bgu.ac.il/~mcodish/Papers/ppapers.html.

17. S. Genaim, J.M. Howe, and M. Codish. Worst-case groundness analysis using definite boolean functions, September 2000.

18. A. Heaton, M. Abo-Zaed, M. Codish, and A. King. A Simple Polynomial Groundness Analysis for Logic Programs. *Journal of Logic Programming*, 45:143–156.

19. J. M. Howe and A. King. Implementing groundness analysis with definite Boolean functions. In G. Smolka, editor, *ESOP*, volume 1782 of *Lecture Notes in Computer Science*. Springer-Verlag, March 2000.

20. A. King, J. G. Smaus, and P. Hill. Quotienting share for dependency analysis. In Doaitse Swierstra, editor, *ESOP*, volume 1576 of *LNCS*, pages 59–73. Springer-Verlag, April 1999.

21. Taisuke Sato and Hisao Tamaki. Enumeration of success patterns in logic programs. *Theoretical Computer Science*, 34(1–2):227–240, November 1984.

22. J. Wunderwald. Memoing evaluation by source-to-source transformation. In Maurizio Proietti, editor, *Proceedings of the Fifth International Workshop on Logic Program Synthesis and Transformation*, volume 1048 of *LNCS*, pages 17–32. Springer.

Author Index

Lecture Notes in Computer Science

For information about Vols. 1–1931
please contact your bookseller or Springer-Verlag